Lecture Notes in Artificial Intelligence   2533

Subseries of Lecture Notes in Computer Science
Edited by J. G. Carbonell and J. Siekmann

Lecture Notes in Computer Science
Edited by G. Goos, J. Hartmanis, and J. van Leeuwen

T0216053

Springer
Berlin
Heidelberg
New York
Barcelona
Hong Kong
London
Milan
Paris
Tokyo

Nicolò Cesa-Bianchi   Masayuki Numao
Rüdiger Reischuk (Eds.)

Algorithmic
Learning Theory

13th International Conference, ALT 2002
Lübeck, Germany, November 24-26, 2002
Proceedings

 Springer

Series Editors

Jaime G. Carbonell, Carnegie Mellon University, Pittsburgh, PA, USA
Jörg Siekmann, University of Saarland, Saarbrücken, Germany

Volume Editors

Nicolò Cesa-Bianchi
Università degli Studi di Milano
Dipartimento di Tecnologie dell'Informazione
via Bramante 65, 26013 Crema (CR), Italy
E-mail: cesa-bianchi@dti.unimi.it

Masayuki Numao
Tokyo Institute of Technology, Department of Computer Science
2-12-1, Ohokayama Meguro Ward, Tokyo 152-8552, Japan
E-mail: numao@cs.titech.ac.jp

Rüdiger Reischuk
Universität zu Lübeck, Institut für Theoretische Informatik
Wallstr. 40, 23560 Lübeck, Germany
E-mail: reischuk@tcs.mu-luebeck.de

Cataloging-in-Publication Data applied for

A catalog record for this book is available from the Library of Congress

Bibliographic information published by Die Deutsche Bibliothek
Die Deutsche Bibliothek lists this publication in the Deutsche Nationalbibliographie;
detailed bibliographic data is available in the Internet at <http://dnd.ddb.de>.

CR Subject Classification (1998): I.2.6, I.2.3, F.1, F.2, F.4.1, I.7

ISSN 0302-9743
ISBN 3-540-00170-0 Springer-Verlag Berlin Heidelberg New York

Springer-Verlag Berlin Heidelberg New York,
a member of BertelsmannSpringer Science+Business Media GmbH

http://www.springer.de

© Springer-Verlag Berlin Heidelberg 2002
Printed in Germany

Typesetting: Camera-ready by author, data conversion by PTP-Berlin, Stefan Sossna e.K.
Printed on acid-free paper   SPIN: 10871518   06/3142   5 4 3 2 1 0

Preface

This volume contains the papers presented at the 13th Annual Conference on Algorithmic Learning Theory (ALT 2002), which was held in Lübeck (Germany) during November 24–26, 2002. The main objective of the conference was to provide an interdisciplinary forum discussing the theoretical foundations of machine learning as well as their relevance to practical applications. The conference was colocated with the Fifth International Conference on Discovery Science (DS 2002).

The volume includes 26 technical contributions which were selected by the program committee from 49 submissions. It also contains the ALT 2002 invited talks presented by Susumu Hayashi (Kobe University, Japan) on "Mathematics Based on Learning", by John Shawe-Taylor (Royal Holloway University of London, UK) on "On the Eigenspectrum of the Gram Matrix and Its Relationship to the Operator Eigenspectrum", and by Ian H. Witten (University of Waikato, New Zealand) on "Learning Structure from Sequences, with Applications in a Digital Library" (joint invited talk with DS 2002). Furthermore, this volume includes abstracts of the invited talks for DS 2002 presented by Gerhard Widmer (Austrian Research Institute for Artificial Intelligence, Vienna) on "In Search of the Horowitz Factor: Interim Report on a Musical Discovery Project" and by Rudolf Kruse (University of Magdeburg, Germany) on "Data Mining with Graphical Models". The complete versions of these papers are published in the DS 2002 proceedings (Lecture Notes in Artificial Intelligence, Vol. 2534).

ALT has been awarding the *E. Mark Gold Award* for the most outstanding paper by a student author since 1999. This year the award was given to Daniel Reidenbach for his paper "A Negative Result on Inductive Inference of Extended Pattern Languages."

This conference was the 13th in a series of annual conferences established in 1990. Continuation of the ALT series is supervised by its steering committee consisting of: Thomas Zeugmann (Univ. Lübeck, Germany) Chair, Arun Sharma (Univ. of New South Wales, Australia) Co-chair, Naoki Abe (IBM T.J. Watson Research Center, USA), Peter Bartlett (Australian National Univ., Australia), Klaus Peter Jantke (DFKI, Germany), Roni Khardon (Tufts Univ., USA), Phil Long (National Univ. of Singapore), Heikki Mannila (Nokia Research Center), Akira Maruoka (Tohoku Univ., Japan), Luc De Raedt (Albert-Ludwigs-Univ., Germany), Takeshi Shinohara (Kyushu Institute of Technology, Japan), and Osamu Watanabe (Tokyo Institute of Technology, Japan).

We would like to thank all individuals and institutions who contributed to the success of the conference: the authors for submitting papers, the invited speakers for accepting our invitation and lending us their insight into recent developments in their research areas and the sponsors for their generous financial support. We are particularly grateful to Mrs. Lisa Dräger for funding the *E. Mark Gold Award* this year.

Furthermore, we would like to express our gratitude to all program committee members for their hard work in reviewing the submitted papers and participating in on-line discussions. We are also grateful to the external referees whose reviews made a considerable contribution to this process.

We are also grateful to DS 2002 chairs Steffen Lange (DFKI GmbH, Germany) and Ken Satoh (National Institute of Informatics, Japan) for their effort in coordinating with ALT 2002, and to Andreas Jakoby and Thomas Zeugmann for their excellent work as the local arrangements chairs. Last, but not least, Springer-Verlag provided excellent support in preparing this volume.

September 2002

Nicolò Cesa-Bianchi
Masayuki Numao
Rüdiger Reischuk

Organization

Conference Chair

Rüdiger Reischuk   Univ. Lübeck, Germany

Program Committee

Nicolò Cesa-Bianchi	(Univ. di Milano, Italy) Co-chair
Masayuki Numao	(Tokyo Inst. of Tech., Japan) Co-chair
Naoki Abe	(IBM T.J. Watson Research Center, USA)
Hussein Al-Muallim	(KFUPM, Saudi Arabia)
Peter Auer	(TU Graz, Austria)
José Balcázar	(Univ. Politecnica de Catalunya, Spain)
Saso Dzeroski	(Jozef Stefan Institute, Slovenia)
Claudio Gentile	(Univ. dell'Insubria, Italy)
Boonserm Kijsirikul	(Chulalongkorn Univ., Thailand)
Robert Schapire	(AT&T Labs., USA)
Kai Ming Ting	(Monash Univ., Australia)
Rolf Wiehagen	(Univ. Kaiserslautern, Germany)

Local Arrangements

Andreas Jacoby   Univ. Lübeck, Germany
Thomas Zeugmann   Univ. Lübeck, Germany

Subreferees

David Albrecht	Jun'ichi Takeuchi
Marta Arias	Montserrat Hermo
Albert Atserias	Gabor Lugosi
Peter Bartlett	Lluis Marquez
Xavier Carreras	Enrique Romero
Jorge Castro	Athasit Surarerks
Prabhas Chongstitvatana	Manfred Warmuth
Ricard Gavalda	Osamu Watanabe

Sponsoring Institutions

DFKI GmbH, Saarbrücken, Germany
Corpo Base, Lübeck
Jessen Lenz, Lübeck
Mrs. Lisa Dräger, Lübeck

Table of Contents

Learning Boolean Functions

Boosting and Margin-Based Learning

Learning with Queries

Learning and Information Extraction

Inductive Inference

Inductive Logic Programming

Language Learning

Statistical Learning

Applications and Heuristics

Author Index

Editors' Introduction

Learning theory is a research area involved in the study, design, and analysis of computer programs that are able to learn from past experiences. Over the last years the idea of learning system has independently emerged in a variety of fields: pattern recognition, theory of repeated games, machine learning, universal prediction and data compression, inductive inference, adaptive optimal control, computational psychology, and others. This is not surprising: on the one hand, the notion of adaptivity is an extremely attractive and powerful tool; on the other hand, the abstract phenomenon of learning is so complex that it is unlikely that a single theory will ever be able to explain it in a fully satisfactory way. Despite their apparent diversity, these learning models present deep connections whose study is an active research area in learning theory.

Another important aspect is the increasingly tight interaction between the theoretical analysis and the practical application of learning. The sharpening of the theoretical tools for designing and analyzing learning techniques, the large amounts of real-world data freely available in digital form, and the growing demand of adaptive techniques for e-commerce, computational biology, and other applications, have stimulated the development of new learning algorithms, some of which are successfully used in commercial and scientific applications.

The papers collected in this volume offer a broad view on the current research in the field, including studies on the most important learning models (inductive inference, statistical learning, large-margin learning techniques, learning with queries, reinforcement learning). The scope of this research is not limited to theory. It also includes algorithm design and analysis, experimental studies of learning heuristics, and application of learning to engineering problems. Moreover, there is an increasing need to learn from semi-structured data that are typically available within the world-wide-web.

The invited lecture for ALT 2002 and DS 2002 by Ian H. Witten presents a solution to the problem of automatically extracting *metadata* for text documents stored in digital libraries. Given that such libraries are usually huge and rapidly expanding, assigning meaningful metadata to the documents stored is crucial for the usability of digital libraries. In his paper, Witten describes a learning paradigm that creates a model from marked-up training text. Then, this model is applied to insert markup into plain text. As a result a plausible hierarchical structure of metadata can be created automatically. Surprisingly, his algorithm works in time linear in the size of the input.

In his invited lecture, Susumi Hayashi develops a mathematics that is based on learning. Traditionally, learning theory is mainly concerned with the learnability of mathematical and logical objects from a finite amount of data. Thus, the main goal is to achieve a better understanding of learning. In contrast, Susumi Hayashi proposes a mathematics that is founded on learning theoretical notions. This research started and is ultimately aimed at testing and debugging formal

N. Cesa-Bianchi et al. (Eds.): ALT 2002, LNAI 2533, pp. 1–6, 2002.

proofs. Interestingly, when the investigations started, learning theory was not involved at all and at the current stage of investigations it is indispensable.

The next invited lecture, given by John Shawe-Taylor and co-authored by Chris Williams, Nello Christianini, and Jaz Kandola, studies the eigenspectrum of the Gram matrix and its relationship to the operator eigenspectrum. It is shown that the difference between the two spectra can be bounded. Moreover, a performance bound on kernel principal component analysis is provided. These results are fundamental for a number of learning algorithms. These algorithms project data into a low dimensional subspace that hopefully will catch most of the variance in the data. Experiments are presented that confirm the theoretical predictions on a real world data set for small projection dimensions.

Data mining with graphical models is presented in the invited lecture for DS 2002 by Rudolf Kruse (co-authored by Christion Borgelt). Graphical models are an important technique for classifier construction and dependency analysis. The paper discusses the main ideas of learning graphical models from datasets of sample cases with an emphasis on probabilistic networks.

The invited lecture for DS 2002 by Gerhard Widmer deals with the complex phenomenon of *expressive music performance*. It is a big challenge to capture this phenomenon by using machine learning techniques and automated discovery methods. The lecture reports the results achieved and identifies a number of important research problems.

Next, we turn our attention to the regular contributions contained in this volume. The first group of papers is concerned with inductive inference. This line of research was pioneered by Gold who introduced his model of learning in the limit [3]. In this model the learner receives a stream of examples of a certain target function and is required to output a sequence of hypotheses converging to this target. The paper by Jain, Menzel, and Stephan investigates whether target classes that are learnable in the limit contain non-trivial subclasses that can be learned in a harder learning model. A related important question, also investigated in this paper, is whether for such target classes there are learners for the full class that are able to learn targets in the subclass under the harder model, too.

The paper by Grieser develops the notion of reflective inductive inference. Reflective learners are able to detect the fact that the sequence of examples contains inconsistent information, but occasionally they may also make detection mistakes. The results determine how learners obeying to different notions of reflection behave in different learning models. It turns out that for some learning models changes in the notion of reflection do not change the learning power, whereas in others the learning power is greatly affected by these changes.

The work by Martin, Sharma, and Stephan goes towards providing a unified view over logic, learning, and topology. The outcome is a notion of parameterized logic, based on topology, that makes use of learning-theoretic notions for its interpretation and application. The framework is also seen to provide a nice interpolation between applications based on induction and deduction. Finally, the paper by Harizanov and Stephan establishes a number of fundamental results relating the learnability properties and algebraic properties of recursive vector spaces. The main result states that for identification in the limit from positive examples only, the learnability properties can be characterized by algebraic properties, whereas for learning from positive and negative examples this is not true anymore.

The second group of papers is concerned with the computationally efficient statistical learning of Boolean functions, a field initiated in theoretical computer science by Valiant who introduced the PAC learning model [4]. In this model examples of the target Boolean function are drawn from an unknown probability distribution, and the learner is required to approximate the target function to within a given accuracy. The paper by Amano and Maruoka deals with the important class of monotone boolean functions. They propose a learning algorithm for weakly PAC learning under the uniform distribution obtaining a lower bound on the accuracy of the weak hypotheses generated.

The paper by Servedio studies the PAC learnability of another important class of Boolean functions: those representable by constant-depth, polynomial-size circuits of unbounded fan-in (the ACC class). A first result relates the efficient learnability of ACC to that of a different class: the embedded midbit functions. Several positive and negative results on the efficient learnability of this latter class, providing important insights on the learnability of ACC, are shown for the PAC model and some of its restrictions.

The last paper in this group is by Bshouty and Burroughs. The main theme is the proof of impossibility results for efficient learning of several subclasses of Boolean functions in an extension of PAC learning called co-agnostic learning. The key proof technique is the construction of reductions between learning problems and well-studied approximability problems for which there exist known hardness results.

The third group of papers applies learning to the problem of information extraction. Information extraction is a rapidly growing applied research area whose goal is the design of systems able to extract meaningful information from structured, semi-structured, and unstructured data sources. Important subareas of information extraction are database mining, web mining, and text analysis.

The paper by Grieser, Jantke, and Lange applies theoretical results from inductive inference to perform wrapper induction; i.e., selecting interesting fragment of web pages (originated from a given source) on the basis of a few learning examples. The paper describes the theoretical framework together with a functioning system called LExIKON.

Suzuki, Shoudai, Uchida, and Miyahara consider algorithms for the efficient learning of ordered tree structures. This rich class of structures is well suited for modeling the parse trees of semi-structured data such as HTML or XML documents.

A further set of paper is concerned with a model where the learning algorithm is allowed to ask certain queries to a teacher. The learning performance is measured by the number and type of queries needed by the learner to identify the target concept. This model of learning with queries was introduced by Angluin [1].

Two papers by Köbler and Lindner present results that characterize the computational complexity of query learning for concept classes satisfying certain structural requirements based on the notion of general dimension. The main focus of the first paper is to understand when learning with a few queries (of a given type) implies learning in a reasonable amount of time. The second paper uses the general dimension to characterize the complexity of learning using queries whose response is a random variable and when the goal is relaxed to the approximate identification of the target concept.

The last paper in this group is by Kalnishkan and Vyugin and investigates the notion of predictive complexity. This quantity is an extension of the Kolmogorov complexity of individual sequences and may be viewed as a measure of learnability of a given data sequence abstracted from any specific learning strategy. Predictive complexity is parameterized by the loss function used to measure the success of learning. The main result of the paper characterizes the set of losses admitting the existence of predictive complexity.

The next group contains five papers belonging to the area of statistical learning. This is a very active research field that has started with the seminal works of Vapnik and others in the seventies on the theory of pattern recognition [5, 6]. Statistical learning may be viewed as an extension of PAC learning where, however, computational complexity issues are disregarded.

The work by Schmitt applies ideas derived from the Descartes' rule of signs to derive upper and lower bounds on the Vapnik-Chervonenkis dimension and pseudodimension of radial basis function networks (a popular family of neural networks) with one input variable.

In the next paper, Vovk studies region predictors. These are on-line learning algorithms for pattern classification parameterized by a confidence value. Whereas usual pattern classification algorithms output a single label as prediction, region predictors output a subset of the possible labels, and the size of the subset may increase as the confidence parameter approaches 1.

The paper by Dasgupta, Pavlov, and Singer investigates provably correct and efficient algorithms for reconstructing images. They define a noisy sampling model for images consisting only of lines in the plane and present an algorithm that reconstructs these lines with high probability.

A method for transforming any multi-class, multi-label, or ranking learning problem into a binary classification problem with linear hypotheses is proposed in the paper by Har-Peled, Roth, and Zimak.

The last paper in this group, by Braess, Forster, Sauer, and Simon, has an information-theoretic flavor: it analyzes the problem of learning a probability distribution over a finite domain of fixed size using the Kullback-Leibler divergence as cost function.

The papers in the next group are concerned with inductive logic programming. In this framework, the goal is to learn concepts using logical formulae (propositional or first-order) as hypotheses. In many cases this is a difficult problem, but the payoff is that logical formulae provide solutions that are generally more understandable than those provided by other classes of functions (like neural networks).

In the first paper, Fürnkranz considers the problem of rule learning using a covering approach; i.e., finding a small set of simple rules that explains (covers) all the positive examples and none of the negative examples. In particular, his work points out a problem in covering strategies that proceed bottom-up (i.e., by generalizing a rule that initially covers a single example) and proposes some techniques to alleviate this problem.

In the second and last paper of this group, Fronhöfer and Yamamoto study the notion of relevant logic. A relevant logic is a logic where a formula may be derived as conclusion only if it is deductively related to all the premises. The main idea of the paper is to use relevance as a notion of appropriateness for hypotheses in inductive logic.

Large-margin learning algorithms, like support vector machines, boosting and their variants, build on results from statistical learning theory to generate linear hypotheses with good generalization abilities. Algorithms of this kind are studied in the next group of papers.

The first one is by Gavinsky who proposes a new boosting method. Boosting [2] is a general technique for obtaining a highly accurate hypothesis by combining hypotheses generated on different reweightings of the training set. Good boosting algorithms are adaptive as they work without need to know any *a priori* lower bound on the accuracy of the individual hypotheses to combine. The price of adaptivity is lack of robustness: traditional boosting is likely to work not so well on noisy data. On the other hand, this new boosting method is the first one able to provide adaptivity together with a certain noise robustness.

The second paper in this group is by Kivinen, Smola, and Williamson and investigates two incremental variants of the support vector machine algorithm. The main result shows that these variants are robust with respect to drift of the target. The performance of both algorithms is shown to degrade in proportion to the amount of drift in the considered time interval and also in proportion to the amount of nonlinearity in the data sequence.

The third paper, by Forster and Simon, is concerned with some fundamental questions about the use of linear-threshold hypotheses. Statistical learning theory ensures that a good generalization error is achieved whenever the sample can be embedded in a space where some linear hypothesis can be found that separates positive examples from negative ones with large margin. The paper proves bounds relating the spectrum of a matrix derived from the sample to the margin which can be obtained via the embedding technique.

The last group of papers is devoted to heuristics and applications of learning to concrete problems. Lindgren and Boström propose an alternative approach to rule-based learning techniques where it may happen that many contradicting rules are applicable to a single example. In these cases, one may weigh each rule by the number of examples covered in the sample or, alternatively, assume rule independence in a naïve Bayes fashion. The solution proposed in this paper is to improve naïve Bayes by taking into account the examples in the intersecting regions of the overlapping rules. The paper also provides experimental validation of the approach proposed.

The last paper in this group is by Coulom and applies neural networks to the solution of a motor control problem. The control problem is modeled using reinforcement learning, a very general framework formalizing the learning of plans and complex strategies. The proposed approach is based on the *temporal difference learning algorithm* coupled with *feedforward neural networks*. Empirical convergence of the resulting algorithm is shown via simulation of a mechanical system consisting of five articulated segments.

References

[1] D. Angluin. Queries and concept learning. *Machine Learning*, 2(4):319–342, 1988.

[2] Y. Freund and R.E. Schapire. A decision-theoretic generalization of on-line learning and an application to boosting. *Journal of Computer and System Sciences*, 55(1):119–139, 1997.

[3] E.M. Gold. Language identification in the limit. *Information and Control*, 10:447–474, 1967.

[4] L. Valiant. A theory of the learnable. *Communications of the ACM*, 27(11):1134–1142, 1984.

[5] V.N. Vapnik. *Estimation of Dependences Based on Empirical Data*. Springer, 1982.

[6] V.N. Vapnik. *The Nature of Statistical Learning Theory*. Springer Verlag, 1999. 2nd edition.

Mathematics Based on Learning

Susumu Hayashi

Kobe University, Rokko-dai, Nada, Kobe 657-8501, Japan,
shayashi@kobe-u.ac.jp, http://www.shayashi.jp

Abstract. Learning theoretic aspects of mathematics and logic have been studied by many authors. They study how mathematical and logical objects are algorithmically "learned" (inferred) from finite data. Although the subjects of studies are mathematical objects, the objective of the studies are learning. In this paper, a mathematics of which foundation itself is learning theoretic will be introduced. It is called *Limit-Computable Mathematics*. It was originally introduced as a means for "Proof Animation," which is expected to make interactive formal proof development easier. Although the original objective was not learning theoretic at all, learning theory is indispensable for our research.

1 Mathematics Based on Learning?

Learning theory of mathematical or logical concepts seem to be one of the main research targets of learning theory and its applications. Shapiro [18] investigated how axioms systems are inductively inferred by ideas of learning theory. We may say that Shapiro studied how logical systems (axiom systems) are learned. Stephan and Ventsov [19] investigated how algebraic structures are learned and have given some interesting learning theoretic characterizations of fundamental algebraic notions.

We may say that they investigated learnability of the mathematical concepts. Contrary to them, we are now developing a mathematics of which semantics and reasoning systems are influenced by ideas from computational learning theory. Let us compare these two lines of research.

In Shaprio's work, the concept of validity and models were the standard ones from Tarski semantics, and learning of axiom systems in Horn-logic from models are investigated. On the other hand, we give semantics of the first order formulas by means of computation in the limit. For example, $\exists y.A(x,y)$, which reads as "there exists y satisfying $A(x,y)$", is interpreted as "the value of y satisfying $A(x,y)$ is computable in the limit from the value of x". We also study proof rules representing the semantics.

Stephan and Ventsov showed that the class of enumerable ideals of a recursive ring is BC-learnable iff every such ideal is finitely generated. They proved it in the standard set theoretical mathematics. We investigate, for example, if the statement "the ideal generated by any sequence of n-variable polynomials with rational coefficients is finitely generated" is valid under our learning-theoretic semantics and is provable by learning-theoretic proof rules.

N. Cesa-Bianchi et al. (Eds.): ALT 2002, LNAI 2533, pp. 7–21, 2002.

Shapiro, Stephan and Ventsov explored learning theoretic aspects of Horn-logic and algebra. In a sense, we study learning theoretic aspects of logical *reasonings* based on learning theoretic semantics of mathematics. Since the large part of contemporary mathematics is "reasoning", it would be fair to say that we are developing mathematics based on learning. The mathematics based on learning is called *Limit-Computable Mathematics*, abbreviated to LCM [16,11]. In this largely expository paper, we will give an introductory account to LCM and raise some open problems.

2   Objectives and Backgrounds

Although the researches are tending very mathematical at this moment, the original objective of my research on LCM was technological and it is still kept as the ultimate goal. The real goal is a methodology of testing and debugging formal proofs. Since the subject of the talk would be foreign to most of ALT audiences and I am completely new to the community, let me explain the background of the research. A more technically detailed accounts of objectives and backgrounds can be found in [11].

Our mathematics was found through an investigation of interactive formal proof developments. The area is mainly known by the names of proof checkers such as NQTHM, HOL PVS, COQ,.... It may be regarded as a branch of the broad area of formal methods, which aims to utilize formal languages, formal semantics, and formal proofs for developments of software and hardware systems. Formal verification, formal specifications, model checking are all branches of the formal methods and formal proof development is a basic technology for the entire area.

In the mid 80's formal methods community realized importance of validation of formal specifications. In the formal verification project of 8-bits Viper chip for military and other safety-critical uses, it was found that errors in large scale specifications are much more serious than expected and the ultimate way to detect them must be somehow informal. Ultimate requirements of systems are in human minds. They are often unclear and even unstable. We will never be able to verify formal things correct with respect to informal things. Thus, informal things must be translated into formal things. However, the errors may be in the translation of informal things into formal things. It is now clear that such errors were underestimated too much. Informal and empirical methodologies are important even in formal methods.

I found similar difficulties in formal proof developments in my own project. In experiments, goals and subgoals (lemmas), and definitions of concepts could be formalized in wrong ways. There was no formal way to detect the wrong formalizations. However, I found that *testing* formal proofs under development is an extremely efficient way to detect such errors on translation of informal things to formal things. My PX proof system [10] designed to extract "certified" functional programs from formal proofs could extract programs finely representing computational contents of intuitionistic proofs. By testing such programs in the usual sense, errors in definitions and lemmas (subgoals) in the formal proofs were quickly detected. Since the technique is similar to a formal method technique "specification animation" testing specification on examples, I called it proof animation, abbreviated to PA.

I proposed to use proof animation to make formal proof developments less costly in [12]. Since the method was applicable only to intuitionistic proofs, I had to find a method applicable to classical proofs. Berardi's semantics [3] approximating classical proofs by finitely restricted version of the proofs was a possible candidate. Just by chance, I found that Berardi's examples are very similar to Hilbert's original reasoning of his famous finite basis theorem proved in the late 19th century (see [11] for details). Akihiro Yamamoto pointed out to me that both are the same as Gold's computation in the limit. After Yamamoto's suggestion, I found that "computation in the limit" or "limiting recursion" correspond to restricted forms of classical principles such as the law of excluded middle applied to an arithmetical formula with a single quantifier, e.g., Σ_1^0-formulas.

I will refer these restricted principles as "semi-classical principles". Logicians including me tend to think that the limit-recursive functions and semi-classical principles would not make a good logic. They look so fragmentary. At first, I doubted even its closure under the usual inference rules.

To my surprise, the logic defined by limiting recursion was very natural, and a remarkably wide realms of mathematical proofs were found to use only these weak classical principles instead of the full power of classical principles. Thus, it seemed possible to develop most formal proofs only with semi-classical principles and animate them by computation in the limit. Since it is based on limit, I named such a mathematics Limit-Computable Mathematics, LCM.

To built LCM-tools for formal proof developments, there are some theoretical questions to be solved. The standard limit notations are not adequate to represent limit-structures of proofs, and so a concurrent calculus of limit processes must be defined and implemented as a kind of programming language. It is not known if impredicative reasonings have LCM-interpretations. Is it possible to extend the proof animation by limit beyond LCM?[1] There are some important and interesting theoretical questions to be solved to build realistic LCM-environments.

LCM is also interesting as a branch of pure mathematics. It seems related to recursion theory, to reverse mathematics [20] and even to computation theories over real numbers [16,22].

Many of mathematical problems of LCM we face seem related to learning theory. Techniques and knowledge of learning theory seem very useful even for implementation of environments. For example, RichProlog [14] seems a correct tool to built a prototype LCM-environment. Thus, we are seeking collaborations from ALT community. On the other hand, our research might be able to provide new insights for learning theory. An open problem which I am eager to

---

[1] Berardi is extending his limit-semantics [4] to Δ_n^0-reasonings. His results suggest that there might be a way to animate proofs by the law of excluded middle applied to any arithmetical formula.

understand and might be interesting for ALT community will be presented in 4.4.

3 Semantics

In this section, we explain LCM by giving its semi-informal semantics. The semantics of LCM given below is a variant of Brouwer-Heyting-Kolmogorov interpretation (BHK interpretation) of intuitionistic mathematics. In the early 20th century, a famed mathematician L.E.J. Brouwer attacked usage of the traditional Aristotelian logic in mathematics. He attacked especially the law of the excluded middle $A \vee \neg A$. Since he interpreted "A or B" as "there is an algorithm deciding A or B", the law was the same to him as saying "all mathematical problems are decidable by a universal algorithm". Thus, he rejected it and created a mathematics which did not employ such principles. He called his mathematics *intuitionistic mathematics* and the usual mathematics was called *classical mathematics*.[2]

Morphologically, intuitionistic mathematics is a subset of classical mathematics in which the law of excluded middle and its equivalents are forbidden. Brouwer had a philosophical reason to reject the law, and to guarantee correctness of other rules. However, his philosophical principle was rather subjective, mysterious and unclear for the rational minds of most mathematicians and logicians.

Later, Heyting and Kolmogorov gave a much clearer and objective interpretation for Brouwer's mathematics without Brouwer's philosophy. The interpretation is now called *BHK-interpretation*. Although BHK-interpretation was much clearer, it was still somehow unclear since the undefined notion of "construction" was employed and the semantics was explained in informal languages. To make it ultimately clear, Kleene replaced "constructions" with partial recursive functions and gave a translation of a formula into a formula representing his version of BHK-interpretation. Kleene named it "realizability interpretation". Introductory accounts of BHK-interpretation and realizabilities are found in [2, 5,21].

Our semantics of LCM given below is obtained from BHK-interpretation by replacing constructions with limiting recursive functions. It will be called *limit-BHK-interpretation*. Since BHK-interpretation is rather informal, there are many different ways to make it formal. Formal versions can be different to each other in some essential ways. The informal semantics (limit-BHK-interpretation) may be regarded as a guideline or a framework such as object oriented modeling paradigm. Thus, it does not specify the details of the semantics. Details must be given by a formal semantics like realizability interpretations, which correspond to actual object oriented programming languages such as Java, C++.

Now we give limit-BHK interpretation of mathematics. We will describe what first order logical formulas of the forms, $\exists x.A(x)$, $\forall x.A(x)$, $A \vee B$, $A \wedge B$, $A \Rightarrow B$

---

[2] Intuitionistic mathematics have many variants. They are called as *constructive mathematics* including Brouwer's mathematics [5].

mean in limit-BHK interpretation for each case. The crucial cases are $A \vee B$ and $\exists x.A(x)$. Brouwer regarded correctness of $A \vee B$ as the ability to *decide* which of A and B is correct and to prove the correct one. For example, if we say "ZF-set theory is consistent or not", we must know which side of the disjunction is correct and must give its proof actually. Since consistency is Π_1^0-statement, there is no general algorithm to decide it and Gödel's incompleteness theorem tells us that it is impossible to assert one of them by a reasonable method, even if we *believe* in the consistency.

In limit-BHK interpretation, the obligation to "decide" A or B is relaxed to "learn" A or B. We say $A \vee B$ is correct in the sense of limit-BHK interpretation iff we have a computable guessing function $g(t)$ such that

1. $g(t)$ converges to 0 or 1,
2. if $\lim_t g(t) = 0$ then, A is correct in limit-BHK-sense,
3. if $\lim_t g(t) = 1$ then, B is correct in limit-BHK-sense

Let $g(t)$ be

$$g(t) = \begin{cases} 1 \text{ if a proof of a code smaller than } t \text{ derives a contradiction} \\ 0 \text{ otherwise} \end{cases}$$

Obviously g satisfies the three conditions above. Thus, the law of the excluded middle applied to the consistency of ZF-set theory is correct in the sense of limit-BHK-interpretation.

Remark 1. What is this guessing function g of? A guessing function of n-ary function is $n + 1$-ary. However, g has only one argument. Thus, it's a guessing function of 0-ary function h such that $h() = x$. Although a guessing function of a 0-ary functions seems rare in learning theory, it is quite useful for LCM.

Note that we need the law of excluded middle to prove the convergence of g. Thus, this does not help to decide if the system is consistent or not at all.[3] "ZF-set theory is consistent or not in limit-BHK-interpretation" means that consistency of ZF-set theory is computable in the limit in Gold's sense. Since we cannot compute the limit in Turing's sense, this does not help to understand consistency of formal systems anyway.

However, limit-BHK-interpretation gives a systematic way to *approximate* a non-computable truth by a guessing function. The approximation given by a guessing function helps to understand computational contents of a class of non-computational or non-constructive proofs. It was the original aim of my Proof Animation technique to give a method by which classical proofs in mathematics are computationally analyzable through actual execution. Although LCM-proofs cannot be executed in Turing's sense, they are approximately executable by guessing functions. And, such approximate executions are adequate for Proof Animation (see [11]).

---

[3] Berardi[3] has given a limit-semantics without this kind of classical reasoning at meta-level. Since the condition of convergence is replaced with a computationally weak one in his semantics, it does not give the limit value either.

The interpretation of $A \vee B$ above has a defect. We have to assert A is correct in limit-BHK-sense, if $\lim_t g(t)$ is 0. Just as the guessing function g approximates the truth of the outermost disjunction of $A \vee B$, a guessing function approximating the truth of A must be given. Technically, it is better to give such a guessing function for A together the guessing function g for the disjunction. The corrected definition of a guessing function of $A \vee B$ is as follows:

1. $g(t)$ is a pair $(g_1(t), g_2(t))$ and $g(t)$ converges as $t \to \infty$,
2. if $\lim_t g_1(t) = 0$ then, g_2 is a guessing function of A,
3. if $\lim_t g_1(t) \neq 0$ then, g_2 is a guessing function of B.

Similarly, asserting the existential statement "$\exists x. A(x)$" is interpreted to give its guessing function $g(t)$ with the following conditions:

1. $g(t)$ is a pair $(g_1(t), g_2(t))$ and $g(t)$ converges as $t \to \infty$,
2. g_2 is a guessing function of $A(m)$, where $m = \lim_t g_1(t)$.

Asserting an existential or disjunctive formula means giving a guessing function by which we can compute in the limit the information on the existential quantifier "x of $\exists x. A(x)$ and information for $A(x)$" or on disjunction "the correct disjunct of $A \vee B$ and information for the disjunct". Such a guessing function will be called a *guessing function of the statement*. In general, giving a limit-BHK-interpretation to a formula is defining the conditions of the guessing functions for the formula. When a guessing function satisfying the conditions exists, the formula is valid or correct in limit-BHK-interpretation. Such a formula will be said to be limit-BHK-correct for short.

The conditions on a guessing function g of a conjunctive statement $A \wedge B$ is given as follows:

1. $g(t)$ is a pair $(g_1(t), g_2(t))$,
2. g_1 is a guessing function of A and g_2 is a guessing function of B.

The condition of a guessing function $g(x, t)$ of a universal statement $\forall x. A(x)$ is

– $g(x, t)$ converges to a guessing function of $A(x)$ for all x.

Similarly the condition of a guessing function $g(x, t)$ of $A \Rightarrow B$ is

– if f is a guessing function of A, then $g(f, t)$ converges to a guessing function of B.

The conditions for the universal quantifier and the implication are somehow problematic, since limits of guessing functions are again guessing functions. There are two major different approaches on functions incidentally corresponding to the approaches to functions in EX-learnability and BC-learnability.

In his original interpretation, Kleene treated functions as "programs" or "indices" as EX-learnability. This approach is called *intensional*. Kreisel's modified realizability interpretation can treat functions as their extensions as in the usual set theoretical mathematics, i.e., two functions are equal iff their graphs are equal. This approach is called *extensional* and apparently corresponds to BC-learnability by Case and Smith. Kleene-style intensional interpretation is given in the appendix. A realizability using extensional approach is possible by the construction in [1]

Finally, we give interpretation of non-logical formulas such as equations and $\perp$. A non-logical atomic formula F is considered limit-BHK-correct iff it is correct in the ordinary sense. Since asserting a statement means giving a guessing function, we have to define guessing functions for F. Since guessing functions are meaningless for this case, we may take any guessing function converging as far as F is correct in the sense of Tarski semantics. The condition on a guessing function $g(t)$ of an atomic non-logical formula F is

- $g(t)$ converges and F holds.

The convergence condition is not very important. We may drop it.

Note that an interpretation of negation $\neg A$ has not been given. It is understood to be an abbreviation of $A \Rightarrow \perp$, and its semantics is given by this formula. $\perp$ is the atomic formula representing a contradiction such as $0 = 1$. By the definition for atomic formulas, there is no guessing function of the formula $\perp$, which never holds. If A and $A \Rightarrow \perp$ both have guessing functions, then it yields a contradiction. Thus if $A \Rightarrow \perp$ has a guessing function, A does not. If A does not have any guessing function, then any function $g(t)$ is a guessing function $A \Rightarrow \perp$ since the condition becomes vacuously true. Namely, $A \Rightarrow \perp$ is limit-BHK-correct iff A cannot have any guessing function.

It would be worth noting that if guessing functions $g(x, t)$ are all trivial, i.e. $g(x, t) = g(x, 0)$, then limit-BHK-interpretation becomes the usual BHK-interpretation of intuitionistic mathematics.

4   Semi-classical Principles

In this section, semi-classical principles of LCM are introduced. A Π_n^0-*formula* is a formula of the form $\forall x_1 \exists x_2 \cdots Q x_n.A$, where A is a formula for a recursive relation. Σ_n^0-*formula* is defined similarly.

- Σ_n^0-LEM is $A \vee \neg A$ for any Σ_n^0-formula A. LEM stands for Law of Excluded Middle.
- Π_n^0-LEM is defined similarly.
- Σ_n^0-DNE is $\neg\neg A \Rightarrow A$ for any Σ_n^0-formula A. DNE stands for Double Negation Elimination.

4.1   Validity of Semi-classical Principles

By the same argument for the consistency of ZF-set theory, Π_1^0-LEM $\forall x.A(x) \vee \neg\forall x.A(x)$ is limit-BHK-correct. Since x is recursively computable when $\exists x.A(x)$ holds, Σ_1^0-LEM $\exists x.A(x) \vee \neg\exists x.A(x)$ is also limit-BHK-correct. Take $T(e, e, x)$ as

$A(x)$, where T is Kleene's T-predicate. Then giving a realizer for Π_1^0-LEM or Σ_1^0-LEM means giving a function answering to Turing's halting problem.

Next we consider Σ_2^0-DNE. Assume $\neg\neg\exists x.\forall y.P(x,y)$ is limit-BHK-correct for a recursive predicate P. Then $\exists x.\forall y.P(x,y)$ holds classically and we can define a guessing function g converging to such an x as follows:

$$g(t) = \pi_0(h(t)),$$
$$h(0) = (0,0),$$
$$h(n+1) = \begin{cases} (\pi_0(h(n)), \pi_1(h(n))+1) & \text{if } P(\pi_0(h(n)), \pi_1(h(n))) \\ (\pi_0(h(n))+1, 0) & \text{if } \neg P(\pi_0(h(n)), \pi_1(h(n))) \end{cases}$$

π_0 and π_1 are projection functions such that $\pi_0(x,y) = x$ and $\pi_1(x,y) = y$. Since a trivial guessing function of $\forall y.P(x,y)$ is given if $\forall y.P(x,y)$ is classically true, it is easy to define a guessing function $k(t)$ for $\exists x.\forall y.P(x,y)$. Thus, Σ_2^0-DNE is limit-BHK-correct with the guessing function $l(x,t)$ defined by $l(x,t) = k$.

4.2 Mind Change Hierarchy of Propositions

In the realizations of semi-classical principles given above, realizers for Σ_1^0- and Π_1^0-LEM are apparently simpler than the realizers for Δ_2^0-DNE. The first guess of the realizer given for Π_1^0-LEM is fixed to $\forall$-side ($\neg\exists$-side) and a mind change happens if a counterexample is found. Thus realizers of Π_1^0-LEM belong to Π_1^{-1} class of Ershov's boolean hierarchy [7,8,9]. On the other hand, the realizers for Σ_2^0-DNE need the full Ershov hierarchy. In this sense, Δ_2^0-DNE is stronger than Σ_1^0- and Π_1^0-LEM, and Σ_1^0- and Π_1^0-LEM have the same strength.

Some mathematical propositions have intermediate strengths. Assume f is a function from the natural numbers to the natural numbers. The minimum number principle(MNP) "there is m such that for all n $f(m) \le f(n)$ holds" is formalized as follows:
$$\exists m.\forall n.f(m) \le f(n).$$
Its natural realizer does at most $f(0)$-time mind changes. (We guess $m = 0$. If we find a smaller $f(i)$ then we change mind to $m = i$ and repeat the process.)

We will define a realizability interpretation of arithmetical formula in the appendix. These examples show that formulas realizable by recursive guessing functions would be classified finely by Ershov's mind change hierarchy or something like that.[4]

4.3 A Hierarchy by Formal Provability

In the previous subsection, we considered the strengths of semi-classical principles via interpretations (semantical hierarchy). There is another kind of hierarchy via derivability (syntactical hierarchy). Hierarchy via derivability is the one

---

[4] Note that our guessing functions are not always converging for all natural numbers. This might make difference from the original Ershov hierarchy, since limiting partial functions of *partial* recursive functions may be beyond Δ_2^0 (see Yamazaki's example in [16]).

used in proof theoretic studies such as reverse mathematics. Some base systems are fixed and logical principles are compared their strength via these systems. Proof checkers are formal systems implemented on computers. Thus this kind of research is quite important for proof animation. It would show which kind of theorems can be animated by PA/LCM-technology, and which kind of semi-classical principles are appropriate to animate a particular theorem. A team of several researchers including me is now developing such a hierarchy theory.[5]

We call it *calibration of classical principles*. Some calibration results have been already known. MNP and Σ_2^0-LEM are provably equivalent in the standard formal system of first order intuitionistic arithmetic augmented with a free function variable. Hilbert's original form of finite basis theorem for polynomial rings is equivalent to Σ_1^0-LEM. A formulation of existence of step functions such as $y = |x|$ over real numbers is equivalent to Σ_2^0-LEM. Etc. etc.

The standard intuitionistic formal systems are too weak to derive Σ_1^0-LEM from Π_1^0-LEM by the lack of ability to prove Σ_1^0-DNE (Markov's principle). Σ_1^0-DNE is realized even by the original Kleene realizability. Thus some intuitionistic systems contain it. However, most systems do not contain it. For example, standard logics of constructive proof checkers as COQ does not include it. Similarly, Δ_2^0-DNE is not derivable from Σ_1^0-LEM. Thus, this hierarchy is not the same as expected in the standard recursion theory. There is a weaker but still natural form of existence statement of Gauss function which is equivalent to Π_1^0-LEM but not to Σ_1^0-LEM. Since the difference actually affects mathematical theory to be formalized, the syntactical hierarchy should be analyzed.

To analyze this hierarchy, proof theoretic techniques are useful [13]. However, recursion theoretic analysis is also important. For example, the unprovability of Π_1^0-LEM from LCM-WKL is shown by a recursion theoretic argument as explained below.

In the syntactical hierarchy in the previsous subsection, MNP and Σ_1^0-LEM are equivalent, since MNP is derivable from Σ_1^0-LEM by mathematical induction [11]. Mathematical induction enables to use Σ_1^0-LEM repeatedly and so mixes up all finite mind changes.

Then a natural question arises. *Is it possbile to make the syntactical hierarchy finer according to mind change hierarchy?* Linear logic is sensible to the number of applications of axioms or assumptions. A finer interpretation we should seek may be an interpretation of linear logic or something like that. A fine hierarchy might be obtained by restricting induction principle as reverse mathematics [20].

4.4 Problem of Weak König Lemma

In the syntactic hierarchy of LCM principles, Weak König Lemma, abbreviated to WKL, is especially interesting. WKL is a theorem for binary tree:

– Any binary-branching tree with infinite many nodes has an infinite path.

---

[5] Current members are Berardi, Hayashi, Ishihara, Kohlenbach, Yamazaki, and Yasugi.

Harvey Friedman found that this principle is logically as weak as Hilbert's finite standpoint, but mathematically strong enough. It is enough to prove many important mathematical theorems such as the completeness theorem of first order predicate logic. On this unexpected finding, Simpson and his colleagues developed an interesting theory of "reverse mathematics" [20]. They calibrated mathematical theorems by means of WKL or related. For example, they identify which theorem is proved by WKL and WKL is necessary to prove it.

The syntactical hierarchy of LCM is very similar to the one of reverse mathematics. Although our hierarchy is finer than the one of reverse mathematics, many techniques developed in reverse mathematics are quite useful to investigate our syntactical hierarchy.[6]

Upon results of reverse mathematics, Kohlenbach and Ishihara found that WKL is important in LCM as well. LCM version of WKL, LCM-WKL is formulated as follows:

- Any computable binary-branching tree with infinite many nodes has an infinite path.

Computable means that recursive or recursive relative to an oracle, which is regarded as an input stream α. To state the principle properly, we need an appropriate second order language in which function variables represent limiting computable functions whose guessing functions are recursive in α. The infinite path is understood as a limiting computable function.

LCM-WKL is intuitionistically equivalent to "Π_1^0-LLPO+Π_1^0-b-AC$_{00}$", where Π_1^0-LLPO is

$$\forall x. \neg(\exists y. A(x,y) \land \exists y. B(x,y)) \Rightarrow \forall y. \neg A(x,y) \lor \forall y. \neg B(x,y)$$

and Π_1^0-b-AC$_{00}$ is a very weak axiom of choice

$$\forall x.(\forall y. A(x,y) \lor \forall y. B(x,y)) \Rightarrow$$
$$\exists f. \forall x.(f(x) = 0 \Rightarrow \forall y. A(x,y)) \land (f(x) = 1 \Rightarrow \forall y. B(x,y))]$$

In these schemes, A and B are predicates with computable characteristic functions.

Π_1^0-LLPO is an LCM version of an intuitionistic principle "Lesser Limited Principles of Omniscience" [5]. LLPO may be regarded as a very weak law of excluded middle. Π_1^0-LEM implies it. Π_1^0-b-AC$_{00}$ is also derivable from Π_1^0-LEM with a help of very weak function principle.

This ultra weak law of excluded middle is still enough to prove many important theorems, e.g., the completeness theorem of predicate logic. Furthermore, these theorems can be used to prove Π_1^0-LLPO and Π_1^0-b-AC$_{00}$ modulo intuitionistic logic. This fact remarkably resembles reverse mathematics [20]. Actually,

---

[6] The axiom of ACA$_0$ of reverse mathematics represents the entire arithmetical hierarchy, i.e. the union of $\mathbf{0}^{(n)}$ for all n. On the other hand, Π_n^0-LEM represents only $\mathbf{0}^{(n)}$.

proofs of corresponding results in reverse mathematics go through in LCM without almost any changes.

We can define a realizability interpretation of second order language, in which interpretation of LCM-WKL coincides with Kreisel's basis theorem (Proposition V.5.31, [17]), which maintains the leftmost infinite branch is a limiting recursive function. However, LCM-WKL can be realized with a degree weaker than $\mathbf{0}'$ by the low basis theorem (Theorem V.5.32, [17]). The low basis theorem maintains that there is an infinite path of which the degree is low. A degree $\mathbf{a}$ is called low iff $\mathbf{a}' = \mathbf{0}'$. Using partial functions with such a degree $\mathbf{a}$ instead of the limiting recursive functions, we can give a realizability interpretation for LCM-WKL in which Π_1^0-LEM is not realizable. Thus, LCM-WKL is strictly weaker than Π_1^0-LEM.

Upon these results which will appear in a joint paper by the calibration team, a question arises. LCM-WKL or Π_1^0-LLPO may be considered as an ultra weak but meaningful form of the law of excluded middle. It is actually weaker than Π_1^0-LEM corresponding to 1-mind change learning. What kind of learning is used in LCM-WKL or Π_1^0-LLPO? Is it possible to explain why these principle are weaker than Π_1^0-LEM learning theoretically?

To learn the disjunction in the conclusion of Π_1^0-LLPO, we guess that two formulas $\forall y.\neg A(x, y)$ and $\forall y.\neg B(x, y)$ are both correct. If we restrict the universal quantifiers to a finite subset as $\forall y < t.\neg A(x, y)$ and $\forall y < t.\neg B(x, y)$, both conjectures are correct for $t = 0$. We start with $t = 0$ and successively increase the value of t to verify our guesses. However, one of two formulas may turn false. Then, we simply drop it and keep the other. It never happens both turn false by the assumption of the principle. In this learning process, we never change our mind completely in a sense. At least one conjecture remains, and it was guessed already at the beginning and is kept forever. We only cut down wrong ones. Is it possible to explain the weakness of Π_1^0-LLPO to Π_1^0-LEM by this kind of learning theoretic considerations?

5   Conclusion

In this paper, we gave an expository account of the foundations of Limit-Computable Mathematics LCM. A semi-formal interpretation of LCM was given by means of guessing functions, and a formal interpretation was given in the appendix. Some relationships to learning theory, open problems likely related to learning theory were discussed.

Researches of LCM has begun recently. The notion was conceived two years ago and there are still plenty of problems to be solved. LCM is a mathematics of approximation in a very wide sense including identification in the limit. In practical mathematics, some kinds of approximations are inevitable. We are trying to relate LCM to practical mathematics like numerical analysis and computer algebra. Theories and techniques developed in learning theory must be very useful and indispensable in these researches.

Investigations of links between learning theory, reverse mathematics and LCM must be fruitful to understand the relationship between learning theory and LCM. There are some interesting resemblances between these three. It has been shown that the ideals of the polynomial ring over the rationals in n variables is EX-learnable with mind change bound ω^n but not less than ω^n [19]. In reverse mathematics, Hilbert finite basis theorem for the same polynomial rings for all n is equivalent to transfinite induction up to ω^ω [20]. In LCM, the same theorem is equivalent to Σ_1^0-LEM. Are there any good reason for this resemblance?

More information on LCM can be found at http://www.shayashi.jp/PALCM/

References

[1] Y. Akama and S. Hayashi, Limiting Cartesian Closed Categories, submitted, 2002.

[2] M. Beeson, Foundations of Constructive Mathematics, Springer, 1985

[3] S. Baratella and S. Berardi, Constructivization via Approximations and Examples, Theories of Types and Proofs, M. Takahashi, M. Okada and M. Dezani-Ciancaglini eds., MSJ Memories **2** (1998) 177–205

[4] S. Berardi, Classical logic as Limit Completion I. Part I: a constructive model for non-recursive maps, submitted, 2001, at http://www.di.unito.it/~stefano/ available.

[5] D. Bridges and F. Richman, Varieties of Constructive Mathematics, 1987, Cambridge University Press.

[6] J. Case and M. Suraj, Inductive Inference of Σ_1^0- vs. Σ_2^0-Definitions of Computable Functions, manuscript, 2002.

[7] Y. Ershov, A hierarchy of sets I, Alg. Log. 7 (1968) 47–74, transl. 7 (1968) 25–43.

[8] Y. Ershov, A hierachy of sets II, Alg. Log. 7 (1968) 15–47, transl. 7 (1968) 212–232.

[9] Y.Ershov, A hierachy of sets III, Alg. Log. 9 (1970) 34–51, transl. 9 (1970) 20–31.

[10] S. Hayashi and H. Nakano, PX: A Computational Logic, 1988, The MIT Press, PDF version is available free for charge at
http://www.shayashi.jp/PXbook.html

[11] S. Hayashi and M. Nakata, Towards Limit Computable Mathematics, in Types for Proofs and Programs, P. Challanghan, Z. Luo, J. McKinna, R. Pollack, eds., Springer Lecture Notes in Computer Science 2277 (2001) 125–144

[12] S. Hayashi, R. Sumitomo and K. Shii, Towards Animation of Proofs – Testing Proofs by Examples –, Theoretical Computer Science, **272** (2002), 177–195

[13] U. Kohlenbach, Proof Interpretations and the Computational Contents of Proofs (draft in progress), BRIC, University of Aarhus, available at
http://www.brics.dk/~kohlenb/

[14] E. Martin, P. Nguyen, A. Sharma, and F. Stephan, Learning in logic with Rich-Prolog, in Logic Programming 18th International Conference, ICLP 2002, Copenhagen, Denmark, July 29 - August 1, 2002 Proceedings, Stuckey, P.J. ed., 2002, Springer.

[15] J. Mitchell, Type systems for programming languages, in Handbook of Theoretical Computer Science, vol.B, van Leeuwen et al. eds., North-Holland, 1990, 365-458

[16] M. Nakata and S. Hayashi, Realizability Interpretation for Limit Computable Mathematics, Scientiae Mathematicae Japonicae, vol.5 (2001), 421–434.

[17] P.G. Odifreddi, Classical Recursion Theory North-Holland, 1989

[18] E.Y. Shapiro, Inductive Inference of Theories from Facts, in Computational Logic: Essays in Honor of Alan Robinson, Lassez, J.L. and Plotkin, G.D. eds., MIT Press, 199–255, 1991

[19] F. Stephan and Y. Ventsov, Learning Algebraic Structures from Text using Semantical Knowledge, in Theoretical Computer Science - Series A, 268:221-273, 2001, Extended Abstract in Proceedings of the Ninth Annual Workshop on Algorithmic Learning Theory - ALT 1998, Springer LNCS 1501, 321-335, 1998.

[20] S.G. Simpson, Subsystems of Second Order Arithmetic, Springer, 1999

[21] A. Troelstra, Realizability, in Handbook of Proof Theory, S. Buss (ed.), Elsevier, Amsterdam, 1998, 407–474

[22] M. Yasugi, V. Brattka, and M. Washihara, Computability aspects of some discontinuous functions, 2001, Scientiae Mathematicae Japonicae, vol.5 (2001), 405–419.

A Realizabilities

In this appendix, a Kleene style realizability for first order LCM and a modified realizability for LCM are given. A realizability similar to the Kleene style realizability has been given in [16]. The one given here is designed in a little bit more learning theoretic way and closer to Berardi's limit-semantic [4].

It should be noted that if guessing functions $g(x,t)$ are all trivial, i.e. $g(x,t) = g(x,0)$, then the realizabilities given below turn to realizability of intuitionistic logic. Then realizers are computable (partial) functions.

A.1 Kleene Style Limit-Realizability

We give a Kleene style limit-realizability interpretation. In this approach, we regard guessing functions as their indices. Thus we assume ϕ an acceptable programming system or an acceptable system of indices of partial recursive functions (see [17]). We assume a standard coding of finite sequences of numbers and write, e.g., $(a_1, ..., a_n)$ for the code of the sequences $a_1, ..., a_n$. A pair is regarded as a sequence with two elements. π_i is a computable function retrieving i-th element of sequence as a code. An index of n-ary function $f(x_1, ..., x_n)$ is regarded as an index of 1-ary function f' such as $f'((x_1, ..., x_n)) = f(x_1, ..., x_n)$. We fix an algorithm to compute p from q, r so that $\phi_p(x) = (\phi_q(x), \phi_r(x))$. p is called the standard paring index of the indices q and r. Although it is not necessary, it make things easier to assume q and r are computable from p. We assume it here.

Let $A_1, ..., A_n, B$ be formulas of first order arithmetic and let $x_1, ..., x_m$ be a finite sequence of variables including all free variables of the $n + 1$ formulas. Furthermore, $r_1, ..., r_n$ is a sequence of fresh n-variables. A tuple

$$[x_1, ..., x_m, A_1, ..., A_n, r_1, ..., r_n, B]$$

is called a formula with context. $[x_1, ..., x_m, A_1, ..., A_n, r_1, ..., r_n]$ is called *context* and B is called *body*. We denote the context by Γ and a formula with context as $[\Gamma, B]$. These notions are borrowed from type theory. They are not really necessary for our definition but make things much clearer.

We define a first order condition "r **r** $[\Gamma, B]$" for each formula with context $[\Gamma, B]$. (r is a new free variable.) Although we will define it in English, it can be formalized by a first order arithmetical formula including function symbol for ϕ of the index system.

The condition "r **r** $[\Gamma, B]$" is called the *realization* or *realizability interpretation* of $[\Gamma, B]$. If $x_1, ..., x_n$ is an enumeration of free variables of B, then the realization of $[x_1, ..., x_n, B]$ is called the realization of B and we write r **r** B. The conditions are defined so that if r **r** B holds, then r is an index of a total recursive functions. Such functions are called *guessing functions* or *guessing realizers* of the formula with context. *It should be noted that the standard concept of "realizers" do not correspond to guessing realizers but correspond to their limits* $\lim_t g$.

The definition of realization is done by cases on B using an induction over the complexity defined as the sum of the logical signs in $A_1, \cdots, A_n$ and B. In the definition, we intend r to be index of $m + n + 1$-ary total recursive guessing function $g(x_1, ..., x_m, r_1, ..., r_n, t)$ of B. Thus, we may regard it as a condition defining "guessing function of B". We will list the definition of realization below. We say *context is realized* when r_i **r** $[x_1, \cdots, x_m, A_i]$ holds for $(i = 1, ..., n)$.

Case 1: B is an atomic formula: r is an index of a total recursive function and $\phi_r(x_1, ..., x_m, r_1, ..., r_n, t)$ converges whenever the context is realized.

Case 2: B is $B_1 \wedge B_2$: r is the standard pairing index of indices s_1 and s_2. If the context is realized, then s_1 **r** $[\Gamma, B_1]$ and s_2 **r** $[\Gamma, B_2]$.

Case 3: B is $B_1 \vee B_2$: r is the standard pairing index of indices s_1 and s_2. If the context is realized, then $\phi_{s_1}(x_1, ..., x_m, r_1, ..., r_n, t)$ converges. Let p be the limit value. If $p = 0$ then s_2 **r** $[\Gamma, B_1]$. If $p \neq 0$ then s_2 **r** $[\Gamma, B_2]$.

Case 4: B is $B_1 \Rightarrow B_2$: r is an index of a total recursive function. We consider a new context Γ_0:

$$[x_1, ..., x_m, A_1, ..., A_n, B_1, r_1, ..., r_n, r_{n+1}].$$

If Γ_0 is realized, then $\phi_r(x_1, ..., x_m, r_1, ..., r_n, r_{n+1}, t)$ converges to a value b and b **r** B_2.

Case 5: B is $\forall x.C$: r is an index of a total recursive function. We consider a new context Γ_1:

$$[x_1, ..., x_m, x, A_1, ..., A_n, r_1, ..., r_n].$$

If Γ_1 is realized, then $\phi_r(x_1, ..., x_m, x, r_1, ..., r_n, t)$ converges to a value b and b **r** $[\Gamma_1, C]$.

Case 6: B **is** $\exists x.C$**:** r is the standard pairing index of indices s_1 and s_2. $\phi_r(x_1, ..., x_m, r_1, ..., r_n, t)$ converges whenever the context is realized. That is,

$$s_2 \; \mathbf{r} \; [\Gamma, C[t/x]],$$

where t is the numeral representing $\lim_t \phi_{s_1}(x_1, ..., x_m, r_1, ..., r_n, t)$.

It is easy to see that a guessing realizer is always a total recursive function. Similarly to the theorem 7 of [16], the soundness theorem holds, i.e., if A is provable in $\mathbf{HA}+\Sigma_2^0$-DNE, then a number p is effectively computable and p $\mathbf{r}$ A. The partial recursive function ϕ_p represents a formal version of guessing function of A in limit-BHK-interpretation.

Without loss of generality, we may assume guessing functions of $\forall x.A(x)$ and $A \Rightarrow B$ are trivial. Namely, $g(x, 0) = g(x, t)$ for all t. Let us assume g be a guessing function of $\forall x.A(x)$. $\lim_t g(x, t)$ converges to an index of guessing function for $A(x)$. To realize A, we compute two nested limits $\lim_t \phi_{\lim_t g(x,t)}(t)$. It is equivalent to a single limit $\lim_t \phi_{g(x,t)}(t)$. Let h be a recursive function such that $\phi_h(x)(t) = \phi_{g(x,t)}(t)$. Then g' defined by $g'(x, t) = h(x)$ can replace g.

The realizability given here is different from the one given in [16] in two respects. The realizability in [16] is based on an axiomatic recursion theory BRFT. Here, acceptable programming systems are used instead. Since acceptable programming systems may have dynamic complexity measures, the problem of limits of partial guessing functions in [16] does not arise. A limit BRFT system whose guessing functions are restricted to total functions can be defined for any BRFT with Blum's dynamic complexity measure (c.f. Lemma 1.1, [6]). Thus, we assumed guessing functions are total as usual.

The other difference is the points where limit are evaluated. As noted above, guessing functions for implication and universal formulas could be trivial. This is not so in [16]. On the other hand, guessing realizer of $\exists x.A$ was defined so that it includes the value of x. A guessing realizer g of $\forall x.\exists y.A(x, y)$ in this paper, may return in the limit an index of a guessing function h of $\exists y.A(x, y)$ for input x. Thus evaluation of limit to retrieve y could be postponed till the limit of h is evaluated. On the other hand, in [16], g was assumed to return a natural number y itself instead of its guessing function h. Thus, g could not avoid evaluation of limit and g could not be trivial in general.

Berardi introduced a semantics based on limit-natural numbers [4]. Limit-natural numbers N^* are 0-ary guessing functions converging to natural numbers. From classical point of view, N^* is isomorphic to the standard natural numbers N. However there is no recursive isomorphism form N^* to N. In this sense, they differ. Berardi has developed constructive theory of non-constructive functions using this trick. The guessing functions of formulas with empty context can be regard his limit-natural numbers. In this respect, ours interpretation may be thought a non-standard semantics of number theory with limit-numbers.

Data Mining with Graphical Models*

Rudolf Kruse and Christian Borgelt

Department of Knowledge Processing and Language Engineering
Otto-von-Guericke-University of Magdeburg
Universitätsplatz 2, D-39106 Magdeburg, Germany
{kruse,borgelt}@iws.cs.uni-magdeburg.de

Abstract. *Data Mining*, or *Knowledge Discovery in Databases*, is a
fairly young research area that has emerged as a reply to the flood of
data we are faced with nowadays. It tries to meet the challenge to develop methods that can help human beings to discover useful patterns in
their data. One of these techniques — and definitely one of the most important, because it can be used for such frequent data mining tasks like
classifier construction and dependence analysis — is learning *graphical
models* from datasets of sample cases. In this paper we review the ideas
underlying graphical models, with a special emphasis on the less well
known possibilistic networks. We discuss the main principles of learning
graphical models from data and consider briefly some algorithms that
have been proposed for this task as well as data preprocessing methods
and evaluation measures.

---

* The full version of this paper is published in the Proceedings of the 5th International
Conference on Discovery Science, Lecture Notes in Artificial Intelligence Vol. 2534

N. Cesa-Bianchi et al. (Eds.): ALT 2002, LNAI 2533, p. 22, 2002.
© Springer-Verlag Berlin Heidelberg 2002

On the Eigenspectrum of the Gram Matrix and Its Relationship to the Operator Eigenspectrum

John Shawe-Taylor[1], Chris Williams[2], Nello Cristianini[3], and Jaz Kandola[1]

[1] Department of Computer Science,
Royal Holloway, University of London
Egham, Surrey TW20 0EX, UK
[2] Division of Informatics,
University of Edinburgh
[3] Department of Statistics,
University of California at Davies

Abstract. In this paper we analyze the relationships between the eigenvalues of the $m \times m$ Gram matrix K for a kernel $k(\cdot, \cdot)$ corresponding to a sample $\mathbf{x}_1, \ldots, \mathbf{x}_m$ drawn from a density $p(\mathbf{x})$ and the eigenvalues of the corresponding continuous eigenproblem. We bound the differences between the two spectra and provide a performance bound on kernel PCA.

1   Introduction

Over recent years there has been a considerable amount of interest in kernel methods such as Support Vector Machines [5], Gaussian Processes *etc* in the machine learning area. In these methods the *Gram matrix* plays an important rôle. The $m \times m$ Gram matrix K has entries $k(\mathbf{x}_i, \mathbf{x}_j)$, $i, j = 1, \ldots, m$, where $\{\mathbf{x}_i : i = 1, \ldots, m\}$ is a given dataset and $k(\cdot, \cdot)$ is a kernel function. For Mercer kernels K is symmetric positive semi-definite. We denote its eigenvalues $\hat{\lambda}_1 \geq \hat{\lambda}_2 \ldots \geq \hat{\lambda}_m \geq 0$ and write its eigendecomposition as $K = V \hat{\Lambda} V'$ where $\hat{\Lambda}$ is a diagonal matrix of the eigenvalues and V' denotes the transpose of matrix V. The eigenvalues are also referred to as the spectrum of the Gram matrix.

A number of learning algorithms rely on estimating spectral data on a sample of training points and using this data as input to further analyses. For example in Principal Component Analysis (PCA) the subspace spanned by the first k eigenvectors is used to give a k dimensional model of the data with minimal residual, hence forming a low dimensional representation of the data for analysis or clustering. Recently the approach has been applied in kernel defined feature spaces in what has become known as kernel-PCA [13]. This representation has also been related to an Information Retrieval algorithm known as latent semantic indexing, again with kernel defined feature spaces [6].

Furthermore eigenvectors have been used in the HITS [9] and Google's PageRank [4] algorithms. In both cases the entries in the eigenvector corresponding to the

N. Cesa-Bianchi et al. (Eds.): ALT 2002, LNAI 2533, pp. 23–40, 2002.

maximal eigenvalue are interpreted as authority weightings for individual articles or web pages.

The use of these techniques raises the question of how reliably these quantities can be estimated from a random sample of data, or phrased differently, how much data is required to obtain an accurate empirical estimate with high confidence. [14] have undertaken a study of the sensitivity of the estimate of the first eigenvector to perturbations of the connection matrix. They have also highlighted the potential instability that can arise when two eigenvalues are very close in value, so that their eigenspaces become very difficult to distinguish empirically.

In this paper we shift the emphasis towards studying the reliability of the estimates gained from a finite sample. In particular if we perform (kernel-) PCA on a random sample and project new data into the k-dimensional space spanned by the first k eigenvectors, how much of the data will be captured or in other words how large will the residuals be. It turns out that this accuracy is not sensitive to the eigenvalue separation, while at the same time being the quantity that is relevant in a practical application of dimensionality reduction.

The second question that motivated the research reported in this paper is the relation between the eigenvalues of the Gram matrix and those of the underlying process. For a given kernel function and density $p(\mathbf{x})$ on a space $\mathcal{X}$, we can also write down the eigenfunction problem

$$\int_{\mathcal{X}} k(\mathbf{x}, \mathbf{y}) p(\mathbf{x}) \phi_i(\mathbf{x}) \, d\mathbf{x} = \lambda_i \phi_i(\mathbf{y}). \tag{1}$$

Note that the eigenfunctions are orthonormal with respect to $p(\mathbf{x})$, i.e.

$$\int_{\mathcal{X}} \phi_i(\mathbf{x}) p(\mathbf{x}) \phi_j(\mathbf{x}) d\mathbf{x} = \delta_{ij}.$$

Let the eigenvalues of the underlying process be ordered so that $\lambda_1 \geq \lambda_2 \geq \dots$. This continuous eigenproblem can be approximated in the following way. Let $\{\mathbf{x}_i : i = 1, \dots, m\}$ be a sample drawn according to $p(\mathbf{x})$. Then

$$\int_{\mathcal{X}} k(\mathbf{x}, \mathbf{y}) p(\mathbf{x}) \phi_i(\mathbf{x}) d\mathbf{x} \simeq \frac{1}{m} \sum_{k=1}^{m} k(\mathbf{x}_k, \mathbf{y}) \phi_i(\mathbf{x}_k) \tag{2}$$

As pointed out in [17], the standard numerical method (see, e.g., [3], chapter 3) for approximating the eigenfunctions and eigenvalues of equation (1) is to use a numerical approximation such as equation (2) to estimate the integral, and then plug in $\mathbf{y} = \mathbf{x}_j$ for $j = 1, \dots, m$ to obtain a matrix eigenproblem

$$\frac{1}{m} \sum_{k=1}^{m} k(\mathbf{x}_k, \mathbf{x}_j) \phi_i(\mathbf{x}_k) = \hat{\lambda}_i \phi_i(\mathbf{x}_j).$$

Thus we see that $\mu_i \stackrel{def}{=} \frac{1}{m} \hat{\lambda}_i$ is an obvious estimator for the ith eigenvalue of the continuous problem. The theory of the numerical solution of eigenvalue problems

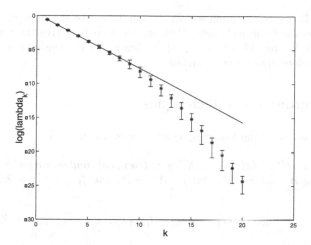

Fig. 1. A plot of the log eigenvalue against the index of the eigenvalue. The straight line is the theoretical relationship. The centre point (marked with a star) in the "error bar" is the log of the average value of μ_k. The upper and lower ends of the error bars are the maximum and minimum values of $\log(\mu_k)$ respectively taken over ten repetitions.

([3], Theorem 3.4) shows that for a fixed k, μ_k will converge to λ_k in the limit as $m \to \infty$.

For the case that $\mathcal{X}$ is one dimensional and $p(x)$ is Gaussian and $k(x,y) = \exp -b(x-y)^2$ (the RBF kernel with lengthscale $b^{-1/2}$), there are analytic results for the eigenvalues and eigenfunctions of equation (1) as given in section 4 of [18]. For this example we can therefore compare the values of μ_i with the corresponding λ_i, as shown in Figure 1. Here $m = 500$ points were used, with parameters $b = 3$ and $p(x) \sim N(0, 1/4)$. As the result depends upon the random points chosen for the sample, this process was repeated ten times. We observe good agreement of the process and matrix eigenvalues for small k, but that for larger k the matrix eigenvalues underestimate the process eigenvalues. One of the by-products of this paper will be bounds on the degree of underestimation for this estimation problem in a fully general setting.

[10] discuss a number of results including rates of convergence of the μ-spectrum to the λ-spectrum. The measure they use compares the whole spectrum rather than individual eigenvalues or subsets of eigenvalues. They also do not deal with the estimation problem for PCA residuals.

In an earlier paper [15] we discussed the concentration of spectral properties of Gram matrices and of the residuals of fixed projections. However, we note that these results gave deviation bounds on the sampling variability of μ_i with respect to $\mathbb{E}[\mu_i]$, but did not address the relationship of μ_i to λ_i or the estimation problem of the residual of PCA on new data.

The paper is organised as follows. In section 2 we give the background results and develop the basic techniques that are required to derive the main results in section 3. We provide experimental verification of the theoretical findings in section 4, before drawing our conclusions.

2 Background and Techniques

We will make use of the following results due to McDiarmid.

Theorem 1. *([12]) Let $X_1, \ldots, X_n$ be independent random variables taking values in a set A, and assume that $f : A^n \to \mathbb{R}$, and $f_i : A^{n-1} \to \mathbb{R}$ satisfy for $1 \leq i \leq n$*

$$\sup_{x_1, \ldots, x_n} |f(x_1, \ldots, x_n) - f_i(x_1, \ldots, x_{i-1}, x_{i+1}, \ldots, x_n)| \leq c_i,$$

then for all $\epsilon > 0$,

$$P\{|f(X_1, \ldots, X_n) - \mathbb{E}f(X_1, \ldots, X_n)| > \epsilon\} \leq 2 \exp\left(\frac{-2\epsilon^2}{\sum_{i=1}^n c_i^2}\right)$$

Theorem 2. *([12]) Let $X_1, \ldots, X_n$ be independent random variables taking values in a set A, and assume that $f : A^n \to \mathbb{R}$, for $1 \leq i \leq n$*

$$\sup_{x_1, \ldots, x_n, \hat{x}_i} |f(x_1, \ldots, x_n) - f(x_1, \ldots, x_{i-1}, \hat{x}_i, x_{i+1}, \ldots, x_n)| \leq c_i,$$

then for all $\epsilon > 0$,

$$P\{|f(X_1, \ldots, X_n) - \mathbb{E}f(X_1, \ldots, X_n)| > \epsilon\} \leq 2 \exp\left(\frac{-2\epsilon^2}{\sum_{i=1}^n c_i^2}\right)$$

We will also make use of the following theorem characterising the eigenvectors of a symmetric matrix.

Theorem 3 (Courant-Fischer Minimax Theorem). *If $M \in \mathbb{R}^{m \times m}$ is symmetric, then for $k = 1, \ldots, m$,*

$$\lambda_k(M) = \max_{\dim(T)=k} \min_{0 \neq \mathbf{v} \in T} \frac{\mathbf{v}'M\mathbf{v}}{\mathbf{v}'\mathbf{v}} = \min_{\dim(T)=m-k+1} \max_{0 \neq \mathbf{v} \in T} \frac{\mathbf{v}'M\mathbf{v}}{\mathbf{v}'\mathbf{v}},$$

with the extrema achieved by the corresponding eigenvector.

The approach adopted in the proofs of the next section is to view the eigenvalues as the sums of squares of residuals. This is applicable when the matrix is positive semi-definite and hence can be written as an inner product matrix $M = X'X$, where X' is the transpose of the matrix X containing the m vectors $\mathbf{x}_1, \ldots, \mathbf{x}_m$ as columns. This is the finite dimensional version of Mercer's theorem, and follows immediately if we take $X = V\sqrt{\Lambda}$, where $M = V\Lambda V'$ is the eigenvalue decomposition of M. There may be more succinct ways of representing X, but we will assume for simplicity (but without loss of generality) that X is a square matrix with the same dimensions as M. To set the scene, we now present a short description of the residuals viewpoint.

The starting point is the singular value decomposition of $X = U\Sigma V'$, where U and V are orthonormal matrices and Σ is a diagonal matrix containing the singular values (in descending order). We can now reconstruct the eigenvalue decomposition of $M = X'X = V\Sigma U'U\Sigma V' = V\Lambda V'$, where $\Lambda = \Sigma^2$. But equally we can construct a matrix $N = XX' = U\Sigma V'V\Sigma U' = U\Lambda U'$, with the same eigenvalues as M.

As a simple example consider now the first eigenvalue, which by Theorem 3 and the above observations is given by

$$\lambda_1(M) = \max_{0\neq v\in\mathbb{R}^m} \frac{v'Nv}{v'v} = \max_{0\neq v\in\mathbb{R}^m} \frac{v'XX'v}{v'v} = \max_{0\neq v\in\mathbb{R}^m} \frac{\|v'X\|^2}{v'v}$$

$$= \max_{0\neq v\in\mathbb{R}^m} \sum_{j=1}^m \|P_v(x_j)\|^2 = \sum_{j=1}^m \|x_j\|^2 - \min_{0\neq v\in\mathbb{R}^m} \sum_{j=1}^m \|P_v^\perp(x_j)\|^2$$

where $P_v(x)$ $(P_v^\perp(x))$ is the projection of x onto the space spanned by v (space perpendicular to v), since $\|x\|^2 = \|P_v(x)\|^2 + \|P_v^\perp(x)\|^2$. It follows that the first eigenvector is characterised as the direction for which sum of the squares of the residuals is minimal.

Applying the same line of reasoning to the first equality of Theorem 3, delivers the following equality

$$\lambda_k(M) = \max_{\dim(V)=k} \min_{0\neq v\in V} \sum_{j=1}^m \|P_v(x_j)\|^2. \tag{3}$$

Notice that this characterisation implies that if v^k is the k-th eigenvector of N, then

$$\lambda_k(M) = \sum_{j=1}^m \|P_{v^k}(x_j)\|^2, \tag{4}$$

which in turn implies that if V_k is the space spanned by the first k eigenvectors, then

$$\sum_{i=1}^k \lambda_i(M) = \sum_{j=1}^m \|P_{V_k}(x_j)\|^2 = \sum_{j=1}^m \|x_j\|^2 - \sum_{j=1}^m \|P_{V_k}^\perp(x_j)\|^2. \tag{5}$$

It readily follows by induction over the dimension of V that we can equally characterise the sum of the first k and last $m - k$ eigenvalues by

$$\sum_{i=1}^{k} \lambda_i(M) = \max_{\dim(V)=k} \sum_{j=1}^{m} \|P_V(\mathbf{x}_j)\|^2 = \sum_{j=1}^{m} \|\mathbf{x}_j\|^2 - \min_{\dim(V)=k} \sum_{j=1}^{m} \|P_V^\perp(\mathbf{x}_j)\|^2,$$

$$\sum_{i=k+1}^{m} \lambda_i(M) = \sum_{j=1}^{m} \|\mathbf{x}_j\|^2 - \sum_{i=1}^{k} \lambda_i(M) = \min_{\dim(V)=k} \sum_{j=1}^{m} \|P_V^\perp(\mathbf{x}_j)\|^2. \qquad (6)$$

Hence, as for the case when $k = 1$, the subspace spanned by the first k eigenvalues is characterised as that for which the sum of the squares of the residuals is minimal.

Frequently, we consider all of the above as occurring in a kernel defined feature space, so that wherever we have written a vector $\mathbf{x}$ we should have put $\psi(\mathbf{x})$, where ψ is the corresponding feature map

$$\psi : \mathbf{x} \in \mathcal{X} \longmapsto \psi(\mathbf{x}) \in F$$

to a feature space F. Hence, the matrix M has entries $M_{ij} = \langle \psi(\mathbf{x}_i), \psi(\mathbf{x}_j) \rangle$. The kernel function computes the composition of the inner product with the feature maps,

$$k(\mathbf{x}, \mathbf{z}) = \langle \psi(\mathbf{x}), \psi(\mathbf{z}) \rangle = \psi(\mathbf{x})'\psi(\mathbf{z}),$$

which can in many cases be computed without explicitly evaluating the mapping ψ. We would also like to evaluate the projections into eigenspaces without explicitly computing the feature mapping ψ.

This can be done as follows. Let $\mathbf{u}_i$ be the i-th singular vector in the feature space, that is the i-th eigenvector of the matrix N, with the corresponding singular value being $\sigma_i = \sqrt{\lambda_i}$ and the corresponding eigenvector of M being $\mathbf{v}_i$. The projection of an input $\mathbf{x}$ onto $\mathbf{u}_i$ is given by

$$\begin{aligned} \psi(\mathbf{x})'\mathbf{u}_i &= (\psi(\mathbf{x})'U)_i \\ &= (\psi(\mathbf{x})'XV)_i\sigma_i^{-1} \\ &= \mathbf{k}'\mathbf{v}_i\sigma_i^{-1}, \end{aligned}$$

where we have used the fact that $X = U\Sigma V'$ and $\mathbf{k}_j = \psi(\mathbf{x})'\psi(\mathbf{x}_j) = k(\mathbf{x}, \mathbf{x}_j)$.

Our final background observation concerns the kernel operator and its eigenspaces. The operator in question is

$$\mathcal{K}(f)(\mathbf{x}) = \int_{\mathcal{X}} k(\mathbf{x}, \mathbf{z})f(\mathbf{z})p(\mathbf{z})d\mathbf{z},$$

where $p(\mathbf{x})$ is the underlying probability density function that governs the occurrence of different examples. Note that we have moved away from a finite set of examples to a potentially uncountably infinite space $\mathcal{X}$.

Provided the operator is positive semi-definite, by Mercer's theorem we can decompose $k(\mathbf{x}, \mathbf{z})$ as a sum of eigenfunctions,

$$k(\mathbf{x}, \mathbf{z}) = \sum_{i=1}^{\infty} \lambda_i \phi_i(\mathbf{x}) \phi_i(\mathbf{z}) = \langle \boldsymbol{\psi}(\mathbf{x}), \boldsymbol{\psi}(\mathbf{z}) \rangle,$$

where $\lambda_i = \lambda_i(\mathcal{K}(f))$ the functions $(\phi_i(\mathbf{x}))_{i=1}^{\infty}$ form a complete orthonormal basis with respect to the inner product $\langle f, g \rangle_p = \int_{\mathcal{X}} f(\mathbf{x}) g(\mathbf{x}) p(\mathbf{x}) d\mathbf{x}$ and $\boldsymbol{\psi}(\mathbf{x})$ is the feature space mapping

$$\boldsymbol{\psi} : \mathbf{x} \longrightarrow (\psi_i(\mathbf{x}))_{i=1}^{\infty} = \left(\sqrt{\lambda_i} \phi_i(\mathbf{x}) \right)_{i=1}^{\infty} \in F.$$

Note that $\phi_i(\mathbf{x})$ has norm 1 and satisfies

$$\phi_i(\mathbf{x}) = \lambda_i \int_{\mathcal{X}} k(\mathbf{x}, \mathbf{z}) \phi_i(\mathbf{z}) p(\mathbf{z}) d\mathbf{z} ,$$

so that

$$\int_{\mathcal{X}^2} k(\mathbf{x}, \mathbf{z}) \phi_i(\mathbf{x}) \phi_i(\mathbf{z}) p(\mathbf{z}) p(\mathbf{z}) d\mathbf{y} d\mathbf{z} = \lambda_i.$$

If we let $\boldsymbol{\phi}(\mathbf{x}) = (\phi_i(\mathbf{x}))_{i=1}^{\infty} \in F$, we can define the unit vector $\mathbf{u}_i \in F$ corresponding to λ_i by

$$\mathbf{u}_i = \int_{\mathcal{X}} \phi_i(\mathbf{x}) \boldsymbol{\phi}(\mathbf{x}) p(\mathbf{x}) d\mathbf{x} = \mathbf{e}_i.$$

For a general function $f(\mathbf{x})$ we can similarly define the vector

$$\mathbf{f} = \int_{\mathcal{X}} f(\mathbf{x}) \boldsymbol{\phi}(\mathbf{x}) p(\mathbf{x}) d\mathbf{x}.$$

Now the expected square of the norm of the projection $P_{\mathbf{f}}(\boldsymbol{\psi}(\mathbf{x}))$ onto the vector $\mathbf{f}$ (assumed to be of norm 1) of an input $\boldsymbol{\psi}(\mathbf{x})$ drawn according to $p(\mathbf{x})$ is given by

$$\mathbb{E}\left[\|P_{\mathbf{f}}(\boldsymbol{\psi}(\mathbf{x}))\|^2 \right] = \int_{\mathcal{X}} \|P_{\mathbf{f}}(\boldsymbol{\psi}(\mathbf{x}))\|^2 p(\mathbf{x}) d\mathbf{x} = \int_{\mathcal{X}} \left(\mathbf{f}' \boldsymbol{\psi}(\mathbf{x}) \right)^2 p(\mathbf{x}) d\mathbf{x}$$

$$= \int_{\mathcal{X}} \int_{\mathcal{X}} \int_{\mathcal{X}} f(\mathbf{y}) \boldsymbol{\phi}(\mathbf{y})' \boldsymbol{\psi}(\mathbf{x}) p(\mathbf{y}) d\mathbf{y} f(\mathbf{z}) \boldsymbol{\phi}(\mathbf{z})' \boldsymbol{\psi}(\mathbf{x}) p(\mathbf{z}) d\mathbf{z} p(\mathbf{x}) d\mathbf{x}$$

$$= \int_{\mathcal{X}^3} f(\mathbf{y}) f(\mathbf{z}) \sum_{j=1}^{\infty} \sqrt{\lambda_j} \phi_j(\mathbf{y}) \phi_j(\mathbf{x}) p(\mathbf{y}) d\mathbf{y} \sum_{\ell=1}^{\infty} \sqrt{\lambda_\ell} \phi_\ell(\mathbf{z}) \phi_\ell(\mathbf{x}) p(\mathbf{z}) d\mathbf{z} p(\mathbf{x}) d\mathbf{x}$$

$$= \int_{\mathcal{X}^2} f(\mathbf{y}) f(\mathbf{z}) \sum_{j,\ell=1}^{\infty} \sqrt{\lambda_j} \phi_j(\mathbf{y}) p(\mathbf{y}) d\mathbf{y} \sqrt{\lambda_\ell} \phi_\ell(\mathbf{z}) p(\mathbf{z}) d\mathbf{z} \int_{\mathcal{X}} \phi_j(\mathbf{x}) \phi_\ell(\mathbf{x}) p(\mathbf{x}) d\mathbf{x}$$

$$= \int_{\mathcal{X}^2} f(\mathbf{y}) f(\mathbf{z}) \sum_{j=1}^{\infty} \lambda_j \phi_j(\mathbf{y}) \phi_j(\mathbf{z}) p(\mathbf{y}) d\mathbf{y} p(\mathbf{z}) d\mathbf{z}$$

$$= \int_{\mathcal{X}^2} f(\mathbf{y}) f(\mathbf{z}) k(\mathbf{y}, \mathbf{z}) p(\mathbf{y}) p(\mathbf{z}) d\mathbf{y} d\mathbf{z}.$$

Since all vectors $\mathbf{f}$ in the subspace spanned by the image of the input space in F can be expressed in this fashion, it follows that the sum of the finite case characterisation of eigenvalues and eigenvectors is replaced by an expectation

$$\lambda_k(\mathcal{K}(f)) = \max_{\dim(V)=k} \min_{0 \neq \mathbf{v} \in V} \mathbb{E}[\|P_{\mathbf{v}}(\boldsymbol{\psi}(\mathbf{x}))\|^2], \tag{7}$$

where V is a linear subspace of the feature space F. Similarly,

$$\sum_{i=1}^{k} \lambda_i(\mathcal{K}(f)) = \max_{\dim(V)=k} \mathbb{E}\left[\|P_V(\boldsymbol{\psi}(\mathbf{x}))\|^2\right]$$

$$= \mathbb{E}\left[\|\boldsymbol{\psi}(\mathbf{x})\|^2\right] - \min_{\dim(V)=k} \mathbb{E}\left[\|P_V^\perp(\boldsymbol{\psi}(\mathbf{x}))\|^2\right],$$

$$\sum_{i=k+1}^{\infty} \lambda_i(\mathcal{K}(f)) = \mathbb{E}\left[\|\boldsymbol{\psi}(\mathbf{x})\|^2\right] - \sum_{i=1}^{k} \lambda_i(\mathcal{K}(f)) = \min_{\dim(V)=k} \mathbb{E}\left[\|P_V^\perp(\boldsymbol{\psi}(\mathbf{x}))\|^2\right] \tag{8}$$

where $P_V(\boldsymbol{\psi}(\mathbf{x}))$ $(P_V^\perp(\boldsymbol{\psi}(\mathbf{x})))$ is the projection of $\boldsymbol{\psi}(\mathbf{x})$ into the subspace V (the projection of $\boldsymbol{\psi}(\mathbf{x})$ into the space orthogonal to V).

We are now in a position to motivate the main results of the paper. We consider the general case of a kernel defined feature space with input space $\mathcal{X}$ and probability density $p(\mathbf{x})$. We fix a sample size m and a draw of m examples $S = (\mathbf{x}_1, \mathbf{x}_2, \ldots, \mathbf{x}_m)$ according to p. We fix the feature space determined by the kernel as given by the mapping $\boldsymbol{\psi}$ using the process eigenfunctions. We can therefore view the eigenvectors of correlation matrices corresponding to finite Gram matrices as lying in this space. Further we fix a feature dimension k. Let $\hat{V}_k$ be the space spanned by the first k eigenvectors of the correlation matrix corresponding to the sample kernel matrix K with corresponding eigenvalues $\hat{\lambda}_1, \hat{\lambda}_2, \ldots, \hat{\lambda}_k$, while V_k is the space spanned by the first k process eigenvectors with corresponding eigenvalues $\lambda_1, \lambda_2, \ldots, \lambda_k$. Similarly, let $\hat{\mathbb{E}}[f(\mathbf{x})]$ denote expectation with respect to the sample,

$$\hat{\mathbb{E}}[f(\mathbf{x})] = \frac{1}{m} \sum_{i=1}^{m} f(\mathbf{x}_i),$$

while as before $\mathbb{E}[\cdot]$ denotes expectation with respect to p.

We are interested in the relationships between the following quantities:

$$\hat{\mathbb{E}}\left[\|P_{\hat{V}_k}(\boldsymbol{\psi}(\mathbf{x}))\|^2\right] = \frac{1}{m} \sum_{i=1}^{k} \hat{\lambda}_i = \sum_{i=1}^{k} \mu_i$$

$$\mathbb{E}\left[\|P_{V_k}(\boldsymbol{\psi}(\mathbf{x}))\|^2\right] = \sum_{i=1}^{k} \lambda_i$$

$$\mathbb{E}\left[\|P_{\hat{V}_k}(\boldsymbol{\psi}(\mathbf{x}))\|^2\right] \text{ and } \hat{\mathbb{E}}\left[\|P_{V_k}(\boldsymbol{\psi}(\mathbf{x}))\|^2\right].$$

Bounding the difference between the first and second will relate the process eigenvalues to the sample eigenvalues, while the difference between the first and third will bound the expected performance of the space identified by kernel PCA when used on new data.

Our first two observations follow simply from equation (8),

$$\hat{\mathbb{E}}\left[\|P_{\hat{V}_k}(\boldsymbol{\psi}(\mathbf{x}))\|^2\right] = \frac{1}{m}\sum_{i=1}^{k}\hat{\lambda}_i \geq \hat{\mathbb{E}}\left[\|P_{V_k}(\boldsymbol{\psi}(\mathbf{x}))\|^2\right], \tag{9}$$

$$\text{and} \quad \mathbb{E}\left[\|P_{V_k}(\boldsymbol{\psi}(\mathbf{x}))\|^2\right] = \sum_{i=1}^{k}\lambda_i \geq \mathbb{E}\left[\|P_{\hat{V}_k}(\boldsymbol{\psi}(\mathbf{x}))\|^2\right] \tag{10}$$

Our strategy will be to show that the right hand side of inequality (9) and the left hand side of inequality (10) are close in value making the two inequalities approximately a chain of inequalities. We then bound the difference between the first and last entries in the chain.

First, however, in the next section we will examine averages over random m samples. We will use the notation $\mathbb{E}_m[\cdot]$ to denote this type of average.

3   Averaging over Samples and Population Eigenvalues

Consider a zero-mean random variable $\mathbf{X} \in \mathbb{R}^p$. Let m samples drawn from $p(\mathbf{X})$ be stored in the $p \times m$ data matrix X. The the sample estimate for the covariance matrix is $S_X = \frac{1}{m}XX'$. Let the eigenvalues of S_X be $\mu_1 \geq \mu_2 \ldots \geq \mu_p$. By the results above these are the same as the eigenvalues of the matrix $\frac{1}{m}X'X$. Note that in the notation of the previous section $\mu_i = (1/m)\hat{\lambda}_i$. The corresponding population covariance be denoted Σ, with eigenvalues $\lambda_1 \geq \lambda_2 \ldots \geq \lambda_p$ and eigenvectors $\mathbf{u}_1, \ldots, \mathbf{u}_p$. Again by the observations above these are the process eigenvalues.

Statisticians have been interested in the sampling distribution of the eigenvalues of S_X for some time. There are two main approaches to studying this problem, as discussed in section 6 of [7]. In the case that $p(\mathbf{X})$ has a multivariate normal distribution, the exact sampling distribution of $\mu_1, \ldots, \mu_p$ can be given [8]. Alternatively, the "delta method" can be used, expanding the sample roots about the population roots. For normal populations this has been carried out by [11] (if there are no repeated roots of the population covariance) and [1] (for the general case), and extended by [16] to the non-Gaussian case.

The following proposition describes how $\mathbb{E}_m[\mu_1]$ is related to λ_1 and $\mathbb{E}_m[\mu_p]$ is related to λ_p. It requires no assumption of Gaussianity.

Proposition 1 (Anderson, 1963, pp 145-146). $\mathbb{E}_m[\mu_1] \geq \lambda_1$ *and* $\mathbb{E}_m[\mu_p] \leq \lambda_p$.

Proof: By the results of the previous section we have

$$\mu_1 = \max_{0 \neq \mathbf{c}}\sum_{i=1}^{m}\frac{1}{m}\|P_{\mathbf{c}}(\mathbf{x}_i)\|^2 \geq \frac{1}{m}\sum_{i=1}^{m}\|P_{\mathbf{u}_1}(\mathbf{x}_i)\|^2 = \hat{\mathbb{E}}\left[\|P_{\mathbf{u}_1}(\mathbf{x})\|^2\right].$$

We now apply the expectation operator $\mathbb{E}_m$ to both sides. On the RHS we get

$$\mathbb{E}_m \hat{\mathbb{E}} \left[\|P_{\mathbf{u}_1}(\mathbf{x})\|^2 \right] = \mathbb{E} \left[\|P_{\mathbf{u}_1}(\mathbf{x})\|^2 \right] = \lambda_1$$

by equation (8), which completes the proof. Correspondingly μ_p is characterized by $\mu_p = \min_{0 \neq \mathbf{c}} \hat{\mathbb{E}} \left[\|P_{\mathbf{c}}(\mathbf{x}_i)\|^2 \right]$ (minor components analysis). $\square$

Interpreting this result, we see that $\mathbb{E}_m[\mu_1]$ *overestimates* λ_1, while $\mathbb{E}_m[\mu_p]$ *underestimates* λ_p.

Proposition 1 can be generalized to give the following result where we have also allowed for a kernel defined feature space of dimension $N_F \leq \infty$.

Proposition 2. *Using the above notation, for any* k, $1 \leq k \leq m$,
$\mathbb{E}_m[\sum_{i=1}^{k} \mu_i] \geq \sum_{i=1}^{k} \lambda_i$ *and* $\mathbb{E}_m[\sum_{i=k+1}^{m} \mu_i] \leq \sum_{i=k+1}^{N_F} \lambda_i$.

Proof: Let V_k be the space spanned by the first k process eigenvectors. Then from the derivations above we have

$$\sum_{i=1}^{k} \mu_i = \max_{V: \dim V = k} \hat{\mathbb{E}} \left[\|P_V(\psi(\mathbf{x}))\|^2 \right] \geq \hat{\mathbb{E}} \left[\|P_{V_k}(\psi(\mathbf{x}))\|^2 \right].$$

Again, applying the expectation operator $\mathbb{E}_m$ to both sides of this equation and taking equation (8) into account, the first inequality follows. To prove the second we turn max into min, P into $P^\perp$ and reverse the inequality. Again taking expectations of both sides proves the second part. $\square$

Furthermore, [11] (section 4) gives the asymptotic relationship

$$\mathbb{E}_m[\mu_i] = \lambda_i + \frac{1}{m} \sum_{j=1, j \neq i}^{p} \frac{\lambda_i \lambda_j}{\lambda_i - \lambda_j} + O(m^{-2}). \tag{11}$$

Note that this is consistent with Proposition 2.

Proposition 2 also implies that

$$\mathbb{E}_{N_F} \left[\sum_{i=1}^{N_F} \mu_i \right] = \sum_{i=1}^{N_F} \lambda_i$$

if we sample N_F points.

We can tighten this relation and obtain another relationship from the trace of the matrix when the support of p satisfies $k(\mathbf{x}, \mathbf{x}) = C$, a constant. For example if the kernel is stationary, this holds since $k(\mathbf{x}, \mathbf{x}) = k(\mathbf{x} - \mathbf{x}) = k(\mathbf{0}) = C$. Thus

$$\text{trace} \left(\frac{1}{m} K \right) = C = \sum_{i=1}^{m} \mu_i.$$

Also we have for the continuous eigenproblem $\int_{\mathcal{X}} k(\mathbf{x}, \mathbf{x}) p(\mathbf{x}) d\mathbf{x} = C$. Using the feature expansion representation of the kernel $k(\mathbf{x}, \mathbf{y}) = \sum_{i=1}^{N_F} \lambda_i \phi_i(\mathbf{x}) \phi_i(\mathbf{y})$ and the orthonormality of the eigenfunctions we obtain the following result

$$\sum_{i=1}^{m} \mu_i = \sum_{i=1}^{N_F} \lambda_i.$$

Applying the results obtained in this section, it follows that $\mathbb{E}_m[\mu_1]$ will overestimate λ_1, and the cumulative sum $\sum_{i=1}^{k} \mathbb{E}_m[\mu_i]$ will overestimate $\sum_{i=1}^{k} \lambda_i$. At the other end, clearly for $N_F \geq k > m$, $\mu_k \equiv 0$ is an underestimate of λ_k.

4   Concentration of Eigenvalues

Section 2 outlined the relatively well-known perspective that we now apply to obtain the concentration results for the eigenvalues of positive semi-definite matrices. The key to the results is the characterisation in terms of the sums of residuals given in equations (3) and (6). Note that these results (Theorems 4 to 6) are reproduced from [15].

Theorem 4. *Let $k(\mathbf{x}, \mathbf{z})$ be a positive semi-definite kernel function on a space X, and let p be a probability density function on X. Fix natural numbers m and $1 \leq k < m$ and let $S = (\mathbf{x}_1, \ldots, \mathbf{x}_m) \in X^m$ be a sample of m points drawn according to p. Then for all $\epsilon > 0$,*

$$P\left\{ \left| \frac{1}{m}\hat{\lambda}_k(S) - \mathbb{E}_m\left[\frac{1}{m}\hat{\lambda}_k(S)\right] \right| \geq \epsilon \right\} \leq 2\exp\left(\frac{-2\epsilon^2 m}{R^4}\right),$$

where $\hat{\lambda}_k(S)$ is the k-th eigenvalue of the matrix $K(S)$ with entries $K(S)_{ij} = k(\mathbf{x}_i, \mathbf{x}_j)$ and $R^2 = \max_{\mathbf{x} \in X} k(\mathbf{x}, \mathbf{x})$.

Proof: The result follows from an application of Theorem 1 provided

$$\sup_{S} \left| \frac{1}{m}\hat{\lambda}_k(S) - \frac{1}{m}\hat{\lambda}_k(S \setminus \{\mathbf{x}_i\}) \right| \leq R^2/m.$$

Let $\hat{S} = S \setminus \{\mathbf{x}_i\}$ and let V ($\hat{V}$) be the k dimensional subspace spanned by the first k eigenvectors of $K(S)$ ($K(\hat{S})$). Let k correspond to the feature mapping ψ. Using equation (3) we have

$$\hat{\lambda}_k(S) \geq \min_{v \in \hat{V}} \sum_{j=1}^{m} \|P_v(\psi(\mathbf{x}_j))\|^2 \geq \min_{v \in \hat{V}} \sum_{j \neq i} \|P_v(\psi(\mathbf{x}_j))\|^2 = \hat{\lambda}_k(\hat{S})$$

$$\hat{\lambda}_k(\hat{S}) \geq \min_{v \in V} \sum_{j \neq i} \|P_v(\psi(\mathbf{x}_j))\|^2 \geq \min_{v \in V} \sum_{j=1}^{m} \|P_v(\psi(\mathbf{x}_j))\|^2 - R^2 = \hat{\lambda}_k(S) - R^2. \ \square$$

Surprisingly a very similar result holds when we consider the sum of the last $m - k$ eigenvalues or the first k eigenvalues.

Theorem 5. *Let $k(\mathbf{x}, \mathbf{z})$ be a positive semi-definite kernel function on a space X, and let p be a probability density function on X. Fix natural numbers m and*

$1 \leq k < m$ and let $S = (\mathbf{x}_1, \ldots, \mathbf{x}_m) \in X^m$ be a sample of m points drawn according to p. Then for all $\epsilon > 0$,

$$P\left\{\left|\frac{1}{m}\hat{\lambda}^{>k}(S) - \mathbb{E}_m\left[\frac{1}{m}\hat{\lambda}^{>k}(S)\right]\right| \geq \epsilon\right\} \leq 2\exp\left(\frac{-2\epsilon^2 m}{R^4}\right),$$

and $$P\left\{\left|\frac{1}{m}\hat{\lambda}^{\leq k}(S) - \mathbb{E}_m\left[\frac{1}{m}\hat{\lambda}^{\leq k}(S)\right]\right| \geq \epsilon\right\} \leq 2\exp\left(\frac{-2\epsilon^2 m}{R^4}\right),$$

where $\hat{\lambda}^{\leq k}(S)$ $(\hat{\lambda}^{>k}(S))$ is the sum of (all but) the largest k eigenvalues of the matrix $K(S)$ with entries $K(S)_{ij} = k(\mathbf{x}_i, \mathbf{x}_j)$ and $R^2 = \max_{\mathbf{x} \in X} k(\mathbf{x}, \mathbf{x})$.

Proof: The result follows from an application of Theorem 1 provided

$$\sup_S \left|\frac{1}{m}\hat{\lambda}^{>k}(S) - \frac{1}{m}\hat{\lambda}^{>k}(S \setminus \{\mathbf{x}_i\})\right| \leq R^2/m.$$

Let $\hat{S} = S \setminus \{\mathbf{x}_i\}$ and let V $(\hat{V})$ be the k dimensional subspace spanned by the first k eigenvectors of $K(S)$ $(K(\hat{S}))$. Let k correspond to the feature mapping $\boldsymbol{\psi}$. Using equation (6) we have

$$\hat{\lambda}^{>k}(S) \leq \sum_{j=1}^m \|P_{\hat{V}}^\perp(\boldsymbol{\psi}(\mathbf{x}_j))\|^2 \leq \sum_{j \neq i} \|P_{\hat{V}}^\perp(\boldsymbol{\psi}(\mathbf{x}_j))\|^2 + R^2 = \hat{\lambda}^{>k}(\hat{S}) + R^2$$

$$\lambda^{>k}(\hat{S}) \leq \sum_{j \neq i} \|P_V^\perp(\boldsymbol{\psi}(\mathbf{x}_j))\|^2 = \sum_{j=1}^m \|P_V^\perp(\boldsymbol{\psi}(\mathbf{x}_j))\|^2 - \|P_V^\perp(\boldsymbol{\psi}(\mathbf{x}_i))\|^2 \leq \lambda^{>k}(S).$$

A similar derivation proves the second inequality. □

Our next result concerns the concentration of the residuals with respect to a fixed subspace. For a subspace V and training set S, we introduce the notation

$$\bar{P}_V(S) = \hat{\mathbb{E}}\left[\|P_V(\boldsymbol{\psi}(\mathbf{x}))\|^2\right].$$

Theorem 6. Let p be a probability density function on X. Fix natural numbers m and a subspace V and let $S = (\mathbf{x}_1, \ldots, \mathbf{x}_m) \in X^m$ be a sample of m points drawn according to a probability density function p. Then for all $\epsilon > 0$,

$$P\{\bar{P}_V(S) - \mathbb{E}_m[\bar{P}_V(S)]| \geq \epsilon\} \leq 2\exp\left(\frac{-\epsilon^2 m}{2R^4}\right).$$

Proof: The result follows from an application of Theorem 2 provided

$$\sup_{S, \hat{\mathbf{x}}_i} |\bar{P}_V(S) - \bar{P}(S \setminus \{\mathbf{x}_i\} \cup \{\hat{\mathbf{x}}_i\})| \leq R^2/m.$$

Clearly the largest change will occur if one of the points $\boldsymbol{\psi}(\mathbf{x}_i)$ and $\boldsymbol{\psi}(\hat{\mathbf{x}}_i)$ is lies in the subspace V and the other does not. In this case the change will be at most R^2/m. □

The concentration results of this section are very tight. In the notation of the earlier sections they show that with high probability

$$\hat{\mathbb{E}}\left[\|P_{\hat{V}_k}(\psi(\mathbf{x}))\|^2\right] = \frac{1}{m}\sum_{i=1}^{k}\hat{\lambda}_i \approx \mathbb{E}_m\left[\hat{\mathbb{E}}\left[\|P_{\hat{V}_k}(\psi(\mathbf{x}))\|^2\right]\right] = \mathbb{E}_m\left[\frac{1}{m}\sum_{i=1}^{k}\hat{\lambda}_i\right]$$

and $$\mathbb{E}\left[\|P_{V_k}(\psi(\mathbf{x}))\|^2\right] = \sum_{i=1}^{k}\lambda_i \approx \hat{\mathbb{E}}\left[\|P_{V_k}(\psi(\mathbf{x}))\|^2\right],\qquad(12)$$

where we have used Theorem 5 to obtain the first approximate equality and Theorem 6 with $V = V_k$ to obtain the second approximate equality.

This gives the sought relationship to create an approximate chain of inequalities

$$\hat{\mathbb{E}}\left[\|P_{\hat{V}_k}(\psi(\mathbf{x}))\|^2\right] = \frac{1}{m}\sum_{i=1}^{k}\hat{\lambda}_i \geq \hat{\mathbb{E}}\left[\|P_{V_k}(\psi(\mathbf{x}))\|^2\right]$$

$$\approx \mathbb{E}\left[\|P_{V_k}(\psi(\mathbf{x}))\|^2\right] = \sum_{i=1}^{k}\lambda_i \geq \mathbb{E}\left[\|P_{\hat{V}_k}(\psi(\mathbf{x}))\|^2\right].\ (13)$$

Notice that using Proposition 2 we also obtain the following diagram of approximate relationships

$$\hat{\mathbb{E}}\left[\|P_{\hat{V}_k}(\psi(\mathbf{x}))\|^2\right] = \frac{1}{m}\sum_{i=1}^{k}\hat{\lambda}_i \geq \qquad \hat{\mathbb{E}}\left[\|P_{V_k}(\psi(\mathbf{x}))\|^2\right]$$
$$\approx \qquad\qquad\qquad \approx$$
$$\mathbb{E}_m\left[\frac{1}{m}\sum_{i=1}^{k}\hat{\lambda}_i\right] \qquad \geq \mathbb{E}\left[\|P_{V_k}(\psi(\mathbf{x}))\|^2\right] = \sum_{i=1}^{k}\lambda_i.$$

Hence, the approximate chain could have been obtained in two ways. It remains to bound the difference between the first and last entries in this chain. This together with the concentration results of this section will deliver the required bounds on the differences between empirical and process eigenvalues, as well as providing a performance bound on kernel PCA.

5   Learning a Projection Matrix

The key observation that enables the analysis bounding the difference between

$$\hat{\mathbb{E}}\left[\|P_{\hat{V}_k}(\psi(\mathbf{x}))\|^2\right] = \frac{1}{m}\sum_{i=1}^{k}\hat{\lambda}_i$$

and $\mathbb{E}\left[\|P_{\hat{V}_k}(\psi(\mathbf{x}))\|^2\right]$ is that we can view the projection norm $\|P_{\hat{V}_k}(\psi(\mathbf{x}))\|^2$ as a linear function of pairs of features from the feature space F.

Proposition 3. *The projection norm* $\|P_{\hat{V}_k}(\psi(\mathbf{x}))\|^2$ *as a linear function* $\hat{f}$ *in a feature space* $\hat{F}$ *for which the kernel function is given by*

$$\hat{k}(\mathbf{x}, \mathbf{z}) = k(\mathbf{x}, \mathbf{z})^2.$$

Furthermore the 2-norm of the function $\hat{f}$ *is* $\sqrt{k}$.

Proof: Let $X = U\Sigma V'$ be the singular value decomposition of the sample matrix X in the feature space. The projection norm is then given by

$$\hat{f}(\mathbf{x}) = \|P_{\hat{V}_k}(\boldsymbol{\psi}(\mathbf{x}))\|^2 = \boldsymbol{\psi}(\mathbf{x})'U_k U_k'\boldsymbol{\psi}(\mathbf{x}),$$

where U_k is the matrix containing the first k columns of U. Hence we can write

$$\|P_{\hat{V}_k}(\boldsymbol{\psi}(\mathbf{x}))\|^2 = \sum_{ij=1}^{N_F} \alpha_{ij}\boldsymbol{\psi}(\mathbf{x})_i\boldsymbol{\psi}(\mathbf{x})_j = \sum_{ij=1}^{N_F} \alpha_{ij}\hat{\boldsymbol{\psi}}(\mathbf{x})_{ij},$$

where $\hat{\boldsymbol{\psi}}$ is the projection mapping into the feature space $\hat{F}$ consisting of all pairs of F features and $\alpha_{ij} = (U_k U_k')_{ij}$. The standard polynomial construction gives

$$\hat{k}(\mathbf{x}, \mathbf{z}) = k(\mathbf{x}, \mathbf{z})^2 = \left(\sum_{i=1}^{N_F} \boldsymbol{\psi}(\mathbf{x})_i\boldsymbol{\psi}(\mathbf{z})_i\right)^2$$

$$= \sum_{i,j=1}^{N_F} \boldsymbol{\psi}(\mathbf{x})_i\boldsymbol{\psi}(\mathbf{z})_i\boldsymbol{\psi}(\mathbf{x})_j\boldsymbol{\psi}(\mathbf{z})_j = \sum_{i,j=1}^{N_F} (\boldsymbol{\psi}(\mathbf{x})_i\boldsymbol{\psi}(\mathbf{x})_j)(\boldsymbol{\psi}(\mathbf{z})_i\boldsymbol{\psi}(\mathbf{z})_j)$$

$$= \left\langle \hat{\boldsymbol{\psi}}(\mathbf{x}), \hat{\boldsymbol{\psi}}(\mathbf{z}) \right\rangle_{\hat{F}}.$$

It remains to show that the norm of the linear function is k. The norm satisfies (note that $\|\cdot\|_F$ denotes the Frobenius norm and $\mathbf{u}_i$ the columns of U)

$$\|\hat{f}\|^2 = \sum_{i,j=1}^{N_F} \alpha_{ij}^2 = \|U_k U_k'\|_F^2 = \left\langle \sum_{i=1}^{k} \mathbf{u}_i\mathbf{u}_i', \sum_{j=1}^{k} \mathbf{u}_j\mathbf{u}_j' \right\rangle_F = \sum_{i,j=1}^{k} (\mathbf{u}_i'\mathbf{u}_j)^2 = k$$

as required. $\square$

We are now in a position to apply a learning theory bound where we consider a regression problem for which the target output is the square of the norm of the sample point $\|\boldsymbol{\psi}(\mathbf{x})\|^2$. We restrict the linear function in the space $\hat{F}$ to have norm $\sqrt{k}$. The loss function is then the shortfall between the output of $\hat{f}$ and the squared norm. If we scale this with a factor $1/R^2$ the output is in the range $[0, 1]$ and we can apply Theorem 17.7 of [2].

Due to space limitations we will not quote a detailed result of this type here. The expected squared residual of a random test point is with probability $1 - \delta$ bounded by

$$O\left(R^2\epsilon + \frac{1}{m}\sum_{i=k+1}^{m} \hat{\lambda}_i\right),$$

where ϵ is chosen so that

$$\epsilon^2 = \frac{c}{m}\left[\frac{k}{\epsilon^2}\log\frac{1}{\epsilon}\log\frac{m}{\epsilon} + \log\frac{1}{\delta}\right],$$

where c is a constant, $R^2 = \max_i k(\mathbf{x}_i, \mathbf{x}_i)$, k is the projection dimension. The second factor is the average residue after the projection of the training set or in other words the sum of the remaining eigenvalues divided by the sample size. The size of the difference between the expected 2-norm residual and the training set estimate depends on the dimension of the projection space and the number of training examples. For a non-trivial bound the number of examples must be much larger than the projection dimension.

6 Experiments

In order to test the concentration results we performed experiments with the Breast cancer data using a cubic polynomial kernel. The kernel was chosen to ensure that the spectrum did not decay too fast.

We randomly selected 50% of the data as a 'training' set and kept the remaining 50% as a 'test' set. We centered the whole data set so that the origin of the feature space is placed at the centre of gravity of the training set. We then performed an eigenvalue decomposition of the training set. The sum of the eigenvalues greater than the k-th gives the sum of the residual squared norms of the training points when we project onto the space spanned by the first k eigenvectors. Dividing this by the average of all the eigenvalues (which measures the average square norm of the training points in the transformed space) gives a fraction residual not captured in the k dimensional projection. This quantity was averaged over 5 random splits and plotted against dimension in Figure 2 as the continuous line. The error bars give one standard deviation. The Figure 2a shows the full spectrum, while Figure 2b shows a zoomed in subwindow. The very tight error bars show clearly the very tight concentration of the sums of tail of eigenvalues as predicted by Theorem 5.

In order to test the concentration results for subsets we measured the residuals of the test points when they are projected into the subspace spanned by the first k eigenvectors generated above for the training set. The dashed lines in Figure 2 show the ratio of the average squares of these residuals to the average squared norm of the test points. We see the two curves tracking each other very closely, indicating that the subspace identified as optimal for the training set is indeed capturing almost the same amount of information in the test points.

7 Conclusions

The paper has shown that the eigenvalues of a positive semi-definite matrix generated from a random sample is concentrated. Furthermore the sum of the last $m - k$ eigenvalues is similarly concentrated as is the residual when the data is projected into a fixed subspace.

Furthermore, we have shown that estimating the projection subspace on a random sample can give a good model for future data provided the number of examples is much larger than the dimension of the subspace. The results provide

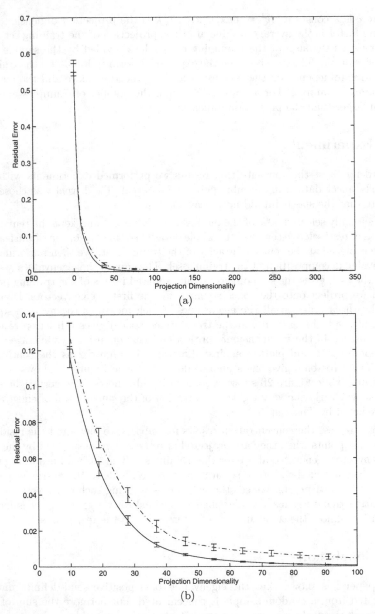

Fig. 2. Plots of the fraction of the average squared norm captured in the subspace spanned by the first k eigenvectors for different values of k. Continuous line is fraction for training set, while the dashed line is for the test set. (a) shows the full spectrum, while (b) zooms in on an interesting portion.

a basis for performing PCA or kernel-PCA from a randomly generated sample, as they confirm that the subset identified by the sample will indeed 'generalise' in the sense that it will capture most of the information in a test sample.

Experiments are presented that confirm the theoretical predictions on a real world data-set for small projection dimensions. For larger projection dimensions the theory is unable to make confident predictions, though in practice the residuals became very small in the examples tested. This phenomenon suggests that the theory is unable to accurately model the case when the residuals are very small but the dimension approaches the training set size.

Further research should look at the question of how the space identified by a subsample relates to the eigenspace of the underlying kernel operator since this is not guaranteed by the bounds obtained.

Acknowledgements. CW thank Matthias Seeger for comments on an earlier version of the paper. We would like to acknowledge the financial support of EPSRC Grant No. GR/N08575, EU Project KerMIT, No. IST-2000-25341 and the Neurocolt working group No. 27150.

References

[1] T. W. Anderson. Asymptotic Theory for Principal Component Analysis. *Annals of Mathematical Statistics*, 34(1):122–148, 1963.

[2] M. Anthony and P. Bartlett. *Learning in Neural Networks: Theoretical Foundations*. Cambridge, England: Cambridge University Press, 1999.

[3] C. T. H. Baker. *The numerical treatment of integral equations*. Clarendon Press, Oxford, 1977.

[4] S. Brin and L. Page. The anatomy of a large-scale hypertextual (web) search engine. In *Proceedings of the Seventh International World Wide Web Conference*, 1998.

[5] N. Cristianini and J. Shawe-Taylor. *An Introduction to Support Vector Machines*. Cambridge University Press, 2000.

[6] Nello Cristianini, Huma Lodhi, and John Shawe-Taylor. Latent semantic kernels for feature selection. Technical Report NC-TR-00-080, NeuroCOLT Working Group, http://www.neurocolt.org, 2000.

[7] M. L. Eaton and D. E. Tyler. On Wielandt's Inequality and Its Application to the Asymptotic Distribution of the Eigenvalues of a Random Symmetric Matrix. *Annals of Statistics*, 19(1):260–271, 1991.

[8] A. T. James. The distribution of the latent roots of the covariance matrix. *Annals of Math. Stat.*, 31:151–158, 1960.

[9] J. Kleinberg. Authoritative sources in a hyperlinked environment. In *Proceedings of 9th ACM-SIAM Symposium on Discrete Algorithms*, 1998.

[10] V. Koltchinskii and E. Gine. Random matrix approximation of spectra of integral operators. *Bernoulli*, 6(1):113–167, 2000.

[11] D. N. Lawley. Tests of Significance for the Latent Roots of Covariance and Correlation Matrices. *Biometrika*, 43(1/2):128–136, 1956.

[12] C. McDiarmid. On the method of bounded differences. In *Surveys in Combinatorics 1989*, pages 148–188. Cambridge University Press, 1989.

[13] S. Mika, B. Schölkopf, A. Smola, K.-R. Müller, M. Scholz, and G. Rätsch. Kernel PCA and de-noising in feature spaces. In *Advances in Neural Information Processing Systems 11*, 1998.

[14] Andrew Y. Ng, Alice X. Zheng, and Michael I. Jordan. Link analysis, eigenvectors and stability. In *To appear in the Seventeenth International Joint Conference on Artificial Intelligence (IJCAI-01)*, 2001.

[15] J. Shawe-Taylor, N. Cristianini, and J. Kandola. On the Concentration of Spectral Properties. In T. G. Diettrich, S. Becker, and Z. Ghahramani, editors, *Advances in Neural Information Processing Systems 14*. MIT Press, 2002.

[16] C. M. Waternaux. Asymptotic Distribution of the Sample Roots for a Nonnormal Population. *Biometrika*, 63(3):639–645, 1976.

[17] C. K. I. Williams and M. Seeger. The Effect of the Input Density Distribution on Kernel-based Classifiers. In P. Langley, editor, *Proceedings of the Seventeenth International Conference on Machine Learning (ICML 2000)*. Morgan Kaufmann, 2000.

[18] H. Zhu, C. K. I. Williams, R. J. Rohwer, and M. Morciniec. Gaussian regression and optimal finite dimensional linear models. In C. M. Bishop, editor, *Neural Networks and Machine Learning*. Springer-Verlag, Berlin, 1998.

In Search of the Horowitz Factor: Interim Report on a Musical Discovery Project*

Gerhard Widmer

Department of Medical Cybernetics and Artificial Intelligence,
University of Vienna, Austria, and
Austrian Research Institute for Artificial Intelligence, Vienna
gerhard@ai.univie.ac.at

Abstract. The paper gives an overview of an inter-disciplinary research project whose goal is to elucidate the complex phenomenon of *expressive music performance* with the help of machine learning and automated discovery methods. The general research questions that guide the project are laid out, and some of the most important results achieved so far are briefly summarized (with an emphasis on the most recent and still very speculative work). A broad view of the discovery process is given, from data acquisition issues through data visualization to inductive model building and pattern discovery. It is shown that it is indeed possible for a machine to make novel and interesting discoveries even in a domain like music. The report closes with a few general lessons learned and with the identification of a number of open and challenging research problems.

---

* The full version of this paper is published in the Proceedings of the 5th International Conference on Discovery Science, Lecture Notes in Artificial Intelligence Vol. 2534

N. Cesa-Bianchi et al. (Eds.): ALT 2002, LNAI 2533, p. 41, 2002.

Learning Structure from Sequences, with Applications in a Digital Library

Ian H. Witten

Department of Computer Science, University of Waikato
Hamilton, New Zealand
ihw@cs.waikato.ac.nz

Abstract. The services that digital libraries provide to users can be greatly enhanced by automatically gleaning certain kinds of information from the full text of the documents they contain. This paper reviews some recent work that applies novel techniques of machine learning (broadly interpreted) to extract information from plain text, and puts it in the context of digital library applications. We describe three areas: hierarchical phrase browsing, including efficient methods for inferring a phrase hierarchy from a large corpus of text; text mining using adaptive compression techniques, giving a new approach to generic entity extraction, word segmentation, and acronym extraction; and keyphrase extraction.

1 Introduction

Digital libraries are focused collections of digital objects (text, audio, video etc.—though we focus here on text) along with methods for access and retrieval of the information in the collection, and methods for selecting, organizing, and maintaining it. The gateway to the contents of a bricks-and-mortar library is *metadata*—the bibliographic information in the library catalog. Manual cataloging takes one to two hours of expert time per document, well beyond the resources of most digital libraries. All the techniques we discuss here are ways of automatically extracting metadata, broadly defined, from the full text of a document collection.

A hierarchy of the phrases that recur in the text allows readers to browse comfortably through a large digital library. A plausible, easily-understood, hierarchical structure can be created automatically from full text on a purely lexical basis. We describe a simple algorithm for inferring a structural hierarchy of phrases, that operates in time linear in the size of the input—an important consideration for multi-gigabyte collections. Not only is this technique practically useful for browsing large information collections, but different formulations lead to alternative methods that raise interesting open questions.

Adaptive compression is a powerful tool for eliciting structure from sequences. We describe a learning paradigm that creates a model from marked-up training text and applies it to insert markup into plain text. Viterbi-style search is used to "correct" the text by inserting markup in a way that maximizes compression.

N. Cesa-Bianchi et al. (Eds.): ALT 2002, LNAI 2533, pp. 42–56, 2002.

This strategy yields excellent results on the word segmentation problem—an important practical problem in digital libraries of Chinese text. It has also proved successful for generic entity extraction. Used in a simpler way, a compression-based evaluation metric works well for recognizing acronyms, and users of our digital collections can now browse automatically-extracted lists of acronyms and their definitions.

The third area is keyphrase extraction. Elementary machine learning techniques (supervised discretization, naive Bayes), with a simple two- or three-attribute set, perform well for both domain-independent and domain-dependent extraction of keyphrases. The results, evaluated in an experiment with human judges, are excellent. Interfaces that use keyphrases for browsing provide a new and absorbing environment for reading and writing within a digital library.

2   Digital Libraries

Digital libraries, whose history spans a mere handful of years, will surely figure amongst the most important and influential institutions of this new century. The information revolution not only supplies the technological horsepower that drives digital libraries, but fuels an unprecedented demand for storing, organizing, and accessing information. If information is the currency of the knowledge economy, digital libraries will be the banks where it is invested. And unlike most technological progress the benefits will accrue not just to technically sophisticated nations. In developing countries digital libraries will prove to be a "killer app" for computers, because traditional publishing and distribution mechanisms have tragically failed the developing world and people there face a desperate scarcity of high-quality, reliable, practical information. Even those from oral cultures who lack basic literacy skills, and are completely disenfranchised by traditional libraries, will enjoy a new-found abundance of knowledge sources, for non-textual documents will gradually achieve first-class status in the digital library and the provocative notion of libraries for the illiterate will eventually take wing [13].

Digital libraries have the potential to be far more flexible than conventional ones. Of course, they are portable: they will be with you whenever you want them to be: in the home, in the plane, at the beach, in a Ugandan village, on the street when you want to play your friends that new song. They will be large, giving access to your personal book collection, your town's public library, your university library. Not only this, but they will ultimately be seamlessly integrated with national and international sources of information—inter-library loan at your fingertips.

But flexibility will extend well beyond matters of physical convenience. Future libraries will surround you with information in ways that we can yet only dimly perceive. When Karl Marx wrote *Das Kapital*, he worked in the reading room of the British Museum library. Not only will tomorrow's writers use their laptop instead of Marx's pen and paper, and sit in the garden, they will work "inside" their digital libraries in a stronger and more visceral sense. Although digital libraries are libraries without walls, they do have boundaries—the very

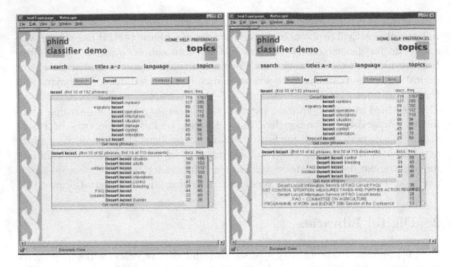

Fig. 1. (a) Browsing for information about *locusts*, (b) Expanding on *desert locust*

notion of a "collection" implies a boundary. Paradoxically, perhaps, in the future we will work inside the digital library with a new sense of "in"-ness that we can barely glimpse today. The library will be an environment that surrounds you in an intellectual, not a physical, sense. But virtual reality means that intellectual experiences can easily be translated into physical ones. More or less immersive (you can choose), the library will be an environment that reacts and responds to what you are doing, making the right kind of information available to you as and when you need it, and in an appropriate form.

3 Generating Phrase Hierarchies

Hierarchical phrase structures, extracted from the full text of a large document collection, suggest a new way of approaching the problem of familiarizing oneself with the contents of a large collection of electronic text [9].

3.1 Browsing a Phrase Hierarchy

Figure 1 shows an interactive interface to a phrase hierarchy that has been extracted automatically from the full text of a document collection, in this case the United Nations Food and Agriculture Organization web site. This interface is designed to resemble a paper-based subject index or thesaurus.

In Figure 1a, the user enters an initial word in the search box at the top—in this case the word *locust*. On pressing the Search button the upper of the two panels appears. This shows the phrases at the top level in the hierarchy that contain the search term. The list is sorted by phrase frequency; on the right is the number of times the phrase appears in the entire document collection, and beside that is the number of documents in which the phrase appears.

Only the first ten phrases are shown, because it is impractical with a web interface to download a large number of phrases, and many of these phrase lists are huge. Clicking the item at the end of the list that reads *Get more phrases* (displayed in a distinctive color) will download another ten phrases, and so on. The interface accumulates the phrases: a scroll bar appears to the right for use when more than ten phrases are displayed. The number of phrases appears above the list: in this case there are 102 top-level phrases that contain the term *locust*.

The lower panel in Figure 1a appears as soon as the user clicks one of the phrases in the upper list. In this case the user has clicked *Desert locust* (which is why the upper panel's first line is highlighted), causing phrases containing the string *Desert locust* to be displayed below.

If you continue to descend through the phrase hierarchy, eventually the leaves will be reached. In this system, any sequence of words is a "phrase" if it appears more than once in the entire document collection. Thus a leaf corresponds to a phrase that occurs in a unique context somewhere in the collection (though the document that contains that contextually unique occurrence may include several other occurrences too). In Figure 1, the text above the lower panel shows that the phrase *Desert locust* appears in 82 longer phrases, and also in 719 documents. These 719 documents each contain the phrase in some unique context. The first few documents are visible when the list is scrolled down, as is shown in Figure 1b.

In effect, both panels show a phrase list followed by a document list. Either list may be empty: in fact, the document list is empty in the upper panel because every context in which the word locust occurs appears more than once in the collection. The document list displays the titles of the documents. Just as you can click *Get more phrases* to increase the number of phrases that are shown in the list, you can, in the lower panels, also click *Get more documents* (again it is displayed at the end of the list in a distinctive color, but to see that entry you must scroll the panel down a little more) to increase the number of documents that are shown.

Clicking on a phrase expands that phrase. The page holds only two panels, and if a phrase in the lower one is clicked the contents of that panel move up to the top to make space for the phrase's expansion. Alternatively, clicking on a document opens that document in a new window. If the user were to click on *Desert Locust Information Service of FAO: Locust FAQs* in Figure 1b, that would bring up a web page with that title. As Figure 1b indicates, that document contains 38 occurrences of the phrase *Desert locust*.

3.2   Generating Phrase Hierarchies

The phrase hierarchies exemplified in Figure 1 reflect the repetition of sequences of words in the document collection. So-called "dictionary" methods of compression also capitalize on repetitions: they represent structure in terms of a set of substrings of the text, and achieve compression by replacing fragments of text by an index into a dictionary. "Hierarchical" dictionary methods extend the dictionary to a non-trivial hierarchical structure which is inferred from the input sequence [7]. As well as fulfilling their original purpose of forming an excellent basis for compression, such hierarchies expose interesting structure in the text that is very useful for supporting information-browsing interfaces.

We describe three algorithms for generating phrase hierarchies that operate in time linear in the length of the input sequence and hence are practical on large volumes of text. This is a severe restriction: apart from standard compression algorithms that produce non-hierarchical structure and tail-recursive hierarchical structure, no linear-time algorithms for detecting hierarchical repetition in sequences were known until recently. These methods form a grammar for a text by replacing each repeated string with a production rule.

3.3 SEQUITUR: **An Online Technique**

"Online" algorithms are ones that process the input stream in a single pass, and begin to emit compressed output long before they have seen all the input. This severely restricts the opportunities for detecting repetitions, for there is no alternative to proceeding in a greedy left-to-right manner. It may be possible to postpone decision-making by retaining a buffer of recent history and using this to improve the quality of the rules generated, but at some point the input must be processed greedily and a commitment made to a particular decomposition.

SEQUITUR is an algorithm that creates a hierarchical dictionary for a given string in a greedy left-to-right fashion [7]. It builds a hierarchy of phrases by forming a new rule out of existing pairs of symbols, including non-terminal symbols. Rules that become non-productive—in that they do not yield a net space saving—can be deleted, and their head replaced by the symbols that comprise the right-hand side of the deleted rules. This allows rules that concatenate more than two symbols to be formed. For example, the string *abcdbcabcdbc* gives rise to the grammar

$$S \to AA$$
$$A \to aBdB$$
$$B \to bc$$

Surprisingly, SEQUITUR operates in time that is linear in the size of the input [8]. The proof sketched here also contains an explanation of how the algorithm works. It operates by reading a new symbol and processing it by appending it to the top-level string and then examining the last two symbols of that string. Zero or more of the three transformations described below are applied, until none applies anywhere in the grammar. Finally, the cycle is repeated by reading in a new symbol.

At any given point in time, the algorithm has reached a particular point in the input string, and has generated a certain set of rules. Let r be one less than the number of rules, and s the sum of the number of symbols on the right-hand side of all these rules. Recall that the top-level string S, which represents the input read so far, forms one of the rules in the grammar; it begins with a null right-hand side. Initially, r and s are zero.

Here are the three transformations. Only the first two can occur when a new symbol is first processed; the third can only fire if one or more of the others has already been applied in this cycle.

1. The digram comprising the last two symbols matches an existing rule in the grammar. Substitute the head of that rule for the digram. s decreases by one; r remains the same.
2. The digram comprising the last two symbols occurs elsewhere on the right-hand side of a rule. Create a new rule for it and substitute the head for both its occurrences. r increases by one; s remains the same (it increases by two on account of the new rule, and decreases by two on account of the two substitutions).
3. A rule exists whose head occurs only once in the right-hand sides of all rules. Eliminate this rule, substituting its body for the head. r decreases by one; s decreases by one too (because the single occurrence of the rule's head disappears).

To show that this operates in linear time, we demonstrate that the total number of rules applied cannot exceed $2n$ where n is the number of input symbols. Consider the quantity $q = s - r/2$. Initially 0, it can never be negative because $r \leq s$. It increases by 1 for each input symbol processed, and it is easy to see that it must decrease by at least $1/2$ for each rule applied. Hence the number of rules applied is at most twice the number of input symbols.

3.4 Most Frequent First

SEQUITUR processes symbols in the order in which they appear. The first-occurring repetition is replaced by a rule, then the second-occurring repetition, and so on. If online operation is not required, this policy can be relaxed. This raises the question of whether there exist heuristics for selecting substrings for replacement that yield better compression performance. One obvious possibility is to replace the most frequent digram first.

The idea of forming a rule for the most frequently-occurring digram, substituting the head of the rule for that digram in the input string, and continuing until some terminating condition is met, was proposed over a quarter century ago by Wolff [14] and has been reinvented many times since then. The most common repeated digram is replaced first, and the process continues until no digram appears more than once. This algorithm operates offline because it must scan the entire string before making the first replacement.

Wolff's algorithm is inefficient: it takes $O(n^2)$ time because it makes multiple passes over the string, recalculating digram frequencies from scratch every time a new rule is created. However, Larsson and Moffat [6] recently devised a clever algorithm, dubbed RE-PAIR, whose time is linear in the length of the input string, which creates just this structure of rules: a hierarchy generated by giving preference to digrams on the basis of their frequency. They reduce execution time to linear by incrementally updating digram counts as substitutions are made, and using a priority queue to keep track of the most common digrams.

3.5   Longest First

A second heuristic for choosing the order of replacements is to process the longest repetition first. Bentley and McIlroy [1] explored the longest-first heuristic for very long repetitions, and removed them using an LZ77 pointer-style approach before invoking *gzip* to compress shorter repetitions. This is not a linear-time solution.

Suffix trees provide an efficient mechanism for identifying longest repetitions. The longest repetition corresponds to the deepest internal node, measured in symbols from the root. The deepest non-terminal can be found by traversing the tree, which takes time linear in the length of the input because there is a one-to-one correspondence between leaf nodes and symbols in the string.

We are left with two problems: how to find all longest repetitions, and how to update the tree after creating a rule. Farach-Colton and Nevill-Manning (private communication) have shown that it is possible to build the tree, and update it after each replacement, in time which is linear overall. The tree can be updated in linear amortized time by making a preliminary pass through it and sorting the depths of the internal nodes. Sorting can be done in linear time using a radix sort, because no repetition will be longer than $n/2$ symbols. The algorithm relies on the fact that the deepest node is modified at each point.

3.6   Discussion

It is interesting to compare the performance of the three algorithms we have described: SEQUITUR, most frequent first, and longest first. It is not hard to devise short strings on which any of the three outperforms the other two. In practice, however, longest-first is significantly inferior to the other techniques; indeed, simple artificial sequences can be found on which the number of rules it produces grows linearly with sequence length whereas the number of rules produced by frequent-first grows only logarithmically. Experiments on natural language text indicate that in terms of the total number of symbols in the resulting grammar, which is a crude measure of compression, frequent-first outperforms SEQUITUR, with longest-first lagging well behind [10].

4   Mining for Metadata

Text mining is about inferring structure from sequences representing natural language text, and may be defined as the process of analyzing text to extract information that is useful for particular purposes—"metadata". Compared with the data stored in databases, text is unstructured, amorphous, and contains information at many different levels. Nevertheless, the motivation for trying to extract information from it is compelling—even if success is only partial. Despite the fact that the problems are difficult to define clearly, interest in text mining is burgeoning because it is perceived to have enormous potential practical utility.

Hand-crafted heuristics are a common practical approach for extracting information from text. However, a general, and generalizable, approach requires adaptive techniques. Compression forms a sound unifying principle that allows many text mining problems to be tackled adaptively, and here we look at how the techniques used in adaptive text compression can be applied to text mining. We develop several examples: locating proper names and quantities of interest in a piece of text, word segmentation, and acronym extraction.

4.1 Compression as a Basis for Text Mining

Character-based compression methods predict each upcoming character based on its preceding context, and use the predictions to compress the text effectively. Accurate predictions mean good compression. These techniques open the door to new ways of mining text adaptively.

For example, character-based language models provide a way of recognizing lexical tokens. Business and professional documents are packed with loosely structured information: phone and fax numbers, street addresses, email addresses and signatures, tables of contents, lists of references, tables, figures, captions, meeting announcements, URLs. In addition, there are countless domain-specific structures—ISBN numbers, stock symbols, chemical structures, and mathematical equations, to name a few. These items of interest in a piece of text are sometimes called "named entities" [2]. The standard approach to extracting them from text is manual: tokenizers and grammars are hand-crafted for the particular data being extracted.

Instead, the tokens can be compressed using models derived from different training data, and classified according to which model supports the most economical representation. We use the well-known PPM text compression scheme [3]. However, the methods and results are not particularly sensitive to the compression scheme used, although character-based prediction is assumed.

4.2 Identifying Tokens in Isolation

In order to indicate the potential of PPM to locate and identify useful tokens, we describe an experiment that was conducted with information items extracted from twenty issues of a 4-page, 1500-word, weekly electronic newsletter. Items of the kind that readers might wish to take action on were classified into ten generic types: people's names; dates and time periods; locations; sources, journals, and book series; organizations; URLs; email addresses; phone numbers; fax numbers; and sums of money. These types are subjective: dates and time periods are lumped together, whereas for some purposes they should be distinguished; personal and organizational names are separated, whereas for some purposes they should be amalgamated. The methodology we describe accommodates all these options: there is no commitment to any particular ontology.

The first question is whether language models can discriminate between different token types when the tokens are taken in isolation. Lists of names, dates, locations, etc. in twenty issues of the newsletter were input to PPM separately, to form ten compression models. Each issue contained about 150 tokens, unevenly distributed over token types. In addition, a plain text model was formed from the full text of all these issues. These eleven models were used to identify each of the tokens in a newsletter that did not form part of the training data, on the basis of which model compresses them the most. Although the plain text model could in principle be assigned to a token, in fact this never occurred.

Of the 200 tokens in the test data, 40% appeared in the training data (with the same label) and the remainder were new. 91% of the total were identified correctly and the remaining 9% incorrectly; all errors were on new symbols. Identifying "old" symbols correctly is not completely trivial; for example some of them contain line breaks that do not appear in the training data. Of course, line breaks could be mapped to white space as a preprocessing step, but this would prevent learning certain kinds of token that depended on the configuration of line breaks. Our intention was to learn how far we could go without making any assumptions whatsoever about the nature of the tokens.

The individual errors on new symbols are easily explained; some do not seem like errors at all. For example, place names are often the same as people's names—only the context can discriminate—and many apparently correct identifications were counted as incorrect.

4.3 Identifying Tokens in Context

When tokens appear in text, contextual information provides additional cues for disambiguating them—e.g., email addresses in this particular corpus are always flanked by angle brackets. Conversely, identification may be foiled by misleading context: e.g., some names are preceded by titles that end in a period (*Dr.*, *Prof.*), which reduces the weight of the capitalization evidence for the following word because capitalization routinely follows a period.

To assess the effect of context we assume that all tokens have been located, and the task is to identify their types *in situ*. If a stretch of text is identified as a token of the appropriate type it will compress better using the specialized model; however, begin- and end-token markers must be coded to indicate this fact. To investigate this, all tokens in the data were replaced by a surrogate symbol that was treated by PPM as a single character (different from all the ASCII characters). A different surrogate was used for each token type. A new model was generated from the modified training data, and the test article was compressed by this model to give a baseline entropy of e_0 bits. Then each token in turn, taken individually, was restored into the test article as plain text and the result recompressed to give entropy e bits. This will be greater than e_0 because the information required to represent the token itself (almost certainly) exceeds that required to represent its type. Suppose e_m is the token's entropy with respect to model m. The net space saved by recognizing this token as belonging to model m is $e - (e_0 + e_m)$ bits. This quantity was evaluated for each model to determine which one classified the token best, or whether it was best left as plain text. The procedure was repeated for each token.

When context is taken into account the error rate actually increases! However, almost all the errors are caused by failure to recognize a token as different from plain text, and the rate of actual mis-recognitions is very low—only two, in fact, both of which are easily understandable.

To mark up a string as a token two extra symbols, *begin-token* and *end-token*, are inserted, and it is this additional overhead that causes the above-noted recognition failures. However, the tradeoff between actual errors and failures to identify can be adjusted by using a threshold when comparing the compression for a particular token with the compression when its characters are interpreted as plain text. This allows a small increase in the number of errors to be sacrificed for a larger decrease in identification failures.

4.4   Locating Tokens in Context

Tokens can be located by considering the input as an interleaved sequence of information from different sources. Every token is to be bracketed by *begin-token* and *end-token* markers; the problem is to "correct" text by inserting such markers appropriately. The markers also identify the type of token in question—thus we have *begin-name-token*, *end-name-token*, etc. Whenever a *begin-token* is encountered, the encoder switches to the compression model appropriate to that token type, initialized to a null prior context. Whenever *end-token* is encountered, the encoder reverts to the plain text model that was in effect before, replacing the token by a single symbol representing that token type.

The algorithm takes a string of text and determines the optimal sequence of models that would produce it, along with their placement. It works Viterbi-style, processing the input characters to build a tree in which each path from root to leaf represents a string of characters that is a possible interpretation of the input. The paths are alternative output strings, and *begin-token* and *end-token* symbols appear on them. The entropy of a path can be calculated by starting at the root and coding each symbol along the path according to the model that is in force when that symbol is reached. The context is re-initialized to a unique starting token whenever *begin-token* is encountered, and the appropriate model is entered. On encountering *end-token*, it is encoded and the context reverts to what it was before.

What causes the tree to branch is the insertion of *begin-token* symbols for every possible token type, and the *end-token* symbol—which must be for the currently active token type so that nesting is properly respected. To expand the tree, a list of open leaves is maintained, each recording the point in the input string that has been reached and the entropy value up to that point. The lowest-entropy leaf is chosen for expansion at each stage. Unless the tree and the list of open leaves are pruned, they grow very large very quickly. A beam search is used, and pruning operations are applied that remove leaves from the list and therefore prevent the corresponding paths from growing further.

To evaluate the procedure for locating tokens in context, we used the training data from the same issues of the newsletter as before, and the same single issue for testing. The errors and mis-recognitions noted above when identifying tokens in context also occur when locating tokens. Inevitably there were a few incorrect positive identifications, where a segment of plain text was erroneously deemed to

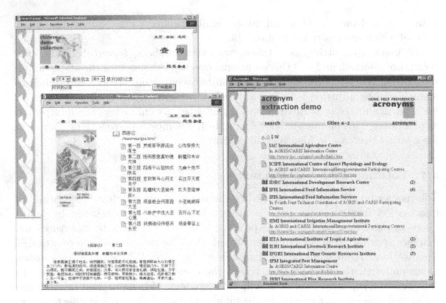

Fig. 2. (a) Chinese digital library collection; (b) browsing based on acronyms

be a token. In addition, some tokens suffered from slightly incorrect boundary placement. Finally, several discrepancies were caused by inadvertent errors in the manual markup.

4.5   Segmentation into Words

Most text mining schemes presuppose that the input has been divided into lexical items, usually words—the methods described above are unique in that they make no such assumption. Although "words" delimited by non-alphanumeric characters provide a natural tokenization for many items in ordinary text, this assumption fails in particular cases. For example, generic tokenization would not allow many date structures to be parsed (e.g. *30Jul98*, which is used throughout the electronic newsletters used as an example above). In general, any prior segmentation into tokens runs the risk of obscuring information.

A special case of the scheme for compression-based entity extraction can be used to segment text into words, based on hand-segmented training data. An excellent application is the problem of segmenting Chinese text, which is written without using spaces. Although Chinese readers are accustomed to inferring the corresponding sequence of words as they read, they must in the process resolve considerable ambiguity in the placement of boundaries. Interpreting a text as a sequence of words is necessary for many information retrieval and storage tasks. For example, Figure 2a illustrates a digital library collection of classic Chinese literature. For effective querying, word segmentation should be performed on the query itself and on all documents in the collection.

Inserting spaces into text can be viewed as a hidden Markov modeling problem. Between every pair of characters lies a potential space. Segmentation can be achieved by training a character-based compression model on pre-segmented text, and using a Viterbi-style algorithm to interpolate spaces in a way that maximizes the overall probability of the text.

Existing techniques for Chinese text segmentation are either word-based, or rely on hand-crafted segmentation rules. In contrast, the compression-based methodology uses character-level models formed adaptively from training text. Such models do not rely on a dictionary and fall back on general properties of language statistics to process novel words. Excellent results have been obtained with the new scheme [11].

4.6   Extracting Acronyms

Identifying acronyms in documents poses a rather different kind of problem. Acronyms are often defined by preceding or following their first use with a textual explanation. Finding all acronyms, along with their definitions, in a particular technical document is a problem that has previously been tackled using *ad hoc* heuristics. The information desired—acronyms and their definitions—is relational, which distinguishes it from the text mining problems discussed above.

We have experimented with coding potential acronyms with respect to the initial letters of neighboring words, and using the compression achieved to signal the occurrence of an acronym and its definition [15]. Our criterion is whether a candidate acronym could be coded more efficiently using a special model than using a regular text compression scheme. A phrase is declared to be an acronym definition if the difference between the number of bits required to code it using a general-purpose compressor and the acronym model exceeds a certain threshold.

Figure 2b shows a list of acronyms automatically extracted from a document collection, along with their definitions. When an acronym is defined in more than one document, a bookshelf is shown, with the number of documents in parentheses. Clicking on the bookshelf brings up the list of documents.

5   Keyphrases

Keyphrases are an important kind of metadata for many documents. They are often used for topic search, or to summarize or cluster documents. Figure 3a shows a hierarchical phrase browser just like that in Figure 1—except that here the phrases are author-assigned keyphrases. Figure 3b shows a different style of interface to a document collection, also based on keyphrases. At the very top the user has typed the word *query*. Underneath are three large panels. The left-hand one displays all keyphrases in the document collection that contain the word *query*. Unlike the earlier displays, this is not hierarchical. The user has selected one of these phrases, *dynamic query*; the number beside it indicates

54   I.H. Witten

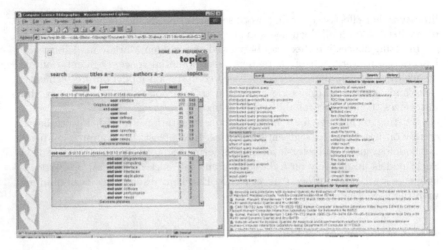

Fig. 3. Browsing interfaces based on keyphrases: (a) hierarchical browser; (b) document explorer

that it has been identified as a keyphrase for eight documents. Clicking on a document icon displays that document.

It is desirable to automate the keyphrase extraction process, for only a small minority of documents have author-assigned keyphrases, and manual assignment of keyphrases to existing documents is very laborious. There are two fundamentally different approaches: keyphrase *assignment* and keyphrase *extraction*. Both use machine learning methods, and require for training purposes a set of documents with keyphrases already identified. In keyphrase assignment, for each keyphrase the training data provides a set of documents associated with it, and a classifier is created from all training documents using the ones associated with it as positive examples and the remainder as negative examples. A new document is processed by each classifier, and is assigned the keyphrases associated with those classifiers that classify it positively [4].

In contrast, keyphrase extraction is treated as a rather different classification task. Each phrase in a document is either a keyphrase or not, and the problem is to correctly classify phrases into one of these two categories. The phrases in a document are "examples" and the learning problem is to find a mapping from the examples to the classes "keyphrase" and "not-keyphrase". Learning techniques generate this mapping automatically from a set of training examples, that is, phrases that have been identified as either being keyphrases or not.

Not all phrases in a document are equally likely to be keyphrases *a priori*, and many phrases can be filtered out before invoking the learning scheme. We have experimented with many ways of doing this, most involving the hierarchical phrase extraction algorithms described above. Following this process, all words are case-folded and stemmed. The final step in preparing the phrases for the learning scheme is to remove all stemmed phrases that occur only once in the document.

Once candidate phrases have been generated from the text, it is necessary to derive selected attributes from them to be used in learning. Several potential attributes immediately spring to mind: the number of words in a phrase, the number of characters, the position of the phrase in the document, etc. However, in our experiments, only two attributes turned out to be useful in discriminating between keyphrases and non-keyphrases: the TF×IDF score of a phrase [12], and the distance into the document of the phrase's first appearance.

Both these attributes are real numbers. We use naive Bayes because it is simple, quick, and effective: it conditions class probabilities on each attribute, and assumes that the attributes are statistically independent. In order to compute conditional probabilities, the attributes are discretized prior to applying the learning scheme. Naive Bayes assumes that the attributes are independent given the class. The probability that a phrase is a keyphrase given that it has discretized TF×IDF value T and discretized distance D is computed from the probability that a keyphrase has TF×IDF score T, the probability that a keyphrase has distance D, the prior probability that a phrase is a keyphrase, and a suitable normalization factor. These probabilities are easily estimated by counting the number of times the corresponding event occurs in the training data.

This procedure generates a Bayes model from a set of training documents for which keyphrases are known (for example, because the author provided them). The resulting model can then be applied in a straightforward way to new documents from which keyphrases are to be extracted [5].

6   Conclusions

Digital libraries will become socially important institutions in a variety of contexts, many of which we can barely envisage. They are focused, organized collections of information, and creative designers will invent new ways of organizing, browsing, and displaying information that transcend our imagination today. Browsing techniques will capitalize on information about the documents—metadata—that is, by and large, extracted automatically from the document text itself, or from related resources. We will see a rich interplay between information extraction by text mining and information display through novel interaction techniques.

Text mining is a burgeoning new area that will underpin these developments. This paper has argued, through examples, that compression forms a sound unifying principle that allows many text mining problems to be tacked adaptively.

Acknowledgments. The research described here has been undertaken in conjunction with many others, particularly Zane Bray, John Cleary, Eibe Frank, Stuart Inglis, Malika Mahoui, Gordon Paynter, Craig Nevill-Manning, Bill Teahan, YingYing Wen and Stuart Yeates.

References

[1] Bentley, J. and McIlroy, D. (1999) "Data compression using long common strings." *Proc Data Compression Conference*, pp. 287–295. IEEE Press, Los Alamitos, CA.

[2] Chinchor, N.A. (1999) "Overview of MUC-7/MET-2." *Proc Message Understanding Conference MUC-7*.

[3] Cleary, J.G. and Witten, I.H. (1984) "Data compression using adaptive coding and partial string matching." *IEEE Trans on Communications*, Vol. 32, No. 4, pp. 396–402.

[4] Dumais, S. T., Platt, J., Heckerman, D. and Sahami, M. (1998) "Inductive learning algorithms and representations for text categorization." In *Proceedings of the 7th International Conference on Information and Knowledge Management*.

[5] Frank, E., Paynter, G.W., Witten, I.H., Gutwin, C. and Nevill-Manning, C. (1999) "Domain-specific keyphrase extraction." *Int Joint Conference on Artificial Intelligence*, Stockholm, Sweden, pp. 668–673.

[6] Larsson, N.J. and Moffat, A. (1999) "Offline dictionary-based compression." *Proc Data Compression Conference*, pp. 296–305. IEEE Press, Los Alamitos, CA.

[7] Nevill-Manning, C.G. and Witten, I.H. (1997) "Identifying hierarchical structure in sequences: a linear-time algorithm." *J Artificial Intelligence Research*, Vol. 7, pp. 67–82.

[8] Nevill-Manning, C.G. and Witten, I.H. (1998) "Phrase hierarchy inference and compression in bounded space," *Proc. Data Compression Conference*, J.A. Storer and M. Cohn (Eds.), Los Alamitos, CA: IEEE Press. 179–188.

[9] Nevill-Manning, C.G., Witten, I.H. and Paynter, G.W. (1999) "Lexically-generated subject hierarchies for browsing large collections." *International Journal of Digital Libraries*, Vol. 2, No. 2/3, pp. 111–123.

[10] Nevill-Manning, C.G. and Witten, I.H. (2000) "Online and offline heuristics for inferring hierarchies of repetitions in sequences," *Proc. IEEE*, Vol. 88, No. 11, pp. 1745–1755.

[11] Teahan, W.J., Wen, Y., McNab, R. and Witten, I.H. (2000) "A compression-based algorithm for Chinese word segmentation." *Computational Linguistics*, Vol. 26, No. 3, pp. 375–393.

[12] Witten, I.H., Moffat, A. and Bell, T.C. (1999) *Managing gigabytes: compressing and indexing documents and images*. Second Edition, Morgan Kaufmann, San Francisco, California.

[13] Witten, I.H. and Bainbridge, D. (2003) *How to build a digital library*. Morgan Kaufmann, San Francisco, California.

[14] Wolff, J.G. (1975) "An algorithm for the segmentation of an artificial language analogue." *British J Psychology*, Vol. 66, pp. 79–90.

[15] Yeates, S., Bainbridge, D. and Witten, I.H. (2000) "Using compression to identify acronyms in text." *Proc Data Compression Conference* (Poster paper). IEEE Press, Los Alamitos, CA. Full version available as Working Paper 00/1, Department of Computer Science, University of Waikato, New Zealand.

On Learning Monotone Boolean Functions under the Uniform Distribution

Kazuyuki Amano and Akira Maruoka

Graduate School of Information Sciences, Tohoku University
Aoba 05, Aramaki, Sendai 980-8579 JAPAN
{ama|maruoka}@ecei.tohoku.ac.jp

Abstract. In this paper, we prove two general theorems on monotone Boolean functions which are useful for constructing an learning algorithm for monotone Boolean functions under the uniform distribution.
A monotone Boolean function is called fair if it takes the value 1 on exactly half of its inputs. The first result proved in this paper is that the single variable function $f(x) = x_i$ has the minimum correlation with the majority function among all fair monotone functions (Theorem 1). This proves the conjecture by Blum, Burch and Langford (FOCS '98) and improves the performance guarantee of the best known learning algorithm for monotone Boolean functions under the uniform distribution proposed by them.
Our second result is on the relationship between the influences and the average sensitivity of a monotone Boolean function. The influence of variable x_i on f is defined as the probability that $f(x)$ differs from $f(x \oplus e_i)$ where x is chosen uniformly from $\{0,1\}^n$ and $x \oplus e_i$ means x with its i-th bit flipped. The average sensitivity of f is defined as the sum of the influences over all variables x_i. We prove that a somewhat unintuitive result which says if the influence of every variable on a monotone Boolean function is small, i.e., $O(1/n^c)$ for some constant $c > 0$, then the average sensitivity of the function must be large, i.e., $\Omega(\log n)$ (Theorem 11). We also discuss how to apply this result to construct a new learning algorithm for monotone Boolean functions.

1 Introduction

A *monotone* Boolean function f maps $\{0,1\}^n$ to $\{0,1\}$ in such a way that $f(x) \leq f(y)$ whenever $x \leq y$. The problem of learning monotone Boolean functions has been widely investigated because they contain a very broad class of Boolean expressions.

For a target function f and a hypothesis function h, we define the error of h for f, denoted by $\text{err}(f, h)$, as the fraction of points x such that $f(x) \neq h(x)$; that is $\Pr[f(x) \neq h(x)]$ where x is chosen uniformly from $\{0,1\}^n$. We sometimes use the closely related concept of *correlation*, which is defined to be $1 - 2 \Pr[f(x) \neq h(x)]$.

The algorithms we discuss in this paper are for learning monotone Boolean functions under the uniform distribution : The algorithm is assumed to have an

N. Cesa-Bianchi et al. (Eds.): ALT 2002, LNAI 2533, pp. 57–68, 2002.

example oracle EXAMPLE for an unknown target function f. When the oracle EXAMPLE is invoked, it produces an example $(x, f(x))$ for a vector x chosen uniformly from $\{0, 1\}^n$. The goal of a learning algorithm is to produce a good approximation to the target f in polynomial time by calling oracle EXAMPLE a polynomial number of times.

The first algorithm for learning monotone Boolean functions under the uniform distribution was proposed by Kearns et al[7]. Their algorithm produces one of the constant-zero, the constant-one or single variable functions that has the highest correlation on the data obtained by calling oracle EXAMPLE. The output produced guarantees error at most $1/2 - \Omega(1/n)$. Subsequently, Bshouty and Tamon[3] gave another algorithm which outputs linear threshold functions as a hypothesis and guarantees error at most $1/2 - \Omega((\log n)^2/n)$. Recently, Blum, Burch and Langford[2] improved on this guarantee. They gave an especially simple algorithm that can achieve error at most $1/2 - \Omega(1/\sqrt{n})$: Draw $O(n)$ examples labeled by a target f. If at least a $1/2 + 0.05/\sqrt{n}$ fraction of samples are labeled by 1 then the algorithm outputs the constant-one function. Likewise if at least a $1/2 + 0.05/\sqrt{n}$ fraction of samples are labeled by 0 then the algorithm outputs the constant-zero function. Otherwise the algorithm blindly outputs as hypothesis the majority function over all the variables. Remarkably, their simple algorithm is nearly the best possible even if the algorithm is allowed to access to a more powerful oracle than EXAMPLE. The membership oracle MEMBER allows the algorithm to query f at arbitrary points of its choosing. They proved that no algorithm can guarantee error $1/2 - \omega(\log n/\sqrt{n})$ provided that the algorithm is allowed to access to oracle MEMBER only a polynomial number of times.

The key of their algorithm is the fact that for every *fair* monotone Boolean function f, the error of the majority function for f is at most $1/2 - \Omega(1/\sqrt{n})$. Here a Boolean function is called *fair* if it takes the value 1 on exactly half of its inputs. In [2], they conjectured that the single variable function has the minimum correlation with the majority function among all fair monotone functions. The first result proved in this paper is that the conjecture is true, i.e., the single variable function is the "farthest" from the majority function among all fair monotone functions. Although our improvement on the error only affects the hidden constant in the Ω notation, we believe that the result is interesting in its own right.

If we apply this result to the learning algorithm described above, it can be seen that the "worst" case occurs when a target function is a single variable function. But we can easily determine whether the target function is well correlated with a single variable. This consideration leads to a new algorithm that outputs the function in $\{0, 1, x_1, \ldots, x_n, \text{majority}\}$ which has the highest observed correlation on examples.

In the second part of the paper, we analyze the performance of this algorithm by applying the ideas from Harmonic analysis and obtain a general theorem on the relationship between the influences and the average sensitivity of a monotone Boolean function. The influence of variable x_i on a Boolean function f is defined as the probability that $f(x)$ differs from $f(x \oplus e_i)$ where x is chosen uniformly from $\{0, 1\}^n$ and $x \oplus e_i$ means x with its i-th bit flipped. The average sensitivity of f is defined as the sum of the influences of all the variables. The analysis of the influences and the average sensitivity of Boolean functions and their application to learning have been widely investigated (e.g. [6,3]).

For every monotone Boolean function f, the influence of x_i on f is identical to the correlation between f and x_i. If a single variable function x_i has high correlation with a target function f on examples then x_i is a good approximation to f, so we are done. We can therefore assume that the target function has small influence for every variable.

The second result we establish in this paper is somewhat unintuitive statement on the relationship between the influences and the average sensitivity of a monotone Boolean function. Our theorem says that if the influence of x_i on a monotone Boolean function f is small, i.e., $O(1/n^c)$ for some constant $c > 0$, for every variable x_i then the average sensitivity of f must be large, i.e., $\Omega(\log n)$. We also observe that a monotone Boolean function having large average sensitivity is likely to be a good approximation to the majority function. We conjecture that the error of the majority function approximating a fair monotone Boolean function with average sensitivity $s(f)$ is at most $1/2 - \Omega(s(f)/\sqrt{n})$. If this conjecture were true, then the new algorithm, proposed in this paper, to learn monotone Boolean functions would achieve the optimal error $1/2 - \Omega(\log n/\sqrt{n})$.

2   Distance between Fair Monotone Function and Majority Function

For $x \in \{0, 1\}^n$, $||x||$ represents the number of 1's in x, i.e., $||x|| = \sum_i x_i$ where x_i denotes the i-th bit of x. For a set S, $\sharp S$ denotes the cardinality of S. For a set of vectors $S \subseteq \{0, 1\}^n$ and an integer $0 \leq k \leq n$, we use S_k to represent the set of vectors that contains k 1's, i.e., $S_k = \{x \in S \mid ||x|| = k\}$. For a natural number n, $[n]$ stands for the set $\{1, 2, \ldots, n\}$. For a Boolean function f, we define $I^f = \{x \mid f(x) = 1\}$ and $O^f = \{x \mid f(x) = 0\}$. For simplicity, we abbreviate $(I^f)_k$ and $(O^f)_k$ as I_k^f and O_k^f, respectively. A Boolean function f is called *fair* if $\sharp I^f = \sharp O^f$ holds. A Boolean function f on n variables is *monotone* if $f(x_1, \ldots, x_n) \leq f(y_1, \ldots, y_n)$ whenever $x_i \leq y_i$ for all i.

The *majority* function on n variables, denoted by MAJ_n, is a function that outputs 1 if and only if the number of 1's in its input is exceed $n/2$, i.e.,

$$\mathrm{MAJ}_n(x) = \begin{cases} 1 & \text{if } ||x|| \geq \lfloor n/2 \rfloor + 1, \\ 0 & \text{if } ||x|| \leq \lfloor n/2 \rfloor. \end{cases}$$

In [2], Blum et al conjectured that any single variable function has the minimum correlation with the majority function among all fair monotone functions. In this section, we prove that their conjecture is true.

Theorem 1 *For any fair monotone Boolean function f on n variables,*

$$\sharp\{x \mid MAJ_n(x) \neq f(x)\} \leq \sharp\{x \mid MAJ_n(x) \neq x_1\} = 2^{n-1} - \binom{n-1}{\lfloor n/2 \rfloor}.$$

□

The single variable function disagrees with the majority function on

$$2^{n-1} - \binom{n-1}{\lfloor n/2 \rfloor} \sim \left(\frac{1}{2} - \frac{1}{\sqrt{2\pi n}}\right) 2^n \sim \left(\frac{1}{2} - \frac{0.4}{\sqrt{n}}\right) 2^n$$

points. Blum et al proved slightly weaker result to guarantee the performance of the learning algorithm for monotone Boolean functions under the uniform distribution described in Section 1.

Theorem 2 (Blum, Burch, Langford[2]) *For any fair monotone Boolean function f on n variables,*

$$\sharp\{x \mid MAJ_n(x) \neq f(x)\} \leq \left(\frac{1}{2} - \frac{0.1}{\sqrt{n}}\right) 2^n.$$

□

To prove Theorem 2, they analyzed the quantities p_k, which is defined as $p_k = \sharp I_k^f / \binom{n}{k}$. The key of the proof of the theorem is to apply the Kruskal-Katona Theorem (e.g., [5,4]) that says the p_k must be increasing with k at a reasonable rate. More specifically, they insisted that, for every monotone Boolean function and for every $0 \leq i < j \leq n$, $(p_i)^i \leq (p_j)^j$ holds ([2, Lemma 2]) as a corollary to the Kruskal-Katona theorem, and applied this to prove the theorem.

Remark :   Unfortunately, the above proposition ([2, Lemma 2]) does not hold for some range of i and j. For $i \geq 2$, define the Boolean function f as

$$f = x_1 \left(\bigvee_{k_2, k_3, \ldots, k_i \in \{2, \ldots, n\}} x_{k_2} x_{k_3} \cdots x_{k_i} \right).$$

It is easy to check that $p_j = \binom{n-1}{j-1} / \binom{n}{j} = j/n$ for every $i \leq j \leq n$. If we set $i = 0.3n$ and $j = 0.4n$, then we have $(p_i)^i = (3/10)^{0.3n} \sim (0.697)^n > (0.693)^n \sim (4/10)^{0.4n} = (p_j)^j$ holds and this contradicts the above proposition. Generally, the above proposition holds when the values of i and j are sufficiently close to $n/2$ (This can be proved by Corollary 4 stated below and a simple calculation) and may not hold for other cases. In the proof of Theorem 2 they applied the above lemma for $i = n/2 - c\sqrt{n}$ and $j = n/2 + c\sqrt{n}$ where c is a small constant. So this error does not affect the correctness of the proof of Theorem 2 in [2].

To prove Theorem 1, we use another version of the Kruskal-Katona Theorem which was introduced by Lovász's([8, Excecises 13.31], [5, Theorem 2]). This is the slightly weaker but much handier form of the Kruskal-Katona Theorem. Intuitively this theorem says that for every monotone Boolean function and for every $1 \leq k \leq n-1$, if $p_k \geq k/n$ then $p_{k+1} \geq (k+1)/n$ holds. This is a stronger statement than the proposition used by Blum et al when k is close to $n/2$.

Now we state the Lovász's version of the Kruskal-Katona Theorem. For $\mathcal{F} \subseteq 2^{[n]}$, define $\Delta(\mathcal{F}) = \{E \subseteq [n] \mid \exists F \in \mathcal{F} \ E \subseteq F, |F - E| = 1\}$.

Lemma 3 (Lovász[8]) *Let l and k be two integers such that $l \geq k \geq 1$. If $\mathcal{F} \subseteq 2_k^{[n]}$ and $\sharp\mathcal{F} = \binom{l}{k}$, then $\sharp\Delta(\mathcal{F}) \geq \binom{l}{k-1}$.* $\square$

An elegant proof of the lemma using so called the *shifting technique* appears in [5].

Corollary 4 *For any monotone Boolean function f on n variables and for any $1 \leq k \leq n-1$, if $\sharp I_k^f \geq \binom{n-1}{k-1}$ then $\sharp I_{k+1}^f \geq \binom{n-1}{k}$.*

Proof. Set $S_x = \{i \in [n] \mid x_i = 0\}$ for $x \in \{0,1\}^n$ and set $\mathcal{F}_{n-k} = \{S_x \mid x \in I_k^f\}$ for $0 \leq k \leq n$. Then there is one to one correspondence between I_k^f and $\mathcal{F}_{n-k}$ and so $\sharp I_k^f = \sharp\mathcal{F}_{n-k}$. By the monotonicity of f, $\Delta(\mathcal{F}_{n-k}) \subseteq \mathcal{F}_{n-k-1}$. Hence if $\sharp I_k^f \geq \binom{n-1}{k-1} = \binom{n-1}{n-k}$, then we have

$$\sharp I_{k+1}^f = \sharp F_{n-k-1} \geq \sharp\Delta(\mathcal{F}_{n-k}) \geq \binom{n-1}{n-k-1} = \binom{n-1}{k}$$

in view of Lemma 3. $\square$

The following lemma follows easily from Corollary 4.

Lemma 5 *For any fair monotone Boolean function f on n variables and for any $1 \leq t \leq n-1$,*

$$\sum_{k=0}^{t} \sharp I_k^f \leq \sum_{k=0}^{t-1} \binom{n-1}{k}, \tag{1}$$

and

$$\sum_{k=t}^{n} \sharp I_k^f \geq \sum_{k=t-1}^{n-1} \binom{n-1}{k}. \tag{2}$$

Proof. First we prove (1). Suppose in contradiction that $\sum_{k=0}^{t} \sharp I_k^f > \sum_{k=0}^{t-1} \binom{n-1}{k}$ for some $1 \leq t \leq n-1$. Let $t' \in [t]$ be the minimum integer such that $\sum_{k=0}^{t'} \sharp I_k^f >$

$\sum_{k=0}^{t'-1} \binom{n-1}{k}$. Then $\sharp I_{t'}^f > \binom{n-1}{t'-1}$ and $\sum_{k=0}^{t'} \sharp I_k^f = \sum_{k=0}^{t'-1} \binom{n-1}{k} + c$ for some integer $c \geq 1$. By Corollary 4, we have

$$\sharp I_{t'+1}^f \geq \binom{n-1}{t'}.$$

By applying Corollary 4 repeatedly, we obtain

$$\sharp I_t^f \geq \binom{n-1}{t-1}$$

for every $t' + 1 \leq t \leq n$. Thus

$$\sharp I^f = \sum_{k=0}^{n} \sharp I_k^f = \sum_{k=0}^{t'} \sharp I_k^f + \sum_{k=t'+1}^{n} \sharp I_k^f$$

$$\geq \sum_{k=0}^{t'-1} \binom{n-1}{k} + c + \sum_{k=t'}^{n-1} \binom{n-1}{k}$$

$$\geq \sum_{k=0}^{n-1} \binom{n-1}{k} + c > 2^{n-1}.$$

This contradicts the assumption that f is fair and thus completes the proof of (1).

Next we prove (2). Let f' be the dual function of f, i.e., $f'(x) = 1 - f(\bar{x})$. It is obvious that f' is monotone and fair. Since $\sharp I_k^f = \sharp O_k^{f'} = \binom{n}{n-k} - \sharp I_{n-k}^{f'}$,

$$(2) \Longleftrightarrow \sum_{k=t-1}^{n-1} \binom{n-1}{k} - \sum_{k=t}^{n} \sharp I_k^f \leq 0$$

$$\Longleftrightarrow \sum_{k=t-1}^{n-1} \binom{n-1}{k} - \sum_{k=t}^{n} \binom{n}{k} + \sum_{k=t}^{n} \sharp I_{n-k}^{f'} \leq 0$$

$$\Longleftrightarrow - \sum_{k=0}^{n-t-1} \binom{n-1}{k} + \sum_{k=0}^{n-t} \sharp I_k^{f'} \leq 0.$$

This is identical to inequality (1) when we replace t by $n - t$. $\square$

Now we proceed to the proof of the theorem.

Proof (of Theorem 1). Let f be a fair monotone Boolean function on n variables. The number of points on which f and the majority function differ can be written as

$$\sharp\{x \in \{0,1\}^n \mid \mathrm{MAJ}_n(x) \neq f(x)\} = \sharp\{x \in \{0,1\}^n \mid \mathrm{MAJ}_n(x) \neq x_1\} + \sharp N - \sharp P,$$

where

$$N = \{x \in \{0,1\}^n \mid (\mathrm{MAJ}_n(x) = x_1) \wedge (\mathrm{MAJ}_n(x) \neq f(x))\}$$

and

$$P = \{x \in \{0,1\}^n \mid (\mathrm{MAJ}_n(x) \neq x_1) \wedge (\mathrm{MAJ}_n(x) = f(x))\}.$$

So it is sufficient to show that $\sharp P \geq \sharp N$. In what follows, x denotes a vector of length n, whereas $\tilde{x}$ denotes a vector of length $n-1$. We have

$$
\begin{aligned}
\sharp N &= \sharp\{x \mid \mathrm{MAJ}_n(x) = 0, x_1 = 0, f(x) = 1\} \\
&\quad + \sharp\{x \mid \mathrm{MAJ}_n(x) = 1, x_1 = 1, f(x) = 0\} \\
&= \sharp\{\tilde{x} \mid \|\tilde{x}\| \leq \lfloor n/2 \rfloor, f(0\tilde{x}) = 1\} \\
&\quad + \sharp\{\tilde{x} \mid \|\tilde{x}\| \geq \lfloor n/2 \rfloor, f(1\tilde{x}) = 0\},
\end{aligned}
\tag{3}
$$

and

$$
\begin{aligned}
\sharp P &= \sharp\{x \mid \mathrm{MAJ}_n(x) = 0, x_1 = 1, f(x) = 0\} \\
&\quad + \sharp\{x \mid \mathrm{MAJ}_n(x) = 1, x_1 = 0, f(x) = 1\} \\
&= \sharp\{\tilde{x} \mid \|\tilde{x}\| \leq \lfloor n/2 \rfloor - 1, f(1\tilde{x}) = 0)\} \\
&\quad + \sharp\{\tilde{x} \mid \|\tilde{x}\| \geq \lfloor n/2 \rfloor + 1, f(0\tilde{x}) = 1)\}.
\end{aligned}
\tag{4}
$$

We denote the first and second terms in (3) by N_0 and N_1, respectively, and the first and the second terms in (4) by P_1 and P_0, respectively. From now on, we prove $\sharp P_1 - \sharp N_0 \geq 0$ and $\sharp P_0 - \sharp N_1 \geq 0$, which implies the theorem since we have $\sharp P - \sharp N = \sharp P_0 + \sharp P_1 - (\sharp N_0 + \sharp N_1) \geq 0$.

For $i \in \{0,1\}$ and for $0 \leq k \leq n-1$, define the sets of vectors of length $n-1$ by $I_k^i = \{x \in 1_k^f \mid f(i\tilde{x}) = 1\}$ and $O_k^i = \{\tilde{x} \in O_k^f \mid f(i\tilde{x}) = 0\}$. Then

$$
\begin{aligned}
\sharp P_1 - \sharp N_0 &= \sum_{k=0}^{\lfloor n/2 \rfloor - 1} \sharp O_k^1 - \sum_{k=0}^{\lfloor n/2 \rfloor} \sharp I_k^0 \\
&= \sum_{k=0}^{\lfloor n/2 \rfloor - 1} \binom{n-1}{k} - \sum_{k=0}^{\lfloor n/2 \rfloor - 1} \sharp I_k^1 - \sum_{k=0}^{\lfloor n/2 \rfloor} \sharp I_k^0 \\
&= \sum_{k=0}^{\lfloor n/2 \rfloor - 1} \binom{n-1}{k} - \sum_{k=0}^{\lfloor n/2 \rfloor} \sharp I_k^f \geq 0.
\end{aligned}
$$

The last inequality follows from (1) in Lemma 5. Similarly,

$$
\begin{aligned}
\sharp P_0 - \sharp N_1 &= \sum_{k=\lfloor n/2 \rfloor + 1}^{n-1} \sharp I_k^0 - \sum_{k=\lfloor n/2 \rfloor}^{n-1} \sharp O_k^1 \\
&= \sum_{k=\lfloor n/2 \rfloor + 1}^{n-1} \sharp I_k^0 - \sum_{k=\lfloor n/2 \rfloor}^{n-1} \binom{n-1}{k} + \sum_{k=\lfloor n/2 \rfloor}^{n-1} \sharp I_1^k \\
&= \sum_{k=\lfloor n/2 \rfloor + 1}^{n} \sharp I_k^f - \sum_{k=\lfloor n/2 \rfloor}^{n-1} \binom{n-1}{k} \geq 0.
\end{aligned}
$$

The last inequality follows from (2) in Lemma 5.   □

To construct an algorithm for learning monotone functions based on our theorem, the following lemma due to Blum et al[2] is useful.

Lemma 6 (Blum, Burch and Langford[2]) *Suppose that there exists an algorithm A for learning fair monotone functions, which uses no samples and outputs a hypothesis with error at most $1/2 - \epsilon$. Then there exists an algorithm A' for learning monotone functions that, for any $\alpha, \delta > 0$, produces a hypothesis with error at most $1/2 - \epsilon/(2 + \alpha)$ with probability $1 - \delta$, accessing the oracle EXAMPLE $\frac{2(2+\alpha)^2}{\alpha\epsilon^2}$ times and calling the algorithm A.*   □

We apply Lemma 6 with $\alpha = 1/2$ and $\epsilon = 0.4/\sqrt{n}$ to get the following corollary which slightly improves on the result of Blum et al.

Corollary 7 *In linear time we can learn monotone Boolean function guaranteeing error at most $1/2 - 0.15/\sqrt{n}$ under the uniform distribution.*   □

3   Relationship between Influences and Average Sensitivity

In the previous section, we proved the single variable function has the minimum correlation with the majority function among all fair monotone Boolean functions. This leads us to consider a new learning algorithm for monotone Boolean functions under the uniform distribution : Draw example enough times and then output the most correlated function in $\{0, 1, x_1, x_2, \ldots, x_n, \mathrm{MAJ}_n\}$ on the examples as a hypothesis.

It is interesting to see whether the above algorithm can achieve error better than $1/2 - \omega(1/\sqrt{n})$. In this section, we analyze the performance of this algorithm by using the ideas from Harmonic analysis.

As in the previous section, we can assume that a target function is fair. Now our problem turns out to be estimating $\max_f \min_{h \in \mathcal{F}} err(f, h)$ for $\mathcal{F} = \{x_1, x_2, \ldots, x_n, \mathrm{MAJ}_n\}$, where the maximum is taken over all fair monotone Boolean functions on n variables.

Because of the hardness result described below and Corollary 7, it can be seen that the above value is lower bounded by $1/2 - O(\log n/\sqrt{n})$.

Theorem 8 (Blum, Burch, Langford[2]) *There are no algorithms, given only a polynomial number of accesses to the oracle MEMBER, can guarantee error $1/2 - \omega(\log n/\sqrt{n})$ for learning monotone Boolean functions under the uniform distribution.*   □

Note that given access to MEMBER, the oracle EXAMPLE is redundant because a randomized learning algorithm can simulate EXAMPLE by simply calling MEMBER on uniform random inputs.

Throughout this section we view Boolean functions as real valued functions which map $\{0,1\}^n$ to $\{-1,1\}$. For $x \in \{0,1\}^n$ and for $1 \le i \le n$, $x \oplus e_i$ denotes x with its i-th bit flipped. For a Boolean function f on n variables, the *influence* of x_i on f, denoted by $L^f(x_i)$, is defined as the probability that $f(x)$ differs from $f(x \oplus e_i)$ when x is drawn from the uniform distribution on $\{0,1\}^n$. That is

$$L^f(x_i) = \Pr[f(x) \ne f(x \oplus e_i)].$$

Note that, for every monotone Boolean function f, $\mathrm{err}(f, x_i) = 1/2(1 - L^f(x_i))$. The *average sensitivity* of f, denoted by $s(f)$, is defined as

$$s(f) = \sum_{i=1}^{n} L^f(x_i).$$

For example, if $f = x_1$ then $L^f(x_1) = 1$, $L^f(x_i) = 0$ for every $i \ne 1$ and $s(f) = 1$. Theorem 1 implies $\mathrm{err}(f, \mathrm{MAJ}_n) = \frac{1}{2} - \Theta(1/\sqrt{n}) = \frac{1}{2} - \Theta(s(f)/\sqrt{n})$. If $f = \mathrm{MAJ}_n$ then $L^f(x_1) = \Theta(1/\sqrt{n})$ for every $1 \le i \le n$, $s(f) = \Theta(\sqrt{n})$ and $\mathrm{err}(f, \mathrm{MAJ}_n) = 0 = \frac{1}{2} - \Theta(s(f)/\sqrt{n})$. Here we consider another example. Let $f = t_1 \vee t_2 \vee \cdots \vee t_m$ be a monotone DNF formula on n variables such that each term t_i is a product of exactly l variables satisfying $(1 - 1/2^l)^m \sim 1/2$ and every variable appears exactly once in f. It is easy to check that f is an almost fair and $L^f(x_i) = \Theta(\log n/n)$ for every $1 \le i \le n$ and so $s(f) = \Theta(\log n)$. A simple but tedious calculation shows $\mathrm{err}(f, \mathrm{MAJ}_n) = \frac{1}{2} - \Theta(\log n/\sqrt{n}) = \frac{1}{2} - \Theta(s(f)/\sqrt{n})$. These observations motivate us to divide our problem into two subproblems.

Problem 9 Is it true that for every fair monotone Boolean function f on n variables

$$\mathrm{err}(f, MAJ_n) = \frac{1}{2} - \Omega\left(\frac{s(f)}{\sqrt{n}}\right)?$$

Problem 10 Let f be a fair monotone Boolean function on n variables. Is it true that if, for every $1 \le i \le n$,

$$\mathrm{err}(f, x_i) = \frac{1}{2} - O\left(\frac{\log n}{\sqrt{n}}\right),$$

which is equivalent to $L^f(x_i) = O(\log n/\sqrt{n})$, then $s(f) = \Omega(\log n)$?

If answers of both problems are true then the above algorithm achieves an optimal error $1/2 - \Omega(\log n/n)$ for learning monotone Boolean functions under the uniform distribution. Problem 10 seems somewhat curious since it says "If the influence of every variable is small then the sum of them is large." In the rest of this section, we prove the answer of Problem 10 is true even if we drop the condition that f is fair and weaken the condition $L^f(x_i) = O(\log n/\sqrt{n})$ to $L^f(x_i) = O(1/n^c)$ for some constant $c > 0$. Unfortunately, we could not solve Problem 9 at the time of writing this paper.

To solve this problem we use the ideas from Harmonic analysis. The Fourier transform of Boolean functions over the uniform distribution is defined as follows (see e.g. [3]). Given any subset $A \subseteq [n]$, the Fourier basis function $\chi_A : \{0,1\} \to \{-1,1\}$ is defined as $\chi_A(x) = (-1)^{|A \cap X|}$, where X is the subset of $[n]$ defined as $i \in X$ if and only if $x_i = 1$. It is well known that the 2^n basis functions χ_A form an orthonormal basis for the vector space of real valued functions on $\{0,1\}^n$. For a subset $A \subseteq [n]$, the Fourier coefficient of the basis χ_A, denoted by $\hat{f}_A$, is given by

$$\hat{f}_A = E[f\chi_A] = \frac{1}{2^n} \sum_x f(x)(-1)^{|A \cap X|}.$$

Note that any function f can be uniquely expressed as $f(x) = \sum_A \hat{f}_A \chi_A(x)$. Because of orthonomality we have Parseval's equation : $\sum_A \hat{f}_A^2 = 1$.

If f is a monotone Boolean function then it is easy to check that $L^f(x_i) = -\hat{f}_{\{i\}} \geq 0$ for every $1 \leq i \leq n$. For $1 \leq i \leq n$, we define function $f^i : \{0,1\}^n \to \{-1,0,1\}$ as

$$f^i(x) = \frac{1}{2}\left(f(x) - f(x \oplus e_i)\right).$$

It is easy to check that if $i \notin A$ then $\hat{f^i}_A = 0$ and if $i \in A$ then $\hat{f^i}_A = \hat{f}_A$. So we have $L^f(x_i) = \sum_x f^i(x)^2/2^n = \sum_{A:i \in A} \hat{f}_A^2$ (See e.g., [3, Lemma 1]). Summing this over all $1 \leq i \leq n$ we obtain

$$s(f) = \sum_{i=1}^n L^f(x_i) = \sum_A |A|\hat{f}_A^2. \tag{5}$$

Now we state our theorem.

Theorem 11 *Let f be a monotone Boolean function on n variables such that $e \leq \Pr[f(x) = 1] \leq 1 - e$ for some constant $e > 0$. If there is a constant $c > 0$ such that $L^f(x_i) < 1/n^c$ for any $1 \leq i \leq n$ then $s(f) = \sum_{i=1}^n L^f(x_i) = \Omega(\log n)$.*   □

Note that the above theorem is the best possible in the sense that there exist a monotone Boolean function f such that $L^f(x_i) = \Theta(\log n/n)$ for every i and $s(f) = \Theta(\log n)$.

The outline of the proof of Theorem 11 is as follows : Because of (5) and Parseval's equation ($\sum_A \hat{f}_A^2 = 1$), it is sufficient to show that $\sum_{A:|A| \geq \Omega(\log n)} \hat{f}_A^2$ is not negligible under the assumption that $L^f(x_i)$ is small for every i. To prove this, we use the idea of the proof of the theorem due to Kahn et al[6, Theorem 3.1] that says the sum of squares of the individual influences is $\Omega((\log n)^2/n)$ for every monotone Boolean function f. To prove this theorem, they applied the inequalities of Beckner[1] to establish a slightly weaker version of our statement without the assumption that the influences are small. As in the proof of their theorem, the next lemma due to Kahn et al[6] is a key of the proof of our theorem.

Lemma 12 (Kahn, Kalai, Linial([6], Lemma 3.4)) *Let g be a function from $\{0,1\}^n$ into $\{-1,0,1\}$. Let t be the probability that $g \neq 0$ and let $g = \sum_A \hat{g}_A \chi_A$ be the Fourier expansion of g. Then,*

$$t^{\frac{2}{1+\delta}} \geq \sum_A \delta^{|A|} \hat{g}_A^2$$

for every $0 \leq \delta \leq 1$. $\square$

Proof (of Theorem 11(Sketch)). If

$$\sharp\left\{i \in [n] \Big| L^f(x_i) \geq \frac{1}{n^{1/2^\alpha + c'}}\right\} \geq n^{1/2^\alpha + c'} \log n$$

for some $\alpha > 0$ and for some $c' > 0$, then $s(f) = \sum_{i=1}^n L^f(x_i) \geq \log n$ holds. Thus, without loss of generality, we can assume that

$$\sharp\left\{i \in [n] \Big| L^f(x_i) \geq \frac{1}{n^{1/2^\alpha + c'}}\right\} < n^{1/2^\alpha + c'} \log n,$$

for any $\alpha > 0$ and for any $c' > 0$. From this and the assumption that $L^f(x_i) < 1/n^c$ for any $1 \leq i \leq n$ we have

$$\sum_{i=1}^n L^f(x_i)^2 < \left(\frac{1}{n^c}\right)^2 n^{1/2^\alpha + c'} \log n$$

$$+ \left(\frac{1}{n^{1/2^\alpha + c'}}\right)^2 n^{1/2^{\alpha-1} + c'} \log n + \cdots + \left(\frac{1}{n^{1/4 + c'}}\right)^2 n^{1/2 + c'} \log n$$

$$+ \left(\frac{1}{n^{1/2 + c'}}\right)^2 n$$

$$= n^{1/2^\alpha - 2c + c'} \log n + (\alpha - 1) n^{-c'} \log n + n^{-2c'}.$$

Let α and c' be two constants satisfying $1/2^\alpha - 2c + c' \leq -c'$. (The condition can be satisfied by putting $\alpha = \log \frac{1}{c}$ and $c' = c/2$.) Then we have

$$\sum_{i=1}^n L^f(x_i)^2 = O(n^{-c'} \log n) = O(n^{-c'/2}). \tag{6}$$

Now we apply Lemma 12 with $g = f^i$. Note that the probability that $f^i \neq 0$ is equal to $L^f(x_i)$. So we have

$$L^f(x_i)^{\frac{2}{1+\delta}} \geq \sum_A \delta^{|A|} (\hat{f^i}_A)^2 = \sum_{A:i \in A} \delta^{|A|} \hat{f}_A^2.$$

Summing this over $1 \leq i \leq n$, we have

$$\sum_{i=1}^n L^f(x_i)^{\frac{2}{1+\delta}} \geq \sum_A \delta^{|A|} |A| \hat{f}_A^2 \geq \delta^b \sum_{A:|A| \leq b} |A| \hat{f}_A^2 \geq \delta^b \Big(\sum_{A:|A| \leq b} \hat{f}_A^2 - \hat{f}_\phi \Big), \tag{7}$$

where b is a parameter which we will choose shortly. From (6) and the Cauchy-Schwartz inequality we obtain

$$\sum_{i=1}^{n} L^f(x_i) \le \sqrt{n} \cdot O(n^{-c'/4}).$$

Since $\frac{2}{1+\delta} < 2$ and the monotonicity of r-th power averages we have

$$\sum_{i=1}^{n} L^f(x_i)^{\frac{2}{1+\delta}} \le \sqrt{n} \cdot O(n^{-c'/4}) \cdot O(n^{-1/2-c'/4})^{\frac{1-\delta}{1+\delta}} = O\left(n^{\frac{2\delta-c'}{2(1+\delta)}}\right). \quad (8)$$

Choose δ to be $c'/4$ and b to be $\frac{c'}{8} \frac{\log n}{\log(4/c')}$. From (7) and (8) we have

$$\sum_{A:|A|\le b} \hat{f}_A^2 \le \left(\frac{1}{\delta}\right)^b \sum_{i=1}^{n} L^f(x_i)^{\frac{2}{1+\delta}} + \hat{f}_\phi^2 \le \left(\frac{4}{c'}\right)^b O\left(n^{-c'/4}\right) + \hat{f}_\phi^2$$

$$\le O\left(n^{c'/8-c'/4}\right) + \hat{f}_\phi^2 \le O\left(n^{-c'/8}\right) + \hat{f}_\phi^2 < c'',$$

where c'' is some constant satisfying $c'' < 1$. The last inequality follows from the fact that $\hat{f}_\phi^2 = (2\Pr[f(x) = 1] - 1)^2 \le (1 - 2e)^2 < 1$. By Parseval's equation $(1 = \sum_A \hat{f}_A^2)$, we have $\sum_{A:|A|>b} \hat{f}_A^2 = \Omega(1)$. Hence

$$s(f) = \sum_A |A|\hat{f}_A^2 \ge \sum_{A:|A|>b} |A|\hat{f}_A^2 > b \sum_{A:|A|>b} \hat{f}_A^2 = \Omega(\log n) \cdot \Omega(1) = \Omega(\log n).$$

This completes the proof of the theorem.   □

References

[1] W. Beckner, "Inequalities in Fourier Analysis", Annals of Mathematics, Vol. 102, pp. 159–182, 1975.

[2] A. Blum, C. Burch and J. Langford, "On Learning Monotone Boolean Functions", Proc. 39th FOCS, pp. 408–415, 1998.

[3] N.H. Bshouty and C. Tamon, "On the Fourier Spectrum of Monotone Functions", JACM, Vol. 43, No. 4, pp. 747–770, 1996.

[4] D.E. Daykin, "A Simple Proof of the Kruskal-Katona Theorem", J. Combinatorial Theory (A), Vol. 17, pp. 252–253, 1974.

[5] P. Frankl, "A New Short Proof for the Kruskal-Katona Theorem", Discrete Mathematics, Vol. 48, pp. 327–329, 1984.

[6] J. Kahn, G. Kalai and N. Linial, "The influence of Variables on Boolean Functions (Extended Abstract)", Proc. 29th FOCS, pp. 68–80, 1988.

[7] M. Kerans, M. Li and L. Valiant, "Learning Boolean Formulas", JACM, Vol. 41, No. 6, pp. 1298–1328, 1994.

[8] L. Lovász, Combinatorial Problems and Exercises, North-Holland, Amsterdam, 1979.

On Learning Embedded Midbit Functions

Rocco A. Servedio

Division of Engineering and Applied Sciences
Harvard University
Cambridge, MA 02138 USA
rocco@deas.harvard.edu
http://www.cs.harvard.edu/~rocco

Abstract. A midbit function on ℓ binary inputs $x_1, \ldots, x_\ell$ outputs the middle bit in the binary representation of $x_1 + \cdots + x_\ell$. We consider the problem of PAC learning *embedded* midbit functions, where the set $S \subset \{x_1, \ldots, x_n\}$ of relevant variables on which the midbit depends is unknown to the learner.

To motivate this problem, we first show that a polynomial time learning algorithm for the class of embedded midbit functions would immediately yield a fairly efficient (quasipolynomial time) PAC learning algorithm for the entire complexity class ACC. We then give two different subexponential learning algorithms, each of which learns embedded midbit functions under any probability distribution in $2^{\sqrt{n} \log n}$ time. Finally, we give a polynomial time algorithm for learning embedded midbit functions under the uniform distribution.

1 Introduction

A central goal of computational learning theory is to understand the computational complexity of learning various classes of Boolean functions. While much research has been devoted to learning syntactic classes such as decision trees, DNF formulas, and constant depth circuits, researchers have also considered various "semantically defined" classes as well. A natural and important class of this sort is the class of *embedded symmetric functions* which was studied by Blum *et al.* [5]. (Recall that a Boolean function is symmetric if its value depends only on the number of input bits which are set to 1.) An embedded symmetric function is a Boolean function which depends only on some subset of its input variables and is a symmetric function on this subset, i.e., it is a symmetric function whose domain is "embedded" in a larger domain containing irrelevant variables.

In this paper we give a detailed PAC learning analysis of an interesting and natural family of embedded symmetric functions, namely the *embedded midbit functions*. An embedded midbit function is defined by a subset $i_1, \ldots, i_s$ of variables from $\{1, \ldots, n\}$. The value of this embedded midbit function on an input $x \in \{0,1\}^n$ is the value of the middle bit in the binary representation of $x_{i_1} + x_{i_2} + \cdots + x_{i_s}$. As described below, we show that the class of embedded midbit functions has many interesting properties from a PAC learning perspective.

N. Cesa-Bianchi et al. (Eds.): ALT 2002, LNAI 2533, pp. 69–82, 2002.

1.1   Our Results

We first give a hardness result (Theorem 2) for learning embedded midbit functions in the standard PAC model of learning from random examples drawn from an arbitrary probability distribution. Using Green et $al.$'s characterization of the complexity class ACC [9], we show that if there is a PAC learning algorithm for the class of embedded midbit functions which runs in polynomial time (or even quasipolynomial time), then the class ACC of constant-depth, polynomial-size circuits of unbounded fanin AND/OR/MOD$_m$ gates can also be PAC learned in quasipolynomial time. This would be a major breakthrough since, as described in Section 3, the fastest PAC learning algorithms to date for even very restricted subclasses of ACC require much more than quasipolynomial time. Our hardness result strengthens an earlier hardness result of Blum et $al.$ for embedded symmetric functions, and establishes an interesting connection between learning the "semantic" class of embedded midbit functions and learning rich syntactic classes.

While Theorem 2 implies that it may be difficult to learn embedded midbit functions efficiently under an arbitrary distribution, this does not mean that PAC learning algorithms for embedded midbit functions must require exponential time. In Section 4 we give two different subexponential time PAC learning algorithms, each of which can learn embedded midbit functions over n variables in time $n^{O(\sqrt{n})}$.

Finally, by means of a careful analysis of the correlation of single variables and pairs of variables with embedded midbit functions, we show in Section 5 that embedded midbit functions can be learned in polynomial time under the uniform distribution. Embedded midbit functions thus give a simple and natural concept class which seems to exhibit a large gap between the complexity of learning in the uniform distribution PAC model and the general (arbitrary distribution) PAC model.

2   Preliminaries

Throughout this paper S denotes a subset of the variables $\{x_1, \ldots, x_n\}$ and s denotes $|S|$. All logarithms are base 2.

Definition 1. *For $S \neq \emptyset$ the embedded midbit function $M_S : \{0,1\}^n \to \{0,1\}$ is defined as $M_S(x) =$ the value of the $\lfloor \log(s)/2 \rfloor$-th bit in the binary representation of $\sum_S x_i$, where we consider the least significant bit to be the 0-th bit. (We take $M_\emptyset(x)$ to be identically 0.) The class C_{mid} of embedded midbit functions is $C_{mid} = \{M_S\}_{S \subseteq \{x_1, \ldots, x_n\}}$.*

We write C_{sym} to denote the class of all embedded symmetric functions on $\{0,1\}^n$ as described in Section 1; note that $C_{mid} \subset C_{sym}$.

Definition 2. *Given an embedded midbit function $M_S(x)$, let $f_s : \{0, 1, \ldots, s\} \to \{0,1\}$ be the unique function such that $M_S(x) = f_s(\sum_S x_i)$ for all $x \in \{0,1\}^n$. We say that f_s is the basis function of $M_S(x)$ and we refer to the $(s+1)$-bit string $f_s(0)f_s(1) \ldots f_s(s)$ as the pattern of f_s.*

If f_s is the basis function for M_S then the pattern for f_s is a concatenation of strings of the form $0^{k(s)}1^{k(s)}$, where $k(s) = 2^{\lfloor \log(s)/2 \rfloor}$ and the concatenation is truncated to be of length precisely $s+1$. It is easy to see that $\sqrt{s}/2 < k(s) \le \sqrt{s}$.

A function f is *quasipolynomial* if $f(n) = 2^{(\log n)^{O(1)}}$. We write $[a \bmod b]$ to denote the unique real number $r \in [0, b)$ such that $a = kb + r$ for some integer k.

2.1   The Learning Model

We work in the standard Probably Approximately Correct (PAC) learning model [17] and the uniform distribution variant of the PAC model. Let C be a class of Boolean functions over $\{0,1\}^n$. In the PAC model, a learning algorithm has access to a random example oracle $EX(c, \mathcal{D})$ which when invoked in one time step provides a labeled example $\langle x, c(x) \rangle \in \{0,1\}^n \times \{0,1\}$ where x is drawn from the distribution $\mathcal{D}$ over $\{0,1\}^n$. An algorithm A is a PAC learning algorithm for class C if the following holds: for all $c \in C$ and all distributions $\mathcal{D}$ over $\{0,1\}^n$, if A is given as input $\epsilon, \delta > 0$ and A is given access to $EX(c, \mathcal{D})$, then with probability at least $1 - \delta$ the output of A is a hypothesis $h : \{0,1\}^n \to \{0,1\}$ such that $\Pr_{x \in \mathcal{D}}[c(x) \ne h(x)] \le \epsilon$. (Strictly speaking, the output of A is some particular representation of h such as a Boolean circuit.) Algorithm A is said to run in time t if (i) the worst case running time of A (over all choices of $c \in C$ and all distributions $\mathcal{D}$) is at most t, and (ii) for every output h of A and all $x \in \{0,1\}^n$, $h(x)$ can be evaluated in time t.

If A satisfies the above definition only for some fixed distribution $\mathcal{D}$ (such as the uniform distribution on $\{0,1\}^n$), then we say that A is a PAC learning algorithm for C under distribution $\mathcal{D}$.

3   Hardness of Learning Embedded Midbit Functions

In this section we show that learning embedded midbit functions is almost as difficult as learning a rich syntactic class which contains decision trees, DNF formulas, and constant depth circuits.

3.1   Background: Hardness of Learning C_{sym}

We first describe a result of Blum *et al.* which gives some evidence that the broader class C_{sym} of embedded symmetric functions may be hard to PAC learn in polynomial time. Let C_{log} denote the class of Boolean functions on n bits which have at most $\log n$ relevant variables. Note that like C_{sym}, the class C_{log} has the property that learning is no more difficult than finding relevant variables – in either case, once the set of relevant variables has been identified, learning is simply a matter of observing and filling in at most n "table entries" which define the function (these entries are the bits of the pattern for a function from C_{sym}, and are the values of the function on all $2^{\log n}$ inputs for a function from C_{log}).

Building on this intuition, Blum *et al.* gave a polynomial time prediction-preserving reduction from C_{log} to C_{sym}, thus showing that if C_{sym} can be PAC learned in polynomial time then C_{log} can also be PAC learned in polynomial time. Since no polynomial time learning algorithm is yet known for C_{log}, this gives some evidence that C_{sym} may not be learnable in polynomial time.

3.2   Hardness of Learning C_{mid}

The class ACC was introduced by Barrington [2] and since been studied by many researchers, e.g. [1,3,4,9,12,18,19]. ACC consists of languages recognized by a family of constant-depth polynomial-size circuits with NOT gates and unbounded fanin AND, OR and MOD_m gates, where m is fixed for each circuit family. In the context of learning theory ACC is quite an expressive class, containing as it does polynomial size decision trees, polynomial size DNF formulas, and the well-studied class AC^0 of constant-depth polynomial-size AND/OR/NOT circuits.

Building on work of Beigel and Tarui [4], Green *et al.* [9] have given the following characterization of ACC :

Theorem 1. *For each $L \in ACC$ there is a depth-2 circuit which recognizes $L \cap \{0,1\}^n$ and has the following structure: the top-level gate computes a midbit function of its inputs, and the bottom level consists of $2^{(\log n)^{O(1)}}$ AND gates each of fanin $(\log n)^{O(1)}$.*

Using this characterization we obtain the following hardness result for learning C_{mid} :

Theorem 2. *If C_{mid} can be PAC learned in polynomial (or even quasipolynomial) time, then ACC can be PAC learned in quasipolynomial time.*

Proof. Let $f : \{0,1\}^n \to \{0,1\}$ be the target ACC function. Let $q(n) = 2^{(\log n)^{O(1)}}$ be an upper bound on the number of AND gates on the bottom level of the Green *et al.* representation for f, and let $\ell(n) = (\log n)^{O(1)}$ be an upper bound on the fanin of each bottom level AND gate. Given an instance $x \in \{0,1\}^n$ we generate a new instance $x' \in \{0,1\}^m$ where $m = 2^{(\log n)^{O(1)}}$ by listing $q(n)$ copies of each AND of at most $\ell(n)$ variables from $x_1, \ldots, x_n$. Theorem 1 implies that there is an embedded midbit function f' on m bits such that $f(x) = f'(x')$ for all $x \in \{0,1\}^n$. By assumption we can PAC learn this function f' in $2^{(\log m)^{O(1)}} = 2^{(\log n)^{O(1)}}$ time, so the theorem is proved.

We note that while our reduction only establishes quasipolynomial time learnability for ACC from learnability of C_{mid}, whereas the Blum reduction would establish polynomial time learnability of C_{log}, the class ACC is likely to be much harder to learn than C_{log}. While C_{log} can be PAC learned in $n^{\log n}$ time by doing an exhaustive search for the set of $\log n$ relevant variables, no learning algorithm for ACC is known which runs in subexponential time. In fact, no such algorithm is known even for the subclass of polynomial-size, depth 3 AND/OR/NOT circuits; to date the most expressive subclass of ACC which is known to be PAC learnable in subexponential time is the class of polynomial-size AND/OR/NOT circuits of depth 2, which has recently been shown by Klivans and Servedio [11] to be PAC learnable in time $2^{\tilde{O}(n^{1/3})}$.

4   Learning Embedded Midbit Functions in $n^{O(\sqrt{n})}$ Time

The results of Section 3 suggest that the class of embedded midbit functions may not be PAC learnable in quasipolynomial time. However, we will show that it is possible to learn this class substantially faster than a naive exponential time algorithm. In this section we describe two different algorithms each of which PAC learns C_{mid} in time $n^{O(\sqrt{n})}$.

4.1   An Algorithm Based on Learning Linear Threshold Functions

Our first approach is a variant of an algorithm given by Blum et al. in section 5.2 of [5].

Definition 3. *Let* $f\colon\{0,1\}^n \to \{0,1\}$ *be a Boolean function and* $p(x_1,\ldots,x_n)$ *a real-valued polynomial. We say that* $p(x)$ *sign-represents* $f(x)$ *if for all* $x \in \{0,1\}^n$, $p(x) \geq 0$ *iff* $f(x) = 1$.

Claim. Let M_S be an embedded midbit function. Then there is a polynomial $p_S(x_1,\ldots,x_n)$ of degree $O(\sqrt{n})$ which sign-represents $M_S(x)$.

Proof. Let f_s be the basis function for M_S. Since $k(s) = \Omega(\sqrt{s})$, the number of "flip" positions in the pattern of f_s where $f_s(i) \neq f_s(i+1)$ is $O(\sqrt{s})$. Since the pattern for f_s has $O(\sqrt{s})$ flips, there is some polynomial $P(X)$ of degree $O(\sqrt{s})$ which is nonnegative on precisely those $i \in \{0,1,\ldots,s\}$ which have $f_s(i) = 1$. This implies that $p_S(x_1,\ldots,x_n) = P(\sum_S x_i)$ sign-represents $M_S(x)$. Since the degree of p_S is $O(\sqrt{s})$ and $s \leq n$ the claim is proved.

Consider the expanded feature space consisting of all monotone conjunctions of at most $O(\sqrt{n})$ variables. (Note that this feature space contains $\sum_{i=1}^{O(\sqrt{n})} n^i = n^{O(\sqrt{n})}$ features.) Claim 4.1 implies that $M_S(x)$ is equivalent to some linear threshold function over this space. Thus we can use known polynomial time PAC learning algorithms for linear threshold functions [6] over this expanded feature space to learn embedded midbit functions in $n^{O(\sqrt{n})}$ time.

Note that one can show that the sign-representing polynomial $p_S(x_1,\ldots,x_n)$ described in Claim 4.1 can be taken without loss of generality to have integer coefficients of total magnitude $n^{O(\sqrt{n})}$. This implies that simple algorithms such as Winnow or Perceptron can be used to learn in $n^{O(\sqrt{n})}$ time (instead of the more sophisticated algorithm of [6] which is based on polynomial time linear programming). We also note that in [13] Minsky and Papert used a symmetrization technique to give a lower bound on the degree of any polynomial which sign-represents the parity function. The same technique can be used to show that the $O(\sqrt{n})$ degree bound of Claim 4.1 is optimal for embedded midbit functions.

4.2   An Algorithm Based on Learning Parities

We have seen that any embedded midbit function is equivalent to some linear threshold function over the feature space of all $O(\sqrt{n})$-size monotone conjunctions. We now show that any embedded midbit function is equivalent to some parity over this feature space as well.

Lemma 1. *Let* $r, \ell \geq 0$. *Then* $\binom{r}{2^\ell}$ *is even if and only if*

$$[r \bmod 2^{\ell+1}] \in \{0, 1, \dots, 2^\ell - 1\}.$$

Proof. By induction on ℓ. The base case $\ell = 0$ is trivial; we suppose that the claim holds for $\ell = 0, \dots, i-1$ for some $i \geq 1$. For the induction step we use the fact (Exercise 5.61 of [8]) that

$$\binom{r}{m} \equiv \binom{\lfloor r/p \rfloor}{\lfloor m/p \rfloor} \binom{[r \bmod p]}{[m \bmod p]} \pmod{p}$$

for all primes p and all $r, m \geq 0$. Taking $p = 2$ and $m = 2^i$, since $i \geq 1$ we have

$$\binom{r}{2^i} \equiv \binom{\lfloor r/2 \rfloor}{2^{i-1}} \binom{[r \bmod 2]}{0} \equiv \binom{\lfloor r/2 \rfloor}{2^{i-1}} \pmod 2$$

By the induction hypothesis this is 0 iff $[\lfloor r/2 \rfloor \bmod 2^i] \in \{0, 1, \dots, 2^{i-1} - 1\}$, which holds if and only if $[r \bmod 2^{i+1}] \in \{0, 1, \dots, 2^i - 1\}$.

Claim. Let M_S be an embedded midbit function. Then $M_S(x)$ is equivalent to some parity of monotone conjunctions each of which contains at most $O(\sqrt{n})$ variables.

Proof. Let $\oplus$ denote the parity function. We have

$$M_S(x) = 0 \iff \lfloor \log(s)/2 \rfloor\text{-th bit of } \sum_S x_i \text{ is } 0$$

$$\iff \left[\sum_S x_i \bmod 2^{\lfloor \log(s)/2 \rfloor + 1} \right] \in \{0, 1, \dots, 2^{\lfloor \log(s)/2 \rfloor} - 1\}$$

$$\iff \binom{\sum_S x_i}{2^{\lfloor \log(s)/2 \rfloor}} = \binom{\sum_S x_i}{k(s)} \text{ is even}$$

$$\iff \bigoplus_{A \subseteq S, |A| = k(s)} \left(\bigwedge_{i \in A} x_i \right) = 0.$$

The third step is by Lemma 1 and the last step is because for any x exactly $\binom{\sum_S x_i}{k(s)}$ of the conjunctions $\{\bigwedge_{i \in A} x_i\}_{A \subseteq S, |A| = k(s)}$ take value 1. Since $k(s) = O(\sqrt{n})$ the claim is proved.

As in the discussion following Claim 4.1, Claim 4.2 implies that we can use known PAC learning algorithms for parity [7,10] over an expanded feature space to learn embedded midbit functions in $n^{O(\sqrt{n})}$ time.

5 A Polynomial Time Algorithm for Learning Embedded Midbits under the Uniform Distribution

In [5] Blum *et al.* posed as an open problem the question of whether embedded symmetric concepts can be learned under the uniform distribution in polynomial time. In this section, we show that embedded midbit functions can be PAC learned under the uniform distribution in polynomial time. This is in strong contrast to the results of Section 3 which indicate that embedded midbit functions probably cannot be PAC learned (in even quasipolynomial time) under arbitrary probability distributions.

Throughout this section we let $t(s)$ denote $\lfloor \frac{s}{k(s)} \rfloor$.

5.1 First Approach: Testing Single Variables

To learn M_S it is sufficient to identify the set $S \subseteq \{x_1, \ldots, x_n\}$ of relevant variables. A natural first approach is to test the correlation of each individual variable with $M_S(x)$; clearly variables not in S will have zero correlation, and one might hope that variables in S will have nonzero correlation. However this hope is incorrect as shown by Lemma 3 below.

For $1 \le i \le n$ define $p_i = \Pr[M_S(x) = 1 | x_i = 1] - \Pr[M_S(x) = 1]$. The following fact is easily verified:

Fact 3 *If $i \notin S$ then $p_i = 0$.*

Lemma 2. *If $i \in S$ then*

$$p_i = \frac{1}{2^s} \sum_{\ell=1}^{t(s)} (-1)^{\ell-1} \binom{s-1}{\ell k(s) - 1}. \tag{1}$$

Proof. Since the distribution on examples is uniform over $\{0,1\}^n$, the probability that exactly ℓ of the s relevant variables are 1 is exactly $\binom{s}{\ell}/2^s$. Hence we have

$$p_i = \frac{1}{2^{s-1}} \sum_{\ell:f_s(\ell)=1} \binom{s-1}{\ell-1} - \frac{1}{2^s} \sum_{\ell:f_s(\ell)=1} \binom{s}{\ell}.$$

Using the identity $\binom{s}{\ell} = \binom{s-1}{\ell-1} + \binom{s-1}{\ell}$ we find that

$$p_i = \frac{1}{2^s} \sum_{f_s(\ell)=1} \left(\binom{s-1}{\ell-1} - \binom{s-1}{\ell} \right).$$

Cancelling terms where possible we obtain (1).

Lemma 3. *There are embedded midbit functions $M_S(x)$ with S a proper subset of $\{x_1, \ldots, x_n\}$ such that $p_i = 0$ for all $1 \le i \le n$.*

Proof. By Fact 3 for $i \notin S$ we have $p_i = 0$. Suppose that $t(s)$ is even and $t(s)k(s) - 1 = s - 1 - (k(s) - 1)$. Then the expression for p_i given in (1) is exactly 0 since the positive and negative binomial coefficients $\pm\binom{s-1}{\ell k(s)-1}$ and $\mp\binom{s-1}{(t(s)-\ell+1)k(s)-1}$ cancel each other out (e.g. take $s = 27, k(s) = 4, t(s) = 6$).

Thus the correlation of individual variables with $M_S(x)$ need not provide information about membership in S. However, we will show that by testing correlations of *pairs* of variables with $M_S(x)$ we can efficiently determine whether or not a given variable belongs to S.

5.2   Second Approach: Testing Pairs of Variables

For $1 \le i, j \le n, i \neq j$ let $p_{i,j} = \Pr[M_S(x) = 1 | x_i = x_j = 1] - \Pr[M_S(x) = 1 | x_j = 1]$. Similar to Fact 3 we have:

Fact 4 *If $i \notin S$ then $p_{i,j} = 0$.*

Lemma 4. *If $i \in S$ and $j \in S$ then*

$$p_{i,j} = \frac{1}{2^{s-1}} \sum_{\ell=1}^{t(s)} (-1)^{\ell-1} \binom{s-2}{\ell k(s)-2}. \tag{2}$$

Proof. We have

$$p_{i,j} = \frac{1}{2^{s-2}} \sum_{\ell:f_s(\ell)=1} \binom{s-2}{\ell-2} - \frac{1}{2^{s-1}} \sum_{\ell:f_s(\ell)=1} \binom{s-1}{\ell-1}.$$

Rearranging the sum as in Lemma 2 proves the lemma.

Our algorithm is based on the fact (Theorem 5 below) that quantities (1) and (2) cannot both be extremely close to 0.

Theorem 5. *Let k be even and $\sqrt{s}/2 < k \le \sqrt{s}$. Let*

$$A = \frac{1}{2^s} \sum_\ell (-1)^{\ell-1} \binom{s-1}{\ell k-1} \quad \text{and} \quad B = \frac{1}{2^{s-1}} \sum_\ell (-1)^{\ell-1} \binom{s-2}{\ell k-2}.$$

Then $\max\{|A|, |B|\} \ge \frac{1}{1000s}$.

The proof of Theorem 5 is somewhat involved and is deferred to Section 5.3.

With Theorem 5 in hand we can prove our main positive learning result for C_{mid}.

Theorem 6. *The class of embedded midbit functions is learnable under the uniform distribution in polynomial time.*

Input: variable $x_i \in \{x_1, \ldots, x_n\}$
Output: either "$x_i \in S$" or "$x_i \notin S$" correct with probability $1 - \frac{\delta}{n}$

1.   let T be a sample of $m = \text{poly}(n, \log \frac{1}{\delta})$ labeled examples $\langle x, M_S(x) \rangle$
2.   let $\hat{p}_i$ be an empirical estimate of p_i obtained from T
3.   **for all** $j \in \{1, \ldots, n\} - \{i\}$
4.   let $\hat{p}_{i,j}$ be an empirical estimate of $p_{i,j}$ obtained from T
5.   **if** $|\hat{p}_i| > \frac{1}{2000n}$ or $|\hat{p}_{i,j}| > \frac{1}{2000n}$ for some $j \in \{1, \ldots, n\} - \{i\}$
6.   **then output** "$i \in S$"
7.   **else output** "$i \notin S$"

Fig. 1. An algorithm to determine whether x_i is relevant for $M_S(x)$.

Proof. Since there are fewer than n^3 midbit functions $M_S(x)$ which have $s \leq 3$ we can test each of these for consistency with a polynomial size random sample in polynomial time, and thus we can learn in polynomial time if $s \leq 3$. We henceforth assume that $s \geq 4$ and thus that $k(s) \geq 2$ is even.

We show that the algorithm in Figure 1 correctly determines whether or not $x_i \in S$ with probability $1 - \frac{\delta}{n}$. By running this algorithm n times on variables $x_1, \ldots, x_n$ we can identify the set S and thus learn M_S correctly with probability $1 - \delta$.

Case 1: $x_i \notin S$. In this case by Facts 3 and 4 we have $p_i = p_{i,j} = 0$. Hence for a suitably chosen value of $m = \text{poly}(n, \log(\frac{1}{\delta}))$ each of the n empirical estimates $\hat{p}_i, \hat{p}_{i,j}$ will satisfy $|\hat{p}_i| < \frac{1}{2000n}$ and $|\hat{p}_{i,j}| < \frac{1}{2000n}$ with probability $1 - \frac{\delta}{n^2}$. Thus in this case the algorithm outputs "$x_i \notin S$" with probability at least $1 - \frac{\delta}{n}$.

Case 2: $x_i \in S$. Since $s \geq 4$ there is some $x_j \neq x_i$ such that $x_j \in S$. Lemmas 2 and 4 and Theorem 5 imply that the true value of at least one of $|p_i|, |p_{i,j}|$ will be at least $\frac{1}{1000s} \geq \frac{1}{1000n}$. As before, for a suitably chosen value of $m = \text{poly}(n, \log(\frac{1}{\delta}))$, each of the n empirical estimates $\hat{p}_i, \hat{p}_{i,j}$ will differ from its true value by less than $\frac{1}{2000n}$ with probability $1 - \frac{\delta}{n}$. Thus in this case the algorithm outputs "$x_i \in S$" with probability at least $1 - \frac{\delta}{n}$.

5.3   Proof of Theorem 5

The following lemma gives a useful expression for sums in the form of (1) and (2).

Lemma 5. *Let* $r, j, k > 0$ *with* k *even. Then*

$$\sum_\ell (-1)^{\ell-1} \binom{r}{\ell k - j} =$$

$$\frac{-2}{k} \left(\sum_{\ell=1,3,5,\ldots,k-1} \left(2 \cos \frac{\ell\pi}{2k} \right)^r \cos \left(\frac{(r+2j)\ell\pi}{2k} \right) \right). \tag{3}$$

Proof. We reexpress the left side as

$$\sum_\ell \binom{r}{\ell(2k) + (k - j)} - \sum_\ell \binom{r}{\ell(2k) - j}. \tag{4}$$

The following well known identity (see e.g. [15,16]) is due to Ramus [14]:

$$\sum_\ell \binom{r}{\ell k - j} = \frac{1}{k} \sum_{\ell=1}^{k} \left(2 \cos \frac{\ell\pi}{k} \right)^r \cos \left(\frac{(r + 2j)\ell\pi}{k} \right).$$

Applying this identity to (4) we obtain

$$\frac{1}{2k} \left(\sum_{\ell=1}^{2k} \left(2 \cos \frac{\ell\pi}{2k} \right)^r \cos \left(\frac{(r - 2k + 2j)\ell\pi}{2k} \right) - \sum_{\ell=1}^{2k} \left(2 \cos \frac{\ell\pi}{2k} \right)^r \cos \left(\frac{(r + 2j)\ell\pi}{2k} \right) \right)$$

Since even terms cancel out in the two sums above, we obtain

$$\frac{-1}{k} \left(\sum_{\ell=1,3,\dots,2k-1} \left(2 \cos \frac{\ell\pi}{2k} \right)^r \cos \left(\frac{(r + 2j)\ell\pi}{2k} \right) \right). \tag{5}$$

Consider the term of this sum obtained when $\ell = 2k - h$ for some odd value h:

$$\left(2 \cos \frac{(2k - h)\pi}{2k} \right)^r \cos \left(\frac{(r + 2j)(2k - h)\pi}{2k} \right)$$

$$= (-1)^{r+(r+2j)} \left(2 \cos \frac{-h\pi}{2k} \right)^r \cos \left(\frac{(r + 2j)(-h)\pi}{2k} \right)$$

$$= \left(2 \cos \frac{h\pi}{2k} \right)^r \cos \left(\frac{(r + 2j)h\pi}{2k} \right)$$

This equals the term obtained when $\ell = h$. Since $k = 2m$ is even we have that (5) equals the right side of (3).

The following two technical lemmas will help us analyze the right hand side of equation (3). No attempt has been made to optimize constants in the bounds.

Lemma 6. *Let r, k be such that $k \geq 4$ is even and $k^2 - 2 \leq r < 4k^2 - 1$. Then*

(i) for $\ell = 1, 3, \dots, k - 3$ we have $0 < \left(\cos \frac{(\ell+2)\pi}{2k} \right)^r < \left(\cos \frac{\ell\pi}{2k} \right)^r / 16$,

(ii) $\left(\cos \frac{\pi}{2k} \right)^r \geq \frac{1}{200}$.

Proof. By considering the Taylor series of $\cos x$ one can show that $1 - \frac{x^2}{2} \leq \cos x \leq 1 - \frac{x^2}{3}$ for all $x \in [0, \frac{\pi}{2}]$.

Part (i): since $0 < \frac{\ell\pi}{2k} < \frac{(\ell+2)\pi}{2k} < \frac{\pi}{2}$, we have

$$\cos \frac{(\ell + 2)\pi}{2k} = \cos \frac{\ell\pi}{2k} \cos \frac{\pi}{k} - \sin \frac{\ell\pi}{2k} \sin \frac{\pi}{k}$$

$$< \left(1 - \frac{\pi^2}{3k^2} \right) \cos \frac{\ell\pi}{2k}$$

and hence

$$\left(\cos\frac{(\ell+2)\pi}{2k}\right)^r \leq \left(1-\frac{\pi^2}{3k^2}\right)^r \left(\cos\frac{\ell\pi}{2k}\right)^r$$

$$\leq \left(1-\frac{\pi^2}{3k^2}\right)^{k^2-2}\left(\cos\frac{\ell\pi}{2k}\right)^r$$

$$\leq \frac{e^{-\pi^2/3}}{(1-\pi^2/(3k^2))^2}\cdot\left(\cos\frac{\ell\pi}{2k}\right)^r$$

$$\leq \frac{1}{16}\cdot\left(\cos\frac{\ell\pi}{2k}\right)^r.$$

Here the third inequality uses $(1-\frac{1}{x})^x \leq e^{-1}$ and the fourth inequality uses $k \geq 4$.

Part (ii): we have

$$\left(\cos\frac{\pi}{2k}\right)^r > \left(\cos\frac{\pi}{2k}\right)^{4k^2}$$

$$> \left(1-\frac{\pi^2}{8k^2}\right)^{4k^2}.$$

This is an increasing function of k so for $k \geq 4$ the value is at least $\left(1-\frac{\pi^2}{128}\right)^{64} \geq \frac{1}{200}$.

Lemma 7. *For all real x and all odd $\ell \geq 3$, we have $|\cos(\ell x)| \leq \ell|\cos x|$.*

Proof. Fix $\ell \geq 3$. Let $y = \frac{\pi}{2} - x$ so $\ell|\cos x| = \ell|\sin y|$ and

$$|\cos(\ell x)| = \left|\cos\frac{\ell\pi}{2}\cos(\ell y) - \sin\frac{\ell\pi}{2}\sin(\ell y)\right|$$

$$= |\sin(\ell y)|$$

(note that we have used the fact that ℓ is odd). Thus we must show that $|\sin(\ell y)| \leq \ell|\sin y|$. This is clearly true if $|\sin y| \geq \frac{1}{\ell}$; otherwise we may suppose that $0 \leq y < \sin^{-1}\frac{1}{\ell}$ (the other cases are entirely similar) so $0 \leq \ell y \leq \frac{\pi}{2}$. Now $\sin(\ell y) \leq \ell\sin y$ follows from the concavity of $\sin y$ on $[0, \frac{\pi}{2}]$ and the fact that the derivative of $\sin y$ is 1 at $y = 0$.

Using these tools we can now prove Theorem 5.

Theorem 5 *Let k be even and $\sqrt{s}/2 < k \leq \sqrt{s}$. Let*

$$A = \frac{1}{2^s}\sum_\ell (-1)^{\ell-1}\binom{s-1}{\ell k-1} \quad \text{and} \quad B = \frac{1}{2^{s-1}}\sum_\ell (-1)^{\ell-1}\binom{s-2}{\ell k-2}.$$

Then $\max\{|A|, |B|\} \geq \frac{1}{1000s}$.

Proof. By Lemma 5 we have

$$A = \frac{-1}{k} \left(\sum_{\ell=1,3,\ldots,k-1} \left(\cos \frac{\ell\pi}{2k} \right)^{s-1} \cos \left(\frac{(s+1)\ell\pi}{2k} \right) \right) \tag{6}$$

and

$$B = \frac{-1}{k} \left(\sum_{\ell=1,3,\ldots,k-1} \left(\cos \frac{\ell\pi}{2k} \right)^{s-2} \cos \left(\frac{(s+2)\ell\pi}{2k} \right) \right). \tag{7}$$

First the easy case: if $k = 2$ then $4 \leq s \leq 15$ and $A = \frac{-1}{2}(\cos \frac{\pi}{4})^{s-1} \cos \left(\frac{(s+1)\pi}{4} \right)$, $B = \frac{-1}{2}(\cos \frac{\pi}{4})^{s-2} \cos \left(\frac{(s+2)\pi}{4} \right)$. Since either $\left| \cos \left(\frac{(s+1)\pi}{4} \right) \right|$ or $\left| \cos \left(\frac{(s+2)\pi}{4} \right) \right|$ must be $\frac{\sqrt{2}}{2}$ we have $\max\{|A|,|B|\} \geq \frac{1}{2^{\frac{s}{2}+1}}$ which is easily seen to be at least $\frac{1}{1000s}$ for $4 \leq s \leq 15$.

Now suppose $k \geq 4$. For $\ell = 3,\ldots,k-1$ we have

$$\left| \left(\cos \frac{\ell\pi}{2k} \right)^{s-1} \cos \left(\frac{(s+1)\ell\pi}{2k} \right) \right| \leq \frac{(\cos \frac{\pi}{2k})^{s-1}}{4^{\ell-1}} \cdot \left| \cos \left(\frac{(s+1)\ell\pi}{2k} \right) \right|$$

$$\leq \left| \frac{\ell}{4^{\ell-1}} \cdot \left(\cos \frac{\pi}{2k} \right)^{s-1} \cos \left(\frac{(s+1)\pi}{2k} \right) \right|$$

where the first inequality is by repeated application of part (i) of Lemma 6 and the second is by Lemma 7. We thus have

$$\sum_{\ell=3,5,\ldots,k-1} \left| \left(\cos \frac{\ell\pi}{2k} \right)^{s-1} \cos \left(\frac{(s+1)\ell\pi}{2k} \right) \right|$$

$$\leq \sum_{\ell=3,5,\ldots,k-1} \left| \frac{\ell}{4^{\ell-1}} \cdot \left(\cos \frac{\pi}{2k} \right)^{s-1} \cos \left(\frac{(s+1)\pi}{2k} \right) \right|$$

$$< \left| \left(\cos \frac{\pi}{2k} \right)^{s-1} \cos \left(\frac{(s+1)\pi}{2k} \right) \right| \cdot \sum_{\ell=3}^{\infty} \frac{\ell}{4^{\ell-1}}$$

$$= \frac{5}{18} \cdot \left| \left(\cos \frac{\pi}{2k} \right)^{s-1} \cos \left(\frac{(s+1)\pi}{2k} \right) \right|.$$

Thus the $\ell = 1$ term in the sum (6) dominates the sum and we have

$$|A| \geq \frac{13}{18} \cdot \frac{1}{k} \left| \left(\cos \frac{\pi}{2k} \right)^{s-1} \cos \left(\frac{(s+1)\pi}{2k} \right) \right|$$

$$\geq \frac{13}{3600k} \cdot \left| \cos \left(\frac{(s+1)\pi}{2k} \right) \right|$$

by part (ii) of Lemma 6. An identical analysis for B shows that

$$|B| \geq \frac{13}{3600k} \cdot \left| \cos \left(\frac{(s+2)\pi}{2k} \right) \right|$$

as well.

We now observe that

$$\max\{ \left| \cos \frac{(s+1)\pi}{2k} \right|, \left| \cos \frac{(s+2)\pi}{2k} \right| \} \geq \cos \left(\frac{\pi}{2} - \frac{\pi}{4k} \right) = \sin \frac{\pi}{4k}.$$

Using Taylor series this is easily seen to be at least $\frac{\pi}{8k}$. Hence we have

$$\max\{|A|, |B|\} \geq \frac{13}{3600k} \cdot \frac{\pi}{8k} > \frac{1}{1000k^2} \geq \frac{1}{1000s}$$

and the theorem is proved.

Acknowledgements. This research was supported by NSF Grant CCR-98-77049 and by an NSF Mathematical Sciences Postdoctoral Research Fellowship.

References

[1] E. Allender and U. Hertrampf. Depth reduction for circuits of unbounded fan-in. *Information and Computation*, 112(2):217–238, 1994.

[2] D. Barrington. Bounded-width polynomial-size branching programs recognize exactly those languages in NC^1. *Journal of Computer and System Sciences*, 38(1):150–164, 1989.

[3] D. Barrington and D. Therien. Finite monoids and the fine structure of NC^1. *J. ACM*, 35(4):941–952, 1988.

[4] R. Beigel and J. Tarui. On *ACC*. *Computational Complexity*, 4:350–366, 1994.

[5] A. Blum, P. Chalasani, and J. Jackson. On learning embedded symmetric concepts. In *Proceedings of the Sixth Annual Conference on Computational Learning Theory*, pages 337–346, 1993.

[6] A. Blumer, A. Ehrenfeucht, D. Haussler, and M. Warmuth. Learnability and the Vapnik-Chervonenkis dimension. *Journal of the ACM*, 36(4):929–965, 1989.

[7] P. Fischer and H.U. Simon. On learning ring-sum expansions. *SIAM Journal on Computing*, 21(1):181–192, 1992.

[8] R. L. Graham, D. E. Knuth, and O. Patashnik. *Concrete Mathematics*. Addison-Wesley, Reading, MA, 1994.

[9] F. Green, J. Kobler, K. Regan, T. Schwentick, and J. Toran. The power of the middle bit of a #P function. *Journal of Computer and System Sciences*, 50(3):456–467, 1998.

[10] D. Helmbold, R. Sloan, and M. Warmuth. Learning integer lattices. *SIAM Journal on Computing*, 21(2):240–266., 1992.

[11] A. Klivans and R. Servedio. Learning DNF in time $2^{\tilde{O}(n^{1/3})}$. In *Proceedings of the Thirty-Third Annual Symposium on Theory of Computing*, pages 258–265, 2001.

[12] P. McKenzie and D. Therien. Automata theory meets circuit complexity. In *Proceedings of the International Colloquium on Automata, Languages and Programming*, pages 589–602, 1989.

[13] M. Minsky and S. Papert. *Perceptrons: an introduction to computational geometry*. MIT Press, Cambridge, MA, 1968.

[14] C. Ramus. Solution générale d'un problème d'analyse combinatoire. *J. Reine Agnew. Math.*, 11:353–355, 1834.

[15] J. Riordan. *An Introduction to Combinatorial Analysis*. Wiley, New York, 1958.

[16] J. Riordan. *Combinatorial Identities*. Wiley, New York, 1968.

[17] L. Valiant. A theory of the learnable. *Communications of the ACM*, 27(11):1134–1142, 1984.

[18] A. Yao. Separating the polynomial time hierarchy by oracles. In *Proceedings of the Twenty-Sixth Annual Symposium on Foundations of Computer Science*, pages 1–10, 1985.

[19] A. Yao. On *ACC* and threshold circuits. In *Proceedings of the Thirty-First Annual Symposium on Foundations of Computer Science*, pages 619–627, 1990.

Maximizing Agreements and CoAgnostic Learning

Nader H. Bshouty[1][*] and Lynn Burroughs[2]

[1] Department of Computer Science, Technion, Haifa, Israel,
bshouty@cs.technion.ac.il,
[2] Department of Computer Science, University of Calgary, Calgary, Alberta, Canada
lynnb@cpsc.ucalgary.ca

Abstract. This paper studies α-CoAgnostic learnability of classes of boolean formulas. To α-CoAgnostic learn C from H, the learner seeks a hypothesis $h \in H$ that *agrees* (rather than disagrees as in Agnostic learning) within a factor α of the best agreement of any $f \in C$. Although 1-CoAgnostic learning is equivalent to Agnostic learning, this is not true for α-CoAgnostic learning for $\frac{1}{2} < \alpha < 1$.

It is known that α-CoAgnostic learning algorithms are equivalent to α-approximation algorithms for maximum agreement problems. Many studies have been done on maximum agreement problems, for classes such as monomials, monotone monomials, antimonotone monomials, halfspaces and balls. We study these problems further and some extensions of them. For the above classes we improve the best previously known factors α for the hardness of α-CoAgnostic learning. We also find the first constant lower bounds for decision lists, exclusive-or, halfspaces (over the boolean domain), 2-term DNF and 2-term multivariate polynomials.

1 Introduction

In this paper we study α-CoAgnostic learnability of classes of boolean formulas. In α-CoAgnostic learning C from H, the learner seeks a hypothesis $h \in H$ that agrees (rather than disagrees as in Agnostic learning) within a factor α of the best hypothesis in class C. Although 1-CoAgnostic learning is equivalent to Agnostic learning, this is not true for α-CoAgnostic learning for $\frac{1}{2} < \alpha < 1$. For $\alpha \le \frac{1}{2}$, a trivial α-CoAgnostic learning algorithm can return a constant formula.

It is known [7] that CoAgnostic learning is equivalent to finding a polynomial time algorithm for the Maximum Agreement (MA) problems. For a Maximum Agreement problem, the goal is to find a hypothesis h from some class C of hypotheses, such that h maximizes the agreements with a training sample S. We also study an extension of MA in which we allow h to be from a larger class of hypotheses $H \supset C$ and we ask $h \in H$ to have an agreement rate at least as

[*] This research was supported by the fund for promotion of research at the Technion. Research no. 120-025. Part of this research was done at the University of Calgary, Calgary, Alberta, Canada.

N. Cesa-Bianchi et al. (Eds.): ALT 2002, LNAI 2533, pp. 83–97, 2002.

good as the best formula in C. We call this problem C/H-MA. An algorithm is an α-approximation algorithm (where $\alpha \leq 1$) if it returns $h \in H$ such that h agrees with at least αOPT examples, where OPT is the maximum agreement achieved by any $f \in C$. Then using similar techniques to the ones used in [9,10, 7,5,4], C/H-MA is equivalent to α-CoAgnostic learning in the following sense: there is an α-approximation algorithm for C/H-MA that runs in time T if and only if there is an α-CoAgnostic PAC-learning algorithm for C from H that runs in time T.

For MA and a variety of simple concept classes it is known that unless P=NP, there is some constant $\alpha > \frac{1}{2}$ such that no polynomial time algorithm can find a formula in the class that approximates the maximum agreement rate to within α [2,9,8,1,5,6]. The classes studied were exclusive-or (Xor), monomials (Mon), monotone monomials (MMon), antimonotone monomials (AMon), all over the boolean $\{0,1\}$ domain, and halfspaces (HS) and balls (Ball) over the $\{0,1,-1\}$ domain.

In this paper we substantially improve on the best previously known constant factors α for the above problems. Where the results in the literature were obtained by reductions from 2SAT, our reductions are from very specific instances of MAXCUT created by [6]. We show that these instances have some nice properties, which we then exploit to produce our improved negative results. Using similar techniques, we also find negative results for other classes such as decision lists (DL), monotone decision lists (MDL), 2-term DNF, and its monotone version (2-term MDNF), and 2-term multivariate polynomial (MP), and its monotone version (2-term MMP) etc. Where the previous results in the literature for halfspaces considered the $\Re$ or $\{0,1,-1\}$ domain, we improve the constant factor and give the first constant factor for the $\{0,1\}$ domain.

We also show that for boolean classes with VC-dimension d if the consistent hypothesis problem (find $h \in H$ consistent with training sample S) is solvable in polynomial time then for any constant c there is a polynomial time $1/2 + c/poly(d)$-approximation algorithm for C/H-MA. So classes with constant VC-dimension have a polynomial-time $(1-\epsilon)$-approximation algorithm for C/H-MA for some constant ϵ. Thus they are α-CoAgnostic learnable for any constant α.

The paper is organized as follows. In the remainder of this section we give the previous results from the literature and list the results of this paper. In section 2 we give definitions and some preliminary results. In section 3 we give a general upper bound for MA. Then in sections 4 and 5 we give our negative results for approximating MA.

1.1   Results

In this subsection we give the results in the literature and our results for C/H-MA and the connection to CoAgnostic learning. It is clear that solving C/H-MA implies PAC learnability of C from H. Therefore all the negative results in the literature for PAC learning of classes C from H will give negative results for C/H-MA. Therefore in this paper we will only consider classes C that are PAC-learnable. When $H = C$ we will just write C-MA.

NP-Hardness and Lower Bounds for MA Angluin and Laird [2] showed that MMon-MA is NP-Hard. Kearns and Li [9] showed that Mon-MA is NP-Hard. Höffgen, Simon and Van Horn [8] showed that AMon/HS-MA, DL/HS-MA and HS-MA are NP-Hard. It follows from results of Håstad [6] that Xor-MA is NP-Hard. Those results imply that there is no learning algorithm that CoAgnostic learns the classes MMon, AMon, Mon, DL, HS and Xor.

Amaldi and Kann [1] showed that if P$\neq$NP there is no poly time $\frac{261}{262}$-approximation algorithm for HS-MA over the $\Re$ domain. Ben-David et. al. [5] improved this ratio to $\frac{415}{418}$ for HS over $\{0, 1, -1\}$ and gave a lower bound of $\frac{767}{770}$ for approximating MMon-MA, AMon-MA and Mon-MA over the Boolean domain and a lower bound of $\frac{415}{418}$ for approximating Ball-MA over $\{0, 1, -1\}$. In this paper we show that if P$\neq$NP then there is no $\frac{84}{85}$-approximation algorithm for HS-MA over the Boolean domain, no $\frac{58}{59}$-approximation algorithm for Mon-MA, AMon-MA and MMon-MA and no $\frac{100}{101}$-approximation algorithm for Ball-MA. For the Xor class, it follows from Håstad [6], that there is no $\frac{1}{2} + \frac{1}{2^{(\log n)^c}}$-approximation algorithm for Xor-MA for some constant c. We extend this result and show that this lower bound is true for Xor/H-MA even if the hypothesis class H includes $2^{\log^c n}$-node decision trees with Xor nodes and $O(\log^c n)$-term DNF (we define H in section 4).

We further extend our results to classes for which no constant lower bounds have yet been shown. We give the first negative results for decision lists, disjunction of two monomials and Xor of two monomials. We show that unless P=NP, there is no $\frac{58}{59}$-approximation algorithm for MDL-MA, no $\frac{64}{65}$-approximation algorithm for DL-MA, no $\frac{58}{59}$-approximation algorithm for 2-term MDNF-MA or 2-term DNF-MA, and no $\frac{37}{38}$-approximation algorithm for 2-term MMP-MA or 2-term MP-MA.

2   Preliminary Results and Definitions

In this section we give some preliminary results and definitions. We start by defining the concept classes we will use in this paper then give some background in the theory of VC-dimension. We then define the extended Maximum Agreement problem and prove a few basic results. Finally we give the learning models we will use in this paper.

2.1   Concept Classes

Let X be a set of *instances* and 2^X be the set of *boolean functions* $f : X \to \{0, 1\}$. Let $C \subset \Sigma^*$ be a class of *formulas* for some alphabet Σ. Each formula $h^* \in C$ represents a boolean function $h : X \to \{0, 1\}$. We will call C the *concept class* over X. The size $|f|_C$ of any boolean function f with respect to C is the minimal length of a formula $h^* \in C$ such that $h \equiv f$. If no such h^* exists then we write $|f|_C = \infty$. We will write $|f|$ when C is known from the context. A parametrized class of representations is $C = \bigcup_{n \geq 1} C_n$ where each C_n is a concept class over X_n. For example, $X_n = \{0, 1\}^n$ and C_n is the set of all Boolean formulas over

n variables with $|f| \leq n^k$ for some fixed constant k. In this case we simply say that C is a concept class over X.

For $X_n = \{0,1\}^n$ we define the following classes. **Mon** is the set of all conjunctions of literals $\{x_1, \ldots, x_n, \bar{x}_1, \ldots, \bar{x}_n\}$ over Boolean variables $\{x_1, \ldots, x_n\}$. **MMon** is the set of monomials with no negated variables, and **AMon** is the set of (antimonotone) monomials with no unnegated variables. **Clause** is the set of all disjunctions of literals over the Boolean variables $\{x_1, \ldots, x_n\}$, and **MClause** is the set of clauses with no negated variables. **2-term MDNF** (resp. **2-term DNF, 2-term ADNF**) is the set of $M_1 \vee M_2$ where M_1 and M_2 are in MMon (resp Mon, AMon). **XOR** is the set of exclusive-ors of literals over the Boolean variables $\{x_1, \ldots, x_n\}$. **MP** (Multivariate Polynomial) is the set of exclusive-ors of Monomials. **MMP** (resp. **AMP**) is the set of exclusive-ors of Monotone (resp. Antimonotone) Monomials. **2-term MMP** (resp **2-term MP, 2-term AMP**) is the set of exclusive-ors of two Monotone Monomials (resp. Monomials, Antimonotone Monomials). **DL** is the set of decision lists $f = (l_1, b_1), \ldots, (l_r, b_r)$ where l_i is a literal for $i < r$, $l_r = 1$ and $b_i \in \{0,1\}$. Then $f(x) = b_i$ if $l_1(x) = l_2(x) = \cdots = l_{i-1}(x) = 0$ and $l_i(x) = 1$. **MDL** is the set of decision lists whose literals are all positive. **HS** is the set of formulas $[a_1 x_1 + \cdots + a_n x_n \geq b]$ where a_i and b are real numbers in $\Re$. Here $[I] = 1$ if I is true and $= 0$ otherwise. Halfspace may also be defined over domain $X_n = \{0, 1, -1\}$. For that domain we define one more class. **Ball** is the set of functions $B : \{0, 1-1\}^n \rightarrow \{0,1\}$ of the form $B(x_1, \ldots, x_n) = [(w_1 - x_1)^2 + \cdots + (w_n - x_n)^2 \leq \theta]$ where $w_1, \ldots, w_n, \theta \in \Re$.

It is known that MMon$\subset$Mon$\subset$DL$\subset$HS and MClause$\subset$Clause$\subset$DL$\subset$HS.

A *labeled example* from X is (x, y) where $x \in X$ and $y \in \{0,1\}$. A *labeled sample* from X is a set $S = \{(x_1, y_1), \ldots, (x_m, y_m)\}$ of labeled examples.

2.2   The Vapnik-Chervonenkis Dimension

Let C be a concept class over X. Let $Y \subseteq X$, and define

$$\Pi_C(Y) = \{Z \subseteq Y \mid \text{there is } g \in C \text{ where } g \text{ is 1 on } Z \text{ and 0 on } Y \backslash Z\}$$

If $\Pi_C(Y) = \mathcal{P}(Y)$, the power set of Y, then we say that Y is *shattered* by C. Vapnik and Chervonenkis in [13] define VCD(C) to be the size of the maximal set shattered by C. It is known that for $X = B_n = \{0,1\}^n$, and classes with VCD$(C) > 2$, we have $\frac{\log|C|}{n} \leq$ VCD$(C) \leq \log|C|$. See [3] for other results in VC-dimension.

2.3   The Maximum Agreement, Minimum Disagreement Problems

Let $S = \{(x_1, y_1), \ldots, (x_m, y_m)\} \subseteq X \times \{0,1\}$ be a labeled sample and $h \in C$. We say that $(x, y) \in X \times \{0,1\}$ *agrees* with h if $h(x) = y$. Otherwise we say that h *disagrees* with (x, y). We define

$$A(S, h) = \frac{|\{i \mid h(x_i) = y_i\}|}{|S|} = \Pr_{(x,y) \in_u S}[h(x) = y],$$

the ratio of points in S that agree with h. If $A(S, h) = 1$ we say h is consistent on S. Define

$$D(S, h) = 1 - A(S, h) = \frac{|\{i \mid h(x_i) \neq y_i\}|}{|S|} = \Pr_{(x,y) \in_U S}[h(x) \neq y],$$

the ratio of points that disagree with h. Define

$$A(S, C) = \max_{h \in C} A(S, h), \quad D(S, C) = \min_{h \in C} D(S, h).$$

It is clear that $A(S, C) = 1 - D(S, C)$.

Let $C \subseteq H$ be two concept classes over X. Define the *Maximum Agreement* (MA) and *Minimum Disagreement* (MD) problems for C/H as follows.

C/H-MA

Input: A sample $S = \{(x_1, y_1), \ldots, (x_m, y_m)\} \subseteq X \times \{0, 1\}$.
Output: A hypothesis h in H where $A(S, h) \geq A(S, C)$.

C/H-MD

Input: A sample $S = \{(x_1, y_1), \ldots, (x_m, y_m)\} \subseteq X \times \{0, 1\}$.
Output: A hypothesis h in H where $D(S, h) \leq D(S, C)$.

For all the classes we have in this paper $\{0, 1\} \subset C$ and therefore $A(S, C) \geq 1/2$. For $\alpha \leq 1$ (resp. $\alpha \geq 1$), an α-approximation algorithm for C/H-MA (resp. C/H-MD) is an algorithm $\mathcal{A}_{C/H}$ that on input S outputs a hypothesis $\mathcal{A}_{C/H}(S) \in H$ such that $A(S, \mathcal{A}_{C/H}(S)) \geq \alpha A(S, C)$ (resp. $D(S, \mathcal{A}_{C/H}(S)) \leq \alpha D(S, C)$).

The *Consistent Hypothesis* (CH) problem for C/H is defined as follows:

C/H-CH

Input: A sample $S = \{(x_1, f(x_1)), \ldots, (x_m, f(x_m))\}$ for some $f \in C$.
Output: A hypothesis h in H where $D(S, h) = 0$. That is, an $h \in H$ that is
             consistent with S.

We will write C-MA (resp. C-MD, C-CH) for the problem C/C-MA (resp. C/C-MD, C/C-CH).

In the next Theorem we demonstrate a connection between the MA and MD problems.

Theorem 1. *We have*

1. *If there is an α-approximation algorithm for C/H-MD that runs in time T then there is an $\frac{1}{2} + \frac{1}{4\alpha-2}$-approximation algorithm for C/H-MA that runs in time T.*

2. *If there is no β-approximation algorithm for C/H-MA that runs in time T then there is no $\frac{\beta}{2\beta-1}$-approximation algorithm for C/H-MD that runs in time T.*

Proof. Let $\mathcal{A}$ be an algorithm that returns a hypothesis $h \in H$ such that $D(S, h) \leq \alpha D(S, C)$. Define an algorithm $\mathcal{B}$ that runs $\mathcal{A}$ to get h, and then outputs $h' \in \{0, 1, h\}$ such that $A(S, h') = \max(A(S, 0), A(S, 1), A(S, h))$. Suppose $D(S, C) = \gamma$. Then $A(S, C) = 1 - \gamma$ and

$$A(S, h') \geq A(S, h) = 1 - D(S, h) \geq \frac{1 - \alpha \gamma}{1 - \gamma} A(S, C).$$

On the other hand

$$A(S, h') \geq \max(A(S, 1), A(S, 0)) \geq \frac{1}{2} \geq \frac{1}{2(1 - \gamma)} A(S, C).$$

The ratio that $\mathcal{B}$ obtains is therefore

$$\min_{0 \leq \gamma \leq 1} \max \left(\frac{1 - \alpha \gamma}{1 - \gamma}, \ \frac{1}{2(1 - \gamma)} \right) \geq \frac{\alpha}{2\alpha - 1} = \frac{1}{2} + \frac{1}{4\alpha - 2}.$$

Now (2) follows from (1).   □

2.4   Composition Lemma and Duality

In this subsection we present composition and duality, which we will use frequently. These two tools allow us to extend our results for one class, to other classes.

Let $X = \bigcup_n X_n$ where $X_n = \{0, 1\}^n$ and C be concept class over X. Let $G_n = (g_1, \ldots, g_{t_n})$ be a sequence of functions $g_i : X_n \to \{0, 1\}$. Define the concept class

$$C(G_n) = \{f(g_1, \ldots, g_{t_n}) \mid f \in C_{t_n}, G_n = (g_1, \ldots, g_{t_n})\}, \text{ and } C(G) = \bigcup_{n \geq 0} C(G_n).$$

We remind the reader that C_t is the set of all functions f in C where $f : \{0, 1\}^t \to \{0, 1\}$. For example, let $L_n = \{x_1, \ldots, x_n, \bar{x}_1, \ldots, \bar{x}_n\}$, the set of literals over $\{0, 1\}^n$. Then $MMon(L_n) = Mon$ and $(MMon \Delta MMon)(L_n, L_n) = Mon \Delta Mon$ for any boolean operation Δ.

Lemma 1. (Composition Lemma) *If C/H-MA (resp. C/H-MD) has an $\alpha(n)$-approximation algorithm that runs in time $T(n)$ then $C(G)/H(G)$-MA (resp. $C(G)/H(G)$-MA) has an $\alpha(t_n)$-approximation algorithm that runs in time $T(t_n)$.*

Proof. Let $\mathcal{A}(n, S)$ be an algorithm that $\alpha(n)$-approximates C/H-MA and runs in time $T(n)$. For $h \in H_{t_n}$ let $h_G = h(g_1(x), \ldots, g_{t_n}(x))$. For $(x, y) \in X_n \times \{0, 1\}$ let $x_G = (g_1(x), \ldots, g_{t_n}(x))$ and $(x, y)_G = (x_G, y)$. Define algorithm $\mathcal{B}(n, S)$ to do the following. On input $S \subseteq X_n \times \{0, 1\}$ (an instance of $C(G)/H(G)$-MA) it builds $S_G = \{((x_i, y_i)_G \mid (x_i, y_i) \in S\}$. It then runs $\mathcal{A}(t_n, S_G)$ to get h, and outputs h_G. Notice that $h_G \in H(G)$. Now $\mathcal{B}(n, S)$ runs in time $T(t_n)$. Since $\mathcal{A}_{t_n}$ is an $\alpha(t_n)$-approximation algorithm, we have $A(S_G, h) \geq \alpha(t_n) A(S_G, C)$. Since $h(x_G) = h_G(x)$ we have $A(S_G, h) = A(S, h_G)$ and $A(S, C(G)) = \min_{f_G \in C(G)} A(S, f_G) = \min_{f \in C} A(S_G, f) = A(S_G, C)$. Therefore, $A(S, h_G) = A(S_G, h) \geq \alpha(t_n) A(S_G, C) = \alpha(t_n) A(S, C(G))$.   □

Define the dual class $C^D = \{f(\bar{x}) \mid f \in C\}$ where $\bar{x} = (\bar{x}_1, \ldots, \bar{x}_n)$. The following dual Lemma is easy to prove.

Lemma 2. (Duality) *If C/H-MA (resp. C/H-MD) has an α-approximation algorithm that runs in time T then C^D/H^D-MA (resp. C^D/H^D-MD) has an α-approximation algorithm that runs in time T.*

Since $MMon^D = MClause$ and $Mon^D = Clause$ all the results in this paper for $MMon$ and Mon are also true for $MClause$ and $Clause$.

2.5   Models of Learning

In learning, a *teacher* has a *target function* $f \in C$ where $f : X \to \{0, 1\}$ and a *target distribution* $\mathcal{D}$ over X. The *learner* knows X and C but does not know distribution $\mathcal{D}$ nor the function f.

The learner can ask the teacher *queries* about the target. The query type we consider in this paper is the **Example Query (Ex)** [12], in which the teacher chooses $x \in X$ according to a distribution $\mathcal{D}$ and returns $(x, f(x))$ to the learner. We say that $h \in C$ is ϵ-*good* hypothesis with respect to f and $\mathcal{D}$ if $\Pr_{x \in \mathcal{D} X}[f(x) \neq h(x)] \leq \epsilon$. The goal of the learner is to output with high probability (probability greater than $1 - \delta$) an ϵ-good hypothesis with respect to f and $\mathcal{D}$.

The learning models we will consider in this paper are

PAC (Probably Approximately Correct) In the PAC learning model we say that an algorithm $\mathcal{A}$ of the learner *PAC learns class* C if for any $f \in C$, any distribution $\mathcal{D}$ and for any $\epsilon, \delta > 0$, algorithm $\mathcal{A}(\epsilon, \delta)$ asks queries from oracle Ex and, with probability at least $1 - \delta$, outputs a hypothesis $h \in C$ that is ϵ-good with respect to f and $\mathcal{D}$. If $\mathcal{A}$ runs in time T (e.g. polynomial, exponential, etc.) in $1/\epsilon, 1/\delta$ and $|f|$ then we say that C is *PAC-learnable* in time T. Here $|f|$ also includes $\log |X|$ when X is finite. For example when $X = \{0, 1\}^n$ then $|f|$ is defined as the length of the representation of f plus n. If we allow h to be from a larger class $H \supset C$ then we say that C is *PAC-learnable from H* in time T.

CoAgnostic PAC [5] In this model an oracle Ex_P produces examples according to a distribution P on $X \times \{0, 1\}$. We say an algorithm $\mathcal{A}$ (of the learner) *Agnostic PAC-learns* the class C if for any distribution P and for any $\epsilon, \delta > 0$, algorithm $\mathcal{A}(\epsilon, \delta)$ asks queries from Ex_P and, with probability at least $1 - \delta$, outputs a hypothesis $h \in C$ that satisfies

$$\Pr_{(x,y) \in_P X \times \{0,1\}}[h(x) = y] \geq \max_{f \in C} \Pr_{(x,y) \in_P X \times \{0,1\}}[f(x) = y] - \epsilon.$$

If $\mathcal{A}$ runs in time T in $1/\epsilon, 1/\delta$ and $|f|$ then we say C is *CoAgnostic PAC-learnable* in time T. If we allow h to be from a larger class H then we say C is *CoAgnostic PAC-learnable* from H in time T. We relax the CoAgnostic PAC-learning model and define α-CoAgnostic PAC-learning. We say that C is α-*CoAgnostic PAC-learnable* from H in time T if

$$\Pr_{(x,y) \in_P X \times \{0,1\}}[h(x) = y] \geq \alpha \max_{f \in C} \Pr_{(x,y) \in_P X \times \{0,1\}}[f(x) = y] - \epsilon.$$

See [5] for some motivation of this definition.

3   General Upper Bounds for MA

In this section we derive two general upper bounds for MA. The first Theorem was implicit in [9], and proved in [4].

Theorem 2. *If C/H-CH is solvable in time T and H is finite, then for any constant c there is a $\left(1 + \frac{\log|H|}{c\log T}\right)$-approximation algorithm for C/H-MD that runs in time $\text{poly}(T)$.*

The next Theorem follows from Theorem 2 and Theorem 1.

Theorem 3. *If C/H-CH is solvable in time T and H is finite then for any constant c with $T \leq |H|^{\frac{1}{4c}}$, there's a $\left(\frac{1}{2} + \frac{c\log T}{\log|H|}\right)$-approximation algorithm for C/H-MA that runs in time $\text{poly}(T)$.*

Corollary 1. *For any constant c there is a polynomial-time $1/2 + (c\log n)/n$-approximation algorithm for MMon-MA, Mon-MA, Xor-MA, 2-term-MDNF-MA, 2-term-DNF-MA, 2-term-MMP-MA and 2-term-MP-MA.*

Proof. All these classes have $|H| = 2^{O(n)}$ and $T = n^{O(1)}$. $\qquad\qquad\square$

For classes with small VC-dimension we have the following.

Theorem 4. *If C/H-CH is solvable in time T then*
1. For any constant c there is an α-approximation algorithm for C/H-MD that runs in time $\text{poly}(T)$ where $\alpha = 1 + \frac{VCD(H)}{c\log T}\log\frac{m\log m}{VCD(H)}$, for sample size m.
2. For any constant c there is an β-approximation algorithm for C/H-MA that runs in time $\text{poly}(T)$ where

$$\beta = \frac{1}{2} + \frac{1}{2 + \frac{VCD(H)}{c\log T}\log\frac{m\log m}{VCD(H)}}.$$

In particular, there is a $1 - \epsilon$-approximation algorithm for C/H-MA that runs in time $m^{VCD(H)}$.

For m and T that are polynomial in n (where $X = \{0,1\}^n$) we have $\alpha = 1 + \frac{VCD(H)}{c}$ and $\beta = 1 - \frac{VCD(H)}{c}$ for any constant c.

Proof. Part 1 is from [4]. Then part 2 follows easily from Theorem 1. $\qquad\square$

Corollary 2. *For any constant c there is a polynomial-time $\frac{1}{2} + \frac{c}{n}$-approximation algorithm for MDL-MA, DL-MA, HS-MA and Ball-MA.*

Proof. We use Theorem 4, the fact that the VC-dimension for monotone decision lists, decision lists, and halfspaces is $n + 1$, and for balls is at most $2n$. $\qquad\square$

Corollary 3. *If C/H-CH is solvable in polynomial time and $VCD(H)$ is constant then C is α-CoAgnostic learnable from H for any constant α.*

4   Improved Lower Bounds for Approximating MA

In this section and section 5 we give all the lower bounds in the paper. This section gives improved lower bounds for previously studied classes. All of our results in sections 4 and 5 are built on the work of Håstad [6], which we describe below. Then we give improved constant lower bounds for classes of monomials and clauses, followed by improved constant lower bounds for halfspaces, and balls.

Our results are derived by reductions from MAXCUT. For the MAXCUT problem we are given a (multi)graph $G = (V, E)$ and must find a subset $S \subset V$ that maximizes the number of cut edges (i.e., edges with exactly one endpoint in S). Håstad [6] showed the following.

Theorem 5. *[6] There exists a method for generating graphs with $20m_0 + 22m_1$ edges, where $m_1 \leq m_0$, such that for some small constants $\epsilon, \delta > 0$, a maximum cut in this graph has size at least $(16 - 2\epsilon)m_0 + (18 - 2\epsilon)m_1$, or size between $(15 + \delta)m_0 + (17 + \delta)m_1$ and $15m_0 + 17m_1$, and it is NP-hard to distinguish the two cases. The graph has maximum degree $d_{max} \leq 4m_0 + 2m_1$.*

The standard technique of exploiting the gap between the two cases to derive an inapproximability result is stated in the following Lemma.

Lemma 3. *[Folklore] If it is NP-hard to distinguish instances of C-MA with optimal agreement rate at least a from those with optimal agreement rate at most b, then C-MA cannot have a polynomial-time α-approximation algorithm for $\alpha > \frac{b}{a}$ unless $P = NP$.*

We use the following notation throughout our proofs.

Notation 1 *Let $p_{uv} \in \{0,1\}^n$ be the n-bit vector with 0s in positions u and v, and 1s elsewhere. Similarly, let $p_u \in \{0,1\}^n$ have a 0 in position u and 1s elsewhere. Let $z_{uv} \in \{0,1\}^n$ have 1s in positions u and v and 0s elsewhere, and let $z_u \in \{0,1\}^n$ have a 1 in position u and 0s elsewhere. For an edge (u, v), define the multisets $X^4_{uv} = \{(p_{uv}, 0), (p_{uv}, 0), (p_u, 1), (p_v, 1)\}$, $X^3_{uv} = \{(p_{uv}, 0), (p_u, 1), (p_v, 1)\}$, and $Y^4_{uv} = \{(z_{uv}, 0), (z_{uv}, 0), (z_u, 1), (z_v, 1)\}$,*

Now we show our results. We start by proving new negative results for the α-approximability of MA for classes of Monomials and Clauses. It was previously shown by [5] that MA could not be approximated within $\frac{767}{770} + \epsilon$ unless P=NP for those classes. We improve this constant substantially to $\frac{58}{59} + \epsilon$.

Theorem 6. *For any $\epsilon' > 0$, it is NP-hard to approximate MMon-MA (and hence AMon-MA and MClause-MA) within a factor of $\frac{58}{59} + \epsilon'$.*

Proof. Given a graph $G = (V, E)$ as described in Theorem 5, the instance of MMon-MA will be $I = \cup_{(u,v) \in E} X^4_{uv}$. Associate with each $M(x_1, \ldots, x_n) \in$ MMon a cut $S_M = \{u \mid M \text{ contains } x_u\}$. Then edge (u, v) is cut by S_M if and only if 3/4 examples in X^4_{uv} agree with M, while edge (u, v) is left uncut by S_M if and only if 2/4 examples in X^4_{uv} agree with M. Thus G has a cut of size k (leaving $|E| - k$ edges uncut) if and only if there is a monomial M that agrees with $k + 2|E|$ examples. Then by Theorem 5 it is NP-hard to distinguish if there is a monomial that agrees with at least $(56 - 2\epsilon)m_0 + (62 - 2\epsilon)m_1$ examples, or no monomial agrees with more than $(55 + \delta)m_0 + (61 + \delta)m_1$ examples. The result then follows from Lemma 3. By Lemmas 1 and 2, this result also applies to AMon-MA and MClause-MA.   □

Theorem 7. *For any $\epsilon' > 0$ it is NP-hard to approximate MMon/Mon-MA, Mon-MA and Clause-MA within a factor of $\frac{58}{59} + \epsilon'$.*

Proof. In the proof of Theorem 6, if $M \in$ Mon has a literal $\overline{x}_u$, then M disagrees with all examples $(p_v, 1)$ in I except possibly those with $v = u$. So M agrees with at most $2|E| + d_{max} < 2|E| + k$ examples, and thus an optimal M is monotone. The result for MMon/Mon-MA and Mon-MA follows from Theorem 6. The result for Clause-MA follows from Lemma 2. $\qquad\square$

Theorem 8. *For any $\epsilon' > 0$ it is NP-hard to approximate (Mon$\cup$Clause)-MA within $\frac{58}{59} + \epsilon'$.*

Proof. Consider sample I in the proof of Theorem 6. If a clause C contains a literal x_w then C disagrees with all examples $(p_{uv}, 0)$ except possibly those with $w \in \{u, v\}$. Then C agrees with at most $2|E| + 2d_{max} < 2|E| + k$ examples.

Now assume C contains only negated variables. For each X_{uv}^4 such that either $\overline{x}_u$ or $\overline{x}_v$ is in C, C will disagree with both copies of $(p_{uv}, 0)$. If neither $\overline{x}_u$ or $\overline{x}_v$ is in C, then C disagrees with both $(p_u, 1)$ and $(p_v, 1)$. So C agrees with at most $2/4$ examples in X_{uv}^4, and thus agrees with at most $2|E|$ in total.

On the other hand, in proving theorem 7 we saw that a monomial M will agree with at least $2|E| + k$ examples. Thus the lower bound for this class follows from the lower bound for monomials. $\qquad\square$

Now we give a negative result for halfspace. Amaldi and Kann [1] proved that unless P=NP, HS-MA could not be approximated within $\frac{261}{262} + \epsilon$ when the domain is $\Re$. Ben-David, Eiron and Long [5] improved this factor to $\frac{415}{418}$ for the $\{0, 1, -1\}$ domain. We improve the constant ratio further to $\frac{84}{85} + \epsilon$, for the $\{0, 1\}$ (and hence also the $\{0, 1, -1\}$ and $\Re$) domain.

Theorem 9. *For any $\epsilon' > 0$ it is NP-hard to approximate HS-MA within a factor of $\frac{84}{85} + \epsilon'$.*

Proof. Given a graph $G = (V, E)$ as described in Theorem 5, we create $4|E| + 25m_0 + 27m_1$ examples: For each edge $(u, v) \in E$, we create the examples Y_{uv}^4. In addition, we create $25m_0 + 27m_1$ copies of the example $(\mathbf{0}, 0)$ where $\mathbf{0}$ is the zero vector.

Let $H = [a_1 x_1 + \cdots + a_n x_n \geq b]$ agree with $(\mathbf{0}, 0)$, which implies $b > 0$. Consider Y_{uv}^4. If $(z_u, 1)$ and $(z_v, 1)$ both agree with H, then $a_u, a_v \geq b > 0$ which implies $H(z_{uv}) = [a_u + a_v \geq b] = 1$. So H disagrees with $(z_{uv}, 0)$ and thus agrees with only $2/4$ examples. If $(z_u, 1)$ agrees with H but $(z_v, 1)$ does not, (or $(z_u, 1)$ disagrees and $(z_v, 1)$ agrees) then H can agree with at most $3/4$ examples. If $(z_u, 1)$ and $(z_v, 1)$ both disagree, then H agrees with at most $2/4$. To maximize the total agreement while maintaining H's agreement with $(\mathbf{0}, 0)$, we need to maximize the number of sets Y_{uv}^4 for which exactly one of $(z_u, 1)$, $(z_v, 1)$ agree with H. Indeed, for an optimal cut S of size k in G, the halfspace $H_S(x_1, \ldots, x_n) = \left[\sum_{u \in S} a_u x_u - \sum_{i \notin S} a_u x_u \geq 0.1\right]$ agrees with an optimal $25m_0 + 27m_1 + 2|E| + k$ examples. By Theorem 5, this is at least $4|E|$, so no better agreement could be achieved by disagreeing with $(\mathbf{0}, 0)$. Then by

Theorem 5, an optimal H agrees with at least $(81-2\epsilon)m_0+(89-2\epsilon)m_1$ examples or at most $(80+\delta)m_0+(88+\delta)m_1$. The result follows from Lemma 3.   □

Now we give a negative result for Ball-MA. Ben-David, Eiron and Long [5] proved if P $\neq$ NP then for any $\epsilon > 0$ there is no polynomial-time $(418/415 - \epsilon)$-approximation algorithm for Ball Maximum Agreement. We improve that ratio to $\frac{100}{101} + \epsilon$ in this next Theorem.

Theorem 10. *For any $\epsilon' > 0$ it is NP-hard to approximate Ball-MA within a factor of $\frac{100}{101} + \epsilon'$.*

Proof. Given a graph $G = (V, E)$ as described in Theorem 5, create for each edge $(u,v) \in E$: one copy of $(z_u, 0)$, one copy of $(z_v, 0)$, two copies of $(z_{uv}, 1)$, and two copies of $(z_{uv}^-, 1)$, where z_{uv}^- is the vector of length n that contains zeros everywhere except for -1s in positions u and v. Call this set of 6 examples W_{uv}^6. Let $B(x_1, \ldots, x_n) = [(w_1 - x_1)^2 + \ldots + (w_n - x_n)^2 \leq \theta]$ and $S = \sum_i (w_i)^2$.

If $(z_{uv}^-, 1)$ agrees with B then we have $S + 2w_u + 2w_v + 2 \leq \theta$. If we also have $w_u, w_v > 0$, this implies $S - 2w_u + 1 \leq \theta$ and $S - 2w_v + 1 \leq \theta$, so both $(z_u, 0)$ and $(z_v, 0)$ disagree with B. Thus if both w_u and w_v are positive, then B can agree with at most 4/6 examples in W_{uv}^6. On the other hand, if $(z_{uv}, 1)$ agrees with B then $S - 2w_u - 2w_v + 2 \leq \theta$. If we also have $w_u < 0$, this implies $S - 2w_v + 1 \leq \theta$ and $(z_v, 0)$ disagrees with B. So B can agree with at most 5/6 examples in W_{uv}^6 and if both w_u and w_v are negative, then B agrees with at most 4/6 examples.

Thus to obtain maximum agreement we maximize the number of W_{uv}^6 with $sign(w_u) \neq sign(w_v)$, which corresponds to a maximum cut in G. For example, given a maximum cut T of size k in G, the ball

$$B_T(x_1, \ldots, x_n) = \left[\sum_{u \in T}(4 - x_u)^2 + \sum_{u \notin T}(-9 - x_u)^2 \leq 18 + 16|T| + 81|V - T| \right]$$

agrees with an optimal $4|E| + k$ examples. Thus by theorem 5, B agrees with at least $(96-2\epsilon)m_0 + (106-2\epsilon)m_1$ examples or at most $(95+\delta)m_0 + (105+\delta)m_1$ examples. The result then follows from Lemma 3.   □

For the next result we define the FL_1 concept class. We can regard any boolean function $f : \{0,1\}^n \to \{0,1\}$ as a function from $\{0,1\}^n$ to $\{-1,+1\}$ where -1 is True (or 1) and 1 is False (or 0). Then any XOR function can be written as $\chi_a(x) = (-1)^{a \cdot x}$ where $a \cdot x = \sum_{i=1}^n a_i x_i$. It is known (see [11] for a good review) that any boolean function f can be written as $f = \sum_{a \in \{0,1\}^n} \hat{f}_a \chi_a(x)$ where $\hat{f}_a = E_{x \in_U \{0,1\}^n}[f(x)\chi_a(x)]$ and $\mathcal{U}$ is the uniform distribution. We define the L_1 norm of a boolean function as $L_1(f) = \sum_a |\hat{f}_a|$. We define the class $FL_1[k]$ to be the set of all boolean functions f with $L_1(f) \leq k$. The next Theorem is proved in [4].

Theorem 11. *Let $c_1^\alpha = (\frac{1}{3} - \alpha) \log \frac{1}{c}$ and $c_2^\alpha = \alpha \log \frac{1}{c}$ where c is a constant. For any constant $\alpha < 1/3$, and for any constant $c_1 < c_1^\alpha$ and $c_2 < c_2^\alpha$, there is no polynomial time $\frac{1}{2} + \frac{1}{2^{(\log n)^{c_2}}}$-approximation algorithm for $Xor/FL_1(2^{(\log n)^{c_2}})$-MA unless NP$\subset$RTIME$(n^{O(\log \log n)})$.*

The class $FL_1(2^{(\log n)^{c_2}})$ contains $2^{(\log n)^{c_2}}$-node decision trees with Xor functions on the nodes. It also contains $(\log n)^{c_2}$-term DNF and $(\log n)^{c_2}$-clause CNF [11]. The result also implies that for almost all the classes C that we study in this paper (and many other classes) it is hard to solve $C\cup$Xor-MA (even, Xor/$C\cup$Xor-MA).

5   New Lower Bounds for Approximating MA

In this section we give the first constant lower bounds for monotone decision lists, decision lists, 2-term DNF and 2-term multivariate polynomials.

Theorem 12. *For any $\epsilon' > 0$ it is NP-hard to approximate MDL-MA within a factor of $\frac{58}{59} + \epsilon'$.*

Proof. Given a graph $G = (V, E)$ as described in Theorem 5, create Y_{uv}^4 for each $(u, v) \in E$. Let $D(x_1, \ldots, x_{|V|}) \in$ MDL agree with a maximum number of examples. We may assume that any pairs $(x_u, 0)$ are at the beginning of the list, since two consecutive pairs $(x_u, 1), (x_v, 0)$ can be swapped without decreasing the total agreement (such a swap only affects X_{uv} if it exists). Furthermore, if $D(x_1, \ldots, x_n) = (x_{u_1}, 0), \ldots, (x_{u_k}, 0), (x_{v_1}, 1), \ldots, (x_{v_\ell}, 1), (1, 0)$, then we can replace it with $D(x_1, \ldots, x_n) = (x_{u_1}, 0), \ldots, (x_{u_k}, 0), (1, 1)$. The replacement only harms examples $(z_{uv}, 0)$ in Y_{uv}^4 where $u, v \notin \{u_1, \ldots, u_k, v_1, \ldots, v_\ell\}$. But the other two examples, $(z_u, 1)$ and $(z_v, 1)$ in Y_{uv}^4 agree now where they did not before. So the total agreement does not decrease.

So assume $D(x_1, \ldots, x_n) = (x_{u_1}, 0), \ldots, (x_{u_k}, 0), (1, 1)$. Let $S = \{u_1, \ldots, u_k\}$. Then D agrees with $3/4$ examples in Y_{uv}^4 if and only if edge (u, v) is cut by S, and D agrees with $2/4$ examples in Y_{uv}^4 if and only if (u, v) is uncut by S. Thus G has a cut of size k if and only if D agrees with $2|E| + k$ examples in total. By Theorem 5 it is thus NP-hard to distinguish instances of MDL-MA such that at most $(55 + \delta)m_0 + (61 + \delta)m_1$ examples agree with D from those such that at least $(56 - 2\epsilon)m_0 + (62 - 2\epsilon)m_1$ agree. The result follows from Lemma 3.   □

Theorem 13. *For any $\epsilon' > 0$ it is NP-hard to approximate DL-MA within a factor of $\frac{64}{65} + \epsilon'$.*

Proof. Consider the sample used in the proof of Theorem 12. Let $T = \{u_1, \ldots, u_\ell\}$ be an optimal cut in G, such that the vertex p of maximum degree is not in T (replace T with $V \setminus T$ if necessary). Let $\{v_1, \ldots, v_j\}$ be the neighbours of p that are not in T. Define the decision list
$$D_T = (x_{u_1}, 0), \ldots, (x_{u_\ell}, 0), (\overline{x}_p, 1), (x_{v_1}, 0), \ldots, (x_{v_j}, 0), (1, 1).$$
Then for each edge (u, v) with $u, v \in T$, two examples in Y_{uv}^4 agree with D_T. For each edge (u, v) with $u \in T, v \notin T$ (or $u \notin T, v \in T$), D_T agrees with three examples in Y_{uv}^4. For each edge (u, v) with $u, v \notin T$ and $p \notin \{u, v\}$, two examples in Y_{uv}^4 agree with D_T. For any edge (u, p) (or (p, u)) with $u \notin T$, D_T agrees with 4 examples in Y_{uv}^4. So D_T agrees with $2(|E| - k - d_p) + 3k + 4d_p = 2|E| + k + 2d_p$ examples, where k is the size of the cut and d_p is the degree of p.

Now, let D be an optimal decision list for the sample. By Theorem 12, and the agreement of D_T, list D is not monotone. However, as before, if $(x_u, 1), (x_v, 0)$ are consecutive in D, they can be swapped. So can $(x_u, 1), (\overline{x}_v, 1)$ and $(x_u, 0), (\overline{x}_v, 0)$. So assume $D = D_1 \circ D_2$ where $D_1 = (x_{u_1}, 0) \ldots, (x_{u_\ell}, 0)$ is the (possibly empty) list containing pairs with positive literals and label 0, and D_2 starts with either $(\overline{x}_r, 1)$ or $(x_{v_1}, 1), \ldots, (x_{v_j}, 1), (\overline{x}_r, 0)$ where $\{v_1, \ldots, v_j\}$ may be empty.

Case 1: D_2 starts with $(\overline{x}_r, 1)$. Let $S = \{u_1, \ldots, u_\ell\}$. Consider Y_{uv}^4. If $u, v \in S$, then 2/4 examples agree with D. If $u \in S, v \notin S$ (or $v \in S$ and $u \notin S$), then at most 3/4 examples agree with D. If $u, v \notin S$ and $r \notin \{u, v\}$ then 2/4 examples agree. If $u, v \notin S$ and $r = u$ then at most 4/4 examples agree. Clearly D is optimized when S is an optimal cut and r has maximum degree. Thus the total agreement is at most the agreement that D_T achieves.

Case 2: $D_2 = (x_{v_1}, 1), \ldots, (x_{v_j}, 1), (\overline{x}_r, 0), \ldots$ Let $S = \{u_1, \ldots, u_\ell\}$ and $T = \{v_1, \ldots, v_j\}$. Consider Y_{uv}^4. If $u, v \in S$ then 2/4 examples agree. If $u \in S, v \notin S$, at most 3/4 agree. If $u, v \notin S$ and $u \in T$ or $v \in T$ at most 2/4 agree. If $u, v \notin S \cup T$ and $r \notin \{u, v\}$, 2/4 agree. If $u, v \notin S \cup T$ and $r \in \{u, v\}$, at most 3/4 agree. The total agreement is at most $2|E| + k + d_p$, less than achieved by D_T.

So w.l.o.g. D_T is the optimal list, and the graph has a cut of size k if and only if there is a list that agrees with $2|E| + k + 2d_{max}$ examples, where d_{max} is the maximum degree of a vertex in G. Thus by Theorem 5, it is NP-hard to distinguish instances of DL-MA such that a decision list agrees with at most $(63 + \delta)m_0 + (65 + \delta)m_1$ examples, or at least $(64 - 2\epsilon)m_0 + (66 - 2\epsilon)m_1$ examples. The result then follows from Lemma 3.   □

Now we provide the first negative results for the approximability of 2-term DNF-MA.

Theorem 14. *For any $\epsilon' > 0$ it is NP-hard to approximate (2-term MDNF)-MA and (2-term ADNF)-MA within a factor of $\frac{58}{59} + \epsilon'$.*

Proof. Given a graph $G = (V, E)$ as described in Theorem 5, create the examples X_{uv}^3 for each edge $(u, v) \in E$. Let $(M_1 \vee M_2)(x_1, \ldots, x_n)$ agree with a maximum number of examples. Suppose some variable x_u appears in both monomials, and consider removing x_u from M_1. The change only harms $(p_{uv}, 0)$ from example sets X_{uv}^3. But for each $(p_{uv}, 0)$ there is a $(p_u, 1)$ that disagreed before and agrees now. So overall there is no decrease in agreement. So assume each x_i appears at most once in $M_1 \vee M_2$ and some x_u is absent from $M_1 \vee M_2$. Then $M_1 \vee M_2$ disagrees with all the $(p_{uv}, 0)$ examples. Add x_u to one of the monomials. Then $M_1 \vee M_2$ still agrees with $(p_u, 1)$ and may also agree with $(p_{uv}, 0)$. There is no decrease in agreement. So w.l.o.g. each variable $x_1, \ldots, x_n$ appears in exactly one of the monomials. Associate with $M_1 \vee M_2$ a cut S with $u \in S$ if and only if x_u is in M_1. Then (u, v) is cut by S if and only if 3/3 examples in X_{uv}^3 agree with $M_1 \vee M_2$, and (u, v) is left uncut by S if and only if 2/3 examples in X_{uv}^3 agree. G has a cut of size k if and only if some $M_1 \vee M_2$ agrees with $2|E| + k$ examples. By Theorem 5, it is NP-hard to distinguish whether an optimal $M_1 \vee M_2$ agrees with at least $(56 - 2\epsilon)m_0 + (62 - 2\epsilon)m_1$ examples, or at most $(55 + \delta)m_0 + (61 + \delta)m_1$ examples. The result follows from Lemma 3. The result for (2-term ADNF)-MA follows from Lemma 1.   □

Theorem 15. *For any $\epsilon' > 0$ it is NP-hard to approximate (2-term MDNF)/(2-term DNF)-MA, (2-term DNF)-MA, and (2-term ADNF)/(2-term DNF)-MA within a factor of $\frac{58}{59} + \epsilon'$.*

Proof. Consider the sample used in the proof of Theorem 14, and recall that a 2-term MDNF can agree with $2|E| + k$ examples where k is the optimal cut size in G. Now let $M_1 \vee M_2 \in$ 2-term DNF agree with a maximum number of examples. If M_1 contains a literal $\overline{x}_u$ and M_2 contains a literal $\overline{x}_v$, then all $(p_w, 1)$ disagree with $M_1 \vee M_2$ except possibly those with $w \in \{u, v\}$. Then by Theorem 5, $M_1 \vee M_2$ agrees with at most $|E| + 2d_{max} < 2|E| + k$ examples.

Now assume M_2 is monotone and M_1 contains a literal $\overline{x}_u$. For each X_{vw}^3 with $w, v \neq u$, we have $M_1(p_w) = M_1(p_v) = 0$. If $M_1 \vee M_2$ agrees with both $(p_v, 1)$ and $(p_w, 1)$, then neither x_v nor x_w are in M_2. But then $(p_{vw}, 0)$ disagrees with $M_1 \vee M_2$. So $M_1 \vee M_2$ agrees with at most $2|E| + d_{max} < 2|E| + k$ examples.

Therefore, in an optimal $M_1 \vee M_2$ both M_1 and M_2 are monotone, and the lower bound of theorem 14 is also a lower bound for (2-term DNF)-MA and (2-term MDNF/2-term DNF)-MA. By the composition Lemma 1, the result also applies to (2-term ADNF/2-term DNF)-MA.   □

Now we show the first negative results for approximating MA over the class of 2-term multivariate polynomials.

Theorem 16. *For any $\epsilon' > 0$ it is NP-hard to approximate (2-term MMP)-MA and (2-term AMP)-MA within a factor of $\frac{37}{38} + \epsilon'$.*

Proof. Given a graph $G = (V, E)$ as described in Theorem 5, create examples X_{uv}^4 for each edge $(u, v) \in E$. Let $M_1 \oplus M_2(x_1, \ldots, x_n) \in$ 2-term MMP agree with a maximum number of examples. Suppose a variable x_u appears in neither monomial and we add x_u to both monomials. Then all examples $(p_u, 1)$ disagreed before and still disagree. Examples $(p_{uv}, 0)$ now agree whether they did before or not. Examples that do not involve u are unaffected by the change. So w.l.o.g. every variable appears somewhere in $M_1 \oplus M_2$.

Now suppose a variable x_u appears in both M_1 and M_2. All $(p_{uv}, 0)$ agree with $M_1 \oplus M_2$, and there are $2d_u$ of these examples where d_u is the degree of vertex u. But none of the d_u examples $(p_u, 1)$ agree with $M_1 \oplus M_2$. Let M_1' be M_1 with x_u removed, and let M_2' be M_2 with x_u removed. Consider $M_1' \oplus M_2$ and $M_1 \oplus M_2'$. Both of these functions agree with all d_u examples $(p_u, 1)$. An example $(p_{uv}, 0)$ will agree with at least one of the two functions, since x_v appears in either M_1 or M_2. Thus one of the two functions agrees with at least half of the examples $(p_{uv}, 0)$, and thus disagrees with at most d_u examples. Therefore either $M_1' \oplus M_2$ or $M_1 \oplus M_2'$ agrees with at least as many examples as $M_1 \oplus M_2$ did and we may assume w.l.o.g. that each variable occurs in exactly one of the monomials M_1, M_2.

Associate with $M_1 \oplus M_2$ a cut S such that $u \in S$ if and only if $x_u \in M_1$. Then edge $(u, v) \in E$ is cut by S if and only if $M_1 \oplus M_2$ agrees with 4 examples in X_{uv}^4. Edge (u, v) is left uncut by S if and only if $M_1 \oplus M_2$ agrees with 2 examples in X_{uv}^4. Therefore G has a cut of size k if and only if $M_1 \oplus M_2$ agrees with $2k + 2|E|$ examples. By theorem 5 this implies that either there exists an

$M_1 \oplus M_2$ that agrees with at least $(72 - 4\epsilon)m_0 + (80 - 4\epsilon)m_1$ examples, or no $M_1 \oplus M_2$ can agree with more than $(70 + \delta)m_0 + (78 + \delta)m_1$ examples, and it is NP-hard to distinguish the two cases. The result then follows from Lemma 3. The result for (2-term AMP)-MA follows from Lemma 1. $\qquad\square$

Theorem 17. *For any ϵ' it is NP-hard to approximate (2-term MMP)/(2-term MP)-MA, (2-term MP)-MA and (2-term AMP)/(2-term MP)-MA within a factor of $\frac{37}{38} + \epsilon'$.*

Proof. Consider the sample used in the proof of Theorem 16. Let $M_1 \oplus M_2 \in$ 2-term MP. Suppose M_1 contains $\overline{x}_u$ and M_2 contains $\overline{x}_v$. Then all examples $(p_w, 1)$ disagree with $M_1 \oplus M_2$ when $w \notin \{u, v\}$. So $M_1 \oplus M_2$ agrees with at most $2|E| + 2d_{max} < 2|E| + 2k$ examples. Now suppose M_1 contains a negated variable $\overline{x}_u$ but M_2 is monotone. For example sets X_{wv}^4 with $w, v \neq u$ we have $M_1(p_{wv}) = M_1(p_w) = M_1(p_v) = 0$. If $(p_{wv}, 0)$ agrees with $M_1 \oplus M_2$ then M_2 must contain either x_w or x_v or both. But then at least one of the examples $(p_w, 1)$ or $(p_v, 1)$ does not agree with $M_1 \oplus M_2$. Then $M_1 \oplus M_2$ agrees with at most $3|E| + d_{max} < 2|E| + 2k$ examples. By Theorem 16, a better agreement rate is achieved by $M_1 \oplus M_2$ where M_1 and M_2 are both monotone. Thus the lower bound follows from Theorem 16. $\qquad\square$

References

[1] E. Amaldi and V. Kann, The complexity and approximability of finding maximum feasible subsystems of linear relations, *Theoretical Computer Science*, 147: 181-210, 1995.

[2] D. Angluin and P. D. Laird, Learning from noisy examples, *ML*, 2:343-370,1988.

[3] M. Anthony and N. Biggs, Computational learning theory, *Cambridge Tracts in Theoretical Computer Science* 30, Cambridge University Press, 1992.

[4] N. H. Bshouty, L. Burroughs. Bounds for the Minimum Disagreement Problem with Applications to Learning Theory. *15th COLT*, 271-286, 2002.

[5] S. Ben-David, N. Eiron, P. M. Long. On the difficulty of approximately maximizing agreement. *13th COLT*, 266-274, 2000.

[6] J. Håstad, Some optimal inapproximability results, *29th STOC*, 1-10, 1997.

[7] D. Haussler, Decision theoretic generalizations of the PAC model for neural net and other learning applications. *Inform. Comput.*, 100(1):78-150, Sept. 1992.

[8] Klaus-U Höffgen, Hans-U. Simon and Kevin S. Van Horn, Robust trainability of single neurons, *JCSS*, 50(1): 114-125, 1995.

[9] M. Kearns and M. Li, Learning in the presence of malicious errors, *SIAM Journal on Computing*, 22(4): 807-837, 1993.

[10] M. Kearns, R. E. Schapire and L. M. Sellie. Toward efficient agnostic learning. *5th COLT*, 341-352, 1992.

[11] Y. Mansour, Learning Boolean Functions via the Fourier Transform. In *Theoretical Advances in Neural Computation and Learning*, (V. P. Roychodhury, K-Y. Siu and A. Orlitsky, ed), 391-424 (1994).

[12] L. G. Valiant, A theory of the learnable, *Comm. of the ACM*, 27(11): 1134-1142, 1984.

[13] V. Vapnik, A. Chervonenkis, On the uniform convergence of relative frequencies of events to their probabilities. *Theory of Probability and its Applications*, 16(2): 264-280, 1971.

Optimally-Smooth Adaptive Boosting and Application to Agnostic Learning

Dmitry Gavinsky

Department of Computer Science
Technion
Haifa, Israel, 32000
demitry@cs.technion.ac.il

Abstract. We construct a boosting algorithm, which is the first both smooth and adaptive booster. These two features make it possible to achieve performance improvement for many learning tasks whose solution use a boosting technique.

Originally, the boosting approach was suggested for the standard PAC model; we analyze possible applications of boosting in the model of agnostic learning (which is "more realistic" than PAC). We derive a lower bound for the final error achievable by boosting in the agnostic model; we show that our algorithm actually achieves that accuracy (within a constant factor of 2): When the booster faces distribution D, its final error is bounded above by $\frac{1}{1/2-\beta}\,\mathrm{err}_D(F) + \zeta$, where $\mathrm{err}_{D'}(F) + \beta$ is an upper bound on the error of a hypothesis received from the (agnostic) weak learner when it faces distribution D' and ζ is any real, so that the complexity of the boosting is polynomial in $1/\zeta$. We note that the idea of applying boosting in the agnostic model was first suggested by Ben-David, Long and Mansour and the above accuracy is an exponential improvement w.r.t. β over their result $\left(\frac{1}{1/2-\beta}\,\mathrm{err}_D(F)^{2(1/2-\beta)^2/\ln(1/\beta-1)} + \zeta\right)$. Eventually, we construct a boosting "tandem", thus approaching in terms of O the lowest number of the boosting iterations possible, as well as in terms of $\tilde{O}$ the best possible smoothness. This allows solving adaptively problems whose solution is based on *smooth* boosting (like noise tolerant boosting and DNF membership learning), preserving the original solution's complexity.

1 Introduction

Boosting is a learning method discovered by Schapire [17]. It proves computational equivalence between two learning models: the model of *distribution-free (strong) PAC-learning* and that of *distribution-free weak PAC-learning* (the PAC-model was first introduced by Valiant in [20], the strong and the weak cases were distinguished by Kearns and Valiant in [15]). This (theoretical) equivalence between the two models may be used to solve various problems in the domain of Learning Theory: Indeed, a number of such problems are currently known whose "strong" solution was achieved by initial construction of a weak learner and then applying a boosting algorithm.

N. Cesa-Bianchi et al. (Eds.): ALT 2002, LNAI 2533, pp. 98–112, 2002.

On the other hand, for many concept classes no weak (PAC) learner has been found so far (e.g., for the class of DNF formulas, see [12]). In such cases one of the possible approaches is to modify the learning model, so that the task of learning would be simpler. For example, in the case of DNF learning a solution is known for the "simplified" PAC model, when the learner is allowed to ask membership queries and the target distribution is always uniform ([12]); at the same time, in its unrestricted form the task is considered rather difficult.

It turns out that the boosting approach, originally developed for the standard PAC model, may me adapted to other more or less similar learning models. For example, the solution suggested in [12] for the DNF learning problem is partially based on a previously known boosting algorithm, adapted for the uniform model with allowed membership queries.

Recently Ben-David, Long and Mansour [6] have shown that the boosting approach may also be utilized in the model of agnostic learning, which is in a sense "more practical" than PAC (see Subsection 1.1 for model description).

In this paper we construct a boosting algorithm whose requirements for some resources are "optimally modest"; as a result, this algorithm may be used in a number of "near-PAC" learning models, achieving the optimal performance.

1.1   Learning Models

All the models considered in this paper have one feature in common: A learner always "communicates" with a D-oracle which produces examples $(x, f(x))$, where f is the target function and x is chosen from the domain X according to the distribution D.

In this paper we will always assume that f is binary-valued to $\{-1, 1\}$. We will sometimes use as a complexity parameter a measure of the representation size of f, which we denote by $I(f)$ (its definition depends on the target class and is usually clear from the context).

Therefore the difference between the following models lies in the requirements for the learner's complexity and for its accuracy.

PAC Learning (Strong) The target function f is assumed to come from some hypotheses class C.

The learner receives parameters ε and δ; its goal is to produce with probability at least $1 - \delta$ a binary hypothesis h_f, satisfying:

$$\varepsilon_{h_f} \triangleq \Pr_D [h(x) \neq f(x)] \leq \varepsilon.$$

(Throughout this paper we will use notation of $\varepsilon_{function}$ to denote the value of $\Pr_D [function(x) \neq f(x)]$.)

The time complexity of the learner should be polynomial in $1/\varepsilon$, $log(1/\delta)$ and $I(f)$. (Sometimes δ is referred to as a *confidence parameter*.)

PAC Learning (Weak) The target function f is assumed to come from some hypotheses class C.

The learner receives a parameter δ; its goal is to produce with probability at least $1 - \delta$ a hypothesis h_f, satisfying:

$$\gamma_{h_f} \triangleq \mathbf{E}_D [h(x) \cdot f(x)] \geq \gamma_{min},$$

where γ_{min} may be inverse-polynomial low in $I(f)$. (Throughout this paper we will use notation of $\gamma_{function}$ to denote the value of $\mathbf{E}_D [function(x) \cdot f(x)]$.) In the context of weak PAC learning we will not demand the produced hypothesis to be binary (it may be real-valued to $[-1,1]$).

The time complexity of the learner should be polynomial in $I(f)$ and $log(1/\delta)$.

Agnostic Learning In the framework of agnostic learning no a priori assumptions regarding the target function f are made; instead we require that the learner's response h_f should be "near to the best possible" up to some parameter.

Formally, agnostic learning means that we define some learning hypotheses class F to be used for learning. For any target function f, the best possible accuracy a hypothesis from F can achieve is either equal or infinitesimal near to

$$\text{err}(F) \triangleq \inf_{h' \in F} \varepsilon_{h'}.^{[1]}$$

The learner receives a parameter δ and has to produce with probability at least $1 - \delta$ a binary hypothesis h_f, satisfying:

$$\varepsilon_{h_f} \leq \underset{D}{\text{err}}(F) + \beta,$$

for some β announced a priori. A learner satisfying this is called a β-optimal learner.

We do not define a general notion of agnostic learning efficiency now.

For a detailed overview of the agnostic learning model, see [14].

1.2   Boosting

A boosting algorithm B is supplied with an auxiliary algorithm WL (the *weak learner*). B "communicates" with WL, performing a number of "sessions": During session i B chooses a distribution D_i over X and emulates for WL a D_i-oracle, answering according to the target function f. In response WL has to learn f w.r.t. D_i, each session ends when WL constructs its hypothesis.

We will denote the total number of performed boosting sessions by T and the weak learner's response to D_i by h_i. We will sometimes refer to individual sessions as "iterations".

---

[1] Note that sometimes the agnostic model is defined so that the class used for accuracy evaluation is allowed to differ from that used to produce approximating hypotheses.

The boosting algorithm itself "faces" some target distribution D, according to which it receives instances from the oracle. After the T'th session is finished, B produces its final hypothesis h_f whose accuracy w.r.t. D is higher than the accuracies of the received weak hypotheses (w.r.t. corresponding D_i-s).

When the boosting is performed in the PAC model, the weak learner is usually a weak PAC-learner and the booster itself is required to satisfy the strong PAC requirements (see Subsection 1.1). In this case the booster is considered efficient when its complexity is polynomial in the γ_{min} parameter of WL, as well as in standard PAC complexity parameters. Note that when WL is an efficient weak PAC learner (i.e., γ_{min} is inverse-polynomial low), the whole tandem $B+WL$ constitutes an efficient strong PAC learner.

For the case of agnostic model (see Subsection 1.1) we will derive efficiency requirements for both B and WL later in the paper. (Since the PAC model is "more natural" for boosting, we will describe and analyze our algorithm as a PAC booster, and then we will separately consider its usage under agnostic settings.)

Boosting by Sampling versus Boosting by Filtering In this paper we consider two boosting modes: boosting "by sampling" and boosting "by filtering".

Boosting *by sampling* means that the learning is performed in two stages. In the first stage the algorithm collects a sufficient number of learning examples (i.e., a subset $S \subset X$ together corresponding values of f) by repeatedly calling the oracle. In the second stage the booster performs learning over this collection of examples only. The training sample S is of polynomial size.

The booster's goal is to achieve some required accuracy over the training set (which is often the absolute accuracy, so that the hypothesis coincides with f for each $x \in S$). Then information-theoretic techniques like VC theory [19] and Occam's Razor [1] may be applied to measure the overall accuracy w.r.t. D of the same hypothesis.

Of course, the hypothesis may be not accurate over whole X even if it is correct over S. Such "switching" from sub-domain S to whole X is sometimes called *generalization*, and the additional error introduced by generalization is called a *generalization error*.

On the other hand, the meaning of boosting *by filtering* is that the booster takes the whole set of instances as its learning domain. The examples received by the booster from the PAC-oracle are not stored, but are "filtered": Each example is either forwarded to WL or "rejected" (i.e., is not used at all).

This approach has two obvious advantages over boosting by sampling: the space complexity is reduced (the examples are not stored) and no generalization error is introduced. At the same time, the analysis and the algorithm itself become slightly more complicated, because now the booster cannot get exact "statistics" by running through all the instances of the domain and needs to use some estimation schemes (based on various statistical "laws of large numbers", like Chernoff bound).

Among the possible reasons for using boosting by sampling is that the booster is not smooth: In general, a distribution which is not polynomially near-D cannot be efficiently simulated using repeated calls to a D-oracle, when X is superpolynomially large.

Smooth Boosting and Adaptive Boosting In this paper we will consider two special features of boosting algorithm: *smoothness* and *adaptiveness*.

The term "adaptiveness" means that the algorithm doesn't require a priori lower bound for γ_i; instead the algorithm "takes advantage" of each single weak hypothesis, as good as it is. More formally, while a non-adaptive booster has its complexity bounds polynomial in $1/\min(\{\gamma_{h_i} | 1 \leq i \leq T\})$, adaptive algorithm's running time is polynomial in

$$1/ \mathop{\mathbf{E}}_{1 \leq i \leq T} [poly(\gamma_{h_i})].$$

(For example, we will derive complexity bounds for our algorithm in terms of $1/\mathbf{E}_{1 \leq i \leq T} [\gamma_i^2]$.)

The term "smoothness" means that the distributions D_i emulated by the booster do not diverge dramatically from the target distribution D of the booster itself. To measure the "smoothness" of a distribution D_i, we define a *smoothness parameter*:

$$\alpha_i \triangleq \sup_{x \in X} \frac{D_i(x)}{D(x)}.$$

We define a smoothness parameter for a boosting algorithm as sup of possible smoothness parameters of distributions emulated by it. A boosting algorithm with smoothness parameter α will be called α-smooth.

For example, if the target distribution is known to be always uniform and the booster is smooth, *WL* will has to deal only with distributions which are near to the uniform (which simplifies its quest sometimes). This idea is basic for the only known solution of DNF membership learning w.r.t. uniform ([12], [13]). Among other known applications for smooth boosting algorithms are noise-tolerant learning ([10], [7], [18]), learning via extended statistical queries ([2]) and agnostic boosting ([6]).

1.3   Our Results

In this paper we construct a boosting algorithm called *AdaFlat*, which is optimal from several points of view.

We show that *AdaFlat* is adaptive and nearly optimally smooth (within a constant multiplicative factor of 2).

Let us assume that the size of the final hypothesis produced by a booster cannot be upper bounded without bounding the running time of the algorithm. (To the best of our knowledge, this is true for all the boosting algorithms known so far.) We claim that under this assumption the two qualities (smoothness and adaptiveness) are essential for performing adaptive boosting over a superpoly-nomially large domain:

Non-smoothness makes it essential to use boosting by sampling. For an adaptive booster, one (in general) cannot know what will the running time be before the boosting process halts, and therefore the size of the future final hypothesis is also unknown. On the other hand, in order to determine required size of the learning sample S, so that the final error (after generalization) would be at most ε, it is essential to have an upper bound for the size of the final hypothesis before the boosting is started (in order to be able to apply generalization techniques, see [19] and [1]).

To the best of our knowledge, $AdaFlat$ is the first both smooth and adaptive booster. An algorithm $MadaBoost$ constructed by Domingo and Watanabe [7] is smooth, but it is adaptive only for a non-increasing sequence of weak hypotheses accuracies (i.e., when $\gamma_{h_{i+1}} \leq \gamma_{h_i}$ for $1 \leq i \leq T - 1$). Besides, their result applies only to the case of binary-valued weak hypotheses, which seems to produce some difficulties when Fourier spectrum approach is used for weak learning ([16], [3], [5]).

Another similar result was achieved by Bshouty and Gavinsky in [4]: their algorithm is smooth, but it is not "completely" adaptive: While their algorithm makes adaptive number of boosting iterations and constructs final hypothesis of adaptive size, the time complexity of each iteration depends upon the value of γ_{min} (which should be provided before the boosting starts).

We show that $AdaFlat$ may be used in the framework of agnostic learning. We derive a lower bound for the final error achievable by agnostic boosting; we show that our algorithm achieves that accuracy (within a constant factor of 2). Our upper bound on the final error is

$$\frac{1}{1/2 - \beta} \operatorname*{err}_D(F) + \zeta,$$

where ζ is any real so that the time complexity of the solution is polynomial in $1/\zeta$.

The idea of applying boosting in the agnostic model is due to Ben-David, Long and Mansour [6]. Our result is an exponential improvement w.r.t. β over the solution suggested in [6], whose error is upper bounded by

$$\frac{1}{1/2 - \beta} \operatorname*{err}_D(F)^{2(1/2-\beta)^2 / \ln(1/\beta - 1)} + \zeta.$$

(In particular, our result answers an open question posed in [6].)

Algorithm $AdaFlat$ performs the lowest possible number of boosting iterations in terms of $O(f(\gamma))$. We construct a "boosting tandem", consisting of $AdaFlat$ "joined" with another boosting algorithm (this approach was first used in [8] and since then became very popular in boosting algorithms' construction). The idea standing behind is to use one booster ($AdaFlat$, in our case) to boost hypotheses from the "weak" accuracy $\frac{1}{2} + \gamma$ to some fixed accuracy $\frac{1}{2} + \mathbf{const}$, and then to amplify ($\frac{1}{2} + \mathbf{const}$)-accurate hypotheses to $1 - \varepsilon$ using another boosting algorithm. Naturally, this approach is used when the first booster is more efficient in terms of γ and the second one is more efficient in terms of ε. Moreover, since the feature of adaptiveness is "expressed" in terms of γ and our tandem has *AdaFlat* in its "bottom level", the tandem itself is adaptive.

Naturally, the final hypothesis structure of the tandem is slightly more complicated. On the other hand, using this approach we achieve in terms of $O(f(\gamma))$ and $O(f(\varepsilon))$ the lowest possible number of boosting iterations and in terms of $\tilde{O}$ the lowest smoothness factor possible. Since our tandem algorithm is smooth and adaptive, it may be used in order to solve adaptively and with optimal number of iterations various boosting tasks, including those requiring that the boosting algorithm be smooth.

2   Preliminaries

For simplicity, in our analysis of boosting schemes we will not allow *WL* to fail.

2.1   Agnostic Boosting Approach

The main idea standing behind agnostic boosting is as follows: Suppose we are given a β-optimal learning algorithm; it will be used as a weak learner and therefore is referred to by *WL*.

Consider some target distribution D. By definition, the weak learner being executed "in a straightforward manner" must provide a $(1 - \text{err}_D(F) - \beta)$-accurate hypothesis in the worst case. Let us modify slightly the target distribution thus achieving a new distribution D_i of smoothness α_i (measured w.r.t. D). Obviously, it holds that

$$\text{err}_{D_i}(F) \leq \alpha_i \cdot \text{err}_D(F),$$

and *WL* must provide a hypothesis h_i whose error is $\alpha_i \cdot \text{err}_D(F) + \beta$, in the worst case.

If distribution D_i was produced by a boosting algorithm on stage i, then in terms of boosting we may write $\alpha_i \cdot \text{err}_D(F) + \beta \geq \varepsilon_i = \frac{1}{2} - \gamma_i$, which leads to

$$\gamma_i \geq \frac{1}{2} - \beta - \alpha_i \cdot \text{err}_D(F). \tag{1}$$

While in [6] agnostic learning is mainly considered in the context of boosting by sampling, our result equally applies to both boosting by sampling and boosting by filtering. In fact, it seems that the main difficulty lies in constructing a weak learner; possible solutions for this determine the applicability and the efficiency of the boosting methods. Some examples of "agnostic weak learners" may be found in [6].

3   Optimally-Smooth Adaptive Boosting

In this section we construct a booster working by sampling and in Section 5 we build a modification of the algorithm which works by filtering. For the construction of *AdaFlat* we modify another algorithm, first introduced by Impagliazzo [11] in a non-boosting context and later recognized as a boosting algorithm by Klivans and Servedio [13].

Algorithm *AdaFlat* is represented in Figure 1, the following notation is used:

$$N_i(s) \triangleq f(s) \cdot \sum_{j=0}^{i-1} l_j \cdot h_j(s), \ N_0(s) \triangleq 0,$$

$$m(N) \triangleq \begin{cases} 1 & N \leq 0 \\ 1 - N & 0 < N < 1 \\ 0 & 1 \leq N \end{cases},$$

$$\mu_i \triangleq \frac{\sum_{s \in S} m(N_i(s))}{|S|}, \ \gamma_i(s) \triangleq \frac{h_i(s) \cdot f(s)}{2}, \ \text{sign}(y) \triangleq \begin{cases} 1 & y \geq 0 \\ -1 & y < 0 \end{cases}.$$

When the domain S is of polynomial size, simulation of D_i-s is straightforward. Note that the number of iterations performed by the algorithm defines the number of weak hypotheses combined in a final hypothesis.

$AdaFlat(WL, S, \varepsilon)$
1.   **set:** $i = 0$
2.   **while** $\Pr[s \in S]h_f(s) \neq f(s) \geq \varepsilon$
3.   **define:** $D_i(s) \triangleq \frac{m(N_i(s))}{\sum_{s \in S} m(N_i(s))}$
4.   **call:** *WL, providing it with distribution D_i;*
         denote the returned weak hypothesis by h_i
5.   **set:** $\gamma_i = \sum_{s \in S} D_i(s) \cdot \gamma_i(s)$
6.   **set:** $l_i = 2\mu_i \gamma_i$
7.   **define:** $h_f(s) \triangleq \text{sign} \left(\sum_{j=0}^{i} l_j \cdot h_j(s) \right)$
8.   **set:** $i = i + 1$
9.   **end-while**
10. *Output the final hypothesis h_f*

Fig. 1. The *AdaFlat(WL, S, ε)* hypothesis boosting algorithm.

3.1   *AdaFlat*'s Analysis

Claim. Algorithm *AdaFlat* executed with parameters (WL, S, ε) performs

$$T \leq \frac{\varepsilon^{-2}}{4 \, \mathbf{E}_{0 \leq i < T} [\gamma_i^2]} \tag{2}$$

boosting iterations and produces a final hypothesis which is accurate over S and possesses the structure of a weighted majority vote of T weak hypotheses. The smoothness parameter of $AdaFlat$ satisfies:

$$\alpha \leq \varepsilon^{-1}. \tag{3}$$

Proof of Claim 3.1   Define the following reward function:

$$B(N) \triangleq \begin{cases} N & N \leq 0 \\ N - \frac{N^2}{2} & 0 < N < 1 \\ \frac{1}{2} & 1 \leq N \end{cases}.$$

As follows from a second-order Taylor expansion, for any $c \in \mathbf{R}$ it holds:

$$B(N + c) \geq B(N) + \frac{dB}{dN} \cdot c + \inf B''(N) \cdot \frac{c^2}{2},$$

where $B''(N) \triangleq \min\{\frac{dB^2}{dN \cdot dN^+}, \frac{dB^2}{dN \cdot dN^-}\}$. By noting that $m(N) = \frac{dB}{dN}$, we get:

$$B(N + c) \geq B(N) + m(N) \cdot c - \frac{c^2}{2}.$$

Further, denote:

$$c_i(s) \triangleq l_i \cdot h_i(s) \cdot f(s) = 2l_i \gamma_i(s), \quad B_i \triangleq \frac{\sum_{s \in S} B(N_i(s))}{|S|}, \quad \Delta_B^i \triangleq B_{i+1} - B_i.$$

Consequently,

$$\Delta_B^i \geq \frac{\sum_{s \in S} m(N_i(s)) \cdot c_i(s)}{|S|} - \frac{\sum_{s \in S} c_i^2(s)}{2|S|} \geq$$
$$\geq 2l_i \frac{\sum_{s \in S} m(N_i(s)) \cdot \gamma_i(s)}{\sum_{s \in S} m(N_i(s))} \cdot \mu_i - \frac{l_i^2}{2} = 2l_i \gamma_i \mu_i - \frac{l_i^2}{2},$$

and using the expression set for l_i by $AdaFlat$, we get:

$$\Delta_B^i \geq 2\gamma_i^2 \cdot \mu_i^2. \tag{4}$$

Since $B(N) \leq \frac{1}{2}$, the last inequality leads to

$$T \leq \frac{1}{4 \, \mathbf{E}_{0 \leq i < T} \left[\gamma_i^2 \cdot \mu_i^2\right]}. \tag{5}$$

Here the adaptiveness is expressed: the number of iterations depends on the value of $\mathbf{E}_{0 \leq i < T} \left[\gamma_i^2\right]$, rather then on $\min_{0 \leq i < T}^2 [\gamma_i]$.

Next, it holds that:

$$\frac{1}{\alpha_i} = \frac{1}{|S|} \cdot \frac{1}{\max_{s \in S} D_i(s)} = \frac{\mu_i}{\max_{s \in S} m(N_i(s))} \geq \mu_i \geq \varepsilon.$$

Since we obviously interrupt the algorithm as soon as $\varepsilon = 0$, it holds that for each i

$$\underset{s \in S}{\operatorname{argmax}} \, m(N_i(s)) = \min_{s \in S} N_i(s) \le 0,$$

and therefore

$$\alpha_i^{-1} = \mu_i \ge \varepsilon, \tag{6}$$

which leads to (3). Combining (6) with (5), we prove statement (2).

The result follows.

■ *Claim 3.1*

4   Agnostic Boosting

In this section we apply *AdaFlat* to agnostic boosting. (We refer to *AdaFlat* which works by sampling and not to *AdaFlat$_{Filt}$* introduced in Section 5; however, algorithm *AdaFlat$_{Filt}$* may be used for agnostic boosting as well.) As a result, we achieve upper bound on final error of

$$\frac{1}{1/2 - \beta} \operatorname*{err}_D(F) + \zeta,$$

where ζ is any real, so that the time complexity of the solution is polynomial in $1/\zeta$, as well as in other standard complexity parameters.

The analysis of our new application is straightforward: Combining (1), (4) and (6) gives us that:

$$\Delta_B^i \ge 2 \left(\frac{\gamma_i}{\alpha_i} \right)^2 \ge \left(\varepsilon \left(\tfrac{1}{2} - \beta \right) - \operatorname*{err}_D(F) \right)^2,$$

$$T \le \tfrac{1}{4} \left(\varepsilon \left(\tfrac{1}{2} - \beta \right) - \operatorname*{err}_D(F) \right)^{-2},$$

$$\varepsilon \le \frac{\frac{1}{2\sqrt{T}} + \operatorname*{err}_D(F)}{\frac{1}{2} - \beta}.$$

That is, applying *AdaFlat* to the task of agnostic boosting allows to get a hypothesis which $\left(\frac{\operatorname*{err}_D(F)}{\frac{1}{2} - \beta} + \zeta \right)$-approximates the target concept. For that, *AdaFlat* needs to perform

$$T \le \frac{1}{4} \left(\zeta \cdot \left(\frac{1}{2} - \beta \right) \right)^{-2}$$

iterations.

Recall that if we straightly apply *WL*, we get a $(\operatorname*{err}_D(F) + \beta)$-approximation. Therefore, our approach actually amplifies *WL* if and only if

$$\operatorname*{err}_D(F) < \beta \cdot \frac{1 - 2\beta}{1 + 2\beta}.$$

Note that evaluating in terms of $O(f)$ would work well for the number of iterations needed, but it is not sufficient for the smoothness estimation (3). That is because the smoothness property determines the "base" for the final error expression $\left(\frac{\text{err}_D(F)}{\frac{1}{2}-\beta}\right)$, which cannot be lowered by performing a larger number of iterations. The same thing holds regarding the parameter β.

In Section 6 we show that *AdaFlat* (and *AdaFlat$_{Filt}$*) are near-optimally smooth up to the constant multiplicative factor of 2, therefore the final hypothesis has half the best possible relative correspondence with the target for the agnostic boosting approach.

5   Boosting Using Filtering

Algorithm *AdaFlat$_{Filt}$* is shown in Figure 2 and its subroutine *Evaluate* in Figure 3. Note that the algorithm receives confidence parameter δ. Recall that now the target distribution is D itself and the instance space is $\{(x, f(x)) \mid x \in X\}$.

$AdaFlat_{Filt}(WL, \varepsilon, \delta)$

   1. **set:** $i = 0$, $\delta_0 = \frac{\delta}{2}$

   2. **while** $\mu'_i(m) \geq \frac{4\varepsilon}{5}$

   3.   **call:** *WL, providing it with distribution generated by $D_i gen$;*
              denote the returned weak hypothesis by h_i

   4.   **set:** $\mu'_i(m) = Evaluate\left(m(N_i(s))|_{s \sim D}, 1, \frac{\delta_i}{2}\right)$

   5.   **set:** $\gamma'_i = Evaluate\left(\left.\left(\gamma_i(s) \cdot m(N_i(s))\right)\right|_{s \sim D}, 1, \frac{\delta_i}{2}\right)$

   6.   **set:** $l'_i = 2\mu'_i(m)\gamma'_i$, $i = i+1$, $\delta_i = \frac{2}{3}l'^2_{i-1} \cdot \delta$

   7. **end-while**

   8. **define:** $h_f(s) \triangleq \text{sign}\left(\sum_{j=0}^{i} l'_j \cdot h_j(s)\right)$

   9. *Output the final hypothesis h_f*

$D_i gen$

   1. **do:**

   2.   *get $(x_j, f(f_j))$ from the oracle; choose $r \sim \mathbf{U}_{0,1}$*

   3.   **if** $(r < m(N_i(s)))$ **then return** $(x_j, f(x_j))$

   4. **end-do**

Fig. 2. The $AdaFlat_{Filt}(WL, \varepsilon, \delta)$ hypothesis boosting algorithm.

The algorithm has two subroutines: $D_i gen$ which is used to produce examples for *WL* and $Evaluate(V, b - a, \delta)$ (shown in Figure 3) which, with probability δ at least, returns a value μ' s.t. $|\mu' - \mathbf{E}[V]| \leq \frac{\mathbf{E}[V]}{5}$ when V receives values from $[a, b]$ and $\mathbf{E}[V] \neq 0$. The latter subroutine is based on Chernoff bound, its time

$Evaluate(V, b - a, \delta)$
1. **set:** $\mu_g = \frac{1}{2}$, $i = 0$, $\sigma = 0$, $\delta = \frac{\delta}{2}$
2. **do:**
3.   **set:** $i = i + 1$, $\sigma = \sigma + < sample\ from\ V >$
4.   **if** $i = \left\lceil \frac{18(b-a)^2 \ln(\frac{2}{\delta})}{\mu_g^2} \right\rceil$ **then**
5.   **set:** $\mu' = \frac{\sigma}{i}$
6.   **if** $|\mu'| \geq \mu_g$ **then return** μ'
7.   **set:** $\mu_g = \frac{\mu_g}{2}$, $\delta = \frac{\delta}{2}$
8.   **end-if**
9. **end-do**

Fig. 3. Subroutine *Evaluate*.

complexity is

$$O\left(\frac{(b-a)^2 \cdot \ln(\delta^{-1}) \cdot \ln((\mathbf{E}\,[V])^{-1})}{(\mathbf{E}\,[V])^2} \right).$$

5.1 *AdaFlat$_{Filt}$*'s Analysis

Denote by $T[WL]$ the time complexity of WL running over the instance space X, and by $Q[WL]$ the corresponding query complexity (i.e., the number of requested examples).

Claim. Suppose algorithm $AdaFlat_{Filt}$ is executed with parameters $(WL, \varepsilon, \delta)$. Then with probability at least δ the following statements hold:

- The algorithm performs

$$T \leq \frac{3}{4\varepsilon^2 \cdot \mathbf{E}_{0 \leq i < T}\,[\gamma_i^2]} \tag{7}$$

  boosting iterations.
- The algorithm produces a final hypothesis possessing the structure of a weighted majority vote of T weak hypotheses whose prediction error over the learning domain (X) is ε at most.
- The smoothness parameter of $AdaFlat_{Filt}$ satisfies

$$\alpha \leq \varepsilon^{-1}.$$

- The query complexity of the algorithm is

$$\tilde{O}\left(\frac{\varepsilon^{-1} \cdot Q[WL] + \mathbf{E}_{0 \leq i < T}\,[\gamma_i^{-2}] + \varepsilon^{-2}}{\varepsilon^2 \cdot \mathbf{E}_{0 \leq i < T}\,[\gamma_i^2]} \right). \tag{8}$$

- The time complexity of the algorithm is

$$\tilde{O}\left(\frac{\varepsilon^{-1} \cdot Q[WL] + T[WL] + \mathbf{E}_{0 \leq i < T}\,[\gamma_i^{-2}] + \varepsilon^{-2}}{\varepsilon^2 \cdot \mathbf{E}_{0 \leq i < T}\,[\gamma_i^2]} \right). \tag{9}$$

6   Optimality of *AdaFlat* and *AdaFlat$_{Filt}$*

In this section we consider the smoothness parameter and the number of iterations performed by our algorithms.

Our algorithms are twice near-optimally smooth and the number of iterations performed are optimally low in terms of $O(f(\gamma))$.

The second fact simply follows from a fact shown by Freund in [9]: The number of desired iterations for any general boosting scheme must satisfy $T = \Theta\left(\gamma^{-2} \cdot \ln \varepsilon^{-1}\right)$.

The fact that $\alpha \leq \varepsilon^{-1}$ is near-optimal up to the multiplicative factor of 2, becomes clear from the following mental experiment. If some algorithm is not allowed to diverge by more than $\frac{1}{2}\varepsilon^{-1} \cdot (1 - 2\gamma)$ from the original distribution D, then it is unable to force the *WL* to reveal any information regarding any (fixed) set of points of total probabilistic weight 2ε. Therefore, the best thing that can be done there is to guess, which leads to the error ε at least in the final hypothesis, and the result follows.

7   Boosting Tandems

In this section we construct a boosting tandem, or combine two boosting algorithm in a kind of hierarchy. The upper level algorithm views the lower level algorithm as its weak learner, while the latter communicates with the "real" weak learner. While in the case of "usual" boosting the weak learner provides a polynomially-accurate weak hypothesis which is afterwards "amplified" by the booster into a polynomially-accurate strong hypothesis, in the boosting tandem model the corresponding evolution is **polynomial weak → constant correspondence → polynomial strong**.

This technique was first used by Freund in [8]. Its advantage is that if one algorithm is more efficient in terms of γ and the other in terms of ε, this approach makes use of the "strong sizes" of the both, setting their "weak" parameters to constants.

Naturally, we are interested to preserve the adaptiveness and efficiency in terms of γ of *AdaFlat$_{Filt}$*, and it will be used as a low level[2]. In this case the smoothness factor of *AdaFlat$_{Filt}$* will be bounded by a constant.

As a high level, we use an algorithm introduced in [8] (and used there for the same purpose). It performs $O(\ln(\varepsilon^{-1}) \cdot f(\gamma))$ iterations and its smoothness is $\tilde{O}(\varepsilon^{-1})$.

Putting everything together, we achieve the number of iterations (i.e., that of calls to the weak learner) bounded by

$$O\left(\frac{\ln(\varepsilon^{-1})}{\mathbf{E}_{0 \leq i < T}[\gamma_i^2]}\right)$$

and smoothness of

$$\alpha = \tilde{O}(\varepsilon^{-1}).$$

---

[2] The same approach works for *AdaFlat* as well.

Note that the resulting algorithm is adaptive. (The whole construction is similar to that made by Klivans and Servedio [13]; their result, however, is not adaptive.)

As mentioned in Section 6, this number of iterations corresponds to the lower bound. The price that we pay for the improvement is further complication of the final hypothesis structure[3], and also a logarithmic in ε^{-1} growth of the smoothness parameter[4]. Notice that for the case of agnostic boosting considered in Section 4, bounding the smoothness strictly was shown to be critical.

An interesting application for the tandem is for near-uniform DNF learning with membership queries. The problem was solved for the first time by Jackson in [12]; The most efficient solution known so far is that by Klivans and Servedio represented in [13], where they use a similar tandem for their construction. Our algorithm possesses the same complexity, and therefore the complexity of the solution equals that achieved in [13]; moreover, our solution it is adaptive. The latter fact directly addresses an open question posed in [12]. Another attempt to use an adaptive algorithm in the context of near-uniform DNF learning was made in [4]; the result received there has weaker complexity bounds and it is adaptive only w.r.t. the size of the final hypothesis, but not w.r.t. the time complexity of the solution.

8   Other Applications and Further Work Directions

As mentioned before, in addition to the contexts of agnostic boosting and near-uniform DNF learning with membership queries, smoothness is critical for noise-tolerant learning ([10], [7], [18]), for learning via extended statistical queries ([2]) and for agnostic learning ([6]).

Our algorithm can be used to solve all these tasks adaptively; the boosting tandem introduced in Section 7 achieves performance as efficient as that of other boosting algorithms known so far.

We based our analysis of the application of *AdaFlat* to agnostic boosting upon the adaptiveness feature of the booster (if we would use a lower bound on γ_i-s instead, the achieved result would be noticeably weaker). An interesting open question is whether this adaptiveness feature can be similarly taken into consideration in the analysis of other smoothness dependent learning tasks, in particular, it would be interesting to gain some performance improvement for the widely studied task of DNF membership learning.

Acknowledgments. I would like to thank Nader Bshouty for his guidance and advice.

---

[3] The final hypothesis generated by the tandem is represented as a majority vote of weighted majority votes, instead of a single weighted majority vote, as generated by *AdaFlat*.

[4] Recall that for *AdaFlat* and *AdaFlat*$_{Filt}$ it was strictly bounded by ε^{-1}.

References

[1] A. Blumer, A. Ehrenfeucht, D. Haussler and M.K. Warmuth. Learnability and the Vapnik-Chervonenkis Dimension. *Journal of the ACM 36(4), pp. 929-965*, 1989.

[2] N. Bshouty and V. Feldman. On Using Extended Statistical Queries to Avoid Membership Queries. *Proceedings of the 14th Annual Conference on Computational Learning Theory, pp. 529-545*, 2001.

[3] A. Blum, M. Furst, J. Jackson, M. Kearns, Y. Mansour and S. Rudich. Weakly learning DNF and characterizing statistical query learning using Fourier analysis. *Proceedings of the 26th Symposium on Theory of Computing, pp. 253-262*, 1994.

[4] N. Bshouty and D. Gavinsky. On Boosting with Optimal Poly-Bounded Distributions. *Proceedings of the 14th Annual Conference on Computational Learning Theory, pp. 490-506*, 2001.

[5] N. Bshouty, J. Jackson and C. Tamon. More efficient PAC-learning of DNF with membership queries under the uniform distribution. *Proceedings of the 12th Annual Conference on Computational Learning Theory, pp. 286-295*, 1999.

[6] S. Ben-David, P.M. Long and Y. Mansour. Agnostic Boosting. *Proceedings of the 14th Annual Conference on Computational Learning Theory, pp. 507-516*, 2001.

[7] C. Domingo and O. Watanabe. MadaBoost: A modification of AdaBoost. *Proceedings of the 13th Annual Conference on Computational Learning Theory, pp. 180-189*, 2000.

[8] Y. Freund. An improved boosting algorithm and its implications on learning complexity. *Proceedings of the 5th Annual Conference on Computational Learning Theory, pp. 391-398*, 1992.

[9] Y. Freund. Boosting a weak learning algorithm by majority. *Information and Computation 121(2), pp. 256-285*, 1995.

[10] Y. Freund. An adaptive version of the boost by majority algorithm. *Proceedings of the 12th Annual Conference on Computational Learning Theory, pp. 102-113*, 1999.

[11] R. Impagliazzo. Hardcore Distributions for Somewhat Hard Problems. *Proceedings of the 36th Annual Symposium on Foundations of Computer Science, pp. 538-545*, 1995.

[12] J. Jackson. An efficient membership-query algorithm for learning DNF with respect to the uniform distribution. *Journal of Computer and System Sciences 55(3), pp. 414-440*, 1997.

[13] A.R. Klivans and R.A. Servedio. Boosting and Hard-Core Sets. *Proceedings of the 40th Annual Symposium on Foundations of Computer Science, pp. 624-633*, 1999.

[14] M.J. Kearns, R.E. Schapire and L. M. Sellie. Towards Efficient Agnostic Learning. *Machine Learning 17, pp. 115-141*, 1994.

[15] M. Kearns and L. Valiant. Cryptographic limitations on learning boolean formulae and finite automata. *Journal of the ACM 41(1), pp. 67-95*, 1994.

[16] Y. Mansour. Learning Boolean Functions via the Fourier Transform. *Theoretical Advances in Neural Computing and Learning, Kluwe Academic Publishers, -*, 1994.

[17] R.E. Schapire. The strength of weak learnability. *Machine Learning 5(2), pp. 197-227*, 1990.

[18] R. Servedio. Smooth Boosting and Learning with Malicious Noise. *Proceedings of the 14th Annual Conference on Computational Learning Theory, pp. 473-489*, 2001.

[19] V.N. Vapnik. Estimation of Dependences Based on Empirical Data. *Springer,* , 1982.

[20] L. Valiant. A theory of learnable. *Communications of the ACM 27(11), pp. 1134-1142*, 1984.

Large Margin Classification for Moving Targets

Jyrki Kivinen, Alex J. Smola, and Robert C. Williamson

Research School of Information Sciences and Engineering
Australian National University
Canberra, ACT 0200, Australia
{Jyrki.Kivinen, Alex.Smola, Bob.Williamson}@anu.edu.au

Abstract. We consider using online large margin classification algorithms in a setting where the target classifier may change over time. The algorithms we consider are Gentile's ALMA, and an algorithm we call NORMA which performs a modified online gradient descent with respect to a regularised risk. The update rule of ALMA includes a projection-based regularisation step, whereas NORMA has a weight decay type of regularisation. For ALMA we can prove mistake bounds in terms of the total distance the target moves during the trial sequence. For NORMA, we need the additional assumption that the movement rate stays sufficiently low uniformly over time. In addition to the movement of the target, the mistake bounds for both algorithms depend on the hinge loss of the target. Both algorithms use a margin parameter which can be tuned to make them mistake-driven (update only when classification error occurs) or more aggressive (update when the confidence of the classification is below the margin). We get similar mistake bounds both for the mistake-driven and a suitable aggressive tuning. Experiments on artificial data confirm that an aggressive tuning is often useful even if the goal is just to minimise the number of mistakes.

1 Introduction

Consider the basic linear classification problem. We are given a set of data points (x_t, y_t) where $x_t \in \mathbb{R}^n$ and $y_t \in \{-1, +1\}$ for $t = 1, \ldots, m$. The task is to find a coefficient vector $w \in \mathbb{R}^n$ such that $w \cdot x_t > 0$ if $y_t = +1$, and $w \cdot x_t < 0$ if $y_t = -1$. In other words, we wish the *margin* $y_t w \cdot x_t$ to be positive for every example (x_t, y_t). Recently a lot of work has been done on large margin classification, where we do not just settle for any linear separator w, but try to find one that achieves the largest possible separation [3]. Maximising the separation can be thought of as maximising the smallest margin over the example set, while keeping the norm of w bounded. This often leads to significant improvements in the generalisation ability of the resulting linear classifier [3].

The discussion above presumes a batch learning scenario: we obtain a set of examples (x_t, y_t) from a source, use that data to induce a classifier w, and then use the classifier to predict the labels y for new instances x coming from the same source. Contrast this with the online scenario: at each time t, the algorithm receives an input x_t, makes its prediction $\hat{y}_t$ using its *current hypothesis* w_t, and

N. Cesa-Bianchi et al. (Eds.): ALT 2002, LNAI 2533, pp. 113–127, 2002.
© Springer-Verlag Berlin Heidelberg 2002

upon seeing the correct outcome y_t updates its hypothesis to $\boldsymbol{w}_{t+1}$. Thus, the algorithm is interleaving predicting and learning. This goes on for some time, and the goal is to minimise the total number of prediction mistakes. The question now is: *can an analogue of large margin classification usefully be applied in an online setting?* In addition to the number of prediction mistakes, we might be interested in the convergence properties of the algorithm, the quality of the final hypothesis produced etc.

Theoretical analyses of mistake bounds of online algorithms are typically done in a worst-case setting. Then it is known that the best mistake bounds are achieved by mistake-driven algorithms, i.e., algorithms that update only after they made a mistake. For linear separation, this means having $y\boldsymbol{w} \cdot \boldsymbol{x} < 0$. The analogue of large margin classification would be to update whenever we have $y\boldsymbol{w} \cdot \boldsymbol{x} < \rho$ for some positive margin $\rho > 0$. If $0 < y\boldsymbol{w} \cdot \boldsymbol{x} < \rho$, we get updates that are not mistake-driven, and thus not useful at least in terms of worst-case mistake bounds. (Of course, if we wish our on-line algorithm to converge to a maximum-margin classifier, as in [12,6], we need to use a positive margin, but this is a somewhat different goal.) Since margins can be changed without affecting the classifications by simply multiplying the weight vector by a scalar, margin-based algorithms usually also employ some kind of regularisation to control the norm of the weight vector.

To get a better idea of the usefulness of large margins and regularisation in online learning, we consider the situation when the target classifier we are trying to learn is allowed to move over time. This is the setting analysed earlier for regression by Herbster and Warmuth [10] and Herbster [9] and for classification with disjunctions as targets by Auer and Warmuth [2]. This previous work also uses norm bounds on the hypothesis, or some other form of regularisation, to deal with having a moving target (even when no margins are involved). More recently, Mesterharm [14] has considered tracking arbitrary linear classifiers with a variant of Winnow [13].

In this paper we establish mistake bounds with moving targets for general linear classification algorithms. We have bounds for two algorithms, a simplified version of Gentile's Approximate Large Margin Algorithm (ALMA) [6], and a new Naive Online Regularised-risk Minimisation Algorithm (NORMA) which is motivated by gradient descent with respect to a regularised risk [11]. We have a special interest in whether using a nonzero margin may help here. As it turns out, the best bounds we can obtain for nonzero margins are identical to those for zero margin (i.e., mistake driven algorithms). This is not really conclusive in any sense, but it does give some evidence that mistake driven algorithms are not the only way to minimise mistakes. On the technical side, our analysis of ALMA is a rather standard application of known techniques. For analysing NORMA we need something a little different to handle the weight decay. The technique requires some additional assumptions, so our bounds for NORMA are less general than for ALMA. However, experiments on artificial data suggest that the actual performance of the algorithms is rather similar.

In Section 2, we describe more formally the online mistake-bounded model and what we mean by moving targets. Section 3 describes the algorithms we study here. The main theoretical results are given in Section 4. Some experiments, which use artificial data to study the actual behaviour of the algorithms, are described in Section 5.

2   Basic Setting

We consider linear classification problems. An example is a pair $(x, y) \in \mathbb{R}^n \times \{-1, +1\}$. We interpret a weight vector $w \in \mathbb{R}^n$ as a linear classifier, which gives for a vector x the classification $+1$ if $w \cdot x > 0$, and otherwise classification -1. We say that w makes a *mistake*, or *classification error*, on example (x, y), if $yw \cdot x \leq 0$. (Thus, we consider $w \cdot x = 0$ as an error.) We generalise this by saying that w makes a *margin error at scale* ρ if $yw \cdot x \leq \rho$. We also define the *hinge loss* as $L_\rho(w, x, y) = \max\{0, \rho - yw \cdot x\}$. The scale parameter ρ, or the *margin*, is usually nonnegative; we omit mentioning it when it is clear from the context. We are basically interested in finding weight vectors w that make few mistakes, or few margin errors, but the continuous-valued hinge loss turns out to be a useful tool in analysing the algorithms. Notice that $L_\rho(w, x, y) \geq \rho$ if and only if w made a mistake on (x, y).

An online linear classification algorithm maintains as its current *hypothesis* a weight vector $w \in \mathbb{R}^n$. We denote the hypothesis at time t by w_t. The initial hypothesis w_1 is typically $\mathbf{0}$, for lack of any other preference. At time t, for $t = 1, \ldots, T$, the algorithm receives an instance $x_t \subset \mathbb{R}^n$ and makes its prediction, which is $+1$ if $w_t \cdot x_t \geq 0$ and -1 otherwise. Then the algorithm receives the correct outcome $y_t \in \{-1, +1\}$ and updates its weight vector into w_{t+1} based on this new information.

Suppose A is some online algorithm. We write $\sigma_t = 1$ if the algorithm made a margin error at trial t ($y_t w_t \cdot x_t \leq \rho$) and $\sigma_t = 0$ otherwise. We denote the total number of margin errors made by A over a sequence of T examples by $\text{ME}_\rho(A) = \sum_{t=1}^{T} \sigma_t$. Similarly, let $\text{Mist}(A)$ be the number of mistakes. We will also use the *cumulative hinge loss* $\text{Loss}_\rho(A) = \sum_{t=1}^{T} L_\rho(w_t, x_t, y_t)$. Notice that $\text{Mist}(A) \leq \text{Loss}_\rho(A)/\rho$.

To prove a mistake bound, we obviously need to assume something about the examples. For instance, the Perceptron Convergence Theorem [15] assumes that some weight vector $u \in \mathbb{R}^n$ separates the examples with margin $\mu > 0$; the mistake bound is then proportional to $(\|u\|_2/\mu)^2$. More generally, given a fixed *comparison vector* $u \in \mathbb{R}^n$, let $\text{Loss}_\mu(u) = \sum_{t=1}^{T} L_\mu(u, x_t, y_t)$ be its cumulative hinge loss with respect to margin μ. Thus, u separates the examples with margin μ if and only if $\text{Loss}_\mu(u) = 0$. Our approach will be to bound the cumulative hinge loss $\text{Loss}_\rho(A)$ of an online algorithm in terms of $\inf_{u \in \mathcal{U}} \text{Loss}_\mu(u)$ where $\mu > \rho$ and $\mathcal{U} \subset \mathbb{R}^n$ is some *comparison class* of vectors. Typical comparison classes consist of vectors of bounded q-norm for some $1 \leq q \leq 2$ [8,7], i.e., $\mathcal{U} = \{u \mid \|u\|_q \leq B\}$ for some $B > 0$. Our loss bounds go to infinity as ρ approaches μ; in other words, we need to give the algorithm a slight advantage by measuring its performance with respect to a smaller margin than that used for the comparison vectors. From a hinge loss bound we can rather easily derive a bound for the number of mistakes or margin errors.

We generalise the setting for moving comparison vectors by considering *comparison sequences* $U = (u_1, \ldots, u_{T+1})$ [10]. The loss of such a comparison sequence is naturally defined as $\text{Loss}_\mu(U) = \sum_{t=1}^{T} L_\mu(u_t, x_t, y_t)$. As in the fixed target scenario, we assume some norm bound $\|u_t\|_q \leq B$ for all the individual comparison vectors u_t. We additionally restrict the amount of movement by the comparison vectors in terms of the total q-norm distance $\sum_t \|u_t - u_{t+1}\|_q$ travelled by the comparison vectors. Thus, we define for parameters $1 \leq q \leq 2$, $B > 0$ and $D \geq 0$ the comparison class

$$\mathcal{U}_q(B, D) = \left\{ (u_1, \ldots, u_{T+1}) \mid \sum_{t=1}^{T} \|u_t - u_{t+1}\|_q \leq D, \|u_t\|_q \leq B \right\} .$$

For technical reasons, we also need to consider bounding the sum of *squared* distances, so we also define

$$\mathcal{U}_q'(B, D_1, D_2) = \left\{ (u_1, \ldots, u_{T+1}) \mid \sum_{t=1}^{T} \|u_t - u_{t+1}\|_q \leq D_1, \right.$$

$$\left. \sum_{t=1}^{T} \|u_t - u_{t+1}\|_q^2 \leq D_2, \|u_t\|_q \leq B \right\} .$$

The meaning of the parameter D_2 is perhaps a little non-intuitive; it will become clearer after Theorem 4 when we discuss how D_2 appears in the loss bounds.

3   The Algorithms

The algorithms we consider are based on the p-norm algorithms introduced by Grove et al. [8] and further studied, e.g., by Gentile and Littlestone [7]. Thus, for the rest of the paper we assume $p \geq 2$ and $2 \geq q > 1$ are such that $1/p + 1/q = 1$, and define

$$f_i(w) = \frac{\text{sign}(w_i)|w_i|^{q-1}}{\|w\|_q^{q-2}} . \tag{1}$$

Notice that f is one-to-one from $\mathbb{R}^n$ onto $\mathbb{R}^n$ with the inverse given by $f_i^{-1}(\theta) = \text{sign}(\theta_i)|\theta_i|^{p-1}/\|\theta\|_p^{p-2}$. The update of the p-norm Perceptron can be written as

$$w_{t+1} = f^{-1}(f(w_t) + \alpha \sigma_t y_t x_t) ,$$

where $\alpha > 0$ is a learning rate parameter. The parameter p can adjusted to change the behaviour of the algorithm. For $p = 2$, the function f is the identity function, and the algorithm is the usual Perceptron algorithm. Setting $p = O(\log n)$ gives an algorithm with performance similar to Winnow [8,7].

The first algorithm we define here is called Naive Online Regularised-Risk Minimisation Algorithm, or NORMA. The algorithm is parameterised by a learning rate $\alpha > 0$, a weight decay parameter $0 \leq \lambda < 1/\alpha$, and a margin $\rho \geq 0$. The update is then

$$w_{t+1} = f^{-1}((1 - \alpha\lambda)f(w_t) + \alpha \sigma_t y_t x_t) , \tag{2}$$

where again $\sigma_t = 1$ if $y_t \boldsymbol{w}_t \cdot \boldsymbol{x}_t \leq \rho$ and $\sigma_t = 0$ otherwise. For $p = 2$ the NORMA update can be seen as a gradient descent step with respect to the regularised risk $R(\boldsymbol{w}) = L_\rho(\boldsymbol{w}, \boldsymbol{x}_t, y_t) + \lambda ||\boldsymbol{w}||^2/2$; see [11] for additional discussion and applications.

We also consider a simplified version of Gentile's Approximate Large Margin Algorithm ALMA [6]. For simplicity, we call our algorithm just ALMA although it omits the parameter tuning method of Gentile's original algorithm. Our version of ALMA has a fixed learning rate parameter $\alpha > 0$, regularisation parameter $B > 0$ and margin $\rho \geq 0$. The update of ALMA has two steps:

Additive step $\boldsymbol{w}'_{t+1} = \boldsymbol{f}^{-1}(\boldsymbol{f}(\boldsymbol{w}_t) + \alpha\sigma_t y_t \boldsymbol{x}_t)$, $\sigma_t = 1_{y_t \boldsymbol{w}_t \cdot \boldsymbol{x}_t \leq \rho}$
Normalisation step $\boldsymbol{w}_{t+1} = \boldsymbol{w}'_{t+1}/\beta_t$ where $\beta_t = \max\{1, ||\boldsymbol{w}'_{t+1}||_q/B\}$

Gentile's original ALMA also includes a method for tuning the parameters α and ρ during learning. The tuning method there has been carefully crafted so that assuming separable data, the algorithm converges to an approximate maximum margin classifier even without advance knowledge of the maximum margin. We use here a cruder version where α and ρ need to be fixed beforehand (and a poor choice may lead to bad performance), since we have not been able to generalise the dynamic tuning method to the moving target scenario.

In the case $p = 2$ (with $\boldsymbol{f}$ the identity function), we see that the hypotheses of NORMA and ALMA can be represented as $\boldsymbol{w}_{T+1} = \sum_{t=1}^{T} a_t \boldsymbol{x}_t$ for some scalar coefficients a_t. Thus, the algorithms allow the standard generalisation to non-linear classification by using kernels to compute dot products. Also the normalisation in the kernel version of ALMA can be accomplished with little computational overhead by keeping track of the changes in $||\boldsymbol{w}_t||$ [6].

Both NORMA and ALMA have been here represented as having three parameters: margin ρ, learning rate α, and a regularisation type parameter (λ or B). However, effectively there are only two parameters, as multiplying all the parameters (except for λ) by any constant will leave the predictions of the algorithm unchanged; also the scaled hinge losses $L_\rho(\boldsymbol{w}_t, \boldsymbol{x}_t, y_t)/\rho$ remain invariant. Thus, without loss of generality we could fix, e.g., $\rho = 1$, but we find it convenient to do the analysis with all the parameters explicitly written out. Although the parameterisations of NORMA and ALMA are quite similar, we find that of NORMA a little more intuitive. The underlying idea of gradient descent with respect to a regularised risk can be easily applied, e.g., in SVM regression using the ν parameterisation [11].

4   Worst-Case Mistake Bounds

We start with some general comments on the kind of bounds we are after. Fix some comparison class $\mathcal{U}$; say $\mathcal{U} = \mathcal{U}_q(B, D)$ for some $B > 0$ and $D \geq 0$. Let $K_* = \inf_{U \in \mathcal{U}} \text{Loss}_\mu(U)$ for some margin $\mu > 0$. Thus if some $U \in \mathcal{U}$ separates the examples with margin μ, i.e., $y_t \boldsymbol{u}_t \cdot \boldsymbol{x}_t > \mu$ for all t, then $K_* = 0$. Otherwise K_* is a measure for the non-separability of the examples at scale μ. An alternative intuition is to think that the data have been obtained by corrupting some (hypothetical) separable data by noise; then K_* would be a measure of the total amount of noise added.

In the case of non-moving targets, one can get bounds of the form $\mathrm{Mist}(A) \leq K_*/\mu + o(K_*)$ ([7]; see also [5]). Here $o(K_*)$ is a term that is sublinear in K_*; we would expect it to depend on the norms of the examples, the bound B, etc. Notice that K_*/μ is an upper bound for the number of mistakes made by the best comparison sequence from $\mathcal{U}$; of course, it may be a quite loose bound. We would expect target movement to result in an additional $O(D)$ term in the mistake bound, analogous to the regression case [10]. In other words, there should be a constant cost per unit target movement. It turns out that with the optimal choice of the parameters, bounds of exactly this form are attainable for ALMA. For NORMA there are some additional considerations about the nature of the target movement.

Choosing the parameters is an issue in the bounds we have. The bounds depend on the choice of the learning rate and margin parameters, and the optimal choices depend on quantities (such as K_*) that would not be available when the algorithm starts. In our bounds, we handle this by assuming an upper bound $K \geq K_*$ that can be used for tuning. By substituting $K = K_*$, we obtain the kind of bound we discussed above; otherwise the estimate K replaces K_* in the bound. In a practical application, we probably prefer to ignore the formal tuning results in the bounds and just tune the parameters by whatever empirical methods we prefer. Recently, online algorithms have been suggested that dynamically tune the parameters to almost optimal values as the algorithm runs [1,6]. Applying such techniques to our analysis remains an open problem.

We now turn to the actual bounds, starting with a margin error bound for ALMA. It will be convenient to give the parameter tunings in terms of the function

$$h(x, R, S) = \sqrt{\frac{S}{R}\left(x + \frac{S}{R}\right)} - \frac{S}{R} ,$$

where we assume x, R and S to be positive. Notice that $0 \leq h(x, R, S) \leq x$ holds, and $\lim_{R \to 0+} h(x, R, S) = x/2$. Accordingly, we define $h(x, 0, S) = x/2$.

Theorem 1. Let $X > 0$ and suppose that $\|\boldsymbol{x}_t\|_p \leq X$ for all t. Fix $K \geq 0$, $D \geq 0$ and $B > 0$, and write

$$C = \frac{p-1}{4} X^2 (B^2 + 2BD) . \tag{3}$$

Consider ALMA with regularisation parameter B, margin parameter ρ and learning rate $\alpha = 2h(\mu - \rho, K, C)/((p-1)X^2)$ where $\mu > \rho \geq 0$. If we have $\mathrm{Loss}_\mu(U) \leq K$ for some $U \in \mathcal{U}_q(B, D)$, then

$$\mathrm{ME}_\rho(\mathrm{ALMA}) \leq \frac{K}{\mu - \rho} + 2\frac{C}{(\mu - \rho)^2} + 2\left(\frac{K}{\mu - \rho} + \frac{C}{(\mu - \rho)^2}\right)^{1/2}\left(\frac{C}{(\mu - \rho)^2}\right)^{1/2} .$$

To prove Theorem 1, we apply Herbster and Warmuth's [10] technique of using a Bregman divergence [4] as a measure of progress. As first suggested by Grove et al. [8], the p-norm family of algorithms is related to the *potential function* $F(\boldsymbol{w}) = ||\boldsymbol{w}||_q^2/2$. (Notice that $\nabla F = \boldsymbol{f}$ where $\boldsymbol{f}$ is as in (1).) Using this, we define the appropriate divergence for $\boldsymbol{u}, \boldsymbol{w} \in \mathbb{R}^n$ as

$$d_q(\boldsymbol{u}, \boldsymbol{w}) = F(\boldsymbol{u}) - F(\boldsymbol{w}) + \boldsymbol{f}(\boldsymbol{w}) \cdot (\boldsymbol{w} - \boldsymbol{u}) \ . \tag{4}$$

See [8,7,6] for basic properties of F and d_q.

The key part of the analysis is the following lower bound on the *progress* the algorithm makes on its tth update.

Lemma 1. *Assume $||\boldsymbol{u}_t||_q \leq B$ and $||\boldsymbol{x}_t||_p \leq X$ for all t. Then at any trial t the update of* ALMA *with regularisation parameter B, margin parameter ρ and learning rate α satisfies*

$$d_q(\boldsymbol{u}_t, \boldsymbol{w}_t) - d_q(\boldsymbol{u}_{t+1}, \boldsymbol{w}_{t+1})$$
$$\geq \alpha L_\rho(\boldsymbol{w}_t, \boldsymbol{x}_t, y_t) - \alpha L_\mu(\boldsymbol{u}_t, \boldsymbol{x}_t, y_t) + \alpha v_t \left(\mu - \rho - \alpha \frac{p-1}{2} X^2 \right)$$
$$+ \frac{1}{2}||\boldsymbol{u}_t||_q^2 - \frac{1}{2}||\boldsymbol{u}_{t+1}||_q^2 - B||\boldsymbol{u}_{t+1} - \boldsymbol{u}_t||_q \ .$$

Proof. We split the progress into three parts:

$$d_q(\boldsymbol{u}_t, \boldsymbol{w}_t) - d_q(\boldsymbol{u}_{t+1}, \boldsymbol{w}_{t+1}) = (d_q(\boldsymbol{u}_t, \boldsymbol{w}_t) - d_q(\boldsymbol{u}_t, \boldsymbol{w}'_{t+1}))$$
$$+ (d_q(\boldsymbol{u}_t, \boldsymbol{w}'_{t+1}) - d_q(\boldsymbol{u}_t, \boldsymbol{w}_{t+1}))$$
$$+ (d_q(\boldsymbol{u}_t, \boldsymbol{w}_{t+1}) - d_q(\boldsymbol{u}_{t+1}, \boldsymbol{w}_{t+1})) \ . \tag{5}$$

Grove et al. [8] have shown that $d_q(\boldsymbol{w}_t, \boldsymbol{w}'_{t+1}) \leq \frac{p-1}{2} \sigma_t \alpha^2 ||\boldsymbol{x}_t||_p^2$. Hence, for the first part of (5) we get

$$d_q(\boldsymbol{u}_t, \boldsymbol{w}_t) - d_q(\boldsymbol{u}_t, \boldsymbol{w}'_{t+1}) = \alpha \sigma_t y_t \boldsymbol{x}_t \cdot (\boldsymbol{u}_t - \boldsymbol{w}_t) - d_q(\boldsymbol{w}_t, \boldsymbol{w}'_{t+1})$$
$$\geq \alpha \sigma_t y_t \boldsymbol{x}_t \cdot (\boldsymbol{u}_t - \boldsymbol{w}_t) - \frac{p-1}{2} \alpha^2 \sigma_t ||\boldsymbol{x}_t||_p^2$$
$$\geq \alpha (\sigma_t \mu - L_\mu(\boldsymbol{u}_t, \boldsymbol{x}_t, y_t)) - \alpha (\sigma_t \rho - L_\rho(\boldsymbol{w}_t, \boldsymbol{x}_t, y_t))$$
$$- \frac{p-1}{2} \alpha^2 \sigma_t ||\boldsymbol{x}_t||_p^2 \ .$$

It is easy to see that $\boldsymbol{w}_{t+1}$ satisfies

$$\boldsymbol{w}_{t+1} = \arg \min_{\boldsymbol{w} \in \mathcal{B}} d_q(\boldsymbol{w}, \boldsymbol{w}'_{t+1})$$

where $\mathcal{B} = \{ \boldsymbol{w} \mid ||\boldsymbol{w}||_q \leq B \}$. Since $\boldsymbol{u}_t \in \mathcal{B}$ and $\mathcal{B}$ is convex, the well-known result about projections with respect to a Bregman divergence (see [10] for details) implies

$$d_q(\boldsymbol{u}_t, \boldsymbol{w}'_{t+1}) - d_q(\boldsymbol{u}_t, \boldsymbol{w}_{t+1}) \geq 0 \ .$$

For the third part we have

$$d_q(\boldsymbol{u}_t, \boldsymbol{w}_{t+1}) - d_q(\boldsymbol{u}_{t+1}, \boldsymbol{w}_{t+1}) = \frac{1}{2}||\boldsymbol{u}_t||_q^2 - \frac{1}{2}||\boldsymbol{u}_{t+1}||_q^2 + (\boldsymbol{u}_{t+1} - \boldsymbol{u}_t) \cdot \boldsymbol{f}(\boldsymbol{w}_{t+1})$$
$$\geq \frac{1}{2}||\boldsymbol{u}_t||_q^2 - \frac{1}{2}||\boldsymbol{u}_{t+1}||_q^2 - B||\boldsymbol{u}_{t+1} - \boldsymbol{u}_t||_q$$

by Hölder's inequality and the fact $\|f(\boldsymbol{w}_{t+1})\|_p = \|\boldsymbol{w}_{t+1}\|_q \leq B$. Substituting the above three estimates to the right-hand side of (5) gives the claim.

The following technical lemma, which is proved by a simple differentiation, is used for choosing the optimal parameters.

Lemma 2. *Given $R > 0$, $S > 0$ and $\gamma > 0$ define $f(z) = R/(\gamma - z) + S/(z(\gamma - z))$ for $0 < z < \gamma$. Then $f(z)$ is maximised for $z = h(\gamma, R, S)$, and the maximum value is*

$$f(h(\gamma, R, S)) = \frac{R}{\gamma} + \frac{2S}{\gamma^2} + 2\left(\frac{R}{\gamma} + \frac{S}{\gamma^2}\right)^{1/2}\left(\frac{S}{\gamma^2}\right)^{1/2} .$$

Proof of Theorem 1. By summing the bound of Lemma 1 over $t = 1, \ldots, T$ we get

$$d_q(\boldsymbol{u}_1, \boldsymbol{w}_1) - d_q(\boldsymbol{u}_{T+1}, \boldsymbol{w}_{T+1})$$

$$\geq \alpha \mathrm{Loss}_\rho(\mathrm{ALMA}) - \alpha \mathrm{Loss}_\mu(\boldsymbol{U}) + \alpha \mathrm{ME}_\rho(\mathrm{ALMA})\left(\mu - \rho - \alpha\frac{p-1}{2}X^2\right)$$

$$+ \frac{1}{2}\|\boldsymbol{u}_1\|_q^2 - \frac{1}{2}\|\boldsymbol{u}_{T+1}\|_q^2 - B\sum_{t=1}^{T}\|\boldsymbol{u}_{t+1} - \boldsymbol{u}_t\|_q .$$

We take $\boldsymbol{w}_1 = \boldsymbol{0}$, so $d_q(\boldsymbol{u}_1, \boldsymbol{w}_1) = \|\boldsymbol{u}_1\|_q^2/2$, and clearly $-d_q(\boldsymbol{u}_{T+1}, \boldsymbol{w}_{T+1}) \leq 0$. On the right-hand side, we use the assumptions about $\boldsymbol{U}$. We get

$$\mathrm{ME}_\rho(\mathrm{ALMA})(\mu - \rho - \alpha(p-1)X^2/2) \leq K - \mathrm{Loss}_\rho(\mathrm{ALMA}) + \frac{1}{\alpha}(BD + B^2/2) . \quad (6)$$

We can of course drop the non-positive term $-\mathrm{Loss}_\rho(\mathrm{ALMA})$. For the value α given in the theorem, we have $\mu - \rho - \alpha(p-1)X^2/2 > 0$, so we get

$$\mathrm{ME}_\rho(\mathrm{ALMA}) \leq \frac{K}{\mu - \rho - \alpha(p-1)X^2/2} + \frac{BD + B^2/2}{\alpha(\mu - \rho - \alpha(p-1)X^2/2)} .$$

The claim follows by applying Lemma 2 with $z = \alpha(p-1)X^2/2$, $\gamma = \mu - \rho$, $R = K$ and $S = C$.

Next, we use the margin error result of Theorem 1 to obtain mistake bounds. It turns out that two ways of choosing the parameter pair (α, ρ) result in the same mistake bound. In particular, the same bound we get for the mistake driven algorithm with $\rho = 0$ also holds for certain positive $\rho > 0$, assuming the learning rate is chosen appropriately.

Theorem 2. *Let $X > 0$ and suppose that $\|\boldsymbol{x}_t\|_p \leq X$ for all t. Fix $K \geq 0$, $B > 0$ and $D \geq 0$. Define C as in (3), and given $\mu > 0$ let $r = h(\mu, K, C)$. Consider ALMA with regularisation parameter B, learning rate $\alpha = 2r/((p-1)X^2)$ and margin set to either $\rho = 0$ or $\rho = \mu - r$. Then for both of these margin settings, if there exists a comparison sequence $\boldsymbol{U} \in \mathcal{U}_q(B, D)$ such that $\mathrm{Loss}_\mu(\boldsymbol{U}) \leq K$, we have*

$$\mathrm{Mist}(\mathrm{ALMA}) \leq \frac{K}{\mu} + \frac{2C}{\mu^2} + 2\left(\frac{C}{\mu^2}\right)^{1/2}\left(\frac{K}{\mu} + \frac{C}{\mu^2}\right)^{1/2} .$$

Proof. For $\rho = 0$ this is a direct corollary of Theorem 1. To get non-zero ρ, we set $\alpha = 2(\mu - \rho)/((p - 1)X^2)$ so that the coefficient in front of $\mathrm{ME}_\rho(\mathrm{ALMA})$ in (6) becomes zero. We then exploit $\mathrm{Mist}(\mathrm{ALMA}) \le \mathrm{Loss}_\rho(\mathrm{ALMA})/\rho$ to get

$$\mathrm{Mist}(\mathrm{ALMA}) \le \frac{K}{\rho} + \frac{(p-1)X^2(BD + B^2/2)}{2\rho(\mu - \rho)} .$$

The claim follows by applying Lemma 2 with $\gamma = \mu$ and $z = \mu - \rho$.

To interpret Theorem 2, let us start with a fixed target $(D = 0)$ and $p = 2$. In the noise-free case $K = 0$, we recover the familiar Perceptron mistake bound X^2B^2/μ^2. Notice that by Theorem 2 we can get this mistake bound also using the positive margin $\rho = \mu/2$ with suitable α. However, a positive margin obviously leads to a larger number of updates; the margin error bound we get from Theorem 1 with this tuning is worse by a factor of 4 compared to $\rho = 0$.

In the noisy case $K > 0$, we get additional terms $K/\mu + O(\sqrt{K/\mu})$ as expected. For a discussion of how different choices of p affect this kind of a bound, see [8] and [7]. If the target movement bound D is non-zero, it will appear linearly in the mistake bound as expected.

Our bounds generalise those of Gentile [6] in that we allow a moving target. Also, Gentile was concerned only with margin error bounds and not obtaining mistake bounds using a nonzero margin. However, in the case of no target movement $(D = 0)$, Gentile gets better bounds than ours by using special techniques we have not been able to apply to the moving target case $(D > 0)$. Also, Gentile's algorithm includes a dynamical tuning of the parameters, unlike the simplified version we here call ALMA.

We now go to bounds for NORMA. Since NORMA does not maintain a bound on the norm of the weight vector, the meaning of margin errors is not as clear as for ALMA. However, the number of margin errors, i.e., updates, is still interesting as a measure of the complexity of the hypothesis produced by the algorithm.

Theorem 3. *Let $X > 0$ and suppose that $\|\boldsymbol{x}_t\|_p \le X$ for all t. Fix $K \ge 0$, $B > 0$, $D_1 \ge 0$ and $D_2 \ge 0$. Write*

$$C = \frac{p-1}{4}X^2 \left(B^2 + B \left(\sqrt{TD_2} + D_1 \right) \right) \tag{7}$$

and, given parameters $\mu > \rho \ge 0$, let $\alpha' = 2h(\mu - \rho, K, C)/((p-1)X^2)$. Consider NORMA *with weight decay parameter*

$$\lambda = \frac{1}{B\alpha'} \sqrt{\frac{D_2}{T}} , \tag{8}$$

learning rate parameter $\alpha = \alpha'/(1 + \alpha'\lambda)$ and margin ρ. If we have $\mathrm{Loss}_\mu(U) \le K$ for some $U \in \mathcal{U}_q'(B, D_1, D_2)$, then

$$\mathrm{ME}_\rho(\mathrm{NORMA}) \le \frac{K}{\mu - \rho} + \frac{2C}{(\mu - \rho)^2}$$
$$+ 2 \left(\frac{C}{(\mu - \rho)^2} \right)^{1/2} \left(\frac{K}{\mu - \rho} + \frac{C}{(\mu - \rho)^2} \right)^{1/2} .$$

Proof. It will be convenient to write $\boldsymbol{\theta}_t = \boldsymbol{f}(\boldsymbol{w}_t)$. We also define $\boldsymbol{\theta}'_{t+1} = \boldsymbol{\theta}_t + \alpha'\sigma_t y_t \boldsymbol{x}_t$, so $\boldsymbol{\theta}_{t+1} = (1 - \alpha\lambda)\boldsymbol{\theta}'_{t+1}$, and let $\boldsymbol{w}'_{t+1}$ be such that $\boldsymbol{\theta}'_{t+1} = \boldsymbol{f}(\boldsymbol{w}'_{t+1})$. As in the proof of Lemma 1, we split the progress into three parts:

$$
\begin{aligned}
d_q(\boldsymbol{u}_t, \boldsymbol{w}_t) - d_q(\boldsymbol{u}_{t+1}, \boldsymbol{w}_{t+1}) &= (d_q(\boldsymbol{u}_t, \boldsymbol{w}_t) - d_q(\boldsymbol{u}_t, \boldsymbol{w}'_{t+1})) \\
&\quad + (d_q(\boldsymbol{u}_t, \boldsymbol{w}'_{t+1}) - d_q(\boldsymbol{u}_t, \boldsymbol{w}_{t+1})) \\
&\quad + (d_q(\boldsymbol{u}_t, \boldsymbol{w}_{t+1}) - d_q(\boldsymbol{u}_{t+1}, \boldsymbol{w}_{t+1})) \ . \quad (9)
\end{aligned}
$$

For the first part we have

$$
\begin{aligned}
d_q(\boldsymbol{u}_t, \boldsymbol{w}_t) - d_q(\boldsymbol{u}_t, \boldsymbol{w}'_{t+1}) \geq{} & \alpha'(\sigma_t\mu - L_\mu(\boldsymbol{u}_t, \boldsymbol{x}_t, y_t)) - \alpha'(\sigma_t\rho - L_\rho(\boldsymbol{w}_t, \boldsymbol{x}_t, y_t)) \\
& - \frac{p-1}{2}\alpha'^2\sigma_t X^2 \ . \quad (10)
\end{aligned}
$$

as in the proof of Lemma 1.

For the second part, the definition of d_q gives

$$
d_q(\boldsymbol{u}_t, \boldsymbol{w}'_{t+1}) - d_q(\boldsymbol{u}_t, \boldsymbol{w}_{t+1}) = d_q(\boldsymbol{w}_{t+1}, \boldsymbol{w}'_{t+1}) + (\boldsymbol{\theta}'_{t+1} - \boldsymbol{\theta}_{t+1}) \cdot (\boldsymbol{w}_{t+1} - \boldsymbol{u}_t) \ .
$$

By using $\boldsymbol{w}_{t+1} = (1 - \alpha\lambda)\boldsymbol{w}'_{t+1}$ and the fact $\boldsymbol{w} \cdot \boldsymbol{f}(\boldsymbol{w}) = \|\boldsymbol{w}\|_q^2$ we get

$$
\begin{aligned}
d_q(\boldsymbol{w}_{t+1}, \boldsymbol{w}'_{t+1}) &= \frac{1}{2}\|(1 - \alpha\lambda)\boldsymbol{w}'_{t+1}\|_q^2 - \frac{1}{2}\|\boldsymbol{w}'_{t+1}\|_q^2 + \alpha\lambda\boldsymbol{w}'_{t+1} \cdot \boldsymbol{\theta}'_{t+1} \\
&= \frac{1}{2}\left(\frac{\alpha\lambda}{1 - \alpha\lambda}\right)^2 \|\boldsymbol{w}_{t+1}\|_q^2 \ .
\end{aligned}
$$

Also, since $\boldsymbol{\theta}'_{t+1} - \boldsymbol{\theta}_{t+1} = \alpha\lambda\boldsymbol{\theta}'_{t+1} = \alpha\lambda\boldsymbol{\theta}_{t+1}/(1 - \alpha\lambda)$, we have

$$
\begin{aligned}
(\boldsymbol{\theta}'_{t+1} - \boldsymbol{\theta}_{t+1}) \cdot (\boldsymbol{w}_{t+1} - \boldsymbol{u}_t) &= \frac{\alpha\lambda}{1 - \alpha\lambda}(\boldsymbol{\theta}_{t+1} \cdot \boldsymbol{w}_{t+1} - \boldsymbol{\theta}_{t+1} \cdot \boldsymbol{u}_t) \\
&= \frac{\alpha\lambda}{1 - \alpha\lambda}(\|\boldsymbol{w}_{t+1}\|_q^2 - \boldsymbol{\theta}_{t+1} \cdot \boldsymbol{u}_t) \ .
\end{aligned}
$$

Hence, recalling the definition of α' and using the fact $\|\boldsymbol{w}\|_q = \|\boldsymbol{f}(\boldsymbol{w})\|_p$, we get

$$
\begin{aligned}
d_q(\boldsymbol{u}_t, & \boldsymbol{w}'_{t+1}) - d_q(\boldsymbol{u}_t, \boldsymbol{w}_{t+1}) \\
&= \left(\alpha'\lambda + \frac{\alpha'^2\lambda^2}{2}\right) \|\boldsymbol{w}_{t+1}\|_q^2 - \alpha'\lambda\boldsymbol{\theta}_{t+1} \cdot \boldsymbol{u}_t \\
&= \left(\alpha'\lambda + \frac{\alpha'^2\lambda^2}{2}\right) \|\boldsymbol{\theta}_{t+1}\|_p^2 - \alpha'\lambda\boldsymbol{\theta}_{t+1} \cdot \boldsymbol{u}_t \ . \quad (11)
\end{aligned}
$$

For the third part of (9) the definition of d_q directly gives

$$
d_q(\boldsymbol{u}_t, \boldsymbol{w}_{t+1}) - d_q(\boldsymbol{u}_{t+1}, \boldsymbol{w}_{t+1}) = \frac{1}{2}\|\boldsymbol{u}_t\|_q^2 - \frac{1}{2}\|\boldsymbol{u}_{t+1}\|_q^2 + (\boldsymbol{u}_{t+1} - \boldsymbol{u}_t) \cdot \boldsymbol{\theta}_{t+1} \ . \quad (12)
$$

Substituting (10), (11) and (12) into (9) gives us

$$
\begin{aligned}
d_q(\boldsymbol{u}_t, & \boldsymbol{w}_t) - d_q(\boldsymbol{u}_{t+1}, \boldsymbol{w}_{t+1}) \\
&\geq \alpha'(\sigma_t\mu - L_\mu(\boldsymbol{u}_t, \boldsymbol{x}_t, y_t)) - \alpha'(\sigma_t\rho - L_\rho(\boldsymbol{w}_t, \boldsymbol{x}_t, y_t)) \\
&\quad - \frac{p-1}{2}\alpha'^2\sigma_t\|\boldsymbol{x}_t\|_p^2 + \frac{1}{2}\|\boldsymbol{u}_t\|_q^2 - \frac{1}{2}\|\boldsymbol{u}_{t+1}\|_q^2 + R(\boldsymbol{\theta}_{t+1}) \quad (13)
\end{aligned}
$$

where

$$R(\boldsymbol{\theta}) = \left(\alpha'\lambda + \frac{\alpha'^2\lambda^2}{2}\right)||\boldsymbol{\theta}||_p^2 - \alpha'\lambda\boldsymbol{\theta}\cdot\boldsymbol{u}_t + (\boldsymbol{u}_{t+1} - \boldsymbol{u}_t)\cdot\boldsymbol{\theta} \ .$$

To bound $R(\boldsymbol{\theta}_{t+1})$ from below, we notice that R is convex. Its gradient is given by

$$\nabla R(\boldsymbol{\theta}) = \left(2\alpha'\lambda + \alpha'^2\lambda^2\right)\boldsymbol{f}^{-1}(\boldsymbol{\theta}) + \boldsymbol{u}_{t+1} - (1 + \alpha'\lambda)\boldsymbol{u}_t$$

where $\boldsymbol{f}^{-1}$ is the inverse of $\boldsymbol{f}$. Therefore, $R(\boldsymbol{\theta}_{t+1}) \geq R(\boldsymbol{\theta}_*)$ where

$$\boldsymbol{f}^{-1}(\boldsymbol{\theta}_*) = \frac{\boldsymbol{u}_t - \boldsymbol{u}_{t+1} + \alpha'\lambda\boldsymbol{u}_t}{2\alpha'\lambda + \alpha'^2\lambda^2} \ .$$

Write $\boldsymbol{w}_* = \boldsymbol{f}^{-1}(\boldsymbol{\theta}_*)$. First using $||\boldsymbol{w}||_q = ||\boldsymbol{f}(\boldsymbol{w})||_p$ and $\boldsymbol{w}\cdot\boldsymbol{f}(\boldsymbol{w}) = ||\boldsymbol{w}||_q^2$ and then observing that $||\boldsymbol{u}_t - \boldsymbol{u}_{t+1} + \alpha'\lambda\boldsymbol{u}_t||_q \leq ||\boldsymbol{u}_t - \boldsymbol{u}_{t+1}||_q + \alpha'\lambda||\boldsymbol{u}_t||_q$ gives us

$$\begin{aligned}
R(\boldsymbol{\theta}_*) &= (\alpha'\lambda + \frac{\alpha'^2\lambda^2}{2})||\boldsymbol{\theta}_*||_p^2 - (2\alpha'\lambda + \alpha'^2\lambda^2)\boldsymbol{w}_* \cdot \boldsymbol{\theta}_* \\
&= -\frac{1}{2}(2\alpha'\lambda + \alpha'^2\lambda^2)||\boldsymbol{w}_*||_q^2 \\
&\leq -\frac{1}{2}\frac{1}{2\alpha'\lambda + \alpha'^2\lambda^2}\left(||\boldsymbol{u}_t - \boldsymbol{u}_{t+1}||_q + \alpha'\lambda||\boldsymbol{u}_t||_q\right)^2 \\
&= -\frac{1}{2}\frac{1}{2 + \alpha'\lambda}\left(\frac{||\boldsymbol{u}_t - \boldsymbol{u}_{t+1}||_q^2}{\alpha'\lambda} + 2||\boldsymbol{u}_t - \boldsymbol{u}_{t+1}||_q||\boldsymbol{u}_t||_q + \alpha'\lambda||\boldsymbol{u}_t||_q^2\right) \ .
\end{aligned}$$

By applying $R(\boldsymbol{\theta}_{t+1}) \geq R(\boldsymbol{\theta}_*)$ in (13) and noticing that $-1/(2 + \alpha'\lambda) > -1/2$, we get

$$\begin{aligned}
d_q(\boldsymbol{u}_t, \boldsymbol{w}_t) &- d_q(\boldsymbol{u}_{t+1}, \boldsymbol{w}_{t+1}) \\
&\geq -\alpha'(\sigma_t\rho - L_\rho(\boldsymbol{w}_t, \boldsymbol{x}_t, y_t)) + \alpha'(\sigma_t\mu - L_\mu(\boldsymbol{u}_t, \boldsymbol{x}_t, y_t)) \\
&- \alpha'^2\sigma_t\frac{p-1}{2}||\boldsymbol{x}_t||_p^2 + \frac{1}{2}||\boldsymbol{u}_t||_q^2 - \frac{1}{2}||\boldsymbol{u}_{t+1}||_q^2 \\
&- \frac{1}{4}\left(\frac{||\boldsymbol{u}_{t+1} - \boldsymbol{u}_t||_q^2}{\alpha'\lambda} + 2||\boldsymbol{u}_t||_q||\boldsymbol{u}_{t+1} - \boldsymbol{u}_t||_q + \alpha'\lambda||\boldsymbol{u}_t||_q^2\right) \ . \quad (14)
\end{aligned}$$

By summing over $t = 1,\ldots,T$ and using the assumption that $U \in \mathcal{U}_q'(B, D_1, D_2)$ we get

$$\begin{aligned}
d_q(\boldsymbol{u}_1, \boldsymbol{w}_1) &- d_q(\boldsymbol{u}_{T+1}, \boldsymbol{w}_{T+1}) \\
&\geq \alpha'\text{Loss}_\rho(\textsc{Norma}) - \alpha'\text{Loss}_\mu(U) \\
&+ \alpha'\text{ME}_\rho(\textsc{Norma})\left(\mu - \rho - \alpha'\frac{p-1}{2}X^2\right) \\
&+ \frac{1}{2}||\boldsymbol{u}_1||_q^2 - \frac{1}{2}||\boldsymbol{u}_{T+1}||_q^2 \\
&- \frac{1}{4}\left(\frac{D_2}{\alpha'\lambda} + 2BD_1 + T\alpha'\lambda B^2\right) \ .
\end{aligned}$$

Now λ appears only in a subexpression $S(\alpha'\lambda)$ where

$$S(z) = -\frac{D_2}{z} - zTB^2 \ .$$

Since $S(z)$ is maximized for $z = \sqrt{D_2/(TB^2)}$, we choose λ as in (8) which gives $S(\alpha'\lambda) = -2B\sqrt{TD_2}$. We assume $\boldsymbol{w}_1 = \boldsymbol{0}$, so $d_q(\boldsymbol{u}_1, \boldsymbol{w}_1) - d_q(\boldsymbol{u}_{T+1}, \boldsymbol{w}_{T+1}) \leq d_q(\boldsymbol{u}_1, \boldsymbol{w}_1) = \|\boldsymbol{u}_1\|_q^2/2$. By moving some terms around and estimating $\|\boldsymbol{u}_{T+1}\|_q \leq B$ and $\mathrm{Loss}_\mu(\boldsymbol{U}) \leq K$ we get

$$\mathrm{Loss}_\rho(\mathrm{NORMA}) + \mathrm{ME}_\rho(\mathrm{NORMA}) \left(\mu - \rho - \alpha' \frac{p-1}{2} X^2 \right)$$

$$\leq K + \frac{B^2 + B(\sqrt{TD_2} + D_1)}{2\alpha'} \ . \tag{15}$$

To get a bound for margin errors, notice that the value α' given in the theorem satisfies $\mu - \rho - \alpha'(p-1)X^2/2 > 0$. We make the trivial estimate $\mathrm{Loss}_\rho(\mathrm{NORMA}) \geq 0$, which gives us

$$\mathrm{ME}_\rho(\mathrm{NORMA}) \leq \frac{K}{\mu - \rho - \alpha'(p-1)X^2/2} + \frac{B^2 + B(\sqrt{TD_2} + D_1)}{2\alpha'(\mu - \rho - \alpha'(p-1)X^2/2)} \ .$$

The bound follows by applying Lemma 2 with $\gamma = \mu - \rho$ and $z = \alpha'(p-1)X^2/2$.

As with ALMA, we can get a mistake bound either by setting $\rho = 0$ in the margin error bound or doing a slightly different analysis that leads to a non-zero margin.

Theorem 4. *Let $X > 0$ and suppose that $\|\boldsymbol{x}_t\|_p \leq X$ for all t. Fix $K \geq 0$, $B > 0$, $D_1 \geq 0$ and $D_2 \geq 0$. Define C as in (7), and given $\mu > 0$ let $\alpha' = 2r/((p-1)X^2)$ where $r = h(\mu, K, C)$. Consider NORMA with weight decay parameter as in (8), learning rate $\alpha = \alpha'/(1 - \alpha'\lambda)$, and margin set to either $\rho = 0$ or $\rho = \mu - r$. Then for both of these margin settings, if there exists a comparison sequence $\boldsymbol{U} \in \mathcal{U}_q'(B, D_1, D_2)$ such that $\mathrm{Loss}_\mu(\boldsymbol{U}) \leq K$, we have*

$$\mathrm{Mist}(\mathrm{NORMA}) \leq \frac{K}{\mu} + \frac{2C}{\mu^2} + 2 \left(\frac{C}{\mu^2} \right)^{1/2} \left(\frac{K}{\mu} + \frac{C}{\mu^2} \right)^{1/2} \ .$$

Proof of Theorem 4 from Theorem 3 is completely analogous with the proof of Theorem 2 from Theorem 1. We omit the details.

Comparing the bounds for the algorithms, we notice that the NORMA bound has a term $\sqrt{TD_2}$ replacing D in the ALMA bound. Suppose the parameters here have been chosen optimally: $D = \sum_{t=1}^T \|\boldsymbol{u}_t - \boldsymbol{u}_{t+1}\|_q$ and $D_2 = \sum_{t=1}^T \|\boldsymbol{u}_t - \boldsymbol{u}_{t+1}\|_q^2$. Then it is easy to see that $\sqrt{TD_2} \geq D$ always holds, with equality if the target speed is uniform ($\|\boldsymbol{u}_t - \boldsymbol{u}_{t+1}\|_q = \|\boldsymbol{u}_{t'} - \boldsymbol{u}_{t'+1}\|_q$ for all t, t'). Thus, the bound for NORMA gets worse if the target speed changes a lot. We believe that this may be due to our proof techniques, since the experiments reported in Section 5 do not show such differences between ALMA and NORMA.

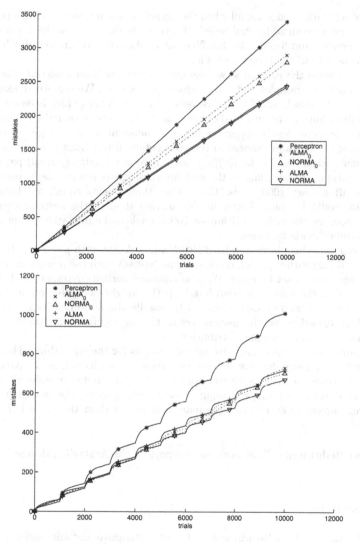

Fig. 1. Mistakes made by the algorithms on drifting (above) and switching (below) data

5   Experiments

The mistake bounds in Section 4 are of course only worst-case upper bounds, and even as such maybe not very tight. Hence, we have performed some preliminary experiments on artificial data to see qualitatively how the bounds relate to the actual performance of the algorithms. Our bounds would suggest that some form of regularisation is useful when the target is moving, and forcing a positive margin may give an additional benefit. Further, the difference in the assumptions of Theorems 1 and 3 suggests that NORMA might not perform so well when the movement rate of the target varies a lot.

To generate the examples, we use one mixture of 2-dimensional Gaussians for the positive examples and another for negative ones. We remove all examples that would be misclassified by the Bayes-optimal classifier (which is based on the actual distribution known to us) or are close to its decision boundary. This gives us data that are cleanly separable using a Gaussian kernel. Target movement takes place as random changes in the parameters of the Gaussians. We use two movement schedules: In the *drifting* case, there is a relatively small parameter change after every ten trials. In the *switching* case, there is a very large parameter change after every 1000 trials. Thus, other things being equal, our bound for NORMA would be much better in the drifting than in the switching case. In either case, we ran each algorithm for 10000 trials and cumulatively summed up the mistakes made by them.

In our experiments we compare NORMA and ALMA with $p = 2$ and the basic Perceptron algorithm (which is the same as NORMA with the margin and weight decay parameters set to zero). We also consider variants $NORMA_0$ and $ALMA_0$ where we fix the margin to zero but keep the weight decay (or regularisation) parameter. We used Gaussian kernels to handle the non-linearity of the data. For these experiments, the parameters of the algorithms were tuned by hand optimally for each example distribution.

Figure 1 shows the cumulative mistake counts for the algorithms. There does not seem to be any decisive differences between the algorithms. In particular, NORMA seems to work quite well also on switching data. In general, it does seem that using a positive margin is better than fixing the margin to zero, and regularisation even with zero margin is better than the basic Perceptron algorithm.

Acknowledgments. This work was support by the Australian Research Council.

References

[1] P. Auer, N. Cesa-Bianchi and C. Gentile. Adaptive and self-confident on-line learning algorithms. Technical Report NC-TR-00-083, NeuroCOLT, 2000.

[2] P. Auer and M. K. Warmuth. Tracking the best disjunction. *Machine Learning*, 32(2):127–150, August 1998.

[3] P. Bartlett and J. Shawe-Taylor. Generalization performance of support vector machines and other pattern classifiers. In B. Schölkopf, C. J. C. Burges and A. J. Smola, editors, *Advances in Kernel Methods: Support Vector Learning*, pages 43–54. MIT Press, 1999.

[4] L. M. Bregman. The relaxation method of finding the common point of convex sets and its application to the solution of problems in convex programming. *USSR Computational Mathematics and Physics*, 7:200–217, 1967.

[5] Y. Freund and R. E. Schapire. Large margin classification using the perceptron algorithm. *Machine Learning*, 37(3):277–296, 1999.

[6] C. Gentile. A new approximate maximal margin classification algorithm. *Journal of Machine Learning Research*, 2:213–242, December 2001.

[7] C. Gentile and N. Littlestone. The robustness of the p-norm algorithms. In *Proc. 12th Annu. Conf. on Comput. Learning Theory*, pages 1–11. ACM Press, New York, NY, 1999.

[8] A. J. Grove, N. Littlestone and D. Schuurmans. General convergence results for linear discriminant updates. *Machine Learning*, 43(3):173–210, 2001.

[9] M. Herbster. Learning additive models online with fast evaluating kernels. In D. Helmbold and B. Williamson, editors, *Proc. 14th Annu. Conf. on Comput. Learning Theory*, pages 444–460. Springer LNAI 2111, Berlin, July 2001.

[10] M. Herbster and M. K. Warmuth. Tracking the best linear predictor. *Journal of Machine Learning Research*, 1:281–309, September 2001.

[11] J. Kivinen, A. J. Smola and R. C. Williamson. Online learning with kernels. In T. G. Dietterich, S. Becker and Z. Ghahramani, editors, *Advances in Neural Information Processing Systems 14*, pages 785–792. MIT Press, Cambridge, MA, 2002.

[12] Y. Li and P. M. Long. The relaxed online maximum margin algorithm. *Machine Learning*, 46(1):361–387, January 2002.

[13] N. Littlestone. Learning quickly when irrelevant attributes abound: A new linear-threshold algorithm. *Machine Learning*, 2(4):285–318, 1988.

[14] C. Mesterharm. Tracking linear-threshold concepts with Winnow. In J. Kivinen and B. Sloan, editors, *Proc. 15th Annu. Conf. on Comput. Learning Theory*, pages 138–152. Springer LNAI 2375, Berlin, July 2002.

[15] A. B. J. Novikoff. On convergence proofs on perceptrons. In *Proceedings of the Symposium on the Mathematical Theory of Automata*, volume 12, pages 615–622. Polytechnic Institute of Brooklyn, 1962.

On the Smallest Possible Dimension and the Largest Possible Margin of Linear Arrangements Representing Given Concept Classes Uniform Distribution[*]

Jürgen Forster and Hans Ulrich Simon

Fakultät für Mathematik, Ruhr-Universität Bochum, D-44780 Bochum, Germany
{forster,simon}@lmi.ruhr-uni-bochum.de

Abstract. This paper discusses theoretical limitations of classification systems that are based on feature maps and use a separating hyper-plane in the feature space. In particular, we study the embeddability of a given concept class into a class of Euclidean half spaces of low dimension, or of arbitrarily large dimension but realizing a large margin. New bounds on the smallest possible dimension or on the largest possible margin are presented. In addition, we present new results on the rigidity of matrices and briefly mention applications in complexity and learning theory.

1   Introduction

During the last decade, there has been a lot of interest in maximal margin classifiers. Learning algorithms that calculate the hyper-plane with the largest margin on a sample and use this hyper-plane to classify new instances have a relatively solid theoretical foundation and have shown excellent empirical performance (e.g., see [4,17,5]). Typically, the instances are mapped (implicitly when a kernel function is used) to some (possibly high-dimensional) feature space before the hyper-plane with maximal margin is calculated.

Recently, several authors [3,8] started to study the theoretical limitations of classification systems that build on embeddings in feature spaces and apply linear separation afterwards. From an abstract point of view, one may represent a finite concept class, consisting of n Boolean concepts over a domain of size m, as a binary matrix $M \in \{-1, +1\}^{m \times n}$, where $M_{i,j} = -1$ indicates that instance i is a negative example for concept j (analogously for positive examples). We may also view matrix M as our prior guess which sign patterns we believe are appropriate for a specific classification task. Anyway, if the classification task can be handled by a classification system of the type described above, there must be an appropriate feature mapping that allows to reproduce the sign patterns in M (at least approximately) by the hypothesis class of half spaces in the feature space. This leads us to the following central

---

[*] This work has been supported in part by the ESPRIT Working Group in Neural, Computational Learning II, NeuroCOLT2, No. 27150 and by the Deutsche Forschungsgemeinschaft Grant SI 498/4-1.

N. Cesa-Bianchi et al. (Eds.): ALT 2002, LNAI 2533, pp. 128–138, 2002.

Definition 1. *A linear arrangement representing a matrix $M \in \mathbb{R}^{m \times n}$ is given by collections of vectors $u_1, \ldots, u_m, v_1, \ldots, v_n \in \mathbb{R}^d$ of Euclidean length $\|u_i\|_2 = \|v_j\|_2 = 1$ such that $\mathrm{sign}\langle u_i, v_j \rangle = \mathrm{sign}M_{i,j}$ for all i, j. Parameter d is called* the *dimension of the arrangement,* $\min_{i,j} \langle u_i, v_j \rangle$ *is the* minimal margin *and* $\frac{1}{mn} \sum_{i,j} \langle u_i, v_j \rangle$ the average margin *realized by the arrangement.*

In this definition, the signum function $\mathrm{sign} : \mathbb{R} \to \mathbb{R}$ is given by

$$\mathrm{sign(x)} = \begin{cases} +1 \;, & x > 0 \;, \\ 0 \;, & x = 0 \;, \\ -1 \;, & x < 0 \;. \end{cases}$$

A few comments are in place here:

- The definition of a linear arrangement representing M depends on M only through the *sign pattern* $(\mathrm{sign}M_{i,j})$ of M. One might ask why we did not simply focus on matrices with entries from $\{-1, 0, +1\}$. It will turn out, however, that some of our dimension- or margin-bounds depend on M *not* only through the sign pattern of M. For this reason, we preferred the more liberal definition.
- We may view vectors u_i as points in $\mathbb{R}^d$ and vectors v_j as normal vectors of the (positive) homogeneous half spaces $\{x \in \mathbb{R}^d : \langle v_j, x \rangle > 0\}$ (or vice versa). The restriction to *homogeneous* half spaces has purely technical reasons and is obviously not essential.
- If $M_{i,j} = +1$, then point u_i should be placed in the (positive) half space with normal vector v_j. The analogous remark is valid for $M_{i,j} = -1$ and negative half spaces. Since we restricted u_i, v_j to vectors of unit length, the absolute value of the scalar product $\langle u_i, v_j \rangle$ is the geometric distance of the point u_i from the boundary of the half space with normal vector v_j (and this distance cannot be trivially increased by scaling).

It should become clear from these remarks that Definition 1 captures our original intention.

Like in the papers [3,8], we are interested in linear arrangements with a "low" dimension or a "large" minimal (or average) margin, because in both cases one could invoke the usual VC-dimension machinery such as to guarantee small generalization errors. If no linear arrangement for M with low dimension or large margin exists, then this indicates that the underlying concept class will suffer from a large generalization error whenever we attempt to learn its concepts by a typical large margin classification system. It should also be mentioned that large lower bounds on the dimension imply small upper bounds on the minimal margin because a linear arrangement with a large minimal margin can be transformed into a linear arrangement of small dimension (and still large minimal margin) by random projection techniques from [14,9,1]. Finally, it should be mentioned that one can always find "trivial arrangements" of dimension $\min\{m, n\}$ with minimal margin $1/\min\{\sqrt{m}, \sqrt{n}\}$. However, this trivial embedding leads to poor bounds on the generalization error. The reader interested in a more detailed discussion is referred to [3,8].

In [3], it was shown by means of counting arguments that almost all matrices of constant VC-dimension do not have linear arrangements being significantly better than the trivial arrangement. These results were complemented by results in [6,8], where methods from functional analysis were used to show the existence or non-existence of nice linear arrangements for *concrete* matrices. In this paper, we complement these results further. In Section 3, we improve on an algebraic lower bound from [6] on the dimension of a linear arrangement of a matrix M in terms of its spectral norm. The new bound is given in terms of the singular values of M. In Section 4, we narrow the gap between the known lower and upper bounds on the smallest possible dimension of a linear arrangement representing Hadamard matrices. This is done by presenting (the first) non-trivial arrangements for these matrices. Section 5 discusses the issue of "matrix-rigidity": how many entries of a given matrix must be changed to lower its rank below a given threshold r? We introduce a new rigidity definition with applications in complexity and learning theory. Then, we present a new lower bound on the rigidity of matrices. Section 6 discusses new upper bounds on the largest possible margin realized by linear arrangements. The paper closes with Section 7, where some open problems are mentioned.

2   Preliminaries

We use the *singular value decomposition* of a matrix $A \in \mathbb{R}^{m \times n}$: Let r be the rank of A. Then there always exist matrices $U \in \mathbb{R}^{m \times r}$ and $V \in \mathbb{R}^{n \times r}$ with orthonormal columns and nonnegative numbers $\sigma_1(A) \geq \ldots \geq \sigma_r(A) > 0$, called the *singular values* of A, such that $A = U\mathrm{diag}(\sigma_1(A), \ldots, \sigma_r(A))V^\top$ (see [12]). We also write $\sigma_i(A) = 0$ for $i > r$.

The *spectral norm* $\|A\|$ of A is the largest singular value of A, i.e., $\|A\| = \sigma_1(A)$. The *Frobenius norm* is

$$\|A\|_\mathrm{F} = \left(\sum_{i,j} A_{i,j}^2 \right)^{1/2} .$$

It is well known (see, e.g., [10]) that

$$\|A\|_\mathrm{F}^2 = \sum_i \sigma_i(A)^2 .$$

It follows that $\|A\| \leq \|A\|_\mathrm{F}$.

The following two results play a central role in our proofs.

Theorem 1 (Fejer's Theorem, [12], Corollary 7.5.4).
A matrix $A \in \mathbb{R}^{m \times m}$ is positive semidefinite if and only if

$$\sum_{i,\ell} A_{i,\ell} B_{i,\ell} \geq 0$$

for all positive semidefinite matrices $B \in \mathbb{R}^{m \times m}$.

Theorem 2 (Hoffman-Wielandt [11] and [10], Section 8.3). *Let A, B be matrices in $\mathbb{R}^{m \times n}$. Then*

$$\sum_i (\sigma_i(A) - \sigma_i(B))^2 \le \|A - B\|_{\mathrm{F}}^2 .$$

We will also make use of the following well known

Fact 1 There exists a d-dimensional linear arrangement representing a matrix $M \in \{-1, +1\}^{m \times n}$ if and only if there is a matrix $\widetilde{M} \in \mathbb{R}^{m \times n}$ of rank d with the same sign pattern as M.

3   An Improved Lower Bound on the Dimension

The following lower bound on the dimension of a linear arrangement was proven by Forster:

Theorem 3 ([6]). *Let $u_1, \dots, u_m, v_1, \dots, v_n \in \mathbb{R}^d$ be a linear arrangement representing a matrix $M \in \{-1, +1\}^{m \times n}$. Then $d \ge \sqrt{mn}/\|M\|$.*

This theorem bounds d from by below in terms of the spectral norm $\|M\| = \sigma_1(M)$. Thus, the bound involves only the largest singular value of M. In this section (building on a powerful lemma from [6]), we derive an improved lower bound that makes use of the full spectrum of singular values. Our main result is as follows:

Theorem 4. *Let $M \in \mathbb{R}^{m \times n}$ be a matrix satisfying $|M_{i,j}| \ge 1$ for all i, j. Let r be the rank and $\sigma_1(M) \ge \cdots \ge \sigma_r(M)$ the singular values of M. For $d \le r$ let $u_1, \dots, u_m, v_1, \dots, v_n \in \mathbb{R}^d$, $\|u_i\|_2 = \|v_j\|_2 = 1$, be a linear arrangement representing M. Then*

$$d \cdot \sum_{i=1}^d \sigma_i^2(M) \ge mn . \tag{1}$$

Proof. It was shown in [6] that any d-dimensional linear arrangement $u_1, \dots, u_m$, $v_1, \dots, v_n$ representing a matrix M can be "normalized" such as to satisfy

$$\frac{1}{mn} \sum_{i=1}^m \sum_{j=1}^n \langle u_i, v_j \rangle^2 \ge \frac{1}{d} . \tag{2}$$

We may therefore assume (2) without loss of generality. Consider the matrix $\widetilde{M} \in \mathbb{R}^{m \times n}$ with entries $\widetilde{M}_{i,j} = \langle u_i, v_j \rangle \in \mathbb{R}^{m \times n}$. From the assumptions of the theorem and (2), the following properties are evident:

Property 1 $\mathrm{sign}\widetilde{M}_{i,j} = \mathrm{sign}M_{i,j}$ and $|\widetilde{M}_{i,j}| \le 1 \le |M_{i,j}|$. This implies that $M_{i,j}\widetilde{M}_{i,j} \ge \widetilde{M}_{i,j}^2$.

Property 2 $\|\widetilde{M}\|_{\mathrm{F}}^2 \ge mn/d$.

Property 3 The rank of $\widetilde{M}$ is bounded by $d \leq r$. This implies that $\sigma_i(\widetilde{M}) = 0$ for $i > d$.

Because of Properties 1 and 2, $\|M - \widetilde{M}\|_{\mathrm{F}}^2$ can be upper-bounded as follows:

$$\|M - \widetilde{M}\|_{\mathrm{F}}^2 = \sum_{i,j} M_{i,j}^2 - 2M_{i,j}\widetilde{M}_{i,j} + \widetilde{M}_{i,j}^2$$

$$\leq \sum_{i,j} M_{i,j}^2 - 2\widetilde{M}_{i,j}^2 + \widetilde{M}_{i,j}^2$$

$$= \|M\|_{\mathrm{F}}^2 - \|\widetilde{M}\|_{\mathrm{F}}^2$$

$$= \sum_{i=1}^{r} \sigma_i^2(M) - \|\widetilde{M}\|_{\mathrm{F}}^2$$

$$\leq \sum_{i=1}^{r} \sigma_i^2(M) - \frac{mn}{d} .$$

Using Property 3 and the Hoffman-Wielandt inequality, $\|M - \widetilde{M}\|_{\mathrm{F}}^2$ can be lower-bounded as follows:

$$\|M - \widetilde{M}\|_{\mathrm{F}}^2 \geq \sum_{i=1}^{d}(\sigma_i(M) - \sigma_i(\widetilde{M}))^2 + \sum_{i=d+1}^{r} \sigma_i^2(M) \geq \sum_{i=d+1}^{r} \sigma_i^2(M) .$$

We conclude that $\sum_{i=d+1}^{r} \sigma_i^2(M) \leq \sum_{i=1}^{r} \sigma_i^2(M) - mn/d$, which is equivalent to (1).   •

Note that $d \cdot \sum_{i=1}^{d} \sigma_i^2(M) \geq mn$ implies

$$d^2\|M\|^2 = d^2\sigma_1^2(M) \geq d \cdot \sum_{i=1}^{d} \sigma_i^2(M) \geq mn ,$$

which, in turn, implies Forster's lower bound $d \geq \sqrt{mn}/\|M\|$. It follows that the new bound improves the old one. Note that both bounds coincide if and only if $\sigma_1(M) = \cdots = \sigma_d(M)$ for the smallest d that satisfies (1). If the first d singular values do not coincide, the new bound yields a strict improvement. The improvement is particularly strong if $\sigma_1(M)$ is relatively large compared to $\sigma_i(M)$ for $i \geq 2$. For instance, if an $(n \times n)$-matrix M with ± 1-entries and full rank n had the spectrum

$$\sigma_1^2(M) = n^{3/2} \text{ and } \sigma_2^2 = \cdots = \sigma_n^2(M) = \frac{n^2 - n^{3/2}}{n-1} < n ,$$

then Forster's lower bound from Theorem 3 would lead to $d \geq n^{1/4}$, whereas the new lower bound from Theorem 4 would lead to $d \geq n^{1/2}/2$ (as an easy evaluation shows).

4   Nontrivial Arrangements for Hadamard Matrices

Hadamard matrices H_n of size $2^n \times 2^n$ can be inductively defined as follows:

$$H_0 = (1)$$

$$H_{n+1} = \begin{pmatrix} H_n & H_n \\ H_n & -H_n \end{pmatrix}$$

Although the conjecture that each linear arrangement representing H_n requires $2^{\Omega(n)}$ Euclidean dimensions was long standing, it was not confirmed until recently [6]: since $\|H_n\| = 2^{n/2}$, an evaluation of Forster's lower bound from Theorem 3 yields that each linear arrangement representing H_n requires at least $2^{n/2}$ Euclidean dimensions. Clearly, 2^n Euclidean dimensions are enough because we may use the trivial embedding. To the best of our knowledge, no nontrivial linear arrangement for H_n is known so far. In this section, we present a non-trivial arrangement for H_n, thereby narrowing (but still not closing) the gap between $2^{n/2}$ and 2^n. For sake of simple exposition, we will restrict ourselves to even n.

Our main result of this section reads as follows:

Lemma 1. *For every even n, there is a matrix $\tilde{H}_n \in \mathbb{R}^{2^n \times 2^n}$ of rank $3^{n/2}$ that has the same sign pattern as the Hadamard matrix H_n.*

Proof. Remember that the *Kronecker product* $A \otimes B$ of two matrices $A \in \mathbb{R}^{m \times n}$, $B \in \mathbb{R}^{p,q}$ is defined as

$$A \otimes B := \begin{pmatrix} A_{1,1}B & \cdots & A_{1,n}B \\ \vdots & & \vdots \\ A_{m,1}B & \cdots & A_{m,n}B \end{pmatrix} \in \mathbb{R}^{mp \times nq} .$$

The rank of the Kronecker product is $\mathrm{rank}(A \otimes B) = \mathrm{rank}(A) \cdot \mathrm{rank}(B)$. (See, e.g., [13], Theorem 4.2.15.) The Hadamard matrix H_n can be written as the n-th Kronecker power of the matrix H_1:

$$H_n = \begin{pmatrix} +1 & +1 \\ +1 & -1 \end{pmatrix}^{\otimes n} = \left(\begin{pmatrix} +1 & +1 \\ +1 & -1 \end{pmatrix} \otimes \begin{pmatrix} +1 & +1 \\ +1 & -1 \end{pmatrix} \right)^{\otimes \frac{n}{2}}$$

$$= \begin{pmatrix} +1 & +1 & +1 & +1 \\ +1 & -1 & +1 & -1 \\ +1 & +1 & -1 & -1 \\ +1 & -1 & -1 & +1 \end{pmatrix}^{\otimes \frac{n}{2}} .$$

Obviously the matrix

$$\tilde{H}_n = \begin{pmatrix} +1 & +1 & +1 & +1 \\ +1 & -1 & +5 & -1 \\ +1 & +5 & -1 & -1 \\ +1 & -1 & -1 & +5 \end{pmatrix}^{\otimes \frac{n}{2}}$$

has the same sign pattern as H_n. The rank of $\tilde{H}_n$ is

$$\mathrm{rank}(\widetilde{\mathrm{H}}_n) = \left(\mathrm{rank} \begin{pmatrix} +1 +1 +1 +1 \\ +1 -1 +5 -1 \\ +1 +5 -1 -1 \\ +1 -1 -1 +5 \end{pmatrix} \right)^{\frac{n}{2}} = 3^{\frac{n}{2}} \ .$$

•

Combining Fact 1 with Lemma 1, we arrive at the following result:

Corollary 1. *For every even n, there exists a $3^{n/2}$-dimensional linear arrangement representing H_n.*

5 Rigidity

The rigidity of a matrix, $\mathcal{R}_M(r)$, is the number of entries of M that must be changed to reduce its rank to at most r. Let $H \in \{-1, +1\}^{N \times N}$ be a Hadamard matrix. Lokam [16] showed that $\mathcal{R}_H(r) \geq N^2/(r+1)^2$. Kashin and Razborov [15] improved this result to $\mathcal{R}_H(r) = \Omega(N^2/r)$ for $r \leq N/2$.

We consider a different definition of the rigidity of a matrix here. The new definition distinguishes between sign-preserving and sign-non-preserving changes of entries. Only sign-non-preserving changes are counted. More formally: $\widetilde{\mathcal{R}}_M(r)$ is the number of entries of M that must be exposed to a sign-non-preserving change to reduce the rank of M to at most r, where we allow arbitrarily many sign-preserving changes as well. Clearly, $\mathcal{R}_M(r) \geq \widetilde{\mathcal{R}}_M(r)$. Thus, lower bounds on $\widetilde{\mathcal{R}}_M(r)$ are harder to obtain than lower bounds on $\mathcal{R}_M(r)$. The main goal of this section is to demonstrate that quite strong lower bounds on $\widetilde{\mathcal{R}}_M(r)$ can be derived (in a surprisingly simple manner) from Theorem 3. For ease of exposition, we restrict ourselves to matrices M without zero-entries in what follows.

We start with a somewhat technical result, which, loosely speaking, tells that zero-substitutions do not help in reducing the rank given that sign-preserving changes are for free.

Lemma 2. *If the rank of $M \in \mathbb{R}^{m \times n}$ can be reduced to r by changing s entries of M in an arbitrary fashion and the remaining entries in a sign-preserving fashion, then this can also be achieved without changing one of the entries to zero.*

Proof. Remember our general assumption that M has no zero-entries. Let $\widetilde{M}$ be a matrix of rank at most r which results from M by changing s entries in an arbitrary fashion (possibly to zero) and the remaining entries in a sign-preserving fashion. It follows from Fact 1 that there exist vectors $u_1, \ldots, u_m, v_1, \ldots, v_n \in \mathbb{R}^r$ such that $\mathrm{sign} \widetilde{M}_{i,j} = \mathrm{sign}\langle u_i, v_j \rangle$ for all i, j. Consider indices i, j of an entry of M that was changed to $\widetilde{M}_{i,j} = 0$. It follows that $\langle u_i, v_j \rangle = 0$, i.e., point u_i lies on the hyper-plane with normal vector v_j. Reversely, each point u_i located on a hyper-plane with normal vector v_j corresponds to an entry of M that was changed to $\widetilde{M}_{i,j} = 0$. We can slightly shift all points being located on hyper-planes such as to avoid scalar products with value zero and such as to preserve the sign of all scalar products with a value different from zero. In this manner, we obtain an r-dimensional linear arrangement of a matrix $\hat{M}$ without zero entries that is still obtained from M by changing s entries in an arbitrary fashion and the remaining entries in a sign-preserving fashion. Applying Fact 1 again, we conclude that the rank of $\hat{M}$ is at most r.   ●

The next result is a simple application of Theorem 3.

Lemma 3. *Let* $M \in \{-1,+1\}^{m \times n}$ *and let* $\widetilde{M}$ *be a matrix without zero entries that is obtained from M by changing s entries to arbitrary new values except zero and by performing (possibly vacuous) sign-preserving changes to the remaining entries. Then*

$$\text{rank}(\widetilde{M}) \geq \frac{\sqrt{mn}}{\|M\| + 2\sqrt{s}} \ . \tag{3}$$

Proof. A change from value $M_{i,j} \in \{-1,+1\}$ to a new value $\widetilde{M}_{i,j} \neq 0$ can be simulated by first performing a (possibly vacuous) sign-change from $M_{i,j}$ to $\text{sign}\widetilde{M}_{i,j}$ and then performing a (cost-free) sign-preserving change from $\text{sign}\widetilde{M}_{i,j}$ to $\widetilde{M}_{i,j}$. Thus, $\widetilde{M}$ has the same sign pattern as a matrix of the form $M' = M - S \in \{-1,+1\}^{m \times n}$ for some matrix S with at most s entries from $\{-2,+2\}$ (representing sign-changes) and with zero-entries everywhere else. Thus,

$$\|M'\| \leq \|M\| + \|S\| \leq \|M\| + \|S\|_{\text{F}} \leq \|M\| + 2\sqrt{s} \ .$$

Applying Theorem 3, the lemma follows.   ●

Because of Lemma 2, the definition of $\widetilde{\mathcal{R}}_M()$ is not affected when we do not allow zero-substitutions. Solving (3) for s leads therefore immediately to

Corollary 2. $\widetilde{\mathcal{R}}_M(r) \geq (\sqrt{mn}/r - \|M\|)^2/4$.

Corollary 2 applied to an $(N \times N)$ Hadamard matrix H with $\|H\| = \sqrt{N}$ yields

Corollary 3. $\widetilde{\mathcal{R}}_H(r) \geq (N^2/r^2 - 2N^{3/2}/r + N)/4$.

This bound is not much worse than the afore-mentioned bounds of Lokam or Kashin and Razborov, although we allowed a much more powerful rank-reduction procedure.

We finally would like to mention an application of Lemma 3. Let $N = 2^n$. It was shown in [7] that the Boolean function induced by the $(N \times N)$-Hadamard matrix H_n (depending on $2n$ Boolean variables) cannot be computed by a 2-layer threshold circuit C_n with polynomially bounded weights in the hidden layer unless the size of C_n grows exponentially in n. Using Lemma 3, it can be shown that this lower bound remains valid when the circuit must only "approximate" H_n in the sense that $2^{(2-\varepsilon)n}$ of the 2^{2n} function values may be computed incorrectly. In a similar fashion, it follows that there is no $d(n)$-dimensional linear arrangement representing an approximation of H_n unless d grows exponentially in n.

6   Upper Bounds on the Margin

Throughout this section, $M \in \{-1, +1\}^{m \times n}$ and $u_1, \ldots, u_m, v_1, \ldots, v_n$ denotes a linear arrangement representing M. The following bounds on the minimal margin (valid for any choice of $u_1, \ldots, u_m, v_1, \ldots, v_n$) are already known:

Theorem 5 ([6]). $\min_{i,j} |\langle u_i, v_j \rangle| \leq \|M\| / \sqrt{m \cdot n}$.

Theorem 6 ([8]). *Let* $\widetilde{M} \in \mathbb{R}^{m \times n}$ *be a matrix with the same sign pattern as* M. *Then the following holds:*

$$
\min_{i,j} |\langle u_i, v_j \rangle| \leq \frac{\sqrt{m} \cdot \|\widetilde{M}\|}{\sqrt{\sum_j \left(\sum_i |\widetilde{M}_{i,j}| \right)^2}} \ . \tag{4}
$$

In the special case $\widetilde{M} = M$, the bound from Theorem 6 coincides with the bound from Theorem 5. However, as demonstrated in [8], the bound in Theorem 6 can be much stronger than the bound in Theorem 5 if $\widetilde{M}$ is cleverly chosen.

It had been observed by Ben-David [2] that the proof of Theorem 5 in [6] implicitly shows a stronger result: the upper bound from this theorem also applies to the average margin. See Corollary 5 below. Although the essential arguments for this observation can already be found in [6], it will be much more convenient to have a proof that addresses the concept of an average margin in a more explicit manner. To this end, we will prove a useful intermediate result (Lemma 4 below) in this section that serves two purposes. First, it leads to a simple proof of Corollary 5. Second, it leads to a bound that is similar to the bound from Theorem 6, but has a somewhat simpler form. See Corollary 4 below.

Lemma 4. *For any matrix* $\widetilde{M} \in \mathbb{R}^{m \times n}$, *the following holds:*

$$
\sum_{i,j} \widetilde{M}_{i,j} \langle u_i, v_j \rangle \leq \sqrt{m \cdot n} \|\widetilde{M}\| \ .
$$

Proof. For every j we have that

$$
\sum_i \widetilde{M}_{i,j} \langle u_i, v_j \rangle = \left\langle \sum_i \widetilde{M}_{i,j} u_i, v_j \right\rangle \overset{\|v_j\|_2 = 1}{\leq} \| \sum_i \widetilde{M}_{i,j} u_i \|_2 \ , \tag{5}
$$

where we used the Cauchy-Schwartz inequality. The lemma can now be derived as follows:

$$
\frac{1}{n} \left(\sum_{i,j} \widetilde{M}_{i,j} \langle u_i, v_j \rangle \right)^2 \leq \sum_j \left(\sum_i \widetilde{M}_{i,j} \langle u_i, v_j \rangle \right)^2
$$

$$
\overset{(5)}{\leq} \sum_j \left\langle \sum_i \widetilde{M}_{i,j} u_i, \sum_\ell \widetilde{M}_{\ell,j} u_\ell \right\rangle
$$

$$= \sum_{i,\ell} \left(\sum_j \widetilde{M}_{i,j} \widetilde{M}_{\ell,j} \right) \langle u_i, u_\ell \rangle$$

$$= \sum_{i,\ell} \left(\widetilde{M} \widetilde{M}^\top \right)_{i,\ell} \langle u_i, u_\ell \rangle$$

$$\overset{(*)}{\leq} \sum_{i,\ell} \left(\|\widetilde{M}\|^2 \, \mathrm{I}_m \right)_{i,\ell} \langle u_i, u_\ell \rangle$$

$$= \|\widetilde{M}\|^2 \sum_i \|u_i\|_2^2 = m \cdot \|\widetilde{M}\|^2$$

The first inequality is obtained when the Cauchy-Schwartz inequality is applied to the vectors $a, b \in \mathbb{R}^n$ given by $a_j = \sum_i \widetilde{M}_{i,j} \langle u_i, v_j \rangle$ and $b_j = 1$. Inequality $(*)$ holds because the matrices $A := \|\widetilde{M}\|^2 \, \mathrm{I}_m - \widetilde{M} \widetilde{M}^\top$ and $B := (\langle u_i, u_\ell \rangle)_{i,\ell}$ are positive semidefinite. Therefore $\sum_{i,\ell} A_{i,\ell} B_{i,\ell} \geq 0$ because of Fejer's Theorem 1. •

Corollary 4. *If $\widetilde{M}$ has the same sign pattern as M, then*

$$\min_{i,j} |\langle u_i, v_j \rangle| \leq \frac{\sqrt{m \cdot n} \, \|\widetilde{M}\|}{\sum_{i,j} |\widetilde{M}_{i,j}|} . \tag{6}$$

Proof. Note that $\langle u_i, v_j \rangle$ has the same sign as $\widetilde{M}_{i,j}$. This implies that $\widetilde{M}_{i,j} \langle u_i, v_j \rangle = |\widetilde{M}_{i,j}| \cdot |\langle u_i, v_j \rangle|$. The corollary now follows from Lemma 4. •

Corollary 5. $\frac{1}{m \cdot n} \sum_{i,j} |\langle u_i, v_j \rangle| \leq \frac{\|M\|}{\sqrt{m \cdot n}}$.

Proof. Note that $\langle u_i, v_j \rangle$ has the same sign as $M_{i,j} \in \{-1, 1\}$. This implies that $M_{i,j} \langle u_i, v_j \rangle = |\langle u_i, v_j \rangle|$. The corollary now follows from Lemma 4 •

Note that (6) is weaker than (4) since it can alternatively be derived from (4) and the Cauchy-Schwarz inequality. However, the bound seems more natural in the simpler form (6). For instance, (6) does not change if we replace $\widetilde{M}$ by its transpose $\widetilde{M}^\top$. Furthermore, it exhibits a comparably simple dependence on $\widetilde{M}$.

7 Open Problems

We would like to close the gap between the lower and the upper bound on the dimension of linear arrangements representing Hadamard matrices. It would be nice to find natural concept classes that exhibit the typical spectrum of singular values that makes our new lower bound on the dimension (depending on *all* singular values) superior to the old lower bound (depending on the *largest* singular value only). The hardest open problem might be to characterize the smallest possible dimension or the largest possible margin of a linear arrangement for an arbitrary given matrix M by general bounds that are (at least approximately) tight. The issue of linear arrangements that *approximately* represent a given matrix was briefly considered in Section 5. It certainly deserves the right of further investigation.

Acknowledgments. Thanks to Shai Ben-David for telling us his observation that Forster's paper [6] implicitly shows an upper bound on the *average* margin. Thanks to Dietrich Braess for pointing us to simplifications based on the clever usage of Fejer's Theorem.

References

[1] Rosa I. Arriaga and Santosh Vempala. An algorithmic theory of learning: Robust concepts and random projection. In *Proceedings of the 40'th Annual Symposium on the Foundations of Computer Science*, pages 616–623, 1999.

[2] Shai Ben-David. Personal Communication.

[3] Shai Ben-David, Nadav Eiron, and Hans Ulrich Simon. Limitations of learning via embeddings in Euclidean half spaces. In *Proceedings of the 14th Annual Workshop on Computational Learning Theory*, pages 385–401. Springer, 2001.

[4] Bernhard E. Boser, Isabelle M. Guyon, and Vladimir N. Vapnik. A training algorithm for optimal margin classifiers. In *Proceedings of the 5th Annual ACM Workshop on Computational Learning Theory*, pages 144–152. ACM Press, 1992.

[5] Nello Christianini and John Shawe-Taylor. *An Introduction to Support Vector Machines.* Cambridge University Press, 2000.

[6] Jürgen Forster. A linear bound on the unbounded error probabilistic communication complexity. In *Proceedings of the 16th Annual Conference on Computational Complexity*, pages 100–106, 2001.

[7] Jürgen Forster, Matthias Krause, Satyanarayana V. Lokam, Rustam Mubarakzjanov, Niels Schmitt, and Hans U. Simon. Relations between communication complexity, linear arrangements, and computational complexity. In *Proceedings of the 21'st Annual Conference on the Foundations of Software Technology and Theoretical Computer Science*, pages 171–182, 2001.

[8] Jürgen Forster, Niels Schmitt, and Hans Ulrich Simon. Estimating the optimal margins of embeddings in Euclidean half spaces. In *Proceedings of the 14th Annual Workshop on Computational Learning Theory*, pages 402–415. Springer, 2001.

[9] P. Frankl and H. Maehara. The Johnson-Lindenstrauss lemma and the sphericity of some graphs. *Journal of Combinatorial Theory (B)*, 44:355–362, 1988.

[10] Gene H. Golub and Charles F. Van Loan. *Matrix Computations.* The John Hopkins University Press, 1991.

[11] A. J. Hoffman and H. W. Wielandt. The variation of the spectrum of a normal matrix. *Duke Mathematical Journal*, 20:37–39, 1953.

[12] Roger A. Horn and Charles R.Johnson. *Matrix Analysis.* Cambridge University Press, 1985.

[13] Roger A. Horn and Charles R.Johnson. *Topics in Matrix Analysis.* Cambridge University Press, 1991.

[14] W. B. Johnson and J. Lindenstrauss. Extensions of Lipshitz mapping into Hilbert spaces. *Contemp. Math.*, 26:189–206, 1984.

[15] B. S. Kashin and A. A. Razborov. Improved lower bounds on the rigidity of Hadamard matrices. *Mathematical Notes*, 63(4):471–475, 1998.

[16] Satyanarayana V. Lokam. Spectral methods for matrix rigidity with applications to size-depth tradeoffs and communication complexity. In *Proceedings of the 36th Symposium on Foundations of Computer Science*, pages 6–15, 1995.

[17] Vladimir Vapnik. *Statistical Learning Theory.* Wiley Series on Adaptive and Learning Systems for Signal Processing, Communications, and Control. John Wiley & Sons, 1998.

A General Dimension for Approximately Learning Boolean Functions*

Johannes Köbler and Wolfgang Lindner

Institut für Informatik, Humboldt-Universität zu Berlin, 10099 Berlin, Germany

Abstract. We extend the notion of general dimension, a combinatorial characterization of learning complexity for arbitrary query protocols, to encompass approximate learning. This immediately yields a characterization of the learning complexity in the statistical query model. As a further application, we consider approximate learning of DNF formulas and we derive close upper and lower bounds on the number of statistical queries needed. In particular, we show that with respect to the uniform distribution, and for any constant error parameter $\varepsilon < 1/2$, the number of statistical queries needed to approximately learn DNF formulas (over n variables and s terms) with tolerance $\tau = \Theta(1/s)$ is $n^{\Theta(\log s)}$.

1 Introduction

A main issue in computational learning theory is to decide whether a concept class can be learned with a polynomial number of interactions with a teacher, regardless of the computational resources required by the learning algorithm. One way of addressing this problem is to apply combinatorial characterizations such as the VC dimension for the PAC learning model [8], or the approximate fingerprint property for the exact learning model with equivalence queries [2]. Further combinatorial characterizations for various query-types in the exact learning model can be found in, e.g., [11,12,5].

In [4], Balcázar et al. introduce the notion of a general dimension as a uniform way to characterize, up to a logarithmic factor, the learning complexity, i.e., the number of queries both necessary and sufficient for exact learning, with any set of queries.

Here we address the question whether the general dimension can be extended to capture approximate learning, where the learning algorithm has to identify the target only with respect to some error parameter ε. We show that the general dimension of [4] can in fact be adapted so that the resulting notion characterizes the learning complexity for approximate learning, provided that the learning algorithm is able to decide (possibly with the help of the teacher) whether a hypothesis is already a sufficiently close approximation of the target. This immediately yields characterizations of the learning complexity in the statistical query model. In contrast to the SQ-dimension of [7], our general dimension for

* Work supported by the DFG under project KO 1053/1-1

N. Cesa-Bianchi et al. (Eds.): ALT 2002, LNAI 2533, pp. 139–148, 2002.
© Springer-Verlag Berlin Heidelberg 2002

statistical queries works for any error parameter ε and any tolerance parameter $\tau \leq \varepsilon$.

As an application, we consider approximate learning of DNF formulas (over n variables and s terms) with statistical queries and we show that with respect to the uniform distribution, and for any constant error parameter $\varepsilon < 1/2$ it is possible to choose the tolerance parameter $\tau = \Theta(1/s)$ such that the number of statistical queries needed to approximately learn DNF formulas with tolerance τ is $n^{\Theta(\log s)}$.

2   Approximate Learning for Arbitrary Query Protocols

In this paper we only consider concept learning of boolean functions of some arity n. We let B_n denote the set of all boolean functions $f : \{0,1\}^n \to \{0,1\}$ and $[n]$ denotes the set $\{1, \ldots, n\}$.

The learning model presented in [4] is a generalization of the query learning model of Angluin [1]. In this model, learning of a concept class $C \subseteq B_n$ can be viewed as a game between a learning algorithm A and a teacher T with respect to some target $f \in C$ that is only known to T. In each round, A asks a query q from a set Q of queries and T responds with a subset $\Lambda \subseteq B_n$ that contains f. Thereby, T provides some partial knowledge about the target f in form of a property Λ shared by f. The communication between A and T is guided by some *protocol* $P \subseteq Q \times 2^{B_n}$, i.e., the teacher is only allowed to respond with an answer Λ such that $\langle q, \Lambda \rangle \in P$. Further, P is required to be *complete* in the sense that for all $f \in B_n$ and for all queries $q \in Q$ there exists an answer $\Lambda \in P_q^f$, where $P_q^f = \{\Lambda \mid \langle q, \Lambda \rangle \in P \wedge f \in \Lambda\}$.

In the approximate learning setting, the goal of the learning algorithm is to collect enough knowledge about f such that every function in C that shares all properties exposed by T is a close approximation to f. As in [6] we formally express the success condition in terms of an arbitrary *pseudo-metric* ϱ on B_n, i.e., ϱ is a function from B_n^2 to non-negative reals satisfying $\varrho(f,f) = 0$, $\varrho(f,g) = \varrho(g,f)$, and $\varrho(f,h) \leq \varrho(f,g) + \varrho(g,h)$, for all functions f, g and h in B_n. We will frequently use pseudo-metrics of the form $\varrho(f,g) = \Pr_D[f(x) \neq g(x)]$, for some distribution D on $\{0,1\}^n$.

In the following we will further use the following notations. The *diameter* of a set of boolean functions $F \subseteq B_n$ is the maximal distance between two members of F, $\varrho(F) = \max_{f,g \in F} \varrho(f,g)$, and for $f \in B_n$ and $\rho \geq 0$, we let $B_\varrho(f,\rho) = \{g \in B_n \mid \varrho(f,g) \leq \rho\}$ denote the *ball* of radius ρ with center f.

Let $C \subseteq B_n$ be a concept class, let $P \subseteq Q \times 2^{B_n}$ be a protocol, and let ϱ be a pseudo-metric on B_n. A teacher T *answers with respect to f using P* if for each query $q \in Q$, T responds with an answer $\Lambda \in P_q^f$. The *current version space* at any stage in the run of a learning algorithm A is the set of all functions in C that are contained in all answers received by A so far. The concept class C is *ε-learnable with at most d queries under P*, if there exists a learning algorithm A such that for all $f \in C$, and for any teacher T which answers with respect to f using P, after at most d queries the current version space is contained in the ball $B_\varrho(f, \varepsilon)$. We define the *learning complexity* of C under P, denoted by $\mathrm{LC}_\varrho(C, P, \varepsilon)$, as the smallest integer $d \geq 0$ such that C is ε-learnable with at most d queries under P. If no such integer d exists, then $\mathrm{LC}_\varrho(C, P, \varepsilon) = \infty$.

Before we proceed, let us consider some examples. The protocol $\mathrm{Eq}(C)$ for equivalence queries with hypotheses from a concept class $C \subseteq B_n$ is the set of all pairs $\langle h, \{f \in B_n \mid f(x) \neq h(x)\}\rangle$, for $h \in C$ and $x \in \{0, 1\}^n$, together with all pairs $\langle h, \{h\}\rangle$ with $h \in C$. The first set of pairs corresponds to the case that a hypothesis h is answered with a counterexample x, and the second set of pairs corresponds to the answer "Yes". Note that, for $\varepsilon = 0$, the learning complexity of C under the protocol $\mathrm{Eq}(C)$ describes precisely the number of queries both necessary and sufficient for exact learning C with proper equivalence queries.

In the model of learning from statistical queries [14], queries are of the form $\chi : \{0, 1\}^n \times \{0, 1\} \to \{0, 1\}$ (i.e., $\chi \in B_{n+1}$) for which we receive an estimate σ of the probability $\mathrm{Pr}_D[\chi(x, f(x)) = 1]$, for a target f a randomly chosen $x \in_D \{0, 1\}^n$ and with respect to some distribution D on $\{0, 1\}^n$. The estimate has to be accurate within an additive error $\tau \geq 0$, which we refer to as the tolerance. Thus, a protocol for statistical queries can be defined as

$$\mathrm{STAT}_D(\tau) = \{\langle \chi, \Lambda_{\chi, \sigma}\rangle \mid \chi \in B_{n+1}, \sigma \in \mathbb{R}^+\},$$

where $\Lambda_{\chi, \sigma}$ is the set of all functions $f \in B_n$ such that

$$\left| \mathrm{Pr}_D[\chi(x, f(x)) = 1] - \sigma \right| \leq \tau.$$

In the less known model of learning by distance [6], a query is a hypothesis $h \in B_n$ for which we get an approximation of the distance between h and the target f with respect to some given pseudo metric ϱ. Thus, the corresponing protocol can be defined as

$$\mathrm{DIST}_\varrho(\tau) = \{\langle h, S_\varrho(h, \rho, \tau)\rangle \mid h \in B_n, \rho \in \mathbb{R}^+\},$$

where $S_\varrho(h, \rho, \tau)$ denotes the *sphere* around h of radius ρ and width τ, $S_\varrho(h, \rho, \tau) = \{f \in B_n \mid |\varrho(f, h) - \rho| \leq \tau\}$.

In order to compare the strength of different protocols, we use the following notion of reducibility between protocols.

Definition 1. *A protocol $P' \subseteq Q' \times 2^{B_n}$ simulates a protocol $P \subseteq Q \times 2^{B_n}$ with at most k queries (in which case we also write $P \leq_k P'$), if for every query $q \in Q$ there exist k queries $q'_1, \ldots, q'_k \in Q'$, such that for all answers $\Lambda'_i \in P'_{q_i}$, $i = 1, \ldots, k$, there exists an answer $\Lambda \in P_{q'}$ such that $\bigcap_{i=1}^k \Lambda'_i \subseteq \Lambda$.*

The following basic properties of the reducibility $\leq_k$ are easily verified.

Proposition 1. *1. $P \leq_k P$, $k \geq 1$,*
2. $P \leq_k P'$ and $P' \leq_l P''$ implies $P \leq_{kl} P''$,
3. $P \leq_k P'$ implies both $\mathrm{LC}_\varrho(C, P', \varepsilon) \leq k\mathrm{LC}_\varrho(C, P, \varepsilon)$ and $\mathrm{Gdim}(C, P', \varepsilon) \leq k\mathrm{Gdim}(C, P, \varepsilon)$.

For a statistical query $\chi(x,y) = y \oplus h(x)$, where $h \in B_n$, it holds that $\Pr_D[\chi(x, f(x)) = 1] = \Pr_D[h(x) \oplus f(x) = 1] = \Pr_D[h \neq f] = \varrho(f, h)$. Hence, any answer to such a query χ is just some sphere $S_\varrho(h, \sigma, \tau)$ around h of radius σ and width τ with respect to the metric $\varrho(f, g) = \Pr_D[f \neq g]$. This means that $\mathrm{DIST}_\varrho(\tau) \leq_1 \mathrm{STAT}_D(\tau)$. On the other hand, arguments from [7] can be used to show that every statistical query can be simulated by two distance queries [9].

Proposition 2. *For any distribution D on $\{0,1\}^n$, and for the metric $\varrho(f, g) = \Pr_D[f \neq g]$, it holds that $\mathrm{DIST}_\varrho(\tau) \leq_1 \mathrm{STAT}_D(\tau) \leq_2 \mathrm{DIST}_\varrho(\tau)$.*

3   General Dimension for Approximate Learning

Now we extend the general dimension of [4] to encompass approximate learning. For a query $q \in Q$ and a subset $T \subseteq P$, T_q denotes the set of all answers Λ such that $\langle q, \Lambda \rangle \in T$, whereas $T_Q = \bigcup_{q \in Q} T_q$. The definition is based on the notion of an *answering scheme* $T \subseteq P$, i.e., T has the property that for all queries $q \in Q$ there exists an answer $\Lambda \in T_q$. Note that in contrast to P, T need not be complete since there might exist a query $q \in Q$ and a function $f \in B_n$ such that no answer $\Lambda \in T_q$ contains f.

Definition 2. *The general dimension $\mathrm{Gdim}_\varrho(C, P, \varepsilon)$ of C under protocol P and pseudo-metric ϱ is the smallest integer $d \geq 0$ such that for all answering schemes $T \subseteq P$ there exists a set $S \subseteq T_Q$ of cardinality at most d such that the diameter of the set*

$$\bigcap S \cap C = \{h \in C \mid (\forall \Lambda \in S)[h \in \Lambda]\}$$

is at most ε. If no such integer d exists, then $\mathrm{Gdim}_\varrho(C, P, \varepsilon) = \infty$.

Lemma 1. $\mathrm{Gdim}_\varrho(C, P, \varepsilon) \leq \mathrm{LC}_\varrho(C, P, \varepsilon)$

Proof. Suppose $\mathrm{Gdim}_\varrho(C, P, \varepsilon) > d$. Then there exists an answering scheme $T \subseteq P$ such that for all $S \subseteq T_Q$ of cardinality at most d it holds that $\varrho(\bigcap S \cap C) > \varepsilon$. Fix some learning algorithm A and consider a run of A where the i-th query q_i of A is answered by some $\Lambda_i \in T_{q_i}$. Since T is an answering scheme, these answers always exist. By the assumption, the version space after d queries contains two functions f and g with $\varrho(f, g) > \varepsilon$. It follows that there is some teacher which answers with respect to f using P such that after d queries, the current version space is not contained in $B_\varrho(f, \varepsilon)$, i.e., $\mathrm{LC}_\varrho(C, P, \varepsilon) > d$. $\square$

In the next lemma we use the following notation. For any set $V \subseteq B_n$ and $f \in B_n$, let $r(f, V, \varepsilon) = \|B_\varrho(f, \varepsilon) \cap V\|$ denote the number of functions $g \in V$ with $\varrho(f, g) \leq \varepsilon$. Further, let $r_{\max}(V, \varepsilon) = \max_{f \in V} r(f, V, \varepsilon)$.

Lemma 2. *Suppose $\mathrm{Gdim}_\varrho(C, P, \varepsilon) = d \geq 1$, and let V be a non-empty subset of C. Then there exists a query $q \in Q$ such that for all $\Lambda \in P_q$ it holds that*

$$\|V \setminus \Lambda\| \geq \frac{\|V\| - r_{\max}(V, \varepsilon)}{d}.$$

Proof. Assume that for any query $q \in Q$ there exists an answer $\Lambda_q \in P_q$ for which

$$\|V \setminus \Lambda_q\| < \frac{\|V\| - r_{\max}(V, \varepsilon)}{d}.$$

Consider the answering scheme $T = \{\langle q, \Lambda_q \rangle \mid q \in Q\}$. For all $S \subseteq T_Q$ with $\|S\| \leq d$ it follows that

$$\left\| V \setminus \bigcap S \right\| = \left\| \bigcup_{\Lambda \in S} (V \setminus \Lambda) \right\| \leq \sum_{\Lambda \in S} \|V \setminus \Lambda\| < \|V\| - r_{\max}(V, \varepsilon).$$

Thus, the set $\bigcap S \cap V$ is larger than $r_{\max}(V, \varepsilon)$, which means that there is a function $f \in \bigcap S \cap V$ such that $\bigcap S \cap V \not\subseteq B_\varrho(f, \varepsilon)$. This, however, implies that $\varrho(\bigcap S \cap C) \geq \varrho(\bigcap S \cap V) > \varepsilon$, contradicting the assumption $\mathrm{Gdim}_\varrho(C, P, \varepsilon) = d$. $\square$

In order to apply Lemma 2, we have to assume that the protocol P allows the learning algorithm to (approximately) check if a hypothesis h is already sufficiently close to the target with respect to some tolerance parameter τ. Formally, we express this assumption by requiring that P is able to simulate the protocol

$$\mathrm{SUCCESS}_\varrho(\varepsilon, \tau) = \{\langle h, B_n \setminus B_\varrho(h, \varepsilon - \tau) \rangle \mid h \in B_n\} \cup \{\langle h, B_\varrho(h, \varepsilon + \tau) \rangle \mid h \in B_n\}.$$

Intuitively, by asking a query h under the protocol $\mathrm{SUCCESS}_\varrho(\varepsilon, \tau)$, the learning algorithm A can determine whether the target is already sufficiently close to h (in case he gets the answer $B_\varrho(h, \varepsilon + \tau)$) or not (in case he gets the answer $B_n \setminus B_\varrho(h, \varepsilon - \tau)$). If $\mathrm{SUCCESS}_\varrho(\varepsilon, \tau) \leq_k P$ holds, then A can also get this information from the teacher by asking k queries under P.

Based on Lemma 2 we can bound the learning complexity by the general dimension as follows.

Lemma 3. *For any protocol P with $\mathrm{SUCCESS}_\varrho(\varepsilon, \tau) \leq_k P$ it holds that $\mathrm{LC}_\varrho(C, P, 2(\varepsilon + \tau)) \leq 2k\mathrm{Gdim}_\varrho(C, P, \varepsilon - \tau)\lceil \ln \|C\| \rceil$.*

Proof. Suppose that $\mathrm{Gdim}_\varrho(C, P, \varepsilon - \tau) = d$. We have to describe a learning algorithm such that the version space after at most $2kd\lceil \ln \|C\| \rceil$ queries is contained in the ball $B_\varrho(f, 2(\varepsilon + \tau))$ around the target $f \in C$.

Given the current version space V, we first compute $r_{\max}(V, \varepsilon - \tau)$.

- If $r_{\max}(V, \varepsilon - \tau) \leq \|V\|/2$, then we use the query of Lemma 2 to discard at least

$$\|V \setminus \Lambda\| \geq \frac{\|V\| - r_{\max}(V, \varepsilon - \tau)}{d} \geq \frac{\|V\|}{2d}$$

hypotheses from V.
- If $r_{\max}(V, \varepsilon - \tau) > \|V\|/2$, then there exists a function $h \in V$ with $r(h, V, \varepsilon - \tau) = \|B_\varrho(h, \varepsilon - \tau) \cap V\| > \|V\|/2$. Since $\mathrm{SUCCESS}_\varrho(\varepsilon, \tau) \leq_k P$, we can find k queries $q_1, \ldots, q_k$ such that the intersection of the corresponding answers $\Lambda_1, \ldots, \Lambda_k$ is either contained in $B_n - B_\varrho(h, \varepsilon - \tau)$ or in $B_\varrho(h, \varepsilon + \tau)$.

In case the intersection $\bigcap_{i=1}^{k} \Lambda_i$ is contained in $B_n - B_\varrho(h, \varepsilon - \tau)$, then the answers $\Lambda_1, \ldots, \Lambda_k$ discard more than half of V, since $\|B_\varrho(h, \varepsilon - \tau) \cap V\| > \|V\|/2$.

In case the intersection $\bigcap_{i=1}^{k} \Lambda_i$ is contained in $B_\varrho(h, \varepsilon+\tau)$, it follows that the version space after the queries $q_1, \ldots, q_k$ is contained in the ball $B_\varrho(f, 2(\varepsilon + \tau))$.

This means that by asking a set of at most k queries we can either get V within the ball $B_\varrho(f, 2(\varepsilon + \tau))$ or reduce the size of V by a fraction of at least $(1 - 1/2d)$. Thus, after at most km queries, where m satisfies the inequality

$$(1 - 1/2d)^m \|C\| \leq 1,$$

V must be contained in the ball $B_\varrho(f, 2(\varepsilon+\tau))$. A simple calculation shows that any $m \geq 2d\lceil \ln \|C\| \rceil$ fulfills the inequality. $\square$

Combining Lemmas 1 and 3 we get the following theorem.

Theorem 1. *For any protocol P with $\mathrm{SUCCESS}_\varrho(\varepsilon, \tau) \leq_k P$ it holds that* $\mathrm{Gdim}_\varrho(C, P, 2(\varepsilon + \tau)) \leq \mathrm{LC}_\varrho(C, P, 2(\varepsilon + \tau)) \leq 2k\mathrm{Gdim}_\varrho(C, P, \varepsilon - \tau)\lceil \ln \|C\| \rceil$.

Next we apply Theorem 1 to the protocols for statistical and distance queries. In order to see how the protocol $\mathrm{SUCCESS}_\varrho(\varepsilon, \tau)$ can be simulated by the protocol $\mathrm{DIST}_\varrho(\tau)$, consider a distance query $h \in B_n$ and an answer $S_\varrho(h, \rho, \tau)$ to h with respect to $\mathrm{DIST}_\varrho(\tau)$. If $\rho \leq \varepsilon$, then the sphere $S_\varrho(h, \rho, \tau)$ is contained in the ball $B_\varrho(h, \varepsilon + \tau)$, and if $\rho > \varepsilon$, then the sphere $S_\varrho(h, \rho, \tau)$ is disjoint from $B_\varrho(h, \varepsilon - \tau)$, and hence contained in $B_n \setminus B_\varrho(h, \varepsilon - \tau)$. This means that $\mathrm{SUCCESS}_\varrho(\varepsilon, \tau) \leq_1 \mathrm{DIST}_\varrho(\tau)$, for any $\varepsilon \geq 0$.

Further, since $\mathrm{DIST}_\varrho(\tau) \leq_1 \mathrm{STAT}_D(\tau)$ for any metric of the form $\varrho(f, g) = \mathrm{Pr}_D[f \neq g]$, it also follows that $\mathrm{SUCCESS}_\varrho(\varepsilon, \tau) \leq_1 \mathrm{STAT}_D(\tau)$ for any $\varepsilon \geq 0$. Thus, as an application of Theorem 1 we get the following characterizations of the learning complexity for statistical and distance queries.

Corollary 1. *For $P \in \{\mathrm{DIST}_\varrho(\tau), \mathrm{STAT}_D(\tau)\}$ and all $\varepsilon \geq 0$ it holds that* $\mathrm{Gdim}_\varrho(C, P, 2(\varepsilon + \tau)) \leq \mathrm{LC}_\varrho(C, P, 2(\varepsilon + \tau)) \leq 2\mathrm{Gdim}_\varrho(C, P, \varepsilon - \tau)\ln\lceil \|C\| \rceil$.

4   The Learning Complexity of DNF Formulas

In this section we give upper und lower bounds for the learning complexity of DNF formulas with respect to distance queries and the metric $\varrho(f, g) = \mathrm{Pr}_U[f \neq g]$, where U denotes the uniform distribution on $\{0, 1\}^n$. The DNF-size of a boolean function f is the minimal number of terms of a DNF formula for f. We use the Fourier transform of boolean functions and basic ideas from [7].

In order to describe the Fourier transform of a boolean function f of arity n, it is convenient to think of f as a mapping from $\{0, 1\}^n$ to $\{-1, +1\}$. Then, for $A \subseteq [n]$, the parity function $\chi_A : \{0, 1\}^n \to \{-1, +1\}$ is defined as

$$\chi_A(x) = (-1)^{\sum_{i \in A} x_i}.$$

The 2^n parity functions $\{\chi_A \mid A \subseteq [n]\}$ form an orthonormal basis for the vector space of all real-valued functions on $\{0,1\}^n$, provided that the inner product is defined as $\langle f, g \rangle = \mathrm{E}[f \cdot g]$ and the norm of f is $\|f\| = \sqrt{\mathrm{E}[f^2]}$, where the expectation is taken with respect to the uniform distribution on $\{0,1\}^n$. Hence, every function $f : \{0,1\}^n \to \mathbb{R}$ can be uniquely expressed as a linear combination $f(x) = \sum_{A \subseteq [n]} \hat{f}(A)\chi_A(x)$, where $\hat{f}(A) = \langle \chi_A, f \rangle$.

A particularly useful fact is *Parseval's identity* which states that for every $f : \{0,1\}^n \to \mathbb{R}$ it holds that $\mathrm{E}[f^2] = \sum_{A \subseteq [n]} \hat{f}(A)^2$. For a boolean function $f : \{0,1\}^n \to \{-1,+1\}$, we thus get $\sum_{A \subseteq [n]} \hat{f}(A)^2 = 1$, which in particular gives us a bound on the number of coefficients exceeding a threshold $\theta > 0$,

$$\|\{A \subseteq [n] \mid \hat{f}(A) > \theta\}\| < 1/\theta^2.$$

This is useful in proving the following lemma which is inspired by a similar result in [9].

Lemma 4. *Let $C \subseteq B_n$ and suppose that $k = \|\{A \subseteq [n] \mid \chi_A \in C\}\| \geq 2$. Then, for $\varrho(f,g) = \Pr_U[f \neq g]$, and for every $\varepsilon < 1/2$ and $\tau \geq 0$ it holds that $\mathrm{Gdim}_\varrho(C, \mathrm{DIST}_\varrho(\tau), \varepsilon) > k\tau^2$.*

Proof. Suppose that $\mathrm{Gdim}_\varrho(C, \mathrm{DIST}_\varrho(\tau), \varepsilon) = d$, let $K = \{A \subseteq [n] \mid \chi_A \in C\}$, and consider the answering scheme $T = \{\langle h, \Lambda_h \rangle \mid h \in B_n\}$, where $\Lambda_h = \{f \mid |\varrho(f,h) - 1/2| \leq \tau\}$. Note that $\mathrm{E}[fg] = 2\Pr[f = g] - 1$ and therefore $\varrho(f,g) - 1/2 = -\langle f, g \rangle/2$. By Parseval's identity, we can bound the number of parity functions that can be eliminated from K by an answer Λ_h by

$$\|\{A \in K \mid \chi_A \notin \Lambda_h\}\| = \|\{A \in K \mid |\varrho(h, \chi_A) - 1/2| > \tau\}\|$$
$$= \|\{A \in K \mid |\langle h, \chi_A \rangle| > 2\tau\}\|$$
$$\leq \|\{A \subseteq [n] \mid |\hat{h}(A)| > 2\tau\}\|$$
$$< 1/4\tau^2.$$

It follows that for any set $S \subseteq T_Q$ of cardinality at most $d \leq k\tau^2$,

$$\|\{A \in K \mid (\forall \Lambda_h \in S)[\chi_A \in \Lambda_h]\}\| = k - \|\{A \in K \mid (\exists \Lambda_h \in S)[\chi_A \notin \Lambda_h]\}\|$$
$$> k - d/4\tau^2$$
$$\geq k - k/4$$
$$> 1.$$

Since $\varepsilon < 1/2$, and since the distance between two parity functions is precisely $1/2$, it follows that $\mathrm{Gdim}_\varrho(C, P, \varepsilon) > k\tau^2$.   □

Every parity function χ_A with $\|A\| \leq \log s$ can be represented by a DNF formula with at most s terms. Together with Lemma 4 we get that for every $\varepsilon < 1/2$,

$$\mathrm{LC}_\varrho(DNF_{s,n}, \mathrm{DIST}_\varrho(\tau)) > \binom{n}{\log s}\tau^2 = n^{\Omega(\log s)}\tau^2,$$

where $DNF_{s,n}$ is the class of n-ary boolean functions that can be represented by a DNF formula with at most s terms. Recall that for a real-valued function f over $\{0,1\}^n$, the norm $L_\infty(f)$ is defined as $\max_{x \in \{0,1\}^n} |f(x)|$.

Theorem 2. *For $\varrho(f,g) = \Pr_U[f \neq g]$, for all $\varepsilon > 0$, s and n, and for $\tau = \Omega(\varepsilon^2/s)$,*

$$LC_\varrho(DNF_{s,n}, \text{DIST}_\varrho(\tau)) = n^{O(\log(s/\varepsilon^2))}.$$

Proof. The proof is based on the fact that every boolean function f of DNF-size s has a large coefficient. In particular, for every Boolean function f of DNF-size s, and for every distribution D on $\{0,1\}^n$ there exists a set $A \subseteq [n]$ of cardinality at most $\log((2s+1)L_\infty(2^n D))$ such that $|E_D[f\chi_A]| \geq 1/(2s+1)$ [7,13,9].

It follows that for any distribution D on $\{0,1\}^n$, and for every target f of DNF-size s, a simple learning algorithm under the protocol $\text{DIST}_\varrho(\tau)$ with respect to $\varrho(f,g) = \Pr_D[f \neq g] = (1 - E_D[fg])/2$ can do an exhaustive search to produce a hypothesis $h \in \{\chi_A, -\chi_A\}$, for some A of cardinality at most $\log((2s+1)L_\infty(2^n D))$, such that h satisfies $E_D[fh] \geq 1/(2s+1) - 4\tau$. Hence, $\Pr_D[f = h] \geq 1/2 + 1/(4s+2) - 2\tau$, and the number of queries required is

$$\binom{n}{\log((2s+1)L_\infty(2^n D))}.$$

Now we can invoke known boosting techniques due to Freund [10] which, as shown by Aslam and Decatur [3], also can be applied to statistical queries as follows. Suppose that there is a learning algorithm WL, such that for every distribution D, and for all $f \in C$, WL uses N_0 queries under the protocol $\text{STAT}_D(\tau_0)$ with respect to $\varrho(f,g) = \Pr_D[f \neq g]$ to output a hypothesis h such that $\Pr_D[h = f] \geq 1/2 + \Omega(1/s)$. Then there is an algorithm B such that for every distribution D, every $f \in C$, and for every $\varepsilon > 0$, B under the protocol $\text{STAT}_D(\tau)$ uses $N = O(N_0 \tau^{-4} \log^2(\varepsilon^{-1}))$ queries to output a hypothesis h such that $\Pr_D[h = f] \geq 1 - \varepsilon$. The required tolerance is $\tau = \Omega(\tau_0 \varepsilon^2)$, and B simulates WL with respect to distributions D_i with $L_\infty(D_i) \leq O(1/\varepsilon^2)L_\infty(D)$.

Since $\text{DIST}_\varrho(\tau) \leq_1 \text{STAT}_D(\tau) \leq_2 \text{DIST}_\varrho(\tau)$, for any distribution D and metric $\varrho(f,g) = \Pr_D[f \neq g]$, this construction can also be applied to the above exhaustive-search algorithm for learning DNF formulas with distance queries. This yields for the uniform distribution a learning algorithm B that for all f of DNF-size s and every $\varepsilon > 0$ uses

$$\binom{n}{O(\log(s/\varepsilon^2))} s^4 \log^2(1/\varepsilon) = n^{O(\log(s/\varepsilon^2))}$$

many queries under the protocol $\text{DIST}_\varrho(\tau)$, where $\tau = \Omega(\varepsilon^2/s)$, and outputs a hypothesis h such that $\Pr_U[h \neq f] \leq \varepsilon$.

Finally, we have to take into account that in our definition of learning complexity, we require that the final version space (consisting of all functions in C not yet discarded by the answers received so far) is contained in the ball $B_\varrho(f, \varepsilon)$. It is clear that the version space of a learning algorithm A that for every $f \in C$

produces a hypothesis h with distance at most ε from f, must be contained in the ball $B_\varrho(f, 2\varepsilon)$ when A outputs the hypothesis (otherwise, there would be a function g left in the final version space whose distance from f is more than 2ε; but since there is no (boolean) function whose distance to both f and g is at most ε, such a function g could be used to fool the algorithm). Thus, the theorem follows by replacing ε by $\varepsilon/2$. $\square$

By combining the upper bound of 2 with the lower bound that can be derived from Lemma 4 and from Corollary 1, we get the following bound on the number of queries needed to approximately learn DNF formulas in the statistical query model as well as in the model of learning by distance.

Corollary 2. *Fix some constant* $0 < \varepsilon_0 < 1/2$. *Then, for all* s *and* n, *there is some* $\tau = \Theta(1/s)$ *such that for* $\varrho(f, g) = \Pr_U[f \neq g]$ *and* $P \in \{\mathrm{DIST}_\varrho(\tau), \mathrm{STAT}_U(\tau)\}$,

$$LC(DNF_{s,n}, P, \varepsilon_0) = n^{\Theta(\log s)}.$$

Acknowledgements. For helpful conversations and suggestions on this work we are very grateful to José Balcázar, Jorge Castro, and Richard Gavaldà.

References

[1] D. Angluin. Queries and concept learning. *Machine Learning*, 2:310 342, 1988.
[2] D. Angluin. Negative results for equivalence queries. *Machine Learning*, 5(2):121–150, 1990.
[3] J. Aslam and S. Decatur. General bounds on statistical query learning and PAC learning with noise via hypothesis boosting. *Information and Computation*, 141(2):85–118, 1998.
[4] J. Balcázar, J. Castro, and D. Guijarro. A general dimension for exact learning. In *Proc. 14th ACM Conference on Computational Learning Theory*, volume 2111 of *Lecture Notes in Artificial Intelligence*, pages 354–367. Springer-Verlag, Berlin Heidelberg New York, 2001.
[5] J. L. Balcázar, J. Castro, D. Guijarro, and H. U. Simon. The consistency dimension and distribution-dependent learning from queries. In *Proc. 10th International Workshop on Algorithmic Learning Theory (ALT'99)*, Lecture Notes in Artificial Intelligence. Springer-Verlag, Berlin Heidelberg New York, 1999.
[6] S. Ben-David, A. Itai, and E. Kushilevitz. Learning by distances. *Information and Computation*, pages 240–250, 1995.
[7] A. Blum, M. Furst, J. Jackson, M. Kearns, Y. Mansour, and S. Rudich. Weakly learning DNF and characterizing statistical query learning using Fourier analysis. In ACM, editor, *Proc. 26thACM Symposium on Theory of Computing*, pages 253–262. ACM Press, 1994.
[8] A. Blumer, A. Ehrenfeucht, D. Haussler, and M. K. Warmuth. Learnability and the Vapnik-Chervonenkis dimension. *Journal of the ACM*, 36(4):929–965, 1989.
[9] N. H. Bshouty and V. Feldman. On using extended statistical queries to avoid membership queries. *Journal of Machine Learning Research*, 2:359–395, 2002.

[10] Y. Freund. Boosting a weak learning algorithm by majority. *Information and Computation*, 121(2):256–285, Sept. 1995.

[11] T. Hegedüs. Generalized teaching dimensions and the query complexity of learning. In *Proceedings of the 8th Annual Conference on Computational Learning Theory (COLT'95)*, pages 108–117. ACM Press, July 1995.

[12] L. Hellerstein, K. Pillaipakkamnatt, V. Raghavan, and D. Wilkins. How many queries are needed to learn? *Journal of the ACM*, 43(5):840–862, 1996.

[13] J. C. Jackson. An efficient membership-query algorithm for learning DNF with respect to the uniform distribution. *Journal of Computer and System Sciences*, 55(3):414–440, 1997.

[14] M. J. Kearns. Efficient noise-tolerant learning from statistical queries. *Journal of the ACM*, 45(6):983–1006, 1998.

The Complexity of Learning Concept Classes with Polynomial General Dimension*

Johannes Köbler and Wolfgang Lindner

Institut für Informatik, Humboldt-Universität zu Berlin, 10099 Berlin, Germany

Abstract. We use the notion of general dimension to show that any p-evaluatable concept class with polynomial query complexity can be learned in polynomial time with the help of an oracle in the polynomial hierarchy, where the complexity of the required oracle depends on the query-types used by the learning algorithm. In particular, we show that for subset and superset queries an oracle in Σ_3^P suffices. Since the concept class of DNF formulas has polynomial query complexity with respect to subset and superset queries with DNF formulas as hypotheses, it follows that DNF formulas are properly learnable in polynomial time with subset and superset queries and the help of an oracle in Σ_3^P. We also show that the required oracle in our main theorem cannot be replaced by an oracle in a lower level of the polynomial-time hierarchy, unless the hierarchy collapses.

1 Introduction

In computational learning theory, one can distinguish between efficient learnability, which is usually modeled as learning in polynomial time, and polynomial query complexity, i.e. the possibility to learn a concept class with only a polynomial number of queries but unbounded computational resources. Clearly, polynomial-time learnability implies polynomial query complexity. On the other hand, in Angluin's query-learning model [2], it is known that for all combinations of equivalence and membership queries, polynomial query complexity implies polynomial-time learnability with additional access to an oracle in a low level of the polynomial-time hierarchy [6,8,11]. Thus, under the unlikely assumption that P = NP, polynomial query complexity in fact coincides with polynomial-time learnability for equivalence and/or membership queries. There are, however, prominent examples such as boolean formulas, which can be learned with a polynomial number of equivalence queries, but there is high evidence that these concept classes cannot be learned in polynomial time (e.g., [9]).

Here we address the question whether similar results hold also for more powerful types of queries, such as subset and superset queries [2]. For equivalence and/or membership queries, the polynomial-time oracle algorithms in [6,8,11] are based on combinatorial characterizations of the corresponding polynomial

---

* Work supported by the DFG under project KO 1053/1-1

N. Cesa-Bianchi et al. (Eds.): ALT 2002, LNAI 2533, pp. 149–163, 2002.
© Springer-Verlag Berlin Heidelberg 2002

query complexity. In [5], Balcázar et al. introduce the notion of the general dimension, a combinatorial measure which can be applied to arbitrary query-types and which characterizes, up to a logarithmic factor, the number of queries needed to learn a concept class. We use this notion to show, as our main result, that any p-evaluatable concept class with polynomial query complexity can be learned in polynomial time with the help of an oracle in the polynomial hierarchy, where the complexity of the required oracle depends on the query-types used by the learning algorithm. Similar as in [11] we use a modification of the majority-based algorithm of [5], where the emerging counting problems are solved by universal hashing techniques. Furthermore, our learning algorithm is proper in the sense that its output is a hypothesis from the concept class in question.

As a consequence, we get that all concept classes that are learnable with a polynomial number of equivalence and/or membership queries can be learned in polynomial time with an oracle in Σ_2^P, subsuming the results shown in [11]. A similar consequence holds also for subset and superset queries using an oracle in Σ_3^P. Since the concept class of DNF formulas has polynomial query complexity with respect to subset and superset queries with DNF formulas as hypotheses [4], it further follows that DNF formulas are properly learnable in polynomial time with subset and superset queries and the help of an oracle in Σ_3^P.

We further consider a concept class of [1] and show that this concept class is not learnable in polynomial time with an oracle in NP using equivalence queries with boolean circuits as hypotheses, unless the polynomial-time hierarchy collapses. This implies that the required oracle in our main theorem cannot be replaced by an oracle in a lower level of the polynomial-time hierarchy, unless the hierarchy collapses.

2   Preliminaries

We let $\mathcal{B}_n$ denote the set of all boolean functions $f : \{0,1\}^n \to \{0,1\}$. We assume the reader to be familiar with definitions and basic properties of the complexity classes in the polynomial-time hierarchy, as can be found in standard text books as, e.g., [12].

Let Σ be an alphabet. For a string $x \in \Sigma^*$, $|x|$ denotes its length. $\Sigma^{[n]}$ denotes the set of all strings $x \in \Sigma^*$ of length $|x| \leq n$. We assume the existence of a pairing function $\langle \cdot, \cdot \rangle : \Sigma^* \times \Sigma^* \to \Sigma^*$ that is computable in polynomial time and has inverses also computable in polynomial time. $\langle \cdot, \cdot \rangle$ can be extended to encode finite sequences $(x_1, \ldots, x_k)$ of strings into a string $\langle x_1, \ldots, x_k \rangle \in \Sigma^*$. For a set A, $\|A\|$ denotes its cardinality.

Let C be a class of sets $A \subseteq \Sigma^*$. Then $\sharp$C denotes the class of functions $f : \Sigma^* \to \mathbb{N}$ such that there is a set $A \in$ C and a polynomial p such that for all $x \in \Sigma^*$,

$$f(x) = \{y \in \Sigma^{p(|x|)} \mid \langle x, y \rangle \in A\}.$$

Let F be a class of functions $f : \Sigma^* \to \mathbb{N}$. Then $\max F$ denotes the class of functions $g : \Sigma^* \to \mathbb{N}$ such that there is a function $f \in F$ and a polynomial p such that for all $x \in \Sigma^*$,

$$g(x) = \max_{|y|=p(|x|)} f(\langle x, y \rangle).$$

The class min F ist defined analogously.

2.1 Learning Complexity and General Dimension

Balcázar et al. [5] introduced the general dimension of a boolean concept class to characterize the learning complexity with respect to arbitrary query protocols. The learning model presented in [5] is a generalization of the query learning model of Angluin [2]. Similar, but less general models have already been considered in [4,13].

In the model of [5], learning of a concept class $C \subseteq \mathcal{B}_n$ can be viewed as a game between a learning algorithm A and a teacher T with respect to some target $f \in C$ that is only known to T. In each round, A asks a query q from a set Q of queries and T responds with a subset $\Lambda \subseteq \mathcal{B}_n$ that contains f. Thereby, T provides some partial knowledge about the target f in form of a *property* Λ shared by f. The communication between A and T is guided by some *protocol* $\mathcal{P} \subseteq Q \times 2^{\mathcal{B}_n}$, i.e., the teacher is only allowed to respond with an answer Λ such that $\langle q, \Lambda \rangle \in \mathcal{P}$. The protocol $\mathcal{P}$ is required to be *complete* in the sense that for all $f \in \mathcal{B}_n$ and for all queries $q \in Q$ there exists an answer $\Lambda \in \mathcal{P}_q^f$ where $\mathcal{P}_q^f = \{\Lambda \mid \langle q, \Lambda \rangle \in \mathcal{P} \wedge f \in \Lambda\}$.

For example, the protocol for equivalence queries with hypotheses from a concept class $C \subseteq \mathcal{B}_n$ is the set of all pairs $(h, \{f \in \mathcal{B}_n \mid f(x) \neq h(x)\})$, for $h \in C$ and $x \in \{0,1\}^n$, together with all pairs $(h, \{h\})$ with $h \in C$. The first set of pairs corresponds to the case that a hypothesis h is answered by giving a counterexample x, and the second set of pairs corresponds to the answer "Yes".

The goal of the learning algorithm is to collect enough knowledge about the target f such that f is the only remaining function in C that shares all properties exposed by T. More precisely, the *current version space* at any stage in the run of a learning algorithm A is the set of all functions in C that are contained in all answers received by A so far, and a concept class $C \subseteq \mathcal{B}_n$ is *learnable* with at most d queries under a protocol $\mathcal{P}$, if there exists a learning algorithm A such that for all targets $f \in C$ and any teacher T that answers each query q with some $\Lambda \in \mathcal{P}_q^f$, the only concept left in the current vesion space after at most d queries is f. The *learning complexity* of C under $\mathcal{P}$, denoted by $\mathrm{LC}(C, \mathcal{P})$, is the smallest integer $d \geq 0$ such that C is learnable with at most d queries under $\mathcal{P}$. If no such integer d exists, then $\mathrm{LC}(C, \mathcal{P}) = \infty$.

In order to characterize the learning complexity of a concept class C under an arbitrary protocol $\mathcal{P}$, Balcázar et al. introduce the *general dimension* of C under $\mathcal{P}$. The definition is based on the notion of an *answering scheme*, i.e., a subset $T \subseteq \mathcal{P}$ such that for all queries $q \in Q$ the set $T_q = \{\Lambda \mid (q, \Lambda) \in T\}$ is non-empty. Note that, in contrast to a protocol $\mathcal{P}$, an answering scheme T need not be complete since there might exist a query $q \in Q$ and a function $f \in \mathcal{B}_n$ such that no answer $\Lambda \in T_q$ contains f. The *general dimension* of C under $\mathcal{P}$, denoted by $\mathrm{Gdim}(C, \mathcal{P})$, is the smallest integer $d \geq 0$ such that for all answering schemes $\mathcal{T} \subseteq \mathcal{P}$ there exists a set $\mathcal{S} \subseteq \bigcup_{q \in \mathcal{Q}} \mathcal{T}_q$ of cardinality at most d such that $\|\{f \in \mathcal{C} \mid (\forall \Lambda \in \mathcal{S})[f \in \Lambda]\}\| \leq 1$. If no such integer d exists, then $\mathrm{Gdim}(\mathcal{C}, \mathcal{P}) = \infty$.

It is shown in [5] that for each concept class $\mathcal{C}$ and protocol $\mathcal{P}$ it holds that $\mathrm{Gdim}(\mathcal{C}, \mathcal{P}) \leq \mathrm{LC}(\mathcal{C}, \mathcal{P}) \leq \mathrm{Gdim}(\mathcal{C}, \mathcal{P}) \lceil \ln \|\mathcal{C}\| \rceil$. Thus, the general dimension is in fact a combinatorial characterization of the learning complexity.

3   Polynomial Learning Complexity and Dimension

To define polynomial learning complexity and, in particular, polynomial-time learnability under an arbitrary protocol, we need to specify a way to represent concept classes and protocols. For concept classes, we use the following notations from [3] adapted to the boolean case.

Definition 1. *Let Σ and Γ be finite alphabets. A* representation *of (boolean) concepts is a set $C \subseteq 0^* \times \Gamma^* \times \Sigma^*$. With respect to any given $n \in \mathbb{N}$, we let $C_n = \{\langle u, x \rangle \mid \langle 0^n, u, x \rangle \in C\}$. The* concept *represented by a* concept name *$u \in \Gamma^*$ is $\kappa_{C_n}(u) = \{x \mid \langle u, x \rangle \in C_n\}$, and the* concept class *represented by C_n is $\mathcal{K}(C_n) = \{\kappa_{C_n}(u) \mid u \in \Gamma^*\}$.*

Here we always assume that $\Sigma = \{0, 1\}$. For the sake of notational brevity we simply write κ_n instead of κ_{C_n} whenever C is clear from the context. Furthermore, by abusing the notation, we identify the set $\kappa_n(u)$ with its characteristic function. Thus, we can view $\mathcal{K}(C_n)$ as a subset of $\mathcal{B}_n$.

The above definition allows us to regard a representation C of concepts as a decision problem. This means that we can express the usual assumption that the concept class represented by C can be evaluated in polynomial time by the fact that C is decidable in the complexity class P.

Example 1. The circuit representation of boolean concepts, denoted by Circ, is the set of all tuples $\langle 0^n, c, x \rangle$ such that c is an encoding of a boolean circuit over the basis $\{\wedge, \vee, \neg\}$ with n input gates, x is a binary string of length n, and the circuit encoded by c accepts x.

Now we define representations of protocols in a similar style as we defined representions of concepts. To illustrate the underlying idea let us reconsider the model of learning with equivalence queries with respect to a representation of concepts C. Here, a query is a concept name h, and the answer is either a counterexample in form of a binary string x, or the token "Yes". A counterexample x as an answer to some query h means that the target concept does not agree with the concept represented by h on x, i.e., the answer x to the query h means that the target is contained in the set of all concepts $\kappa_n(u)$ such that x is contained in the symmetric difference of $\kappa_n(u)$ and $\kappa_n(h)$. Similarly, the answer "Yes" to a query h means that the target is contained in the singleton set $\{\kappa_n(h)\}$. Consequently, with respect to some fixed arity n, we represent a protocol $\mathcal{P}$ as a set P of triples $\langle 0^n, q, a, u \rangle$, where $q \in \Delta^*$ is a *query* and $a \in \Delta^*$ is an *answer*, for an additional finite alphabet Δ, and $u \in \Gamma^*$ is a concept name. An answer a together with a query q determine a set of concept names u satisfying $\langle 0^n, q, a, u \rangle \in P$, which, when interpreted with respect to a given represention of concepts C, describes the property associated with q and a.

Definition 2. *Let C be a representation of concepts, and let Δ be a finite alphabet. A representation of a (boolean) protocol with respect to C is a set $P \subseteq 0^* \times \Delta^* \times \Delta^* \times \Gamma^*$ which satisfies the following conditions for all $n \in \mathbb{N}$.*

1. *For all concept names u, and for all queries q, there exists an answer a such that $\langle 0^n, q, a, u \rangle \in P$.*
2. *For all concept names u and v, and for all queries q and answers a it holds that if $\langle 0^n, q, a, u \rangle \in P$ and $\kappa_n(u) = \kappa_n(v)$, then $\langle 0^n, q, a, v \rangle \in P$.*

With respect to any given integer $n \in \mathbb{N}$, we let $P_n = \{ \langle q, a, u \rangle \mid \langle 0^n, q, a, u \rangle \in P \}$, and for a query q and an answer a we let $P_n(q, a) = \{ u \mid \langle q, a, u \rangle \subset P_n \}$. The property associated with the pair $\langle q, a \rangle$ is $\Lambda_{P_n}(q, a) = \{ \kappa_n(u) \mid u \in P_n(q, a) \}$ which we also denote by $\Lambda_n(q, a)$, and the protocol represented by P_n is $\mathcal{K}(P_n) = \{ (q, \Lambda_n(q, a)) \mid q, a \in \Delta^* \}$.

By the first condition, we have that $\mathcal{K}(P_n)$ is *complete* with respect to $\mathcal{K}(C_n)$ in the sense that for all $f \in \mathcal{K}(C_n)$ and for all queries $q \in \Delta^*$, there exists an answer $a \in \Delta^*$ with $f \in \Lambda_n(q, a)$. Clearly, completeness with respect to some proper subset $\mathcal{K}(C_n)$ of $\mathcal{B}_n$ is a strictly weaker condition than completeness with respect to $\mathcal{B}_n$ as required in [5]. It is, however, easy to see that the combinatorial characterization of [5] also holds if $\mathcal{K}(P_n)$ is only complete with respect to $\mathcal{K}(C_n)$.

The second condition is merely for the sake of notational convenience and implies that a concept $\kappa_n(u)$ is in the property $\Lambda_n(q, a)$ if and only if $\langle q, a, u \rangle \in P_n$.

Example 2. Let $C \subseteq 0^* \times \Gamma^* \times \Sigma^*$ be a representation of concepts.

- The representation of the protocol for equivalence queries to C is the set $\mathrm{Eq}(C) = \{ \langle 0^n, h, x, u \rangle \mid h, u \in \Gamma^*, x \in \kappa_n(h) \triangle \kappa_n(u) \} \cup \{ \langle 0^n, h, \text{"Yes"}, u \rangle \mid h, u \in \Gamma^*, \kappa_n(h) = \kappa_n(u) \}$.
- The representation of the protocol for membership queries is the set $\mathrm{Mem}(C) = \{ \langle 0^n, x, \text{"Yes"}, u \rangle \mid u \in \Gamma^*, x \in \kappa_n(u) \} \cup \{ \langle 0^n, x, \text{"No"}, u \rangle \mid u \in \Gamma^*, x \notin \kappa_n(u) \}$.
- The representation of the protocol for subset queries to C is the set $\mathrm{Sub}(C) = \{ \langle 0^n, h, x, u \rangle \mid h, u \in \Gamma^*, x \in \kappa_n(h) \setminus \kappa_n(u) \} \cup \{ \langle 0^n, h, \text{"Yes"}, u \rangle \mid h, u \in \Gamma^*, \kappa_n(h) \subseteq \kappa_n(u) \}$.
- The representation of the protocol for subset and superset queries to C is the set $\mathrm{Sub}(C) \oplus \mathrm{Sup}(C) = \{ \langle 0^n, 0h, a, u \rangle \mid h, u \in \Gamma^*, \langle 0^n, h, a, u \rangle \in \mathrm{Sub}(C) \} \cup \{ \langle 0^n, 1h, a, u \rangle \mid h, u \in \Gamma^*, \langle 0^n, h, a, u \rangle \in \mathrm{Sup}(C) \}$, where $\mathrm{Sup}(C)$ is the representation for superset queries which is similarly defined as $\mathrm{Sub}(C)$.

We now define polynomial learning complexity by imposing a polynomial bound both on the number of queries and the length of queries required for successful learning.

Definition 3. *Let C be a representation of concepts, and let P be a protocol representation with respect to C. Then C has* polynomial learning complexity *under P if there exist polynomials p and m, and an algorithm A which gets inputs s and n and may ask queries q of size at most $m(s,n)$, such that for all concept names u of size at most s, the following implication holds: If A always receives an answer a for each of its queries q satisfying $\kappa_n(u) \in \Lambda_n(q,a)$, then after at most $p(s,n)$ queries, A eventually halts and outputs a concept name h with $\kappa_n(h) = \kappa_n(u)$.*

In contrast to the definition of learning complexity, where the success condition is expressed in terms of the current version space, in the definition of polynomial learning complexity we require that a successful learning algorithm has to produce a concept name h for the target $\kappa_n(u)$. It is, however, easy to see that in the resource unbounded setting, both success conditions are equivalent.

Next we consider the corresponding notion of polynomial general dimension. We call a set $T \subseteq \Delta^{[m]} \times \Delta^*$ an *answering scheme for the length bound m*, if for each query q of length at most m there is an answer a with $\langle q, a \rangle \in T$. We further use $C_{s,n} = C_n \cap (\Gamma^{[s]} \times \Sigma^n)$ to denote the representation of concepts of size at most s.

Definition 4. *Let C be a representation of concepts, and let P be a protocol representation with respect to C. Then C has* polynomial general dimension *under P if there exist polynomials p and m, such that for all size bounds s, for all n, and for all answering schemes $T \subseteq \Delta^{[m(s,n)]} \times \Delta^*$ for the length bound $m(s,n)$ there exists a set $S \subseteq T$ of cardinality at most $p(s,n)$ such that $\|\{f \in \mathcal{K}(C_{s,n}) \mid (\forall \langle q, a \rangle \in S)[f \in \Lambda_n(q,a)]\}\| \le 1$.*

Now we can use the arguments of [5] to show that polynomial learning complexity is equivalent to polynomial general dimension. The implication from polynomial general dimension to polynomial learning complexity is based on the fact that there always exists an inverse polynomially good query q for the current version space of any learning algorithm, where a good query q (with respect to C and P) is defined as follows.

Definition 5. *A query q is δ-good for a set of concepts $\mathcal{V}$ if each answer a to q eliminates at least a δ-fraction from $\mathcal{V}$, i.e. $\|\{f \in \mathcal{V} \mid f \notin \Lambda_n(q,a)\}\| \ge \delta \|\mathcal{V}\|$.*

Lemma 1 (cf. [5]). *Suppose that C has polynomial general dimension under P, and let p and m be the corresponding polynomials. Then, for all s and n, and for all non-empty sets $\mathcal{V} \subseteq \mathcal{K}(C_{s,n})$, there exists a query q of length at most $m(s,n)$ that is $(1 - 1/\|\mathcal{V}\|)/p(s,n)$-good for $\mathcal{V}$.*

By Lemma 1, for any set S of queries and answers received thus far, we can find a query q of polynomial length such that any answer to q eliminates at least an inverse polynomial fraction from the current version space $\mathcal{V} = \{f \in \mathcal{K}(C_{s,n}) \mid (\forall \langle q, a \rangle \in S)[f \in \Lambda_n(q,a)]\}$. Hence, after at most a polynomial number of queries, the only concept left in $\mathcal{V}$ is the target. This shows that polynomial general dimension implies polynomial learning complexity and we have the following equivalence.

Theorem 1. *Let C be a representation of concepts, and let P be a protocol representation with respect to C. Then the following are equivalent.*

1. *C has polynomial learning complexity under P.*
2. *C has polynomial general dimension under P.*

4   Polynomial-Time Learning with an Oracle in the Polynomial Hierarchy

In this section we show that any representation of concepts $C \in \mathrm{P}$ with polynomial general dimension under some representation P of a protocol can be learned in polynomial time with the help of an oracle whose complexity depends on the complexity of the decision problem P. We consider the following time-bounded analogue of polynomial learning complexity.

Definition 6. *A representation of concepts C is* polynomial-time learnable *under a protocol representation P if there is an algorithm A which fulfills all the conditions required in Definition 3, and whose running time is polynomially bounded in s and n.*

Obviously, any polynomial-time learning algorithm should be able to read the complete answer received at any stage. Thus, it is natural to require a polynomial bound on the possible answers in a protocol P.

Definition 7. *A representation of a protocol P is* polynomially (p-) honest *if there exists some polynomial l such that $|a| \le l(n, |q|)$ for all $\langle q, a, u \rangle \in P_n$.*

As we will see below, if P can be decided in NP, then we get polynomial-time learnability with an oracle in Σ_2^P. In fact, we only need that the restriction of P specifying the properties $\Lambda_n(q, a)$ with $\|\Lambda_n(q, a)\| > 1$ can be decided in NP. This allows us to apply our theorem also to the important case of equivalence queries, where, in general, the part of P specifying "Yes" answers can only be decided in coNP.

Definition 8. *Let P be a protocol representation with respect to some representation of concepts C. An* admissible subset *of P is a set $P^* \subseteq P$ satisfying the following conditions for all n, q and a.*

1. *If $\|\Lambda_n(q, a)\| \ne 1$, then $P_n^*(q, a) = P_n(q, a)$.*
2. *If $\|\Lambda_n(q, a)\| = 1$, then $P_n^*(q, a) = P_n(q, a)$ or $P_n^*(q, a) = \emptyset$.*

Note that if $C \in \mathrm{P}$, then the protocol representation $\mathrm{Eq}(C)$ as given in Example 2 is p-honest. Moreover, $\mathrm{Eq}(C)$ is decidable in coNP and has the admissible subset $\{\langle 0^n, h, x, u \rangle \mid h, u \in \Gamma^*, x \in \kappa_n(h) \triangle \kappa_n(u)\}$ that is decidable in P.

Now we are ready to present our main theorem.

Theorem 2. *Let $C \in \mathrm{P}$ be a representation of concepts, and let $P \in \Sigma_2^P$ be a p-honest protocol representation with respect to C with an admissible subset $P^* \in \mathrm{NP}$. If C has polynomial general dimension under P, then C is polynomial-time learnable under P with an oracle in Σ_2^P.*

Before we proceed to the proof of Theorem 2, let us first discuss some consequences. By the remark above, it follows that for all representations $C \in \mathrm{P}$, C has polynomial learning complexity with respect to equivalence queries if and only if C is polynomial-time learnable with equivalence queries and an oracle in Σ_2^P. This holds also for equivalence and membership queries, and for membership queries alone. Thus, Theorem 2 subsumes all the results shown in [11].

Since Theorem 2 holds relative to any oracle A we get the following corollary.

Corollary 1. *Let $i \geq 1$, let $C \in \mathrm{P}$ be a representation of concepts, and let $P \in \Sigma_{i+1}^P$ be a p-honest protocol representation with respect to C with an admissible subset $P^* \in \Sigma_i^P$. If C has polynomial general dimension under P, then C is polynomial-time learnable under P with an oracle in Σ_{i+1}^P.*

For any $C \in \mathrm{P}$, the protocol representation $\mathrm{Sub}(C) \oplus \mathrm{Sup}(C)$ for subset and superset queries can be decided in $\Delta_2^P \subseteq \Sigma_2^P$. Hence, for all $C \in \mathrm{P}$, C has polynomial learning complexity with respect to subset and superset queries if and only if C is polynomial-time learnable with subset and superset queries and an oracle in Σ_3^P. Since the concept class of DNF-formulas can be learned with polynomial subset and superset queries (with DNF-formulas as hypotheses) [4], we get that this can be done also in polynomial time with an oracle in Σ_3^P.

Corollary 2. DNF *is polynomial-time learnable under* $\mathrm{Sub}(\mathrm{DNF}) \oplus \mathrm{Sup}(\mathrm{DNF})$ *relative to an oracle in* Σ_3^P.

4.1 Proof of Theorem 2

Let C be a representation of concepts with polynomial general dimension under a p-honest protocol representation $P \in \Sigma_2^P$ with an admissible subset $P^* \in \mathrm{NP}$. We have to show that C can be learned under P in polynomial time and with the help of an oracle in Σ_2^P.

Our algorithm will proceed similarly as the algorithm for Theorem 1 in the resource-unbouded setting. That is, for a given set S of queries and answers received thus far, we will try to find an inverse polynomially good query q such that any answer to q eliminates at least an inverse polynomial fraction from the current version space

$$V_{s,n}(S) = \{u \in \Gamma^{[s]} \mid (\forall \langle q, a \rangle \in S)[\langle q, a, u \rangle \in P_n]\}.$$

Then after a polynomial number of queries, the only concept left in $\mathcal{V}_{s,n}(S) = \{\kappa_n(u) \mid u \in V_{s,n}(S)$ is the target.

To compute such a good query q in polynomial time with an oracle in Σ_2^P, we will use well-known approximate counting techniques based on universal hashing, as already be done in [5,11] for the specific case of equivalence queries. For this, however, we will have to consider the fraction of concept *names* rather than the fraction of concepts that are eliminated by any answer to q. That is, we will try to find an inverse polynomially good query q for the set $V_{s,n}(S)$ of concept names.

Definition 9. *A query q is δ-good for a set of concept names V if each answer a to q eliminates at least a δ-fraction from V, i.e. $\|\{u \in V \mid \langle q, a, u \rangle \notin P_n\}\| \geq \delta \|V\|$ for all $a \in \Delta^*$.*

Because the fraction of a set of concepts in $V_{s,n}(S)$ might be very different from the fraction of the corresponding set of concept names in $V_{s,n}(S)$, we cannot use Lemma 1 directly to guarantee the existence of a sufficiently good query for V. For the specific case of equivalence queries, it is shown in [11] that an analogue of Lemma 1 also works for concept names rather than concepts. In the general case, however, the goodness of the query q depends on the maximal size of the equivalence classes $[u] = \{v \mid \kappa_n(v) = \kappa_n(u)\}$, $u \in V_{s,n}(S)$. We use the following notation.

Definition 10. *Let V be a finite set of concept names. The weight of a concept name u in V is $\mu(u) = \|[u] \cap V\|/\|V\|$. The bias of V is $\mu = \max_{u \in V} \mu(u)$.*

Now we can show the following analogue of Lemma 1 for concept names rather than concepts.

Lemma 2. *Suppose that C has polynomial general dimension under P via the polynomials p and m. Then, for all s and n, and for all non-empty sets $V \subseteq \Gamma^{[s]}$ with bias μ, there is a query q of length at most $m(s, n)$ that is $(1-\mu)/p(s,n)$-good for V.*

Proof. Fix s and n, some non-empty set $V \subseteq \Gamma^{[s]}$, and assume that no query q of length at most $m(s, n)$ is $(1 - \mu)/p(s, n)$-good for V, i.e., for all queries q of length at most $m(s, n)$ there exists an answer a_q such that

$$\|\{u \in V \mid \langle q, a_q, u \rangle \notin P_n\}\| < \frac{\|V\| - \max_{u \in V}\|[u] \cap V\|}{p(s,n)}.$$

Consider the answering scheme $T = \{\langle q, a_q \rangle \mid q \in \Delta^{[m(s,n)]}\}$. Then, for any subset $S \subseteq T$ of cardinality at most $p(s, n)$, it follows that

$$\|\{u \in V \mid (\exists \langle q, a \rangle \in S)[\langle q, a, u \rangle \notin P_n]\}\| \leq \sum_{\langle q, a \rangle \in S} \|\{u \in V \mid \langle q, a, u \rangle \notin P_n\}\|$$
$$< \|V\| - \max_{u \in V}\|[u] \cap V\|,$$

which implies that

$$\|\{u \in V \mid (\forall \langle q, a \rangle \in S)[\langle q, a, u \rangle \in P_n]\}\| > \max_{u \in V}\|[u] \cap V\|$$

and hence

$$\|\{\kappa_n(u) \mid u \in V \wedge (\forall \langle q, a \rangle \in S)[\langle q, a, u \rangle \in P_n]\}\| > 1.$$

Since the set of concepts $\{\kappa_n(u) \mid u \in V\}$ is contained in $\mathcal{K}(C_{s,n})$, this contradicts the assumption that C has polynomial general dimension under P. $\square$

If the bias μ is not to large, i.e., $1 - \mu$ is at least inverse polynomial, then Lemma 2 guarantees the existence of an inverse polynomially good query for V, and as we will see below, we then are able to compute such a query in polynomial time with an oracle in Σ_2^P. Thus, the remaining obstacle is to treat also the case when μ is large. This is the main departure from the special case of equivalence queries and the algorithm in the resource-unbouded setting.

However, if μ is large, then there exists a concept name u of large weight in V. Hence, if we replace the whole equivalence class $[u]$ with the single concept name u within V, then we eliminate a large fraction of concept names from V, and this does not effect the set of concepts $\mathcal{V}$ represented by V. To implement this idea, we maintain an additional set W of concept names, and we represent the current version space $\mathcal{V}_{s,n}(S)$ by the set

$$V_{s,n}(S,W) = (V_{s,n}(S) \cap W) \cup (V_{s,n}(S) \setminus \bigcup_{w \in W} [w]$$

$$= V_{s,n}(S) \cap \{u \in \Gamma^{[s]} \mid (\forall w \in W \setminus \{u\})[\kappa_n(u) \neq \kappa_n(w)]\}$$

of concept names $u \in V_{s,n}(S)$ that are not equivalent to some $w \in W \setminus \{u\}$. This means, that for all concept names $u \in W$, $V_{s,n}(S,W)$ contains at most one concept name from the equivalence class $[u]$. By moving some u from V to W, we can discard $\|[u]\| - 1$ elements from $V_{s,n}(S,W)$ without changing the set of concepts represented by $V_{s,n}(S,W)$.

Now we are ready to describe our algorithm. We initially set $S = W = \emptyset$. Then we repeat the following steps until $\|\mathcal{V}\| = 1$, and thus the current version space is reduced to the target. In each loop, we first compute an approximation $\tilde{\mu}$ of the bias μ satisfying $|\mu - \tilde{\mu}| \leq 1/12$. If $\tilde{\mu} \leq 2/3$, then $\mu \leq 2/3 + 1/12 = 3/4$, and hence, by Lemma 2, there exists a $(1/4p(s,n))$-good query. We then compute a $(1/6p(s,n))$-good query, and thus any answer to q eliminates at least a $(1/6p(s,n))$-fraction of concept names form V. If $\tilde{\mu} > 2/3$, then $\mu > 2/3 - 1/12 = 7/12$, and we proceed by computing a concept name u of weight $\mu(u) \geq 1/2$ in V. Note that $\mu > 7/12$ implies $\|V\| \geq 3$, and hence by adding u to W we eliminate at least $[u] - 1 \geq \|V\|/2 - \|V\|/3 = \|V\|/6$ concept names from V. Thus, in both cases, we eliminate at least a $1/6p(s,n)$-fraction of concept names form V, and it follows that after at most polynomially many queries, the only concept left in the current version space is the target. We then compute a concept name u in V and output u.

In the remainder of this section we have to show that each step in our learning algorithm can be done in polynomial time with an oracle in Σ_2^P.

First note that we only ask queries of length $m(s,n)$, and the honesty condition on P implies that all answers a we receive have length at most $l(n)$. Thus, the set S contains at most polynomially many pairs of queries and answers of polynomial length. Also note that the set W contains at most polynomially many concept names of length bounded by s.

To analyze the uniform comlexity of our algorithm, let $V_{s,n}^*(S,W)$ denotes the set $V_{s,n}(S,W)$ with the admissible subset $P^* \in \mathrm{NP}$ in place of $P \in \Sigma_2^P$, and consider the sets $V = \{\langle 0^s, 0^n, S, W, u \rangle \mid u \in V_{s,n}(S,W)\}$ and

$V^* = \{\langle 0^s, 0^n, S, W, u \rangle \mid u \in V_{s,n}^*(S, W)\}$. Note that since $C \in \mathrm{P}$, V is in Σ_2^P and V^* is in NP. Further note that if $\|V_{s,n}(S)\| > 1$, then $V_{s,n}(S, W)$ coincides with $V_{s,n}^*(S, W)$. It follows that $\|V_{s,n}(S)\| > 1$ if and only if $V_{s,n}^*(S, W)$ contains two concept names u and v with $\kappa_n(u) \neq \kappa_n(v)$. Thus, we can test whether there is more than one concept left in $V_{s,n}(S, W)$ in polynomial time relative to an oracle in NP.

The final construction of a concept name $u \in V_{s,n}(S, W)$, when $\|V_{s,n}(S)\| = 1$, can be done by prefix search in polynomial time with an oracle in Σ_2^P that contains all tuples $\langle 0^s, 0^n, S, W, u' \rangle$ such that there exists some u extending u' with $\langle 0^s, 0^n, S, W, u' \rangle \in V$.

For the remaining steps we use the already mentioned approximate counting techniques, which we summarize in the following two lemmas (cf. [10]).

Lemma 3. *Let $f \in \min\max \sharp \mathrm{NP}$. Then there exists an oracle $A \in \Sigma_2^P$ such that for all $x \in \Sigma^*$, and for all integers $a \geq 0$ and $e \geq 1$:*

1. $\langle x, a, 0^e \rangle \in A \Longrightarrow f(x) \leq (1 + \frac{1}{e})a$
2. $\langle x, a, 0^e \rangle \notin A \Longrightarrow f(x) > a$.

Lemma 4. *Let $f \in \min\max \sharp \mathrm{NP}$. Then there exists a function $\tilde{f} \in \mathrm{FP}(\Sigma_2^P)$ such that for all $x \in \Sigma^*$, and for all integers $e \geq 1$, $f(x) \leq \tilde{f}(x, 0^e) \leq (1 + \frac{1}{e})f(x)$.*

For all integers s, n, for all S and W, and for $\tau = \langle 0^s, 0^n, S, W \rangle$ let $t(\tau)$ be the cardinality of the set $V_{s,n}^*(S, W)$. Since V^* is in NP, $t(\tau)$ is in $\sharp \mathrm{NP}$, and it follows immediately from Lemma 4 that we can compute an approximation $\tilde{t}(\tau, 0^e)$ of $t(\tau)$ in polynomial time and with an oracle in Σ_2^P, such that for all $e \geq 1$, $t(\tau) \leq \tilde{t}(\tau, 0^e) \leq (1 + \frac{1}{e})t(\tau)$.

Claim. For all integers s, n and $e \geq 1$, for all S and W, and for $\tau = \langle 0^s, 0^n, S, W \rangle$ it is possible to compute an approximation $\tilde{\mu}(\tau, 0^e)$ of the bias $\mu(\tau)$ of $V_{s,n}^*(S, W)$ satisfying $|\tilde{\mu}(\tau, 0^e) - \mu(\tau)| \leq 1/e$ for all $e \geq 1$ in polynomial time with an oracle in Σ_2^P.

Proof. Let $t(\tau)$ and $\tilde{t}(\tau, 0^e)$ as above, and consider the $\min \sharp \mathrm{NP}$-function

$$b(\tau) = \min_{v \in \Gamma^{[s]}} \|V_{s,n}^*(S, W) \setminus [v]_n\|.$$

By Lemma 4 there is an approximation $\tilde{b}(\tau, 0^e)$ computable in polynomial time with an oracle in Σ_2^P such that $b(\tau) \leq \tilde{b}(\tau, 0^e) \leq (1 + \frac{1}{e})b(\tau)$.

Clearly, the bias $\mu(\tau)$ can be expressed as $\mu(\tau) = 1 - \frac{b(\tau)}{t(\tau)}$. Setting $\tilde{\mu}(\tau, 0^e) = 1 - \frac{\tilde{b}(\tau, 0^e)}{\tilde{t}(\tau, 0^e)}$, it follows that

$$\tilde{\mu}(\tau, 0^e) = \frac{\tilde{t}(\tau, 0^e) - \tilde{b}(\tau, 0^e)}{\tilde{t}(\tau, 0^e)} \leq \frac{t(\tau) + t(\tau)/e - b(\tau)}{t(\tau)} = \mu(\tau) + \frac{1}{e}$$

and since $b(\tau) \leq t(\tau)$ it also holds that

$$\tilde{\mu}(\tau, 0^e) \geq 1 - \frac{b(\tau) + b(\tau)/e}{t(\tau)} \geq \mu(\tau) - 1/e.$$

□

Now let us see how to construct a concept name of large weight in $V_{s,n}^*(S,W)$.

Claim. For all integers s, n and $e \geq 1$, for all S and W, and for $\tau = \langle 0^s, 0^n, S, W \rangle$, it is possible to compute a concept name u of weight $\mu(\tau, u) \geq \mu(\tau) - 1/e$ in $V_{s,n}^*(S,W)$ in polynomial time with an oracle in Σ_2^P.

Proof. Let $b(\tau)$ and $\tilde{b}(\tau, 0^e)$ as in the proof of the previous claim, and consider the $\sharp$NP-function

$$b(\tau, u) = \|V_{s,n}^*(S,W) \setminus [u]_n\|.$$

Applying Lemma 3 we get an oracle A in Σ_2^P such that for all integers $a \geq 0$ and $e \geq 1$, we have that

1. $\langle \tau, u, a, 0^e \rangle \in A \Longrightarrow b(u) \leq (1 + \frac{1}{e})a$
2. $\langle \tau, u, a, 0^e \rangle \notin A \Longrightarrow b(u) > a$

Let A' be the oracle consisting of all tuples $\langle \tau, u', a, 0^e \rangle$ for which there exists some $u \in \Gamma^{[s]}$ with prefix u' and $\langle \tau, u, a, 0^e \rangle \in A$. Since there exists some concept name u with $b(\tau, u) \leq b(\tau) \leq \tilde{b}(\tau, 0^e)$, and hence $\langle \tau, u, \tilde{b}, 0^e \rangle \in A$, it follows that we can construct a concept name u with $\langle \tau, u, \tilde{b}, 0^e \rangle \in A$ by prefix search in polynomial time and with the help of the oracle A' in Σ_2^P. Since for the resulting u it holds that $\langle \tau, u, \tilde{b}(\tau), 0^e \rangle \in A$, it follows that

$$b(\tau, u) \leq (1 + \frac{1}{e})\tilde{b}(\tau) \leq (1 + \frac{1}{e})^2 b(\tau) \leq (1 + \frac{3}{e})b(\tau)$$

and since $b(\tau) \leq t(\tau)$ we get

$$\mu(\tau, u) = 1 - \frac{b(\tau, u)}{t(\tau)} \geq 1 - \frac{b(\tau) + 3b(\tau)/e}{t(\tau)} \geq \mu(\tau) - \frac{3}{e}.$$

□

As our final application of Lemmas 3 and 4 we show how to construct a good query q.

Claim. For all integers s, n and $e \geq 1$, for all S and W such that for $\tau = \langle 0^s, 0^n, S, W \rangle$ it holds that $\mu(\tau) \leq \frac{3}{4}$, it is possible to compute a query q of length $m(s,n)$ that is $(\frac{1}{4p(s,n)} - 1/e)$-good for $V_{s,n}^*(S,W)$ in polynomial time with an oracle in Σ_2^P.

Proof. Consider the max $\sharp$NP-function

$$c(\tau, q) = \max_{a \in \Delta^{[l(n,|q|)]}} \|\{u \in V_{s,n}^*(S,W) \mid \langle q, a, u \rangle \in P_n^*\}\|$$

and let A be the oracle in Σ_2^P provided by Lemma 3 such that for all integers $a \geq 0$ and $e \geq 1$, we have that

1. $\langle \tau, q, a, 0^e \rangle \in A \Longrightarrow c(\tau, q) \leq (1 + \frac{1}{e})a$,
2. $\langle \tau, q, a, 0^e \rangle \notin A \Longrightarrow c(\tau, q) > a$.

By Lemma 2, the assumption $\mu \leq \frac{3}{4}$ implies that there exists a query q of length $m(s, n)$ such that q is $1/4p(s, n)$-good for $V_{s,n}^*(S, W)$. This means that for all answers a it holds that

$$\|\{u \in V_{s,n}^*(S, W) \mid \langle q, a, u \rangle \in P_n^*\}\| \leq \|\{u \in V_{s,n}^*(S, W) \mid \langle q, a, u \rangle \in P_n\}\|$$
$$\leq (1 - \frac{1}{4p(s, n)})t(\tau)$$

and hence $c(\tau, q) \leq (1 - 1/4p(s, n))t(\tau) \leq (1 - 1/4p(s, n))\tilde{t}(\tau, 0^e)$. Setting $a = (1 - 1/4p(s, n))\tilde{t}(\tau, 0^e)$ it follows that $\langle \tau, q, a, 0^e \rangle \in A$, and similarly as in the previous claim we can construct query q in polynomial time and with the help of an oracle in Σ_2^P such that $\langle \tau, q, a, 0^e \rangle \in A$. Now, $\langle \tau, q, a, 0^e \rangle \in A$ implies

$$c(\tau, q) \leq (1 + \frac{1}{e})a = (1 + \frac{1}{e})(1 - \frac{1}{4p(s, n)})\tilde{t}(\tau, 0^e) \leq (1 + \frac{1}{e})^2(1 - \frac{1}{4p(s, n)})t(\tau)$$
$$\leq (1 - \frac{1}{4p(s, n)} + \frac{3}{e})t(\tau).$$

Since $c(\tau, q)$ is defined in terms of P^* rather than P, this only means that for all answers a with $\|A_n(q, a)\| > 1$ it holds that

$$\|\{u \in V_{s,n}^*(S, W) \mid \langle q, a, u \rangle \in P_n\}\| = \|\{u \in V_{s,n}^*(S, W) \mid \langle q, a, u \rangle \in P_n^*\}\|$$
$$\leq (1 - \frac{1}{4p} + \frac{3}{e})t(\tau).$$

The assumption $\mu \leq \frac{3}{4}$ implies that also for all answers a with $\|A_n(q, a)\| = 1$ it holds that $\|\{u \in V^* \mid \langle q, a, u \rangle \in P_n\}\| \leq \mu(\tau)t(\tau) \leq (\frac{3}{4})t(\tau)$. □

5   Non-learnability with an Oracle in NP

In this section we show that the Σ_2^P oracle in our main theorem cannot be replaced by an oracle in NP, unless the polynomial hierarchy collapses to Δ_2^P. This computational hardness result is based on the *representation problem* REP(C) [14,1] for a representation C,

$$\mathrm{REP}(C) = \{\langle 0^s, 0^n, c \rangle \mid (\exists u \in \Gamma^{[s]})[\kappa_{C_n}(u) = \kappa_{\mathrm{Circ}_n}(c)]\},$$

where Circ is the circuit representation for boolean functions.

Aizenstein et al. [1] showed that there is a representation $K \in P$ such that its representation problem REP(K) is complete for Σ_2^P. The representation K can be described as follows. Concept names are of the form $c \vee t$, where c is a boolean circuit over an even number of variables $x_1, \ldots, x_n$, and t is a conjunction containing exactly one literal for each of the first $n/2$ variables $x_1, \ldots, x_{n/2}$. The concept represented by $c \vee t$ is the set of all $x \in \{0,1\}^n$ such that c accepts x or t is true under the assignment x. (In [1] a 3CNF formula is used in place of a circuit as above. This, however, does not affect the Σ_2^P-completeness of REP(K).)

Let us first consider the complexity of learning K with equivalence queries to K. By answering each query $c \vee t$ with a counterexample x that fulfills the conjunction t it is easy to see that any learner under Eq(K) needs at least $2^{n/2} - 1$ queries to identify the target.

Proposition 1. K *does not have polynomial learning complexity under* Eq(K).

If we allow arbitrary circuits as hypotheses, then in contrast to the previous proposition, K is learnable with a polynomial number of queries by using a simple majority-vote strategy.

Proposition 2. K *has polynomial learning complexity under* Eq(Circ).

Recall that in our definition of polynomial learning complexity for a representation of concepts C, we insist that the learning algorithm A outputs a concept name h such that independently of the protocol, the concept represented by h with respect to C is equivalent to the target. This allows us to proof that if K is polynomial-time learnable under Eq(Circ) with an oracle in NP, then the representation problem for K is in Δ_2^P. Combining this with the Σ_2^P-completeness of REP(K) we get the following theorem.

Theorem 3. K *is not polynomial-time learnable under* Eq($Circ$) *with an oracle in* NP, *unless the polynomial-time hierarchy collapses to* Δ_2^P.

Thus we have found representations C and P satisfying the conditions of Theorem 2 but C is not polynomial-time learnable under P relative to an oracle in NP, unless the polynomial hierarchy collapses to Δ_2^P. In fact, by Theorem 2, K is polynomial-time learnable under Eq($Circ$) with an oracle in NP if and only if the polynomial-time hierarchy collapses to Δ_2^P.

The non-learnability of K under Eq($Circ$) with an oracle in NP relies on the fact, that we allow equivalence queries that are arbitrary circuits but we insist that the output is of the form $c \vee t$. For a similar non-learnability result for K where both the output and the hypothesis are of the form $c \vee t$, we now consider learning with *projective* equivalence queries [7,4]. A projective equivalence query with respect to a representation C of hypotheses is a pair of the form $\langle \alpha, h \rangle$, where $\alpha \in \{0,1,*\}^n$. The *partial assignment* α describes the hypercube G_α consisting of all strings $x \in \{0,1\}^n$ such that x coincides with α on all positions where α is not $*$. In response to a query $\langle \alpha, h \rangle$, the answer is "Yes" if $\kappa_n(h)$ coincides with the target on all strings in the hypercube G_α. Otherwise, the answer consists of a string x in the hypercube G_α for which $\kappa_n(h)$ does not agree with the target. Let Proj-Eq(C) denote a representation of the corresponding protocol. By adapting the proof in [11] that boolean circuits are polynomial-time learnable under Eq($Circ$) with an oracle in Σ_2^P we can show the following theorem.

Theorem 4. K *is polynomial-time learnable under* Proj-Eq(K) *relative to an oracle in* Σ_2^P.

Similarly as in Theorem 3, the learnability of K under Proj-Eq(K) with an oracle in NP implies that the representation problem from K is in Δ_2^P.

Theorem 5. K *is not polynomial-time learnable under* Proj-Eq(K) *relative to an oracle in* NP, *unless the polynomial-time hierarchy collapses to* Δ_2^P.

Acknowledgements. For helpful conversations and suggestions on this work we are very grateful to José Balcázar, Jorge Castro, Richard Gavaldà, and David Guijarro.

References

[1] H. Aizenstein, T. Hegedüs, L. Hellerstein, and L. Pitt. Complexity theoretic hardness results for query learning. *Computational Complexity*, 7:19–53, 1998.

[2] D. Angluin. Queries and concept learning. *Machine Learning*, 2:319–342, 1988.

[3] D. Angluin and M. Kharitonov. When won't membership queries help? *Journal of Computer and System Sciences*, 50:336–355, 1995.

[4] J. Balcázar, J. Castro, and D. Guijarro. Abstract combinatorial characterizations of exact learning via queries. In *Proc. 13th ACM Conference on Computational Learning Theory*, pages 248–254. Morgan Kaufmann, 2000.

[5] J. Balcázar, J. Castro, and D. Guijarro. A general dimension for exact learning. In *Proc. 14th ACM Conference on Computational Learning Theory*, volume 2111 of *Lecture Notes in Artificial Intelligence*, pages 354–367. Springer-Verlag, Berlin Heidelberg New York, 2001.

[6] N. Bshouty, R. Cleve, R. Gavaldà, S. Kannan, and C. Tamon. Oracles and queries that are sufficient for exact learning. *Journal of Computer and System Sciences*, 52:421–433, 1996.

[7] L. Hellerstein and M. Karpinsky. Learning read-once formulas using membership queries. In *Proc. 2nd ACM Conference on Computational Learning Theory*, pages 146–161. Morgan Kaufmann, 1989.

[8] L. Hellerstein, K. Pillaipakkamnatt, V. Raghavan, and D. Wilkins. How many queries are needed to learn? *Journal of the ACM*, 43(5):840–862, 1996.

[9] M. J. Kearns and L. G. Valiant. Cryptographic limitations on learning boolean formulae and finite automata. *Journal of the ACM*, 41:67–95, 1994.

[10] J. Köbler. Lowness-Eigenschaften und Erlernbarkeit von Booleschen Schaltkreis-klassen. Habilitationsschrift, Universität Ulm, 1995.

[11] J. Köbler and W. Lindner. Oracles in Σ_2^p are sufficient for exact learning. *International Journal of Foundations of Computer Science*, 11(4):615–632, 2000.

[12] C. Papadimitriou. *Computational Complexity*. Addison-Wesley, 1994.

[13] O. Watanabe. A framework for polynomial time query learnability. *Mathematical Systems Theory*, 27:211–229, 1994.

[14] O. Watanabe and R. Gavaldà. Structural analysis of polynomial time query learnability. *Mathematical Systems Theory*, 27:231–256, 1994.

On the Absence of Predictive Complexity for Some Games

Yuri Kalnishkan and Michael V. Vyugin

Department of Computer Science, Royal Holloway,
University of London, Egham, Surrey, TW20 0EX,
United Kingdom
{yura, misha}@cs.rhul.ac.uk

Abstract. This paper shows that if the curvature of the boundary of the set of superpredictions for a game vanishes in a nontrivial way, then there is no predictive complexity for the game. This is the first result concerning the absence of complexity for games with convex sets of superpredictions. The proof is further employed to show that for some games there are no certain variants of weak predictive complexity. In the case of the absolute-loss game we reach a tight demarcation between the existing and non-existing variants of weak predictive complexity.

1 Introduction

In this paper we consider on-line prediction protocols. An on-line prediction algorithm $\mathfrak{A}$ receives elements of a sequence one by one and tries to predict each element before it actually sees it. The discrepancy between the prediction and the outcome is measured by a loss function and loss over several trials sums up to the total loss $\mathrm{Loss}_{\mathfrak{A}}$. A particular environment of this kind is called a game.

Predictive complexity was introduced in [VW98] as a natural development of the theory of prediction with expert advice. Predictive complexity bounds from below the cumulative error suffered by any on-line learning algorithm on a sequence. It may be considered as an inherent measure of 'learnability' of a string in the same way as Kolmogorov complexity reflects the 'simplicity' of a string.

We investigate the problem of the existence of predictive complexity. Papers [Vov90,VW98] introduce a property of a game called mixability, which is shown to be sufficient for the existence of predictive complexity for the game. It remains an open problem to show whether this is a necessary condition or to formulate other necessary conditions.

The first (rather trivial) result along this line was obtained in [KVV01]. It was proved that if the set of superpredictions for a game is not convex, then there is no predictive complexity for the game. In fact, the convexity of the set of superpredictions is a very weak condition. Most of the interesting games satisfy it anyway. An example of a game that satisfies it but is not mixable is given by the absolute-loss game.

N. Cesa-Bianchi et al. (Eds.): ALT 2002, LNAI 2533, pp. 164–172, 2002.

The main result of the paper is a sufficient condition for the absence of predictive complexity. This sufficient condition can apply to games with convex sets of superpredictions as well. This development is based on a characterisation of mixable games given in [KV02]. It is shown in [KV02] that, provided some natural conditions hold, a game is mixable if and only if the curvature of the nontrivial part of the boundary of the set of superpredictions does not vanish. In this paper we prove that if the curvature vanishes, there is no predictive complexity for the game. The absolute-loss game provides an example.

The results of [KV02] and this paper lead to a new open problem. If there is no predictive complexity for a game, what is the strongest weak complexity for this game? Our results allow us to give a complete result for the absolute-loss game, which has predictive complexity up to the square root of the length of a string.

2 Preliminaries

2.1 Games and Complexities

A *game* $\mathfrak{G}$ is a triple $(\mathbb{B}, [0,1], \lambda)$, where $\mathbb{B} = \{0,1\}$ is an *outcome space*[1], $[0,1]$ is a *prediction space*, and $\lambda : \mathbb{B} \times [0,1] \to [0,+\infty]$ is a *loss function*. We suppose that λ is continuous w.r.t. the extended topology of $[-\infty, +\infty]$ and computable. The *square-loss* game with $\lambda(\omega, \gamma) = (\omega - \gamma)^2$, the *absolute-loss* game with $\lambda(\omega, \gamma) = |\omega - \gamma|$, and the *logarithmic* game with

$$\lambda(\omega, \gamma) = \begin{cases} -\log(1 - \gamma) & \text{if } \omega = 0 \\ -\log \gamma & \text{if } \omega = 1 \end{cases},$$

where log stands for the binary logarithm $\log_2$, are examples of games.

A prediction algorithm $\mathfrak{A}$ works according to the following protocol:

```
FOR t = 1, 2, ...
   (1) 𝔄 chooses a prediction γt ∈ [0, 1]
   (2) 𝔄 observes the actual outcome ωt ∈ 𝔹
   (3) 𝔄 suffers loss λ(ωt, γt)
END FOR.
```

Over the first T trials, $\mathfrak{A}$ suffers the total loss

$$\text{Loss}_{\mathfrak{A}}^{\mathfrak{G}}(\omega_1, \omega_2, \ldots, \omega_T) = \sum_{t=1}^{T} \lambda(\omega_t, \gamma_t) .$$

By definition, put $\text{Loss}_{\mathfrak{A}}(\Lambda) = 0$, where Λ denotes the empty string.

A *loss process* is a function $\text{Loss}_{\mathfrak{A}} : \mathbb{B}^* \to [0, +\infty]$, where $\mathfrak{A}$ is some prediction algorithm. Our goal is to find a universal process. Unfortunately, the set of

---

[1] In this paper we restrict ourselves to binary games of this kind. A more general definition is possible.

loss processes does not contain natural universal elements except for degenerate games. We need to extend the class of loss processes to the class of superloss processes, which exhibits nicer properties.

We say that a pair $(s_0, s_1) \in [-\infty, +\infty]^2$ is a *superprediction* w.r.t. $\mathfrak{G}$ if there exists a prediction $\gamma \in [0, 1]$ such that $s_0 \geq \lambda(0, \gamma)$ and $s_1 \geq \lambda(1, \gamma)$. If we let $P = \{(p_0, p_1) \in [-\infty, +\infty]^2 \mid \exists \gamma \in [0, 1] : p_0 = \lambda(0, \gamma) \text{ and } p_1 = \lambda(1, \gamma)\}$ (cf. the canonical form of a game in [Vov98]), the set S of all superpredictions is the set of points that lie 'north-east' of P.

A function $L : \mathbb{B}^* \to \mathbb{R} \cup \{+\infty\}$ is called a *superloss process* w.r.t. $\mathfrak{G}$ (see [VW98]) if

- $L(\Lambda) = 0$,
- for every $x \in \mathbb{B}^*$, the pair $(L(x0) - L(x), L(x1) - L(x))$ is a superprediction w.r.t. $\mathfrak{G}$, and
- L is semicomputable from above.

Now we can define different variants of predictive complexity. A superloss process $\mathcal{K}$ w.r.t. a game $\mathfrak{G} = \langle \mathbb{B}, [0, 1], \lambda \rangle$ is called *(simple) predictive complexity* w.r.t. $\mathfrak{G}$ if for every other superloss process L w.r.t. $\mathfrak{G}$ there is a constant C such that the inequality $\mathcal{K}(x) \leq L(x) + C$ holds for every $x \in \mathbb{B}^*$.

The definition can be relaxed as follows. A superloss process $\mathcal{K}$ is *predictive complexity up to* $f(n)$, where $f : \mathbb{N} \to [0, +\infty)$, if for every other superloss process L there is a constant C such that the inequality $\mathcal{K}(x) \leq L(x) + Cf(|x|)$ holds for every $x \in \mathbb{B}^*$ ($|x|$ denotes the length of a string x). The definition makes sense if $f(n) = o(n)$ as $n \to +\infty$.

2.2   Mixability and the Existence of Complexity

For games $\mathfrak{G}$ of the type $(\mathbb{B}, [0, 1], \lambda)$ the condition of mixability can be formulated in the following way. Let S be the set of superpredictions for $\mathfrak{G}$. For every $\beta \in (0, 1)$ consider the homeomorphism $\mathfrak{B}_\beta : [-\infty, \infty]^2 \to [0, +\infty]^2$ specified by the formulae

$$\begin{cases} x \to \beta^x \\ y \to \beta^y \ . \end{cases}$$

We say that $\mathfrak{G}$ is β-mixable if the image $\mathfrak{B}_\beta(S)$ is convex. The game $\mathfrak{G}$ is mixable if it is β-mixable for some $\beta \in (0, 1)$.

Proposition 1 ([VW98]). *If a game $\mathfrak{G}$ is mixable, then there exists simple predictive complexity $\mathcal{K}^\mathfrak{G}$ w.r.t. $\mathfrak{G}$.*

Remark 1. The concept of mixability originated from the theory of prediction with expert advice (see [Vov98] for details). This theory addresses the following problem. Suppose there are n experts $\mathcal{E}_1, \mathcal{E}_2, \ldots, \mathcal{E}_N$ that work according to the same on-line protocol but on each trial they output their predictions earlier than the prediction algorithm $\mathfrak{A}$. The prediction algorithm observes their predictions and then makes its own. No restrictions are imposed on the behaviour of the experts; they do not have to be computable, independent, or satisfy any assumptions like i.i.d. The goal of the prediction algorithm is to suffer loss that in not much worse than the loss of the best expert.

The papers [Vov90] and [Vov98] proposed a strategy called *the Aggregating Algorithm* for the learner $\mathfrak{A}$. This strategy is optimal in some sence. Using this strategy, it may be shown that a game $\mathfrak{G}$ is mixable if and only if for any positive integer N there is a constant C_N such that for all sets of experts $\mathcal{E}_1, \mathcal{E}_1, \ldots, \mathcal{E}_N$, all integers T and all sequences of outcomes $\omega_1, \omega_2, \ldots, \omega_T$ the learner $\mathfrak{A}$ achieves the loss satisfying the inequality

$$\mathrm{Loss}_{\mathfrak{A}}^{\mathfrak{G}}(\omega_1, \omega_2, \ldots, \omega_T) \leq \mathrm{Loss}_{\mathcal{E}_i}^{\mathfrak{G}}(\omega_1, \omega_2, \ldots, \omega_T) + C_N$$

for any $i = 1, 2, \ldots, n$. If the game is β-mixable, we can take $C_N = \ln N / \ln(1/\beta)$.

If a game is mixable, then the real part of the set of superpredictions $S \cap \mathbb{R}^2$ is convex. However convexity does not imply mixability since the absolute-loss game is not mixable.

The paper [KV02] contains a partial characterisation of mixable games. We will discuss it here briefly.

Consider the real boundary the $\partial(S \cap \mathbb{R}^2)$. It consists of, perhaps, one or two open half-lines and a curve. The case when both half-lines are present is especially important. If λ is bounded, then this situation occurs. Conversely, if ∂S contains a vertical and a horizontal half-line, it can be specified by a game with a bounded loss function. We will call such games *bounded*.

Let this be the case, i.e., let $\partial(S \cap \mathbb{R}^2)$ consist of two half-lines and a curve A. Suppose that $S \cap \mathbb{R}^2$ is convex and A is twice continuously differentiable all the way including the endpoints. If the curvature of A vanishes at an internal point of A, the game is not mixable. If the curvature vanishes at an endpoint and the corresponding half-tangent at that endpoint is neither vertical nor horizontal, the game is not mixable either. On the other hand, if the curvature never vanishes, the game is mixable. The case of the curvature vanishing at an endpoint where A touches a horizontal or vertical line is trickier and is partly an open problem.

These considerations immediately imply that the square-loss game is mixable and the absolute-loss game is not.

Remark 2. Suppose that two games, $\mathfrak{G}_1$ and $\mathfrak{G}_2$, have sets of superpredictions S_1 and S_2 that differ by a shift, i.e., there is a pair of numbers $(x_0, y_0) \in \mathbb{R}^2$ such that $S_2 = \{(x + x_0, y + y_0) \in [-\infty, +\infty]^2 \mid (x, y) \in S_1\}$. Clearly, there is predictive complexity w.r.t. $\mathfrak{G}_1$ if and only if there is predictive complexity w.r.t. $\mathfrak{G}_2$. Indeed, there is a one-to-one correspondence between superloss processes for the games. If L_1 is a superloss process w.r.t. $\mathfrak{G}_1$, then L_2, defined by the formula $L_2(x) = L_1(x) + x_0 r + y_0 s$, where r is the number of 0s and s is the number of 1s in x, is a superloss process w.r.t. $\mathfrak{G}_2$.

A shift can alter the set of superpredictions S in such a way that it will no longer be contained in $[0, +\infty]^2$. This does not present an obstacle to the theory of predictive complexity. The definition of a loss function λ can be relaxed to allow λ to accept values from $[a, +\infty]$, where $a \in \mathbb{R}$ is an arbitrary number. All definitions and results from this paper remain valid.

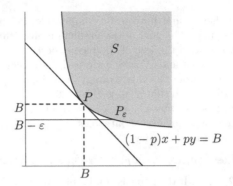

Fig. 1. Construction of the strategy L_ε for Theorem 1.

3   Main Results

Our main result states that if the curvature of ∂S vanishes, the game does not define predictive complexity. The proof works if the boundary is a smooth curve at least on one side of a point P where the curvature vanishes; when speaking about the derivatives at P, we mean one-sided derivatives. Therefore the theorem can be applied to endpoints of bounded games. The only restriction is that the tangent at P should be neither vertical nor horizontal. The situation with horisontal and vertical tangents remain an open problem much in the same way as in [KV02].

Theorem 1. *Let* $\mathfrak{G} = (\mathbb{B}, [0,1], \lambda)$ *be a game with the set of superpredictions* S *and let* P *be an endpoint of an arc* $A \subseteq \partial(S \cap \mathbb{R}^2)$ *such that* A *is a curve that is twice continuously differentiable all the way from one point to another and thrice differentiable at* P *and the corresponding half-tangent at* P *is neither vertical nor horizontal. If the curvature vanishes at* P, *then there is no predictive complexity w.r.t.* $\mathfrak{G}$.

Proof. Assume the converse. Let $\mathcal{K}$ be (simple) predictive complexity w.r.t. the game $\mathfrak{G}$.

Without restricting the generality, it can be assumed that $P = (B, B)$ for some positive B, since the games with sets of superpredictions that differ by a shift of the extended plane $[-\infty, +\infty]^2$ specify predictive complexities simultaneously. Figure 1 illustrates the proof.

Consider the half-tangent from the condition of the theorem. We can assume that S lies above the straight line since otherwise $S \cap \mathbb{R}^2$ is not convex; it was shown in [KV02] that if $S \cap \mathbb{R}^2$ is not convex, then there is no predictive complexity. The equation of the line can be reduced to the form $(1-p)x+py = B$, where $p \in (0,1)$.

Consider random variables $\xi_1^{(p)}, \ldots, \xi_n^{(p)}$ that are outcomes of independent Bernoulli trials with the probability of 1 being equal to p. We need Lemma 3 from [Kal02] to bound the expectations of $\mathcal{K}(\xi_1^{(p)} \ldots \xi_n^{(p)})$ from below. According to the lemma, since S lies above the line $(1 - p)x + py = B$, we have

$$\mathbf{E}\mathcal{K}(\xi_1^{(p)} \ldots \xi_n^{(p)}) \geq Bn \tag{1}$$

for all $n = 1, 2, \ldots$.

We now proceed to constructing an upper bound. Take $\theta > 0$ and let

$$P_\theta(n) = \Pr(\text{more than } np + \theta\sqrt{n} \text{ variables among } \xi_1^{(p)}, \ldots, \xi_n^{(p)} \text{ equal 1}) \ . \tag{2}$$

It follows from the DeMoivre-Laplace Limit Theorem (see, e.g., [Fel68]) that $P_\theta(n) = \delta + o(1)$ as $n \to \infty$, where δ is a number from the interval $(0, 1)$.

Suppose that P is the 'upper' end of the arc A; the other case can be treated in a similar manner. Consider the point $(B + \frac{p}{1-p}\varepsilon, B - \varepsilon)$, where $\varepsilon > 0$. We need to approximate it by a point from S. For the sake of being definite, take the point $P_\varepsilon \in \partial(S \cap \mathbb{R}^2)$ with the second coordinate $B - \varepsilon$. Suppose that P_ε is thus defined for each $\varepsilon \in (0, \varepsilon_0]$.

Let $\mathfrak{A}_\varepsilon$, where $\varepsilon \in (0, \varepsilon_0]$, be the strategy that outputs a prediction corresponding to P_ε and let L_ε be the loss of this strategy. Consider a string x of length n with more than $np + \theta\sqrt{n}$ elements equal to 1. It is easy to see that there are positive numbers α and K such that

$$L_\varepsilon(x) \leq (B + \alpha\varepsilon^3)n - \varepsilon\theta\sqrt{n} + K \tag{3}$$

as $\varepsilon \to 0$. Indeed, consider a pseudo strategy that suffers loss $B + \frac{p}{1-p}\varepsilon$ on $\omega = 0$ and $B - \varepsilon$ on $\omega = 1$. If the number of 1s in y of length n is exactly pn, this pseudo strategy suffers loss Bn on y; on each step $\mathfrak{A}_\varepsilon$ would suffer loss different by no more than $O(\varepsilon^3)$. If the number of 1s in x is greater than $pn + \theta\sqrt{n}$, the loss on x is less by $\varepsilon\theta\sqrt{n}$.

We also need the trivial strategy $\mathfrak{A}_0$ that always makes the prediction corresponding to the point P; let L_0 be the loss of $\mathfrak{A}_0$.

Now let us construct the strategy $\mathfrak{A}$. Consider a very rapidly increasing sequence of natural numbers. For definiteness sake, let it be the sequence defined recursively by $n_1 = 1$ and $n_{i+1} = 2^{n_i}$, $i = 1, 2, \ldots$. Let i_0 be minimal such that $n_{i_0} \geq s/\sqrt[4]{\varepsilon_0}$ (s will be specified below). The strategy $\mathfrak{A}$ works as follows. While the number t of the trial is less than or equal to n_{i_0}, it imitates $\mathfrak{A}_0$. If t is such that $n_i < t \leq n_{i+1}$ and $i \geq i_0$, the strategy $\mathfrak{A}$ imitates $\mathfrak{A}_{\varepsilon_{i+1}}$ with $\varepsilon_{i+1} = s/\sqrt[4]{n_{i+1}}$, where the value of s will be specified below. Let L be the loss of $\mathfrak{A}$.

We can now construct the upper bound for the expectation. It follows from the definition of predictive complexity that there is a positive constant C such that the inequalities

$$\mathcal{K}(x) \leq \text{Loss}_{\mathfrak{A}_0}(x) + C, \tag{4}$$

$$\mathcal{K}(x) \leq \text{Loss}_{\mathfrak{A}}(x) + C \tag{5}$$

hold. Consider $n = n_i$, $i > i_0$. Take $\varepsilon_i = s/\sqrt[4]{n_i}$. For each string $\boldsymbol{x}$ of length n the difference between $L_{\varepsilon_i}(\boldsymbol{x})$ and $L(\boldsymbol{x})$ is bounded in the absolute value by $Rn_{i-1} = R\log n$, where R is independent of i (indeed, all points $(\lambda(0,\gamma), \lambda(1,\gamma))$ for the predictions we have considered in building strategies are confined to a certain finite velocity of the point P).

We will use (5) to estimate $\mathcal{K}(\boldsymbol{x})$ on strings $\boldsymbol{x}$ of length n with more than $Bn + \theta\varepsilon\sqrt{n}$ elements equal to 1 and (4) on the rest of strings of length n. We get

$$\mathbf{E}\mathcal{K}(\xi_1^{(p)} \ldots \xi_n^{(p)}) \leq (1 - P_\theta(n))(Bn + C) + P_\theta(n)\left(\left(B + \alpha s^3 \frac{1}{n^{3/4}}\right)n\right.$$
$$\left. - \frac{1}{n^{1/4}}\theta sn^{1/2} + K + R\log n + C\right).$$

It is easy to see that the constant s can be chosen in such a way as to ensure that the term $\theta sn^{1/4}$ dominates and therefore there are positive constants α_1 and $\tilde{R}$ such that

$$\mathbf{E}\mathcal{K}(\xi_1^{(p)} \ldots \xi_n^{(p)}) \leq Bn - \alpha_1 n^{1/4} + \tilde{R}\log n + C . \tag{6}$$

Comparing (6) against (1) yields

$$C \geq \alpha_2 n^{1/4} \tag{7}$$

for some positive α_2, where n obtains infinitely many values n_i, $i > i_0$. The contradiction proves the theorem. $\square$

Compared with the results of [KV02], this theorem allows us to claim that, under certain conditions, mixability is equivalent to the existence of predictive complexity.

Corollary 1. *Let* $\mathfrak{G} = (\mathbb{B}, [0, 1], \lambda)$ *be a bounded game with the set of superpredictions* S. *Let the boundary* $\partial(S \cap \mathbb{R}^2)$ *consists of two half-lines and a curve* A *which is thrice differentiable all the way including endpoints. Suppose that each endpoint satisfy the following condition: either the curvature does not vanish or the half-tangent is neither vertical nor horizontal. Then* $\mathfrak{G}$ *is mixable if and only if there exists predictive complexity w.r.t.* $\mathfrak{G}$.

4 Weak Complexities

The definition of predictive complexity given in Subsect. 2.1 can be relaxed in the following way. Let $\mathfrak{G}$ be a game as in Subsect. 2.1. A superloss process $\mathcal{K}$ is *predictive complexity up to* $f(n)$, where $f : \mathbb{N} \to [0, +\infty)$, if for every other superloss process L there is a constant C such that the inequality $\mathcal{K}(\boldsymbol{x}) \leq L(\boldsymbol{x}) + Cf(|\boldsymbol{x}|)$ holds for every $\boldsymbol{x} \in \mathbb{B}^*$ ($|\boldsymbol{x}|$ denotes the length of a string $\boldsymbol{x}$). The definition makes sense if $f(n) = o(n)$ as $n \to +\infty$. (Simple) predictive complexity is complexity up to a constant.

The paper [KV02] contains a number of sufficient conditions for a game to specify weak predictive complexity. It is shown that for every bounded game having the set of superpredictions S with the convex real part $S \cap \mathbb{R}^2$ there is weak predictive complexity up to some $f(n) = o(n)$. Under certain conditions (e.g., under the conditions of Corollary 1) it may be shown that the game have complexity up to $\sqrt{n}$.

The problem of finding a general criterion for the existence of complexity can thus be generalised to the following problem. Given a game, what is the strongest variant of predictive complexity it specifies?

The proof of Theorem 1 can be modified to prove the following.

Corollary 2. *Under the conditions of Theorem 1, if $f(n) = o(n^{1/4})$ as $n \to +\infty$, then there is no predictive complexity up to $f(n)$ w.r.t. $\mathfrak{G}$.*

Proof. The constant C in the proof of Theorem 1 can be replaced by a function in the length of a string. Inequality (7) transforms into the inequality $C(n) \geq \alpha_2 n^{1/4}$ that holds for infinitely many $n \in \mathbb{N}$. □

This result can be strengthened in the following way. Suppose that ∂S is smooth in a vicinity of P, i.e., smooth on both sides of this point. Let g be the function whose graph represents ∂S in a vicinity of $P = (B, B)$. If the curvature vanishes at P, then $g''(B) = 0$. However if $S \cap \mathbb{R}^2$ is convex, the third derivative $g^{(3)}(B)$ should vanish too.

Corollary 3. *Let $\mathfrak{G} = (\mathbb{B}, [0, 1], \lambda)$ be a game having the set of superpredictions S with the convex real part $S \cap \mathbb{R}^2$ and let P be an internal point of an arc $A \subseteq \partial(S \cap \mathbb{R}^2)$ such that A is a curve that is thrice continuously differentiable all the way and four times differentiable at P and the tangent at P is neither vertical nor horizontal. If the curvature vanishes at A and $f(n) = o(n^{1/3})$ as $n \to +\infty$, then there is no predictive complexity up to $f(n)$ w.r.t. $\mathfrak{G}$.*

Proof. The above remark shows that when choosing P_ε in the proof of Theorem 1, we can achieve better approximation. It is possible to ensure the existence of constants α and K such that (3) can be replaced by

$$L_\varepsilon(\boldsymbol{x}) \leq (B + \alpha\varepsilon^4)n - \varepsilon\theta\sqrt{n} + K \tag{8}$$

as $\varepsilon \to 0$. On trials t such that $n_i < t \leq n_{i+1}$ the strategy $\mathfrak{A}$ should imitate $\mathfrak{A}_{\varepsilon_i}$ with $\varepsilon_i = 1/\sqrt[6]{n_{i+1}}$. We finally get a tighter inequality instead of (7). □

Our construction yields the strongest results for games with ∂S containing line segments.

Corollary 4. *Let $\mathfrak{G} = (\mathbb{B}, [0, 1], \lambda)$ be a game having the set of superpredictions S with the convex real part $S \cap \mathbb{R}^2$. If $\partial(S \cap \mathbb{R}^2)$ contains a line segment that is neither vertical nor horizontal and there is predictive complexity up to $f(n)$ w.r.t. $\mathfrak{G}$, then $f(n) = \Omega(\sqrt{n})$.*

Proof. It is sufficient to consider $\mathfrak{A}_\varepsilon$ from the proof of Theorem 1 with a small fixed ε. □

The known results on the existence of complexity (see [KV02]) allow us to formulate the following statements:

Corollary 5. *For the absolute-loss game there is predictive complexity up to $\sqrt{n}$. If there is predictive complexity for the absolute-loss game up to $f(n)$, then $f(n) = \Omega(\sqrt{n})$.*

Corollary 6. *Let $\mathfrak{G} = (\mathbb{B}, [0,1], \lambda)$ be a bounded game with the set of superpredictions S. Let the boundary $\partial(S \cap \mathbb{R}^2)$ consists of two half-lines and a curve A which is thrice differentiable all the way including endpoints. Suppose that each endpoint satisfy the following condition: either the curvature does not vanish or the half-tangent is neither vertical not horizontal. Then one of the following cases holds:*

- *there is (simple) predictive complexity w.r.t. $\mathfrak{G}$*
- *there is predictive complexity up to $\sqrt{n}$ w.r.t. $\mathfrak{G}$ but if $f = o(\sqrt[4]{n})$ then there is no predictive complexity up to $f(n)$ w.r.t. $\mathfrak{G}$.*

Our demarcation for general games is not tight; to determine the best $f(n)$ remains an open problem.

References

[Fel68]   W. Feller. *An Introduction to Probability Theory and Its Applications*, volume I. John Wiley & Sons, Inc, 3rd edition, 1968.

[Kal02]   Y. Kalnishkan. General linear relations among different types of predictive complexity. *Theoretical Computer Science*, 271:181–200, 2002.

[KV02]   Y. Kalnishkan and M. V. Vyugin. Mixability and the existence of weak complexities. In Jyrki Kivinen and Robert H. Sloan, editors, *Computational Learning Theory, 15th Annual Conference on Computational Learning Theory, COLT 2002, Sydney, Australia, July 8-10, 2002, Proceedings*, volume 2375 of *Lecture Notes in Artificial Intelligence*, pages 105–120. Springer, 2002.

[KVV01]   Y. Kalnishkan, M. Vyugin, and V. Vovk. Losses, complexities and the Legendre transformation. In Naoki Abe, Roni Khardon, and Thomas Zeugmann, editors, *Proceedings of the 12th International Conference on Algorithmic Learning Theory, ALT 2001*, volume 2225 of *Lecture Notes in Artificial Intelligence*. Springer-Verlag, 2001.

[Vov90]   V. Vovk. Aggregating strategies. In M. Fulk and J. Case, editors, *Proceedings of the 3rd Annual Workshop on Computational Learning Theory*, pages 371–383, San Mateo, CA, 1990. Morgan Kaufmann.

[Vov98]   V. Vovk. A game of prediction with expert advice. *Journal of Computer and System Sciences*, 56:153–173, 1998.

[VW98]   V. Vovk and C. J. H. C. Watkins. Universal portfolio selection. In *Proceedings of the 11th Annual Conference on Computational Learning Theory*, pages 12–23, 1998.

Consistency Queries in Information Extraction

Gunter Grieser[1], Klaus P. Jantke[2], and Steffen Lange[2]

[1] Technische Universität Darmstadt, Fachbereich Informatik,
Alexanderstr. 10, 64283 Darmstadt, Germany,
`grieser@informatik.tu-darmstadt.de`
[2] Deutsches Forschungszentrum für Künstliche Intelligenz,
Stuhlsatzenhausweg 3, 66123 Saarbrücken, Germany,
`{jantke,lange}@dfki.de`

Abstract. A new formal framework of learning – learning by consistency queries – is introduced and studied. The theoretical approach outlined here is implemented as the core technology of a prototypical development system named LExIKON which supports interactive information extraction in practically relevant cases exactly in the way described in the present paper.

The overall scenario of learning by consistency queries for information extraction is formalized and different constraints on the query learners are discussed and formulated. The principle learning power of the resulting types of query learners is analyzed by comparing it to the power of well-known types of standard learning devices including unconstrained inductive inference machines as well as consistent, total, finite, and iterative learners.

1 Motivation

The development of tools and technologies for information extraction (IE) from the Internet is an urgent need to cope with the current flood of Internet pages rapidly approaching the amount of 3 billions. There is an enormous variety of approaches mostly aiming at indexing techniques which allow for a focussed selection of source documents. Computational linguistics is frequently involved.

The authors are currently engaged in a rather different innovative endeavour of developing, investigating, and applying inductive inference technologies for IE (cf. [4,5]), a project named LExIKON. In the next subsection, some selected screenshots from an experimental session with the LExIKON development system, version 1.2, are presented that may help to illustrate the application-oriented origins of the theoretical work presented.

1.1 Knowledge Extraction in the LExIKON Development System

Imagine the user is searching the Internet for bibliographic information about computational learning theory. What she finds on a certain source page are a collection of files prepared for download together with some describing textual

N. Cesa-Bianchi et al. (Eds.): ALT 2002, LNAI 2533, pp. 173–187, 2002.

information (see the lefthand frame in Fig 1). In such a situation, it might be highly desirable to provide tool support for extracting the relational information about file names and descriptions and for feeding this information into the enterprise's knowledge management infrastructure.

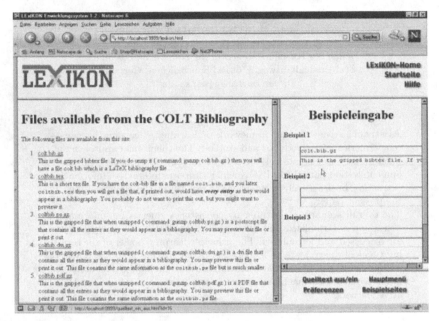

Fig. 1. Feeding the LExIKON system with a document and pointing to an example of information pieces of interest by insertion into the system's entry list "Beispieleingabe"

In the LExIKON system, a user is providing documents and, by pointing to information pieces of interest in a document under inspection, exemplifying what she is interested in. Fig. 1 displays a screenshot where the user is providing a single example of information which should be extracted from the document contained in the lefthand frame.

The information (i.e., a document together with a few examples to be extracted from this document) is fed into a learning engine. This engine is performing an inductive program synthesis task. It generates so-called wrappers, i.e., programs that extract, when applied to a document, a set of extracted information pieces. Naturally, the wrapper generated by the learning engine is hypothetical, since it originates from few examples only and may be the subject of further revisions in subsequent steps.

Whereas specialists may inspect the wrappers generated and have permission to download and, perhaps, modify these programs for their individual purposes, the vast majority of users must not be confronted with those technicalities. Instead, the hypothetical result of the LExIKON learning engine is communicated to the user by illustrating the power of the learnt wrapper on the underlying document. Instead of showing the current wrapper (written in some cumbersome programming language), the user is shown what the wrapper is extracting from the current document.

In the LExIKON development system, the user simply receives a list of all information pieces that are extracted from the underlying document (see Fig. 2).

As the current wrapper is generated on the basis of very limited information, in some cases it might happen that the wrapper is not doing what the user expects. In these cases, the user is not required to specify abstractly what is wrong with the system's hypothesis. It is sufficient, instead, if she provides either an example that illustrates what is missing in the extraction results of the system or an example that illustrates what has been extracted erroneously.

In our example, the name of the last file and the describing textual information are missing. In Fig. 3, the corresponding example is provided. The final screenshot displayed in Fig. 4 demonstrates the LExIKON system's learning success.

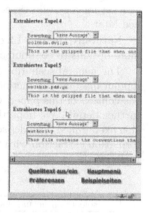

Fig. 2. The system returns the current extraction result to the user

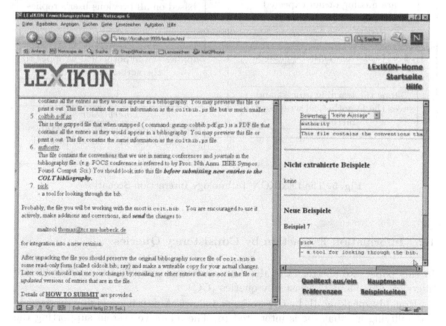

Fig. 3. Providing an example that is missed

When the user is satisfied with the result achieved on a sample document, she may proceed on another document or, alternatively, interrupt the learning process and adopt the generated wrapper, at least for a certain time. Learning may be continued later.

Naturally, in the LExIKON system there are more options to communicate with the system.

The general scenario of the LExIKON system's human-machine-interaction is surveyed in Fig. 5. In the context of this paper, we do not want to go into further details. We hope that the experimental session exemplified provides some impression of how information extraction with the LExIKON technology really works.

Fig. 4. The final wrapper extracts correctly

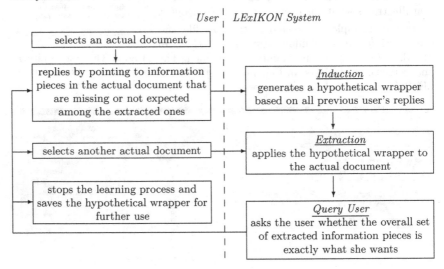

Fig. 5. The LExIKON Technology Interaction Scenario

1.2   Information Extraction by Consistency Queries

In this paper, we abstract the above scenario and introduce a novel inductive inference idea named consistency queries (CQ).

Roughly speaking, IE by CQ works as follows. A user is providing documents exemplifying in what she is interested in. The adaptive system supporting the user in IE contains a query learner as a core component which generates wrappers.

As discussed in the last subsection, the hypothetical results of machine learning for IE are not shown to the user. Instead, the wrappers are communicated by illustrating the power of the current wrapper by applying it on the underlying document, i.e., it is demonstrated which information pieces the wrapper is extracting from the current document.

In slightly more formal terms, the system is asking whether or not its current hypothesis is consistent with the user's expectations on some given document – a consistency query. The user either accepts the extraction results of the system or rejects them by providing a counter-example which is a information piece from the symmetric difference of the extraction results of the system and the extraction results the user expected.

When the user is satisfied with the result achieved on a sample document, she proceeds on another document.

IE by CQ is ultimately implemented by inductive program synthesis, but the computer programs synthesized are intentionally hidden from the user. Humans are not expected to evaluate computer-generated programs, but to express their (dis)satisfaction about a program's behaviour in particular application cases.

To sum up, the paper on hand accentuates two main aspects: On the one hand, we demonstrate how new concepts of recursion-theoretic inductive inference grow out from application-oriented research and development projects, what seems preferable to growing large varieties of definitions in the ivory tower of pure theory. On the other hand, the theoretical concepts carefully derived from application scenarios and from a truly implemented application system's behaviour allow for relating the system's power to well-studied hierarchies of learning problems. The potentials of the approach become understandable and can be circumscribed clearly.

The remaining part of of the present paper is organized as follows. In Section 2, we provide basic knowledge from inductive inference. The basic scenario of IE by QCs is formalized in Section 3. In Sections 4 and 5, the learning power of the different types of learning by CQs and of standard identification types is compared to one another. While Section 4 paraphrases the main results, Section 5 contains the relevant technical details. Finally, some conclusions are presented (see Section 6) and the relevant literature is given.

2   Basic Concepts from Inductive Inference

All unspecified notions can be found in [7].

$\mathbb{N}$ denotes the set of all natural numbers and $\wp(\mathbb{N})$ denotes the powerset of $\mathbb{N}$, i.e., the collection of all finite subsets of $\mathbb{N}$. Moreover, let $(F_i)_{i \in \mathbb{N}}$ be the canonical enumeration of all finite subsets of $\mathbb{N}$, where, by convention, F_0 equals the empty set $\emptyset$.

Let σ be an infinite sequence. Then, σ_n is the initial segment of length $n + 1$ and $\sigma(n)$ is the $(n + 1)$-st element of σ. σ_n^+ denotes the set of all elements contained in σ_n. Moreover, for any two finite sequences τ and ρ, we denote by $\tau \diamond \rho$ the concatenation of τ and ρ.

By $\mathcal{P}$ and $\mathcal{R}$ we denote the set of all partial recursive and all total recursive functions, respectively. Let $f \in \mathcal{P}$ and $x \in \mathbb{N}$. We write $f(x) \downarrow$ to indicate that $f(x)$ is defined. For the rest of this paper, we let φ be a fixed GÖDEL numbering of all partial recursive functions, where $\varphi_0(x) = 0$ for all $x \in \mathbb{N}$.

Let $f \in \mathcal{R}$. An infinite sequence $\sigma = ((x_n, f(x_n)))_{n \in \mathbb{N}}$ constitutes a representation of f, if $\{x_n \mid n \in \mathbb{N}\} = \mathbb{N}$. In case where $x_n = n$ for all $n \in \mathbb{N}$, σ is said to be the canonical representation of f. $Seq(f)$ is the collection of all representations of f.

The learning types defined below (cf. Definitions 1 and 2) have their origins in the standard inductive inference literature (cf., e.g., [3,6]).

As usual, we distinguish learning from all representations and learning from canonical representations.

Definition 1. *Let $\mathcal{C} \subseteq \mathcal{R}$ and let M be an IIM. Then, $\mathcal{C} \subseteq Lim^{arb}(M)$ iff for all $f \in \mathcal{C}$ and all $\sigma \in Seq(f)$:*
1. *For all $n \in \mathbb{N}$, $M(\sigma_n) \downarrow$.*
2. *There is a $j \in \mathbb{N}$ with $\varphi_j = f$ such that, for almost all $n \in \mathbb{N}$, $j = M(\sigma_n)$.*

By Lim^{arb} we denote the collection of all $\mathcal{C}' \subseteq \mathcal{R}$ for which there is an IIM M' such that $\mathcal{C}' \subseteq Lim^{arb}(M')$.

If $f \in Lim^{arb}(M)$, then M is said to learn f from all its representations. We write $f \in Lim(M)$, if M learns f from its canonical representation. Accordingly, Lim denotes the collection of all $\mathcal{C} \subseteq \mathcal{R}$ for which there is an IIM M that meets $f \in Lim(M)$ for all $f \in \mathcal{C}$. We adopt these conventions for the definitions below.

Next, in case when it is decidable whether or not M's actual hypothesis is correct, then M is a finite learner. Moreover, M is a consistent learner, if every hypothesis of M correctly reflects the information it was built upon, while M is said to be total, if every of its hypotheses is defined for all inputs. If M builds its actual hypothesis exclusively on the basis of its last hypothesis and the new example, M is said to work in an iterative manner. The corresponding learning models are denoted by *Fin*, *Total*, *Cons*, and *It*, respectively.

Definition 2. *Let $Idt \in \{Fin, Total, Cons, It\}$, let M be an IIM, and let $\mathcal{C} \subseteq Lim^{arb}(M)$. Then, $\mathcal{C} \subseteq Idt^{arb}(M)$ iff for all $f, f' \in \mathcal{C}$, all $\sigma \in Seq(f)$ all $\sigma' \in Seq(f')$, and all $n, m \in \mathbb{N}$, the corresponding defining constraint is fulfilled:*

Idt	Defining Constraint
Fin	$M(\sigma_n) = M(\sigma_{n+1})$ implies $\varphi_{M(\sigma_n)} = f$.
Total	$\varphi_{M(\sigma_n)} \in \mathcal{R}$.
Cons	For all $(x, f(x)) \in \sigma_n^+$, $\varphi_{M(\sigma_n)}(x) = f(x)$.
It	$M(\sigma_n) = M(\sigma'_m)$ and $\sigma(n+1) = \sigma'(m+1)$ imply $M(\sigma_{n+1}) = M(\sigma'_{m+1})$.

The following theorem summarizes the known relations between the identification types defined above (cf., e.g., [6]).

Theorem 1.
1. *For all $Idt \in \{Fin, Total, Lim\}$: $Idt^{arb} = Idt$.*
2. *$Fin \subset Total \subset Cons^{arb} \subset Cons \subset It \subset Lim$.*
3. *$Fin \subset It^{arb} \subset It$.*
4. *$Cons \mathbin{\#} It^{arb}$.*
5. *$Total \mathbin{\#} It^{arb}$.*

3 Learning for Information Extraction

In a characteristic scenario of system-supported IE, the user is taking a source document and is highlighting representative information pieces that are of interest. It is left to the system to understand how these information pieces are wrapped into syntactic expressions and to learn a procedure (henceforth called wrapper) that allows for an extraction of these information pieces.

3.1 Notions and Notations

A wrapper is a function that, given a document, returns a finite set of information pieces contained in the document. In our formal treatment, we use natural numbers to describe both documents as well as the information pieces extracted. Thus, a wrapper can be seen as a computable mapping from $\mathbb{N}$ to $\wp(\mathbb{N})$.

The rest of the paper relies on the following formalization which allows for a much simpler treatment. A wrapper is considered to be a computable mapping f from $\mathbb{N}$ to $\mathbb{N}$, where, for all $x \in \mathbb{N}$ with $f(x) \downarrow$, $f(x)$ is interpreted to denote the finite set $F_{f(x)}$. (* Recall that $(F_i)_{i \in \mathbb{N}}$ is the canonical enumeration of all finite subsets of $\mathbb{N}$, where $F_0 = \emptyset$. *) If $f(x) = 0$, the wrapper f fails to extract anything of interest from the document x.

3.2 Scenarios for Information Extraction

The figure below depicts an adaptive system for information extraction.

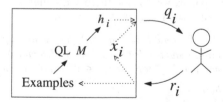

Fig. 6. A query learner as the core component of an adaptive system for IE

A query learner (QL, for short) constitutes the core component of an adaptive system for IE. Depending on the overall history of the interaction between the system and the user, the query learner generates a wrapper that is stored in the system. The system interacts with the user by asking consistency queries.

Via consistency queries, the system provides the user information about the behaviour of the stored wrapper in a user-friendly way. It presents exactly the information pieces (subsequently called data, for short) which can be extracted when applying the stored wrapper to the most recent document. The user answers a consistency query either by indicating that, focussing on the most recent document, the stored wrapper meets her expectations or by providing a counterexample that witnesses the weakness of the wrapper.

More formally speaking, the interaction between the system and the user takes place in accordance with the following rules.

Initially, the system starts with a default wrapper $h_0 = 0$ which does not extract any data from any document. (* Recall that $\varphi_0(x) = 0$ for all $x \in \mathbb{N}$ and that $F_0 = \emptyset$. *) Furthermore, the user selects an initial document d and presents d to the system.

The system applies the most recently stored wrapper h_i to the current document x_i, where $x_0 = d$. Let $F_{h_i(x_i)}$ be the set of data that has have been extracted from x_i by the wrapper h_i. (* Here, it has to be demanded that the wrapper h_i is defined on input x_i. Otherwise, the interaction between the system and the user will definitely crash. *) Now, the consistency query $q_i = (x_i, F_{h_i(x_i)})$ is presented to the user for evaluation.

Depending on whether or not $F_{h_i(x_i)}$ is correct (i.e., $F_{h_i(x_i)}$ contains only interesting data) and complete (i.e., $F_{h_i(x_i)}$ contains all interesting data), the user is going to answer the consistency query q_i. If her expectations are met, she signals that the wrapper h_i is accepted for the current document x_i. In doing so, she selects another document d' which is subject to further interrogation and returns the accepting reply $r_i = d'$. Otherwise, she selects either a data item n_i which was erroneously extracted from x_i (i.e., a negative example) or a data item p_i which is of interest in x_i and which was not extracted (i.e., a positive example). As a result, she returns the rejecting reply $r_i = (n_i, -)$ or $r_i = (p_i, +)$.

Now, the system stores and analyses the user's response. Based on all previous interactions, the last consistency query q_i, and the corresponding reply r_i, the query learner generates the wrapper h_{i+1} that is stored as its new hypothesis. Afterwards, the process continues as described above.

In the rest of the paper, we do not further distinguish between the system and its core component – the integrated query learner.

Definition 3. *Let $d \in \mathbb{N}$ and $I = ((q_i, r_i))_{i \in \mathbb{N}}$ be an infinite sequence. I is said to be an interaction sequence between a query learner M and a user U with respect to a target wrapper f iff for every $i \in \mathbb{N}$ the following conditions hold:*

1. $q_i = (x_i, E_i)$, *where*
   - $x_0 = d$ *and* $E_0 = \emptyset$.
   - $x_{i+1} = r_i$, *if* r_i *is an accepting reply.*
   - $x_{i+1} = x_i$, *if* r_i *is a rejecting reply.*
   - $E_{i+1} = F_{\varphi_{M(I_i)}(x_{i+1})}.$[1]

---

[1] Recall that it assumed that $\varphi_{M(I_i)}(x_{i+1}) \downarrow$. Since M has seen the document x_{i+1} before computing its hypothesis $M(I_i)$, it can exploit this *a priori* knowledge when determining $M(I_i)$. The latter guarantees the appropriateness of this assumption.

2. If $F_{f(x_i)} = E_i$, then r_i is an accepting reply, i.e., $r_i \in \mathbb{N}$.
3. If $F_{f(x_i)} \neq E_i$, then r_i is a rejecting reply, i.e., it holds either $r_i = (n_i, -)$ with $n_i \in E_i \setminus F_{f(x_i)}$ or $r_i = (p_i, +)$ with $p_i \in F_{f(x_i)} \setminus E_i$.

Next, we formulate requirements that make the interaction between the system and the user a reasonable one. In doing so, we formulate constraints on both, the user and the query learner.

Let $\mathcal{C}$ be a class of wrappers.

A query learner M is said to be *open-minded* with respect to $\mathcal{C}$ iff for all users U, all wrappers $f \in \mathcal{C}$, and all interaction sequences $I = ((q_i, r_i))_{i \in \mathbb{N}}$ between M and U with respect to f there are infinitely many $i \in \mathbb{N}$ such that r_i is an accepting reply.

An open-minded query learner does not get stuck in a single document. Conversely, if M is not open-minded, it might happen that the user does not get the opportunity to inform the system adequately about her expectations.

On the other hand, a query learner can only be successful in case when the user illustrates her intentions on various different documents. Consequently, a user U is said to be *co-operative* with respect to $\mathcal{C}$ iff for all open-minded query learners M, for all wrappers $f \in \mathcal{C}$, all interaction sequences $I = ((q_i, r_i))_{i \in \mathbb{N}}$ between M and U with respect to f, and all $x \in \mathbb{N}$ there is an accepting request r_i with $r_i = x$.

Definition 4. Let $\mathcal{C} \subseteq \mathcal{R}$ and let M be an open-minded query learner. $\mathcal{C} \subseteq LimCQ(M)$ iff for all co-operative users U, all wrappers $f \in \mathcal{C}$, and all interaction sequences I between M and U with respect to f there is a $j \in \mathbb{N}$ with $\varphi_j = f$ such that, for almost all $n \in \mathbb{N}$, $j = h_{n+1} = M(I_n)$.

By $LimCQ$ we denote the collection of all $\mathcal{C}' \subseteq \mathcal{R}$ for which there is an open-minded query learner M' such that $\mathcal{C}' \subseteq LimCQ(M')$.

Let M be an open-minded query learner and let $\mathcal{C} \subseteq LimCQ(M)$. Analogously to Definition 2, M witnesses $\mathcal{C} \in FinCQ$, if it is decidable whether or not the wrapper generated by M is correct. Moreover, M witnesses $\mathcal{C} \in ConsCQ$, if every wrapper generated by M correctly reflects the information it was built upon, while M witnesses $\mathcal{C} \in TotalCQ$, if every wrapper generated by M is defined for all inputs. Finally, M shows that $\mathcal{C} \in IncCQ$, if M builds its actual wrapper exclusively on the basis of its last wrapper and on the interactions that concern the actual document.

For a formal definition, we need the following notions. Let σ be a prefix of any interaction sequence between a query learner M and a user U with respect to some wrapper f. Then, $content^+(\sigma)$ is the set of all pairs (x, y) such that there is a consistency query (x, E) in σ that receives the rejecting reply $(y, +)$ or there is a consistency query (x, E) in σ that receives an accepting reply and $y \in E$. Additionally, $content^-(\sigma)$ is the set of all pairs (x, y') such that there is a consistency query (x, E) in σ that receives the rejecting reply $(y', -)$ or there is a consistency query (x, E) in σ that receives an accepting reply and $y' \notin E$.

Definition 5. *Let* $Idt \in \{Fin\,CQ, Total\,CQ, Cons\,CQ, It\,CQ\}$, *let* M *be an open-minded query learner, and let* $C \subseteq Lim\,CQ(M)$. *Then,* $C \subseteq Idt(M)$ *iff for all co-operative users* U, U', *for all* $f, f' \in C$, *all interaction sequences* I *and* I' *between* M *and* U *with respect to* f *resp. between* M *and* U' *with respect to* f', *and all* $n, m \in \mathbb{N}$, *the corresponding defining constraint is fulfilled:*

Idt	Defining Constraint
Fin CQ	$M(I_n) = M(I_{n+1})$ *implies* $\varphi_{M(I_n)} = f$.
Total CQ	$\varphi_{M(I_n)} \in \mathcal{R}$.
Cons CQ	*For all* $(x,y) \in content^+(I_n)$ *and all* $(x,y') \in content^-(I_n)$, *it holds* $y \in F_{\varphi_{M(I_n)}(x)}$ *and* $y' \notin F_{\varphi_{M(I_n)}(x)}$.
It CQ	$M(I_n) = M(I'_m)$ *and* $I(n+1) = I'(m+1)$ *imply* $M(I_{n+1}) = M(I'_{m+1})$.

4   Results and Messages

In the last section, a model of learning by consistency queries has been introduced which is the immediate formalization of information extraction as it takes
place in the LExIKON technology and system. Opposite to other query types
investigated in learning theory (cf. [1,2]), consistency queries concern only local
properties of the learner's actual hypothesis. Moreover, since learning is embedded into a surrounding process certain additional requirements have to be
taken into consideration. For instance, it is required that the involved players
(query learner and user) have to meet fairness constraints (see the notions open-
mindedness and co-operativeness) and, according to the role of the user in the
overall scenario, the user is only willing (perhaps, even only capable) to process
implicit information about the learning progress made. The latter has the following implication: although two different query learners may generate completely
different sequences of hypotheses, the resulting interaction sequences may be
identical, and therefore the user cannot distinguish both learners.

Fig. 7 relates the considered identification types to one another. Each identification type is represented by a vertex in a directed graph. A directed edge
(or path) from vertex A to vertex B indicates that the identification type A is
strictly less powerful than the identification type B, i.e., A constitutes a proper
subset of B. Moreover, no edge (or path) between A and B indicates that both
identification types are incomparable. In this picture, the term $Idt\,CQ$ is used as
a shorthand for the learning types $Total\,CQ$, $Cons\,CQ$, and $Lim\,CQ$, respectively,
which coincide.

The identification type $Lim\,CQ$ describes unconstrained learning by consistency queries. Consequently, it is the first key question to relate $Lim\,CQ$. There
are at least three insights worth to be explicated.

First, $Lim\,CQ$ is situated quite far below in a larger hierarchy of identification
types well-studied before (cf., e.g., [6]). That means, IE as focussed here is quite
ambitious and doomed to fail in situations where other more theoretical learning

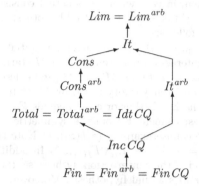

Fig. 7. The relation of standard identification and learning with consistency queries

approaches still work. However, second, $LimCQ$ is nicely characterized to coincide with the known identification type $Total$, i.e., the power of IE as considered here is well-understood. Third, there is the practically truly relevant discovery that IE as supported by the LExIKON technology can always be *consistent* and can return *fully defined* wrappers that work on every document potentially given.

Further key insights refer to the strength of more properties which might be desirable from a practical point of view. Can IE as focussed here always work incrementally by taking wrappers developed before and just presenting a few new samples? Can a query learner decide when the work is done? The corresponding formalizations are called $IncCQ$ and $FinCQ$, respectively.

The one insight is that all those desirable properties turn out to be restrictions. The desired property cannot always be guaranteed. The other insight is that, however, an incremental process can be realized in cases where the system does not know about its potential success, i.e., $IncCQ$ properly exceeds $FinCQ$. Finally, $FinCQ$ is well-characterized by the identification type Fin already known beforehand.

To sum up, the formal investigations to be reported below provide a deep and systematic understanding of IE according to the LExIKON technology.

5   Ideas, Constructions, and Insights

A first new theorem in this section shows that ordinary IIMs are able to simulate query learners.

Theorem 2. *For all $Idt \in \{Fin, Total, Cons, Lim\}$: $IdtCQ \subseteq Idt^{arb}$.*

Proof. Let M be a query learner and let $Idt \in \{Fin, Total, Cons, Lim\}$. We define an IIM M' such that $IdtCQ(M) \subseteq Idt^{arb}(M')$. Let $f \in IdtCQ(M)$ and let $((x_j, f(x_j)))_{j \in \mathbb{N}}$ be any representation of f. The main idea is that M' uses the information which it receives about the graph of f in order to interact with

M on behalf of a user. Then, in case where M's actual consistency query will receive an accepting reply, M' takes over the actual hypothesis generated by M. The relevant details are as follows:

Initially, for the input $(x_0, f(x_0))$, M' presents x_0 as initial document to M, and the first round of the interaction between M' and M starts. In general, the $(i+1)$-st round of the interaction between M' and M can be described as follows. Let (x_i, E_i) be the actual consistency query posed by M. (* Initially, this is the query $(x_0, \emptyset)$. *) Now, M' checks whether or not E_i equals $F_{f(x_i)}$. In case it does not, M' determines the least element z from the symmetrical difference of E_i and $F_{f(x_i)}$ and returns the counterexample $(z, b(z))$. (* Note that $b(z) = +$, if $z \in F_{f(x_i)} \setminus E_i$, and $b(z) = -$, if $z \in E_i \setminus F_{f(x_i)}$. *) In addition, M' and M continue the $(i+1)$-st round of their interaction. Otherwise, the actual round is finished and M' takes over M's actual hypothesis. Moreover, M' answers M's last consistency query with the accepting reply x_{i+1} and the next round of the interaction between M' and M will begin.

It should be obvious that M' learns as required and that M' meets all the constraints which M fulfills. We omit the details.   □

When finite learning is concerned, the opposite inclusion holds as well, i.e., every finite IIM can be replaced by an equally powerful finite query learner.

Theorem 3. $Fin^{arb} \subseteq FinCQ$.

Proof. First, we need some additional notion.

Recall that, in case where a consistency query (x_i, E_i) receives an accepting response, one knows for sure that $f(x_i)$ equals y_i, where y_i is the unique index with $F_{y_i} = E_i$. Moreover, the element $(x_i, f(x_i))$ from the graph of f can be effectively determined. In the rest of the paper, we use the following notion. For any initial segment τ of an interaction sequence I between a query learner M and a user U with respect to some target wrapper f, $content(\tau)$ is the set of all pairs $(x, f(x))$ from the graph of f that can be determined according to the accepting responses in τ.

Let an IIM M be given and let $f \in Fin^{arb}(M)$. The required query learner M' works as follows. Let τ be the most recent initial segment of the resulting interaction sequence between M and U with respect to f. (* Initially, τ is empty. *) First, M' arranges all elements in $content(\tau)$ in lexicographical order. Let σ be the resulting sequence. Now, M' simulates M when fed σ. If M outputs a final hypothesis, say j, M' generates the hypothesis j. Past that point, M' will never change its mind and will formulate all consistency queries accordingly to φ_j. (* To see the appropriateness of this approach, recall that, since M finitely learns f, φ_j equals f. *) Otherwise, M' starts a new interaction cycle with U. Let x_i be either the document that was initially presented or the document that M' received as its last accepting response. Informally speaking, in order to find $f(x_i)$, M' subsequently asks the consistency queries $(x_i, F_0), (x_i, F_1), \ldots$ until it receives an accepting reply. Obviously, this happens, if M' queries $(x_i, F_{f(x_i)})$. At this point, the actual interaction cycle between M' and U is finished and M'

continues as described above, i.e., M' determines σ based on the longer initial segment of the interaction sequence.

Since U is a co-operative user and since M finitely learns f, one directly sees that M' learns f as required. □

The idea used in the last proof can also be adapted for total learning:

Theorem 4. $Total^{arb} \subseteq TotalCQ$.

Every query learner M can be replaced by a learner M' of the same learning power that exclusively generates wrappers being defined for all input documents.

Theorem 5. $LimCQ \subseteq TotalCQ$.

Proof. First, we have to introduce some notions and notations.

Let M be an open-minded query learner and let τ be an initial segment of any interaction sequence. Then, τ^l is the last element of τ and τ^{-1} is the initial segment of τ without τ^l. For the rest of the proof, we fix some effective enumeration $(\rho_i)_{i \in \mathbb{N}}$ of all non-empty finite initial segments of all possible interaction sequences which end with a query q that received an accepting reply $r \in \mathbb{N}$. By $\#\tau$ we denote the least index of τ in this enumeration. Let $i \in \mathbb{N}$. We call ρ_i a candidate stabilizing segment for τ iff (i) $content(\rho_i) \subseteq content(\tau)$, (ii) $M(\rho_i^{-1}) = M(\rho_i)$, and (iii) $M(\rho_j) = M(\rho_i^{-1})$ for all ρ_j with $j \le \#\tau$ that meet $content(\rho_j) \subseteq content(\tau)$ and that have the prefix ρ_i^{-1}.

The required query learner M' works as follows. Let τ be the most recent initial segment of the interaction sequence between M' and a user U. Let x be the most recent document. (* Initially, τ is the empty sequence and x is the first document presented by U. *) First, M' searches for the least index $i \le \#\tau$ such that ρ_i is a candidate stabilizing segment for τ.

Case A. No such index is found.

Now, M' simply generates an index j as auxiliary hypothesis such that φ_j is a total function that meets $\varphi_j(x) = \varphi_{M(\tau)}(x)$. (* Note that, by the constraints on a query learner (see also Definition 3), $\varphi_{M(\tau)}(x)$ has to be defined. *)

Case B. Otherwise.

Now, M determines an index of a total function as follows. Let $\rho_i^l = (q, r)$. (* Note that, by the constraints on a query learner (see also Definition 3), $\varphi_{M(\rho_i^{-1} \diamond (q,x))}(x)$ and $\varphi_{M(\tau)}(x)$ have to be defined. Thus, it can effectively be determined whether or not both values are equal. *)

Subcase B1. $\varphi_{M(\rho_i^{-1} \diamond (q,x))}(x) = \varphi_{M(\tau)}(x)$.

M determines an index k of a function that meets $\varphi_k(z) = \varphi_{M(\rho_i^{-1} \diamond (q,z))}(z)$ for all $z \in \mathbb{N}$. (* Note that, by the constraints on a query learner (see also Definition 3), $M(\rho_i^{-1} \diamond (q,z))$ is defined for all $z \in \mathbb{N}$, since ρ_i ends with an accepting reply. *)

Subcase B2. $\varphi_{M(\rho_i^{-1} \diamond (q,x))}(x) \ne \varphi_{M(\tau)}(x)$.

M generates an index j of a total function as in Case A.

It remains to show that M' is an open-minded query learner with $f \in TotalCQ(M')$.

So, let I be the resulting interaction sequence between M and U with respect to f.

First, by definition of M', M' obviously outputs exclusively indices of total functions (see the corresponding remarks in the description of Case A and Subcases B1 and B2.).

Second, we show that M' is an open-minded query learner. Let x be the most recent document. By definition, it is guaranteed that the most recent hypotheses of M and M''s yield the same output on document x. Hence, the interaction sequence I equals the corresponding interaction sequence between M and U, although M' may generate a sequence of hypotheses that is different from that one produced by M. Since M is an open-minded learner, we may easily conclude that M' is open-minded, too.

Third, we show that M' learns as required. Since $f \in LimCQ(M)$, there is a locking interaction sequence σ of M for f, i.e., $\varphi_{M(\sigma^{-1})} = f$ and for all interaction sequences I' of M and U with respect to f and all $n \in \mathbb{N}$, we have that $M(I'_n) = M(\sigma)$ provided that σ is an initial segment of I'_n. Let ρ_i be the least locking interaction sequence of M for f that ends with an accepting reply (* least with respect to $(\rho_i)_{i \in \mathbb{N}}$ *). Moreover, since I equals an interaction sequence between M and U with respect to f, M has to stabilize on I. Moreover, since M' is open-minded, there is an n such that $content(\rho_i) \subseteq content(I_n)$ and M outputs its final hypothesis when fed I_n. Hence, past this point, M' always forms its actual hypothesis according to Subcase B1. Finally, taking into account that M stabilizes on I to $M(I_n)$, that $\varphi_{M(I_n)} = f$, and that $\varphi_{M(\rho_i^{-1})} = f$, we may easily conclude that $\varphi_{M'(I_n)} = f$. Consequently, M' learns as required, and thus we are done.   □

By applying ideas similar to those used in the demonstration of Theorem 2, it can be shown that every incremental query learner can be simulated by an equally powerfull iterative IIM. Hence, we obtain:

Theorem 6. $IncCQ \subseteq It^{arb}$.

Finally, using the same idea as in the proof of Theorem 3, it can be shown that $FinCQ \subseteq IncCQ$. Moreover, standard ideas can be exploited to show that incremental query learners may outperfom finite query learners and that unconstrained query learners are more powerful than incremental ones.

Theorem 7. $FinCQ \subset IncCQ \subset LimCQ$.

6   Conclusions

Our efforts to bring inductive inference theory to application lead to the development and implementation of the LExIKON technology for information extraction from semi-structured documents. Did the theory benefit in any way from this application oriented work? Does the application development truly depend on our theoretical background?

The answer to both questions is clearly yes. The present paper does bring the community of theoreticians a new concept – *consistency queries*, and the investigations and results presented here have set up the stage for implementational work that aims at automatically learning wrappers that work always consistently and that are defined everywhere. The solvability of this practical task is justified by theoretical results of the present paper.

Future work should be directed towards a formal modelling that captures the underlying information extraction approach even closer. This might lead to refined insights. Here is a prototypical example.

When any document page is given, we currently consider the space of potentially extractable information as being finite. The reason is that we extract only pieces of information which are substrings of the given document. Though the number of combinations may be usually huge, it is bounded in dependence on the document size.

In formal terms, there is a computable function ct, where the ct refers to the fact that it is estimating the *content* of any given document. Functions f to be identified are constrained by $f(x) \subseteq ct(x)$ for every document x.

Because this provides additional information, the identification types based on consistency queries might become more comprehensive. In case this really happens, it points to an extra power to be exploited within practical information extraction. These theoretical questions deserve further investigations.

References

[1] D. Angluin. Queries and concept learning. *Machine Learning*, 2:319–342, 1988.

[2] D. Angluin. Queries revisited. In *Proc. 12th International Conference on Algorithmic Learning Theory*, Lecture Notes in Artificial Intelligence 2225, pages 12–31, Springer–Verlag, 2001.

[3] E. M. Gold. Language identification in the limit. *Information and Control*, 14:447–474, 1967.

[4] G. Grieser, K. P. Jantke, S. Lange, and B. Thomas. A unifying approach to HTML wrapper representation and learning. In *Proc. 3rd International Conference on Discovery Science*, Lecture Notes in Artificial Intelligence 1967, pages 50–64. Springer–Verlag, 2000.

[5] G. Grieser and S. Lange. Learning approaches to wrapper induction. In *Proc. 14th International Florida AI Research Symposium Conference*, pages 249–253. AAAI-Press, 2001.

[6] K. P. Jantke and H.-R. Beick. Combining postulates of naturalness in inductive inference. *Journal of Information Processing and Cybernetics (Elektronische Informationsverarbeitung und Kybernetik)*, 17(8/9):465–484, 1981.

[7] H. Rogers jr. *Theory of Recursive Functions and Effective Computability*. McGraw-Hill, 1967.

Ordered Term Tree Languages which Are Polynomial Time Inductively Inferable from Positive Data

Yusuke Suzuki[1], Takayoshi Shoudai[1], Tomoyuki Uchida[2], and Tetsuhiro Miyahara[2]

[1] Department of Informatics, Kyushu University, Kasuga 816-8580, Japan
{y-suzuki,shoudai}@i.kyushu-u.ac.jp
[2] Faculty of Information Sciences,
Hiroshima City University, Hiroshima 731-3194, Japan
{uchida@cs,miyahara@its}.hiroshima-cu.ac.jp

Abstract. In the fields of data mining and knowledge discovery, many semistructured data such as HTML/XML files are represented by rooted trees t such that all children of each internal vertex of t are ordered and t has edge labels. In order to represent structural features common to such semistructured data, we propose a regular term tree which is a rooted tree pattern consisting of ordered tree structures and internal structured variables. For a regular ordered term tree t, the term tree language of t, denoted by $L(t)$, is the set of all trees which are obtained from t by substituting arbitrary trees for all variables in t.

In this paper, we consider a polynomial time learnability of the class $\mathcal{OTTL} = \{L(t) \mid t \in \mathcal{OTT}\}$ from positive data, where $\mathcal{OTT}$ denotes the set of all regular ordered term trees. First of all, we present a polynomial time algorithm for solving the minimal language problem for $\mathcal{OTT}$ which is, given a set of labeled trees S, to find a term tree t in $\mathcal{OTT}$ such that $L(t)$ is minimal among all term tree languages which contain all trees in S. Moreover, by using this algorithm and the polynomial time algorithm for solving the membership problem for $\mathcal{OTT}$ in our previous work [15], we show that $\mathcal{OTTL}$ is polynomial time inductively inferable from positive data. This result is an extension of our previous results in [14].

1 Introduction

In the fields of data mining and knowledge discovery, many researchers have developed techniques based on machine learning for analyzing electronic data. Many semistructured data such as HTML/XML files have no rigid structure but have tree structures. Such semistructured data are called tree structured data, in general. Tree structured data are represented by rooted ordered trees t such that all children of each inner vertex of t are ordered and t has edge labels [1]. As examples of a representation of tree structured data, we give rooted ordered trees T and T' in Fig. 1. In order to extract structural features from tree

N. Cesa-Bianchi et al. (Eds.): ALT 2002, LNAI 2533, pp. 188–202, 2002.

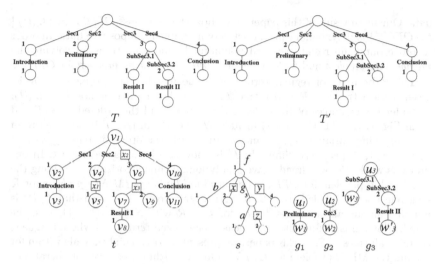

Fig. 1. Ordered trees T, T', g_1, g_2 and g_3, and ordered term trees t and s. The ordered term tree s represents the tree pattern $f(b, x, g(a, z), y)$. A variable is represented by a box with lines to its elements. The label of a box is the variable label of the variable. The number in the left side of a vertex denotes the ordering on its siblings.

structured data, we propose an ordered tree pattern, called an *ordered term tree*, which is a rooted tree pattern with ordered children consisting of tree structures and internal structured variables. A variable in an ordered term tree consists of some number of vertices and it can be substituted by an arbitrary tree. An ordered term tree is more powerful than a standard tree pattern, which is also called a first order term in formal logic, in computational learning theory [2]. For example, in Fig. 1, the tree pattern $f(b, x, g(a, z), y)$ can be represented by the ordered term tree s, but the ordered term tree t can not be represented by any standard tree pattern because of the existence of internal structured variables represented by x_2 and x_3 in t. An ordered term tree t is said to be *regular* if all variable labels in t are mutually distinct. For a set Λ of edge labels, $OTT_\Lambda^{L,K}$ denotes the set of all regular ordered term trees t with edge labels in Λ such that each variable in t consists of at most $L + 1$ vertices for some $L \geq 1$ and any path from the root to a leaf in t has at most K variables for some $K \geq 1$. For a set Λ of edge labels, let $OTT_\Lambda^{L,*} = \bigcup_{K \geq 1} OTT_\Lambda^{L,K}$ and $OTT_\Lambda^{*,*} = \bigcup_{L \geq 1} OTT_\Lambda^{L,*}$. For a set Λ of edge labels, the *term tree language* of a term tree t, denoted by $L_\Lambda(t)$, is the set of all labeled trees which are obtained from t by substituting arbitrary labeled trees for all variables in t.

In this paper, we consider polynomial time learnability of the class of regular term tree languages from positive data. In our previous work [14], we showed that the two fundamental classes $OTTL_\Lambda^{1,1} = \{L_\Lambda(t) \mid t \in OTT_\Lambda^{1,1}\}$ and $OTTL_\Lambda^{1,*} = \{L_\Lambda(t) \mid t \in OTT_\Lambda^{1,*}\}$ are polynomial time inductively inferable from positive data. Our main result of this paper is to show that the class $\mathcal{OTTL}_\Lambda^{*,*} = \{L_\Lambda(t) \mid t \in \mathcal{OTT}_\Lambda^{*,*}\}$ is polynomial time inductively inferable from positive data. In order to prove our main result, we need polynomial time algorithms for solving the *membership problem* and for solving the *minimal language problem* for $\mathcal{OTT}_\Lambda^{*,*}$.

Let $\mathcal{R}$ be a set of regular term trees. The membership problem for $\mathcal{R}$ is, given a term tree $t \in \mathcal{R}$ and a tree T, to decide whether or not $T \in L_\Lambda(t)$. Consider the examples of the ordered term tree t and the ordered trees T and T' in Fig. 1. It holds that $L_\Lambda(t)$ includes T and T'. In fact T is obtained from t by replacing variables x_1, x_2 and x_3 in t with the ordered trees g_1, g_2 and g_3 in Fig. 1, respectively. Similarly T' is shown to be obtained from t. In our previous work [15], we already gave a polynomial time algorithm for solving the membership problem for $\mathcal{OTT}_\Lambda^{*,*}$. The *minimal language (MINL) problem* for $\mathcal{R}$ is, given a set of labeled trees S, to find a term tree $t \in \mathcal{R}$ such that $L_\Lambda(t)$ is minimal among all languages $L_\Lambda(t')$ for $t' \in \mathcal{R}$ with $S \subseteq L_\Lambda(t')$. That is, the MINL problem is to find one of the least generalized term trees whose language contains all trees in S. In this paper, we present a polynomial time algorithm for solving the MINL problem for $\mathcal{OTT}_\Lambda^{*,*}$. Our algorithm uses a set of operations, which are sometimes called refinement operators [5,11].

As previous works, in [6,12], we gave some sets of *unrooted* regular term trees with *unordered* children whose languages are polynomial time inductively inferable from positive data. In [7,13], we considered the complexities of the membership problem and the MINL problem for a set of rooted regular term trees with unordered children. In [13], we gave a polynomial time algorithm for solving the MINL problem for regular unordered term trees and showed that two MINL problems with optimizing the size of an output term tree are NP-complete. In [8,9], we gave data mining systems having special types of *rooted* regular term trees with unordered children and ordered children as knowledge representations, respectively. As the other related works, the works [2,4] show the learnabilities of extended tree patterns in query learning models.

This paper is organized as follows. In Section 2, we propose ordered term trees as tree structured patterns. In Section 3, we define formally the membership problem and the MINL problem for $\mathcal{OTT}_\Lambda^{*,*}$. As our main result of this paper, we show that $\mathcal{OTT}_\Lambda^{*,*}$ is polynomial time inductively inferable from positive data for any set of edge labels Λ. In Section 4, we give a polynomial time algorithm for the MINL problem for $\mathcal{OTT}_\Lambda^{*,*}$.

2   Preliminaries – Ordered Term Trees

Let $T = (V_T, E_T)$ be an ordered tree with a vertex set V_T and an edge set E_T. A list $h = [u_0, u_1, \ldots, u_\ell]$ of vertices in V_T is called a *variable* of T if $u_1, \ldots, u_\ell$ is a sequence of consecutive children of u_0, i.e., u_0 is the parent of $u_1, \ldots, u_\ell$ and u_{j+1} is the next sibling of u_j for j with any $1 \leq j < \ell$. We call u_0 the *parent port* of the variable h and $u_1, \ldots, u_\ell$ the *child ports* of h. Two variables $h = [u_0, u_1, \ldots, u_\ell]$ and $h' = [u_0', u_1', \ldots, u_{\ell'}']$ are said to be *disjoint* if $\{u_1, \ldots, u_\ell\} \cap \{u_1', \ldots, u_{\ell'}'\} = \emptyset$.

Definition 1. Let $T = (V_T, E_T)$ be an ordered tree and H_T a set of pairwise disjoint variables of T. An *ordered term tree obtained from T and H_T* is a triplet $t = (V_t, E_t, H_t)$ where $V_t = V_T$, $E_t = E_T - \bigcup_{h=[u_0,u_1,\ldots,u_\ell] \in H_T} \{\{u_0, u_i\} \in E_T \mid 1 \le i \le \ell\}$, and $H_t = H_T$. For two vertices $u, u' \in V_t$, we say that u is the *parent* of u' in t if u is the parent of u' in T. Similarly we say that u' is a *child* of u in t if u' is a child of u in T. In particular, for a vertex $u \in V_t$ with no child, we call u a *leaf* of t. We define the order of the children of each vertex u in t as the order of the children of u in T. We often omit the description of the ordered tree T and variable set H_T because we can find them from the triplet $t = (V_t, E_t, H_t)$.

For example, the ordered term tree t in Fig. 1 is obtained from the tree $T = (V_T, E_T)$ and the set of variables H_T defined as follows. $V_T = \{v_1, \ldots, v_{11}\}$, $E_T = \{\{v_1, v_2\}, \{v_2, v_3\}, \{v_1, v_4\}, \{v_4, v_5\}, \{v_1, v_6\}, \{v_6, v_7\}, \{v_7, v_8\}, \{v_6, v_9\}, \{v_1, v_{10}\}, \{v_{10}, v_{11}\}\}$ with the root v_1 and the sibling relation displayed in Fig. 1. $H_T = \{[v_4, v_5], [v_1, v_6], [v_6, v_7, v_9]\}$.

For any ordered term tree t, a vertex u of t, and two children u' and u'' of u, we write $u' <_u^t u''$ if u' is smaller than u'' in the order of the children of u. We assume that every edge and variable of an ordered term tree is labeled with some words from specified languages. A label of a variable is called a *variable label*. Λ and X denote a set of edge labels and a set of variable labels, respectively, where $\Lambda \cap X = \phi$. An ordered term tree $t = (V_t, E_t, H_t)$ is called *regular* if all variables in H_t have mutually distinct variable labels in X.

Note. In this paper, we treat only regular ordered term trees, and then we call a regular ordered term tree a *term tree*, simply. In particular, an ordered term tree with no variable is called a *ground term tree* and considered to be a tree with ordered children.

For a term tree t and its vertices v_1 and v_i, a *path* from v_1 to v_i is a sequence $v_1, v_2, \ldots, v_i$ of distinct vertices of t such that for any j with any $1 \le j < i$, v_j is the parent of v_{j+1}. $\mathcal{OT}_\Lambda$ denotes the set of all ground term trees with Λ as a set of edge labels. Let $L \ge 1$ and $K \ge 1$ be integers. Let $\mathcal{OTT}_\Lambda^{L,K}$ be the set of all term trees t with Λ as a set of edge labels such that each variable in t has at most L child ports and any path from the root to a leaf in t has at most K variables. Let $\mathcal{OTT}_\Lambda^{*,*} = \bigcup_{L \ge 1} \bigcup_{K \ge 1} \mathcal{OTT}_\Lambda^{L,K}$.

Let $f = (V_f, E_f, H_f)$ and $g = (V_g, E_g, H_g)$ be term trees. We say that f and g are *isomorphic*, denoted by $f \equiv g$, if there is a bijection φ from V_f to V_g such that (i) the root of f is mapped to the root of g by φ, (ii) $\{u, u'\} \in E_f$ if and only if $\{\varphi(u), \varphi(u')\} \in E_g$ and the two edges have the same edge label, (iii) $[u_0, u_1, \ldots, u_\ell] \in H_f$ if and only if $[\varphi(u_0), \varphi(u_1), \ldots, \varphi(u_\ell)] \in H_g$, and (iv) for any vertex u in f which has more than one child, and for any two children u' and u'' of u, $u' <_u^f u''$ if and only if $\varphi(u') <_{\varphi(u)}^g \varphi(u'')$.

Let f and g be term trees with at least two vertices. Let $h = [v_0, v_1, \ldots, v_\ell]$ be a variable in f with the variable label x and $\sigma = [u_0, u_1, \ldots, u_\ell]$ a list of $\ell + 1$ distinct vertices in g where u is the root of g and $u_1, \ldots, u_\ell$ are leaves of g. The form $x := [g, \sigma]$ is called a *binding* for x. A new term tree $f' = f\{x := [g, \sigma]\}$ is obtained by applying the binding $x := [g, \sigma]$ to f in the following way. For the

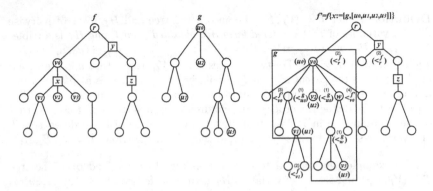

Fig. 2. The new ordering on vertices in the term tree $f' = f\{x := [g, [u_0, u_1, u_2, u_3]]\}$.

variable $h = [v_0, v_1, \ldots, v_\ell]$, we attach g to f by removing the variable h from H_f and by identifying the vertices $v_0, v_1, \ldots, v_\ell$ with the vertices $u_0, u_1, \ldots, u_\ell$ of g in this order. We define a new ordering $<^{f'}_v$ on every vertex v in f' in the following natural way. Suppose that v has more than one child and let v' and v'' be two children of v in f'. We note that $v_i = u_i$ for any $0 \le i \le \ell$. (1) If $v, v', v'' \in V_g$ and $v' <^g_v v''$, then $v' <^{f'}_v v''$. (2) If $v, v', v'' \in V_f$ and $v' <^f_v v''$, then $v' <^{f'}_v v''$. (3) If $v = v_0 (= u_0)$, $v' \in V_f - \{v_1, \ldots, v_\ell\}$, $v'' \in V_g$, and $v' <^f_v v_1$, then $v' <^{f'}_v v''$. (4) If $v = v_0 (= u_0)$, $v' \in V_f - \{v_1, \ldots, v_\ell\}$, $v'' \in V_g$, and $v_\ell <^f_v v'$, then $v'' <^{f'}_v v'$. In Fig. 2, we give an example of the new ordering on vertices in a term tree.

A *substitution* θ is a finite collection of bindings $\{x_1 := [g_1, \sigma_1], \cdots, x_n := [g_n, \sigma_n]\}$, where x_i's are mutually distinct variable labels in X. The term tree $f\theta$, called the *instance* of f by θ, is obtained by applying all the bindings $x_i := [g_i, \sigma_i]$ on f. Lastly we define the root of the resulting term tree $f\theta$ as the root of f. Consider the examples in Fig. 1. Let $\theta = \{x_1 := [g_1, [u_1, w_1]], x_2 := [g_2, [u_2, w_2]], x_3 := [g_3, [u_3, w_3, w'_3]]\}$ be a substitution, where g_1, g_2, and g_3 are trees. Then the instance $t\theta$ of the term tree t by θ is the tree T.

Definition 2. Let Λ be a set of edge labels. The *term tree language* $L_\Lambda(t)$ of a term tree $t \in \mathcal{OTT}^{*,*}_\Lambda$ is defined as $\{s \in \mathcal{OT}_\Lambda \mid s \equiv t\theta$ for a substitution $\theta\}$. The class $\mathcal{OTTL}^{*,*}_\Lambda$ of term tree languages is defined as $\{L_\Lambda(t) \mid t \in \mathcal{OTT}^{*,*}_\Lambda\}$.

3 Polynomial Time Inductive Inference of Ordered Term Tree Languages from Positive Data

We give the framework of inductive inference from positive data [3,10] and show our main theorem. Let U be a recursively enumerable set to which we refer as a *universal set*. We call $L \subseteq U$ a *concept*. An *indexed family of recursive concepts* or a *class* is a triplet $\mathcal{C} = (C, R, \gamma)$, where C is a family of nonempty concepts, R is a recursively enumerable set, each element in R is called a *representation*, γ is a surjection from R to C, and there exists a recursive function $f : U \times R \to \{0, 1\}$ such that $f(w, r) = 1$ if $w \in \gamma(r)$, 0 otherwise. A class $\mathcal{C} = (C, R, \gamma)$ *has finite thickness* if for any nonempty finite set $T \subseteq U$, the cardinality of $\{L \in C \mid T \subseteq L\}$ is finite. For a class $\mathcal{C} = (C, R, \gamma)$, when the family of concepts C and the surjection γ are clear from the context, we write only the representation R for the class $\mathcal{C}$.

An *inductive inference machine* (IIM, for short) for $\mathcal{C}$ is an effective procedure which requests inputs from time to time and produces elements in R from time to time. The outputs produced by the machine are called *hypotheses*. A *positive presentation* of a nonempty concept L is an infinite sequence $\rho = w_1, w_2, \ldots$ of elements in L such that $\{w_1, w_2, \ldots\} = L$. We denote by $\rho[n]$ the ρ's initial segment of length $n \geq 1$ and by $M(\rho[n])$ the last hypothesis produced by M which is successively presented $w_1, w_2, \ldots, w_n$ on its input requests. An IIM is said to *converge to a representation* r for a positive presentation ρ, if there is an $n \geq 1$ such that for any $m \geq n$, $M(\rho[m])$ is r. An IIM M *infers a class* $\mathcal{C}$ *in the limit from positive data* if for any $L \in \mathcal{C}$ and any positive presentation ρ of L, M converges to a representation r for ρ such that $L = \gamma(r)$. A class $\mathcal{C}$ is said to be *inferable in the limit from positive data* if there is an IIM which infers $\mathcal{C}$ in the limit from positive data. An IIM M is *consistently working* if for any $L \in C$, any positive presentation $\rho = w_1, w_2, \ldots$ of L and any $n \geq 1$ with $M(\rho[n]) \in R$, we have $\{w_1, \ldots, w_n\} \subseteq \gamma(M(\rho[n]))$. And an IIM M is *responsively working* if for any $L \in \mathcal{C}$, any positive presentation ρ of L and any $n \geq 1$, we have $M(\rho[n]) \in R$. Moreover, an IIM is *conservatively working* if for any $L \in \mathcal{C}$, any positive presentation ρ of L and any n, m with $1 \leq n < m$ such that $M(\rho[n]), M(\rho[m]) \in R$ and $M(\rho[n]) \neq M(\rho[m])$, we have $\{w_1, \ldots, w_m\} \not\subseteq \gamma(M(\rho[n]))$. A class $\mathcal{C}$ is *polynomial time inductively inferable from positive data* if there exists a consistently, responsively and conservatively working IIM for $\mathcal{C}$ which outputs hypotheses in polynomial time with respect to the length of the input read so far, and infers $\mathcal{C}$ in the limit from positive data.

For a class $\mathcal{C} = (C, R, \gamma)$, let S be a nonempty finite set of U. We say that a representation $r \in R$ is *minimal for* $(S, \mathcal{C})$ if $S \subseteq \gamma(r)$ and $\gamma(s) \subsetneq \gamma(r)$ implies $S \not\subseteq \gamma(s)$ for any $s \in R$. Then, we define the following problems for $\mathcal{C}$:

Membership Problem for $\mathcal{C}$
   Instance: An element $w \in U$ and a representation $r \in R$.
   Question: Is w included in $\gamma(r)$?

Minimal Language Problem (MINL) for $\mathcal{C}$
   Instance: A nonempty finite subset S of U.
   Question: Find a representation $r \in R$ which is minimal for $(S, \mathcal{C})$.

Angluin [3] and Shinohara [10] showed that if $\mathcal{C}$ has finite thickness, and the membership problem and the minimal language problem for $\mathcal{C}$ are computable in polynomial time then $\mathcal{C}$ is polynomial time inductively inferable from positive data. Let Λ be a finite or infinite alphabet of edge labels. In this paper, we consider the class $\mathcal{OTTL}_{\Lambda}^{*,*}$ a target of inductive inference. In this setting, the universal set U is the set $\mathcal{OT}_{\Lambda}$ of all ground term trees, and $\gamma(t)$ is the term tree language $L_{\Lambda}(t)$ for a term tree $t \in \mathcal{OTT}_{\Lambda}^{*,*}$. It is easy to see that the class $\mathcal{OTTL}_{\Lambda}^{*,*}$ has finite thickness. In [15], we gave an algorithm for the membership problem for $\mathcal{OTT}_{\Lambda}^{*,*}$ which runs in $O(nN)$ time where n and N are the numbers of vertices of an input term tree and an input tree, respectively. In Section 4, we give a polynomial time algorithm for the minimal language problem for $\mathcal{OTT}_{\Lambda}^{*,*}$. Therefore, we show the following main result.

Theorem 1. *For any set of edge labels Λ, the class $\mathcal{OTTL}_{\Lambda}^{*,*}$ is polynomial time inductively inferable from positive data.*

4   A Polynomial Time Algorithm for Solving the MINL Problem for $\mathcal{OTT}_{\Lambda}^{*,*}$

4.1   Algorithm MINL

In this section, we give an algorithm, called MINL (Fig. 3), which outputs a term tree $t \in \mathcal{OTT}_{\Lambda}^{*,*}$ which generates a minimal language for an input set of ordered trees $S = \{T_1, \ldots, T_M\}$. For a set S, the number of elements in S is denoted by $|S|$.

The algorithm MINL consists of three procedures, VARIABLE-EXTENSION1, VARIABLE-EXTENSION2 and EDGE-REPLACING. The algorithm MINL starts with a term tree consisting of two vertices and one variable connecting those two vertices. VARIABLE-EXTENSION1 and 2 extend this initial term tree while the temporary term tree matches all trees in S. After these stages terminate, the third stage EDGE-REPLACING begins to put an edge in the place of each variable with one child of the temporary term tree if the new term tree still matches all trees in S. In Fig. 3, we describe an algorithm for $|\Lambda| = 1$ and show the correctness of the case below. We can give an algorithm for the other case $|\Lambda| \geq 2$ that is easier than the case $|\Lambda| = 1$.

Lemma 1 and 2 describe special features of our problem. We omit the proofs.

Lemma 1. *Let t be a term tree which has an edge $\{u,v\}$ (we assume that u is the parent of v) such that the previous and next siblings of v connect to u by variables and v connects to its children by exactly one variable (Fig. 4). A term tree t' is obtained by replacing the edge $\{u,v\}$ with a variable $[u,v]$ of one child port (Fig. 4). If $|\Lambda| = 1$ then $L_{\Lambda}(t') = L_{\Lambda}(t)$.*

A variable surrounded by other variables like the variable $[u,v]$ of t' in Fig. 4 is called a *surrounded variable*. Similarly an edge surrounded by variables like the edge $\{u,v\}$ of t in Fig. 4 is called a *surrounded edge*.

Lemma 2. *Let g be a term tree which has a vertex v such that v connects to its parent by a variable and has exactly two children connecting to v by a variable of two child ports (Fig. 4). A term tree g' is obtained by replacing the variable of two child ports with two variables of one child port (Fig. 4). Then $L_{\Lambda}(g) = L_{\Lambda}(g')$.*

Algorithm MINL;
input: a set of trees $S = \{T_1, \ldots, T_M\} \subseteq \mathcal{OT}_\Lambda$;
begin
    $V_t := \{u, v_1\}$; $E_t := \emptyset$; $H_t := \{h = [u, v_1]\}$; $t := (V_t, E_t, H_t)$; $i := 2$;
    while *true* **do begin**
      Let v_i be a new vertex;
      $t' := (V_t \cup \{v_i\}, E_t, H_t \cup \{[u, v_1, \ldots, v_i]\} - \{[u, v_1, \ldots, v_{i-1}]\})$;
      if $S \subseteq L_\Lambda(t')$ **then begin** $t := t'$; $i := i + 1$ **end else break**
    end;
    VARIABLE-EXTENSION1$(t, S, h = [u, v_1, \ldots, v_{i-1}])$;
    foreach variable $h \in H_t$ **do** VARIABLE-EXTENSION2(t, S, h);
    Let $r[t]$ be the root of t;
    EDGE-REPLACING$(t, S, r[t])$;
    output t
end.

Fig. 3. Algorithm MINL

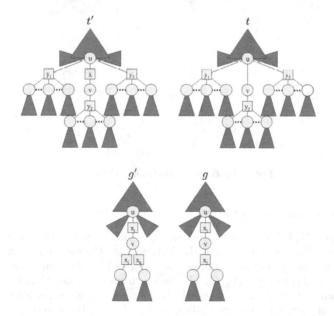

Fig. 4. $L_\Lambda(t') = L_\Lambda(t)$ if $|\Lambda| = 1$ (Lemma 1) and $L_\Lambda(g') = L_\Lambda(g)$ (Lemma 2). The shaded regions represent sub term trees. The difference between t and t' is only the link between u and v, and the difference between g and g' is the variables connecting to v.

Procedure VARIABLE-EXTENSION1;
   input: a term tree $t = (V_t, E_t, H_t) \in \mathcal{OTT}_{\Lambda}^{*,*}$, a set of trees S, and
      a variable $h = [v, c_1, \ldots, c_m]$;
begin
  $\ell := 1$;
  for $i := 1$ **to** m **do**
    for $j := m$ **to** i **do begin**
      Let c'_ℓ be a new vertex and h'_ℓ a new variable $[c'_\ell, c_i, \ldots, c_j]$;
      $t' := (V_t \cup \{c'_\ell\}, E_t,$
          $H_t \cup \{h'_\ell, [v, c'_1, \ldots, c'_\ell, c_{j+1}, \ldots, c_m]\} - \{[v, c'_1, \ldots, c'_{\ell-1}, c_i, \ldots, c_m]\});$
      if $S \subseteq L_\Lambda(t')$ **then begin** $t := t'$; $i := j$; $\ell := \ell + 1$; **break end**
    end;
  if $\ell \geq 2$ **then foreach** $h' \in \{h'_1, \ldots, h'_{\ell-1}\}$ **do**
    VARIABLE-EXTENSION1(t, S, h');
  output t
end;

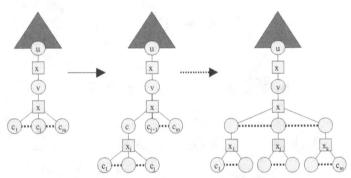

Fig. 5. Procedure VARIABLE-EXTENSION1

4.2 The Correctness of MINL

Let $t = (V_t, E_t, H_t)$ be a term tree and V'_t a subset of V_t. The *least common ancestor* of V'_t is the vertex that is the furthest from the root that is an ancestor of all vertices in V'_t. The least common ancestor of V' is denoted by $lca(V')$. Let $f = (V_f, E_f, H_f)$ and $g = (V_g, E_g, H_g)$ be two term trees. Let f' and g' be term trees obtained from f and g, respectively, by replacing all edges with variables of one child port, and then we write $g \approx f$ if $g' \equiv f'$. For a vertex $v \in V_t$, we denote the number of the children of v by $ch_t(v)$ and the subtree of t rooted at a vertex v by $t[v]$. Moreover we denote the number of the leaves of t by $lf(t)$. Let $v^k[t]$ be the kth vertex of t in the depth first order and $r[t]$ the root of t.
  We show that the algorithm correctly outputs a desired term tree.

Procedure VARIABLE-EXTENSION2;
    input: a term tree $t = (V_t, E_t, H_t) \in \mathcal{OTT}_\Lambda^{*,*}$, a set of trees S, and
      a variable $h = [v, c_1, \ldots, c_m]$;
begin
    if h has more than one child port **then begin**
      $i := 1$;
      for $j := 1$ **to** $m - 1$ **do begin**
        $t' := (V_t, E_t, H_t \cup \{[v, c_i, \ldots, c_j], [v, c_{j+1}, \ldots, c_m]\} - \{[v, c_i, \ldots, c_m]\})$;
        if $S \subseteq L_\Lambda(t')$ **then begin** $t := t'$; $i := j + 1$ **end**
      end
    end;
    output t
end;

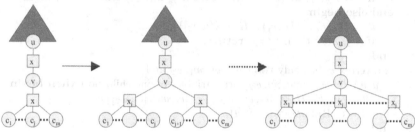

Fig. 6. Procedure VARIABLE-EXTENSION2

Lemma 3. *Let t be the output term tree of* MINL *for an input S. If there exists a term tree t' such that $S \subseteq L_\Lambda(t') \subseteq L_\Lambda(t)$, then $t \approx t'$.*

Proof. From Lemma 1, we assume that t' has no surrounded edge. Let t_1 and t_2 be the outputs of VARIABLE-EXTENSION1 and VARIABLE-EXTENSION2 (Fig. 7), respectively. It is easy to see that $ch(v^k(t_1)) = ch(v^k(t_2))$ for all k. Moreover we easily see that $t_2 \approx t$. Thus we show that $ch(v^k(t')) = ch(v^k(t_1))$ for all k and $t' \approx t_2$. Since $lf(t)$ does not vary after the while-loop of MINL and $L_\Lambda(t') \subseteq L_\Lambda(t)$, we have the following claim:

Claim 1. $lf(t) = lf(t')$.

    VARIABLE-EXTENSION1 calls itself recursively to attempt to add some new vertices and variables (Fig. 5). Let t_1^k be the term tree just after the double for-loop of VARIABLE-EXTENSION1, called a *variable-division stage*, for the kth variable $h = [v, c_1, \ldots, c_m]$ finishes. We note that $v = v^k[t]$. We suppose that a *variable-division stage* divides $h = [v, c_1, \ldots, c_m]$ into one upper variable $h_0 = [v, c'_1, \ldots, c'_{m'}]$ and ℓ lower variables $h_i = [c'_{j_i}, c_{i1}, \ldots, c_{im_i}]$ for i ($1 \le i \le \ell$) where $1 \le j_1 < \cdots < j_\ell \le m'$ and $m_1 + \cdots + m_\ell + m' - \ell = m$. Let $v' = v^k[t']$. Then we have the following two claims:

Procedure EDGE-REPLACING;
  input: a term tree $t \in \mathcal{OTT}_\Lambda^{*,*}$, a set of trees S, and a vertex u;
begin
  if u is a leaf **then return**;
  Let $v_1, \ldots, v_k$ be the children of u;
  for $i := 1$ **to** k **do** EDGE-REPLACING(t, S, v_i);
  for $i := 1$ **to** k **do begin**
    if $\langle u, v_i \rangle$ is not a variable of one child port **then return**
    else if $\langle u, v_i \rangle$ is a surrounded variable and
    $\langle u, v_{i+1} \rangle$ is a variable of one child port **then begin**
        $t_1 := (V_t, E_t \cup \{\{u, v_i\}, \{u, v_{i+1}\}\}, H_t - \{[u, v_i], [u, v_{i+1}]\});$
        $t_2 := (V_t, E_t \cup \{\{u, v_{i+1}\}\}, H_t - \{[u, v_{i+1}]\});$
        $t_3 := (V_t, E_t \cup \{\{u, v_i\}\}, H_t - \{[u, v_i]\});$
        if $S \subseteq L_\Lambda(t_1)$ **or** $(S \subseteq L_\Lambda(t_3)$ **and** $S \not\subseteq L_\Lambda(t_2))$ **then** $t := t_3$ **return**
    end else begin
        $t' := (V_t, E_t \cup \{\{u, v_i\}\}, H_t - \{[u, v_i]\});$
        if $S \subseteq L(t')$ **then** $t := t'$ **return**
    end;
    if a vertex v_i has only two children w_1, w_2 and
    $\langle u, v_i \rangle, \langle v_i, w_1 \rangle$ and $\langle v_i, w_2 \rangle$ are variables of one child port **then begin**
        $t = (V_t, E_t, H_t \cup \{[v_i, w_1, w_2]\} - \{[v_i, w_1], [v_i, w_2]\});$
        EDGE-REPLACING(t, S, u)
    end
  end;
  output t
end;

Fig. 7. Procedure EDGE-REPLACING

Claim 2. $ch_{t'}(v') = m'.$

  We prove this by an induction on k. Let t_1^0 be the first input for VARIABLE-EXTENSION1. From *Claim 1*, $lf(t_1^0) = lf(t')$. We assume that the claim holds for $v^{k-1}[t_1]$ and $v^{k-1}[t']$. Since $L_\Lambda(t') \subseteq L_\Lambda(t)$ and a *variable division stage* attempts to divide the variable h so that v has a smaller number of children, it is not difficult to see that $ch_t(v) \le ch_{t'}(v')$. If $ch_t(v) < ch_{t'}(v')$ then t_1^k can not represent the ordered tree of the smallest size obtained from t', denoted by T, because there is no substitution θ such that $t\theta \equiv T$, $lf(t)$ does not increase and the vertex of $t\theta$ corresponding to v' of T has exactly $ch_{t'}(v')$ children. Thus, $ch_t(v) = ch_{t'}(v')$.

Claim 3. Let c_j'' be the jth child of v' $(1 \le j \le m')$. $lf(t'[c_{j_i}'']) = m_i$ $(1 \le i \le \ell)$ and $lf(t'[c_j'']) = 1$ for $j \notin \{j_1, \ldots, j_\ell\}$.

  It is not difficult to see that $lf(t[c_j']) \ge lf(t'[c_j''])$ for all j $(1 \le j \le m')$. If $lf(t[c_j']) > lf(t'[c_j''])$ for some j, there exists an integer p such that the pth leaf w of t is a leaf of the subtree rooted at c_j' but the pth leaf w' of t' is not a leaf of the subtree rooted at c''_i. Let C (resp. C') be the set of the leaves of the subtree rooted at c'_j (resp. c''_j). Obviously the depth of $lca(\{w'\} \cup C')$ is less than the depth of c''_j but the depth of $lca(\{w\} \cup C)$ $(= lca(C))$ is greater than or equal to the depth of c'_j. Therefore $L_\Lambda(t') \subseteq L_\Lambda(t)$ does not hold. Thus we have $lf(t[c'_j]) = lf(t'[c''_j])$ for all j $(1 \le j \le m')$.

From *Claims 2* and *3*, we have $ch_{t'}(v^k[t']) = ch_{t_1}(v^k[t_1]) = ch_{t_1}(v^k[t_2])$ for all k.

Claim 4. $t' \approx t_2$.

Let v and v' be vertices of t_2 and t' with m children, respectively. Let $C(i) = \{c_{i1}, \ldots, c_{ij_i}\}$ (resp. $C'(i) = \{c'_{i1}, \ldots, c'_{ij'_i}\}$) be the set of the children of v (resp. v') which connect to v (resp. v') by the ith variable or edge. Thus $j_1 + j_2 + \cdots = j'_1 + j'_2 + \cdots = m$. We show that $|C(i)| = |C'(i)|$. Since VARIABLE-EXTENSION2 attempts to divide a variable so that the parent port of it has a larger number of variables, we have $|C(i)| \le |C'(i)|$. If $|C(i)| < |C'(i)|$ then $L_\Lambda(t') \subseteq L_\Lambda(t)$ does not hold except for the case of Lemma 2. For the case of Lemma 2, if v is not the leaf of t_2 and $ch_{t_2}(v) = 2$, $(|C(1)|, |C(2)|) = (1, 1)$ and $(|C(1)|) = (2)$ are considered to be identical. Therefore $|C(i)| = |C'(i)|$. Thus $t' \approx t_2$.

From these claims, we have $t' \approx t$. $\square$

Lemma 4. *Let S be an input set for Algorithm* MINL. *Let $t = (V_t, E_t, H_t)$ be an output term tree by Algorithm* MINL *and $t' = (V_{t'}, E_{t'}, H_{t'})$ a term tree such that $S \subseteq L_\Lambda(t') \subseteq L_\Lambda(t)$. Then $t \equiv t'$.*

Proof (Sketch) From Lemma 1, we assume that t' has no surrounded edge. Let t_0 be the term tree just after the last VARIABLE-EXTENSION2 finishes. Let h_k be the kth variable of one child port which EDGE-REPLACING attempts to replace with an edge. Let t_k be the term tree just after EDGE-REPLACING works on h_k. We prove this by an induction on k. From Lemma 3, $t_0 \approx t'$. Then there exists a bijection ξ from $V_{t'}$ to V_t which realizes $t_0 \approx t'$. Suppose that the statement holds for t' and t_{k-1}. We show that for any $u', v' \in V_{t'}$, $[u', v'] \in H_{t'}$ if and only if $[\xi(u'), \xi(v')] \in H_{t_k}$. The proof depends on the edges and variables around u' and v'. We have the following three special cases (Fig. 9). The first case is not a problem because EDGE-REPLACING always tries t' before t.

1. u' has exactly one child v' which connects to u' by an edge and v' has one variable of two child ports (*Case 1* in Fig. 9).

Let x be the variable label of $[u', v']$. The most cases can be proved by showing that if $[\xi(u'), \xi(v')] \notin H_{t_k}$ then $\{t'\theta_A, t'\theta_B, t'\theta_C, t'\theta_D\} \not\subseteq L_\Lambda(t_k)$ (these substitutions are described in Fig. 8). When $|\Lambda| = 1$, we have the two cases which possibly satisfy that $\{t'\theta_A, t'\theta_B, t'\theta_C, t'\theta_D\} \subseteq L_\Lambda(t_k)$ even if $[\xi(u'), \xi(v')] \notin H_{t_k}$. Let v'_{i-1} and v'_{i+1} be the previous and the next sibling of v', respectively.

2. $[u', v'_{i-1}] \in H_{t'}$, v' has one child w' with $[v', w'] \in H_{t'}$ and $\{u', v'_{i+1}\} \in E_{t'}$ (*Case 2* in Fig. 9).

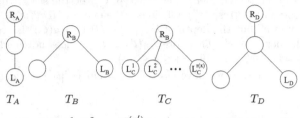

$$\theta_A = \{x' := [T_C, [R_C, L_C^1, L_C^2, ..., L_C^{r(x')}]] \mid x' \in H_{t'} - \{x\}\} \cup \{x := [T_A, [R_A, L_A]\},$$

$$\theta_B = \{x' := [T_C, [R_C, L_C^1, L_C^2, ..., L_C^{r(x')}]] \mid x' \in H_{t'} - \{x\}\} \cup \{x := [T_B, [R_B, L_B]\},$$

$$\theta_C = \{x' := [T_C, [R_C, L_C^1, L_C^2, ..., L_C^{r(x')}]] \mid x' \in H_{t'}\}\},$$

$$\theta_D = \{x' := [T_C, [R_C, L_C^1, L_C^2, ..., L_C^{r(x')}]] \mid x' \in H_{t'} - \{x\}\} \cup \{x := [T_D, [R_D, L_D]\}.$$

Fig. 8. Substitutions: let $r(x)$ denote the number of child ports of the variable labeled with x.

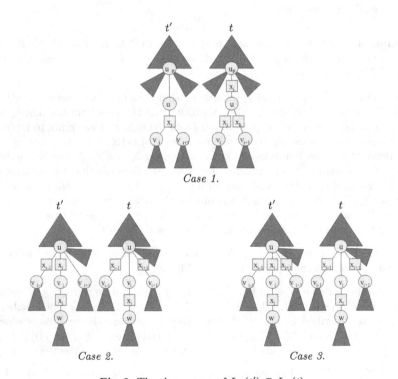

Case 1.

Case 2.   Case 3.

Fig. 9. The three cases of $L_\Lambda(t') \subsetneq L_\Lambda(t)$

3. $\{[u', v'_{i-1}], [u', v'_{i+1}]\} \subseteq H_{t'}$, v' has one child w' with $[v', w'] \in H_{t'}$ and $\{u', v'_{i+1}\} \in E_{t'}$ (*Case 3* in Fig. 9).

For the case 2, *Edge-Replacing* tries t' before t_k and replaces with an edge. Therefore $[\xi(u'), \xi(v')]$ is in H_{t_k}. For the case 3, *Edge-Replacing* does not replace $[\xi(u'), \xi(v')]$ with an edge. Then $[\xi(u'), \xi(v')]$ is in H_{t_k}.   □

We can immediately show the next lemma from Lemma 4.

Lemma 5. *Let S be an input set of trees and t an output term tree of* Algorithm MINL. *Then $L_\Lambda(t)$ is minimal for $(S, \mathcal{OTTL}_\Lambda^{*,*})$.*

Theorem 2. *Minimal Language Problem for $\mathcal{OTT}_\Lambda^{*,*}$ is computable in polynomial time.*

Proof. The correctness follows Lemma 5. Let M be the number of trees in S. Let $N_{\max}$ and $N_{\min}$ be the maximum and minimum numbers of vertices of trees in S, respectively. Let $\Lambda_S = \{a \in \Lambda \mid a \text{ appears on trees in } S\}$. Let $\text{MAT}(N, n)$ be the time complexity of solving a membership problem for a tree with N vertices and a term tree with n vertices. Since any variable of the output term tree t has at most $N_{\min}$ child ports, we need $O(MN_{\min}\text{MAT}(N_{\max}, N_{\min}))$ time for dividing one variable into two variables. Since t has at most $N_{\min}$ variables, *Variable-Extension1* and *2* totally need $O(MN_{\min}^2\text{MAT}(N_{\max}, N_{\min}))$ time. *Edge-Replacing* also computes M membership problems for each labeled edge replacement. Then it needs $O(M|\Lambda_S|N_{\min}\text{MAT}(N_{\max}, N_{\min}))$ time to find a final term tree. Then the total time complexity of the algorithm MINL is $O(M(|\Lambda_S| + N_{\min})N_{\min}\text{MAT}(N_{\max}, N_{\min}))$. By using the membership algorithm in [15] which runs in $\text{MAT}(N, n) = O(Nn)$ time, the algorithm MINL runs in $O(M(|\Lambda_S| + N_{\min})N_{\min}^2 N_{\max})$ time.   □

5   Conclusions

We have presented a polynomial time algorithm for solving the MINL problem for $\mathcal{OTT}_\Lambda^{*,*}$. Then, we have shown that $\mathcal{OTTL}_\Lambda^{*,*}$ is polynomial time inductively inferable from positive data. In order to construct effective data mining tools for semistructured data, we need to show the learnability of regular ordered term tree languages on other learning models from the view point of machine learning. Moreover, as an application of our results in this paper to data mining and knowledge discovery, we are constructing effective data mining tools for real world tree structured data such as HTML/XML files.

References

[1] S. Abiteboul, P. Buneman, and D. Suciu. *Data on the Web: From Relations to Semistructured Data and XML*. Morgan Kaufmann, 2000.

[2] T. R. Amoth, P. Cull, and P. Tadepalli. Exact learning of unordered tree patterns from queries. *Proc. COLT-99, ACM Press*, pages 323–332, 1999.

[3] D. Angluin. Finding patterns common to a set of strings. *Journal of Computer and System Science*, 21:46–62, 1980.

[4] H. Arimura, H. Sakamoto, and S. Arikawa. Efficient learning of semi-structured data from queries. *Proc. ALT-2001, Springer-Verlag, LNAI 2225*, pages 315–331, 2001.

[5] H. Arimura, T. Shinohara, and S. Otsuki. Finding minimal generalizations for unions of pattern languages and its application to inductive inference from positive data. *Proc. STACS-94, Springer-Verlag, LNCS 775*, pages 649–660, 1994.

[6] S. Matsumoto, Y. Hayashi, and T. Shoudai. Polynomial time inductive inference of regular term tree languages from positive data. *Proc. ALT-97, Springer-Verlag, LNAI 1316*, pages 212–227, 1997.

[7] T. Miyahara, T. Shoudai, T. Uchida, K. Takahashi, and H. Ueda. Polynomial time matching algorithms for tree-like structured patterns in knowledge discovery. *Proc. PAKDD-2000, Springer-Verlag, LNAI 1805*, pages 5–16, 2000.

[8] T. Miyahara, T. Shoudai, T. Uchida, K. Takahashi, and H. Ueda. Discovery of frequent tree structured patterns in semistructured web documents. *Proc. PAKDD-2001, Springer-Verlag, LNAI 2035*, pages 47–52, 2001.

[9] T. Miyahara, Y. Suzuki, T. Shoudai, T. Uchida, K. Takahashi, and H. Ueda. Discovery of frequent tag tree patterns in semistructured web documents. *Proc. PAKDD-2002, Springer-Verlag, LNAI 2336*, pages 341–355, 2002.

[10] T. Shinohara. Polynomial time inference of extended regular pattern languages. In *Springer-Verlag, LNCS 147*, pages 115–127, 1982.

[11] T. Shinohara and S. Arikawa. Pattern inference. *GOSLER Final Report, Springer-Verlag, LNAI 961*, pages 259–291, 1995.

[12] T. Shoudai, T. Miyahara, T. Uchida, and S. Matsumoto. Inductive inference of regular term tree languages and its application to knowledge discovery. *Information Modeling and Knowledge Bases XI, IOS Press*, pages 85–102, 2000.

[13] T. Shoudai, T. Uchida, and T. Miyahara. Polynomial time algorithms for finding unordered tree patterns with internal variables. *Proc. FCT-2001, Springer-Verlag, LNCS 2138*, pages 335–346, 2001.

[14] Y. Suzuki, R. Akanuma, T. Shoudai, T. Miyahara, and T. Uchida. Polynomial time inductive inference of ordered tree patterns with internal structured variables from positive data. *Proc. COLT-2002, Springer-Verlag, LNAI 2375*, pages 169–184, 2002.

[15] Y. Suzuki, K. Inomae, T. Shoudai, T. Miyahara, and T. Uchida. A polynomial time matching algorithm of structured ordered tree patterns for data mining from semistructured data. *Proc. ILP-2002, Springer-Verlag, LNAI (to appear)*, 2002.

Reflective Inductive Inference of Recursive Functions

Gunter Grieser

Technische Universität Darmstadt, Fachbereich Informatik,
Alexanderstr. 10, 64283 Darmstadt, Germany,
grieser@informatik.tu-darmstadt.de

Abstract. In this paper, we investigate reflective inductive inference of recursive functions. A reflective IIM is a learning machine that is additionally able to assess its own competence.

First, we formalize reflective learning from arbitrary example sequences. Here, we arrive at four different types of reflection: reflection in the limit, optimistic, pessimistic and exact reflection.

Then, for learning in the limit, for consistent learning of three different types and for finite learning, we compare the learning power of reflective IIMs with each other as well as with the one of standard IIMs.

Finally, we compare reflective learning from arbitrary input sequences with reflective learning from canonical input sequences. In this context, an open question regarding total-consistent identification could be solved: it holds $T\text{-}CONS^a \subset T\text{-}CONS$.

1 Motivation and Introduction

Learning theory aims to model and investigate the scenario that a learner has to identify a target object from indirect information, i.e. examples, about it. Consequently, since there are potentially infinitely many examples about an object, sequences of hypotheses have to be considered. Gold [3] introduced the model of learning in the limit where the learner (here called IIM) is required to converge in the sense that there exists a point in time at which the learner has identified the object and, furthermore, the learner's guesses do not change any more.

However, the point in time at which the stabilization happens, is unknown and in general even undecidable. Therefore, since the early days of learning theory, alternative models has been developed to support the user of a learning device. One of the most strongest forms here is finite learning [3,18] where the user gets told the point when learning is finished.

However, from a user's point of view, even this model has a drawback. Usually, learning is considered with respect to a set $\mathcal{C}$ of target objects. Correct behaviour of an IIM is only required when presenting information about an object of $\mathcal{C}$. Outside of this scope, the IIM may behave arbitrarily. In the worst case, the IIM pretends to learn correctly while in reality its outputs are rubbish. However, a user relying on such an IIM cannot recognize this fact.

N. Cesa-Bianchi et al. (Eds.): ALT 2002, LNAI 2533, pp. 203–217, 2002.

1.1   Machine Self-Assessment

Therefore, models to prevent this behaviour has been developed. Reliable inference machines [1,14] do only converge if they really learn an object. Kinber and Zeugmann [9,10,22] generalized this model by letting an IIM explicitly output some kind of error messages. Still, the messages output by such machines are limiting recursive in character.

Mukouchi and Arikawa [15] developed the model of refutable inference. Here, the learner is required either to identify the target object or to recognize that it is not contained in its hypothesis space and therefore to refute this hypothesis space. This allows the user to recognize a failure of the IIM and to react in some way. This basic idea has been refined in many different directions. For example, in [11], the cases in which a refutation has to take place, has been tailored towards more realistic needs. Jain *et al.* [6] considered weaker variants of refutation. Also, a lot of other investigations of the model of refutation as well as applications in other scenarios took place (cf., e.g., [5,12,13,16]).

In parallel to that evolution, Jantke [7] changed the focus from refuting hypothesis spaces to assessing the competence of an IIM. Whereas in the model of refutable learning, the IIM has to signal if the object to be learnt does not belong to the target class, the competence of an IIM is defined with respect to the information available. Here, a given chunk of information may be rejected when recognizing that this information does not describe any of the target objects. Such information pieces are called inacceptable in this paper.

In [4], the author consequently extended Jantke's ideas and arrived at four so called reflection types: exact, pessimistic, optimistic and limit-reflection. We also underly these models in the present paper. An IIM which is exactly reflecting has to reject an inacceptable information immediately. On the other hand, if some information piece is acceptable (which means, that it is consistent with at least one of the target objects), such an IIM must not reject this information. Pessimistic and optimistic IIMs are allowed to make one-sided errors. A pessimistic IIM may underestimate its competence, i.e. it may erroneously reject acceptable information. In turn, an optimistic IIM may overestimate its competence, i.e. it may sometimes accept inacceptable information. Limit-reflecting machines, finally, are allowed both types of error. However, in the limit all types of reflecting machines have to converge to the correct assessment.

In this paper, we investigate the influence of the four reflection types to learning of recursive functions from arbitrary example sequences. Here, we consider learning in the limit, different variants of consistent learning, and finite learning.

1.2   Results and Messages

The main results are as follows. (A complete overview over the relations of the identification types investigated is displayed in figure 2.)

For learning in the limit (denoted as *LIM*, cf. definition 1), the actual choice of the reflection type doesn't influence the learning power (cf. corollary 1). More precisely, a class of functions is reflectively learnable in the limit iff it is embedded in an initially complete learnable class. This has the following consequences. First, there are learnable classes for which there exists no reflective IIM. Second, reflective learning in the limit is only possible in cases when reflection is not necessary at all, since every information piece is acceptable and hence the IIM never has to reject something.

For finite learning (called *FIN*, cf. definition 2), the picture changes completely. Here, depending on which reflection requirement we demand the IIM to fulfill, we arrive at different learning power (cf. corollary 7). Also, there are classes which are finitely learnable but any IIM for it can not correctly assess its own competence.

Finally, we consider consistent identification. Here, three different formalizations of consistency has been published in the literature which turned out to be of different expressiveness. Surprisingly, these small differences heavily influence the reflecting abilities of consistent IIMs.

An IIM is said to work total-consistently (called *T-CONS*, cf. definition 2), if it is defined for every input and, furthermore, each hypothesis is consistent with the information it was constructed from. Every such IIM can easily be enriched by reflecting abilities (cf. corollary 2). However, this result is of the same quality as the one for learning in the limit since a class of functions is reflectively total-consistently learnable iff it is embedded in an initially complete learnable class.

Whereas for total-consistent identification consistency is required for any hypothesis, in the other two models of consistent learning this is weakened. Here, consistency is demanded for hypotheses built from acceptable information only. Whereas in the model *R-CONS* (see definition 2) the IIM still needs to be defined on any input, a CONS-IIM (cf. definition 2) may be undefined on inacceptable information. For both models, enlarging the IIMs by reflecting abilities has nearly the same effects (cf. corollaries 5 and 6). First, exact and pessimistic reflection are of the same power. Second, these two are less powerful than optimistic reflection which itself is weaker than limit-reflection. Also here, there are IIMs which cannot be made reflective.

To sum up, there is a subtle interplay between learning and reflection requirements. The demand that an IIM additionally has to reflect about its own competence is orthogonal to the classical identification requirements. In some learning models, there is no difference between the reflection types. In other models, the differences are huge. Of special interest here is the relationship between optimistic and pessimistic behaviour. There is no unique trend, which of both is stronger than the other one. However, there seems to appear some tendency that exact and pessimistic reflection as well as optimistic and limit-reflection are similar in spirit. This nicely coincides with the well-known observation that proving something is much harder than disproving it. In our model, pessimistic and exact reflections have to prove that some information is acceptable whereas optimistic or limit-reflective ones have to disprove this fact.

Moreover, we learnt that in most cases a system cannot correctly assess its competence. If this is possible, then such a system is very constrained. There is no universal reflection mechanism.

The remaining paper is structured as follows. In section 2, we provide basic knowledge from inductive inference. The scenario of reflection is introduced in section 3. In section 4, we investigate the learning power of reflective IIMs. This is done in that we compare different types of reflective identification types with each other as well as with standard identification types. Furthermore, we show some closedness properties. Moreover, we investigate whether reflective IIMs can draw benefits from the knowledge that they know in advance the order in which the information is presented. Here, we prove a long outstanding theorem about total-consistent learning. Finally, the relevant literature is given.

2   Inductive Inference

Most notion is adopted from [17]. $I\!N$ denotes the set of natural numbers. We consider recursive functions on $I\!N$. The set of all unary partial and all unary total-recursive functions is denoted by $\mathcal{P}$ and $\mathcal{R}$, respectively.

For the rest of the paper, we fix a Gödel numbering φ of all partial recursive functions as well as a corresponding Blum complexity measure ϕ (cf. [17,2]). Let $i \in I\!N$ and $x \in I\!N$. By φ_i we denote the ith function in φ. If the computation of φ_i terminates on input x, we write $\varphi_i(x)\!\downarrow$.

Let $f \in \mathcal{R}$. An example for f is a pair $(x, f(x))$. Let $\sigma = ((x_n, f(x_n)))_{n \in I\!N}$ be an infinite sequence of examples for f. σ is called a representation for f if $\{x_n \mid n \in I\!N\} = I\!N$. By σ^n we denote the initial segment $(x_0, f(x_0)), \ldots, (x_n, f(x_n))$. σ is in canonical order if $x_n = n$, for all n. $Repr(f)$ denotes the set of all representations of f. Furthermore, by $[f]$ we denote the set of all initial segments of representations from $Repr(f)$. $Repr(\cdot)$ and $[\cdot]$ are canonically extended to function classes $\mathcal{C} \subseteq \mathcal{R}$ as well as to sets $\mathcal{ID} \subseteq \wp(\mathcal{R})$ of function classes. By $[\cdot]^c$ we denote the set of all initial segments of canonical representations of $\cdot$.

An inductive inference machine (IIM) receives finite segments of a representation of recursive functions as input and outputs natural numbers. For technical reasons, we prefer to let an IIM map from $I\!N$ to $I\!N$. For this, we implicitly assume that any finite segment $\tau \in [\mathcal{R}]$ is encoded into a natural number using Cantors pairing function $\langle \cdot, \cdot \rangle$ and identify a segment with its encoding.

Let σ be an infinite and let τ and τ' be two finite sequences. By τ^+ we denote the set of all elements of τ. $\tau \diamond \tau'$ and $\tau \diamond \sigma$ denote the concatenations.

An infinite sequence of natural numbers $(h_n)_{n \in I\!N}$ is said to *converge in the limit* to h (denoted by $\lim_n h_n = h$) iff for all but finitely many n it holds $h_n = h$.

Definition 1. [3] *Let $f \in \mathcal{R}$ and $M \in \mathcal{P}$ be an IIM. M is said to LIM^a-identify f (denoted by $f \in LIM^a(M)$) iff for every $\sigma \in Repr(f)$ it holds:*
1. *$M(\sigma^n)\!\downarrow$, for all $n \in I\!N$.*
2. *There exists an h such that $\lim_n M(\sigma^n) = h$ with $\varphi_h = f$.*

M LIM^a-identifies a class $\mathcal{C} \subseteq \mathcal{R}$ iff M LIM^a-identifies every $f \in \mathcal{C}$.
LIM^a denotes the set of all classes that are LIM^a-identifiable by any IIM.

In the above definition, *LIM* stands for learning in the limit and the superscript a stands for learning from arbitrary representations.

Consistent and finite identification are defined as follows.

Definition 2. [1,3,8,18,20] *Let* $C \subseteq R$ *and* $ID \in \{CONS^a, R\text{-}CONS^a, T\text{-}CONS^a, FIN^a\}$. $C \in ID$ *iff there is an IIM* $M \in P$ *with* $C \subseteq LIM^a(M)$ *such that the following corresponding condition is fulfilled.*

$CONS^a$:   *For all* $\tau \in [C]$ *and for all* $(x, y) \in \tau^+$ *it holds* $\varphi_{M(\tau)}(x) = y$.
$R\text{-}CONS^a$: $M \in R$ *and* $C \subseteq CONS^a(M)$.
$T\text{-}CONS^a$: $M \in R$ *and, for all* $\tau \in [R]$ *and all* $(x, y) \in \tau^+$, *it holds*
          $\varphi_{M(\tau)}(x) = y$.
FIN^a: *There exists a* $d \in R$ *such that for all* $f \in C$ *and all* $\tau \in [f]$, *it*
          holds $d(\tau) = 1$ *iff* $\varphi_{M(\tau)} = f$ *holds.*[1]

Finally, $C \subseteq R$ is exactly enumerable ($C \in NUM!$), if there exists a $g \in R$ with $C = \{\varphi_{g(n)} \mid n \in \mathbb{N}\}$. *NUM* is the smallest superset of *NUM!* that is closed under subsets.

Theorem 1 [1,8,19,20]
1. $NUM! \subset NUM \subset T\text{-}CONS^a \subset R\text{-}CONS^a \subset CONS^a \subset LIM^a$.
2. $FIN^a \subset R\text{-}CONS^a$.
3. $FIN^a \# T\text{-}CONS^a$.
4. $FIN^a \# NUM!$.

3   Reflective Inductive Inference

We want to enrich IIMs by the ability of assessing its own competence. So, first, we have to define what competence of an IIM means. Opposite to the approach of refutable learning (cf. [15]), where competence is defined with respect to complete representations, we define it based on initial segments.

Let M be an IIM and ID be any identification type.

Let $\tau \in [R]$ and $\sigma \in Repr(R)$. τ is said to be acceptable if $\tau \in [ID(M)]$, inacceptable otherwise. σ is acceptable iff $\sigma \in Repr(ID(M))$. σ is inacceptable if it has an initial segment which is inacceptable. The reader should note that by this definition some sequences may neither be acceptable nor inacceptable.

A reflection R for M with respect to ID is a total-computable function $Repr(R) \to \{0, 1\}$ that satisfies the following constraints:
1. On every acceptable sequence σ, R converges to 1, i.e. $\lim_n R(\sigma^n) = 1$.
2. On every inacceptable sequence σ, R converges to 0, i.e. $\lim_n R(\sigma^n) = 0$.
R works optimistically, if, for any $\tau \in [R]$, $R(\tau) = 0$ implies that τ is inacceptable. R works pessimistically, if, for any $\tau \in [R]$, $R(\tau) = 1$ implies that τ is acceptable. Finally, R is exact, if it both works optimistically and pessimistically.

If a reflection outputs 0 for some input τ, we say that R rejects τ. Analogously, R agrees with τ if it outputs 1.

Reflective IIMs are pairs of an ordinary IIM and a corresponding reflection.

---
[1] We call any hypothesis $M(\tau)$ with $d(\tau)$ a final hypothesis.

Definition 3. *Let* $C \subseteq \mathcal{R}$, $M \in \mathcal{P}$ *be an IIM,* $R \in \mathcal{R}$ *be a reflection, and* $\mathcal{ID}$ *be an identification type.*
$C \subseteq \mathcal{ID}\text{-}Refl(M, R)$ *iff* $C \subseteq \mathcal{ID}(M)$ *and* R *is a reflection for* M *with respect to* $\mathcal{ID}$.
$C \subseteq \mathcal{ID}\text{-}oRefl(M, R)$ *[$C \subseteq \mathcal{ID}\text{-}pRefl(M, R)$, $C \subseteq \mathcal{ID}\text{-}eRefl(M, R)$] iff* $C \subseteq \mathcal{ID}(M)$ *and* R *is an optimistic [pessimistic, exact] reflection for* M *with respect to* $\mathcal{ID}$.

As usual, $\mathcal{ID}\text{-}Refl$ is the set of all classes C for which there are an IIM M and a corresponding reflection R with $C \subseteq \mathcal{ID}\text{-}Refl(M, R)$. For any $\lambda \in \{o, p, e\}$, $\mathcal{ID}\text{-}\lambda Refl$ is defined analogously.

The relations between these four reflection types which hold by definition are as follows.

$$\mathcal{ID}\text{-}Refl$$

$$\mathcal{ID}\text{-}oRefl \qquad\qquad \mathcal{ID}\text{-}pRefl$$

$$\mathcal{ID}\text{-}eRefl$$

Fig. 1. The basic relations between the reflective identification types

Moreover, for any identification type $\mathcal{ID}$ we know $\mathcal{ID}\text{-}Refl \subseteq \mathcal{ID}$.

Depending on the underlying identification type, each of the above inclusions may be proper or not. So, as first question, we are interested in the actual instances of these relations for the learning types introduced.

In general, we are interested in the hierarchy of reflective identification types as well as their relation to the standard models.

4   Results

Now, we are ready to investigate reflective learning from arbitrary input sequences.

The results achieved are summarized in figure 2. Here, a line (or a path) between two identification types depicts that the lower one is a proper[2] subset of the upper one. If there is no connection, they are incomparable[2].

Before going into the investigations of the single identification types, it is useful to have the following lemma, which should be obvious.

Lemma 1.
Let $\mathcal{ID}_1, \mathcal{ID}_2 \in \{LIM^a, CONS^a, R\text{-}CONS^a, T\text{-}CONS^a, FIN^a\}$ *with* $\mathcal{ID}_1 \subseteq \mathcal{ID}_2$. *Then, we it holds* $\mathcal{ID}_1\text{-}\lambda Refl \subseteq \mathcal{ID}_2\text{-}\lambda Refl$ *for all* $\lambda \in \{e, p, o, \varepsilon\}$.

---

[2] The exact relationship between $R\text{-}CONS^a\text{-}oRefl$ and $R\text{-}CONS^a\text{-}Refl$ as well as $CONS^a\text{-}oRefl$ and $R\text{-}CONS^a\text{-}Refl$ is still open until now, we just know $R\text{-}CONS^a\text{-}oRefl \subseteq R\text{-}CONS^a\text{-}Refl$ and $CONS^a\text{-}oRefl \setminus R\text{-}CONS^a\text{-}Refl \neq \emptyset$.

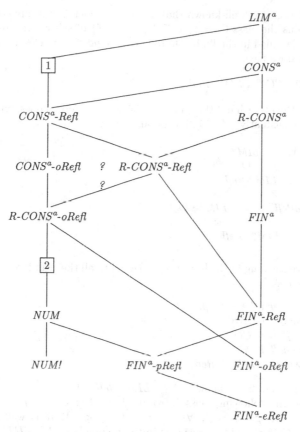

$\boxed{1}$: LIM^a-$Refl = LIM^a$-$oRefl = LIM^a$-$pRefl = LIM^a$-$eRefl$

$\boxed{2}$: T-$CONS^a = T$-$CONS^a$-$Refl = T$-$CONS^a$-$oRefl =$
T-$CONS^a$-$pRefl = T$-$CONS^a$-$eRefl = R$-$CONS^a$-$pRefl =$
R-$CONS^a$-$eRefl = CONS^a$-$pRefl = CONS^a$-$eRefl$

Fig. 2. The relation of the reflective and standard identification types

4.1   Learning in the Limit

Jantke [7] already proved LIM^a-$oRefl = LIM^a$-$eRefl$. In fact, he showed
LIM^a-$oRefl = \mathcal{IC}(LIM^a)$, where we call $\mathcal{IC}(\mathcal{ID})$ the initially complete core
of an identification type $\mathcal{ID}$. For any $\mathcal{ID} \subseteq \wp(R)$, $\mathcal{IC}(\mathcal{ID})$ is the largest subset
of $\mathcal{ID}$ such that every class contained in it is initially complete. The technique
used in [7] can easily be adapted to show LIM^a-$Refl \subseteq \mathcal{IC}(LIM^a)$. Hence, we
arrive at LIM^a-$\lambda Refl = \mathcal{IC}(LIM^a)$, for all $\lambda \in \{e, p, o, \varepsilon\}$.

Furthermore, it is well-known that any class, which is initially complete and which contains the class $C_s = \{f \in \mathcal{R} \mid \varphi_{f(0)} = f\}$ of self-referencing functions can not be identified in the limit. On the other hand, C_s can clearly be identified finitely, hence we have:

Theorem 2 $FIN^a \setminus LIM^a\text{-}Refl \neq \emptyset$.

Since on the other hand there exists initially complete classes, which can not be learned consistently (cf. [19,21]), we also know:

Corollary 1.

$$LIM^a$$
$$\cup$$
$$LIM^a\text{-}Refl$$
$$\text{\textit{//}} \qquad\qquad \text{\textbackslash\textbackslash}$$
$$LIM^a\text{-}oRefl \quad = \quad LIM^a\text{-}pRefl$$
$$\text{\textbackslash\textbackslash} \qquad\qquad \text{\textit{//}}$$
$$LIM^a\text{-}eRefl$$

Reflective learning in the limit is orthogonal to all the standard identification types below LIM^a.

Theorem 3 *For all* $\lambda \in \{e, p, o, \varepsilon\}$,
1. $LIM^a\text{-}\lambda Refl \# CONS^a$.
2. $LIM^a\text{-}\lambda Refl \# R\text{-}CONS^a$.
3. $LIM^a\text{-}\lambda Refl \# FIN^a$.
4. $CONS^a\text{-}\lambda Refl \subset LIM^a\text{-}\lambda Refl$.

Proof. By theorem 2, we know $FIN^a \setminus LIM^a\text{-}Refl \neq \emptyset$.

Consider the following class introduced in [19]: $C = \{f \in \mathcal{R} \mid \exists n \in I\!N : f(n) > 1, \ \varphi_{f(n)} = f, \ \forall m > n : f(m) < 1\}$. It is well-known that $C \in LIM^a \setminus CONS^a$ holds. Since C is initially complete, $C \in LIM^a\text{-}\lambda Refl$ holds as well. Together with theorem 1 and lemma 1 this yields the theorem. $\qquad\square$

4.2   Consistent Learning

Next, we investigate the initially complete cores of the different types of consistent learning: If constrained to initially complete classes, all types coincide.

Theorem 4 $I\!C(T\text{-}CONS^a) = I\!C(R\text{-}CONS^a) = I\!C(CONS^a) = T\text{-}CONS^a$.

Proof. Clearly, an IIM that consistently learns an initially complete class, is consistent on any input segment. Hence, $I\!C(CONS^a) \subseteq T\text{-}CONS^a$ holds.

On the other hand, $T\text{-}CONS^a$ is closed under finite union (cf. [1,21]). Since the class C_{ffs} of all functions of finite support is clearly $T\text{-}CONS^a$-identifiable, for every class $C \in T\text{-}CONS^a$ there exists a superclass C' in $T\text{-}CONS^a$, namely $C \cup C_{ffs}$. Hence, $T\text{-}CONS^a \subseteq I\!C(T\text{-}CONS^a)$, and the theorem follows. $\qquad\square$

This directly yields that all types of reflective $T\text{-}CONS^a$-learning coincide.

Corollary 2.

$$T\text{-}CONS^a$$
$$\parallel$$
$$T\text{-}CONS^a\text{-}Refl$$

$T\text{-}CONS^a\text{-}oRefl$ $=$ $T\text{-}CONS^a\text{-}pRefl$

$$T\text{-}CONS^a\text{-}eRefl$$

Since $T\text{-}CONS^a$ and FIN^a are incomparable, theorem 2 yields the following insights.

Corollary 3. *For all* $\lambda \in \{e, p, o, \varepsilon\}$,
1. $CONS^a\text{-}\lambda Refl \# FIN^a$.
2. $R\text{-}CONS^a\text{-}\lambda Refl \# FIN^a$.
3. $T\text{-}CONS^a\text{-}\lambda Refl \# FIN^a$.
4. $FIN^a\text{-}\lambda Refl \subset T\text{-}CONS^a\text{-}\lambda Refl$.

For $R\text{-}CONS^a$ and $T\text{-}CONS^a$-learning, the initially complete core exactly describes the exact and pessimistic reflective learnable classes.

Theorem 5
1. $R\text{-}CONS^a\text{-}pRefl = R\text{-}CONS^a\text{-}eRefl = \mathcal{IC}(R\text{-}CONS^a)$.
2. $CONS^a\text{-}pRefl = CONS^a\text{-}eRefl = \mathcal{IC}(CONS^a)$.

Proof. By theorem 4, it suffices to prove $CONS^a\text{-}pRefl \subseteq \mathcal{IC}(CONS^a)$.

Let $\mathcal{C} \subseteq CONS^a\text{-}pRefl(M, R)$. Then, an IIM M' that consistently identifies an initially complete superclass of $\mathcal{C}$ can work as follows.

On input τ, determine $R(\tau)$. If $R(\tau) = 1$, determine M's hypothesis h on input τ and output h. Otherwise, i.e. if $R(\tau) = 0$, output a fixed program for the function f_τ. Here, f_τ denotes the 'smallest' function of finite support consistent with τ, i.e. $f_\tau(x) = y$ for any $(x, y) \in \tau^+$ and $f_\tau(x) = 0$, otherwise.

It is not hard to see that M' works as required, i.e. $\mathcal{C} \subseteq CONS^a(M')$ and $CONS^a(M') \in \mathcal{IC}(CONS^a)$ hold. We omit the details. $\square$

We next investigate optimistic reflection.

Theorem 6
1. $R\text{-}CONS^a\text{-}oRefl \setminus T\text{-}CONS^a \neq \emptyset$.
2. $CONS^a\text{-}oRefl \setminus R\text{-}CONS^a \neq \emptyset$.

Proof. The proof idea is similar to the one usually used for diagonalization of consistent IIMs (cf. [21], e.g.). First, we define two function classes $\mathcal{C}_g$ and $\mathcal{C}_h$ as follows. Let $i, j \in I\!N$. Start with Stage 0.

Stage 0: Set $\tau = (0, i)(1, j)$ and $x = 2$. Define $g_{i,j}(0) = h_{i,j}(0) = i$ and $g_{i,j}(1) = h_{i,j}(1) = j$. Goto Stage 1.

Stage $n > 0$: Determine $a = \varphi_i(\tau)$, $b = \varphi_i(\tau \diamond (x, 1))$, and $c = \varphi_i(\tau \diamond (x, 2))$. Set $k = \langle \phi_i(\tau), \phi_i(\tau \diamond (x, 1)), \phi_i(\tau \diamond (x, 2)) \rangle$. Set y_g and y_h according to the following cases:

- If $a \neq b$, set $y_g = 1$ and $y_h = 1$.
- If $a = b$ and $a \neq c$, set $y_g = 2$ and $y_h = 2$.
- If $a = b = c$, set $y_g = 1$ and $y_h = 2$.

Define $g_{i,j}(x) = y_g$, $h_{i,j}(x) = y_h$, and $g_{i,j}(x+1) = h_{i,j}(x+1) = k$. Set $\tau = \tau \diamond (x, y_g)(x+1, k)$, $x = x + 2$, and goto Stage $n + 1$.

We now let $\mathcal{C}_g$ and $\mathcal{C}_h$ be the sets of all functions $g_{i,j}$ and $h_{i,j}$, respectively, which are defined everywhere, i.e. $\mathcal{C}_g = \{g_{i,j} \mid i, j \in \mathbb{N},\ g_{i,j} \in \mathcal{R}\}$ and $\mathcal{C}_h = \{h_{i,j} \mid i, j \in \mathbb{N},\ h_{i,j} \in \mathcal{R}\}$. Obviously, $\mathcal{C}_g$ as well as $\mathcal{C}_h$ is not empty.

By construction, it holds $\mathcal{C}_g \notin T\text{-}CONS^a$ as well as $\mathcal{C}_g \cup \mathcal{C}_h \notin R\text{-}CONS^a$ (see [21], e.g., for a discussion of this technique).

On the other hand, both classes can be optimistically reflected. This is due to the fact that $g_{i,j}$'s as well as $h_{i,j}$'s value for every odd input $x > 2$ carries complexity information which, together with the knowledge about the results for the inputs $0, \ldots, x - 2$, is sufficient to verify the output for $x - 1$. The reflection simply agrees with an input segment τ as long as consistency of τ with the corresponding $g_{i,j}$ resp. $h_{i,j}$ has not been disproved.

$CONS^a$-identification of $\mathcal{C}_g \cup \mathcal{C}_h$ as well as $R\text{-}CONS^a$-identification of $\mathcal{C}_g$ is trivial. The corresponding IIMs M_1 and M_2 may work as follows.

Let τ be any representation segment. Until i and j can be determined from τ, both machines output temporary hypotheses. When knowing i and j, M_1 tests consistency of $g_{i,j}$ with τ. If this consistency test does not terminate, also M_1 does not. If $g_{i,j}$ is consistent with τ, M_1 outputs a program for $g_{i,j}$, otherwise a program for $h_{i,j}$.

M_2 always hypothesizes $g_{i,j}$.

Clearly, $\mathcal{C}_g \cup \mathcal{C}_h = CONS^a(M_1)$ and $\mathcal{C}_g = R\text{-}CONS^a(M_2)$. Since $\mathcal{C}_g \cup \mathcal{C}_h$ as well as $\mathcal{C}_g$ can be optimistically reflected, we have $\mathcal{C}_g \in R\text{-}CONS^a\text{-}oRefl \setminus T\text{-}CONS^a$ as well as $\mathcal{C}_g \cup \mathcal{C}_h \in CONS^a\text{-}oRefl \setminus R\text{-}CONS^a$.   □

This allows for the following conclusions.

Corollary 4.

1. $R\text{-}CONS^a\text{-}oRefl \subset CONS^a\text{-}oRefl$.
2. $R\text{-}CONS^a\text{-}Refl \subset CONS^a\text{-}Refl$.
3. $CONS^a\text{-}oRefl \# R\text{-}CONS^a$.
4. $CONS^a\text{-}Refl \# R\text{-}CONS^a$.

Finally, we can also prove a separation between optimistic $CONS^a$ reflection and reflection in the limit.

Theorem 7 $CONS^a\text{-}Refl \setminus CONS^a\text{-}oRefl \neq \emptyset$.

Proof. We show this by diagonalizing against all potential optimistic computable reflections. Let $(\alpha_n)_{n \in \mathbb{N}}$ be a computable enumeration of $[\mathcal{R}_{i,j}]^c$, where $\mathcal{R}_{i,j} = \{f \in \mathcal{R} \mid f(0) = i, f(1) = j\}$. For any $i, j \in \mathbb{N}$, a function $r_{i,j}$ is defined as follows.

Search for the least n such that $\varphi_j(\alpha_n) = 0$. If this computation does not terminate, $r_{i,j}$ is undefined everywhere. If the least n with $\varphi_j(\alpha_n) = 0$ has been found, we define $r_{i,j}(x) = y$ for all $(x, y) \in \alpha_n^+$ and $r_{i,j}(x) = 0$ otherwise.

Again, we set $\mathcal{C}_r = \{r_{i,j} \mid i, j \in I\!N, \; r_{i,j} \in \mathcal{R}\}$.

An IIM that $CONS^a$-identifies exactly $\mathcal{C}_g \cup \mathcal{C}_r$ can be defined analogously to M_1 in the previous proof.

Clearly, $\mathcal{C}_r$ can be pessimistically reflected by simulating the search for α_n. Since the class $\mathcal{C}_g \cup \mathcal{C}_r$ is discrete, $\mathcal{C}_g \cup \mathcal{C}_r$ can be reflected in the limit. Hence, we have $\mathcal{C}_g \cup \mathcal{C}_r \in CONS^a\text{-}Refl$.

By construction, $\mathcal{C}_g \cup \mathcal{C}_r \notin CONS^a\text{-}oRefl$. This can be seen by assuming the contrary, let $\mathcal{C}_g \cup \mathcal{C}_r \in CONS^a\text{-}oRefl(M, R)$. Let i and j be such that $\varphi_i = M$ and $\varphi_j = R$. Now, we distinguish two cases. First, if $r_{i,j} \in \mathcal{R}$ holds, one directly sees that R does not work optimistically since it rejects an acceptable segment, namely α_n which is used to define $r_{i,j}$.

Therefore, we now assume that $r_{i,j}$ is undefined for some input. Since $R \in \mathcal{R}$, this implies $R(\tau) = 1$, for any $\tau \in [\mathcal{R}_{i,j}]^c$. However, since then every $\tau \in [\mathcal{R}_{i,j}]^c$ is acceptable, M is defined on every $\tau \in [\mathcal{R}_{i,j}]^c$, which in turn implies $g_{i,j} \in \mathcal{R}$ and $h_{i,j} \in \mathcal{R}$. However, by construction of $g_{i,j}$ and $h_{i,j}$, M cannot consistently identify both functions. Thus, at least one of its canonical initial segments is not acceptable, which violates our assumption on R.

Hence, $\mathcal{C}_g \cup \mathcal{C}_r$ can not be optimistically reflected wrt. a consistent IIM.   □

Finally, by putting all these insights together, the structure of reflective $CONS^a$- and $R\text{-}CONS^a$-identification is as follows, where the properness of $R\text{-}CONS^a\text{-}oRefl \subseteq R\text{-}CONS^a\text{-}Refl$ is still open.

Corollary 5.
$$CONS^a$$
$$\cup$$
$$CONS^a\text{-}Refl$$
$$\begin{array}{ccc} & \cup & \\ CONS^a\text{-}oRefl & \supset & CONS^a\text{-}pRefl \\ & \cup & \nparallel \\ & CONS^a\text{-}eRefl & \end{array}$$

Corollary 6.
$$R\text{-}CONS^a$$
$$\cup$$
$$R\text{-}CONS^a\text{-}Refl$$
$$\begin{array}{ccc} & \cup & \\ R\text{-}CONS^a\text{-}oRefl & \supset & R\text{-}CONS^a\text{-}pRefl \\ & \cup & \nparallel \\ & R\text{-}CONS^a\text{-}eRefl & \end{array}$$

4.3   Finite Learning

It is well-known that there does not exist any finitely learnable initially complete class. So, $\mathcal{IC}(FIN^a) = \emptyset$. But clearly, there exist function classes in $FIN^a\text{-}eRefl$, hence $\mathcal{IC}(FIN^a) \subset FIN^a\text{-}eRefl$. Nevertheless, the requirement that a class can both be finitely identified and pessimistically reflected is very strong.

Theorem 8 $FIN^a\text{-}pRefl \subseteq NUM$.

Proof. Let $C \in FIN^a\text{-}pRefl(M, R)$ and let $(\alpha_n)_{n \in I\!\!N}$ be a computable enumeration of $[\mathcal{R}]^c$. A mechanism g enumerating C can be defined as follows. Let $n \in I\!\!N$.

First, on input n, compute $R(\alpha_n)$. If $R(\alpha_n) = 1$, then compute $M(\alpha_n)$ and $d(\alpha_n)$ (which has to be defined if $R(\alpha_n) = 1$). If $d(\alpha_n) = 1$, then output $M(\alpha_n)$. In all other cases, output some default value.

The correctness of this construction should be obvious.   □

By the last proof, one is tempted to guess $FIN^a\text{-}pRefl \subseteq NUM!$. However, this is not the case since $NUM!$ is not closed under subsets, whereas this is the case for $FIN^a\text{-}pRefl$.

For optimistic reflection, the learnable classes become much more powerful.

Theorem 9 $FIN^a\text{-}oRefl \setminus T\text{-}CONS^a \neq \emptyset$.

Proof. In fact, the IIM M_2 defined in the proof of Theorem 6 finitely identifies C_g. Since $C_g \notin T\text{-}CONS^a$, we are done.   □

For all the identification types $\mathcal{ID}$ considered until now, always $\mathcal{ID}\text{-}pRefl \subseteq \mathcal{ID}\text{-}oRefl$ holds. For finite learning, this is no longer the case. The construction from [4] can be adapted to arbitrary information sequences yielding the following result.

Theorem 10 $FIN^a\text{-}pRefl \setminus FIN^a\text{-}oRefl \neq \emptyset$.

Proof. The construction from [4] also applies to arbitrary representation order. We prove the theorem by reducing the halting problem. We define $C_c = \{f \in \mathcal{R} \mid i = f(0), \ \varphi_i(i)\!\downarrow, \ card\{x \in I\!\!N \mid f(x) > 0\} = \phi_i(i)\}$. $C_c \in FIN^a\text{-}pRefl$ obviously holds. On input τ, a reflection may simply determine $i = f(0)$ as well as $k = card\{(x, y) \in \tau^+ \mid y > 0\}$. Only if $\phi_i(i) = k$ holds, it agrees with τ.

Now, assume to the contrary that $C_c \in FIN^a\text{-}oRefl(M, R)$. Then, R can be used to decide the halting problem as follows: Let $i \in I\!\!N$. Search for a $\tau \in \mathcal{R}_i$ with $R(\tau) = 0$. (Since R is an optimistic reflection of M and since M finitely identifies C_c, such a τ must exist.) Now determine $k = card\{(x, y) \in \tau^+ \mid y > 0\}$. If $\phi_i(i) \leq k$, set $\chi_K(i) = 1$, otherwise set $\chi_K(i) = 0$.   □

Standard techniques can be applied to show the following relations.

Theorem 11 *For all $\lambda \in \{e, p, o, \varepsilon\}$, $\lambda_1 \in \{e, p\}$, and $\lambda_2 \in \{o, \varepsilon\}$,*
1. $FIN^a\text{-}\lambda Refl \mathbin{\#} NUM!$.
2. $FIN^a\text{-}\lambda_1 Refl \subset NUM$.
3. $FIN^a\text{-}\lambda_2 Refl \mathbin{\#} NUM$.
4. $FIN^a\text{-}\lambda_2 Refl \mathbin{\#} T\text{-}CONS^a$.

Finally, the complete picture regarding reflective finite learning is as follows.

Corollary 7. FIN^a
$$\cup$$
$$FIN^a\text{-}Refl$$
$$\subset \qquad \supset$$
$$FIN^a\text{-}oRefl \quad \# \quad FIN^a\text{-}pRefl$$
$$\supset \qquad \subset$$
$$FIN^a\text{-}eRefl$$

4.4 Closedness Properties

Next, we study whether the reflective identification types are closed under union.

It is not hard to verify the following propositions, most of them directly follow from the characterizations we achieved above.

Theorem 12 *Let $\lambda \in \{e, p, o, \varepsilon\}$, $\lambda_1 \in \{e, p\}$, and $\lambda_2 \in \{o, \varepsilon\}$.*
1. LIM^a-$\lambda Refl$ is not closed under finite union.
2. T-$CONS^a$-$\lambda Refl$ is closed under recursively enumerable union.
3a. $CONS^a$-$\lambda_1 Refl$ and R-$CONS^a$-$\lambda_1 Refl$ are closed under recursively enumerable union.
3b. $CONS^a$-$\lambda_2 Refl$ and R-$CONS^a$-$\lambda_2 Refl$ are not closed under finite union.
4. FIN^a-$\lambda Refl$ is not closed under finite union.

4.5 Influence of Information Order

Originally, learning of recursive functions has been considered from canonical representations, only. For any of the identification types $\mathcal{ID}^a$ defined above, we let $\mathcal{ID}$ denote the resulting identification type where we require the conditions of the definitions 1 and 2 for canonical representations, only.

The next theorem summarizes the known relations from the literature.

Theorem 13 [8]
1. $LIM^a = LIM$.
2. $CONS^a \subset CONS$.
3. R-$CONS^a \subset R$-$CONS$.
4. $FIN^a = FIN$.

For total-consistent learning, the relation was still open.

Theorem 14 T-$CONS^a \subset T$-$CONS$.

Proof. T-$CONS^a \subseteq T$-$CONS$ holds by definition. We use a diagonalization technique to prove T-$CONS \setminus T$-$CONS^a \neq \emptyset$. Let $i \in \mathbb{N}$. We now define a function t_i in stages as follows. Start with Stage 0.

Stage 0: Set $\tau = (0, i)$, $x = 1$ and define $t_i(0) = i$. Goto Stage 1.
Stage $k > 0$: Search for the least $c \in \mathbb{N}$ and the least $l \leq c$ such that the following conditions are fulfilled: (1) $\phi_i(\tau) \leq c$, (2) $\phi_i(\tau') \leq c$, and (3) $\varphi_i(\tau') \neq \varphi_i(\tau)$, where $\tau' = \tau \diamond (x + 1, l)$.
    If such c and l has been found, we define $t_i(x) = c$ as well as $t_i(x + 1) = l$ and set $\tau = \tau \diamond (x + 1, l)(x, c)$. Set $x = x + 2$ and goto Stage $k + 1$.

We now let $\mathcal{C}_t$ be the set of all functions t_i which are defined everywhere, i.e. $\mathcal{C}_t = \{t_i \mid i \in \mathbb{N}, t_i \in \mathcal{R}\}$. Obviously, $\mathcal{C}_t$ is not empty.

First, we see that that $\mathcal{C}_t \in T$-$CONS$. This is due to the fact that $[\mathcal{C}_t]^c$ is recursive, i.e. for every initial segment τ of the canonical representation of any $f \in \mathcal{R}$ it is decidable whether τ is consistent with some function $t_i \in \mathcal{C}_t$. For this, we can exploit the fact that t_i's value for every odd input x carries complexity information which, together with the knowledge about $t_i(0), \ldots, t_i(x - 1)$, is sufficient to verify t_i's outputs for $x + 1$ as well as for x.

Second, assume $C_t \subseteq T\text{-}CONS^a(M)$ for some $M \in \mathcal{R}$. Select i with $\varphi_i = M$.

Now, first, assume $t_i \notin C_t$. This implies that some stage, say k, in t_i's definition is never left. Let τ be the segment used in Stage k. Then, we know $M(\tau \diamond (2k, 0)) = M(\tau \diamond (2k, 1))$. Hence, at least one of both hypotheses is inconsistent which contradicts our assumption on M.

Therefore, $t_i \in C_t$ holds. On the other hand, by construction, M changes infinitely often its hypothesis on a representation of t_i, namely on $(0, t_i(0)), (2, t_i(2))$ $(1, t_i(1)), (4, t_i(4))(3, t_i(3)), \ldots$ Hence, M cannot identify t_i, and we finally arrive at $C_t \in T\text{-}CONS \setminus T\text{-}CONS^a$. $\square$

Theorem 15 *Select $\mathcal{ID} \in \{LIM,\ CONS,\ R\text{-}CONS,\ T\text{-}CONS,\ FIN\}$ and $\lambda \in \{e, p, o, \varepsilon\}$. Let $\circ$ be the relation in the corresponding cell (i.e. $\circ \in \{=, \subset\}$):*

	LIM	CONS	R-CONS	T-CONS	FIN
ε	$=$			$\subset$	$=$
o	$=$			$\subset$	$=$
p	$=$	$\subset$	$\subset$	$\subset$	$=$
e	$=$	$\subset$	$\subset$	$\subset$	

Then, $\mathcal{ID}^a\text{-}\lambda Refl \circ \mathcal{ID}\text{-}\lambda Refl$ holds.

Proof. Having theorems 13 and 14 in mind, for $\mathcal{ID} \in \{LIM,\ CONS,\ R\text{-}CONS, T\text{-}CONS\}$ the relations are direct consequences from the former results.

For finite IIMs, the proof is a little more involved. First, it is easy to see that any IIM M finitely learning from canonical representations can be transformed into an IIM M' which identifies exactly the same class, i.e. $FIN(M) = FIN^a(M')$ holds.

Hence, it suffices to show that any reflection of some type λ working on canonical input sequences can be transformed into a λ-reflection for arbitrary input sequences.

In the following, we need some notation. Let $\tau \in [\mathcal{R}]$. By τ^c we denote the longest initial segment of a canonical representation which is contained in τ.

First, we consider optimistic reflection. So, let M be a finite IIM with predicate d and let R be an optimistic reflection for M. Furthermore, let M' (and its predicate d') be such that $FIN(M) = FIN^a(M')$. Then, we define a reflection R' as follows. On input τ, determine τ^c and $R(\tau^c)$. Output $R(\tau^c)$.

It is obvious that R' is an optimistic reflection which works on arbitrary input sequences, hence $FIN^a\text{-}oRefl(M, R) = FIN\text{-}oRefl(M', R')$ holds.

Analogously, $FIN^a\text{-}Refl = FIN\text{-}Refl$ can be verified.

For proving $FIN^a\text{-}pRefl = FIN\text{-}pRefl$, let M be a finite IIM with predicate d and let R be a pessimistic reflection for M. Let M' be as above. Then, the following reflection R' obviously pessimistically reflects $FIN^a(M')$ from arbitrary input sequences: On input τ, determine τ^c and $R(\tau^c)$. If $R(\tau^c) = 0$ output 0.

Otherwise, i.e. if $R(\tau^c) = 1$, determine $M(\tau^c)$ and $d(\tau^c)$. If $d(\tau^c) = 0$, output 0. Otherwise, test whether or not $M(\tau^c)$ is consistent with τ. In case $M(\tau^c)$ is consistent with τ, output 1, otherwise output 0. □

References

[1] L. Blum and M. Blum. Toward a mathematical theory of inductive inference. *Inf. & Control*, 28:125–155, 1975.

[2] M. Blum. A machine-independent theory of the complexity of recursive functions. *Journal of the ACM*, 14:322–336, 1967.

[3] E.M. Gold. Language identification in the limit. *Inf. & Control*, 10:447–474, 1967.

[4] G. Grieser. Reflecting inductive inference machines and its improvement by therapy. In *Proc. ALT '96*, LNAI 1160, pp. 325–336, Springer 1996.

[5] S. Jain. Learning with refutation. *J. Comput. Syst. Sci.*, 57:356–365, 1998.

[6] S. Jain, E. Kinber, R. Wiehagen, and T. Zeugmann. Learning recursive functions refutably. In *Proc. ALT '01*, LNAI 2225, pp. 283–298, Springer 2001.

[7] K.P. Jantke. Reflecting and self-confident inductive inference machines. In Proc. *ALT '95*, LNAI 997, pp. 282–297, Springer 1995.

[8] K.P. Jantke and H.R. Beick. Combining postulates of naturalness in inductive inference. *EIK*, 17(8/9):465–484, 1981.

[9] E.B. Kinber and T. Zeugmann. Inductive inference of almost everywhere correct programs by reliably working strategies. *EIK*, 21(3):91–100, 1985.

[10] E. Kinber and T. Zeugmann. One-sided error probabilistic inductive inference and reliable frequency identification. *Inform. & Comput.*, 92(2):253–284, 1991.

[11] S. Lange and P. Watson. Machine Discovery in the presence of incomplete or ambiguous data. In *Proc. AII '94 and ALT '94*, LNAI 872, pp. 438–452 Springer Verlag 1994.

[12] S. Matsumoto and A. Shinohara. Refutably probably approximately correct learning. In *Proc. AII '94 and ALT '94*, LNAI 872, pp. 469–483, Springer-Verlag 1994.

[13] W. Merkle and F. Stephan. Refuting learning revisited. In *Proc. ALT '01*, LNAI 2225, pp. 299–314, Springer 2001.

[14] E. Minicozzi. Some natural properties of strong-identification in inductive inference. *Theoret. Comput. Sci.*, 2:345–360, 1976.

[15] Y. Mukouchi and S. Arikawa. Towards a mathematical theory of machine discovery from facts. *Theoret. Comput. Sci.*, 137(1):53-84, 1995.

[16] Y. Mukouchi and M. Sato. Refutable language learning with a neighbor system. In *Proc. ALT '01*, LNAI 2225, pp. 267–282, Springer 2001.

[17] H. Rogers, Jr. *Theory of Recursive Functions and Effective Computability.* McGraw–Hill, New York, 1967.

[18] B. A. Trakhtenbrot and J.M. Bārzdiņš. *Finite Automata, Behavior and Synthesis* North Holland, Amsterdam, 1973.

[19] R. Wiehagen. Limes-Erkennung rekursiver Funktionen durch spezielle Strategien. *EIK*, 12(1/2):93–99, 1976.

[20] R. Wiehagen and W. Liepe. Charakteristische Eigenschaften von erkennbaren Klassen rekursiver Funktionen. *EIK*, 12(8/9):421–438, 1976.

[21] R. Wiehagen and T. Zeugmann. Learning and consistency. In *Algorithmic Learning for Knowledge-Based Systems*, LNAI 961, pp. 1–24, Springer 1995.

[22] T. Zeugmann. Algorithmisches Lernen von Funktionen und Sprachen. Habilitationsschrift, Technische Hochschule Darmstadt, Fachbereich Informatik, 1993.

Classes with Easily Learnable Subclasses

Sanjay Jain[1*], Wolfram Menzel[2], and Frank Stephan[3**]

[1] National University of Singapore, Singapore 119260, sanjay@comp.nus.edu.sg
[2] Institut für Logik, Komplexität und Deduktionssysteme, Universität Karlsruhe,
76128 Karlsruhe, Germany, EU, menzel@ira.uka.de
[3] Mathematisches Institut, Universität Heidelberg, Im Neuenheimer Feld 294,
69120 Heidelberg, Germany, EU, fstephan@math.uni-heidelberg.de

Abstract. Let Ex denote the explanatory model of learning [3,5]. Various more restrictive models have been studied in the literature, an example is finite identification [5]. The topic of the present paper are the natural variants (a) and (b) below of the classical question whether a given learning criteria is more restrictive than Ex-learning. (a) Does every infinite Ex-identifiable class have an infinite subclass which can be identified according to a given restrictive criterion? (b) If an infinite Ex-identifiable class S has an infinite finitely identifiable subclass, does it necessarily follow that some appropriate learner Ex-identifies S as well as finitely identifies an infinite subclass of S? These questions are also treated in the context of ordinal mind change bounds.

1 Introduction

Gold [5] introduced a model of learning computable functions, where a learner receives increasing amounts of data about an unknown function and outputs a sequence of hypotheses. The learner has learned or identified the function, if it converges to a single explanation, i.e. a program, for the function at hand. This concept of explanatory or Ex-learning has been widely studied [3,5,7,9].

An explanatory learner is often not aware of the fact whether it has already learned the function f or whether the current hypothesis is a preliminary one which must be revised later. It is well-known that, for various restrictive learning criteria, there is a class S which is explanatorily learnable but cannot be learned according to the more restrictive learning type. One might ask, whether there are at least sufficiently large subclasses U of S with better learnability properties. For example, one could impose that the learner on functions from U follows the criterion of finite learning [5] and never replaces any hypothesis. That is, the learner knows after outputting the first hypothesis that either the hypothesis is correct or the data is from a function $f \notin U$. So the learner is aware of the

---

* Sanjay Jain was supported in part by NUS grant number R252-000-127-112.
** Frank Stephan was supported by the Deutsche Forschungsgemeinschaft (DFG) Heisenberg grant Ste 967/1-1.

N. Cesa-Bianchi et al. (Eds.): ALT 2002, LNAI 2533, pp. 218–232, 2002.

fact when learning is completed — this is not possible in the general setting of explanatory learning.

A well-behaved learner only outputs hypotheses which are extended by total functions from the class to be learned. Furthermore such a learner is consistent whenever it outputs a hypothesis. Theorem 2.5 states that there is an infinite well-behaved learnable class which has only finite intersections with recursively enumerable classes of total functions. On the other hand, every recursively enumerable class of total functions has a well-behaved learner and by Theorem 3.1 there is such a class without any infinite finitely learnable subclass. Confidently learnable classes generalize finitely learnable classes and Theorem 3.1 provides even an example of an infinite recursively enumerable class of total functions which does not have an infinite intersection with any confidently learnable class.

Sublearning deals with questions like the following: Is there a learner M which explanatorily learns a class S and – at the same time – finitely learns an infinite subclass U? In Theorem 4.1 it is shown that there is an explanatorily learnable class S which has an infinite finitely learnable subclass but which does not have a sublearner.

Ordinal counters are used to introduce a hierarchy of mind changes within the concept of confident learning. It turns out that ordinals which are a power of ω, in the way defined in Remark 1.4, play a special role in this theory. Theorem 3.6 states that for a recursive ordinal $\alpha = \omega^\gamma$, with $\gamma \geq 1$, the following holds: There is an infinite class, which has a learner using α mind changes, but no infinite subclass of this class can be learned by a learner using β mind changes, for $\beta < \alpha$. For other recursive ordinals $\alpha \geq 2$ such a class does not exist. The case $\alpha - 1 - \omega^0$ is omitted as it is too sensitive to the definition of ordinal counters: if one would count hypotheses instead of mind changes and define that exactly the empty class can be learned with 0 hypotheses, then one could omit the condition "$\alpha \geq 2$" in Theorem 3.6. Theorem 4.4 is the version of Theorem 3.6 in the context of sublearning.

Notation 1.1. Recursion theoretic notation mainly follows the books of Odifreddi [9] and Soare [12]. Let $\mathbb{N} = \{0, 1, \ldots\}$ be the set of natural numbers. For any set $A \subseteq \mathbb{N}$, A^* is the set of finite strings over A and A^∞ the set of total functions from $\mathbb{N}$ to A (viewed as infinite strings). Furthermore, sets are often identified with their characteristic functions, so we may write $A(n) = 1$ for $n \in A$ and $A(n) = 0$ for $n \in \overline{A}$. For a function f, $f[n]$ denotes the string $f(0)f(1)f(2)\ldots$ $f(n-1)$. λ denotes the empty sequence. $\sigma\tau$ denotes the concatenation of strings σ and τ. σa^m denotes the function coinciding with σ on the domain of σ, taking the value a on the next m inputs and being undefined after that in the case of $m < \infty$; σa^∞ is total. Strings are viewed upon as partial functions; $\sigma \subseteq \psi$ denotes that ψ extends σ as a partial function. $\sigma \subset \tau$ denotes that τ extends σ properly. Let φ be a standard acceptable numbering, and φ_e denote the e-th partial recursive function in this numbering.

Definition 1.2 (Explanatory Learning and Mind Changes). A *learner* is a total recursive function mapping finite sequences of natural numbers to $\mathbb{N} \cup \{?\}$.

An output of M is called *hypothesis* if it is different from ?. Hypotheses are viewed upon as indices for partial recursive functions according to our underlying acceptable numbering φ.

A learner M *Ex-learns* (= *Ex-identifies*) [5] a recursive function f if the limit $e = \lim_{n \to \infty} M(f[n])$ exists, is different from ? and is a code for f, that is, $\varphi_e = f$. In this respect, we say that M converges on f to e, iff for all but finitely many n, $M(f[n]) = e$. We say that M Ex-identifies a class S of recursive functions if and only if M Ex-identifies each function in the class. Ex denotes the family of classes that are learnable by a recursive Ex learner. "Ex" stands for "explanatory learning".

Note that the symbol ? stands for the case that the learner cannot make up its mind about what hypothesis to output. The concept of Ex-learning itself does not need this special symbol but additional requirements like bounds on the number of mind changes below will make use of ? in order to avoid mind changes caused by the lack of data which shows up later. Here we say that a learner M makes a *mind change* on f at n, if there is an $m < n$ such that $M(f[n]) \neq M(f[k])$ for $k = m, m+1, \ldots, n-1$ and $M(f[n]), M(f[m])$ are both different from ?. A class of recursive functions S is in Ex_m, if there is a recursive learner that Ex-learns every $f \in S$ by making at most m mind changes on f [3]. Ex_0-learning without any mind changes is also called *finite learning*.

Definition 1.3 (Further Learning Criteria). A learner M, learning a class S, is said to be *consistent* [1], if for all $f \in S$, for all n, $\varphi_{M(f[n])}$ is an extension of $f[n]$. A learner M is said to be *globally consistent* [13], if for all strings $\sigma \in \mathbb{N}^*$, $\varphi_{M(\sigma)}$ is an extension of σ, even if σ is not extended by any $f \in S$.

M is *reliable* [2,8] iff, for all total f, M Ex-identifies f whenever M converges on f to some index. A learner M is *prudent* [11] if it Ex-identifies φ_i, for each i in its range. In particular, all hypotheses output by a prudent learner are indices of total functions. A learner M is said to be *an exact learner* for S, if it identifies all functions in S, and no other function [11]. A learner M is said to be *confident* [11] if it converges on every total function, even the non-recursive functions.

Remark 1.4 (Ordinals). Let $<_0, <_1, \ldots$ be an enumeration of all recursively enumerable partial orders. If an ordering $<_e$ is a well-ordering, it is called a *notation for ordinals*. The natural numbers equipped with $<_e$ are isomorphic to an initial segment of the class of all countable ordinals and one can identify every number x with that ordinal α for which $\{y : y <_e x\}$ and $\{\beta : \beta < \alpha\}$ are order-isomorphic sets.

Cantor introduced a *non-commutative* addition $+$ on the ordinals which is invertible: if $\alpha \leq \beta$, there is a γ such that $\alpha + \gamma = \beta$. This difference γ is denoted as $\beta - \alpha$. Halmos [6, Section 21] gives an overview on ordinal arithmetic. If $<_e$ is a notation for ordinals having a representative x for α, then there is a notation $<_{e'}$ such that whenever y represents an ordinal $\alpha + \beta$ with respect to $<_e$ then y represents the ordinal β with respect to $<_{e'}$. The ordering $<_{e'}$ is constructed by shifting the part of the ordering strictly below x to the top so that $<_{e'}$ still is a well-ordering and x represents 0:

$$y <_{e'} z \Leftrightarrow (x \leq_e y <_e z) \vee (y <_e z <_e x) \vee (z <_e x \leq_e y)$$

where $x \leq_e y$ stands for $x = y \vee x <_e y$.

Furthermore, Cantor introduced the formal powers of ω, the first infinite ordinal. Cantor showed that one can represent every non-null ordinal by a finite sum

$$\alpha = a_1 \omega^{\alpha_1} + a_2 \omega^{\alpha_2} + \ldots + a_n \omega^{\alpha_n}$$

where $0 \leq \alpha_n < \ldots < \alpha_2 < \alpha_1$ as ordinals and $a_1, a_2, \ldots, a_n$ are non-null natural numbers [10, page 280].

This representation permits to look upon the ordinals as a semimodule over the semiring of the natural numbers with pointwise operations $\oplus, \ominus, \otimes$. Given ordinal α and natural number c, one can define $c \otimes \alpha$ as follows. If $c = 0$ or $\alpha = 0$ then $c \otimes \alpha$ is just 0. Otherwise α has the unique representation $a_1 \omega^{\alpha_1} + a_2 \omega^{\alpha_2} + \ldots + a_n \omega^{\alpha_n}$ and one defines $c \otimes \alpha = (a_1 c) \omega^{\alpha_1} + (a_2 c) \omega^{\alpha_2} + \ldots + (a_n c) \omega^{\alpha_n}$. Similarly, one can define the pointwise addition $\alpha \oplus \beta$ which is different from $+$ as it is commutative but has the minimum compatibility $\alpha \oplus 1 = \alpha + 1$. Note that $\alpha \ominus \beta$, the pointwise subtraction, can be undefined even in the case that $\beta < \alpha$: for example, $\omega \ominus 1$ is undefined.

Definition 1.5 [4]. A class S is Ex_α-identifiable for a recursive ordinal α iff there is an Ex-learner M and a notation for ordinals $<_e$ permitting to represent α and a total recursive function ord mapping $\mathbb{N}^*$ to $\mathbb{N}$ such that the following hold.

(a) M Ex-identifies every $f \in S$.
(b) $\mathrm{ord}(\lambda) = \alpha$.
(c) For all total f and m, n such that $m < n$, $\mathrm{ord}(f[n]) \leq_e \mathrm{ord}(f[m])$.
(d) For all $f \in S$ and m, n such that $m < n$ and $M(f[n]), M(f[m])$ are different hypotheses, $\mathrm{ord}(f[n]) <_e \mathrm{ord}(f[m])$.

Remark 1.6. Freivalds and Smith postulated that (d) holds also for all function $f \notin S$. The resulting concept is the same, but in the present paper the restrictions to functions in S will be necessary for studying simultaneous learners. For example, we will consider the case where a learner M simultaneously Ex-identifies R and Ex_α-identifies some $S \subseteq R$. As this class R might not be Ex_α-identifiable itself, the existence of such a simultaneous learner is only possible in a setting where condition (d) is defined as above.

Note that for some $\alpha \geq \omega$ and some classes $S \in \mathrm{Ex}_\alpha$, one must carefully choose the adequate notation for ordinals in order to construct a recursive Ex_α-learner using this notation. If the notation is chosen inadequately, the corresponding learner cannot be recursive.

2   Well-Behaved Learners

This section introduces the notion of well-behaved learners, which combines the properties of exact, prudent and globally consistent learners.

Definition 2.1. A learner M is well-behaved for S iff

(a) M Ex-identifies S;
(b) Whenever M outputs a hypothesis e (a hypothesis is by definition not the symbol ?) then there is a function $f \in S$ which extends φ_e;
(c) On every input σ, $M(\sigma)$ is either the symbol ? or a hypothesis e such that φ_e extends σ.

Furthermore, a learner M is almost well-behaved if M satisfies (a) and (b). M is globally consistent if M satisfies (a) and (c).

Note that condition (c) is equivalent to the notion of consistency as defined by Jain, Royer, Osherson and Sharma [7] – the notable difference is that these authors do not permit the case that $M(\sigma) =?$. One can repair this problem without destructing the Ex-learnability of S by considering a modified learner outputting the same hypothesis as M if $M(\sigma) \neq?$ and outputting any hypothesis for $\sigma 0^\infty$ if $M(\sigma) =?$. The condition (b) is a variant of the notion prudence as given by Osherson, Stob and Weinstein [11]. The definition implies that a well-behaved learner is also reliable in the sense that, on every input function f, M converges to an index e iff $f \in S$. Therefore, M learns only functions in S and so M is also an exact learner [11].

A class is dense if, for every string σ, there is a function f in the class which extends σ. Almost well-behaved learners are very powerful as every dense and Ex-identifiable class has also an almost well-behaved Ex-learner. This relation is lost in the case of mind change bounds, as the following result shows that only recursively enumerable classes can have (but may not have) almost well-behaved Ex_0-learners. Note that there are many Ex_0-identifiable classes which are not in Num and in particular not recursively enumerable.

Definition 2.2. A class S of recursive functions is in *Num*, if some superset S' of S is a recursively enumerable class of recursive functions.

Proposition 2.3. *If an almost well-behaved learner Ex_0-identifies S, then S is recursively enumerable.*

Proof. If M is an almost well-behaved Ex_0-learner and M outputs on σ a hypothesis e such that φ_e extends σ, then M learns some $f \in S$ extending φ_e and hence extending σ. As M does not revise the hypothesis on input f, e must already be an index for f. Thus the equation

$$S = \{\varphi_e : (\exists \sigma)\, [M(\sigma) = e \wedge \sigma \subseteq \varphi_e]\}$$

witnesses that S is a recursively enumerable class of total functions.   ∎

Proposition 2.4. *There is a class R having an almost well-behaved Ex_1-learner but no well-behaved Ex-learner.*

Proof. Consider the class R containing all functions f satisfying one of the following conditions.

- $f = \sigma 0^\infty$ for some $\sigma \in \{1,2\}^*$;
- $f = \varphi_e$ and $f \in \{1^e 2\} \cdot \{1,2\}^\infty$.

Claim 1. *There is no well-behaved Ex-learner for R.*

For given well-behaved M and number e, construct the following function f_e:

$$f_e(x) = \begin{cases} 1 & \text{if } x < e \text{ or } (x > e \text{ and } M(f_e[x]) = M(f_e[x]2)); \\ 2 & \text{if } x = e \text{ or } (x > e \text{ and } M(f_e[x]) \neq M(f_e[x]2)). \end{cases}$$

Assume now that $x > e$ and $M(f_e[x])$ is the hypothesis e'. By condition (c) of the definition of a well-behaved Ex-learner, there is at most one $a \in \{1,2\}$ such that $M(f_e[x]a)$ outputs e'. If $a = 2$, then $f_e(x) = 1$; if $a = 1$, then $f_e(x) = 2$. So $M(f_e[x+1]) \neq e'$. Thus M_e does not converge to a hypothesis on any of the functions f_e. But, by the Fixed-Point Theorem [9, Theorem II.2.10], there is an e such that $f_e = \varphi_e$. Since $f_e \in 1^e 2 \cdot \{1,2\}^\infty$, it follows that $f_e \in R$ and M does not Ex-learn R. So R does not have a well-behaved learner.

Claim 2. *There is an almost well-behaved Ex_1-learner N for R.*

As long as the input is in $\{1\}^*$ the learner N outputs ?. On input $\sigma \in \{1^e 2\} \cdot \{1,2\}^*$ the learner N outputs the index e' given by

$$\varphi_{e'}(x) = \begin{cases} \varphi_e(x) & \text{if } \varphi_e(y){\downarrow} \in \{1,2\} \text{ for all } y \leq x; \\ \uparrow & \text{otherwise.} \end{cases}$$

On input of the form $\sigma 0^k$ with $\sigma \in \{1,2\}^*$, the output is a canonical index for $\sigma 0^\infty$. On all other inputs, N outputs ?.

It is easy to verify that N Ex_1-identifies R. Furthermore, every function output by N on input $\{1,2\}^*$ is either a finite function $\tau \in \{1,2\}^*$ or a total self-describing and $\{1,2\}$-valued function. In the first case, the extension $\tau 0^\infty$ is in R. In the second case, the function $\varphi_{e'}$ is equal to φ_e, is total and is in R itself. If the input is of the form $\sigma 0^k$ with $\sigma \in \{1,2\}^*$, the hypothesis is also in R. So N is an almost well-behaved learner for R. ∎

Although almost well-behaved learners are more general than well-behaved ones, there are also classes which can be learned by a well-behaved learner, but which are not in Num.

Theorem 2.5. *There is an infinite class S, which is Ex-identifiable by a well-behaved learner, such that intersection of S with any class in Num is finite.*

Proof. Let $\sigma_0, \sigma_1, \ldots$ be enumeration of all strings. Let $\Phi_0, \Phi_1, \ldots$ be the step counting functions associated with $\varphi_0, \varphi_1, \ldots$ such that $\Phi_e(x)$ is the number of steps needed to compute $\varphi_e(x)$, if $\varphi_e(x)$ is defined, and $\Phi_e(x) = \infty$ otherwise. Now define for every e the value a_e as

$$a_e = \min(\{\infty\} \cup \{x : \Phi_e(x) = \infty \vee (\exists y < x)\, [\Phi_e(x) < \Phi_e(y)]\}).$$

The a_e's can be approximated from below; that is, there is a total recursive mapping $e, s \to a_{e,s}$ such that $a_{e,s} \leq a_{e,s+1}$ for all e, s and $a_e = \lim_s a_{e,s}$. Note that one can without loss of generality have that $a_{e,s} \leq s$ and thus the approximation never takes the value ∞. Now let

$$\Psi_e(x) = \begin{cases} \sigma_e(x) & \text{if } x \in \text{domain}(\sigma_e); \\ \max(\{0\} \cup \{\Phi_d(y) : d \leq e \wedge y < \min(\{1+x, a_d\})\}) & \text{otherwise.} \end{cases}$$

We cannot recursively know the values $a_0, a_1, \ldots$ but can only approximate them in the limit. So we consider the following enumeration of partial functions containing all the Ψ_e. For each tuple $(b_0, b_1, \ldots, b_e) \in (\mathbb{N} \cup \{\infty\})^*$, let

$$\Theta_{(b_0, b_1, \ldots, b_e)}(x) = \begin{cases} \sigma_e(x) & \text{if } x \in \text{domain}(\sigma_e); \\ \max(B \cup \{0\}) & \text{if the following conditions hold:} \\ & \quad \text{(I) } B = \{\Phi_d(y) : d \leq e \wedge y < \min(\{1+x, b_d\})\} \\ & \qquad \text{exists and can be completely enumerated,} \\ & \quad \text{(II) } a_{d,x} \leq b_d \text{ for all } d \leq e, \\ & \quad \text{(III) } \Phi_d(y) \leq \Phi_d(y+1), \\ & \qquad \text{for all } y < \min(\{1+x, b_d\}) - 1 \text{ and } d \leq e, \\ & \quad \text{(IV) } x \notin \text{domain}(\sigma_e); \\ \uparrow & \text{otherwise.} \end{cases}$$

Note that in (I) above, B exists if $b_d \leq a_d$, for all $d \leq e$.

On the one hand, one can show that the set

$$\{(b_0, b_1, \ldots, b_e, x, y) : x < \infty \wedge y < \infty \wedge \Theta_{(b_0, b_1, \ldots, b_e)}(x) = y\}$$

is recursive. Therefore, there exists a learner M which consistently learns the class of all total $\Theta_{(b_0, b_1, \ldots, b_e)}$, where M outputs only hypotheses for functions of the form $\Theta_{(b_0, b_1, \ldots, b_e)}$. As $\Theta_{(b_0, b_1, \ldots, b_e)}$ is total iff $a_0 = b_0 \wedge a_1 = b_1 \wedge \ldots \wedge a_e = b_e$, it follows that the total functions in this list are exactly the functions Ψ_e and so M is a consistent learner for $S = \{\Psi_0, \Psi_1, \ldots\}$. In particular, M satisfies conditions (a) and (c) in Definition 2.1 of well-behaved learner.

Furthermore, if some $b_k \neq a_k$ for $k \leq e$, then $\Theta_{(b_0, b_1, \ldots, b_e)}$ is equal to a finite string $\sigma_{e'}$ and the function $\Psi_{e'}$ extends $\sigma_{e'}$. As all indices output by M are indices for functions of form $\Theta_{(b_0, b_1, \ldots, b_e)}$, one can conclude that condition (b) in Definition 2.1 of well-behaved learner is also satisfied.

On the other hand, if $f_0, f_1, \ldots$ is a recursive enumeration of total functions, then the function g given by

$$g(x) = f_0(x) + f_1(x) + \ldots + f_x(x) + 1$$

dominates all these functions and there is a total and ascending function Φ_e dominating g. It follows that the functions $\Psi_e, \Psi_{e+1}, \ldots$ are different from all functions $f_0, f_1, \ldots$ and so the intersection of S and any class in Num is finite. ∎

3 Subclasses of Confidently Learnable Classes

Recall from Definition 1.3 that Osherson, Stob and Weinstein [11] defined that a learner M is *confident* iff M always comes up with a final hypothesis about the data seen in the input, that is,

$$(\forall f)\,(\exists e)\,(\forall^\infty n)\,[M(f[n]) = e].$$

So a confident learner converges on every input function, even if this function is not recursive and therefore cannot be learned at all. Thus, confident learning is a generalization of learning with mind change bounds. The first result below shows that some learnable classes do not have infinite confidently learnable subclasses; the further results deal with the question when Ex_α-identifiable classes have infinite Ex_β-identifiable subclasses for $\beta < \alpha$.

Theorem 3.1. *There is an infinite recursively enumerable class GEN such that intersection of GEN with any confidently learnable class is finite.*

Proof. Recall that a 1-generic set G has the property that for every recursive set U of strings there is a k such that either the string $G(0)G(1)\ldots G(k)$ itself is in U or no extension of $G(0)G(1)\ldots G(k)$ is in U. One can choose G such that G is Turing reducible to K [10, Section XI.2]. Therefore, there is a recursive enumeration $f_0, f_1, \ldots$ of $\{0,1\}$-valued recursive functions pointwise converging to (the characteristic function of) the set G. Let $GEN = \{f_0, f_1, \ldots\}$ for these functions. As G is not recursive and differs from every function f_k, the set GEN is infinite.

Now consider any class S with a confident learner M. By confidence, M converges on G. Thus there exists a $\sigma \subseteq G$ such that $M(\eta) = M(\sigma)$ whenever $\sigma \subseteq \eta \subseteq G$. As G is 1-generic and as G does not contain any string of the recursive set $\{\eta : \eta \supseteq \sigma \wedge M(\eta) \neq M(\sigma)\}$, there is a τ with $\sigma \subseteq \tau \subseteq G$ and $M(\eta) = M(\sigma)$ for all $\eta \supseteq \tau$. Furthermore, using the nonrecursiveness of G, one may assume that τ is long enough, so that the hypothesis $M(\sigma)$ does not compute an extension of τ.

As the functions f_k approximate the set G, and $\tau \subseteq G$, almost all f_k extend τ. Thus the set $\{f_k : f_k = \varphi_{M(\sigma)} \vee \tau \not\subseteq f_k\}$ is finite and also contains all functions in the intersection of S and $\{f_0, f_1, \ldots\}$. Theorem follows. ∎

As all recursively enumerable classes have a well-behaved learner, the following corollary is immediate.

Corollary 3.2. *There is a class R having a well-behaved Ex-learner such that $R \cap S$ is finite for every confidently learnable class S.*

Theorem 3.3. *If an infinite class S has a confident and well-behaved learner, then S has an infinite recursively enumerable subclass U which is Ex_0-identifiable.*

Proof. Let M be a confident and well-behaved learner for S such that $M(\lambda)$ outputs a hypothesis for the everywhere undefined function. Now consider the tree $T \subseteq \mathbb{N}^*$, with root λ, defined as follows. A node σ of T has as successors all the nodes $\tau \supset \sigma$ such that M outputs at τ for the first time a hypothesis different from $M(\sigma)$; that is, (I) $M(\tau) \notin \{M(\sigma), ?\}$ and (II) $M(\eta) \in \{M(\sigma), ?\}$ for all η with $\sigma \subseteq \eta \subset \tau$. An invariant of this construction is that M never outputs ? on the nodes of T. The tree T is well-founded as M converges on all functions, that is, the tree does not have infinite branches. By König's Lemma, T would be finite if T is finitely branching. As S is infinite and every hypothesis of M is also in the range of T, T must be infinite. So there is a node $\sigma \in T$ having infinitely many successors $\tau_0, \tau_1, \ldots$ and there is a recursive enumeration producing them. The subclass U is generated from these τ_k as follows.

The function f_k is the limit of strings η_l, where $\eta_0 = \tau_k$ and η_{l+1} is the first string found (in some standard search) such that $\eta_l \subset \eta_{l+1}$ and $M(\eta_{l+1}) \neq ?$.

To see that all f_k are total, assume by way of contradiction that for some f_k, the process terminates at some η_l. Then it would hold that $(\forall \tau \supset \eta_l) [M(\tau) = ?]$ and M would not Ex-identify any extension of η_l. However $M(\eta_l)$, by condition (c) in Definition 2.1, computes a partial function extending η_l and, by condition (b), some total extension of $\varphi_{M(\eta_l)}$, which is also a total extension of η_l, is in S. A contradiction. Thus each f_k is total.

The definition of f_k ensures that M outputs on f_k infinitely often a hypothesis. As M is confident, M converges on f_k to a hypothesis e. The consistency condition (c) from Definition 2.1 implies that φ_e extends infinitely many $\sigma \subseteq f_k$ and so $\varphi_e = f_k$. As φ_e is total, $\varphi_e \in S$ and thus $\{f_0, f_1, \ldots\} \subseteq S$.

An Ex_0-learner for $\{f_0, f_1, \ldots\}$ can be built as follows: on input σ, the learner outputs a hypothesis e_k for f_k whenever $\tau_k \subseteq \sigma \subseteq f_k$ for some k. Otherwise the learner outputs ?. ∎

Freivalds and Smith [4, Theorem 6] showed that classes of step functions like the below separate the various levels of the hierarchy for learning with an ordinal bound on the number of mind changes.

Proposition 3.4 [4]. *For every ordinal α represented by an element y_0 with respect to a suitable notation $<_e$ of ordinals, define the class $DEC_{\alpha,e}$ to be the set of all decreasing functions $f : \mathbb{N} \to \mathbb{N}$ with $f(0) = y_0$ and $(\forall x) [f(x+1) \leq_e f(x)]$. Then $DEC_{\alpha,e}$ is Ex_α-identifiable, but not Ex_β-identifiable for any $\beta < \alpha$.*

Proof. $DEC_{\alpha,e}$ contains only functions which are decreasing with respect to a well-ordering. So they can properly decrease only finitely often and are thus eventually constant. So the class $DEC_{\alpha,e}$ consists of recursive functions which is a precondition for being learnable.

$DEC_{\alpha,e}$ has an Ex_α-learner M defined as follows. On input λ, $M(\lambda) = ?$ and the ordinal is initialized as y_0. On input $y_0 y_1 \ldots y_n$ with $y_0 \geq_e y_1 \geq_e \cdots \geq_e y_n$ let m be the minimal number with $y_m = y_n$. Then M outputs the canonical index for $y_0 y_1 \ldots y_m (y_m)^\infty$ and the value of the ordinal counter is y_m, that is, the counter is counted down iff $m = n > 0$. On all other inputs, M outputs ? and does not change its ordinal counter.

Now we show that there is no Ex_β-learner for $DEC_{\alpha,e}$ as follows. Suppose by way of contradiction that there exists such a learner N with ordinal counter ord using some notation $<_{e'}$. Define that $y <' z$ if the ordinal represented by y with respect to $<_e$ is below that represented by z with respect to $<_{e'}$, similarly define $y =' z$ and $y \leq' z$.

We construct a counterexample f to N being an Ex_β-learner for $DEC_{\alpha,e}$. In this construction, we use that without loss of generality, N updates its ordinal only if necessary, that is, N outputs a new hypothesis on some $f \in DEC_{\alpha,e}$ and there had already been a previous hypothesis. We now define the diagonalizing f inductively and start with $f(0) = y_0$. Assume that $f[x]$ is defined and $x > 0$. If there is a b such that

(I) For every y, z such that $y < z \leq x$ and $N(f[y]), N(f[z])$ are neither equal nor ?, $\text{ord}(f[z]) <_{e'} \text{ord}(f[y])$;
(II) $b =' \text{ord}(f[x])$ and $b <_e f(x-1)$;
(III) $\varphi_{N(f[x])}$ extends $f[x]$ but does not extend $(f[x])b$;

then let $f(x) = b$ else let $f(x) = f(x-1)$.

It is easy to see that the resulting function f is total and in $DEC_{\alpha,e}$. Now we look at the behaviour of N on f assuming that N satisfies (I) on f.

Note the following invariant of the above construction: ordinal represented by $\text{ord}(f[x])$ (in $<_{e'}$ notation) is not greater than the ordinal represented by $f(x)$ (in $<_e$ notation).

Let y be the first number with $f(z) = f(y)$ for all $z > y$ and x be the first number with $N(f[x])$ being the final hypothesis of N. Let b be the number with $b =' \text{ord}(f[x])$.

If $y = 0$ then $N(f[x])$ is not a hypothesis for the function $(y_0)^\infty$ since otherwise (I), (II) and (III) would be satisfied as $y_0 >' \text{ord}(f[x])$.

If $y > 0$ and $x \leq y$ then $N(f[x]) = N(f[y])$ and $\varphi_{N(f[x])}$ does not extend $f[y+1]$, so N does not learn f.

If $x > y > 0$ then $\text{ord}(f[x]) <_{e'} \text{ord}(f[y])$. It follows, using invariant stated above, that $b <_e f(x)$. As $f(x) \neq b$, (III) must be violated and whenever $\varphi_{N(f[x])}$ extends $f[x]$, it also extends $f[x]b$ and is thus different from f.

This case-distinction is complete and in all cases, N does not Ex_β-learn f. Thus N is not Ex_β-learnable. ∎

Freivalds and Smith [4, Theorem 10] showed that $\bigcup_\alpha Ex_\alpha$ is closed under union, where the number of mind changes needed to show the closure can go up. If one does not require the new learner to be recursive, one can get very tight bounds. Recall the definitions of $\oplus$ and $\otimes$ from Remark 1.4.

Fact 3.5 [4]. *If S_1 is Ex_α-identifiable and S_2 is Ex_β-identifiable then $S_1 \cup S_2$ has a not necessarily recursive $Ex_{\alpha \oplus \beta \oplus 1}$-learner. In particular, if $S_1, S_2, \ldots, S_n$ are Ex_α-identifiable then $S_1 \cup S_2 \cup \ldots \cup S_n$ has a not necessarily recursive $Ex_{(n \otimes \alpha) \oplus (n \ominus 1)}$-learner.*

Theorem 3.6. *Let $\alpha \geq 2$ be a recursive ordinal. If $\alpha = \omega^\gamma$ for some γ*

Then there is an infinite Ex_α-identifiable class S_α such that for every $\beta < \alpha$, S_α does not have an infinite Ex_β-identifiable subclass,
Else there is a $\beta < \alpha$ such that every infinite Ex_α-identifiable class S has an infinite Ex_β-identifiable subclass.

Proof. Then-Case. Let e be such that $<_e$ is a notation for ordinals having a representative for α. Now one constructs $S_\alpha \subseteq DEC_{\alpha,e}$ as follows.

Let $M_1, M_2, \ldots$ be a (not necessarily recursive) list of all recursive learners equipped with an ordinal mind change counter. Let β_k be the initial value of the ordinal counter of M_k. If $\beta_k < \alpha$ then let S_k be the set of all functions Ex_{β_k}-learned by M_k and if $\beta_k \geq \alpha$ then let $S_k = \emptyset$. Without loss of generality, $\beta_0 = 1$. As $\alpha = \omega^\gamma$, the expression $(k \oplus 1) \otimes \max(\{\beta_l : l \leq k \wedge \beta_l < \alpha\}) \oplus k$ is again strictly below α. So it follows from Fact 3.5 that there is a not necessarily recursive learner N_k which Ex_δ-identifies $R_k = S_0 \cup S_1 \cup \ldots \cup S_k$ for some $\delta < \alpha$. The negative part of Proposition 3.4 does not use the fact that the Ex_β-learner is recursive. So it follows that there is a function $f_k \in DEC_{\alpha,e}$ which is not Ex_δ-learned by N_k and thus $f_k \notin S_0 \cup S_1 \cup \ldots \cup S_k$. Now let $S_\alpha = \{f_0, f_1, \ldots\}$ for these functions f_k.

As $S_\alpha \subseteq DEC_{\alpha,e}$ it follows that S_α is clearly Ex_α-identifiable. On the other hand, every Ex_β-identifiable class with $\beta < \alpha$ has an Ex_β-learner M_k. Thus every Ex_β-identifiable class with $\beta < \alpha$ is contained in some S_k. It follows from the construction that M_k can Ex_β-identify only functions f_l with $l < k$. Thus S_α has no infinite Ex_β-identifiable subclass. This completes the first part of the proof.

Else-Case. The ordinal α can be represented as $c\omega^\gamma + \delta$ for some ordinal γ with $c > 0$ and $\omega^\gamma > \delta$. If $\delta = 0$ then let $\beta = (c-1)\omega^\gamma$ else let $\beta = c\omega^\gamma$. Note that in both possible definitions it holds that $\beta < \alpha \leq \beta + \beta$ as the first one implicitly requires $c > 1$ by $\alpha \neq \omega^\gamma$. Let M be an Ex_α-learner for a given class S and ord be its ordinal counter. Let U be the set of all $f \in S$ such that $\text{ord}(f[x]) \geq \beta$ for all x. Now consider the following two subcases.

Subcase U finite. We define the following Ex_β-learner N for the whole class S, and the associated ordinal counter ord' as follows:

If $\text{ord}(\sigma)$ is at least β, then $\text{ord}'(\sigma) = \beta$. If exactly one function in U is consistent with the input σ, then N outputs an index for this function. Otherwise N outputs ?.

If $\text{ord}(\sigma)$ is below β, then $\text{ord}'(\sigma) = \text{ord}(\sigma)$, and $N(\sigma) = M(\sigma)$.

It is easy to see that N Ex_β-identifies all the functions in U, as well as all the functions in S on which the ordinal counter of M eventually goes below β. Thus M Ex_β-identifies the whole class S.

Subcase U infinite. One takes the same learner M but adjusts the mind change counter to the following ord'. Let x be the representative of β with respect to $<_e$ and let $<_{e'}$ be such that whenever y represents $\beta + \epsilon$ with respect to $<_e$ then y represents ϵ with respect to $<_{e'}$. Now the new ordinal counter does the following.

If $\mathrm{ord}(\sigma) \geq_e x$ then $\mathrm{ord}(\sigma)$ represents some ordinal $\beta + \epsilon$ with respect to $<_e$. Now $\mathrm{ord}'(\sigma) = \mathrm{ord}(\sigma)$ and represents the ordinal ϵ with respect to $<_{e'}$.

Otherwise $\mathrm{ord}(\sigma) <_e x$ and the data is from a function not in U. Then let $\mathrm{ord}'(\sigma) = x$ and note that x represents 0 with respect to $<_{e'}$.

As a consequence, M is an Ex_β-learner for the infinite class U using that ord' starts with an ordinal less or equal β with respect to the notation $<_{e'}$ and that the Ex-learning capabilities are the same. As long as the data is from functions in U, each mind change is accompanied by counting down the ordinal.

This completes the proof for the second (Else) part of the theorem. ∎

Note that, in the above Theorem, in Then case, one cannot have that S_α has a well-behaved Ex_α-learner (as, by Theorem 3.3, S_α would then have an infinite Ex_0-identifiable subclass).

4   Sublearners

The main question considered in this section is the following: Given an Ex-identifiable class S satisfying some additional constraints, is there an infinite subclass U and an Ex-learner M for S such that M Ex_β-identifies U? One additional constraint is that S has an infinite Ex_0-identifiable subclass. As confidently learnable classes are Ex_α-identifiable for some α, Theorem 3.1 has been adapted into this section as follows. There is a class $S = GEN \cup \{g_0, g_1, \ldots\}$, where GEN is from Theorem 3.1, such that $\{g_0, g_1, \ldots\}$ is Ex_0-identifiable, S is Ex-identifiable and no Ex-learner M for S is at the same time an Ex_α-learner for an infinite subclass of S.

Theorem 4.1. *There exists an infinite class S such that*

(a) *S is Ex-identifiable;*
(b) *S contains an infinite Ex_0-identifiable subclass;*
(c) *For any learner M which Ex-identifies S, for any α, M does not Ex_α-identify an infinite subset of S.*

Proof. Let G and $f_0, f_1, \ldots$ be as in the proof of Theorem 3.1. Furthermore, let $g_k = f_k(0)f_k(1)\ldots f_k(k)2^\infty$, that is, g_k coincides with f_k on $0, 1, \ldots, k$ and takes the constant 2 from then on. Let $S = \{f_0, g_0, f_1, g_1, f_2, g_2, \ldots\}$. The class of all g_k is an infinite subclass of $\{0,1\}^* \cdot \{2\}^\infty$ which is clearly Ex_0-identifiable. Now consider any Ex-learner M for S equipped with an ordinal counter. As M learns all functions f_k, it follows from the proof of Theorem 3.1 that M makes on the characteristic function of G infinitely many mind changes. Thus there is a number l such that M has made a mind change on the input $G(0)G(1)\ldots G(l)$ without counting down the ordinal. As almost all functions f_k and g_k extend the string $G(0)G(1)\ldots G(l)$, M can Ex_α-identify only finitely many functions in S. ∎

Theorem 4.2. *For every infinite class S having a confident and well-behaved learner M, there is a class U and a learner N such that*

- $U \subseteq S$ and U is infinite and U is recursively enumerable;
- N is an Ex_1-learner for U;
- N is a confident and well-behaved learner for S.

Proof. This is a generalization of the proof of Theorem 3.3. In the proof of Theorem 3.3, we defined strings σ and $\tau_0, \tau_1, \ldots$ and functions $f_0, f_1, \ldots \in S$ with the following properties.

(I) The τ_k's are recursively enumerable and pairwise incomparable.
(II) For any k, $\sigma \subseteq \tau_k$ and $M(\tau_k) \notin \{M(\sigma), ?\}$. Furthermore, for all k and all η with $\sigma \subset \eta \subset \tau_k$, $M(\eta) \in \{M(\sigma), ?\}$.
(III) For all k, f_k extends τ_k and belongs to S. Furthermore, there is a program p_k for f_k which can be obtained effectively from k.
(IV) For all τ, if $\sigma \subseteq \tau$ and $M(\tau) \notin \{M(\sigma), ?\}$, then there exists a k such that $\tau_k \subseteq \tau$.

We now define our learner N as follows.

$$N(\tau) = \begin{cases} ?, & \text{if } \tau \subseteq \sigma; \\ p_k, & \text{for the unique } k \text{ with } \tau_k \subseteq \tau \subseteq f_k, \text{ if there is such a } k; \\ M(\tau), & \text{otherwise.} \end{cases}$$

We argue that the second clause above can be recursively decided. Note that the τ_k are the places after σ where M outputs its first hypothesis not in $\{M(\sigma), ?\}$. Also the τ_k and f_k have both an effective enumeration. Thus, we can determine effectively from τ, whether there exists a k (and find such a k if it exists) such that $\tau_k \subseteq \tau$, and then use this k to check whether the data seen so far is consistent with f_k. It is now easy to verify that N Ex_1-identifies each f_k — N only outputs $M(\sigma)$ and then p_k on f_k; it is easy to assign the corresponding ordinal counter to N. Furthermore, if the input is incomparable to any f_k, then N follows M. Thus, N inherits the property of being a well-behaved and confident learner for S from M. ∎

Note that in the above theorem, we are not able to achieve Ex_0 instead of Ex_1, as shown by the following theorem.

Theorem 4.3. *There exists a class S, such that*

- *some well behaved learner Ex_1-identifies S;*
- *no learner which Ex-identifies S, can Ex_0-identify an infinite subset of S.*

Proof. Let $S = \{f : f(x) \neq 0 \text{ for at most one } x\}$. It is easy to verify that S can be Ex_1-identified by a well-behaved learner. On the other hand, any Ex-learner for S has to identify 0^∞ and can thus Ex_0-identify only finitely many functions in S. The theorem follows. ∎

Theorem 4.4. Let $\alpha \geq 2$ be a recursive ordinal. If $\alpha = \omega^\gamma$ for some γ, then there is a class R_α satisfying

(a) R_α is infinite and Ex_α-identifiable;
(b) R_α has an Ex_0-identifiable infinite subclass;
(c) if M Ex-identifies R_α, then for every $\beta < \alpha$, M does not Ex_β-identify an infinite subset of R_α.

If α is not of the form ω^γ, there is no class satisfying all three conditions (a), (b), (c).

Proof. Assume that $\alpha = \omega^\gamma$ for some γ. The construction of R_α to satisfy (a), (b) and (c) is parallel to the construction in Theorem 3.6.

R_α is defined as the union of two sets $\{f_0, f_1, \ldots\}$ and $\{g_0, g_1, \ldots\}$ where the functions f_k are exactly as in Theorem 3.6. For each function f_k, there is a number a_k such that, whenever some M_l with $l \leq k$ makes a mind change on f_k without counting down the ordinal, then this happens for the first time at some place before $f_k[a_k]$. Without loss of generality suppose 0 also represents the ordinal 0. The function g_k is taken to be $f[a_k + 1]0^\infty$.

(a): R_α is clearly infinite. As $R_\alpha \subseteq DEC_{\alpha,e}$ for some e, R_α is Ex_α-identifiable.

(b): The class $\{g_0, g_1, \ldots\}$ is Ex_0-identifiable as a learner can wait for the first 0 to show up in the input function g_k, and then knows the whole function as every 0 is followed by only 0 thereafter (for functions in the class R_α).

(c): Consider any $\beta < \alpha$ and any Ex_β-learner. Such a learner is equal to some M_k with $\beta_k \leq \beta < \alpha$. Suppose M_k Ex-identifies the whole class R_α, and consider $l \geq k$. The learner M_k Ex-identifies, but does not Ex_{β_k}-identify, f_l. Therefore, the counter of M_k is not counted down at some mind change occurring before it sees $f_l[a_l]$. As a consequence, M_k also does not Ex_β-identify g_l. Therefore, M_k can Ex_β-identify only finitely many functions in R_α, namely only some of those f_l and g_l, with $l < k$. This completes the first part of the proof.

If $\alpha \neq \omega^\gamma$ for all γ, then there is an ordinal $\beta < \alpha$ such that the corresponding part of the proof of Theorem 3.6 shows the following. One can construct from a given Ex_α-learner for a given infinite class S a further Ex-learner for S which at the same time is an Ex_β-learner for an infinite subclass of S — if the construction goes according to the first subcase, that subclass is the original class S, if the construction goes according to the second subcase, the learner is not modified but only the ordinal counter. So one cannot satisfy (a) and (c) simultaneously for any class. ∎

Remark 4.5. The negative results made use of the fact that the subclass has to be infinite. Indeed, dropping this constraint destroys all negative results. Given any finite subclass $U \subseteq S$ and any Ex-learner M for S, one can transform M into an Ex-learner N for S, such that N is also an Ex_0-learner for U: There is a number n such that M has converged on every $f \in U$ to the final index for f by the time it has seen $f[n]$. In particular, $M(f[m+1]) = M(f[m])$ for all $m \geq n$ and $f \in U$. The new learner N given by

$$N(\sigma) = \begin{cases} ? & \text{if } |\sigma| < n; \\ M(\sigma) & \text{if } |\sigma| \geq n; \end{cases}$$

has the desired properties: N Ex-identifies the same functions as M but on the functions $f \in U$, N only outputs the symbol ? before outputting the correct hypothesis $M(f[n])$.

Acknowledgement. The authors thank anonymous referees of the conference ALT 2002 for suggestions and comments.

References

[1] Janis Bārzdiņš. Inductive inference of automata, functions and programs. In *Int. Math. Congress, Vancouver*, pages 771–776, 1974.

[2] Lenore Blum and Manuel Blum. Toward a mathematical theory of inductive inference. *Information and Control*, 28:125–155, 1975.

[3] John Case and Carl Smith. Comparison of identification criteria for machine inductive inference. *Theoretical Computer Science*, 25:193–220, 1983.

[4] Rūsiņš Freivalds and Carl Smith. On the role of procrastination in machine learning. *Information and Computation*, 107:237–271, 1993.

[5] E. Mark Gold. Language identification in the limit. *Information and Control*, 10:447–474, 1967.

[6] Paul R. Halmos. *Naive Set Theory*. Springer-Verlag, NY, 1994.

[7] Sanjay Jain, Daniel Osherson, James S. Royer and Arun Sharma. *Systems that Learn: An Introduction to Learning Theory*. MIT Press, Cambridge, Mass., second edition, 1999.

[8] Eliana Minicozzi. Some natural properties of strong identification in inductive inference. *Theoretical Computer Science*, 2:345–360, 1976.

[9] Piergiorgio Odifreddi. *Classical Recursion Theory*. North-Holland, Amsterdam, 1989.

[10] Piergiorgio Odifreddi. *Classical Recursion Theory*, volume II. Elsevier, Amsterdam, 1999.

[11] Daniel Osherson, Michael Stob and Scott Weinstein. *Systems that Learn: An Introduction to Learning Theory for Cognitive and Computer Scientists*. MIT Press, 1986.

[12] Robert Soare. *Recursively Enumerable Sets and Degrees*. Springer-Verlag, 1987.

[13] Rolf Wiehagen and Walter Liepe. Charakteristische Eigenschaften von erkennbaren Klassen rekursiver Funktionen. *Journal of Information Processing and Cybernetics* (EIK), 12:421–438, 1976.

On the Learnability of Vector Spaces

Valentina S. Harizanov[1]⋆ and Frank Stephan[2]⋆⋆

[1] The Department of Mathematics, The George Washington University, Funger Hall,
2201 G Street, Washington, DC, 20052, USA, harizanv@gwu.edu.
[2] Mathematisches Institut, Universität Heidelberg, Im Neuenheimer Feld 294,
69120 Heidelberg, Germany, EU, fstephan@math.uni-heidelberg.de.

Abstract. The central topic of the paper is the learnability of the recursively enumerable subspaces of V_∞/V, where V_∞ is the standard recursive vector space over the rationals with countably infinite dimension,
and V is a given recursively enumerable subspace of V_∞. It is shown that
certain types of vector spaces can be characterized in terms of learnability properties: V_∞/V is behaviourally correct learnable from text iff
V is finitely dimensional, V_∞/V is behaviourally correct learnable from
switching type of information iff V is finite-dimensional, 0-thin, or 1-thin.
On the other hand, learnability from an informant does not correspond
to similar algebraic properties of a given space. There are 0-thin spaces
W_1 and W_2 such that W_1 is not explanatorily learnable from informant
and the infinite product $(W_1)^\infty$ is not behaviourally correct learnable,
while W_2 and the infinite product $(W_2)^\infty$ are both explanatorily learnable from informant.

1 Introduction

A central theme in inductive inference is the relation between learning from all
data, that is, learning from informant, and learning from positive data only, that
is, learning from text. Learning from text is much more restrictive than learning
from informant, as shown by Gold [7]. Gold proved that the collection consisting of an infinite set together with all of its finite subsets can be learned from
informant, but not from text. Sharma [23] showed that combining learning from
informant with a restrictive convergence requirement, namely, that the first hypothesis is already the correct one, implies learnability from text, provided that
the usual convergence requirement is applied and the hypothesis may be changed
finitely often before converging to the correct one.

Hence it is natural to investigate what reasonable notions might exist between these two extremes. Using nonrecursive oracles as additional tools cannot
completely close the gap. Even the most powerful oracles do not permit learning
all sets [9], while the oracle K, the halting set, does for learning from informant.

⋆ Valentina Harizanov was partially supported by the UFF grant of the George Washington University.
⋆⋆ Frank Stephan was supported by the Deutsche Forschungsgemeinschaft (DFG) Heisenberg grant Ste 967/1-1.

N. Cesa-Bianchi et al. (Eds.): ALT 2002, LNAI 2533, pp. 233–247, 2002.

Restrictions on texts reduce their nonregularity and allow them to provide further information implicitly [21,26]. Texts can be strengthened by permitting additional queries [13] to retrieve information not contained in standard texts. Ascending texts allow the learner to reconstruct complete negative information in the case of infinite sets, but might fail to do so in the case of finite sets. Thus, the class consisting of an infinite set together with all of its finite subsets remains unlearnable even for learning from ascending text.

Motoki [16] and later Baliga, Case and Jain [3] added to the positive information on the language L to be learned some, but not all, negative information They considered two ways of supplying negative data: (a) there is a finite set of negative information $S \subseteq \overline{L}$ such that the learner always succeeds in learning the set L from input S plus a text for L; (b) there is a finite set $S \subseteq \overline{L}$ such that the learner always succeeds in learning the set L from a text for L plus a text for a set H, disjoint from L and containing S, that is, satisfying $S \subseteq H \subseteq \overline{L}$. Since in case (a) one can learn all recursively enumerable sets by a single learner, the notion (b) is more interesting.

Jain and Stephan [10] treated positive and negative data symmetrically and defined notions less powerful than the ones in [3] that we discussed. The most convenient way to introduce these notions is to use the idea of a minimum adequate teacher as, for example, described by Angluin [2]. Among the learning concepts considered by Jain and Stephan [10], the following one turned out to be most important. A learner requests positive or negative data items from a teacher who has, whenever almost all requests are of the same type, to eventually reveal all information of that type.

In the present work, this type of information is applied to a natural model-theoretic setting: learning recursively enumerable subspaces of a given recursive vector space. Such a subspace is given as the quotient space of the standard recursive infinitely dimensional space over the rationals with the dependence algorithm, V_∞, and its recursively enumerable subspace V. Alternatively, this can be viewed as learning the following class of vector spaces: $\mathcal{L}(V) = \{W : V \subseteq W \subseteq V_\infty \wedge (W \text{ is recursively enumerable})\}$. This class forms a filter in the lattice $\mathcal{L}(V_\infty)$ of all recursively enumerable subspaces of V_∞. Stephan and Ventsov [25] have previously shown that, in the case of learning all ideals of a recursive ring, learnability from text has strong connections to the algebraic properties of the ring. Here, it also turns out that the two notions of learnability of the class $\mathcal{L}(V)$, from positive data or from switching type of information, have corresponding algebraic characterizations. On the other hand, we show that supplying complete information, that is, learning from informant, no longer gives such nice algebraic characterizations. The reason is that while switching type of information provides more learning power than giving positive information only, it is still much weaker than providing information from informant.

Note that some of the proofs in this version are omitted due to size constraints. You can obtain the complete paper as Forschungsberichte Mathematische Logik 55 / 2002, Mathematisches Institut, Universität Heidelberg, Heidelberg, 2002.

2   Preliminaries

Notions from Recursion Theory. Let $\mathbb{N}$ be the set of natural numbers. Sets are often identified with their characteristic functions, so we may write $X(n) = 1$ for $n \in X$ and $X(n) = 0$ for $n \in \overline{X}$. A subset of $\mathbb{N}$ is *recursive* if its characteristic function is recursive. A set of natural numbers is *recursively enumerable* if it is the domain of a partial recursive function or, equivalently, the range of a partial (even total) recursive function. Let $\varphi_0, \varphi_1, \varphi_2, \ldots$ be a fixed effective enumeration of all unary partial recursive functions on $\mathbb{N}$, where φ_e is computed by the Turing program with Gödel index (code) e. We write $\varphi_{e,s}(x) = y$ if $x, y, e < s$ and y is the output of $\varphi_e(x)$ in up to s steps of the Turing program with code e. For $e, s \in \mathbb{N}$, let W_e be the domain of φ_e and $W_{e,s}$ be the domain of the finite function $\varphi_{e,s}$. Then $W_0, W_1, W_2, \ldots$ is a fixed effective enumeration of all recursively enumerable subsets of $\mathbb{N}$. A Turing degree is recursively enumerable if it contains a recursively enumerable set. Let $\langle \cdot, \cdot \rangle$ be a fixed recursive 1-1 pairing function. We define the set $K = \{\langle e, x \rangle : e \in \mathbb{N} \wedge x \in W_e\}$, where $\langle e, x \rangle$ is the natural number that codes the pair (e, x). The set K is a version of the universal halting problem. It is a recursively enumerable and nonrecursive set. Its Turing degree is $\mathbf{0}'$. A Turing degree $\mathbf{a} \leq \mathbf{0}'$ is *high* if its jump has the highest possible value, that is $\mathbf{a}' = \mathbf{0}''$. A set $M \subseteq \mathbb{N}$ is called *maximal* if M is recursively enumerable and its complement $\overline{M}$ is cohesive. A set $\overline{M}$ is *cohesive* if it is infinite and there is no recursively enumerable set W such that $W \cap \overline{M}$ and $(\mathbb{N} - W) \cap \overline{M}$ are both infinite. Every maximal set has a high Turing degree. Conversely, every recursively enumerable high Turing degree contains a maximal set. This characterization was established by Martin. For more information, see [12,22,24].

We consider only countable algebraic structures and computable first-order languages. A countable structure for a computable language is *recursive* if its domain is recursive and its operations and relations are uniformly recursive. An example of a recursive structure is the field $(Q, +, \cdot)$ of rational numbers.

Notions from Algebra. Let $(F, +, \cdot)$ be a fixed recursive field. Then $(V_\infty, +, \cdot)$ is a computable $\aleph_0$-dimensional vector space over $(F, +, \cdot)$, consisting of all finitely nonzero infinite sequences of elements of F, under pointwise operations. Metakides and Nerode [14] showed that the study of recursive and other algorithmic vector spaces can be reduced to the study of V_∞ and its subspaces. A standard (default) basis for V_∞ is $\{\epsilon_0, \epsilon_1, \ldots\}$, where ϵ_i is the infinite sequence with the i-th term 1 and all other terms 0. Having a recursive basis is equivalent to having a recursively enumerable basis, or to the existence of a dependence algorithm. A *dependence algorithm* decides whether any finite subset of vectors is linearly dependent. If B is a basis and v a vector, then the *support* of v with respect to B is defined to be the least subset of B whose linear closure (span) contains v.

Every vector in V_∞ can be identified with its Gödel code, so the set V_∞ can be identified with $\mathbb{N}$. A subspace V of V_∞ is recursive (recursively enumerable, respectively) if its domain is a recursive (recursively enumerable, respectively) subset of the set V_∞. In that case, we also say that the quotient space V_∞/V is recursive (recursively enumerable, respectively). Let $W_0, W_1, \ldots$ be an effective enumeration of all recursively enumerable subsets of V_∞. For every e, let V_e be the vector space generated by W_e, that is, the linear closure of W_e. Then $V_0, V_1, \ldots$ is an effective enumeration of all recursively enumerable subspaces of V_∞. The set of all recursively enumerable vector subspaces of V_∞ is denoted by $\mathcal{L}(V_\infty)$. The class $\mathcal{L}(V_\infty)$, together with the operations of intersection and the direct sums of vector spaces, forms a modular nondistributive lattice. Let V be a fixed recursively enumerable subspace of V_∞. By $\mathcal{L}(V)$ we denote the lattice of all recursively enumerable spaces W such that $V \subseteq W \subseteq V_\infty$. These spaces can be viewed as representatives of the corresponding classes of recursively enumerable subspaces of V_∞/V. For more information see [19]. In the next two sections we assume that the field $(F, +, \cdot)$ is infinite. Without loss of generality, we can assume that it is $(Q, +, \cdot)$.

Vector spaces are special cases of the so-called closure systems or matroids. A matroid consists of a set X equipped with a closure operator Φ, which satisfies certain axioms. In the case of vector spaces, the closure operator is the linear closure of vector spaces. The full axiomatization of matroids will be given in Section 5.

Notions from Learning Theory. The main setting in *inductive inference* is that a learner receives more and more data on an object to be learned, and outputs a sequence of hypotheses that converges to the description of the object. In general, learning can be viewed as a dialogue between a teacher and a learner, where the learner must succeed in learning, provided the teacher satisfies a certain protocol. The formalization has two aspects: convergence behaviour and teacher constraints.

Definition 2.1 [7,10]. A class $\mathcal{L}$ of subsets of V_∞ is learnable according to the criteria specified below iff there is a (total) recursive M, which alternately requests new data items and outputs hypotheses, and which learns every $W \in \mathcal{L}$, whenever the corresponding teacher meets the following requirements.

- All models of learning have in common that the learner makes infinitely many requests that are always either of type 0 (requesting negative data) or of type 1 (requesting positive data). The teacher answers to each request of type y, either by giving a pause symbol or a data item x such that $W(x) = y$.
- Learning from *Text*: The learner requests only information of type 1, and the teacher provides eventually all x with $W(x) = 1$.
- Learning from *Negative Text*: The learner requests only information of type 0, and the teacher provides eventually all x with $W(x) = 0$.
- Learning from *Switching Type of Information*: Whenever the learner almost always requests information of the same type y, the teacher eventually gives all x with $W(x) = y$.

- Learning from *Informant*: The learner alternately requests information of type 0 and type 1, and the teacher eventually provides every $x \in V_\infty$ after some request of the type $W(x)$.

The hypotheses output by the learner are indices in the enumeration of recursively enumerable subspaces of V_∞. Following the above protocol of the dialogue with the teacher, the learner M has to converge in one of the models below, where $e_0, e_1, \ldots$ is the infinite sequences of hypotheses output by M during the learning dialogue.

- *Explanatory* Learning: For almost every n, e_n is the same hypothesis e, which is the index of an enumeration of W.
- *Behaviourally Correct* Learning: For almost every n, the hypothesis e_n is the index of an enumeration of W, although these indices are permitted to be different (syntactically).

Txt, *Sw*, and *Inf* stand for the protocols of learning from text, switching type of information, and informant, respectively. *Ex* and *BC* stand for explanatorily and behaviourally correct learning. For example, $\mathcal{L}$ is *SwBC*-learnable iff there is a recursive M which for every $W \in \mathcal{L}$ and every teacher for W, respecting the constraints for the dialogue with the learner, outputs almost always a hypothesis for W.

Jain and Stephan [10] introduced three main notions for switching protocols. Among these three notions, the one denoted by *NewSw* in [10] turned out to be most appropriate to model switching types of information. Since the other notions are not considered here, *NewSwEx* and *NewSwBC* are just denoted by *SwEx* and *SwBC*, respectively.

Theorem 2.2. Assume that there is $W \in \mathcal{L}$ such that for every finite set D, there are $U, U' \in \mathcal{L}$ such that $U \subset W \subset U'$ and $D \cap U = D \cap W = D \cap U'$. Then $\mathcal{L}$ cannot be *SwBC*-learned.

Proof. Let M be a given *SwBC*-learner and let $\leq$ be the ordering induced by some fixed recursive 1-1 enumeration of V_∞, that is, $x \leq y$ iff x is enumerated before y or $x = y$. Then there is a teacher who knows M and might be nonrecursive doing the following.

- If the current hypothesis of M is correct and there is a finite sequence of answers of some length k, a sequence $x_1, x_2, \ldots, x_k$, corresponding to requests $y_1, y_2, \ldots, y_k$ of M, such that after the hypothesis of M is incorrect, the teacher gives x_1 from one of the shortest such sequences.
- If the current hypothesis is incorrect and y is the request, then output the least x, with respect to the ordering $\leq$, such that x has not yet appeared in any output and $W(x) = y$.
- In the remaining case, all future answers to requests consistent with W result in hypotheses for W. One considers the following two subcases.

- If U and U' have already been chosen, then take the least x, with respect to the ordering $\leq$, which has not yet appeared in the data given by the teacher, and which satisfies $x \in U$ in the case of a request of type 1, and $x \notin U'$ in the case of a request of type 0. If such x does not exist or U, U' have not been chosen, then give the pause symbol $\#$.
- Otherwise, one chooses U, U' and gives to the learner the symbol $\#$. Let D be the set of examples given to the learner so far. Now, one just chooses U, U' according to the condition in the statement of the Theorem: $U \subset W \subset U'$ and $D \cap U = D \cap W = D \cap U'$.

For the verification, assume that M infinitely often conjectures a false hypothesis. Then the second case applies infinitely often and the teacher gives either all elements or all nonelements of W to the corresponding requests. Otherwise, the learner ends up in the third case and eventually chooses U and U' such that $U \subset W \subset U'$. If infinitely often a data item of type 1 is required, then M sees all elements of U and some nonelements of U'. If infinitely often a data item of type 0 is required, then M sees all nonelements of U' and some elements of U. In the first case, M is expected to learn U, in the second case, M is expected to learn U'. However, by choice, M in both cases almost always conjectures the set W, and hence M does not learn $\mathcal{L}$ from switching type of information. Note that this proof holds for both criteria, $SwEx$ and $SwBC$. ∎

This condition also implies $SwBC$-nonlearnability with respect to general learners, which are not required to be recursive. The reason is that the proof does not use the fact that M is recursive, and, thus, also works for nonrecursive learners.

3   Learnability and Types of Quotient Spaces

For the criteria of learning from text and learning from switching type of information, it is possible to characterize learnability in terms of algebraic properties of the recursively enumerable subspaces of the quotient space V_∞/V.

Theorem 3.1. The following statements are equivalent for any recursively enumerable subspace $V \subseteq V_\infty$.

(a) The dimension of V_∞/V is finite.
(b) The class $\mathcal{L}(V)$ is $TxtEx$-learnable.
(c) The class $\mathcal{L}(V)$ is $TxtBC$-learnable.
(d) The class $\mathcal{L}(V)$ is $SwEx$-learnable.

Proof. (a) $\Rightarrow$ (b): Since the dimension of V_∞/V is finite, there is an algorithm that can check for every finite set $D \subset V_\infty$ and every vector x, whether x is in the linear closure of $V \cup D$. As a consequence, the following learner is recursive.

- Initially set $D = \emptyset$.
- The current hypothesis of M is always the linear closure of $V \cup D$, the hypothesis changes iff a new element is put into D.

- Whenever the teacher provides a data item x, M checks whether x is in the linear closure of $V \cup D$.
- If yes, M does not change D and, therefore, keeps the current hypothesis.
- Otherwise, M updates D to $D \cup \{x\}$ and then also updates its hypothesis.

Since the dimension of V_∞/V is finite, every space in $\mathcal{L}(V)$ is generated by $V \cup D$ for some finite set D. It is easy to verify that the algorithm finds this D in the limit. Furthermore, M makes a mind change iff the hypothesis is properly increased. Thus, M does not make more mind changes than the dimension of V_∞/V, and so the algorithm converges.

(b) $\Rightarrow$ (c) and (d): This follows directly from the definition.

(c) $\rightarrow$ (a): Assume $V \neq V_\infty$. Let $v_0, v_1, \dots$ be a recursive enumeration of V_∞ and U_n be the vector space generated by $V \cup \{v_0, v_1, \dots, v_n\}$. Clearly, V_∞ is the ascending union of all spaces U_n. If follows from the basic results on learning from text [7], that the class can only be learned if this ascending chain is finite, that is, there is m with $U_n = U_m$ for all $m \geq n$. It follows that $V_\infty = U_m$ and the dimension of V_∞/V is at most $m + 1$, and hence finite.

(d) $\Rightarrow$ (a): Below, the construction from Theorem 2.2 is adapted to show that V is recursive. Thus, if V_∞/V is recursive, one can find a recursive basis $\{w_0, w_1, \dots\}$ of a vector space U with $U \cap V = \{0\}$. Let W be the linear closure of $V \cup \{w_x : x \in K\}$. The space W is not recursive, and one could now use the argument below to show that $\mathcal{L}(W)$ and, hence, also $\mathcal{L}(V)$ are not $SwEx$-learnable.

Thus, let V be a nonrecursive, but recursively enumerable subspace of V_∞. Let M be a given recursive learner and let $\leq$ be the ordering defined on V_∞ as in Theorem 2.2. There is a teacher who knows M and who does the following.

- If the current hypothesis of M is old and there is a finite sequence $x_1, x_2, \dots, x_k$ of answers, corresponding to requests $y_1, y_2, \dots, y_k$ of M, such that M changes its hypothesis, then the teacher gives x_1 from the shortest such sequence.
- If the current hypothesis is new, then the teacher returns on a request of a datum of type y, the least x, with respect to $\leq$, such that x has not yet been given to the learner and $V(x) = y$.

If the protocol continues, then the learning process goes infinitely often through both cases. It follows that the learner has made infinitely many hypotheses, and that the teacher has either given all elements of V on requests of type 1, or all elements of $\overline{V}$ on requests of type 0. Thus, the learner is given the required information on V, without converging syntactically. Hence, M does not $SwEx$-learn $\mathcal{L}(V)$, and so this case need not be considered.

Therefore, there is a situation without further mind changes when data consistent with V are fed continuously. One can assume that the current hypothesis is a hypothesis for V, since, otherwise, M would not learn V. Now, there are two cases.

- In every situation the learner can find itself, one can give some elements of V such that later a data item of type 0 is requested. This permits the teacher to take some recursively enumerable superspace W of V, and at every request for a datum of type 0, to feed into the learner the least $x \notin W$ that the learner had not seen so far. Then the learner does not identify the space W, although it has seen an infinite data sequence for this space.
- Otherwise, one can feed into M finitely many data consistent with V, such that M never later requests data of type 0. Let D be the set of data of type 0 seen so far. Now, one can enumerate $\overline{V}$ as follows: $x \notin V$ iff one can either continue to feed M with data from the linear closure of $V \cup \{x\}$ until a mind change occurs, or data of type 0 is requested, or some element of D is enumerated into the linear closure of $V \cup \{x\}$. This contradicts the fact that V is nonrecursive.

This completes the proof that if the dimension of V_∞/V is infinite, then $\mathcal{L}(V)$ is not $SwEx$-learnable. ∎

Metakides and Nerode [14] defined a (recursively enumerable) space $V \in \mathcal{L}(V_\infty)$ to be maximal if the dimension of V_∞/V is infinite and for every recursively enumerable space W such that $V \subseteq W \subseteq V_\infty$, we have that either V_∞/W is finitely dimensional or W/V is finitely dimensional. Metakides and Nerode used Friedberg's e-state method to construct a maximal space. Shore (see [14]) established that every maximal subset of a recursive basis of V_∞ generates a maximal subspace of V_∞.

Kalantari and Retzlaff [11] defined a space $V \in \mathcal{L}(V_\infty)$ to be supermaximal if the dimension of V_∞/V is infinite and for every recursively enumerable space $W \supseteq V$, either $W = V_\infty$ or W/V is finitely dimensional. Let $k \geq 0$ be a natural number. Kalantari and Retzlaff [11] further introduced the concept of a k-thin space, and showed its existence. A space $V \in \mathcal{L}(V_\infty)$ is k-thin if the dimension of V_∞/V is infinite and for every recursively enumerable subspace $W \supseteq V$, either the dimension of V_∞/V is $\leq k$ or the dimension of W/V is finite, and there exists $U \in \mathcal{L}(V_\infty)$ such that $U \supseteq V$ and the dimension of V_∞/U is k. Hence supermaximal spaces are also called 0-thin.

Hird [8] introduced a concept of a strongly supermaximal space. A space $V \in \mathcal{L}(V_\infty)$ is strongly supermaximal if the dimension of V_∞/V is infinite and for every recursively enumerable subset $X \subseteq V_\infty - V$, there exists a finite subset $D \subseteq V_\infty$ such that the set X is contained in the linear closure of $V \cup D$. Hird showed that strongly supermaximal spaces exist. He also established that every strongly supermaximal space is supermaximal, and that not every supermaximal space is strongly supermaximal. Downey and Hird [4] showed that strongly supermaximal spaces exist in every nonzero recursively enumerable Turing degree.

Theorem 3.2. The class $\mathcal{L}(V)$ is $SwBC$-learnable iff either V_∞/V is finite dimensional or V is 0-thin or 1-thin.

Proof. First assume that V_∞/V has infinite dimension, and that V is neither 0-thin nor 1-thin. Then there is a recursively enumerable space W such that $V \subset W \subset V_\infty$, the quotient space W/V has infinite dimension, and V_∞/W has dimension at least 2. In particular, there are vectors $x_1, x_2 \notin W$ that are linearly independent over W. Now, for every finite set D of vectors, one can choose a positive integer n such that none of the vectors in $D - W$ is in the linear closure of $W \cup \{x_1 + nx_2\}$. Furthermore, the linear closure of $V \cup (W \cap D)$ has finite dimension over V, and thus is different from W. So the condition in Theorem 2.2 is satisfied, and hence $\mathcal{L}(V)$ is not $SwBC$-learnable.

To prove the converse, we have to consider only the cases of 0-thin and 1-thin spaces, since Theorem 3.1 deals with the case when the dimension of V_∞/V is finite. In these two cases, there is a minimal space W such that $V \subseteq W$ and W/V is infinitely dimensional. Furthermore, if V is 0-thin, we have that $W = V_\infty$. If V is 1-thin, we have that $W \subset V_\infty$ and there is no other such recursively enumerable vector space U with the quotient space U/V having infinite dimension. This property allows us to give the following learning algorithm.

- The learner M requests examples of type 0 until one of them is enumerated into W. The hypothesis is V_∞ while no example of type 0 (except pause signs) has shown up, and W otherwise.
- If some example of type 0 has shown up so far, then M requests examples of type 1 and the current hypothesis is the linear closure of $V \cup E$, where E is the set of all examples of type 1 seen so far.

In the cases of V_∞ and W, the learner requests only information of type 0. If none is supplied, the hypothesis V_∞ is correct, if some examples are given, but they are all outside W, then the hypothesis W is correct. Otherwise, the vector space to be learned is the linear closure of $V \cup D$, for some finite set D. As that space cannot cover W, an example of type 0 and inside W shows up and causes that, from that time on, M only requests data of type 1. So the teacher has eventually to reveal all elements of the linear closure of $V \cup D$ and, from some time on, D is contained in the set E of current examples used in the hypothesis. ∎

4   Learning Vector Spaces from Informant

The two notions of learning from informant do not seem to have similar algebraic characterizations. In the case of 0-thin vector spaces, the class $\mathcal{L}(V)$ consists just of V_∞ and the vector spaces that are the linear closures of V together with finitely many other vectors. Nevertheless, it depends on the actual choice of V whether the class $\mathcal{L}(V)$ is $InfEx$-learnable. Furthermore, the infinite product of 0-thin spaces (as formalized in Definition 4.3) can be $InfEx$-learnable, as well as nonlearnable. Unfortunately, due to size limitations, this section had to be shortened and we just state its major results.

Theorem 4.1. There is a recursively enumerable vector space V such that $\overline{K}$, the complement of the halting problem, is uniformly enumerable relative to every recursively enumerable vector space W with $V \subseteq W \subset V_\infty$. In particular, $\mathcal{L}(V)$ is $InfEx$-learnable.

Theorem 4.2. There is a strongly supermaximal (and hence 0-thin) vector space V such that the class $\mathcal{L}(V)$ is not $InfEx$-learnable.

Definition 4.3. For $i \in \mathbb{N}$, let l_i be the linear mapping defined by $l_i(\epsilon_j) = \epsilon_{\langle i,j \rangle}$ for every $j \in \mathbb{N}$. Let V_{lp} be the linear closure of the union $l_0(V) \cup l_1(V) \cup \dots$ of linear projections and let, as usual, $\mathcal{L}(V_{lp})$ be the class of all recursively enumerable superspaces of V_{lp}.

Theorem 4.4. There is a 0-thin vector space V such that the class $\mathcal{L}(V_{lp})$ is $InfEx$-learnable. On the other hand, there is also a 0-thin vector space W such that the class $\mathcal{L}(W_{lp})$ is even not $InfBC$-learnable.

5   Generalizing the Results

The previous results hold when the vector space V_∞ is over any infinite recursive field F. If V_∞ is over a finite recursive field, then one of the results changes, namely, the characterization of $SwBC$-learnable classes of superspaces.

Proposition 5.1. Assume that V_∞ is over a finite field F. Let V be a recursively enumerable subspace of V_∞.

(a) $\mathcal{L}(V)$ is $SwEx$-learnable iff V_∞/V is finite dimensional.
(b) $\mathcal{L}(V)$ is $SwBC$-learnable if either V_∞/V is finite dimensional or V is k-thin.
(c) $\mathcal{L}(V)$ is not $SwBC$-learnable if there is a recursively enumerable subspace W such that $V \subset W \subset V_\infty$ and the quotient spaces V_∞/W and W/V both have infinite dimension.

Proof. Part (a) follows from the proof of Theorem 3.1 since the proof does not use the fact that V is vector space over an infinite field.

Part (b), in the case when V_∞/V is finitely dimensional, is proven using the same learning algorithm as in the case of an infinite field. So let V be k-thin and let $W \in \mathcal{L}(V_\infty)$ be such that V_∞ is the closure of $W \cup \{w_1, w_2, \dots, w_k\}$, for some $w_1, w_2, \dots, w_k \in V_\infty$. The set U of linear combinations of $w_1, w_2, \dots, w_k$ is finite. Now one applies the following learning algorithm.

  — As long as no element of W shows up, the learner asks for negative examples and considers the set $\tilde{U}$ of those elements of U that have not appeared so far as negative examples in the data. Then the current hypothesis is the linear closure of $W \cup \tilde{U}$.
  — Otherwise, that is, when some element of W had been returned as a negative example, the learner starts requesting positive examples and always conjectures the linear closure of $W \cup E$, where E is the set of positive examples seen so far.

The extension of learning $\mathcal{L}(V)$ from the case of a 1-thin space V to an arbitrary k-thin space V is based on the fact that, due to the finiteness of U, the set $\tilde{U}$ can be completely determined in the limit. The subspace being learned is generated by $W \cup \tilde{U}$, unless a negative example belonging to W is found. Besides this fact, the verification is the same as in the case of a vector space over an infinite field.

Part (c) is proven using Theorem 2.2 and the fact that the dimensions of the spaces V_∞/W and W/V are infinite. Let $\{v_0, v_1, \ldots\}$ be a linearly independent set over W, that is, no v_i is in the closure of $W \cup \{v_j : j < i\}$. Then W is the lower bound of the linear closures of the sets $W \cup \{v_k\}$, $k \in \mathbb{N}$. Moreover, W is the upper bound of the linear closures of $V \cup \{u_0, u_1, \ldots, u_i\}$, where $u_0, u_1, \ldots$ is an enumeration of W. Both sequences of spaces converge pointwise to W, from above and from below, and consist of members of $\mathcal{L}(V)$. Thus, $\mathcal{L}(V)$ is not $SwBC$-learnable by Theorem 2.2. ∎

A more general approach to learning recursively enumerable substructures of a recursive structure with the dependence relations is to consider, instead of V_∞, recursive matroids (see [5,17,18]). A matroid consists of a set X and of a closure operator Φ that maps the power set of X into itself and satisfies certain axioms [15]. If we consider recursive infinite matroids, without loss of generality, we can identify X with $\mathbb{N}$. The closure operator in matroids corresponds to the linear closure in vector spaces.

Definition 5.2. We say that an infinite set X and an operator Φ define a recursive matroid (X, Φ) if Φ maps recursively enumerable subsets of X to recursively enumerable subsets of X and satisfies the following axioms:

(a) If $Y \subseteq Z$ then $\Phi(Y) \subseteq \Phi(Z)$;
(b) We have that $Y \subseteq \Phi(Y)$ and $\Phi(\Phi(Y)) = \Phi(Y)$;
(c) For all $x \in \Phi(Y)$, there is a finite subset $D \subseteq Y$ with $x \in \Phi(D)$;
(d) If $Y = \Phi(Y)$ and $x, y \notin Y$ and $x \in \Phi(Y \cup \{y\})$, then $y \in \Phi(Y \cup \{x\})$;
(e) There is a recursive function f with $\Phi(W_e) = W_{f(e)}$ for all e.

The axiom (e) can sometimes be strengthened by requiring that one can compute from x and a finite set D, whether $x \in \Phi(D)$. However, this condition does not always hold for vector spaces considered here, and we are interested in a generalization of the classes $\mathcal{L}(V)$ for $V \in \mathcal{L}(V_\infty)$. Thus, we adopt only the weaker version (e). The set $\Phi(D)$ generalizes the concept of the linear closure after adding V to D, and so $x \in V$ iff $x \in \Phi(\emptyset)$. Thus the axiom (e) corresponds to the case where V is recursively enumerable, while the discussed strengthened version corresponds to V being decidable. Decidability of V is equivalent to the existence of a dependence algorithm over V, and implies recursiveness of V as a set (see [14]).

The axiom (d) given here is omitted by some authors. The following remark is a consequence of axiom (d) and shows that matroids are sufficiently similar to vector spaces. In particular, one can for submatroids Y, Z of X with $Y \subseteq Z$ introduce a dimension of Z over Y. Here, Y is a submatroid of X if $Y \subseteq X$ and $Y = \Phi(Y)$. As it is understood that the operator on the submatroid is the restriction of Φ to Y, the operator is omitted from the submatroid and the submatroid is identified with its domain Y.

Remark 5.3. Assume that Y, Z are submatroids of a matroid (X, Φ). Furthermore, assume that $Y \subseteq Z$. One says that Z/Y has dimension n if there is a set D with n elements, but not one with fewer than n elements, such that $Z = \Phi(Y \cup D)$. The space Z/Y has finite dimension iff there is such a set D of finite cardinality.

If $n > 0$, $z \in Z - Y$ and Z/Y has dimension n, then $Z/(\Phi(Y \cup \{z\}))$ has dimension $n - 1$. To see this, first note that there is no set E of cardinality strictly less than $n - 1$ such that $Z = \Phi(Y \cup E \cup \{z\})$, so the dimension of $Z/(\Phi(Y \cup \{z\}))$ is at least $n - 1$. On the other hand, there is a maximal set $F \subset D$ such that $z \notin \Phi(Y \cup F)$. Then $d \in \Phi(Y \cup F \cup \{z\})$ for all $d \in D - F$. It follows that $Z = \Phi(Y \cup F \cup \{z\})$ and the dimension of $Z/(\Phi(Y \cup \{z\}))$ is at most the cardinality of F, in particular at most $n - 1$.

A consequence is that for every submatroid Y, where X/Y has finite dimension, and for every set $U \subseteq X - Y$, there is a finite set D such that $\Phi(Y \cup D) \cap U = \emptyset$ and $\Phi(Y \cup D \cup U) = X$. Note that D is not empty iff $\Phi(Y \cup U) \subset X$.

In the following proposition, we consider the class $\mathcal{L}$ of recursively enumerable submatroids of a given matroid. Furthermore, general learners which do not have to be computable are considered. Adleman and Blum [1] proposed to measure the complexity of such learners in terms of their Turing degrees. Together with Theorem 2.2, one has that, whenever a general $SwEx$-learner exists, this learner can be chosen so that it is computable relative to the halting problem K.

Theorem 5.4. Given a matroid (X, Φ), let $\mathcal{L}$ be the class of its recursively enumerable submatroids. Relative to the halting-problem K, the following conditions are equivalent:

(a) the class $\mathcal{L}$ is $SwEx$-learnable relative to K;
(b) the class $\mathcal{L}$ is $SwBC$-learnable relative to K;
(c) the condition of Theorem 2.2 does not hold.

Proof. The part (a) $\Rightarrow$ (b) follows directly from the definition, and (b) $\Rightarrow$ (c) follows from the proof of Theorem 2.2 since it does not use the property that the learner M is recursive. So it also works with general learners which are recursive in K or even in a more powerful oracle. The part (c) $\Rightarrow$ (a) is shown using the following learning algorithm. Here Φ is defined as in the statement of the theorem, $L_i = \Phi(W_i)$ is the i-th recursively enumerable submatroid of X, and D_j is the j-th finite subset of X. Furthermore, there are recursive functions f and g such that $W_{f(i)} = \Phi(W_i)$ and $W_{g(j)} = D_j$. Let X_s consist of the first s elements of X with respect to some recursive default enumeration.

Algorithm. After having seen s input examples, let P consist of the examples of type 1 and N be the examples of type 0 seen so far. Find the first triple (i, j, pos) or (i, j, neg) from an enumeration of all triples such that the triple satisfies the following condition.

(pos) $i = g(j)$ and $\Phi(D_j) = \Phi(P)$;
(neg) $N \subseteq \overline{L_i}$ and $P \subseteq L_i$ and $X_s \subseteq \Phi(L_i \cup D_j)$ and $D_j \subseteq \Phi(L_i \cup N)$.

Output the index $f(i)$. In the case of (pos), request positive data, otherwise, request negative data.

Verification. Note that $\Phi(D_j) = \Phi(P)$ iff $D_j \subseteq \Phi(P)$ and $P \subseteq \Phi(D_j)$. So the algorithm only checks whether explicitly given finite sets are contained in some recursively enumerable sets or their complements. Thus the learner is K-recursive. Since there is a triple (i, j, pos) such that $D_j = P$ and $i = g(j)$, the search always terminates and the learner is total.

Assume that Y is the submatroid to be learned. If the dimensions of X/Y and $Y/\Phi(\emptyset)$ are both infinite, then the condition of Theorem 2.2 is satisfied since for every finite set D, there is a finite set E such that $\Phi(Y \sqcap D) \subset Y \subset \Phi(Y \cup E)$ and $D \cap \Phi(Y \cup E) = D \cap Y$. So Y could be approximated from below and from above by pointwise convergent series of sets different from Y. Since this cannot happen, at least one of the dimensions X/Y and $Y/\Phi(\emptyset)$ is finite.

Assume that the algorithm takes at some stage s the triple (i, j, pos). Then $L_i = \Phi(D_j) = \Phi(P)$ and the output is consistent with the input. Since $P \subseteq Y$, one has that $L_i \subseteq Y$. Furthermore, the algorithm will then continue to request positive data until some example outside L_i is seen. This happens eventually iff $Y \neq L_i$.

Assume that the algorithm takes at some stage s the triple (i, j, neg). Then the algorithm will keep this index until it either becomes clear that $X \not\subseteq \Phi(Y \cup W_j)$ or a negative example in $Y - L_i$ shows up. In the first case, D_j does not witness that the dimension of X/Y is finite, in the second case, $Y \neq L_i$.

To see that the algorithm converges, let N' and P' be the sets of all negative and positive examples seen by the learner throughout the overall running time of the algorithm. If the dimension of $\Phi(P')/\Phi(\emptyset)$ is finite, then there is a triple (i, j, pos) such that $i = g(j)$ and $\Phi(D_j) = \Phi(P')$. From some time on, enough data has been seen so that this triple will be used unless some of the finitely many triples before it is used almost always. Otherwise, the dimension of $\Phi(P')/\Phi(\emptyset)$ is infinite and the dimension of X/Y is finite. Then the dimension of $Y/\Phi(\emptyset)$ is infinite since $P' \subseteq Y$. It follows that the dimension of X/Y is finite. By Remark 5.3, there is a finite set E such that $N' \cap \Phi(Y \cup E) = \emptyset$ and $X = \Phi(Y \cup E \cup N')$. There is a triple (i, j, neg) such that $L_i = \Phi(Y \cup E)$ and $D_j \cap L_i = \emptyset$ and $X = \Phi(L_i \cup D_j)$. Again, this triple will be used almost always unless some of the finitely many triples before it is used almost always. So it follows that the algorithm converges to one triple that is used almost always. In the paragraphs of the verification preceding this one, it has been shown that whenever a triple is used almost always, then the learner converges to the correct hypothesis. ∎

Each of the $SwBC$-learnable classes of subspaces required only one switch. First, the learner observed negative examples. If these examples ruled out a fixed subspace W, then the learner switched to positive data, and never again abandoned this type of data requests. The following examples give some matroids, where infinitely many switches are required. This situation is more analogous to the general case, for which Jain and Stephan [10] showed that there is a real hierarchy of learnability, depending on the number of switches allowed.

Furthermore, the examples below show that there are classes witnessing both extremes. The class in Example 5.5 has a recursive $SwEx$-learner, while every $SwBC$-learner and thus also every $SwEx$-learner of the class in Example 5.6 needs a K-oracle.

Example 5.5. There is a recursive matroid such that every recursively enumerable submatroid is either finite or cofinite. The class of these submatroids can be $SwEx$-learned, but not with any bound on the number of switches.

Proof. Let $X = \mathbb{N}$. Let A be a maximal subset of X [20, Definition III.4.13]. For any given set Y, let

$$\Phi(Y) = \{x : (\exists y \in Y)\,[y = x \lor (y < x \land \{y, y+1, \ldots, x-1\} \subseteq A)$$
$$\lor (y > x \land \{x, x+1, \ldots, y-1\} \subseteq A)]\,\}.$$

Clearly, $\Phi(Y)$ is recursively enumerable whenever Y is.

Let $a_0, a_1, \ldots$ be the ascending (and nonrecursive) enumeration of all elements of $\overline{A}$. Let $A_0 = \{0, 1, \ldots, a_0\}$ and $A_n = \{a_{n-1} + 1, a_{n-1} + 2, \ldots, a_n\}$ for any $n > 0$. Then $\Phi(Y)$ is the union of all sets A_n that meet Y. If Y is finite, so is $\Phi(Y)$. If Y is infinite, then Y meets infinitely many sets A_n; in particular, $\Phi(Y) - A$ is infinite. If Y is in addition recursively enumerable, then the maximality of A implies that $\Phi(Y)$ contains almost all numbers a_n. For these n, the corresponding sets A_n are subsets of $\Phi(Y)$. In particular, $\Phi(Y)$ is cofinite. So whenever Y is recursively enumerable, $\Phi(Y)$ is either finite or cofinite.

Thus, one can $SwEx$-learn all recursively enumerable submatroids, by $SwEx$-learning all finite and cofinite sets, as it is done in [10]. ∎

Example 5.6. There is a recursive matroid whose class of all recursively enumerable submatroids can be $SwBC$-learned with the help of an K-oracle but not with the help of any oracle $A \not\geq_T K$.

References

[1] Lenny Adleman and Manuel Blum. Inductive inference and unsolvability. *The Journal of Symbolic Logic*, 56(3):891–900, 1991.
[2] Dana Angluin. Learning regular sets from queries and counter-examples. *Information and Computation*, 75:87–106, 1987.
[3] Ganesh Baliga, John Case and Sanjay Jain. Language learning with some negative information. *Journal of Computer and System Sciences*, 51(5):273–285, 1995.
[4] Rod G. Downey and Geoffrey R. Hird, Automorphisms of supermaximal spaces. *The Journal of Symbolic Logic*, 50(1):1–9, 1985.
[5] Rod G. Downey and Jeffrey B. Remmel, Computable algebras and closure systems: coding properties. In: *Handbook of Recursive Mathematics*, volume 2, pages 977–1039. Elsevier, Amsterdam, 1998.
[6] Lance Fortnow, William Gasarch, Sanjay Jain, Efim Kinber, Martin Kummer, Stuart Kurtz, Mark Pleszkoch, Theodore Slaman, Robert Solovay and Frank Stephan. Extremes in the degrees of inferability. *Annals of Pure and Applied Logic*, 66:231–276, 1994.
[7] E. Mark Gold. Language identification in the limit. *Information and Control*, 10: 447–474, 1967.

[8] Geoffrey R. Hird. Recursive properties of relations on models. *Annals of Pure and Applied Logic*, 63:241–269, 1993.

[9] Sanjay Jain and Arun Sharma. On the non-existence of maximal inference degrees for language identification. *Information Processing Letters*, 47:81–88, 1993.

[10] Sanjay Jain and Frank Stephan. Learning by switching type of information. In: *Algorithmic Learning Theory: Twelfth International Conference (ALT 2001)*, volume 2225 of *Lecture Notes in Artificial Intelligence*, pages 205–218. Springer-Verlag, Heidelberg, 2001.

[11] Iraj Kalantari and Allen Retzlaff. Maximal vector spaces under automorphisms of the lattice of recursively enumerable vector spaces. *The Journal of Symbolic Logic*, 42(4):481–491, 1977.

[12] Michael Machtey and Paul Young. *An Introduction to the General Theory of Algorithms*. North Holland, New York, 1978.

[13] Wolfgang Merkle and Frank Stephan. Refuting learning revisited. Technical Report Forschungsberichte Mathematische Logik 52/2001, Mathematisches Institut, Universität Heidelberg, 2001.

[14] George Metakides and Anil Nerode, Recursively enumerable vector spaces. *Annals of Mathematical Logic*, 11:147–171, 1977.

[15] George Metakides and Anil Nerode, Recursion theory on fields and abstract dependence. *Journal of Algebra*, 65:36–59, 1980.

[16] Tatsuya Motoki. Inductive inference from all positive and some negative data. *Information Processing Letters*, 39(4):177–182, 1991.

[17] Anil Nerode and Jeffrey Remmel, Recursion theory on matroids. In: *Patras Logic Symposium, Studies in Logic and the Foundations of Mathematics*, volume 109, pages 41–65. North-Holland, 1982.

[18] Anil Nerode and Jeffrey Remmel, Recursion theory on matroids II. In: *Southeast Asian Conference on Logic*, pages 133–184. North-Holland, 1983.

[19] Anil Nerode and Jeffrey Remmel, A survey of lattices of r.e. substructures. In: *Proceedings of Symposia in Pure Mathematics*, volume 42, pages 323–375. American Mathematical Society, 1985.

[20] Piergiorgio Odifreddi. *Classical Recursion Theory*. North-Holland, Amsterdam, 1989.

[21] Daniel Osherson, Michael Stob and Scott Weinstein. *Systems that Learn: An Introduction to Learning Theory for Cognitive and Computer Scientists*. MIT Press, 1986.

[22] Hartley Rogers. *Theory of Recursive Functions and Effective Computability*. McGraw-Hill, 1967. Reprinted, MIT Press, 1987.

[23] Arun Sharma. A note on batch and incremental learnability. *Journal of Computer and System Sciences*, 56(3):272–276, 1998.

[24] Robert I. Soare. *Recursively Enumerable Sets and Degrees*. Springer-Verlag, Heidelberg, 1987.

[25] Frank Stephan and Yuri Ventsov. Learning Algebraic Structures from Text using Semantical Knowledge. *Theoretical Computer Science – Series A*, 268:221-273, 2001.

[26] Rolf Wiehagen. Identification of formal languages. In: *Mathematical Foundations of Computer Science*, volume 53 of *Lecture Notes in Computer Science*, pages 571–579. Springer-Verlag, 1977.

[27] C. E. M. Yates. Three theorems on the degree of recursively enumerable degrees. *Duke Mathematical Journal*, 32:461–468, 1965.

Learning, Logic, and Topology in a Common Framework

Eric Martin[1], Arun Sharma[1], and Frank Stephan[2]

[1] School of Computer Science and Engineering, The University of New South Wales,
Sydney, NSW 2052, Australia, {emartin, arun}@cse.unsw.edu.au
[2] Universität Heidelberg, 69121 Heidelberg, Germany,
fstephan@math.uni-heidelberg.de

Abstract. Many connections have been established between learning and logic, or learning and topology, or logic and topology. Still, the connections are not at the heart of these fields. Each of them is fairly independent of the others when attention is restricted to basic notions and main results. We show that connections can actually be made at a fundamental level, and result in a parametrized logic that needs topological notions for its early developments, and notions from learning theory for interpretation and applicability.

One of the key properties of first-order logic is that the classical notion of logical consequence is compact. We generalize the notion of logical consequence, and we generalize compactness to β-weak compactness where β is an ordinal. The effect is to stratify the set of generalized logical consequences of a theory into levels, and levels into layers. Deduction corresponds to the lower layer of the first level above the underlying theory, learning with less than β mind changes to layer β of the first level, and learning in the limit to the first layer of the second level. Refinements of Borel-like hierarchies provide the topological tools needed to develop the framework.

1 Introduction

There is an immediate similarity between the compactness theorem of first-order logic and finite learning. Indeed, let T be a (possibly infinite) first-order theory and let φ be a first-order formula. If φ is a logical consequence of T, then φ is a logical consequence of a finite subset of T, which means that if all members of T are enumerated then after some finite time, a learner can discover that $T \models \varphi$ and will not have to change its mind. This simple observation could have initiated a common destiny for logic and learning, but the story of their developments is different. Finite learning is hardly considered as learning, and learning theory thrived over more complex criteria of learnability. On the other hand, classical first-order logic promoted the view that the compactness theorem significantly accounts for its successfulness. So the analogy between the compactness theorem and finite learning seems more like a case for an early divorce than for a natural union of logic and learning.

N. Cesa-Bianchi et al. (Eds.): ALT 2002, LNAI 2533, pp. 248–262, 2002.

The idea of a logic of induction has had advocates before formal deductive logic was invented, even if the term 'logic' applied to induction could either mean a framework that closely follows the line of deductive logic—define a syntax, a semantics and a proof theory—or a framework based on probability theory, hence quite different in nature from Frege's creation. In any case, a 'logic of induction' is generally opposed to deductive logic: for instance, the former should be based on nonmonotonic forms of reasoning [13] contrary to the latter. But is there a natural formal system that would encompass both deduction and induction? Such a system or *paradigm* $\mathcal{P}$ would be based on a notion of generalized logical consequence that would not be compact. We would identify the 'deductive consequences' (w.r.t. $\mathcal{P}$) of a theory T with the generalized logical consequences of T that enjoy the compactness property. And we could hope that a weaker form of compactness would be the hallmark of the 'inductive consequences' (w.r.t. $\mathcal{P}$) of T [16]. As will be seen, this idea can be refined and results in a notion of 'β-weak compactness' that has a natural interpretation by the notion of learning with less than β mind changes [1,6,9,23]. Such a correspondence is appealing, and not just because the notion of β-weak compactness is formally amazingly simple. It can also provide characterizations of the syntax of the hypotheses that can be learned with less than β mind changes, and related to what is known in topology as the difference hierarchy [10]. This kind of characterization has been obtained when β is an integer [5], together with other results that relate various learning paradigms derived from [8] to some topological spaces [12,19,20,22]. For instance, it has been pointed out that learnability in the limit can be related to being Δ_2 in the Borel hierarchy defined over some topological space [7,22]. We will reestablish and extend these connections in a more systematic and general setting (in particular, for an arbitrary set of possible data), where logic, topology and learning are interrelated.

We proceed as follows. We define the logical notions in Section 2, add the topological notions in Section 3, and finally the notions from learning theory in Section 4. We give some of the results that bind the notions together, but space limitations force us to omit some we would like to present. In particular, effective versions of our results are not provided: our aim here is to provide the reader with an overview of the concepts of this framework at a fundamental level. We conclude in Section 5.

2 A Generalized Logic

2.1 Paradigms

Rather than one logic, our framework defines a *parametrized* logic, or set of six parameters, called a *paradigm*. Classical first-order logic is a particular paradigm, and some classical learning paradigms are other examples of paradigms. We now define the six parameters. A vocabulary is a set of predicate symbols and function symbols (constants are 0-ary function symbols), possibly containing equality.

Notation 1 *We denote by S a countable vocabulary.*

All syntactic notions are defined using S. The natural classes of languages to be dealt with in this framework are (maybe not proper) extensions of first-order languages, called *countable fragments of* $\mathcal{L}_{\omega_1\omega}$ [14]. We denote by $\mathcal{L}_{\omega\omega}^S$ the set of formulas built from S and a countable set of first-order variables using negation, disjunction and conjunction of (possibly empty) finite sets of formulas, and quantification. We denote by $\mathcal{L}_{\omega_1\omega}^S$ the extension of $\mathcal{L}_{\omega\omega}^S$ that accepts conjunctions and disjunctions of countable sets of formulas. A *fragment of* $\mathcal{L}_{\omega_1\omega}^S$ is a subset $\mathcal{L}$ of $\mathcal{L}_{\omega_1\omega}^S$ that extends $\mathcal{L}_{\omega\omega}^S$, all of whose members contain at most finitely many distinct free variables, and such that $\mathcal{L}$ is closed under subformulas, substitution of free variables by terms, boolean operators, and quantification.

Notation 2 *We denote by $\mathcal{L}$ a countable fragment of* $\mathcal{L}_{\omega_1\omega}^S$.

We refer to the members of $\mathcal{L}$ as *formulas*, to closed formulas as *sentences*, and to subsets of $\mathcal{L}$ as *theories*. Given $\varphi \in \mathcal{L}$, we represent the negation of the universal closure of φ by $\sim \varphi$. The third parameter is a *metalanguage*. We identify a member φ of $\mathcal{L}_{\omega_1\omega}^S$ with the *elementary* metaformula $\ulcorner\varphi\urcorner$. The sets $\mathcal{M}_{\omega\omega}^S$ and $\mathcal{M}_{\omega_1\omega}^S$ of metaformulas, whose elementary members are respectively $\{\ulcorner\varphi\urcorner \mid \varphi \in \mathcal{L}_{\omega\omega}^S\}$ and $\{\ulcorner\varphi\urcorner \mid \varphi \in \mathcal{L}_{\omega_1\omega}^S\}$, are obtained by successive applications of negation, and disjunction and conjunction over sets that are finite if dealing with $\mathcal{M}_{\omega\omega}^S$, or countable if dealing with $\mathcal{M}_{\omega_1\omega}^S$. It is then possible to define the *countable fragments of* $\mathcal{M}_{\omega_1\omega}^S$ *based on* $\mathcal{L}$, that are the natural metalanguages of the framework.

Notation 3 *We denote by $\mathcal{M}$ a countable fragment of* $\mathcal{M}_{\omega_1\omega}^S$ *based on* $\mathcal{L}$.

Details of what counts as a countable fragment of $\mathcal{M}_{\omega_1\omega}^S$ are omitted. For this paper, it is only essential to understand that if φ is a member of $\mathcal{L}$, then $\neg\ulcorner\varphi\urcorner$ is a member of $\mathcal{M}$; it is a *metalogical consequence* of a theory T iff φ is not a logical consequence of T. Negation as failure [3] is an instance of the metarule: from $\neg\ulcorner\varphi\urcorner$ derive $\neg\varphi$. The fourth parameter is a class of structures (over S). Of particular importance is the class of *Henkin structures*, all of whose individuals are the nonempty sets of closed terms that they interpret, and the class of *Herbrand structures* that is, Henkin structures all of whose individuals are singletons. Suppose for instance that $S = \{P\} \cup \{\bar{n} \mid n \in \mathbb{N}\}$ where P is a unary predicate symbol and for all $n \in \mathbb{N}$, $\bar{n}$ is a constant. Obviously, $\varphi = \forall x P(x)$ is not a logical consequence of $T = \{P(\bar{n}) \mid n \in \mathbb{N}\}$, but every *Herbrand* model of T is a model of φ. The latter could be a definition of 'φ is a generalized logical consequence of T' (w.r.t. the class of Herbrand structures), and arguably, we could expect that φ would even be an inductive consequence of T. Moreover, we claim that when learning theory is cast in a logical framework, the intended interpretations consist of Herbrand or Henkin interpretations only. *E.g.*, consider learning paradigms where the aim is to identify an r.e. set of integers. Only standard integers are considered, nonstandard models of arithmetics are implicitly ruled out.

Notation 4 *We denote by $\mathcal{W}$ a class of structures. Given a set T of formulas, we denote by* $\mathrm{Mod}_{\mathcal{W}}(T)$ *the class of models of T in $\mathcal{W}$.*

Members of W will be referred to as *possible worlds*. The fifth parameter is a set of formulas called set of *possible evidence*.

Notation 5 *We denote by $\mathcal{E}$ a set of formulas.*

Classical first-order logic, being purely hypothetico-deductive, basically sets $\mathcal{E}$ to $\emptyset$. On the other hand, $\mathcal{E}$ is one of the key parameters of any paradigm in learning theory. It corresponds to the set of possible data. Natural choices for $\mathcal{E}$ are the set of atomic sentences and their negations (when learning from both positive and negative data), or the set of atomic sentences (when learning from positive data only) [15]. In general, no condition is imposed on $\mathcal{E}$. In the realm of classical logic, the notion of possible evidence is void, but every set of formulas can be the starting point for logical investigation. This means that every formula is a *possible axiom*. In learning theory on the other hand, either it is assumed that there is no possible axiom, because a learner has access only to data from the environment, or a possible axiom can be conceived of as a member of some background knowledge, that could consist of formulas of a given kind, for instance, definite Horn clauses [18]. The set of possible axioms is the last parameter of the framework. For convenience, a possible evidence is a possible axiom.

Notation 6 *We denote by $\mathcal{A}$ a set of formulas containing $\mathcal{E}$.*

We now have all the ingredients of our framework.

Notation 7 *The sextuple $(S, \mathcal{L}, \mathcal{M}, \mathcal{W}, \mathcal{E}, \mathcal{A})$ is denoted $\mathcal{P}$.*

We refer to $\mathcal{P}$, the paradigm under investigation, as a (logical) *paradigm*.

2.2 Generalized Logical Consequence

Given a structure $\mathfrak{M}$, the $\mathcal{E}$-*diagram of* $\mathfrak{M}$, denoted $D_\mathcal{E}(\mathfrak{M})$, is the set of all members of $\mathcal{E}$ that are true in $\mathfrak{M}$ [11]. Intuitively, in case $\mathcal{A} = \mathcal{E}$, a learner will be presented with an enumeration of $D_\mathcal{E}(\mathfrak{M})$ for some $\mathfrak{M} \in \mathcal{W}$, and the $\mathcal{E}$-diagrams of the possible worlds will be the *possible theories*. In classical logic, where $\mathcal{E} = \emptyset$, a *possible theory* should be any (consistent) set of formulas. More generally, we now have to answer two key questions: how does $\mathcal{P}$ determine the kind of theory we want to consider? And how does $\mathcal{P}$ determine a notion of generalized logical consequence? We start with the first question. The basic idea is to generalize the notion of minimal Herbrand model of a set of definite clauses [4]. It is in accordance with the fact that in learning theory, all possible data that do not occur in a text e are tacitly false in the world for which e is a text.

Definition 8 *Let a theory T and a structure $\mathfrak{M}$ be given. We say that $\mathfrak{M}$ is an $\mathcal{E}$-minimal model of T in $\mathcal{W}$ just in case $\mathfrak{M} \in \mathrm{Mod}_\mathcal{W}(T)$ and for all $\mathfrak{N} \in \mathrm{Mod}_\mathcal{W}(T)$, $D_\mathcal{E}(\mathfrak{N}) \not\subset D_\mathcal{E}(\mathfrak{M})$.*[1]

---

[1] Inclusion is denoted by $\subseteq$, and strict inclusion by $\subset$.

Since $\mathcal{W}$ and $\mathcal{E}$ are arbitrary, a theory can have a unique $\mathcal{E}$-minimal model in $\mathcal{W}$, many of them, or none at all.

Notation 9 *Given $T \subseteq \mathcal{L}$, we denote by $\mathrm{Mod}_{\mathcal{W}}^{\mathcal{E}}(T)$ the class of all $\mathcal{E}$-minimal models of T in $\mathcal{W}$.*

We then define a possible theory as the $\mathcal{E}$-diagram of a possible world, possibly complemented with some possible axioms. This is achieved by the next definition and notation.

Definition 10 *Given a theory T, we say that T is $\mathcal{E}$-minimally invariant in $\mathcal{W}$ iff $\mathrm{Mod}_{\mathcal{W}}^{\mathcal{E}}(T) \neq \emptyset$ and for all $\mathfrak{M} \in \mathrm{Mod}_{\mathcal{W}}^{\mathcal{E}}(T)$, $D_{\mathcal{E}}(\mathfrak{M}) \subseteq T$.*

Notation 11 *We denote by $\mathcal{T}$ the set of all subsets of $\mathcal{A}$ that are $\mathcal{E}$-minimally invariant in $\mathcal{W}$. We call $\mathcal{T}$ the set of possible theories.*

Property 12 *$\mathcal{T}$ consists of the theories of the form $D_{\mathcal{E}}(\mathfrak{M}) \cup A$ for some $\mathfrak{M} \in \mathcal{W}$ and $A \subseteq \mathcal{A}$ with $\mathfrak{M} \models A$.*

Note that every possible theory has at least one $\mathcal{E}$-minimal model in $\mathcal{W}$: for all $\mathfrak{M} \in \mathcal{W}$ and $A \subseteq \mathcal{A}$ with $\mathfrak{M} \models A$, $D_{\mathcal{E}}(\mathfrak{M})$ is an $\mathcal{E}$-minimal model of $D_{\mathcal{E}}(\mathfrak{M}) \cup A$ in $\mathcal{W}$. Since the class of $\mathcal{E}$-minimal models of a possible theory T is the class of intended models of T, it is natural to define generalized logical consequences as follows.

Definition 13 *Given a theory T and $\varphi \in \mathcal{L}_{\omega_1\omega}^{S}$, we say that φ is an $\mathcal{E}$-minimal logical consequence of T in $\mathcal{W}$ iff $\mathrm{Mod}_{\mathcal{W}}^{\mathcal{E}}(T) \subseteq \mathrm{Mod}_{\mathcal{W}}(\varphi)$.*

Notation 14 *Given a theory T and $\varphi \in \mathcal{L}_{\omega_1\omega}^{S}$, we write $T \models_{\mathcal{W}}^{\mathcal{E}} \varphi$ when φ is an $\mathcal{E}$-minimal logical consequence of T in $\mathcal{W}$. We set $\mathrm{Cn}_{\mathcal{W}}^{\mathcal{E}}(T) = \{\varphi \in \mathcal{L} \mid T \models_{\mathcal{W}}^{\mathcal{E}} \varphi\}$.*

Classical first-order logic and fundamental learning paradigms are particular cases of, respectively, *axiomatic* and *evidential* paradigms, defined next.

Definition 15 *$\mathcal{P}$ is said to be axiomatic if $\mathcal{E} = \emptyset$, and evidential if $\mathcal{A} = \mathcal{E}$.*

2.3 Hierarchies of Generalized Logical Consequences

Let T be a possible theory. The notion $T \models_{\mathcal{W}}^{\mathcal{E}} \varphi$ is not necessarily compact. This suggests the stratification of $\mathrm{Cn}_{\mathcal{W}}^{\mathcal{E}}(T)$ into a hierarchy of formulas, with the 'compact' generalized logical consequences of T just above T. Above that first layer, we will find the 'β-weakly compact' generalized logical consequences of T on layer β, where β is a nonnull ordinal. Weak compactness can be viewed as compactness weakened with a notion of 'refutability' [21]. All these layers make up the first level of the hierarchy. Reiterating the process will create levels above the first level, indexed by an ordinal α, partitioned into layers indexed by β. Let us denote the class of all ordinals by Ord. Given $\alpha, \beta, \alpha', \beta' \in$ Ord, we write $(\alpha, \beta) \prec (\alpha', \beta')$ iff (α, β) is lexicographically before (α', β'), *i.e.*, either $\alpha < \alpha'$, or $\alpha = \alpha'$ and $\beta < \beta'$. The hierarchies of generalized logical consequences of T are defined next, with $(\star)$ capturing the notion of β-weak compactness.

Definition 16 *Set $\Lambda_0^P(T) = T$ for all $T \in \mathcal{T}$. Given nonnull $\alpha \in$ Ord, $\beta \in$ Ord, $T \in \mathcal{T}$ and $\varphi \in \mathcal{L}$, φ belongs to $\Lambda_{\alpha,\beta}^P(T)$ iff there is a finite $A \subseteq T$ and a finite $H \subseteq \bigcup_{(\alpha',\beta') \prec (\alpha,0)} \Lambda_{\alpha',\beta'}^P(T)$ such that for all $T' \in \mathcal{T}$, $\varphi \in \mathrm{Cn}_{\mathcal{W}}^{\mathcal{E}}(T')$ whenever:*

$$(\star) \quad A \subseteq T', \ H \subseteq \mathrm{Cn}_{\mathcal{W}}^{\mathcal{E}}(T') \ and \sim \varphi \notin \bigcup_{\beta' < \beta} \Lambda_{\alpha,\beta'}^P(T').$$

Note that compactness in first-order logic corresponds to $\mathcal{L} = \mathcal{L}_{\omega\omega}^S$, $\mathcal{M}$ irrelevant, $\mathcal{W}$ equal to all structures, $\mathcal{E} = \emptyset$, $\mathcal{A} = \mathcal{L}$, $\alpha = 1$, and $\beta = 0$: all logical consequences of a possible theory T are in $\Lambda_{1,0}^P(T)$. In full generality, we also define similarly, hierarchies of metaformulas that are 'generalized metalogical consequences' of T. This is the natural notion for an extremely general class of paradigms, that encompasses evidential paradigms. For evidential paradigms on the other hand, it is always possible to enrich the language and obtain a hierarchy of formulas that is basically the same as the hierarchy of metaformulas. The 'logical complexity' (in $\mathcal{P}$) of a formula φ is then naturally defined as follows.

Definition 17 *Let nonnull ordinals α, β and a formula φ be given. We say that φ is $\Sigma_{\alpha,\beta}^P$ just in case for all $T \in \mathcal{T}$ such that $\varphi \in \mathrm{Cn}_{\mathcal{W}}^{\mathcal{E}}(T)$, $\varphi \in \Lambda_{\alpha,\gamma}^0(T)$ for some ordinal $\gamma < \beta$. We say that φ is $\Delta_{\alpha,\beta}^P$ iff both φ and $\sim \varphi$ are $\Sigma_{\alpha,\beta}^P$.*

The following property can immediately be derived from Definitions 16 and 17. When $\alpha = 1$, it will also characterize learnability with less than β mind changes, yielding a natural interpretation for the notion of β-weak compactness.

Property 18 *Let nonnull ordinals α, β and $\varphi \in \mathcal{L}$ be such that for all $T \in \mathcal{T}$, either $T \vdash_{\mathcal{W}}^{\mathcal{E}} \varphi$ or $T \models_{\mathcal{W}}^{\mathcal{E}} \sim \varphi$. Then φ is $\Delta_{\alpha,\beta}^P$ iff there exists a sequence $(\beta_T)_{T \in \mathcal{T}}$ of ordinals smaller than β such that for all $T \in \mathcal{T}$, there exists a finite subset A of T and a finite subset H of $\bigcup_{(\alpha',\beta') \prec (\alpha,0)} \Lambda_{\alpha',\beta'}^P(T)$ with the following property. For all $T' \in \mathcal{T}$, $\varphi \in \mathrm{Cn}_{\mathcal{W}}^{\mathcal{E}}(T')$ iff $\varphi \in \mathrm{Cn}_{\mathcal{W}}^{\mathcal{E}}(T)$ whenever:*

$$A \subseteq T', \ H \subseteq \mathrm{Cn}_{\mathcal{W}}^{\mathcal{E}}(T) \ and \ \beta_T \leq \beta_{T'}.$$

3   Topological Notions

The Borel hierarchy is usually defined over topological spaces whose closed sets are countable intersections of open sets. This condition is not appropriate when $\mathcal{E}$ is not closed under $\sim$ (hence for learning from positive data only). So we need the following adjustments. Let a set X and a set B of subsets of X be given. When we consider the topology over X generated by B, yielding a topological space $\mathcal{X}$, we call the sets built from B by finite unions and finite intersections, the Π_0 *Borel* sets of $\mathcal{X}$. Their complements are the Σ_0 *Borel* sets of $\mathcal{X}$. Let $\alpha > 0$ be given. The Σ_α *Borel* sets of $\mathcal{X}$ are built from the Π_β Borel subsets of X, with $\beta < \alpha$, by countable unions. Their complements are the Π_α *Borel* sets of $\mathcal{X}$. Subsets Y of X such that both Y and $X \setminus Y$ are Σ_α Borel in $\mathcal{X}$, are said to be Δ_α *Borel in* $\mathcal{X}$. The difference hierarchy introduces a further granularity in the Borel hierarchy. The natural way to introduce the difference hierarchy in this framework is as follows.

Definition 19 *Let $\alpha > 0$ and $Z \subseteq X$ be given. We say that Z is $\Sigma_{\alpha,1}$ Borel in $\mathcal{X}$ iff Z is Σ_α Borel in $\mathcal{X}$. Given $\beta > 1$, we say that Z is $\Sigma_{\alpha,\beta}$ Borel in $\mathcal{X}$ iff there exists two families $(A_i)_{i \in \mathbb{N}}$ and $(Z_i)_{i \in \mathbb{N}}$ of subsets of X and a family $(\beta_i)_{i \in \mathbb{N}}$ of nonnull ordinals smaller than β such that the following holds.*

- *For all $i \in \mathbb{N}$, A_i is Σ_α Borel in $\mathcal{X}$ and Z_i is Σ_{α,β_i} Borel in $\mathcal{X}$.*
- *For all $i, i' \in \mathbb{N}$ and $x \in A_i \cap A_{i'}$, $x \in Z_i$ iff $x \in Z_{i'}$.*
- $Z = \bigcup_{i \in \mathbb{N}} (A_i \setminus Z_i)$.

The previous definition is equivalent to the classical definition (see [10]) of the difference hierarchy over the Σ_α Borel sets of $\mathcal{X}$ for a given $\alpha > 0$.

Proposition 20 *Let a topological space $\mathcal{X}$ over a set X be second countable. For all $\alpha, \beta > 0$ and $Z \subseteq X$, Z is $\Sigma_{\alpha,\beta}$ Borel in $\mathcal{X}$ iff there exists a $\subseteq$-increasing sequence $(Y_\gamma)_{\gamma < \beta}$ of Σ_α subsets of X with the following property. For all $x \in X$, x belongs to Z iff $x \in \bigcup_{\gamma < \beta} Y_\gamma$ and the parity of the least $\gamma < \beta$ such that $x \in Y_\gamma$ is opposite to the parity of β.*

The following topological space is an essential tool to study the hierarchies of generalized logical consequences (for the hierarchies of metaformulas, another topological space, built over $\mathcal{T}$, also needs to be introduced).

Definition 21 *The canonical topological space of type $(\mathcal{W}, \mathcal{E})$, denoted $\mathbb{W}$, is the topological space over $\mathcal{W}$ generated by $\{\mathrm{Mod}_\mathcal{W}(\varphi) \mid \varphi \in \mathcal{E}\}$.*

Some formulas represent Σ_α Borel sets over $\mathbb{W}$, in the following sense.

Definition 22 *Let $\varphi \in \mathcal{L}$ be given. We say that φ is $\Sigma_0^\mathcal{L}$ (respect. $\Pi_0^\mathcal{L}$) Borel in $\mathbb{W}$ iff $\mathrm{Mod}_\mathcal{W}(\varphi)$ is Σ_0 (respect. Π_0) Borel in $\mathbb{W}$. Let $\alpha > 0$ be given, and let X be the set of sentences that are $\Pi_\beta^\mathcal{L}$ (respect. $\Sigma_\beta^\mathcal{L}$) Borel in $\mathbb{W}$ for some $\beta < \alpha$. We say that φ is $\Sigma_\alpha^\mathcal{L}$ (respect. $\Pi_\alpha^\mathcal{L}$) Borel in $\mathbb{W}$ iff $\mathrm{Mod}_\mathcal{W}(\varphi) = \mathrm{Mod}_\mathcal{W}(\psi)$ for some sentence ψ built from X using $\bigvee$ (respect. $\bigwedge$) only.*

Some formulas represent $\Sigma_{\alpha,\beta}$ Borel sets over $\mathbb{W}$, in the following sense.

Definition 23 *Let $\alpha > 0$ and a formula φ be given. We say that φ is $\Sigma_{\alpha,1}^\mathcal{L}$ Borel in $\mathbb{W}$ iff φ is $\Sigma_\alpha^\mathcal{L}$ Borel in $\mathbb{W}$. Given $\beta > 1$, we say that φ is $\Sigma_{\alpha,\beta}^\mathcal{L}$ Borel in $\mathbb{W}$ iff there exists two families $(\psi_i)_{i \in \mathbb{N}}$ and $(\varphi_i)_{i \in \mathbb{N}}$ of sentences and a family $(\beta_i)_{i \in \mathbb{N}}$ of nonnull ordinals smaller than β such that the following holds.*

- *For all $i \in \mathbb{N}$, ψ_i is $\Sigma_\alpha^\mathcal{L}$ Borel in $\mathbb{W}$ and φ_i is $\Sigma_{\alpha,\beta_i}^\mathcal{L}$ Borel in $\mathbb{W}$.*
- *For all $i, i' \in \mathbb{N}$, $\mathrm{Mod}_\mathcal{W}(\psi_i \wedge \psi_{i'}) \subseteq \mathrm{Mod}_\mathcal{W}(\varphi_i \leftrightarrow \varphi_{i'})$.*
- $\mathrm{Mod}_\mathcal{W}(\varphi) = \mathrm{Mod}_\mathcal{W}(\bigvee_{i \in \mathbb{N}} \psi_i \wedge \neg\varphi_i)$.

The previous notions have a syntactic counterpart, a *normal form* that is more natural in this framework than disjunctive or conjunctive normal forms. We do not give the definition of normal form for a (possibly infinitary) formula, but we describe what is the normal form of a finite formula. Let $\alpha > 0$ be given. Let Z be a set of finite S-sentences in Σ_α prenex form, and let $\varphi \in \mathcal{L}_{\omega\omega}^S$ be a boolean combination of members of Z. Let T be the (unique) tree over the set of finite subsets of Z with the following properties.

- The children of the empty sequence are the $\subseteq$-minimal finite subsets of Z of the form $D_Z(\mathfrak{M})$ for some model $\mathfrak{M}$ of φ.
- Let $\sigma \in T$ and a structure $\mathfrak{M}$ be such that $D = D_Z(\mathfrak{M})$ is the set of formulas occurring in σ. For all finite $E \subseteq Z$, $\sigma \star E$ is a child of σ in T iff:
  - $D \cap E = \emptyset$ and $D \cup E$ is the Z-diagram of some structure $\mathfrak{N}$ such that $\mathfrak{M} \models \varphi$ iff $\mathfrak{N} \not\models \varphi$;
  - for all structures $\mathfrak{N}$ with $D \subseteq D_Z(\mathfrak{N}) \subset D \cup E$, $\mathfrak{M} \models \varphi$ iff $\mathfrak{N} \models \varphi$.

Given $\sigma \in T$ and $D \subseteq Z$ with $\sigma \star D \in T$, we inductively define $\varphi_{\sigma \star D}$ as follows.

- Suppose that $\sigma \star D$ is a leaf in T. Then $\varphi_{\sigma \star D} = \bigwedge D$.
- Suppose that $\sigma \star D$ is not a leaf in T. Let Y be the set of children of $\sigma \star D$ in T. Then $\varphi_{\sigma \star D} = \bigwedge D \wedge \neg \bigvee \{\varphi_\tau \mid \tau \in Y\}$.

Finally we set $\varphi^\star = \bigvee \{\varphi_\sigma \mid \sigma$ is a child of the empty sequence$\}$. The formula $\varphi^\star$ is in normal form. Clearly, $\varphi^\star$ is logically equivalent to φ. The syntactic complexity of a formula in normal form can then be related to its complexity in terms of generalized logical consequence, in terms of the topological set it represents, and in terms of its learnability when it is viewed as a hypothesis. The next result shows that the topological hierarchy is embedded in the logical hierarchy:

Proposition 24 *Given $\alpha, \beta > 0$, a formula that is $\Sigma^{\mathcal{L}}_{\alpha,\beta}$ Borel in $\mathbb{W}$, is $\Sigma^{\mathcal{P}}_{\alpha,\beta}$.*

Proof. Proof is by double induction on ordinals, and uses the following lemmas.

Lemma 25 *Let nonnull $\alpha \in \mathrm{Ord}$, $\beta \in \mathrm{Ord}$, and $T \in \mathcal{T}$ be given. For all $\varphi \in \mathcal{L}$, $\varphi \in \Lambda^{\mathcal{P}}_{\alpha,\beta}(T)$ iff there exists finite $A \subseteq T$ and finite $H \subseteq \bigcup_{(\alpha',\beta') \prec (\alpha,0)} \Lambda^{\mathcal{P}}_{\alpha',\beta'}(T)$ such that for all $T' \in \mathcal{T}$, the following holds.*

- *$A \subseteq T'$ and $T' \models^{\mathcal{E}}_{\mathbb{W}} H$ iff $A \subseteq T'$ and $H \subseteq \bigcup_{(\alpha',\beta') \prec (\alpha,0)} \Lambda^{\mathcal{P}}_{\alpha',\beta'}(T')$.*
- *φ belongs to $\mathrm{Cn}^{\mathcal{E}}_{\mathbb{W}}(T')$ whenever $A \subseteq T'$, $H \subseteq \mathrm{Cn}^{\mathcal{E}}_{\mathbb{W}}(T')$, and $\sim \varphi \notin \bigcup_{\beta' < \beta} \Lambda^{\mathcal{P}}_{\alpha,\beta'}(T')$.*

Lemma 26 *Let φ be a formula that is $\Sigma^{\mathcal{L}}_\alpha$ Borel in $\mathbb{W}$ for some ordinal α. For all $T \in \mathcal{T}$, $\varphi \in \mathrm{Cn}^{\mathcal{E}}_{\mathbb{W}}(T)$ or $\sim \varphi \in \mathrm{Cn}^{\mathcal{E}}_{\mathbb{W}}(T)$.*

To prove the proposition, we first note that the following holds for all $\alpha > 0$.

Assume that for all nonnull $\alpha' < \alpha$, all formulas that are $\Sigma^{\mathcal{L}}_{\alpha',2}$ Borel in $\mathbb{W}$ are $\Sigma^{\mathcal{P}}_{\alpha',2}$. Then all formulas that are $\Sigma^{\mathcal{L}}_\alpha$ Borel in $\mathbb{W}$ are $\Sigma^{\mathcal{P}}_\alpha$.

Let $\alpha > 0$ and $\beta > 1$ be given, and assume that for all $\alpha', \beta' > 0$ with $(\alpha',\beta') \prec (\alpha,\beta)$, all formulas that are $\Sigma^{\mathcal{L}}_{\alpha',\beta'}$ Borel in $\mathbb{W}$ are $\Sigma^{\mathcal{P}}_{\alpha',\beta'}$. Given $i \in \mathbb{N}$, let a sentence ψ_i, a nonnull ordinal $\beta_i < \beta$, and a sentence χ_i be such that the following holds.

- For all $i \in \mathbb{N}$, ψ_i is $\Sigma^{\mathcal{L}}_\alpha$ Borel in $\mathbb{W}$ and χ_i is $\Sigma^{\mathcal{L}}_{\alpha,\beta_i}$ Borel in $\mathbb{W}$.
- For all $i, i' \in \mathbb{N}$, $\mathrm{Mod}_{\mathbb{W}}(\psi_i \wedge \psi_{i'}) \subseteq \mathrm{Mod}_{\mathbb{W}}(\chi_i \leftrightarrow \chi_{i'})$.

Let φ be a sentence such that $\text{Mod}_{\mathcal{W}}(\varphi) = \text{Mod}_{\mathcal{W}}(\bigvee_{i \in \mathbb{N}} \psi_i \wedge \neg \chi_i)$. We show that φ is $\Sigma^{\mathcal{P}}_{\alpha,\beta}$. Let $T \in \mathcal{T}$ be such that $T \models^{\mathcal{E}}_{\mathcal{W}} \varphi$. By Lemma 26, we can choose $p \in \mathbb{N}$ such that $T \models^{\mathcal{E}}_{\mathcal{W}} \psi_p \wedge \neg \chi_p$. By inductive hypothesis, ψ_p is $\Sigma^{\mathcal{P}}_\alpha$ and χ_p is $\Sigma^{\mathcal{P}}_{\alpha,\beta_i}$. Since ψ_p is $\Sigma^{\mathcal{P}}_\alpha$, Lemma 25 implies that there exists a finite $A \subseteq T$ and a finite $H \subseteq \bigcup_{(\alpha',\beta') \prec (\alpha,0)} \Lambda^{\mathcal{P}}_{\alpha',\beta'}(T)$ such that for all $T' \in \mathcal{T}$:

- $A \subseteq T'$ and $T' \models^{\mathcal{E}}_{\mathcal{W}} H$ iff $A \subseteq T'$ and $H \subseteq \bigcup_{(\alpha',\beta') \prec (\alpha,0)} \Lambda^{\mathcal{P}}_{\alpha',\beta'}(T')$;
- if $A \subseteq T'$ and $H \subseteq \text{Cn}^{\mathcal{E}}_{\mathcal{W}}(T')$ then $\psi_p \in \text{Cn}^{\mathcal{E}}_{\mathcal{W}}(T')$.

Set $\mathcal{T}' = \{T' \in \mathcal{T} \mid A \subseteq T'$ and $H \subseteq \text{Cn}^{\mathcal{E}}_{\mathcal{W}}(T')\}$. We prove that:

(∗)   For all $T' \in \mathcal{T}'$ and $\beta' \in \text{Ord}$, $\neg \chi_p \in \Lambda^{\mathcal{P}}_{\alpha,\beta'}(T')$ iff $\varphi \in \Lambda^{\mathcal{P}}_{\alpha,\beta'}(T')$, and $\chi_p \in \Lambda^{\mathcal{P}}_{\alpha,\beta'}(T')$ iff $\neg\varphi \in \Lambda^{\mathcal{P}}_{\alpha,\beta'}(T')$.

Let $T' \in \mathcal{T}'$ be given. Assume that $T' \models^{\mathcal{E}}_{\mathcal{W}} \varphi$. By Lemma 26 again, we can choose $q \in \mathbb{N}$ such that $T' \models^{\mathcal{E}}_{\mathcal{W}} \psi_q \wedge \neg \chi_q$. Hence $T' \models^{\mathcal{E}}_{\mathcal{W}} \psi_p \wedge \psi_q$, and we infer that $T' \models^{\mathcal{E}}_{\mathcal{W}} \neg\chi_p$. Conversely, if $T' \models^{\mathcal{E}}_{\mathcal{W}} \neg\chi_p$ then $T' \models^{\mathcal{E}}_{\mathcal{W}} \varphi$. It is then easy to verify (∗) by induction on β'. Let $T' \in \mathcal{T}$ be such that $T' \not\models^{\mathcal{E}}_{\mathcal{W}} \varphi$. From (∗) and the fact that χ_p is $\Sigma^{\mathcal{P}}_{\alpha,\beta_p}$, we infer that $\neg\varphi \in \Lambda^{\mathcal{P}}_{\alpha,\beta_p}(T)$. We conclude that φ is $\Sigma^{\mathcal{P}}_{\alpha,\beta}$.

For evidential paradigms, the embedding is actually an equivalence. To prove this result, we need a few preliminary definitions and lemmas.

Definition 27 *A* trace *is a sequence that is empty or of the form* $((\alpha_0, \beta_0, H_0), \ldots, (\alpha_i, \beta_i, H_i))$ *where* $i \in \mathbb{N}$, $H_0, \ldots, H_i$ *are nonempty, finite subsets of formulas, and* $\alpha_0, \beta_0 \ldots, \alpha_i, \beta_i$ *are ordinals such that for all* $j < i$, $(\alpha_j, \beta_j) \prec (\alpha_{j+1}, \beta_{j+1})$. *The* height bound *of a trace that ends with a triple of the form* (α, β, H) *is equal to* (α, β).

Definition 28 *A* derivation *is a trace of the form* $\sigma \star ((\alpha, \beta, \{\varphi\}))$ *for some* $\alpha, \beta \in \text{Ord}$, $\varphi \in \mathcal{L}$, *and trace* σ *which is either empty or whose height bound is smaller than* $(\alpha, 0)$. *If* σ *is a derivation of the form* $\tau \star ((\alpha, \beta, \{\varphi\}))$ *then we say that* σ *is a* derivation of φ.

Definition 29 *Let a possible theory* T *be given. The empty trace is* from T *(in* $\mathcal{P}$*). A trace* $((\alpha_0, \beta_0, H_0), \ldots, (\alpha_i, \beta_i, H_i))$ *is* from T *(in* $\mathcal{P}$*) just in case (1) if* $\alpha_0 = 0$ *then* $H_0 \subseteq T$ *and (2)* $\bigcup_{j \leq i} H_j \subseteq \text{Cn}^{\mathcal{E}}_{\mathcal{W}}(T)$.

Notation 30 *We denote by* $\mathfrak{D}$ *the maximal set of traces with the following property. Let a trace* σ *be an initial segment of a member of* $\mathfrak{D}$ *ending with* (α, β, H) *for some* $\alpha > 0$, $\beta \in \text{Ord}$ *and* $H \subseteq \mathcal{L}$. *Denote by* τ *the longest initial segment of* σ *whose height bound is smaller than* $(\alpha, 0)$. *For all* $\varphi \in H$, *the following holds.*

- $\tau \star ((\alpha, \beta, \varphi)) \in \mathfrak{D}$.
- *Let* $T \in \mathcal{T}$ *be such that* τ *is from* T. *If* $\varphi \notin \text{Cn}^{\mathcal{E}}_{\mathcal{W}}(T)$ *then* $\mathfrak{D}$ *contains a derivation of* $\sim \varphi$ *from* T *whose height bound is greater than or equal to* $(\alpha, 0)$, *and smaller than* (α, β).

Lemma 31 *Let a possible theory T be given. For all nonnull ordinals α, ordinals β and formulas φ, $\varphi \in \Lambda^{\mathcal{P}}_{\alpha,\beta}(T)$ iff there exists a derivation of φ from T in $\mathfrak{D}$ whose height bound is (α, β) at most.*

Lemma 32 *Suppose that $\mathcal{P}$ is evidential. Let nonnull ordinal α, ordinal β, trace σ, and formula φ be such that the height bound of σ is smaller than $(\alpha, 0)$, σ is from a member of T, and $\sigma \star ((\alpha, \beta, \varphi))$ is a derivation in $\mathcal{P}$. Let D be the set of formulas that occur in σ.*

- *$\bigwedge D$ is $\Sigma^{\mathcal{L}}_{\alpha}$ Borel in $\mathbb{W}$.*
- *If $\beta = 0$ then $\mathrm{Mod}_{\mathbb{W}}(D) \subseteq \mathrm{Mod}_{\mathbb{W}}(\varphi)$. If $\beta > 0$ then there exists a sentence χ such that χ is $\Sigma^{\mathcal{L}}_{\alpha,\beta}$ Borel in $\mathbb{W}$ and $\mathrm{Mod}_{\mathbb{W}}(D) \subseteq \mathrm{Mod}_{\mathbb{W}}(\varphi \leftrightarrow \neg\chi)$.*

Proof. Proof is by double induction on ordinals. Given a trace τ in $\mathfrak{D}$, denote by D_τ the set of formulas occurring in τ. Let nonnull ordinal α and ordinal β be given. Assume that for all nonnull $\alpha' \in \mathrm{Ord}$, $\beta' \in \mathrm{Ord}$, traces σ' and formulas φ', if $(\alpha', \beta') \prec (\alpha, \beta)$, the height bound of σ' is smaller than $(\alpha', 0)$, $\sigma' \star ((\alpha', \beta', \varphi'))$ belongs to $\mathfrak{D}$, and σ' is from a member of T then the following holds.

- *$\bigwedge D_{\sigma'}$ is $\Sigma^{\mathcal{L}}_{\alpha'}$ Borel in $\mathbb{W}$.*
- *If $\beta' = 0$ then $\mathrm{Mod}_{\mathbb{W}}(D_{\sigma'}) \subseteq \mathrm{Mod}_{\mathbb{W}}(\varphi')$. If $\beta' > 0$ then there is a sentence χ such that χ is $\Sigma^{\mathcal{L}}_{\alpha',\beta'}$ Borel in $\mathbb{W}$ and $\mathrm{Mod}_{\mathbb{W}}(D_{\sigma'}) \subseteq \mathrm{Mod}_{\mathbb{W}}(\varphi' \leftrightarrow \neg\chi)$.*

Let a trace σ and a formula φ be such that the height bound of σ is smaller than $(\alpha, 0)$, σ is from a member of T, and $\sigma \star ((\alpha, \beta, \varphi))$ belongs to $\mathfrak{D}$. We first verify that $\bigwedge D_\sigma$ is $\Sigma^{\mathcal{L}}_{\alpha}$ Borel in $\mathbb{W}$. If the height bound of σ is equal to $(0, \beta')$ for some $\beta' \in \mathrm{Ord}$, then $D_\sigma \subseteq \mathcal{E}$, and $\bigwedge D_\sigma$ is trivially $\Sigma^{\mathcal{L}}_{\alpha}$ Borel in $\mathbb{W}$. Suppose that the height bound of σ is equal to (α', β') for some $\alpha' > 0$ and $\beta' \in \mathrm{Ord}$. Let σ' be the largest initial segment of σ whose height bound is smaller than $(\alpha', 0)$. Let trace σ'' be such that $\sigma = \sigma' \star \sigma''$. It follows from the inductive hypothesis that for all formulas ψ that occur in σ'', $\bigwedge D_{\sigma'} \wedge \psi$ is $\Sigma^{\mathcal{L}}_{\alpha,\beta''}$ Borel in $\mathbb{W}$ for some ordinal $\beta'' \leq \beta'$, hence is $\Sigma^{\mathcal{L}}_{\alpha}$ Borel in $\mathbb{W}$. So $\bigwedge D_\sigma$ is logically equivalent to a finite conjunction of formulas that are $\Sigma^{\mathcal{L}}_{\alpha}$ Borel in $\mathbb{W}$, hence is $\Sigma^{\mathcal{L}}_{\alpha}$ Borel in $\mathbb{W}$.

Let X be the set of all traces τ whose height bound is smaller than $(\alpha, 0)$, that are from a member of T, and such that $\tau \star ((\alpha, \gamma, \sim \varphi))$ belongs to $\mathfrak{D}$ for some $\gamma < \beta$. Set $Y = \{\bigwedge D_\tau \wedge \sim \varphi \mid \tau \in X\}$. We show that $\mathrm{Mod}_{\mathbb{W}}(D_\sigma)$ is included in $\mathrm{Mod}_{\mathbb{W}}(\varphi \leftrightarrow \neg\bigvee Y)$. (Note that in case $\beta = 0$, this yields $\mathrm{Mod}_{\mathbb{W}}(D_\sigma) \subseteq \mathrm{Mod}_{\mathbb{W}}(\varphi)$.) For a contradiction, choose $\mathfrak{M} \in W$ with $\mathfrak{M} \models D_\sigma \cup \{\neg\bigvee Y, \sim \varphi\}$. Using Lemma 26 together with the hypothesis that $\mathcal{P}$ is evidential, the derived fact that $\bigwedge D_\sigma$ is $\Sigma^{\mathcal{L}}_{\alpha'}$ Borel in $\mathbb{W}$ for some $\alpha' \in \mathrm{Ord}$, and the choice of $\mathfrak{M}$ as a model of D_σ, it can be easily derived that σ is from $D_{\mathcal{E}}(\mathfrak{M})$. It follows that there exists a trace τ and $\gamma < \beta$ such that $\tau \star ((\alpha, \gamma, \sim \varphi))$ is a derivation from $D_{\mathcal{E}}(\mathfrak{M})$ in $\mathfrak{D}$. Then $\bigwedge D_\tau \wedge \sim \varphi \in Y$, hence $\mathfrak{M} \models \neg\bigwedge D_\tau \vee \varphi$. But $\mathfrak{M} \not\models \varphi$ by the choice of $\mathfrak{M}$, and $\mathfrak{M} \not\models \neg\bigwedge D_\tau$ since τ is from $D_{\mathcal{E}}(\mathfrak{M})$, contradiction. Conversely, it is clear that if $\mathfrak{M}$ is a model of $D_\sigma \cup \{\varphi\}$ then $\mathfrak{M}$ is a model of $\neg\bigvee Y$. So we have shown that $\mathrm{Mod}_{\mathbb{W}}(D_\sigma) \subseteq \mathrm{Mod}_{\mathbb{W}}(\varphi \leftrightarrow \neg\bigvee Y)$. Now assume that $\beta > 0$.

To complete the proof of the lemma, it suffices to show that $\bigvee Y$ is $\Sigma^{\mathcal{L}}_{\alpha,\beta}$ Borel in $\mathbb{W}$. Let $\psi \in D_\sigma$ be given. Let $\alpha', \beta' \in \mathrm{Ord}$ be such that (α', β', ψ) occurs in σ. If $\alpha' = 0$ then $\psi \in \mathcal{E}$. Let $\tau \in X$ be given. The hypothesis that $\mathcal{P}$ is evidential implies immediately that all members of D_τ are $\Sigma^{\mathcal{L}}_\alpha$ Borel in $\mathbb{W}$. We distinguish two cases.

Case 1: $\beta = 1$. By inductive hypothesis, for all $\tau \in X$, $\bigwedge D_\tau$ is $\Sigma^{\mathcal{L}}_\alpha$ Borel in $\mathbb{W}$ and $\mathrm{Mod}_{\mathcal{W}}(\bigwedge D_\tau \wedge \sim \varphi) = \mathrm{Mod}_{\mathcal{W}}(D_\tau)$. It follows immediately that $\bigvee Y$ is $\Sigma^{\mathcal{L}}_\alpha$ Borel in $\mathbb{W}$.

Case 2: $\beta > 1$. Without loss of generality, we can assume that for all $\tau \in X$, the height bound of τ is of the form (α, γ) where γ is nonnull. By inductive hypothesis, for all $\tau \in X$, $\bigwedge D_\tau$ is $\Sigma^{\mathcal{L}}_\alpha$ Borel in $\mathbb{W}$ and there exists a sentence χ_τ and a nonnull ordinal $\gamma < \beta$ such that such that χ_τ is $\Sigma^{\mathcal{L}}_{\alpha,\gamma}$ Borel in $\mathbb{W}$ and $\mathrm{Mod}_{\mathcal{W}}(\bigwedge D_\tau \wedge \sim \varphi) = \mathrm{Mod}_{\mathcal{W}}(\neg \chi_\tau)$. Moreover, for all $\tau, \tau' \in X$ and for all members $\mathfrak{M}$ of $\mathrm{Mod}_{\mathcal{W}}(D_\tau \cup D_{\tau'})$, $\mathfrak{M} \models \chi_\tau$ iff $\mathfrak{M} \models \varphi$ iff $\mathfrak{M} \models \chi_{\tau'}$. Also note that $\mathrm{Mod}_{\mathcal{W}}(\bigvee Y) = \mathrm{Mod}_{\mathcal{W}}(\bigvee \{\bigwedge D_\tau \wedge \neg \chi_\tau \mid \tau \in X\})$. We conclude immediately that $\bigvee Y$ is $\Sigma^{\mathcal{L}}_{\alpha,\beta}$ Borel in $\mathbb{W}$.

We can now state and prove the main result that relates logical and topological complexity in the context of evidential paradigms.

Proposition 33 *Let $\varphi \in \mathcal{L}$ be such that for all $T \in \mathcal{T}$, $T \models^{\mathcal{E}}_{\mathcal{W}} \varphi$ or $T \models^{\mathcal{E}}_{\mathcal{W}} \neg \varphi$. If $\mathcal{P}$ is evidential then for all $\alpha, \beta > 0$, φ is $\Sigma^{\mathcal{P}}_{\alpha,\beta}$ iff φ is $\Sigma^{\mathcal{L}}_{\alpha,\beta}$ Borel in $\mathbb{W}$.*

Proof. Let $\alpha, \beta > 0$ be given. Proposition 24 implies one direction of the equivalence. Conversely, suppose that φ is $\Sigma^{\mathcal{P}}_{\alpha,\beta}$. Let X be the set of all possible theories T such that $T \models^{\mathcal{E}}_{\mathcal{W}} \varphi$. Given $T \in X$, choose a trace σ_T from T whose height bound is smaller than $(\alpha, 0)$ and such that $\sigma \star ((\alpha, \beta, \varphi))$ belongs to $\mathfrak{D}$. For all $T \in X$, let D_T denote the set of formulas that occur in σ_T. Set $\psi = \bigvee \{\bigwedge D_T \wedge \varphi \mid T \in X\}$. Clearly, $\mathrm{Mod}_{\mathcal{W}}(\varphi) = \mathrm{Mod}_{\mathcal{W}}(\psi)$, so it suffices to show that ψ is $\Sigma^{\mathcal{L}}_{\alpha,\beta}$ Borel in $\mathbb{W}$. By Lemma 32, for all $T \in X$, $\bigwedge D_T$ is $\Sigma^{\mathcal{L}}_{\alpha,\beta}$ Borel in $\mathbb{W}$. We distinguish two cases.

Case 1: $\beta = 1$. By Lemma 32 again, $\mathrm{Mod}_{\mathcal{W}}(\psi) = \mathrm{Mod}_{\mathcal{W}}(\bigvee \{\bigwedge D_T \mid T \in X\})$, and we conclude immediately that ψ is $\Sigma^{\mathcal{L}}_{\alpha,\beta}$ Borel in $\mathbb{W}$.

Case 2: $\beta > 1$. By Lemma 32 again, for all $T \in X$, there exists a sentence χ_T and a nonnull $\gamma < \beta$ such that χ_T is $\Sigma^{\mathcal{L}}_{\alpha,\gamma}$ Borel in $\mathbb{W}$ and $\mathrm{Mod}_{\mathcal{W}}(\neg \chi_T) = \mathrm{Mod}_{\mathcal{W}}(\bigwedge D_T \wedge \varphi)$. Moreover, for all $T, T' \in X$ and $\mathfrak{M} \in \mathrm{Mod}_{\mathcal{W}}(D_T \cup D_{T'})$, $\mathfrak{M} \models \chi_T$ iff $\mathfrak{M} \models \sim \varphi$ iff $\mathfrak{M} \models \chi_{T'}$. Also note that $\mathrm{Mod}_{\mathcal{W}}(\psi)$ is equal to $\mathrm{Mod}_{\mathcal{W}}(\bigvee \{\bigwedge D_T \wedge \neg \chi_T \mid T \in X\})$. We conclude immediately that ψ is $\Sigma^{\mathcal{L}}_{\alpha,\beta}$ Borel in $\mathbb{W}$.

4   Notions from Learning Theory

Notation 34 *We extend $\mathcal{L}$ with a new element represented by $\natural$. Given $X \subseteq \mathcal{L}$, we denote by X^* the set of finite sequences of members of $X \cup \{\natural\}$. Given $X \subseteq \mathcal{L}$ and a sequence e (finite or infinite) of members of $X \cup \{\natural\}$, we denote by $\mathrm{cnt}(e)$ the set of members of X that occur in e.*

In full generality, learners output sets of metaformulas. For simplification we fix a single formula φ, and we now define all notions from φ.

Definition 35 *A* learner *is a mapping f from $\mathcal{L}^*$ into the set of subsets of $\{\ulcorner\varphi\urcorner, \neg\ulcorner\varphi\urcorner\}$ such that for all $\sigma, \tau \in \mathcal{L}^*$, if $\sigma \subseteq \tau$ and $f(\sigma) \neq \emptyset$ then $f(\tau) \neq \emptyset$.*

The notion of mind change is captured by the following definition. First remember that if R be a well founded binary relation over a set X, then the length of R denotes the range of the unique function from X into Ord such that for all $x \in X$, $\rho_R(x) = \sup\{\rho_R(y) + 1 \mid y \in X, \; R(y,x)\}$.

Definition 36 *Let a learner f be given. Let R be the binary relation over $\mathcal{L}^*$ such that for all $\sigma, \tau \in \mathcal{L}^*$, $R(\sigma, \tau)$ iff $f(\tau) \neq \emptyset$, $\tau \subset \sigma$, and $f(\gamma) \neq f(\tau)$ for some $\gamma \in \mathcal{L}^*$ with $\tau \subset \gamma \subseteq \sigma$. The ordinal complexity of f is undefined if R is not well founded, and is equal to the length of R otherwise.*

The analogue and generalization of 'texts' or 'informants' in this framework is defined as follows.

Definition 37 *Given a theory T, we call a member e of $(T \cup \{\sharp\})^{\mathbb{N}}$ such that $\mathrm{cnt}(e) = T$, an* environment *for T.*

Learnability in the limit and learnability with less than β mind changes are formalized in Definitions 38 and 39 respectively.

Definition 38 *Given a learner f, we say that φ is Σ_2^f iff for all $T \in \mathcal{T}$ and environments e for T, $\varphi \in \mathrm{Cn}_{\mathcal{W}}^{\mathcal{E}}(T)$ iff $f(e[k]) \neq \{\ulcorner\varphi\urcorner\}$ for finitely many $k \in \mathbb{N}$.*

Definition 39 *Given a learner f and $\beta \in$ Ord, we say that φ is $\Sigma_{1,\beta}^f$ iff φ is Σ_2^f and the ordinal complexity of f is smalller than β.*

When the set of possible theories is countable, we obtain a characterization of learnability in the limit that generalizes the finite tell-tale condition [2]:

Proposition 40 *If $\mathcal{T}$ is countable then for all $\varphi \in \mathcal{L}$, (A) is equivalent to (B).*

(A) *There exists a learner f such that φ is Σ_2^f.*
(B) *For all $T \in \mathcal{T}$ with $\varphi \in \mathrm{Cn}_{\mathcal{W}}^{\mathcal{E}}(T)$, there is a finite $A \subseteq T$ such that for all $T' \in \mathcal{T}$, if $A \subseteq T' \subseteq T$ then $\varphi \in \mathrm{Cn}_{\mathcal{W}}^{\mathcal{E}}(T')$.*

By the following proposition, learnability in the limit is at least as general as being Σ_2 in the logical hierarchy.

Proposition 41 *Every formula that is $\Sigma_2^{\mathcal{P}}$, is Σ_2^f for some learner f.*

Both notions are actually equivalent, provided that the language is rich enough.

Proposition 42 *There exists a countable fragment $\mathcal{L}'$ of $\mathcal{L}_{\omega_1\omega}^S$ that extends $\mathcal{L}$ such that for all $\varphi \in \mathcal{L}'$, φ is Σ_2^f for some learner f iff φ is $\Sigma_2^{\mathcal{P}'}$, where $\mathcal{P}'$ is $\mathcal{P}$ with $\mathcal{L}$ replaced by $\mathcal{L}'$.*

Proposition 42 is an immediately consequence of the following proposition.

Proposition 43 *There exists a countable fragment $\mathcal{L}'$ of $\mathcal{L}^S_{\omega_1\omega}$ that extends $\mathcal{L}$ such that for all $\varphi \in \mathcal{L}'$, (A) and (B) are equivalent.*

(A) *There exists a learner f such that φ is Σ^f_2.*
(B) *For all $T \in \mathcal{T}$ with $T \models^{\mathcal{E}}_W \varphi$, there exists a finite $A \subseteq T$ and $\chi \in \mathcal{L}'$ such that $T \models^{\mathcal{E}}_W \chi$, χ is $\Pi^{\mathcal{L}'}_1$ Borel in $\mathbb{W}$, and for all $T' \in \mathcal{T}$:*

$$\text{if } A \subseteq T' \text{ and } T' \models^{\mathcal{E}}_W \chi \text{ then } T' \models^{\mathcal{E}}_W \varphi.$$

Proof. We use the definition and lemma below.

Definition 44 *Given a learner f, a theory T, $X \subseteq \mathcal{M}$, and $\sigma \in \mathcal{L}^*$, we say that σ is a locking sequence for f, X and T iff $\mathrm{cnt}(\sigma) \subseteq T$ and for all $\tau \in T^*$, $f(\sigma \star \tau) \cap X = f(\sigma) \cap X$.*

Lemma 45 *Let $T \subseteq \mathcal{L}$, $X \subseteq \mathcal{M}$, and a learner f be such that for every environment e for T, $f(e[k]) \cap X \neq f(e[k+1]) \cap X$ for finitely many $k \in \mathbb{N}$. For all $\sigma \in T^*$, there exists a locking sequence for f, X and T that extends σ.*

For the proof of Proposition 43, let a formula φ and a learner f be such that φ is Σ^f_2 for f. It suffices to exhibit a countable set Z of members of $\mathcal{L}^S_{\omega_1\omega}$ such that if $\mathcal{L}'$ is the smallest countable fragment of $\mathcal{L}^S_{\omega_1\omega}$ that contains $\mathcal{L} \cup Z$, then the following holds.

– All subformulas of the members of Z are $\Pi^{\mathcal{L}'}_1$ Borel in $\mathbb{W}$.
– For all $T \in \mathcal{T}$ with $T \models^{\mathcal{E}}_W \varphi$, there exists a finite $A \subseteq T$ and $\chi \in Z$ such that for all $T' \in \mathcal{T}$, if $A \subseteq T'$ and $T' \models^{\mathcal{E}}_W \chi$ then $T' \models^{\mathcal{E}}_W \varphi$.

Given $\sigma \in \mathcal{L}^*$, set $\psi_\sigma = \bigwedge \mathrm{cnt}(\sigma)$. Let X be the set of all $\sigma \in \mathcal{L}^*$ that are locking sequences for f, $\{\ulcorner\varphi\urcorner, \sim\ulcorner\varphi\urcorner\}$ and some member of $\mathcal{T}$. We can assume that $X \neq \emptyset$ (otherwise, it follows from Lemma 45 that $T \not\models^{\mathcal{E}}_W \varphi$ for all $T \in \mathcal{T}$, and the result is trivial). Given $\sigma \in X$, let X_σ be the set of all $\tau \in \mathcal{E}^*$ such that $f(\sigma \star \tau) \cap \{\ulcorner\varphi\urcorner, \sim\ulcorner\varphi\urcorner\} \neq \{\ulcorner\varphi\urcorner\}$. For all $\sigma \in X$ with $X_\sigma = \emptyset$, set $\chi_\sigma = \psi_\sigma$. For all $\sigma \in X$ with $X_\sigma \neq \emptyset$, set $\chi_\sigma = \bigwedge_{\tau \in X_\sigma} \neg\psi_\tau$. Define Z as $\{\chi_\sigma \mid \sigma \in X\}$. Let $\mathcal{L}'$ be the smallest countable fragment of $\mathcal{L}^S_{\omega_1\omega}$ that contains $\mathcal{L} \cup Z$. Clearly, every member of Z is $\Pi^{\mathcal{L}'}_1$ Borel in $\mathbb{W}$. Let $T \in \mathcal{T}$ be such that $T \models^{\mathcal{E}}_W \varphi$. By Lemma 45, let $\sigma \in \mathcal{L}^*$ be a locking sequence for f, $\{\ulcorner\varphi\urcorner, \sim\ulcorner\varphi\urcorner\}$ and T. It is immediately verified that $\mathrm{cnt}(\sigma) \subseteq T$ and $T \models^{\mathcal{E}}_W \chi_\sigma$. Let $T' \in \mathcal{T}$ be such that $\mathrm{cnt}(\sigma) \subseteq T'$ and $T' \models^{\mathcal{E}}_W \chi_\sigma$. To complete the proof of the proposition, it suffices to show that $T' \models^{\mathcal{E}}_W \varphi$. Suppose for a contradiction that $T' \not\models^{\mathcal{E}}_W \varphi$. Set $T'' = \mathrm{cnt}(\sigma) \cup (T' \cap \mathcal{E})$. Clearly, $T'' \models^{\mathcal{E}}_W \chi_\sigma$ and $T'' \not\models^{\mathcal{E}}_W \varphi$. Let e be an infinite sequence of members of $\mathcal{E}^*$ such that $\sigma \star e$ is an environment for T''. Since φ is Σ^f_2 for f, there exists $k \in \mathbb{N}$ such that $f(\sigma \star e[k]) \cap \{\ulcorner\varphi\urcorner, \sim\ulcorner\varphi\urcorner\} \neq \{\ulcorner\varphi\urcorner\}$. Hence $e[k] \in X_\sigma$ and $T'' \models^{\mathcal{E}}_W \psi_{e[k]}$. Hence $T'' \not\models^{\mathcal{E}}_W \chi_\sigma$. Contradiction.

Moreover, the notion of β-weak compactness is naturally related to learnability with less than β mind changes:

Proposition 46 *Suppose that for all $T \in \mathcal{T}$, either $T \models_{\mathcal{W}}^{\mathcal{E}} \varphi$ or $T \models_{\mathcal{W}}^{\mathcal{E}} \neg\varphi$. Given $\beta \in \mathrm{Ord}$, φ and $\sim \varphi$ are $\Sigma_{1,\beta}^{f}$ for a learner f iff φ is $\Delta_{1,\beta}^{P}$.*

Proof. Given a learner f and $\sigma \in \mathcal{L}^{*}$, we denote by $\mathrm{Ord}(f, \sigma)$ the ordinal complexity of f_{σ} where f_{σ} is the learner such that for all $\tau \in \mathcal{L}^{*}$, $f_{\sigma}(\tau) = f(\sigma \star \tau)$. Let $\beta \in \mathrm{Ord}$ be given. By Property 18, it suffices to show that the first clause is equivalent to the following.

$(*)$ There exists a sequence $(\beta_{T})_{T \in \mathcal{T}}$ of ordinals smaller than β and for all $T \in \mathcal{T}$, there is a finite $A \subseteq T$ such that for all $T' \in \mathcal{T}$:

$$\text{if } A \subseteq T' \text{ and } \beta_{T} \leq \beta_{T'}, \text{ then } \varphi \in \mathrm{Cn}_{\mathcal{W}}^{\mathcal{E}}(T) \text{ iff } \varphi \in \mathrm{Cn}_{\mathcal{W}}^{\mathcal{E}}(T').$$

Let a learner f be such that φ and $\sim \varphi$ are $\Sigma_{1,\beta}^{f}$. Given $T \in \mathcal{T}$, let β_{T} be the least ordinal γ such that there exists σ in T^{*} with $\mathrm{Ord}(f, \sigma) = \gamma$ and $f(\sigma) = \{\ulcorner\varphi\urcorner\}$ if $\varphi \in \mathrm{Cn}_{\mathcal{W}}^{\mathcal{E}}(T)$, and $f(\sigma) = \{\neg\ulcorner\varphi\urcorner\}$ otherwise. Let $T \in \mathcal{T}$ be given. Choose $\sigma \in T^{*}$ such that $\mathrm{Ord}(f, \sigma) = \beta_{T}$ and $f(\sigma) = \{\ulcorner\varphi\urcorner\}$ iff $\varphi \in \mathrm{Cn}_{\mathcal{W}}^{\mathcal{E}}(T)$. Suppose that there exists $T' \in \mathcal{T}$ such that $\mathrm{cnt}(\sigma) \subseteq T'$, $\beta_{T} \leq \beta_{T'}$, and $\varphi \in \mathrm{Cn}_{\mathcal{W}}^{\mathcal{E}}(T)$ iff $\varphi \notin \mathrm{Cn}_{\mathcal{W}}^{\mathcal{E}}(T')$. Choose an environment e for T' that begins with σ. Since φ and $\sim \varphi$ are $\Sigma_{1,\beta}^{f}$ for f, there is $k > |\sigma|$ such that $f(e[k]) = \{\ulcorner\varphi\urcorner\}$ iff $\varphi \in \mathrm{Cn}_{\mathcal{W}}^{\mathcal{E}}(T')$. We then infer that $\mathrm{Ord}(f, e[k]) < \mathrm{Ord}(f, \sigma) \leq \beta_{T'}$, which contradicts the definition of $\beta_{T'}$. So we have shown that the first clause of the proposition implies $(*)$.

Conversely, assume that $(*)$ holds. Define a learner f as follows. Let $\sigma \in \mathcal{L}^{*}$ be given. Suppose that there exists a least ordinal γ such that for some $T \in \mathcal{T}$, $A_{T} \subseteq \mathrm{cnt}(\sigma)$ and $\gamma = \beta_{T}$; then $f(\sigma) = \{\ulcorner\varphi\urcorner\}$ if $\varphi \in \mathrm{Cn}_{\mathcal{W}}^{\mathcal{E}}(T)$, and $f(\sigma) = \{\neg\ulcorner\varphi\urcorner\}$ otherwise, where T is a member of $\mathcal{T}$ with $A_{T} \subseteq \mathrm{cnt}(\sigma)$ and $\gamma = \beta_{T}$. Otherwise $f(\sigma) = \emptyset$. It follows from $(*)$ that f is well defined. It is easy to verify that $\mathrm{Ord}(f) \leq \beta$. So to complete the proof of the proposition, it suffices to show that φ and $\sim \varphi$ are $\Sigma_{1,\beta}^{f}$ for f. Let $T \in \mathcal{T}$ and environment e for T be given. Let $n \in \mathbb{N}$ be such that $A_{T} \subseteq \mathrm{cnt}(e[n])$. Using $(*)$ and the definition of f, we infer that $f(e[k]) = \{\ulcorner\varphi\urcorner\}$ iff $\varphi \in \mathrm{Cn}_{\mathcal{W}}^{\mathcal{E}}(T)$, and we are done.

5   Conclusion

Though many connections have been established between logic, learning and topology, there has been no attempt to unify the fields, or at least, part of them. Still the connections are tight and natural at a fundamental level, and can result in a parametrized logic that needs topological notions for its early developments, and notions from learning theory for interpretation and applicability. It is essential to observe the same kind of connection when the framework presented here is cast in a computable setting that can also address complexity issues. This is work in progress, and results have already been obtained in this direction, with relativizations of the properties that can be proved in the more general setting at the heart of which is the notion of β-weak compactness described in this paper.

One of our goals is to provide a theoretical foundation for a declarative programming language for applications in Artificial Intelligence, whose nature could be purely deductive or inductive, but more often, would combine deductive and inductive aspects. A prototype of a system—whose development is driven by the theoretical considerations presented here— that employs such a programming language has been designed and implemented [17].

References

[1] Ambainis, A., Jain, S., Sharma, A.: *Ordinal mind change complexity of language identification.* Theoretical Computer Science. **220(2)** (1999) 323–343
[2] Angluin, D.: *Inductive Inference of Formal Languages from Positive Data.* Information and Control. **45** (1980) 117–135
[3] Apt, K., Bol, R.: *Logic Programming and Negation: A Survey.* Journal of Logic Programming. **19/20** (1994) 177–190
[4] Doets, K.: *From Logic to Logic Programming.* The MIT Press. (1994)
[5] Ershov, Yu.: *A hierarchy of sets I, II, III.* Algebra and Logika. **7(1)** (1968) 47–74. **7(4)** (1968) 15–47. **9(1)** (1969) 34–51
[6] Freivalds, R., Smith, C.: *On the role of procrastination for machine learning.* Information and Computation. **107(2)** (1993) 237–271
[7] Gasarch, W., Pleszkoch, M., Stephan, F., Velauthapillai, M.: *Classification using information.* Annals of Mathematics and Artificial Intelligence. Selected papers from ALT 1994 and AII 1994. **23** (1998) 147–168
[8] Gold, E.: *Language Identification in the Limit.* Information and Control. **10** (1967) 447–474
[9] Jain, S., Sharma, A.: *Elementary formal systems, intrinsic complexity, and procrastination.* Information and Computation. **132(1)** (1997) 65–84
[10] Kechris, A.: *Classical Descriptive Set Theory.* Graduate Texts in Mathematics 156. Springer-Verlag. (1994)
[11] Keisler, H.: *Fundamentals of Model Theory.* In Barwise, J., ed.: Handbook of Mathematical Logic, Elsevier. (1977)
[12] Kelly, K.: *The Logic of Reliable Inquiry.* Oxford University Press. (1996).
[13] Lukaszewicz, W.: *Non-Monotonic Reasoning, formalization of commonsense reasoning.* Ellis Horwood Series in Artificial Intelligence. (1990)
[14] Makkai, M.: *Admissible Sets and Infinitary Logic.* In Barwise, J., ed.: Handbook of Mathematical Logic, Elsevier. (1977)
[15] Martin, E., Osherson, D.: *Elements of Scientific Inquiry.* The MIT Press. (1998)
[16] Martin, E., Sharma, A., Stephan, F.: *A General Theory of Deduction, Induction, and Learning.* In Jantke, K., Shinohara, A.: Proceedings of the Fourth International Conference on Discovery Science. Springer-Verlag. (2001) 228–242
[17] Martin, E., Nguyen, P., Sharma, A., Stephan, F.: *Learning in Logic with RichProlog.* Proceedings of the Eighteenth International Conference on Logic Programming. To appear. (2002)
[18] Nienhuys-Cheng, S., de Wolf, R.: *Foundations of Inductive Logic Programming.* Lecture Notes in Artificial Intelligence, Springer-Verlag. (1997)
[19] Odifreddi, P.: *Classical Recursion Theory.* North-Holland. (1989)
[20] Osherson, D., Stob, M., Weinstein, S. *Systems that learn.* The MIT Press. (1986)
[21] Popper, K.: *The Logic of Scientific Discovery.* Hutchinson. (1959)
[22] Stephan, F.: *On one-sided versus two-sided classification* Archive for Mathematical Logic. **40** (2001) 489–513.
[23] Stephan, F., Terwijn, A.: *Counting extensional differences in BC-learning.* In Proccedings of the 5th International Colloquium Grammatical Inference, Lisbon, Portugal. Springer-Verlag. (2000) 256–269

A Pathology of Bottom-Up Hill-Climbing in Inductive Rule Learning

Johannes Fürnkranz

Austrian Research Institute for Artificial Intelligence
Schottengasse 3, A-1010 Vienna, Austria
juffi@oefai.at

Abstract. In this paper, we close the gap between the simple and straight-forward implementations of top-down hill-climbing that can be found in the literature, and the rather complex strategies for greedy bottom-up generalization. Our main result is that the simple bottom-up counterpart to the top-down hill-climbing algorithm is unable to learn in domains with dispersed examples. In particular, we show that guided greedy generalization is impossible if the seed example differs in more than one attribute value from its nearest neighbor. We also perform an empirical study of the commonness of this problem is in popular benchmark datasets, and present average-case and worst-case results for the probability of drawing a pathological seed example in binary domains.

1 Introduction

Despite its popularity, it is quite well-known that top-down hill-climbing is a problematic rule learning strategy for cases where the target concept contains a set of conditions which are highly relevant as a conjunction but where each of them appears to be irrelevant in isolation (as, e.g., in the parity problem). For such cases, it is often suggested to use a bottom-up strategy, i.e., to generalize a single example by greedily deleting conditions from the corresponding most specific rule. Despite this fact, no description of this simple and efficient form of bottom-up learning can be found in the literature.

Some time ago, we intended to close this gap and started to implement a bottom-up hill-climbing algorithm, only to find out that a straight-forward prototype implementation failed to learn a simple parity concept with a few irrelevant attributes. Thus the intended improvement over top-down hill-climbing did not materialize. As the idea for such a bottom-up procedure is fairly obvious, we consider it quite likely that other researchers have tried similar approaches and encountered a similar failure.

This paper tries to explain this negative experience by pointing out a pathology in bottom-up hill-climbing that inhibits learning in certain domains. We start with a brief survey of hill-climbing in rule learning, primarily focusing on the top-down algorithm that forms the core of many heuristic rule learning algorithms (Section 2). In Section 3, we discuss some weaknesses of top-down approaches which are commonly used for motivating the use of bottom-up search strategies,

N. Cesa-Bianchi et al. (Eds.): ALT 2002, LNAI 2533, pp. 263–277, 2002.

---

procedure SEPARATEANDCONQUER*(Examples)*

Theory = ∅
while POSITIVE*(Examples)* ≠ ∅
    Rule = FINDBESTRULE*(Examples)*
    Theory = *Theory* ∪ *Rule*
    Examples = *Examples* \ COVER*(Rule,Examples)*
return*(Theory)*

Fig. 1. The top-level loop of separate-and-conquer rule-learning algorithms.

before we present the simple bottom-up counter-part to these top-down algorithms and discuss its relation to other bottom-up approaches in the literature. Section 4 presents the main result of the paper and discusses its commonness based on average-case and worst-case analyses of datasets, as well as its limitations. Finally, we also sketch that our result may point to a way for improving bottom-up algorithms by replacing the random selection of seed examples with a bias that prefers examples in comparably dense regions of the example space.

2   Top-Down Hill-Climbing

Rule learning typically follows the so-called *separate-and-conquer* or *covering* strategy, which learns rules successively. The examples covered by previously learned rules are removed from the training set (*separated*) before subsequent rules are learned (before the rest of the training set is *conquered*). The basic algorithm is shown in Fig. 1.

This learning strategy has its roots in the early days of machine learning in the AQ family of rule learning algorithms (Michalski, 1969; Kaufman and Michalski, 2000). It is fairly popular in *propositional rule learning* (cf. CN2 [5, 4] or Ripper [6]) as well as in *inductive logic programming (ILP)* (cf. Foil [23] and its successors [10, 11, 8, 25] or Progol [21]). A detailed survey of this large family of algorithms can be found in [13].

Various approaches that adhere to this framework differ in the way single rules are learned, i.e., in the implementation of the FINDBESTRULE procedure of Fig. 1. The vast majority of algorithms uses a heuristic top-down hill-climbing strategy, i.e., they learn a rule by successively specializing the current best rule. The prevalent specialization operator is to greedily add the most promising condition to the body of the rule. A simple version of this algorithm is shown in Fig. 2.

The algorithm starts with the most general rule (the rule with the body TRUE which covers all training examples), from which it computes all refinements that can be obtained by adding single conditions to the body of the rule. These refinements specialize the rule, i.e. the rule will in general cover less examples than it did without the additional condition. If the excluded examples are

---

```
procedure TOPDOWN(Examples)

BestRule = {true}
BestEval = EVALUATERULE(BestRule,Examples)
loop
    Refinements = ADDCONDITION(BestRule)
    MaxEval = 0
    foreach Refinement ∈ Refinements
        Evaluation = EVALUATERULE(Refinement,Examples)
        if Evaluation > MaxEval
            MaxRule = Refinement
            MaxEval = Evaluation
    if MaxEval ≥ BestEval
        BestRule = MaxRule
        BestEval = MaxEval
    else
        return(BestRule)
```

Fig. 2. A top-down hill-climbing implementation of FINDBESTRULE

mainly negative, the proportion of positive examples among the covered examples will increase, which will be reflected by an increase of the heuristic value of the rule (for which various heuristics can be found in the literature; Fürnkranz 13, Lavrač et al. 17). If the best refinement has a higher evaluation than its predecessor, it replaces it, and the search continues with the refinements of the new best rule. Otherwise, the previous best rule is a local optimum and the search stops. In the worst case, this will happen when no further refinement of the best rule is possible.

More advanced versions of this algorithm differ from this simple version mostly by adding additional mechanisms for preventing overfitting of the training data, for example by decoupling the stopping of the specialization process from the used quality measure or by generalizing overly specialized rules in a separate *pruning* phase [12].

3   Bottom-Up Hill-Climbing

Despite the fact that most algorithms search the rule space in a top-down fashion, we have not seen any convincing argument against bottom-up induction, i.e., against algorithms that successively generalize from a most specific rule (typically a single training example) instead of successively specializing the most general rule. Quite in contrary, there is evidence of situations where bottom-up induction may be the preferable approach (cf. Section 3.1). Nevertheless, no counterpart to the algorithm shown in Fig. 2 can be found in the literature. In the remainder of this section, we will discuss such an algorithm in detail (Section 3.2), and also briefly survey related work in bottom-up hill-climbing in rule learning (Section 3.3).

3.1   Motivation: Pathologies of Top-Down Hill-Climbing

Top-down hill-climbing algorithms like the one discussed in the previous sections are quite popular and reasonably successful. However, a fundamental shortcoming of this approach is that it only evaluates the value of single conditions in isolation (or in the context of all previously added conditions of a rule). The problem with this is that there are cases where a conjunction of conditions may be strongly relevant, while each of its member terms in isolation may appear to be irrelevant.

The best-known examples for this problem are XOR or parity problems. A *parity problem* consists of a few relevant and several irrelevant binary attributes. The class label of each example is 1 if there is an even number of ones among the values of the relevant attributes, and 0 otherwise. For a top-down learner, the individual attributes are indiscriminable because each condition that tests the value of one of the binary attributes will cover approximately half positive and half negative examples. Hence, there is no information that can be used for guiding the search for an appropriate refinement.

Similarly, many top-down ILP algorithms such as Foil [23] have the problem that they cannot learn relations which introduce new variables, because such relations often do not contain any information that helps to discriminate between positive and negative examples. A typical example would be the literal parent(X,Z), which is necessary for learning the concept grandparent(X,Y). As every person X has two parents Z (irrespective of whether Y is her grandparent or not), this literal does not help to discriminate between positive and negative examples. However, its addition is necessary for learning the target concept. Many systems are able to handle a subset of these problems by adding so-called *determinate literals* (literals that have at most one valid binding and therefore do not blow up the number of possible derivations for the clause; Quinlan 24) to the clause even if they do not have any value, but the principal problem remains.

Finally, Chevaleyre and Zucker [3] show a convincing argument that top-down hill-climbing may have severe problems in multi-instance learning problems, i.e., in problems where examples are not described with single feature vectors but with *bags* of feature vectors. The problem occurs when each possible value of an attribute is assumed by at least one instance of each bag. In this case, every condition that tests on values of this attribute covers all examples, positive or negative. Thus, a target concept that consists of a conjunction of values of two (or more) of such attributes cannot be learned because each individual attribute will appear to be completely irrelevant. A detailed example can be found in [3]. As multi-instance learning is a special case of ILP [7], this problem is also relevant to ILP in general. It may occur whenever multiple variable bindings are possible for an unbound existentially quantified variable in the body of a rule.[1]

---

[1] The problem may also be viewed as a generalization of the problem discussed in the previous paragraph.

```
procedure BOTTOMUP(Examples)

BestRule = SELECTRANDOMEXAMPLE(POSITIVE(Examples))
BestEval = EVALUATERULE(BestRule,Examples)
loop
    Refinements = DELETECONDITION(BestRule)
    MaxEval = 0
    foreach Refinement ∈ Refinements
        Evaluation = EVALUATERULE(Refinement,Examples)
        if Evaluation > MaxEval
           MaxRule = Refinement
           MaxEval = Evaluation
    if MaxEval > BestEval
       BestRule = MaxRule
       BestEval = MaxEval
    else
       return(BestRule)
```

Fig. 3. A bottom-up hill-climbing implementation of FINDBESTRULE

In all of the above cases, the conjunction of several conditions is relevant, while some or all of the conditions in isolation may appear to be irrelevant, and will therefore not be selected by a top-down hill-climbing strategy. On the other hand, a bottom-up search strategy could naturally deal with such cases because it starts from most specific rules (basically single examples) and successively generalizes these. As all conjunctions of the target rule must also be present in the examples covered by the rule, bottom-up strategies are therefore not prone to this type of problem. Consequently, it is frequently suggested to use a bottom-up search strategy to cope with such pathologies of top-down search.

3.2   The Basic Algorithm

The bottom-up algorithm of Fig. 3 differs only in three points from the top-down algorithm of Fig. 2. First, it uses a different procedure for computing the refinements of a rule: while TOPDOWN successively *specializes* its best rule by adding conditions, BOTTOMUP successively *generalizes* its best rule by deleting conditions. Naturally, it also has to use a different initialization from which it can start its search, namely it initializes its best rule to a random positive example. The third difference is that TOPDOWN stops its search when the best refinement of a rule does not improve upon its predecessor, while BOTTOMUP generalizes as long as the best refinement is *no worse* than its predecessor. Thus, both methods implement a preference bias for shorter rules.

The above algorithm may be generalized by extending DELETECONDITION to consider not only the deletion of single conditions, but also all possible pairs, triples, etc. We refer to this generalization as **n-step look-ahead hill-climbing**, where n denotes the maximum number of conditions that are considered for deletion in one refinement step.

3.3   Alternative Approaches to Bottom-Up Rule Learning

The simple and straight-forward hill-climbing algorithm of Fig. 3 has a fundamental problem, which we will discuss in section 4. Nevertheless, a variety of successful bottom-up approaches can be found in the rule learning literature. These will be briefly discussed in the remainder of this section.

AQ-based approaches: AQ [18] and its successors [e.g., 19, 20, 1, 15] learn bottom-up in the sense that they search the space of generalizations of a single randomly selected seed example. However, this space of generalizations is searched top-down, i.e., the seed example is only used for constraining the search space, but not as the starting point of the search. In ILP, an equivalent strategy is used in **Progol**, where the seed example is minimally generalized with respect to the available background knowledge and a given maximum inference depth, and the resulting *bottom clause* is then again used for constraining the search space for a subsequent top-down best-first search for the best generalization [21].

lgg-**based Approaches:** Most algorithms that search in a bottom-up fashion do not generalize from single examples, but generalize from pairs of examples. The prototype of this type of algorithm is the ILP system **Golem** [22], which constructs minimal generalizations of pairs of examples, so-called (relative) *least general generalizations (lggs)*. Similar ideas have subsequently also been used in propositional rule learning, for example in **DLG** [26, 27] and **RISE** [9].

The main problem with this approach is its quadratic computational complexity resulting from the fact that in each generalization step, the current rule has to be generalized with each training example and the resulting rules have to be tested on all training examples. **Golem** addresses this problem by restricting its attention to a fixed number of generalizations constructed from a randomly drawn subsample of all example pairs. **DLG** uses a greedy version of the algorithm that incrementally generalizes the first example with all examples in succession, replacing the current rule with the generalization when the heuristic evaluation improves. Thus it finds a final rule in a single pass through the examples (with quadratic effort) but the obtained generalization depends on the (randomized) order of the training examples.

Pruning Algorithms: The only case we know of where bottom-up hill-climbing of the type shown in Fig. 3 is used in rule learning is for pruning, i.e., for simplifying previously learned rules by successively generalizing them. For example, the incremental reduced error pruning strategy [14], which forms the basis of **Ripper** [6], generalizes a rule by greedily deleting single conditions immediately after it has been learned. The problem with bottom-up hill-climbing, which we

Table 1. A pathological example where bottom-up hill-climbing cannot find the target concept $A_1 = 1 \rightarrow +$.

A_1	A_2	A_3	Class
1	1	1	+
1	0	0	+
0	1	0	−
0	0	1	−

will discuss in the following section, does not apply to this scenario for reasons that will be discussed further below.

4   A Pathology of Bottom-Up Hill-Climbing

Consider the sample database shown in Table 1. The target concept $A_1 = 1 \rightarrow +$ is quite obvious and can be found without problems by top-down hill-climbing algorithms. However, one can easily verify that it can only be found by chance by a bottom-up hill-climbing algorithm of the type shown in Fig. 3 (in the remainder of this section, we will only be concerned with this type). Assume, e.g., that the first example is picked as the seed example. The corresponding rule would be $A_1 = 1 \land A_2 = 1 \land A_3 = 1 \rightarrow +$.

If the learner now tries to generalize this rule by deleting the first condition, the resulting rule $A_2 = 1 \land A_3 = 1 \rightarrow +$ does not cover any additional examples. This is good because we obviously do not want to drop the condition $A_1 = 1$. However, the situation is analogous for the other two conditions: no matter what condition is deleted from the rule, the resulting generalization does not cover any additional examples, positive or negative. Also note that this situation does not depend on the choice of the seed example: the same problem occurs for picking any of the other three examples as a seed example.

The basic question at this point is, whether this is simply a carefully constructed example with only minor relevance for practical applications, or whether this a prototypical case that illustrates a common problem. In the following, we will argue for the latter.

4.1   The Problem

The following simple observation shows that the above-mentioned pathology occurs whenever the seed example differs from every other example in at least two attributes.

Theorem 1. *Bottom-up hill-climbing with n-step look-ahead is unable to discriminate between generalizations of an example if the example differs from its nearest neighbour in at least $n + 1$ attribute values.*

Proof. Let E be the training examples, each of them described with m symbolic attributes $A_1, ..., A_m$, $s = (s_1, ..., s_m) \in E$ a randomly chosen seed example, and H be the Hamming distance between two examples, i.e,

$$H(e, f) = \sum_{i=1...m} \delta(e_i, f_i) \text{ for } e, f \in E \text{ where } \delta(a, b) = \begin{cases} 0 & \text{if } a = b \\ 1 & \text{if } a \neq b \end{cases}$$

Let us first consider a one-step look-ahead, i.e., $n = 1$: Then all candidate generalizations of the conjunction $A_1 = s_1 \wedge ... \wedge A_m = s_m$ are obtained by deleting single conditions $A_i = s_i, 1 \leq i \leq m$. Obviously, all of them constrain the examples they cover to be identical to s except for the value of attribute A_i, which could take an arbitrary value. Consequently, no other example $e \neq s$ can be covered by a candidate rule because all covered examples e may differ from s in at most $n = 1$ attribute values (i.e., $H(s, e) \leq 1$), while we assumed that each example $e \neq s$ differs from s in at least $n + 1 = 2$ attributes values, i.e., $\min_{e \in E, e \neq s} H(s, e) \geq 2$.

The generalization of this argument to general $n > 1$ is quite straight-forward. In this case, the candidate generalizations of the conjunction are obtained by deleting (up to) n conditions from the rule. Thus, no generalization of the seed example can cover additional examples iff the seed differs from all examples in at least $n + 1$ attribute values. □

In particular, this theorem states that simple bottom-up hill-climbing will not work well whenever the chances are high that a seed example is picked that has a distance of ≥ 2 to its nearest neighbor. In the following section, we will discuss how common this situation is.

4.2   Commonness of the Problem

In order to estimate how common this problem is in real-world applications we analyzed 13 benchmark datasets with respect to the distribution of distances between nearest neighbor pairs. The datasets are all datasets with less than 10,000 examples and only symbolic attributes among the datasets that are used within the METAL project.[2] Most of them originate from the UCI repository [2]. For each dataset, we computed the distance of each example to its nearest neighbor. Neighbors with distance 0 (i.e., duplicate examples) were ignored for this computation because they are already covered by the most specific rule (the rule that conditions on all values of the example) and therefore also by all its generalizations. The last column of Table 2 shows the proportion of such examples.[3]

---

[2] We ignored trivial variants of datasets (e.g., *vote/vote1*) as well as artificial domains for which the dataset consists of a complete enumeration of the sample space (e.g., *monk, parity*). More on the latter can be found further below.

[3] This is out of the scope of this paper, but we were surprised to find that some domains contain quite a significant portion of duplicate examples. For some commonly used benchmark sets (e.g., *vote* or *soybean*) this begs the question whether in these domains hold-out (or cross-validation) error estimates are optimistically biased because of their lack of independence of the training and test sets.

Table 2. Partial histograms of minimum example distances in 13 symbolic domains with less than 10,000 examples (training and test sets are pooled together). The fourth column (in bold font) shows the proportion of examples that have a nearest neighbor with distance 1. The two following columns show the proportions of distances 2 and > 2. The penultimate column shows the maximum distance between an example and its nearest neighbor in this dataset. The final column shows the proportion of examples that have a duplicate in the dataset (examples with distance = 0 are ignored for computing the nearest neighbor).

dataset	#exs	#atts	$\min_e H(s,e)$ = 1	= 2	> 2	$\max_s$ $\min_e H$	duplicates
titanic	2201	3	**1.000**	0.000	0.000	1	1.000
car	1728	6	**1.000**	0.000	0.000	1	0.000
led7	3200	7	**1.000**	0.000	0.000	1	0.996
mushrooms	8124	22	**1.000**	0.000	0.000	1	0.000
solar flares(x,c,m)	1389	10	**0.986**	0.014	0.000	2	0.866
kr vs. kp	3196	36	**0.958**	0.036	0.006	5	0.000
vote	300	16	**0.553**	0.217	0.230	6	0.223
soybean	683	35	**0.483**	0.253	0.264	8	0.139
acetylation	1511	50	**0.142**	0.068	0.790	42	0.097
splice	3190	60	**0.020**	0.020	0.961	47	0.097
led24	3200	24	**0.018**	0.146	0.836	6	0.001
dna-splice	3186	180	**0.008**	0.015	0.977	53	0.097
tic-tac-toe	958	9	**0.000**	1.000	0.000	2	0.000

The resulting probability estimates are shown (in bold face) in the fourth column of Table 2: these probabilities denote the chance of picking a seed example for which bottom-up hill-climbing (with 1-step look-ahead) can perform no meaningful generalization because no candidate generalization will cover an additional example. In some domains (e.g., *mushrooms* or *titanic*, which has only 3 attributes, but 2201 examples) this does not seem to be a problem, while it seems to become increasingly more problematic with a growing number of attributes. A particularly interesting case is the *tic-tac-toe* domain (bottom line of Table 2), whose special properties prevent the use of bottom-up hill-climbing entirely. This database encodes all won positions of a tic-tac-toe game, with the same player on the move. It is easy to see that, if both players make a move, the board position will change on two squares, and that therefore pairs of positions with the same player to move will always differ in at least two attributes.

Also of interest is the discrepancy between the *led7* and the *led24* domains, which differ only in the fact that *led24* contains an additional 17 irrelevant attributes. This completely reverses the picture: While *led7* is conveniently over-sampled (there are only $2^7 = 128$ unique examples in this domain[4]), it is practically impossible to learn *led24* with bottom-up hill-climbing.

---

[4] It should be noted that there is a designated train/test-split for this domain where only a fraction of the 3200 examples are actually used for training.

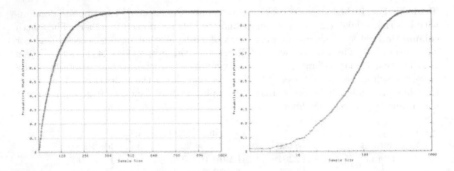

Fig. 4. Probability for drawing an example that has a neighbor at distance 1 over different training set sizes for a domain with 10 binary attributes (estimated from 100 different sequences of nested subsets; regular plot and plot with logarithmic scale for sample sizes).

This is interesting because with the same argument it can be shown that it is practically impossible to learn a parity problem of similar proportions, i.e., it defeats one of the main motivations for considering bottom-up hill-climbing. Fig. 4 illustrates this situation for a domain with 10 Boolean attributes, such as *led10*. The graphs show the probability distribution for picking an example that has a nearest neighbor at distance 1 over the size of subset (shown on a logarithmic scale in the graph to the right). The function is estimated by counting the proportion of such examples in 100 sequences of nested subsets from 2 examples up to all 1024 examples of the domain. If approximately half of the examples are present, one can be quite certain that bottom-up hill-climbing will work. Thereafter, the probability starts to decrease slowly for lower example sizes, and the decline picks up pace at about 250 examples.

Fig. 5 shows a similar plot for subsets of size up to 4800 for a binary domain with 24 attributes (like *led24*). While 4800 appears to be a reasonable training set size for a domain with 24 attributes (there are 200 examples per attribute), this is still a very low number in comparison to the $2^{24} = 16,777,216$ examples of the full domain. The curve shown in Fig. 5 is still in the quasi-linear ascent at the beginning (compare with Fig. 4), and the probability estimates are still below 0.01, i.e. there is not even a 1% chance that bottom-up hill-climbing will pick a suitable example. This explains the difference between the *led7* and *led24* results in Table 2, and shows that bottom-up hill-climbing is very sensitive to the addition of irrelevant attributes.

While above analysis was concerned with the average case, it is fairly straightforward to derive a tight worst-case bound for the largest dataset that can be constructed so that each pair of examples has a distance ≥ 2:

Theorem 2. *The largest dataset for a binary domain with n attributes for which all pairs of examples differ in at least two attributes contains 2^{n-1} examples.*

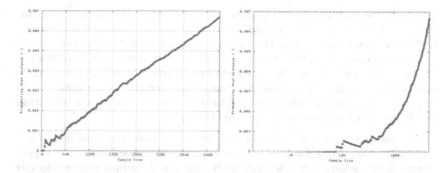

Fig. 5. Probability estimates for drawing an example that has a neighbor at distance 1 over different training set sizes for a domain with 24 binary attributes (estimated from 100 different sequences of nested subsets with size ≤ 4800; regular plot and plot with logarithmic scale for sample sizes).

Proof. There are 2^{n-1} examples with $n-1$ attributes. We extend each example with an n-th attribute as a parity value (i.e., we add 0 for an even number of 1's in the first $n-1$ attributes and 1 for an odd number). Clearly, examples that had a distance of 1 with $n-1$ attributes, now have a distance of 2 because they will in addition differ in the parity attribute. Thus, we have training set with 2^{n-1} examples and pairwise examples distances ≥ 2.

There can also be no larger set because each additional example must share the first $n-1$ attributes with one of the examples in the original dataset. Thus it can only differ in the last attribute, and the distance to its nearest neighbor is ≤ 1. $\square$.

4.3   Discussion

A few comments are at hand to put the above results into the right perspective. First, it should be noted that our results only deal with symbolic and possibly with integer domains. Attributes with continuous value ranges typically have to be generalized to an interval, which may increase chances of covering additional examples. However, this may also result in an undesirable bias that favors generalization of continuous attributes over generalization of symbolic attributes, in case the examples are fairly scattered in the projection to the symbolic subspace.

We also tacitly assumed that bottom-up hill-climbing *can* make a useful generalization if there is at least one other examples that differs in only one value. Obviously, this needs not be the case, because the distribution of positive and negative class labels can be more or less arbitrary at such small samples.

Furthermore, the above-mentioned limitations only apply to bottom-up hill-climbing that starts from the most specific rule, i.e., the equivalent of a single example. Bottom-up hill-climbing of the type shown in Fig. 3 *is* successfully used for pruning, i.e., for simplifying previously learned rules (cf. Section 3.3). It can work there because generalization starts at a point where the last specialization step (i.e., the last addition of a condition to the rule) has decreased the coverage of the rule on the training set. Thus, even if no generalization of the learned rule increases its coverage on the validation set (where the pruned rule is evaluated), the information about the order in which the conditions have been added in the specialization phase may be used for making a reasonable tie-breaking choice. Typically, the conditions added first will be more relevant and more reliable than conditions that have been added towards the end.

It is also unclear whether these results can be carried over to other uses of hill-climbing in machine learning. An obvious candidate would be backwards wrapper feature subset selection, which starts with a full set of features and successively considers individual features for elimination [16]. However, the situation here is somewhat different. Although it can be expected that many features look alike (at least if highly selective inducers like decision trees or rule learners are used), there will be some differences that can be used for guiding the search (e.g., one can expect that the use of a different root attribute in a decision tree, which is guaranteed to happen in this process, will lead to different performance estimates).

There are several extensions to basic hill-climbing that one could expect to help with our type of problem. We already discussed the case of *deeper look-aheads* (i.e., to generalize several steps at the same time) and showed that increasing the look-ahead by one step increases the allowable minimum example distance by one. Thus, the examples may be less dense in the domain. However, Table 2 shows that a 2-step look-ahead could in most cases (a notable exception is *tic-tac-toe*) only marginally improve the situation (the probabilities of failure are the sum of the columns '= 1' and '= 2 (or one minus the values of the column '> 2'). These small improvements have to be paid with a quadratic increase of candidate generalizations that must be considered. Moreover, the penultimate column of Table 2 shows that there are several domains that contain examples whose nearest neighbor differs in five or more attributes, in the DNA-related domains even more than 40 attributes. The exponential growth in the search space makes such deep look-aheads prohibitive.

Another technique for fighting the myopic behavior of hill-climbing is the use of *beam search*. At each generalization step, beam search not only remembers the option that appears to be best (as in hill-climbing), but instead remembers the best b options (where b is the size of the beam). Again, it cannot solve the principal problem that all candidate generalizations will look alike, but by remembering more than one candidate, it increases the chance that a correct generalization is among those remembered. Of course, if the beam is made large enough to remember all possible candidates, we end up with exhaustive search.

It should also be noted that our analysis is only concerned with the counterpart of the popular top-down algorithm. More elaborate generalization operators, such as the use of *lggs* can be employed successfully, as many implementations demonstrate. However, these operators are also quite costly. *lggs*, for example, compute a generalization for each pair of examples instead of each single example, and, for this reason, are often combined with subsampling (cf. Section 3.3).

If one is willing to deal with such quadratic worst-case costs, our results may also lead to a constructive way for selecting good seed examples for bottom-up hill-climbing, namely examples that have a number of neighbors that are fairly close. A similar technique is used in RISE [9] for picking the best pair of examples for an *lgg*-based generalization step. The advantage would be that pairwise example differences are only needed for picking the seed example (instead of at each generalization step, as would be the case for *lggs*). Also, the algorithm may not need to compute all pairwise differences because it may stop as soon as it has discovered a candidate seed example that lies in a reasonably dense neighborhood. Whether such an approach could lead to a competitive bottom-up hill-climber remains subject to future work.

5   Conclusions

In this paper, we closed a gap in the literature on hill-climbing approaches in rule learning. While the simple top-down hill-climbing approach prevails in rule learning, and a few more complex bottom-up algorithms can be found as well, we do not know of any paper that discusses the simple bottom-up dual of the popular top-down approach. Our negative result shows that such an algorithm will fail to generalize in cases where the selected seed example is fairly distant from all its neighbors. For propositional domains, we show that the likeliness of such a pathological case increases with the number of attributes, and that several thousand examples are not sufficient to facilitate greedy bottom-up generalization for some twenty Boolean attributes.

Our results do not touch upon bottom-up approaches previously studied in the literature, but these have to buy the additional power of their generalization operator with a considerably larger number of investigated hypotheses (most approaches rely on generalization from pairs of examples instead of single examples). However, if one does not eschew quadratic run-time complexities, our results may also point to a way of improving future bottom-up systems by replacing the random selection of seed examples with a guided search for examples in denser neighborhoods of the example space.

Acknowledgements. I would like to thank the participants (and the organizers!) of the Leuven-Freiburg workshop 2002 for valuable comments and discussions.

The Austrian Research Institute for Artificial Intelligence is supported by the Austrian Federal Ministry of Education, Science and Culture. This work was supported by an APART stipend of the *Austrian Academy of Sciences* and by the Austrian *Fonds zur Förderung der Wissenschaftlichen Forschung (FWF)* under grant no. P12645-INF.

References

[1] Zhang] F. Bergadano, S. Matwin, R. S. Michalski, and J. Zhang. Learning two-tiered descriptions of flexible concepts: The POSEIDON system. *Machine Learning*, 8:5–43, 1992.

[2] C. L. Blake and C. J. Merz. UCI repository of machine learning databases. http://www.ics.uci.edu/~mlearn/MLRepository.html, 1998. Department of Information and Computer Science, University of California at Irvine, Irvine CA.

[3] Y. Chevaleyre and J.-D. Zucker. A framework for learning rules from multiple instance data. In L. D. Raedt and P. Flach, editors, *Proceedings of the 12th European Conference on Machine Learning (ECML-01)*, pages 49–60, Freiburg, Germany, 2001. Springer-Verlag.

[4] P. Clark and R. Boswell. Rule induction with CN2: Some recent improvements. In *Proceedings of the 5th European Working Session on Learning (EWSL-91)*, pages 151–163, Porto, Portugal, 1991. Springer-Verlag.

[5] P. Clark and T. Niblett. The CN2 induction algorithm. *Machine Learning*, 3(4): 261–283, 1989.

[6] W. W. Cohen. Fast effective rule induction. In A. Prieditis and S. Russell, editors, *Proceedings of the 12th International Conference on Machine Learning (ML-95)*, pages 115–123, Lake Tahoe, CA, 1995. Morgan Kaufmann.

[7] L. De Raedt. Attribute value learning versus inductive logic programming: The missing links (extended abstract). In D. Page, editor, *Proceedings of the 8th International Conference on Inductive Logic Programming (ILP-98)*, pages 1–8. Springer-Verlag, 1998.

[8] L. De Raedt and W. Van Laer. Inductive constraint logic. In *Proceedings of the 5th Workshop on Algorithmic Learning Theory (ALT-95)*. Springer-Verlag, 1995.

[9] P. Domingos. Unifying instance-based and rule-based induction. *Machine Learning*, 24:141–168, 1996.

[10] S. Džeroski and I. Bratko. Handling noise in Inductive Logic Programming. In S. H. Muggleton and K. Furukawa, editors, *Proceedings of the 2nd International Workshop on Inductive Logic Programming (ILP-92)*, number TM-1182 in ICOT Technical Memorandum, pages 109–125, Tokyo, Japan, 1992. Institue for New Generation Computer Technology.

[11] J. Fürnkranz. FOSSIL: A robust relational learner. In F. Bergadano and L. De Raedt, editors, *Proceedings of the 7th European Conference on Machine Learning (ECML-94)*, volume 784 of *Lecture Notes in Artificial Intelligence*, pages 122–137, Catania, Italy, 1994. Springer-Verlag.

[12] J. Fürnkranz. Pruning algorithms for rule learning. *Machine Learning*, 27(2): 139–171, 1997.

[13] J. Fürnkranz. Separate-and-conquer rule learning. *Artificial Intelligence Review*, 13(1):3–54, February 1999.

[14] J. Fürnkranz and G. Widmer. Incremental Reduced Error Pruning. In W. Cohen and H. Hirsh, editors, *Proceedings of the 11th International Conference on Machine Learning (ML-94)*, pages 70–77, New Brunswick, NJ, 1994. Morgan Kaufmann.

[15] K. A. Kaufman and R. S. Michalski. An adjustable rule learner for pattern discovery using the AQ methodology. *Journal of Intelligent Information Systems*, 14:199–216, 2000.

[16] R. Kohavi and G. H. John. Wrappers for feature subset selection. *Artificial Intelligence*, 97(1–2):273–324, 1997. Special Issue on *Relevance*.

[17] N. Lavrač, P. Flach, and B. Zupan. Rule evaluation measures: A unifying view. In S. Džeroski and P. Flach, editors, *Ninth International Workshop on Inductive Logic Programming (ILP'99)*, volume 1634 of *Lecture Notes in Artificial Intelligence*, pages 174–185. Springer-Verlag, June 1999.

[18] R. S. Michalski. On the quasi-minimal solution of the covering problem. In *Proceedings of the 5th International Symposium on Information Processing (FCIP-69)*, volume A3 (Switching Circuits), pages 125–128, Bled, Yugoslavia, 1969.

[19] R. S. Michalski. Pattern recognition and rule-guided inference. *IEEE Transactions on Pattern Analysis and Machine Intelligence*, 2:349–361, 1980.

[20] R. S. Michalski, I. Mozetič, J. Hong, and N. Lavrač. The multi-purpose incremental learning system AQ15 and its testing application to three medical domains. In *Proceedings of the 5th National Conference on Artificial Intelligence (AAAI-86)*, pages 1041–1045, Philadelphia, PA, 1986.

[21] S. H. Muggleton. Inverse entailment and Progol. *New Generation Computing*, 13 (3,4):245–286, 1995. Special Issue on Inductive Logic Programming.

[22] S. H. Muggleton and C. Feng. Efficient induction of logic programs. In *Proceedings of the 1st Conference on Algorithmic Learning Theory*, pages 1–14, Tokyo, Japan, 1990.

[23] J. R. Quinlan. Learning logical definitions from relations. *Machine Learning*, 5: 239–266, 1990.

[24] J. R. Quinlan. Determinate literals in inductive logic programming. In *Proceedings of the 8th International Workshop on Machine Learning (ML-91)*, pages 442–446, 1991.

[25] J. R. Quinlan and R. M. Cameron-Jones. Induction of logic programs: FOIL and related systems. *New Generation Computing*, 13(3,4):287–312, 1995. Special Issue on Inductive Logic Programming.

[26] G. I. Webb. Learning disjunctive class descriptions by least generalisation. Technical Report TR C92/9, Deakin University, School of Computing & Mathematics, Geelong, Australia, September 1992.

[27] G. I. Webb and J. W. M. Agar. Inducing diagnostic rules for glomerular disease with the DLG machine learning algorithm. *Artificial Intelligence in Medicine*, 4: 419–430, 1992.

Minimised Residue Hypotheses in Relevant Logic

Bertram Fronhöfer[1] and Akihiro Yamamoto[2]

[1] Artificial Intelligence Institute, Department of Computer Science
Technische Universität Dresden
D-01062 Dresden GERMANY
Bertram.Fronhoefer@inf.tu-dresden.de
[2] MemeMedia Laboratory, Hokkaido University
N 13 W 8, Sapporo 060-8628 JAPAN
yamamoto@meme.hokudai.ac.jp

Abstract. In the field of deductive logic, relevant logic has been investigated for a long time, as a means to derive only conclusions which are related to all premises. Our proposal is to apply this concept of relevance as a criterion of appropriateness to hypotheses in inductive logic, and in this paper we present some special hypotheses called residue hypotheses, which satisfy such kind of appropriateness. This concept of relevance is different from those often introduced in the field of Inductive Logic Programming. While those aimed at the reduction of search spaces, which went hand in hand with postulating criteria which restricted the appropriateness of formulae as hypotheses, the relevance concept presented in this paper can be regarded as 'logical smallness' of hypotheses, in contrast to 'syntactical smallness'. We also give a further refinement, so-called minimized residue hypotheses, which constitute an interesting trade-off between these two types of smallness. We also give some results on bottom clauses and relevance.

1 Introduction

Finding appropriate hypotheses to explain observations is a central activity towards discovering new theories. In the field of Inductive Logic Programming (ILP), concepts of relevance between logical formulae have often and independently been used for reduction of search spaces, which went hand in hand with postulating criteria which restricted the appropriateness of formulae as hypotheses [LGJ99,Mid99]. On the other hand, relevance has been investigated for a long time in the field of deductive logic. A formula is derived as a conclusion in relevant logic only if it is deductively related to all premises. This means that relevance is a criterion of appropriateness concerning conclusions. Our proposal is to see the relevance concept in deductive logic as a criterion of appropriateness to hypotheses in inductive logic, and in this paper we present some special hypotheses— called residue hypotheses and minimized residue hypotheses—which satisfy such appropriateness.

N. Cesa-Bianchi et al. (Eds.): ALT 2002, LNAI 2533, pp. 278–292, 2002.

We understand ILP as a form of hypothesis finding, i.e., as a process of logical inference aiming at the deductive derivation of *hypotheses* from *observational examples* and *background knowledge* where all three are logical formulae. We adopt the following quite general definition.

Definition 1. *We define a* **hypothesis finding problem** *(HFP) as a pair* $(\mathfrak{B}, \mathfrak{E})$ *of two formulae* $\mathfrak{B}$ *and* $\mathfrak{E}$, *where we assume that* $\mathfrak{B} \not\models \mathfrak{E}$. *A* **solution** *to the* $\mathrm{HFP}(\mathfrak{B}, \mathfrak{E})$ *is given by any formula* $\mathfrak{H}$, *such that* $\mathfrak{B} \wedge \mathfrak{H} \models \mathfrak{E}$. ($\mathfrak{B}$, $\mathfrak{E}$ *and* $\mathfrak{H}$ *are called* **background theory**, **example** *and* **hypothesis** *respectively.*)

As in the seminal work of Plotkin [Plo71], we treat positive examples only. Obviously, we will disallow inconsistent formulae as hypotheses.

Looking quite generally at different solutions of a HFP, it turns out that an appropriate hypothesis $\mathfrak{H}$ should be distinguished by the following *hypothesis criteria*: $\mathfrak{H}$ should be

(C1) *'logically small'* in order to avoid 'overstrengthening' or 'overspecializing' of $\mathfrak{B}$ when adding $\mathfrak{H}$ and

(C2) *'syntactically small'* in order to prevent an explosion of iteratively constructed background theories $\mathfrak{B} \wedge \mathfrak{H}$.

A borderline between these two types of criteria might be drawn as follows: A criterion is *syntactical* if it depends on the hypothesis itself — e.g. we might think of the length of a formula, its Kolmogorov complexity, instantiation depth, etc. — while a criterion is *logical* if it concerns the relationship of a hypothesis to other formulae — e.g. subsumption of other hypotheses, properties of its relationship to $\mathfrak{B}$ and $\mathfrak{E}$, etc. Note that the two hypotheses $\mathfrak{E}$ and $\mathfrak{B} \to \mathfrak{E}$ are close to the extremes: Each satisfies one of these two criteria, but not the other. We decided to adopt 'relevant entailment' instead of 'classical entailment' as our 'logical smallness concept', because this way these extremes are avoided in general.

This lead to the definition of *residue hypotheses* and *minimized residue hypotheses* in [FY98,YF00]. They were defined by means of the *Connection Method*[Bib87] and derived from the non-complementary paths in the matrix obtained from $\mathfrak{B} \to \mathfrak{E}$. In the present paper we show that *residue hypotheses* and *minimized residue hypotheses* — denoted by $\mathfrak{H}^w$ and $\mathfrak{H}^{\underline{W}}$ respectively — constitute a trade-off between the mentioned criteria : They are still classically semantically 'smallest', while $\mathfrak{H}^{\underline{W}}$ is constructed by further reductions of the size of $\mathfrak{H}^w$ and is therefore syntactically smaller. They can both be seen as solutions in Multiplicative Relevant Logic.

We also show that under certain conditions our new hypothesis concepts generalize the earlier hypotheses generated by the Bottom Method in [Yam99b]. Since this method is an extension of both the Saturation Method and the abduction methods as well as a restriction of the Inverse Entailment Method, the result we show relates our new hypothesis finding methods also to those earlier methods.

The paper is organized as follows: In Section 2 we review the fundamentals of the Connection Method and its application to Multiplicative Relevant Logic.

In Section 3 we introduce the concepts of *residue hypothesis* and of *minimized residue hypothesis*. We also show that we may call hypotheses of both types relevant hypotheses. In Section 4 we compare the Bottom Method and the relevant hypothesis concepts.

Due to reasons of space, proofs of some theorems and lemmata — as well as several more detailed explanations — are not in this paper. The complete version of the paper will be made available in a technical report on the web cite http://ca.meme.hokudai.ac.jp/people/yamamoto/tr.html.

2   The Connection Method

We will give in this section a rough outline of the Connection Method [Bib87] with special attention to its use for characterizing theoremhood in Multiplicative Relevant Logic. In order to simplify the presentation we will restrict ourselves to what is indispensable for the following sections. In particular, we will only deal with normal form matrices, although non-normal form matrices are mandatory for dealing with Multiplicative Relevant Logic in general.

2.1   Matrices and Connections

We define a (normal form) *matrix* as a set of sets (*columns*) of occurrences of literals. (*Literals* are propositional variables or their negations. In matrices we denote negation by overlining, i.e. we write $\overline{P}$ instead of $\neg P$ (with P a propositional variable or a literal).)

The need to distinguish different *occurrences of literals* stems from Relevant Logic (see Section 2.2) (Different occurrences of (logical) literals will be distinguished by upper indices. We will sometimes omit the upper index if no confusion may arise, e.g. if there are no different occurrences which must be distinguished. If we speak of literals in (parts of) matrices, we usually refer to occurrences, otherwise not.)

It is convenient to denote by $\Subset$ the reflexive transitive closure of $\in$ (set membership), and thus writing $L \Subset \mathcal{M}$ when we want to speak about an occurrence of a literal in a column of $\mathcal{M}$.

We denote by $\mathfrak{m}$ the usual translation of a formula into a set of clauses. However — following a tradition of the Connection Method — in contrast to the traditional *refutative* translation, we will not negate the formula, and thus translate in an *affirmative* way. Consequently our normal form matrices don't represent a conjunction of disjunctions, but a disjunction of conjunctions.

Two (logical) literals K and L are called *complementary*, if there is a propositional variable P and $K = P$ and $L = \overline{P}$ or vice versa. Since for an arbitrary formula F holds that $\neg\neg F$ is equivalent to F ($\overline{\overline{F}}$ equivalent to F), we make the convention that $\overline{K}$ denotes the literal being *complementary* to the literal K, where K may be a propositional variable or its negation. A *connection* in a matrix $\mathcal{M}$ is an unordered pair of occurrences of complementary literals $L \Subset \mathcal{M}$ and $K \Subset \mathcal{M}$, denoted by (L, K) or (K, L). We denote by $\mathfrak{S}_\mathcal{M}$

the **set of all connections** of the matrix $\mathcal{M}$. A **path** $\mathfrak{p}$ in a matrix $\mathcal{M}$ is a set of literals where we choose exactly one literal from each column of $\mathcal{M}$. A path $\mathfrak{p}$ in a matrix $\mathcal{M}$ is a **complementary path** with respect to a set of connections $\mathfrak{S}$, if $\mathfrak{p}$ **contains a connection** of $\mathfrak{S}$, i.e. there are occurrences of literals $L \in \mathcal{M}$ and $K \in \mathcal{M}$ with $(K, L) \in \mathfrak{S}$ and $K, L \in \mathfrak{p}$. A set of connections $\mathfrak{S}$ is called **spanning** for a matrix $\mathcal{M}$ iff every path in $\mathcal{M}$ contains at least one connection from $\mathfrak{S}$.

The Main Theorem of the Connection Method for classical logic [Bib87] says that a formula F is a theorem iff for the matrix $\mathrm{m}(F)$ the set of all connections is spanning.

Example 1. For the formula $F := ((C \rightarrow P) \wedge (S \wedge P \rightarrow K)) \rightarrow (C \rightarrow K)$ we get the matrix $\mathrm{m}(F) = \{\{C, \overline{P}\}, \{S, P, \overline{K}\}, \ \overline{C}, K\}$. The propositional variables C, P, S, and K respectively mean *cuddly*, *pet*, *small*, and *cat*. This matrix can be presented graphically as follows:

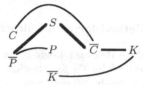

This matrix has the paths $\{C, S, \overline{C}, K\}, \{C, P, \overline{C}, K\}, \{C, \overline{K}, \overline{C}, K\}, \{\overline{P}, S, \overline{C}, K\}, \ldots$. The set of all connections are depicted by curved lines. The matrix is not complementary as there is the non-complementary path $\{\overline{P}, S, \overline{C}, K\}$ depicted by thick straight lines.   ∎

For classical logic holds that if there is a **spanning set of connections** for a matrix, then the set of all connections is also spanning. More generally, the property 'spanning' of a set of connections is inherited by all supersets. Unfortunately, this inheritance by supersets does not hold for the properties minimality and acyclicity which we will define below and which are essential for characterizing Relevant Logic. For this reason we cannot simply always consider the set of all connections, but we have to state more explicitly for a given matrix which set of connections we are dealing with. This leads to the concept of a **matrix graph** $(\mathcal{M}, \mathfrak{S})$, i.e. a pair consisting of a matrix $\mathcal{M}$ and a particular subset $\mathfrak{S}$ of $\mathfrak{S}_{\mathcal{M}}$. A **complementary matrix graph** is a matrix graph $(\mathcal{M}, \mathfrak{S})$ such that $\mathfrak{S}$ is a spanning set of connections for $\mathcal{M}$. Moreover, the consideration of different sets of connections for a given matrix leads to the distinction between **absolute properties** of a matrix $\mathcal{M}$ which are valid in $(\mathcal{M}, \mathfrak{S}_{\mathcal{M}})$ and **properties relative** to a set $\mathfrak{S}$ of connections, i.e. properties which are valid in the matrix graph $(\mathcal{M}, \mathfrak{S})$.

We call a connection (K, L) **superfluous** in a matrix graph $(\mathcal{M}, \mathfrak{S})$ iff every path $\mathfrak{p}$ in $\mathcal{M}$ with $K, L \in \mathfrak{p}$ contains a further connection from $\mathfrak{S}$. A matrix graph $(\mathcal{M}, \mathfrak{S})$ is **minimal complementary** iff it is complementary and none of the connections in $\mathfrak{S}$ is superfluous. In this case we also say that $\mathfrak{S}$ is a **minimal spanning set** of connections for $\mathcal{M}$. A set of connections $\mathfrak{S} \subset \mathfrak{S}_{\mathcal{M}}$ is

subspanning for the matrix $\mathcal{M}$ iff all absolutely complementary paths in $\mathcal{M}$— i.e. all paths which are complementary in $(\mathcal{M}, \mathfrak{S}_{\mathcal{M}})$—are also complementary in $(\mathcal{M}, \mathfrak{S})$. A subspanning set of connections $\mathfrak{S} \subset \mathfrak{S}_{\mathcal{M}}$ is ***minimal subspanning*** for the matrix $\mathcal{M}$ iff none of its connections is superfluous, i.e. for every connection in $\mathfrak{S}$ exists a path in $\mathcal{M}$ which contains no further connection from $\mathfrak{S}$.

A literal in a matrix graph $(\mathcal{M}, \mathfrak{S})$ is ***connected*** iff it is part of a connection in $\mathfrak{S}$. Otherwise it is ***unconnected***. We define the ***degree of connectedness*** of (an occurrence of) a literal L in a set of connections $\mathfrak{S}$ as the number of connections it is involved in:

$$\#_{\mathfrak{S}}(L) := card(\{K \mid (L, K) \in \mathfrak{S}\})$$

We omit the subscript and just write $\#(L)$ if $\mathfrak{S}$ is clear from the context. In case of $\#(L) > 1$ we will say that L is ***multiply connected***. A part of a matrix graph—e.g. a row, column, path, etc.—is ***connected*** iff it contains a connected literal, it is ***totally connected*** iff all its literals are connected, and it is ***isolated*** iff none of its literals is connected.

2.2 The Connection Method for Multiplicative Relevant Logic

A convenient way to introduce Relevant Logic is via dropping the ***Weakening Rule*** from ***sequent systems*** [Gen35] for classical logic. As well known, this destroys the equivalence of formally different ways to introduce connectives, and we get the ***multiplicative*** and the ***additive fragment*** depending on the form of the chosen sequent rules. The multiplicative fragment of Relevant Logic— which we consider in the following—is based on the choice of those rules where the contexts may be different and are concatenated. The connectives are usually denoted by $\multimap$, $\otimes$, $\sharp$ and $\neg$ referring to implication, conjunction, disjunction and negation respectively, but we will keep the ordinary notation $\rightarrow$, $\wedge$, $\vee$ and $\neg$ as we don't consider additive connectives as well from which we have to distinguish the multiplicative ones. Moreover, we don't include (propositional) constants.

Due to the lack of distributive and idempotence laws in the multiplicative fragment (without weakening), for the general characterization of theorems of Multiplicative Relevant Logic by means of the Connection Method we have to use—in contrast to classical logic— non-normal form matrices, multi-occurrences of literals and—as already mentioned in the previous subsection—we have to consider suitably selected subsets of the set of all connections. The use of non-normal form can be avoided by reaxiomatizing our hypothesis finding problems into a classically equivalent disjunction of conjunctions.

In our context we don't care about the general case and just need the following weaker theorem:

Theorem 1 *Given a normal form matrix*

$$\mathcal{M} = \{\{L_{11}, \ldots, L_{n1}\}, \ldots, \{L_{1m}, \ldots, L_{nm}\}\}$$

which can be obtained as translation of the formula $F = (L_{11} \wedge \ldots \wedge L_{n1}) \vee \ldots \vee (L_{1m} \wedge \ldots \wedge L_{nm})$. *Then* F *is a theorem of* Multiplicative Relevant Logic *if there is a totally connected and minimal complementary matrix graph* $(\mathcal{M}^*, \mathfrak{S})$, *where* $\mathcal{M}^*$ *has been obtained from* $\mathcal{M}$ *through horizontal copying of columns.*

A matrix graph $(\mathcal{M}, \mathfrak{S})$ is **linear/totally connected** iff each literal in $\mathcal{M}$ is involved in at most/least one connection of $\mathfrak{S}$, and $(\mathcal{M}, \mathfrak{S})$ is **uniquely connected** iff it is linear and totally connected. **Horizontal copying** means to replace a column $\mathcal{N}$ by a series of copies of $\mathcal{N}$. (For details see [Fro96, Def. 109].)

Example 2. If we take the matrix from our previous examples and make two copies of the second column and three copies of the forth, then we get:

$$
\begin{array}{c}
S^1 \quad S^2 \\
C \\
P^1 \quad P^2 \quad \overline{C} \quad K^1 \quad K^2 \quad K^3 \\
\overline{P} \\
\overline{K}^1 \quad \overline{K}^2
\end{array}
$$

∎

3 Relevant Hypotheses

In this section we define residue hypotheses in the context of the Connection Method and then introduce minimized residue hypotheses [1]. We show their existence and justify why we call them relevant hypotheses.

In order to solve a given Hypothesis Finding Problem we have to extend the matrix graph obtained from the background theory and the example in order to get all still non complementary paths complementary. An easy way to do this is by adding the negated non complementary paths as additional columns. This leads to the following definition.

Definition 2. *Given arbitrary well-formed formulae* $\mathfrak{B}$ *(background theory) and* $\mathfrak{E}$ *(Example) of (classical) propositional logic. In addition, we assume* $\mathfrak{B} \not\models \mathfrak{E}$.

We obtain from $\mathfrak{B}$ *and* $\mathfrak{E}$ *the respective* normal form matrices $B := \mathfrak{m}(\neg\mathfrak{B})$ *and* $\mathcal{E} := \mathfrak{m}(\mathfrak{E})$, *and we denote by* $\widehat{\mathcal{M}}$ *the matrix* $B \sqcup \mathcal{E}$, *i.e.* $\widehat{\mathcal{M}} = \mathfrak{m}(\mathfrak{B} \to \mathfrak{E})$.

With $\mathfrak{p}_i = \{L_{i1}, \dots, L_{in}\}$ $(i = 1, \dots, m)$, *where* n *is the number of columns of the matrix* $\widehat{\mathcal{M}}$, *the set* $\mathfrak{P}^-_{\widehat{\mathcal{M}}}$ *of absolutely non-complementary paths in* $\widehat{\mathcal{M}}$, *we define the* **residue hypothesis** $\mathfrak{H}^w$ *as the formula*

$$(L_{11} \vee \dots \vee L_{1n}) \wedge \dots \wedge (L_{m1} \vee \dots \vee L_{mn})$$

We define the matrix $\mathcal{H}^w := \{\overline{\mathfrak{p}_i} \mid \mathfrak{p}_i \in \mathfrak{P}^-_{\widehat{\mathcal{M}}}\} = \{\{\overline{L_{11}}, \dots, \overline{L_{1n}}\}, \dots, \{\overline{L_{m1}}, \dots, \overline{L_{mn}}\}\}$ *i.e.* $\mathcal{H}^w$ *is a matrix translation of* $\neg\mathfrak{H}^w$ *where we preserve different occurrences of literals, and define the matrix* $\mathcal{M}^w := \widehat{\mathcal{M}} \cup \mathcal{H}^w$. *In addition we get a mapping* $\Gamma : \overline{L_{ij}} \to L_{ij}$ *of the literals in* $\mathcal{H}^w$ *to the literals in the* $\mathfrak{p}_i$ *in* $\mathfrak{P}^-_{\widehat{\mathcal{M}}}$. *For a minimal subspanning* $\mathfrak{S} \subset \mathfrak{S}_{\widehat{\mathcal{M}}}$ *we define* $\mathfrak{S}^w := \mathfrak{S} \cup \mathfrak{T}^w_{\widehat{\mathcal{M}}}$ *with* $\mathfrak{T}^w_{\widehat{\mathcal{M}}} := \{(L, \Gamma(L)) \mid L \in \mathcal{H}^w\}$.

---

[1] In our earlier paper [YF00], residue hypotheses were defined in terms of the Resolution Principle.

Example 3. We will discuss Definition 2 for the background theory $\mathfrak{B}_{cat} :=$ $(C \to P) \wedge (S \wedge P \to K)$ and the example $\mathfrak{E}_{cat} := C \to K$.

Let us look at the matrix $\widehat{\mathcal{M}}_{cat} := \{\{C, \overline{P}\}, \{S, P, \overline{K}\}, \overline{C}, K\}$ —which we obtain as $\mathfrak{m}(\mathfrak{B}_{cat} \to \mathfrak{E}_{cat})$—and the set $\mathfrak{S}_{\widehat{\mathcal{M}}_{cat}}$ of all its possible connections. This matrix graph has been considered already in Example 1. It has exactly one absolutely non-complementary path which corresponds to the residue hypothesis $\neg P \vee S \vee \neg C \vee K$ according to Definition 2.   ∎

The following theorems make essential statements about $\mathfrak{H}^w$: Theorem 3 motivates why the residue hypothesis substantializes the logical smallness of hypotheses, and Theorem 4—based on Theorem 2—motivates why we call it a relevant hypothesis.

Theorem 2 *Given a normal form matrix $\mathcal{M}$ which is not absolutely complementary, we get for every minimal subspanning $\mathfrak{S} \subset \mathfrak{S}_{\mathcal{M}}$ that the matrix graph $(\mathcal{M}^w, \mathfrak{S}^w)$ is minimal complementary and totally connected.*

Proof: The matrix graph $(\mathcal{M}^w, \mathfrak{S}^w)$ is *complementary*, because every path $\mathfrak{p}$ in $\mathcal{M}^w$ is either the continuation of an already complementary path in $(\mathcal{M}, \mathfrak{S})$ or the continuation of a non-complementary path $\mathfrak{p}'$ in $(\mathcal{M}, \mathfrak{S})$. As each path $\mathfrak{p}$ must go through a literal L in $\overline{\mathfrak{p}'} \in \mathcal{H}^w$, we obtain with $\Gamma(L) \in \mathfrak{p}'$, that $\mathfrak{p}$ contains the connection $(L, \Gamma(L)) \in \mathfrak{S}^w$.

For showing *total connectedness* of $(\mathcal{M}^w, \mathfrak{S}^w)$ we assume that there is a literal $L \not\in \mathcal{M}^w$ which is isolated in $(\mathcal{M}^w, \mathfrak{S}^w)$. L cannot be in $\mathcal{H}^w$, because $(L, \Gamma(L)) \in \mathfrak{S}^w$ for all literals $L \not\in \mathcal{H}^w$. Therefore, $L \not\in \mathcal{M}$. Since $(\mathcal{M}, \mathfrak{S})$ is not complementary, there exists a non-complementary path $\mathfrak{p}$. We define $\mathfrak{p}' := (\mathfrak{p} \setminus (\mathfrak{p} \cap \mathcal{C})) \cup \{L\}$ where $L \in \mathcal{C} \in \mathcal{M}$. $\mathfrak{p}'$ is neither complementary in $(\mathcal{M}, \mathfrak{S})$, because L is isolated. Consequently, there must exist a column $\overline{\mathfrak{p}'} \in \mathcal{H}^w$ and a connection in $\mathfrak{S}^w$ between L and a literal in $\overline{\mathfrak{p}'}$ in contradiction to the assumption that L is isolated in $(\mathcal{M}^w, \mathfrak{S}^w)$.

For *minimality* we have to show that for each connection $(K, L) \in \mathfrak{S}^w$ exists a path in $\mathcal{M}^w$ which contains no further connection from $\mathfrak{S}^w$.

If $(K, L) \in \mathfrak{S}$ then exists a path $\mathfrak{p}$ in $\mathcal{M}$ which contains no further connection from $\mathfrak{S}$, because $\mathfrak{S}$ is minimal subspanning. Since $\mathfrak{p}$ must be different from each non complementary path $\mathfrak{p}_i$ in $(\mathcal{M}, \mathfrak{S})$ by at least one literal $L_i \in \mathfrak{p}_i$ and $L_i \not\in \mathfrak{p}$, the continuation of $\mathfrak{p}$ through the corresponding literals in the columns of $\mathcal{H}^w$ which correspond to the $\mathfrak{p}_i$ contains no further connection.

Similarly, for each connection $(L, \Gamma(L)) \in \mathfrak{S}^w \setminus \mathfrak{S}$ exists a non complementary path $\mathfrak{p}$ in $(\mathcal{M}, \mathfrak{S})$ with $\Gamma(L) \in \mathfrak{p}$ such that its extension by the literal $L \not\in \mathcal{H}^w$ contains only the connection $(L, \Gamma(L))$. Since all non complementary paths in $(\mathcal{M}, \mathfrak{S})$ must differ by at least one literal, and consequently the continuation through the corresponding literal in the corresponding column in $\mathcal{H}^w$ doesn't contain a further connection from $\mathfrak{S}^w$.   ∎

Theorem 3 (Logical Smallness) *Under the assumptions of Definition 2, the formula $\mathfrak{H}^w$ is the least general hypothesis in the sense that it is implied by all other hypotheses $\mathfrak{H}$ for which exists a complementary matrix graph of $\mathfrak{B} \wedge \mathfrak{H} \to \mathfrak{E}$. I.e. $\mathfrak{H} \to \mathfrak{H}^w$ is valid.*

Proof: We prove first that $\mathfrak{H}^w$ is an admissible hypothesis w.r.t. $\mathfrak{B}$ and $\mathfrak{E}$, i.e. that $\mathfrak{B} \wedge \mathfrak{H}^w \to \mathfrak{E}$ holds. From the formula $\mathfrak{B} \wedge \mathfrak{H}^w \to \mathfrak{E}$ we get the matrix $\mathcal{M}^w = \mathfrak{m}_o^2(\mathfrak{B} \wedge \mathfrak{H}^w \to \mathfrak{E})$ which contains the columns $\{\overline{L}_{i1}, \ldots, \overline{L}_{ik_i}\}$ for $i = 1, \ldots, m$. Ths implies that for $i = 1, \ldots, m$ the continuations of the (non-complementary) paths $\{L_{i1}, \ldots, L_{ik_i}\}$ through the respective columns $\{\overline{L}_{i1}, \ldots, \overline{L}_{ik_i}\}$ is complementary w.r.t. $\mathfrak{S}_{\mathcal{M}^w}$, and consequently, the matrix graph $(\mathcal{M}^w, \mathfrak{S}_{\mathcal{M}^w})$ is complementary.

We show next that $\mathfrak{H}^w$ is a least general hypothesis:

If $\mathfrak{B} \wedge \mathfrak{H} \to \mathfrak{E}$ is valid, there must exist a complementary matrix graph $(\mathcal{M}_*, \mathfrak{S}_*)$ with $\mathcal{M}_* = \mathfrak{m}_o^2(\neg\mathfrak{B} \vee \neg\mathfrak{H} \vee \mathfrak{E})$. We define $\widehat{\mathcal{M}} := \mathfrak{m}_o^2(\neg\mathfrak{B} \vee \mathfrak{E})$ and $\mathcal{H}_* := \mathfrak{m}_o^2(\neg\mathfrak{H})$, both understood as subsets of $\mathcal{M}_*$.

For every non-complementary path $\mathfrak{p}$ in $\widehat{\mathcal{M}}$ we get through vertical restriction in $(\mathcal{M}_*, \mathfrak{S}_*)$ the complementary matrix graph $(\mathfrak{p} \cup \mathcal{H}_*, \mathfrak{S}_{\mathfrak{p}})$ with $\mathfrak{S}_{\mathfrak{p}} := \mathfrak{S}_*|_{\mathfrak{p} \cup \mathcal{H}_*}$ (Iterative application of Lemma [Fro96, Lemma 24]).

With $\mathfrak{p}_1, \ldots, \mathfrak{p}_n$ the set of all non-complementary paths in $\widehat{\mathcal{M}}$ we get the complementary (non-normal form) matrix graph $(\mathcal{M}_{**}, \mathfrak{S}_{**})$ with $\mathcal{M}_{**} := \{\{\mathfrak{p}_1, \ldots, \mathfrak{p}_n\}\} \cup \mathcal{H}_*$ and $\mathfrak{S}_{**} := \bigcup_{i=1}^n \mathfrak{S}_{\mathfrak{p}_i}$. According to Definition 2 the matrix $\{\{\mathfrak{p}_1, \ldots, \mathfrak{p}_n\}\}$ is a representation of $\mathfrak{H}^w$. With $\mathcal{H}_*$ a matrix representation of $\mathfrak{H}$, the matrix $\{\{\mathfrak{p}_1, \ldots, \mathfrak{p}_n\}\} \cup \mathcal{H}_*$ can be understood as a representation of $\neg\mathfrak{H} \vee \mathfrak{H}^w$. Together with the complementarity of $(\mathcal{M}_{**}, \mathfrak{S}_{**})$ we get that $\mathfrak{H} \to \mathfrak{H}^w$ holds. ∎

Theorem 4 (Relevant Logic Link) *Under the assumptions of Definition 2, the matrix graph $(\mathcal{M}^w, \mathfrak{S}^w)$ implies that the formula $\mathfrak{B}^* \vee \neg\mathfrak{H}^w \vee \mathfrak{E}^*$, with $\mathfrak{B}^*$ and $\mathfrak{E}^*$ disjunctive normal form formulae equivalent to $\neg\mathfrak{B}$ resp. to $\mathfrak{E}$, is a theorem of Multiplicative Relevant Logic.*

Proof: We know from Theorem 2 that the matrix graph $(\mathcal{M}^w, \mathfrak{S}^w)$ is minimal complementary and totally connected. Therefore our claims follow with Theorem 1. ∎

Remark 1. Let us add to Theorem 4 that the passage from $\mathfrak{B}$ and $\mathfrak{E}$ to the classically equivalent $\mathfrak{B}^*$ and $\mathfrak{E}^*$ respectively—i.e. a reaxiomatisation of the hypothesis finding problem—is necessary, because for $\mathfrak{B}$ and $\mathfrak{E}$ a 'relevant hypothesis' might not exist. ∎

Examples show that in many cases the residue hypothesis can be further reduced. Often a large number of literals can be deleted from the Residue Hypothesis without loosing the total connectedness nor the minimal complementarity of the resulting matrix graph, and consequently the link to Relevant Logic is preserved as well. For this deletion process—called minimization—we need some 'preparation' of the matrix graph $(\mathcal{M}^w, \mathfrak{S}^w)$.

Given a matrix graph $(\mathcal{M}, \mathfrak{S})$ with $\mathcal{M}$ in normal form. A list

$$\mathcal{C} = \Big[[L_1, K_1], \ldots, [L_n, K_n]\Big]$$

of ordered pairs of (occurrences of) literals from $\mathcal{M}$ such that $\{(L_1, K_1), \ldots, (L_n, K_n)\} \subset \mathfrak{S}$ is called a **connection chain** iff for $i = 1, \ldots, n-1$ holds that K_i and L_{i+1} are in the same column of $\mathcal{M}$.

If K_n and L_1 are in a common column as well, then the connection chain is called **closed**. A closed connection chain is called a **cycle** iff all its literals are different (as occurrences in the matrix) and the vertical pairs K_i and L_{i+1} (and also K_n and L_1) are all in different columns.

If a matrix graph contains no cycle, then it is called **acyclic**.

Lemma 1. *If $(\mathcal{M}, \mathfrak{S})$ is a normal-form matrix graph which is minimal complementary and totally connected, then there exists a matrix graph $(\mathcal{M}', \mathfrak{S}')$, where $\mathcal{M}'$ is obtained from $\mathcal{M}$ by horizontal copying of columns, which in addition to being minimal complementary and totally connected, is also acyclic.*

Proof: We create $(\mathcal{M}', \mathfrak{S}')$ from $(\mathcal{M}, \mathfrak{S})$ as follows:

Decomposition: We choose a cycle in $(\mathcal{M}, \mathfrak{S})$ and a column $\mathcal{C} \in \mathcal{M}$, $\mathcal{C} = \{L_1, \ldots, L_n\}$, which contains a vertical pair of literals of the chosen cycle. We build the vertical restrictions $\{L_i\} \cup (\mathcal{M} \setminus \{\mathcal{C}\})$ $(i = 1, \ldots, n)$ of $(\mathcal{M}, \mathfrak{S})$. For each of these matrices we chose a minimal spanning set of connections $\mathfrak{S}_i$ from $\mathfrak{S}|_{\{L_i\} \cup (\mathcal{M} \setminus \{\mathcal{C}\})}$ and define $\mathcal{N}_i$ as the set of columns from $\mathcal{M} \setminus \{\mathcal{C}\}$ which are connected by $\mathfrak{S}_i$. Then all the matrix graphs $(\mathcal{N}_i, \mathfrak{S}_i)$ are minimal complementary and totally connected.

Composition: If none of the matrix graphs $(\{L_i\} \cup \mathcal{N}_i, \mathfrak{S}_i)$ contains a cycle, we define $(\mathcal{M}', \mathfrak{S}') := (\{\mathcal{C}\} \cup \bigcup_{i=1}^{n} \mathcal{N}_i, \bigcup_{i=1}^{n} \mathfrak{S}_i)$ (with respective copies of the literal occurrences).

If some of the matrix graphs $(\mathcal{N}_i, \mathfrak{S}_i)$ contain cycles, we continue applying decomposition steps to them. Since the number of cycles per single matrix graph decreases with each step, the decomposition process will eventually end.

When composing the obtained matrix graphs into bigger ones, the problem may occur that instead of a matrix $\{L_i\} \cup \mathcal{N}_i$ we have $\{L_i^1, \ldots, L_i^k\} \cup \mathcal{N}_i$. In this case we may replace the different $L_i^1, \ldots, L_i^k$ by a single occurrence L_i^0 which takes all the connections. This is possible, because no cycle can be created this way (no increase of vertical relationships).   ∎

Definition 3. *With the assumptions and notations of Definition 2, we get with Lemma 1 from $(\mathcal{M}^w, \mathfrak{S}^w)$ a matrix graph $(\mathcal{M}^W, \mathfrak{S}^W)$ which is minimal complementary, totally connected and acyclic.*

*We call a **minimization step** the deletion of a literal L in the $\mathfrak{H}$-part $\mathcal{H}^W$ of $\mathcal{M}^W$, whose connection partner—i.e. the unique literal $K \in \mathcal{M}^W$ with $(L, K) \in \mathfrak{S}^W$—is multiply connected in $\mathfrak{S}^W$.*

*Iterative application of minimization steps until no further literal in $\mathcal{H}^W$ can be deleted leads finally to the so-called **minimized residue matrix graph** $(\mathcal{M}^{\underline{W}}, \mathfrak{S}^{\underline{W}})$ with $\mathfrak{H}$-part $\mathcal{H}^{\underline{W}}$.*

*We call the formula $\mathfrak{H}^{\underline{W}}$, constructed from $\mathcal{H}^{\underline{W}}$ in the same way as we constructed $\mathfrak{H}^w$ from $\mathcal{H}^w$ in Definition 2, the **minimized residue hypothesis**.*

Example 4. Let us apply Definition 3 to the residue matrix graph $(\mathcal{M}_{cat}^w, \mathfrak{S}_{cat}^w)$ from Example 1. It is already acyclic, therefore $(\mathcal{M}_{cat}^W, \mathfrak{S}_{cat}^W) := (\mathcal{M}_{cat}^w, \mathfrak{S}_{cat}^w)$.

We may now delete iteratively all literals of its $\mathfrak{H}$-part excluding $\overline{S}$. (Deletion is indicated in the matrix graph below by putting the respective literals in boxes.) We obtain the Minimized Residue Hypothesis $\mathfrak{H}_{cat}^{\underline{W}} := S$.

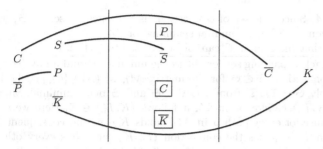

In order to preserve total connectedness, it is obvious that we have to require in Definition 3 that the literal K is multiply connected. That this single requirement is sufficient shows the next theorem, which also maintains the motivation for $\mathfrak{H}^{\underline{W}}$ being called a relevant hypothesis.

Lemma 2. *Given a minimal complementary acyclic normal form matrix graph* $(\mathcal{M}, \mathfrak{S})$ *and a connection* $(K, L_0) \in \mathfrak{S}$ *such that* $\#_{\mathfrak{S}}(K) = 1$ *and* $\#_{\mathfrak{S}}(L_0) > 1$.
Then with $\mathcal{M}'$ *the matrix obtained from* $\mathcal{M}$ *by deleting* K *and with* $\mathfrak{S}' := \mathfrak{S} \setminus \{(K, L_0)\}$, *the matrix graph* $(\mathcal{M}', \mathfrak{S})$ *is minimal complementary.*
(Quite trivially, it is again acyclic and in normal form.)

Proof: Let us first introduce some more notation:
There are columns $\mathcal{C}, \mathcal{C}_K \in \mathcal{M}$ with $K \in \mathcal{C}_K$ and $L_0 \in \mathcal{C}$. We assume $\mathcal{C}$ to be of the form $\{L_0, L_1, \dots, L_n\}$ $(n \geq 0)$ and we define $\mathcal{C}'_K := \mathcal{C}_K \setminus \{K\}$. In addition, we define $\mathcal{N} := \mathcal{M} \setminus \{\mathcal{C}\}, \mathcal{N}' := \mathcal{M}' \setminus \{\mathcal{C}\}$, and for $i = 0, \dots, n$ $\mathcal{N}_i := \{L_i\} \cup \mathcal{N}, \mathcal{N}'_i := \{L_i\} \cup \mathcal{N}'$.

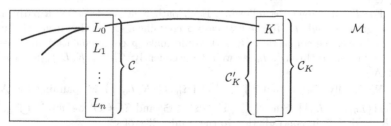

That $(\mathcal{M}', \mathfrak{S}')$ is complementary follows from vertical restriction ([Fro96, Lemma 24]). In order to show minimality we assume that $\mathfrak{S}'$ is not minimal spanning for $\mathcal{M}'$. Then exists a subset $\mathfrak{T}' \subset \mathfrak{S}'$, $\mathfrak{T}' \neq \mathfrak{S}'$, which is minimal spanning for $\mathcal{M}'$. Obviously, for all $i = 0, \dots, n$ the matrix graphs $(\mathcal{N}'_i, \mathfrak{T}'|_{\mathcal{N}'_i})$ are complementary (due to vertical restriction) and we may choose for each $i = 0, \dots, n$ a subset $\mathfrak{T}'_i \subset \mathfrak{T}'|_{\mathcal{N}'_i}$ which is minimal spanning for $\mathcal{N}'_i$.

Our intention is to show that

$$\bigcup_{i=0}^{n} \mathfrak{T}'_i \cup \{(K, L_0)\}$$

is spanning for $\mathcal{M}$. Since this set of connections is a proper subset of $\mathfrak{S}$, we have a contradiction to $\mathfrak{S}$ being minimal spanning for $\mathcal{M}$.

We show first that the column $\mathcal{C}$ cannot be isolated in $(\mathcal{M}', \mathfrak{T}')$:

Obviously, we get a spanning set for $\mathcal{M}$ as the union of $\mathfrak{T}'$ and an arbitrary spanning set of connections $\mathfrak{T} \subset \mathfrak{S}$ for the matrix $\mathcal{M}_K := (\mathcal{M} \setminus \{\mathcal{C}_K\}) \cup \{K\}$. We get immediately $\mathfrak{S} = \mathfrak{T} \cup \mathfrak{T}'$ from $\mathfrak{T} \cup \mathfrak{T}' \subset \mathfrak{S}$ and $\mathfrak{S}$ being minimal. Since the connection (K, L_0) cannot be in $\mathfrak{T}'$, it follows $(K, L_0) \in \mathfrak{T}$. Here we get $\#_{\mathfrak{T}}(L_0) = 1$, because for every path $\mathfrak{p}$ in $\mathcal{M}_K$ holds $K \in \mathfrak{p}$, and consequently, every path $\mathfrak{p}$ with $L_0 \in \mathfrak{p}$ has the connection (L_0, K), and thus every other connection with L_0 would be superfluous. Now $\#_{\mathfrak{S}}(L_0) > 1$ implies $\#_{\mathfrak{T}'}(L_0) > 0$.

We show that for $i = 0, \ldots, n$ the literals L_i cannot be isolated in $(\mathcal{N}'_i, \mathfrak{T}'_i)$:

If there exists a $j \in \{0, \ldots, n\}$ with L_j isolated in $(\mathcal{N}'_j, \mathfrak{T}'_j)$, the set of connections $\mathfrak{T}'_j$ would be spanning for $\mathcal{N}'$. Consequently, $\mathfrak{T}'_j$ would be spanning for $\mathcal{M}'$, and $\mathcal{C}$ would be isolated in $(\mathcal{M}', \mathfrak{T}'_j)$. Since $\mathfrak{T}'$ is minimal spanning for $\mathcal{M}'$, we would get $\mathfrak{T}'_j = \mathfrak{T}'$ and $\mathcal{C}$ would be isolated in $(\mathcal{M}', \mathfrak{T}')$ in contradiction to what we showed before.

For all $i > 0$ the column $\mathcal{C}'_K \in \mathcal{N}'_i$ is isolated w.r.t. $\mathfrak{T}'_i$:

If for some $j \in \{1, \ldots, n\}$ the column $\mathcal{C}'_K$ were not isolated in $(\mathcal{N}'_j, \mathfrak{T}'_j)$, then would exist a regular connection chain $\mathbb{C}$ from L_j to a literal in $\mathcal{C}'_K$ ([Fro96, Lemma 32]). However this would imply the cycle $\mathbb{C} + \left[[K, L_0] \right]$ in $\mathfrak{S}$ in contradiction to being assumed acyclic.

We come to the conclusion:

Since for all $i = 1, \ldots, n$ the column $\mathcal{C}'_K$ is isolated in $(\mathcal{N}'_i, \mathfrak{T}'_i)$, $\mathfrak{T}'_i$ is also spanning for the matrix $\mathcal{N}_i$. (The isolated column $\mathcal{C}'_K$ is replaced by $\mathcal{C}_K = \mathcal{C}'_K \cup \{K\}$.)

For $i = 0$ we get the following: Each path $\mathfrak{p}$ in $\mathcal{N}_0$ is *either* a path in $\mathcal{N}'_0$ *or* it goes through K. In the first case $\mathfrak{p}$ contains a connection from $\mathfrak{T}'_0$. In the second case, the connection (K, L_0) would make $\mathfrak{p}$ complementary, because all paths in $\mathcal{N}_0$ go through L_0 as well. Consequently, $\mathfrak{T}'_0 \cup \{(K, L_0)\}$ is spanning for $\mathcal{N}_0$.

We finally obtain that $\bigcup_{i=1}^{n} \mathfrak{T}'_i \cup \left(\mathfrak{T}'_0 \cup \{(K, L_0)\} \right)$ is spanning for $\mathcal{M} = \mathcal{N} \cup \{\{L_0, \ldots, L_n\}\}$. Since $\bigcup_{i=0}^{n} \mathfrak{T}'_i \subset \mathfrak{T}' \subset \mathfrak{S}'$ and $\mathfrak{T}' \neq \mathfrak{S}'$ we obtain $\bigcup_{i=0}^{n} \mathfrak{T}'_i \cup \{(K, L_0)\} \neq \mathfrak{S}$ in contradiction to the minimality of $\mathfrak{S}$.   ∎

Theorem 5 *Under the assumptions of Definition 2 a (normal-form) matrix graph $(\mathcal{M}^{\underline{W}}, \mathfrak{S}^{\underline{W}})$ constructed iteratively according to Definition 3 is minimal complementary and totally connected.*

The formula $\mathfrak{B}^* \vee \neg \mathfrak{H}^{\underline{W}} \vee \mathfrak{E}^*$, with $\mathfrak{B}^*$ and $\mathfrak{E}^*$ disjunctive normal form formulae equivalent to $\neg\mathfrak{B}$ resp. to $\mathfrak{E}$, is a theorem of Multiplicative Relevant Logic.

Proof: The mentioned matrix properties are preserved because we get the following for each minimization step: *Complementarity* is preserved according to the properties of vertical restriction ([Fro96, Lemma 24]). *Total connectedness* is preserved due to the requirement that L_0 must be multiply connected. *Minimality* follows with iterative application of Lemma 2.

The proof of the statement on Relevant Logic goes analogously as in Theorem 4.   ■

For lifting our relevant hypothesis concepts to first-order logic we will present first the respective extension of the Connection Method. This goes as usual via Herbrand's Theorem (see [Bib87,YF00]). We transform a first-order formula into Skolem normal form[2] which is then transformed into clausal form, thus obtaining a matrix. We next instantiate a suitable set of copies of columns (with renaming of variables) with ground terms, which yields a so-called **compound (ground) instance**. Since such a compound instance is a ground matrix, all concepts defined for propositional matrices carry over in a straightforward manner.

The Main Theorem of the Connection Method for classical first-order logic says that a formula F is a theorem iff for a compound instance of the matrix $\mathrm{m}(F)$ *the set of all connections is spanning.*

On this basis our hypothesis finding approach can be lifted to the first-order level as follows.

Definition 4. *For a first-order* $\mathsf{HFP}(\mathfrak{B}, \mathfrak{E})$ *we proceed as follows:*

- *We create a compound ground instance* $\widehat{\mathcal{M}}$ *of the matrix* $\mathrm{m}(\mathfrak{B} \to \mathfrak{E})$.
- *We generate a minimized residue hypothesis* $\mathcal{H}^{\underline{w}}$ *from* $\widehat{\mathcal{M}}$.
- *We generalize* $\mathcal{H}^{\underline{w}}$ *through anti-instantiation, i.e. we facultatively replace consistently in each column certain terms by variables.*

Example 5. We consider the $\mathsf{HFP}(\mathfrak{B}_{nat}, \mathfrak{E}_{nat})$ with $\mathfrak{B}_{nat} := \mathsf{even}(0) \wedge (\mathsf{odd}(x) \to \mathsf{even}(s(x)))$ and $\mathfrak{E}_{nat} := \mathsf{odd}(s(s(s(0))))$ in the domain of natural numbers which we represent as successors of 0.

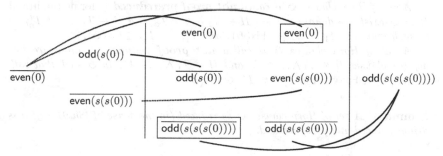

We can get the hypothesis $\mathfrak{H}_{nat} = \mathsf{even}(y) \to \mathsf{odd}(s(y))$ which is desired from our knowledge by means of:

---

[2] Due to not negating the formula we have to Skolemise the universally quantified variables.

- Suitable instantiation of the non-unit column of the matrix $\widehat{\mathcal{M}}$ with $x \leftarrow s(0)$ ($\mathfrak{S}_{\widehat{\mathcal{M}}}$ is minimal subspanning).
- Suitable minimization according to Definition 3 — the residue matrix graph is acyclic.
- Suitable anti-instantiation $0 \to y$ and $s(s(0)) \to y$ respectively of the two hypothesis columns.

∎

4   Bottoms and Relevant Hypotheses

In this section we will show a relationship between the previously introduced Relevant hypotheses and the **Bottom Method** (or **Bottom Generalization Method**) [Yam99a, Yam99b] invented by one of the authors.

Definition 5. *The **bottom** for a pair consisting of a background theory $\mathfrak{B}$ and an example $\mathfrak{E}$ is the disjunction of all literals whose negation is a logical consequence of $\mathfrak{B} \wedge \neg \mathfrak{E}$.*

Example 6. Let us consider the pair $\mathfrak{B}_{cat}$ and $\mathfrak{E}_{cat}$ in Example 3. All literals which are logical consequences of $\mathfrak{B} \wedge \neg \mathfrak{E}$ are: $P, \overline{S}, C, \overline{K}$. Therefore the bottom is $\neg P \vee S \vee \neg C \vee K$.   ∎

Sometimes we have a coincidence, as in Example 3, where the bottom is the residue hypothesis. In general, this is not true. However, we get good correspondence results if we consider the special sets of formulae suggested by Shinohara's concept of reduced Horn sets [Shi91]. This concept covers several different issues and, consequently, it can be broken down as follows:

Definition 6. *A set of Horn clauses $\mathfrak{G}$ is called **not axiom reduced** iff there is a definite clause $H \leftarrow T_1 \wedge \ldots \wedge T_n$ in $\mathfrak{G}$ such that $T_1, \ldots, T_n \not\subseteq \mathsf{Fix}(\mathfrak{G})$.*

*A set of Horn clauses $\mathfrak{G}$ is called **not proof prereduced** iff for no tail literal H in $\mathfrak{G}$ exist two definite clauses $H \leftarrow T_1 \wedge \ldots \wedge T_n$ and $H \leftarrow T'_1 \wedge \ldots \wedge T'_{n'}$ in $\mathfrak{G}$ such that both $T_1, \ldots, T_n \subset \mathsf{Fix}(\mathfrak{G})$. and $T'_1, \ldots, T'_{n'} \subset \mathsf{Fix}(\mathfrak{G})$.*

*A set of Horn clauses $\mathfrak{G}$ is called **not proof reduced** iff there are two definite clauses $H \leftarrow T_1 \wedge \ldots \wedge T_n$ and $H \leftarrow T'_1 \wedge \ldots \wedge T'_{n'}$ in $\mathfrak{G}$ such that both $T_1, \ldots, T_n \subset \mathsf{Fix}(\mathfrak{G})$ and $T'_1, \ldots, T'_{n'} \subset \mathsf{Fix}(\mathfrak{G})$.*

Lemma 3. *A set of Horn clauses $\mathfrak{G}$ is reduced (in the sense of [Shi91]) iff it is axiom reduced and proof reduced.*

Remark 2. We will present in the following some lemmata about Horn formulae and need to make some remarks about their matrix representation. A theorem to be proved usually consists of a conjunction of axioms which imply a further formula. Quite frequently, theorem proving problems specified by Horn formulae are (already) given as a set of Horn clauses, which can be understood as a conjunction of disjunctions. (The disjunction is sometimes written as implication) This means that the theorem to be proved has already been preprocessed for the application of a refutation procedure, i.e. it has been negated. As with the connections method we use to work with the unnegated problem specification we will not follow this 'negation practice', and will understand a set of Horn clauses as the problem $\bigwedge \mathfrak{G}_D \to \bigvee \mathfrak{G}_G$ where $\mathfrak{G}_D \subset \mathfrak{G}$ is the subset of definite Horn clauses and $\mathfrak{G}_G \subset \mathfrak{G}$ the set of negative clauses. Consequently, we will consider the translation of $\neg \bigwedge \mathfrak{G}_D$ into normal form matrices as the 'natural' matrix representations of $\mathfrak{G}_D$.

Recall that the only difference between this matrix and the usual set of clauses (in set notation) is that all positive literals are negated and vice versa. ∎

With the introduced terminology we get the following correspondence results between the Bottom Method and the relevant hypotheses.

Theorem 6 *Given a Hypothesis Finding Problem whose Background Theory $\mathfrak{B}$ consists of a set of definite Horn clauses and whose Example $\mathfrak{E}$ consists of a disjunction of literals, such that $\mathfrak{B} \not\models \mathfrak{E}$. (In the following, we understand $\neg \mathfrak{E}$ as a set of unit clauses.)*

1. *If the Horn set $\mathfrak{B} \cup \neg \mathfrak{E}$ is axiom reduced, then the Residue Hypothesis $\mathfrak{H}^w$ is a disjunction of literals from the bottom of the pair $\mathfrak{B}$ and $\mathfrak{E}$, where each of these literal occurs at least once.*
2. *If the Horn set $\mathfrak{B} \cup \neg \mathfrak{E}$ is reduced, then the residue hypothesis $\mathfrak{H}^w$ is a disjunction of literals from the bottom of the pair $\mathfrak{B}$ and $\mathfrak{E}$, where each of these literal occurs exactly once.*
3. *If the Horn set $\mathfrak{B} \cup \neg \mathfrak{E}$ is axiom reduced and proof prereduced, and if the matrix obtained from $\mathfrak{B} \cup \neg \mathfrak{E}$ contains at least one absolute connection, then the minimized residue hypothesis $\mathfrak{H}^{\underline{W}}$ is definitely smaller than $\mathfrak{H}^w$.*
4. *If the Horn set $\mathfrak{B} \cup \neg \mathfrak{E}$ is reduced, and if the matrix obtained from $\mathfrak{B} \cup \neg \mathfrak{E}$ contains at least one absolute connection, then the minimized residue hypothesis $\mathfrak{H}^{\underline{W}}$ is definitely smaller than the union of bottom and (unit) goal clauses.*

Let us illustrate Theorem 6 by an example:

Example 7. Let us again consider our running example. Note that the Background Theory $\mathfrak{B}_{cat}$ consists of definite Horn clauses and is reduced. Due to $C \to K \equiv \neg C \vee K$ the Example $\mathfrak{E}_{cat}$ can be understood as a disjunction of literals.

The residue hypothesis (see Example 3) and the Bottom (see Example 6) are both $\neg P \vee S \vee \neg C \vee K$. The minimized residue hypothesis S (see Example 4) is definitely smaller. ∎

5 Conclusion

With the minimized residue hypothesis we have created a hypothesis concept which – as suggested by Theorem 6 – might be an interesting alternative to hypothesis generation with the Bottom Method, as it outperforms the latter hypotheses in view of the syntactical smallness of hypotheses postulated in the introduction.

In addition, in contrast to many others our approach is not based on concepts of subsumption (subsumption is only used for analysis of the produced hypotheses). Instead of comparing different possible hypothesis clauses of which the desired one is computed via subsumption we argue on the level of certain properties of proofs. Thus the focus switches from the generated clauses to the concentration on various types of 'irredundant exhaustive reasoning' captured by minimality and total connectedness of matrix graphs.

Let us finally point out that in contrast to existing approaches we are not restricted to clauses — neither concerning the background theory nor the example or the hypotheses to be generated — but we may work with problems stated by formulae of arbitrary shape.

Acknowledgements. This work was carried out while Bertram Fronhöfer spent some months as a visiting researcher at MemeMedia Laboratory, Hokkaido University during winter 1998, 1999, and 2000. It is partly supported by the Grant-in-Aid for Scientific Research from Japan Society for the Promotion of Science.

References

[Bib87]   W. Bibel. *Automated Theorem Proving.* Vieweg, 1987. (second edition).

[Fro96]   B. Fronhöfer. *The Action-as-Implication Paradigm: Formal Systems and Application,* volume 1 of *Computer Science Monographs.* CSpress, München, Germany, 1996. (revised version of Habilitationsschrift, TU München 1994).

[FY98]   B. Fronhöfer and A. Yamamoto. Generating the Weakest Hypotheses. In *Proc. of the 12th Annual Conference of JSAI,* pages 314–317, 1998. (written in Japanese).

[Gen35]   G. Gentzen. Untersuchungen über das logische Schließen. *Math. Zeitschrift,* 39:176–210 and 405–431, 1935.

[LGJ99]   N. Lavrač, D. Gamberger, and V. Jovanoski. A Study of Relevance for Learning in Deductive Databases. *Journal of Logic Programming,* 40:215–249, 1999.

[Mid99]   H. Midelfart. A Bounded Search Space of Cluasal Theories. In *Proc. of the 9th International Workshop on Inductive Logic Programming (LNAI 1634),* pages 210–221, 1999.

[Plo71]   G. D. Plotkin. *Automatic Methods of Inductive Inference.* PhD thesis, Edinburgh University, 1971.

[Shi91]   T. Shinohara. Inductive Inference of Monotonic Formal Systems from Positive Data. *New Generation Computing,* 8:371–384, 1991.

[Yam99a]   A. Yamamoto. An Inference Method for the Complete Inverse of Relative Subsumption. *New Generation Computing,* 17(1):99–117, 1999.

[Yam99b]   A. Yamamoto. Revising the Logical Foundations of Inductive Logic Programming Systems with Ground Reduced Programs. *New Generation Computing,* 17(1):119–127, 1999.

[YF00]   A. Yamamoto and B. Fronhöfer. Hypothesis Finding via Residue Hypotheses with the Resolution Principle. In *Proc. of the 11th International Workshop on Algorithmic Learning Theory (LNAI 1968),* pages 156–165, 2000.

Compactness and Learning of Classes of Unions of Erasing Regular Pattern Languages

Jin Uemura and Masako Sato

Department of Mathematics and Information Sciences
Osaka Prefecture University Sakai, Osaka 599-8531, Japan
{jin, sato}@mi.cias.osakafu-u.ac.jp

Abstract. A *regular pattern* is a string of constant symbols and distinct variables. A semantics of a set P of regular patterns is a union $L(P)$ of *erasing* pattern languages generated by patterns in P. The paper deals with the class $\mathcal{RP}^k$ of sets of at most k regular patterns, and an efficient learning from positive examples of the language class defined by $\mathcal{RP}^k$. In efficient learning languages, the complexity for the MINL problem to find one of minimal languages containing a given sample is one of very important keys. Arimura et al.[5] introduced a notion of *compactness w.r.t. containment* for more general framework, called generalization systems, than $\mathcal{RP}^k$ of language description which guarantees the equivalence between the semantic containment $L(P) \subseteq L(Q)$ and the syntactic containment $P \sqsubseteq Q$, where $\sqsubseteq$ is a syntactic subsumption over the generalization systems.
Under the compactness, the MINL problem reduces to finding one of *minimal sets* in $\mathcal{RP}^k$ for a given sample under the subsumption $\sqsubseteq$. They gave an efficient algorithm to find such minimal sets under the assumption of compactness and some conditions.
We first show that for each $k \geq 1$, the class $\mathcal{RP}^k$ has compactness if and only if the number of constant symbols is greater than $k+1$. Moreover, we prove that for each $P \in \mathcal{RP}^k$, a finite subset $S_2(P)$ is a *characteristic set* of $L(P)$ within the class, where $S_2(P)$ consists of strings obtained from P by substituting strings with length two for each variable. Then our class $\mathcal{RP}^k$ is shown to be polynomial time inferable from positive examples using the efficient algorithm of the MINL problem due to Arimura et al.[5], provided the number of constant symbols is greater than $k + 1$.

1   Introduction

A *pattern* is a string (possibly the *empty* string) consisting of constant symbols in a fixed alphabet Σ and variables. For example, $p = axby$ and $q = axbx$ are patterns, where $a, b \in \Sigma$ and x, y are different variables. The language $L(p)$ generated by a pattern p is the set of all constant strings obtained from p by substituting constant strings (possibly the *empty* string) for each variable. A language L is an *erasing* (or *extended*) pattern language if $L = L(p)$ for some p. On the other hand, L is a *nonerasing* pattern language if it consists of strings obtained from some pattern p by substitutions but not allowing empty string.

N. Cesa-Bianchi et al. (Eds.): ALT 2002, LNAI 2533, pp. 293–307, 2002.
© Springer-Verlag Berlin Heidelberg 2002

The class of nonerasing pattern languages was introduced by Angluin[1] as a class inductively inferable from positive examples based on *identification in the limit* due to Gold[6]. She showed that the class has *finite thickness* to be a sufficient condition for inferability. On the other hand, the class of erasing pattern languages first introduced by Shinohara[14] does not have finite thickness and it is still open whether the class is inferable from positive examples. Shinohara[14] dealt with the subclass $\mathcal{RPL}$ of erasing *regular* pattern languages, and showed that the subclass is polynomial time inferable from positive examples. A pattern is *regular* if each variable appears at most once in the pattern. In the above example, p is regular but not q.

The present paper considers the class $\mathcal{RP}^k$ consisting of sets of at most k regular patterns. For a set $P \in \mathcal{RP}^k$, the language $L(P)$ is defined as the union of *erasing* regular pattern languages generated by patterns in P. We deal with an efficient learning of the language class $\mathcal{RPL}^k$ of such unions from positive examples. The class $\mathcal{RPL}$ has finite thickness as well as that of nonerasing regular pattern languages([14], [2]). A notion of *finite elasticity* due to Wright[16] is a more general sufficient condition, called *finite elasticity*, than finite thickness for inferability, and is preserved under various class operations such as union, concatenation and so on([10], [9], [12]). Hence the class $\mathcal{RPL}^k$ has also finite elasticity, and thus is inferable from positive examples. For a class with finite elasticity, if both of the membership problem and the MINL problem (to find one of minimal languages containing a given sample) for the class are polynomial time computable, then the class is known to be polynomial time inferable from positive examples([1], [5]). A pattern q is a *generalisation* of a pattern p, denoted by $p \preceq q$, if p is obtained by substituting some pattern (possibly the *empty* string) to each variable in q. Thus $p \preceq q$ implies $L(p) \subseteq L(q)$. Shinohara[14] showed that $L(p) \subseteq L(q)$ if and only if $p \preceq q$, and the membership problem for erasing regular pattern languages is polynomial time computable. Thus that problem for $\mathcal{RPL}^k$ is also polynomial time computable.

On the other hand, Arimura et al.[5] gave an efficient algorithm of the MINL problem for unions of *nonerasing* regular pattern languages from positive examples in more general framework which works well under conditions such as compactness mentioned below. For sets $P, Q \in \mathcal{RP}^k$, we define $P \sqsubseteq Q$ if for each p there is $q \in Q$ such that $p \preceq q$. Clearly the syntactic containment $P \sqsubseteq Q$ implies the semantic containment $L(P) \subseteq L(Q)$, but not always the converse. The class $\mathcal{RP}^k$ has *compactness w.r.t. containment* if the converse is always valid for any P, Q in the class.

In this paper, we first show that the class has compactness if and only if the cardinality of Σ is greater than $k + 1$. Moreover, a particular subset $S_2(P)$ of $L(P)$ is shown to be a characteristic set for $L(P)$ within $\mathcal{RPL}$, where $S_2(P)$ is a set of strings obtained from P by substituting constant strings with length *two* to variables in patterns in P. Then by these results, we show that the class $\mathcal{RPL}^k$ is polynomial time inferable from positive examples, provided the cardinality of Σ is greater than $k + 1$.

2   Erasing Regular Pattern Languages

Let N be the set of nonnegative integers. For a set S, by $\sharp S$ we denote the cardinality of S. Let Σ be a fixed alphabet of *constant* symbols. Let X be a countable set of *variables*, whose elements are denoted by $x, x_1, x_2, \cdots, y, y_1, y_2, \cdots$. Assume that $\Sigma \cap X = \phi$. A *pattern* is a finite string (possibly the empty string) over $\Sigma \cup X$. The symbol ε denotes the empty string. A string w is a constant string if $w \in \Sigma^*$. A sample is a finite set of constant strings. For a pattern p, the *length* of p, denoted by $|p|$, is the number of symbols in p. The set of patterns is denoted by $\mathcal{P}$. As mentioned above, $\varepsilon \in \mathcal{P}$.

A *substitution* θ is a homomorphism from $\mathcal{P}$ to $\mathcal{P}$ which maps every constant symbol to itself. A set of replacements $\{x_1 := p_1, \cdots, x_n := p_n\}$ is the substitution that maps each variable x_i to the pattern p_i and any other variables to themselves. For a pattern p and a substitution θ, the image of p by θ is denoted by $p\theta$. In particular, $c(p)$ denotes the image of p by the substitution of mapping each variable in p to ε. Clearly $c(p) \in \Sigma^*$.

For patterns p and q, q is a *generalization* of p or p is an *instance* of q, denoted by $p \preceq q$, if there is a substitution θ such that $p = q\theta$. Patterns p and q are *equivalent*, denoted by $p \equiv q$, if $p \preceq q$ and $q \preceq p$. Note that $p \equiv q$ does not always imply $p = q$. For instance, $x_1 \preceq x_1 x_2$ and $x_1 x_2 \preceq x_1$ imply $x_1 \equiv x_1 x_2$ but $x_1 \neq x_1 x_2$. For a pattern p, the language generated by p is defined by $L(p) = \{w \in \Sigma^* \mid w \preceq p\}$. Clearly $p \preceq q$ implies $L(p) \subseteq L(q)$, and so $p \equiv q$ implies $L(p) = L(q)$.

A language L over Σ is an *erasing pattern language* or *extended pattern language* if there is a pattern p such that $L(p) = L$. The term of *extended pattern* language was named by Shinohara[14] who first introduced it, and that of *erasing pattern* language is used in comparison to *nonerasing pattern* language allowing only nonempty substitutions defined by Angluin[1].

A pattern p is *regular* if each variable occurs at most once in p. Let $\mathcal{RP}$ and $\mathcal{RPL}$ be the classes of regular patterns and erasing regular pattern languages, respectively.

In what follows, we confine ourselves to regular patterns and erasing regular pattern languages, and say patterns and pattern languages, simply, respectively.

A pattern p is a *substring* (or *subpattern*) of a pattern q if $q = q_1 p q_2$ for some strings q_1 and q_2. Particularly, p is a *prefix* of q if $q = pq'$ for some q' and a *suffix* of q if $q = q''p$ for some q''. A string $w \in \Sigma^*$ is a *subsequence* of $u \in \Sigma^*$, denoted by $w \preceq' u$, if w is obtained by deleting some constant symbols from u. Clearly every substring of u becomes its subsequence but not always the converse.

The next result is essential in our results obtained here.

Theorem 1 (Shinohara[14]). *Let p and q be patterns.*
(i) $L(p) \subseteq L(q)$ if and only if $p \preceq q$, provided that $\sharp \Sigma \geq 3$.
(ii)   If $p \preceq q$, then $c(q) \preceq' c(p)$ holds, but not always the converse.

A pattern p is of *canonical form* if $p = w_0 x_1 w_1 x_2 \cdots w_{n-1} x_n w_n$ for some $n \geq 0$, $w_0, w_n \in \Sigma^*$ and $w_i \in \Sigma^+ (i = 1, \cdots, n-1)$. As easily seen, any pattern equivalent to p has a form $w_0\chi_1 w_1 \cdots w_{n-1}\chi_n w_n$, where χ_i is a nonempty string over X. In this sense, we identify p and q if $p \equiv q$, and thus $\mathcal{RP}$ is a partially ordered set under the relation $\preceq$. Hereafter, we assume that $\sharp\Sigma \geq 3$.

3   Conditions for $p \preceq q$

In this section, we deal with finite and simple sets of patterns denoted by D such that $p_1 x p_2 \preceq q$ if and only if $p_1 r p_2 \preceq q$ for all $r \in D$, which are useful for proving the compactness theorem derived in the next section.

Lemma 1. *Let* $a, b, a_i, b_i \in \Sigma$ *for* $i = 1, 2$ *and* $v, w \in \Sigma^*$.

        (i)   If $aw = wb$, *then* $a = b$ *and* $w = a^{|w|}$.
        (ii) If $a_1 b_1 w = w a_2 b_2$, *then* $a_1 b_1 = a_2 b_2$ *or* $b_2 a_2$.
        (iii) If $v a_1 b_1 w = w a_2 b_2 v$, *then* $a_1 b_1 = a_2 b_2$ *or* $b_2 a_2$.
        (iv) If $v a_1 b_1 w = b_2 w v a_2$, *then* $a_1 b_1 = a_2 b_2$ *or* $b_2 a_2$.

Proof. We prove only the assertion (iii). Assume $|v| \geq |w|$ for the pair (v, w) given in the assertion (iii). As easily seen, $a_1 b_1 = a_2 b_2$ if $|v| = |w|$, and $a_1 b_1 = b_2 a_2$ if $|v| = |w| + 1$. Thus we consider a case of $|v| \geq |w| + 2$. Let $|v| = n \times (|w| + 2) + l$ for some $n \in N$ and $0 \leq l < |w| + 2$. Then by $v a_1 b_1 w = w a_2 b_2 v$, it can be shown that there are strings u_1, u_2 such that

$$|u_1| = l, \quad |u_2| = |w| + 2 - l, \quad v = (u_1 u_2)^n u_1, \quad a_1 b_1 w = u_2 u_1, \quad w a_2 b_2 = u_1 u_2.$$

As easily seen, if $|u_2| = 0$ or 1, then the assertion (ii) or (i) implies the assertion (iii). Let $|u_2| \geq 2$, and so $|u_1| \leq |w|$. Then by the above equations, $(u_1 u_2 u_1 =)u_1 a_1 b_1 w = w a_2 b_2 u_1$ holds, and thus the new pair (u_1, w) satisfies the equation given in the assertion (iii). We should note that $|u_1| \leq |w| < |v|$. By repeating the above, the pair (v, w) can be reduced to $v = \varepsilon$, $w = \varepsilon$ or $||v| - |w|| < 2$.   □

    Let p and q be patterns and let $p \preceq q$. A sequence $(p_1 \preceq q_1, p_2 \preceq q_2, \cdots, p_t \preceq q_t)$ of relations for patterns is *a division sequence* for $p \preceq q$, if $p = p_1 p_2 \cdots p_t$, $q = q_1 q_2 \cdots q_t$ and $p_i \preceq q_i$ for each i. If $p \preceq q$, there is a division sequence $(p_1 \preceq q_1, \cdots, p_t \preceq q_t)$ for $p \preceq q$, where $p = p_1 p_2 \cdots p_t$ and $q = q_1 q_2 \cdots q_t$.

    Let $p \preceq q$ and r be nonempty substring of p and $p = p_1 r p_2$. The substring r in $p_1 r p_2$ is *generable by variable substitution* for q, if there is a division sequence $(p_1' \preceq q_1, p_1'' r p_2' \preceq y, p_2'' \preceq q_2)$ for $p \preceq q$ such that $p_1 = p_1' p_1''$ and $p_2 = p_2' p_2''$. If the substring r in $p_1 r p_2$ is generable by variable substitution for q, clearly $p_1 x p_2 \preceq q$ holds. Clearly every variable in p is always generable by variable substitution for q. By the above definition, it immediately follows that:

Lemma 2. *Let* $p = p_1 x p_2$ *and* q *be patterns such that* $p \not\preceq q$.
    (i)   If $p_1 a p_2 \preceq q$ *for a constant symbol* $a \in \Sigma$, *then the substring* a *in* $p_1 a p_2$ *is not generable by variable substitution for* q, *and for any substitution* θ *with* $q\theta = p_1 a p_2$, *there is a division sequence* $(p_1 \preceq q_{\theta,1}, a \preceq a, p_2 \preceq q_{\theta,2})$ *for* $p_1 a p_2 \preceq q(= q_{\theta,1} a q_{\theta,2})$.

(ii)   If $p_1axp_2 \preceq q$ for a constant symbol $a \in \Sigma$, then the substring a in p_1axp_2 is not generable by variable substitution for q, and for any substitution θ with $q\theta = p_1axp_2$, there is a division sequence $(p_1 \preceq q_{\theta,1}, a \preceq a, xp_2 \preceq yq_{\theta,2})$ for $p_1ap_2 \preceq q(= q_{\theta,1}ayq_{\theta,2})$.

(iii)   If $p_1xbp_2 \preceq q$ for a constant symbol $b \in \Sigma$, then the substring b in p_1xbp_2 is not generable by variable substitution for q, and for any substitution θ with $q\theta = p_1xbp_2$, there is a division sequence $(p_1x \preceq q_{\theta,1}y, a \preceq a, p_2 \preceq q_{\theta,2})$ for $p_1ap_2 \preceq q(= q_{\theta,1}yaq_{\theta,2})$.

(iv)   If $p_1(ab)p_2 \preceq q$, $p_1(ax)p_2 \not\preceq q$ and $p_1(xb)p_2 \not\preceq q$ for constant symbols $a, b \in \Sigma$, then the substrings a, b and ab in $p_1(ab)p_2$ are not generable by variable substitution for q, and for any substitution θ with $q\theta = p_1(ab)p_2$, there is a division sequence $(p_1 \preceq q_{\theta,1}, ab \preceq q', p_2 \preceq q_{\theta,2})$ for $p_1(ab)p_2 \preceq q(= q_{\theta,1}q'q_{\theta,2})$.

Lemma 3. Let $p = p_1xp_2$ and $q = q_1q_2q_3$ be patterns. If $p_1 \preceq q_1q_2$ and $p_2 \prec q_2q_3$ but $p \not\preceq q$, then q_2 contains no variable, i.e., $q_2 \in \Sigma^*$.

Proof. Assume that the pattern q_2 contains some variable, say y, and put $q_2 = q_2'yq_2''$ for some q_2', q_2''. Then by $p_1 \preceq q_1q_2(= q_1q_2'yq_2'')$ and $p_2 \preceq q_2q_3(= q_2'yq_2''q_3)$, there are division sequences

$$(p_1' \preceq q_1q_2', p_1'' \preceq yq_2'') \text{ for } p_1 \preceq q_1q_2 \quad \text{and} \quad (p_2' \preceq q_2'y, p_2'' \preceq q_2''q_3) \text{ for } p_2 \preceq q_2q_3$$

where $p_1 = p_1'p_1'', p_2 = p_2'p_2''$ for some $p_i', p_i'' (i = 1, 2)$. Since $p = (p_1'p_1'')x(p_2'p_2'') = p_1'(p_1''xp_2')p_2''$ and $q = (q_1q_2')y(q_2''q_3)$, by the above division sequences, the sequence $(p_1' \preceq q_1q_2', p_1''xp_2' \prec y, p_2'' \prec q_2''q_3)$ gives a division sequence for $p \preceq q$, and a contradiction.   □

Lemma 4. Let $t \geq 2$ and $w_i \in \Sigma^+ (i = 1, 2, \cdots, t)$, and let $p = p_1xp_2$ and $q = q_1w_1q_2 \cdots q_tw_tq_{t+1}$ be patterns such that $p \not\preceq q$. If $p_1w_ip_2 \preceq q$ and there is a division sequence $(p_1 \preceq q_1w_1 \cdots w_{i-1}q_i, w_i \preceq w_i, p_2 \preceq q_{i+1}w_{i+1} \cdots q_{t+1})$ for $p_1w_ip_2 \preceq q (i = 1, \cdots, t)$ then for $i = 2, \cdots, t$, (i) $q_i \in \Sigma^*$, (ii) $w_1q_2 \cdots w_{i-1}q_i$ is a suffix of p_1 and (iii) $q_{i+1}w_{i+1} \cdots w_t$ is a prefix of p_2.

The following result can be shown similarly to that of nonerasing regular patterns given by Sato et al.[13]:

Lemma 5. Let $p = p_1xp_2$ and q be patterns. Then $p \preceq q$ if and only if there are distinct constants $a_1, a_2, a_3 \in \Sigma$ such that $p_1a_ip_2 \preceq q$ for $i = 1, 2, 3$.

The above lemma is not always valid for a case of $p_1a_ip_2 \preceq q$ only for distinct constants a_1 and a_2. Indeed, consider patterns $p = a_1xa_2$ and $q = xa_1a_2y$. Clearly $p\{x := a_1\} = a_1a_1a_2 \preceq xa_1a_2y$ and $p\{x := a_2\} = a_1a_2a_2 \preceq xa_1a_2y$ but $p \not\preceq q$.

Lemma 6. Let $p = p_1xp_2$ and q be patterns. Then $p \preceq q$ if and only if there are distinct constants $a_1, a_2 \in \Sigma$ such that $p_1rp_2 \preceq q$ for all $r \in D$, where $D = \{a_1x_1, a_2x_2\}$ or $\{x_1a_1, x_2a_2\}$.

Proof. We prove only the *if* part for a case of $D = \{a_1x_1, a_2x_2\}$ with $a_1 \neq a_2$. The other case can be proved similarly.

Let $p_1rp_2 \preceq q$ for each $r \in D$. Suppose $p \not\preceq q$. By Lemma 2(ii), the pattern q is of form $q = q_1(a_1y_1q'a_2y_2)q_2$ for some patterns q_1, q', q_2, and two division sequences are given by

$$(p_1 \preceq q_1, \qquad\qquad a_1 \preceq a_1, x_1p_2 \preceq (y_1q'a_2y_2)q_2) \text{ for } p_1(a_1x_1)p_2 \preceq q$$
$$(p_1 \preceq q_1(a_1y_1q'), a_2 \preceq a_2, x_2p_2 \preceq y_2q_2) \qquad\qquad \text{ for } p_1(a_2x_2)p_2 \preceq q.$$

By the above, we have $p_1 \preceq q_1a_1(y_1q')$ and $p_2(\preceq x_1p_2) \preceq (y_1q')a_2y_2q_2$. Since $p \not\preceq q$, by appealing Lemma 3, $y_1q' \in \Sigma^*$ must hold. It is a contradiction since y_1 is a variable. $\qquad\square$

Note that the above lemma is not always sufficient for $p \preceq q$ if $D = \{ax_1, x_2b\}$ for distinct constants $a, b \in \Sigma$. In fact, let $p = bxa$ and $q = y_1bay_2$ for $a \neq b$. Then clearly both $p\{x := ax_1\} = bax_1a$ and $p\{x := x_2b\} = bx_2ba$ are instances of q but $p \not\preceq q$. Concerning with this type, the next result follows:

Lemma 7. *Let $p = p_1xp_2$ and q be patterns, and let $p \not\preceq q$. If $p_1(a_1x_1)p_2 \preceq q, p_1(x_2b_1)p_2 \preceq q$ and $p_1(a_2b_2)p_2 \preceq q$ for some constants $a_1, a_2(\neq a_1), b_1, b_2(\neq b_1)$, then $a_1b_1 = b_2a_2$ holds.*

Proof. Let $p_1rp_2 \preceq q$ for all $r \in \{a_1x_1, x_2b_1, a_2b_2\}$ but $p_1xp_2 \not\preceq q$, where $a_1 \neq a_2$ and $b_1 \neq b_2$. Then by Lemma 2(ii) and (iii), the following three cases are possible for some q_1, q', q_2, where the case 3 is possible for $a_1 = b_1(= c)$:

Case 1. $q = q_1(a_1y_1)q'(y_2b_1)q_2$ and there are division sequences
$$(p_1 \preceq q_1, \qquad\qquad a_1 \preceq a_1, x_1p_2 \preceq (y_1q'y_2b_1)q_2) \text{ for } p_1(a_1x_1)p_2 \preceq q \text{ and}$$
$$(p_1 \preceq q_1(a_1y_1q'y_2), b_1 \preceq b_1, p_2 \preceq q_2) \qquad\qquad \text{ for } p_1(x_2b_1)p_2 \preceq q.$$

Case 2. $q = q_1(y_2b_1q'a_1y_1)q_2$, and there are division sequences
$$(p_1 \preceq q_1(y_2b_1q'), a_1 \preceq a_1, x_1p_2 \preceq y_1q_2) \qquad \text{ for } p_1(a_1x_1)p_2 \preceq q \text{ and}$$
$$(p_1x_2 \preceq q_1y_2, \quad b_1 \preceq b_1, p_2 \preceq (q'a_1y_1)q_2) \text{ for } p_1(x_2b_1)p_2 \preceq q.$$

Case 3. $q = q_1(y_2cy_1)q_2$, and there are division sequences
$$(p_1 \preceq q_1y_2, \quad c \preceq c, x_1p_2 \preceq y_1q_2) \text{ for } p_1(cx_1)p_2 \preceq q \text{ and}$$
$$(p_1x_2 \preceq q_1y_2, c \preceq c, p_2 \preceq y_1q_2) \quad \text{ for } p_1(x_2c)p_2 \preceq q.$$

Hereafter, we show that case 1 or case 3 does not happen, and case 2 leads the equation $a_1b_1 = b_2a_2$.

Case 1. Similarly to the proof of Lemma 6, by Lemma 3, $y_1q'y_2 \in \Sigma^*$ holds, and a contradiction.

Case 2. By two devision sequences of case 2, $p_1 \preceq (q_1y_2b_1)q'$ and $p_2 \preceq q'(a_1y_1q_2)$ hold, and thus by Lemma 3 and $p \not\preceq q$, $q' \in \Sigma^*$ holds. Moreover, by Lemma 4,

$$(*)\ b_1q' \text{ is a suffix of } p_1 \text{ and } q'a_1 \text{ is a prefix of } p_2.$$

Next, we consider another condition of $p_1(a_2b_2)p_2 \preceq q$. By $p \not\preceq q$ and Lemma 6, $p_1(a_2x_1)p_2 \not\preceq q$ and $p_1(x_2b_2)p_2 \not\preceq q$. Hence by Lemma 2(iv), q contains a string q'' with $q'' = a_2b_2$ or a_2yb_2 as a substring, and there is a division sequence $(p_1 \preceq q_1', a_2b_2 \preceq q'', p_2 \preceq q_2')$ for $p_1(a_2b_2)p_2 \preceq q$, where $q = q_1y_2(b_1q'a_1)y_1q_2 = q_1'q''q_2'$.

Claim. The substring q'' of $q = q_1'(q'')q_2'$ is contained in the substring $b_1q'a_1$ of $q = q_1y_2(b_1q'a_1)y_1q_2$.

The proof of the claim. It is enough to show that $|q_1'| \geq |q_1y_2|$ and $|q_2'| \leq |y_1q_2|$. Suppose that $|q_1'| < |q_1y_2|$.

A case of $q'' = a_2b_2$. In this case, $q_1'q''$ is a prefix of q_1y_2. It means $q_1y_2 = (q_1'q'')q_3$ for some q_3. Let us put $q_3' = (b_1q'a_1)y_1q_2$. Then we have $q_2' = q_3q_3'$ and $q = q_1'q''q_3q_3'$. Note that $q_3 \neq \varepsilon$ and the last letter of q_3 is the variable y_2 since the last letter of q'' is b_2 but not variable. By two devision sequences for $p_1(x_2b_1)p_2 \preceq q$ and $p_1(a_2b_2)p_2 \preceq q$, we have

$$p_1(\preceq p_1x_2) \preceq q_1y_2(= q_1'q''q_3) \quad \text{and} \quad p_2 \preceq q_2'(= q_3q_3').$$

By Lemma 3 and $p \not\preceq q$, we have $q_3 \in \Sigma^*$, and a contradiction. Similarly, the case of $q'' = a_2yb_2$ can be shown to lead the contradiction. Hence the claim is valid.

By the claim and $b_1q'a_1 \in \Sigma^+$, it implies that q'' does not contain any variable, i.e., $q'' = a_2b_2$. Let $b_1q'a_1 = w_1(a_2b_2)w_2$ for some $w_1, w_2 \in \Sigma^*$. Then the devision sequence for $p_1(a_2b_2)p_2 \preceq q(= q_1y_2w_1(a_2b_2)w_2y_1q_2)$ is given as follows: $(p_1 \preceq q_1y_2w_1, a_2b_2 \preceq a_2b_2, p_2 \preceq w_2y_1q_2)$. Thus by $(*)$, it follows that:

(1) both b_1q' and w_1 are suffixes of p_1, and so w_1 is a suffix of q'
(2) both $q'a_1$ and w_2 are prefixes of p_2, and so w_2 is a prefix of q'

Since $b_1q'a_1 = w_1(a_2b_2)w_2$, $|q'| = |w_1| + |w_2|$ holds, and by the above, $q' = w_2w_1$. Consequently, we have $b_1(w_2w_1)a_1 = w_1(a_2b_2)w_2$. By Lemma 1(iv), $a_1b_1 = a_2b_2$ or b_2a_2. By $a_1 \neq a_2$, we have $u_1b_1 = b_2u_2$.

Case 3. As noted above, this case is possible for $a_1 = b_1(= c)$. Since $p_1(a_1x_1)p_2$, $p_1(x_2b_1) \preceq q$ and Lemma 6, $p_1(a_2x_1)p_2, p_1(x_2b_2) \not\preceq q$. Moreover, $p_1(a_2b_2)p_2 \preceq q$ and $p \not\preceq q$ are true, so by Lemma 2(iv), there is a division sequence

$$(p_1 \preceq q_1', a_2b_2 \preceq q'', p_2 \preceq q_2') \quad \text{for} \quad p_1(a_2b_2)p_2 \preceq q,$$

where $q'' = a_2b_2$ or a_2yb_2. Similarly to the case 2, since $c \neq a_2, b_2$, it can be shown that q_1' is a prefix of q_1 or q_2' is a suffix of q_2. For any case, by Lemma 3, it leads a contradiction. This completes the proof. $\square$

Lemma 8. Let $p = p_1xp_2$ and q be patterns, and $a, b \in \Sigma$.
(i) If $p_1(ax_1)p_2 \preceq q$ but $p_1(x_2b')p_2 \not\preceq q$ for any $b' \in \Sigma$, then there are not strings $a_ib_i(i = 1, 2)$ such that $p_1(a_ib_i)p_2 \preceq q$ for $i = 1, 2$, a, a_1, a_2 are distinct and $b_1 \neq b_2$.
(ii) If $p_1(x_2b)p_2 \preceq q$ but $p_1(a'x_1)p_2 \not\preceq q$ for any $a' \in \Sigma$, then there are not strings $a_ib_i(i = 1, 2)$ such that $p_1(a_ib_i)p_2 \preceq q$ for $i = 1, 2$, $a_1 \neq a_2$ and b, b_1, b_2 are distinct.

Proof. We prove only for a case (i). Let $p_1(ax_1)p_2 \preceq q$ but $p_1(x_2b')p_2 \not\preceq q$ for any $b' \in \Sigma$. By the latter, $p \not\preceq q$ holds. Suppose there are strings $a_ib_i(i = 1, 2)$ such that $p_1(a_ib_i)p_2 \preceq q$ for $i = 1, 2$, and a, a_1, a_2 are distinct and $b_1 \neq b_2$.

Then by $p \npreceq q$, $a_i \neq a$ and Lemma 6, $p_1(a_ix_2)p_2 \npreceq q$ satisfies for $i = 1, 2$. Since $p_1(x_2b_i)p_2 \npreceq q$ for $i = 1, 2$, by Lemma 2(iv), it implies that q has a form of $q_1(a_1b_1)w(a_2b_2)q_2$ or $q_1(a_1b_1b_2)q_2$ for some $w \in \Sigma^*$ and for some q_1, q_2, and there are the corresponding division sequences as given in Lemma 2(iv). Note that $w \in \Sigma^*$ follows by applying Lemma 3 to the division sequences. The latter form for q is possible only for $b_1 = a_2$. We prove only for the former case, i.e., $q = q_1(a_1b_1)w(a_2b_2)q_2$. By Lemma 2(iv) and Lemma 4, it follows that:

$$(*) \quad (a_1b_1)w \text{ is a suffix of } p_1 \text{ and } w(a_2b_2) \text{ is a prefix of } p_2$$

On the other hand, since $p_1(ax_1)p_2 \preceq q$, by Lemma 2(ii), $q = q_1'(ay_1)q_2'$ for some q_1', q_2'', and there is a division sequence $(p_1 \preceq q_1', a \preceq a, x_1p_2 \preceq y_1q_2')$ for $p_1(ax_1)p_2 \preceq q$. Since $q_1'(ay_1)q_2' = q = q_1(a_1b_1wa_2b_2)q_2$, the following cases are possible: (1) $q_1'ay_1$ is a prefix of q_1, (2) ay_1q_2' is a suffix of q_2 and (3) $a = b_2$ and $y_1q_2' = q_2$.
For the case (1), Lemma 3 brings a contradiction.
For the case (2), by Lemma 3, $q_2 = w'(ay_1)q_2'$ for some $w' \in \Sigma^*$, and so $q_1' = q_1(a_1b_1wa_2b_2)w'$. By $(*)$ and the above division sequence for $p_1(ax_1)p_2 \preceq q$, it implies that

$$(2 - 1) \quad a_1b_1w \text{ and } a_1b_1wa_2b_2w' \text{ are suffixes of } p_1 \text{ and}$$
$$(2 - 2) \quad wa_2b_2 \text{ and } w'a \text{ are prefixes of } p_2.$$

Suppose $|w| \geq |w'|$. Then $w = w_1w' = w'w_2$ holds for some $w_1, w_2 \in \Sigma^*$, and $(2-1)$ implies $a_1b_1(w_1w') = w_2(a_2b_2)w'$, and so $a_1b_1w_1 = w_2a_2b_2$. If $w_1 = \varepsilon$, then $w_2 = \varepsilon$ and $a_1 = a_2$ and a contradiction. Thus $w_1, w_2 \neq \varepsilon$, and so the first symbol of w_2 is a_1. By $(2 - 2)$, however, the symbol must be a, and a contradiction. Similarly we can prove the case of $|w| < |w'|$. The case (3) is impossible because of $a \neq b_2$. From the above, there are not strings $a_ib_i (i = 1, 2, 3)$ satisfying the conditions in our lemma. This completes the proof. $\square$

Lemma 9. *Let $p = p_1xp_2$ and q be patterns. If $p_1(ax_1)p_2 \npreceq q$ and $p_1(x_2b)p_2 \npreceq q$ for any $a, b \in \Sigma$, then there are not constants $a_i, b_j (i, j = 1, 2, 3)$ such that $p_1(a_ib_i)p_2 \preceq q, a_i \neq a_j$ and $b_i \neq b_j$ for $i \neq j (i, j = 1, 2, 3)$.*

Proof. We omit the proof for lack of space. It is similarly done to Lemma 8.

4   Characteristic Sets and Compactness

For a positive integer k, let $\mathcal{RP}^k$ be the class of sets of at most k regular patterns, and let $\mathcal{RPL}^k$ be the class of unions of languages generated by at most k regular patterns, i.e., $\mathcal{RPL}^k = \{L(P) \mid P \in \mathcal{RP}^k\}$, where $L(P) = \bigcup_{p \in P} L(p)$.

We define a syntactic relation $\sqsubseteq$ over the class of finite subsets of $\mathcal{RP}$ as follows: for finite subsets $P, Q \subseteq \mathcal{RP}$, $P \sqsubseteq Q \iff \forall p \in P, \exists q \in Q \text{ s.t. } p \preceq q$.

Clearly $P \sqsubseteq Q$ implies $L(P) \subseteq L(Q)$ but not always the converse. The notion of compactness was introduced by Arimura et al.[5] and defined as follows:

Definition 1. *Let $k \geq 1$. The class $\mathcal{RP}^k$ has compactness w.r.t. containment, if for any $P, Q \in \mathcal{RP}^k$, $L(P) \subseteq L(Q) \iff P \sqsubseteq Q$.*

Definition 2 (Angluin[3]). *Let $\mathcal{L}$ be a class of languages and L be a language in $\mathcal{L}$. A finite set $S \subseteq L$ is a characteristic set of L within $\mathcal{L}$, if $L' \in \mathcal{L}$, $S \subseteq L'$ implies $L \subseteq L'$.*

For a pattern p and $n \in N$, $S_n(p)$ denotes the set of strings obtained from p by substituting constant strings with length n to variables in p. Thus we have $S_0(p) = \{c(p)\}$. For a set $P \in \mathcal{RP}^k$, we define $S_n(P) = \bigcup_{p \in P} S_n(p)$. Then, by Lemma 5, we obtain the following two results which play an important role in inductive inference of pattern languages from positive examples.

Theorem 2. *Suppose $\sharp\Sigma \geq 2k + 1$. Let $P, Q \in \mathcal{RP}^k$. Then the following three statements are equivalent: (i) $S_1(P) \subseteq L(Q)$, (ii) $L(P) \subseteq L(Q)$, (iii) $P \sqsubseteq Q$.*

Corollary 1. *Suppose $\sharp\Sigma \geq 2k + 1$. Let $P \in \mathcal{RP}^k$. Then the set $S_1(P)$ is a characteristic set of $L(P)$ within the class $\mathcal{RPL}^k$.*

Theorem 3. *Suppose $\sharp\Sigma \geq k + 2$. Let $P, Q \in \mathcal{RP}^k$. Then the following three statements are equivalent: (i) $S_2(P) \subseteq L(Q)$, (ii) $L(P) \subseteq L(Q)$, (iii) $P \sqsubseteq Q$.*

Proof. Clearly (ii) implies (i) and (iii) implies (ii). Thus we prove (i) implies (iii). It suffices to show that for any pattern p and for any $Q \in \mathcal{RP}^k$ with $\sharp Q = k$, $S_2(p) \subseteq L(Q)$ implies $p \preceq q$ for some $q \in Q$ under the assumption $\sharp\Sigma \geq k + 2$. The proof is done by mathematical induction on the number $n (\geq 0)$ of variables in p. Clearly it is valid for case of $n = 0$. Assume that it is valid for n. Let p be a regular pattern with $(n + 1)$ variables such that $S_2(p) \subseteq L(Q)$.

Suppose that $p \not\preceq q$ for any $q \in Q$. Let x be a variable in p and $p = p_1 x p_2$ for some p_1, p_2. Let $Q = \{q_1, q_2, \cdots, q_k\}$ and $K = \{1, 2, \cdots, k\}$. By $\sharp\Sigma \geq k + 2$, there are $k + 2$ distinct constant symbols in Σ, say, $a_1, a_2, \cdots, a_{k+2}$. Let $I = \{1, 2, \cdots, k + 2\}$ and $M = I \times I$. Put $p_{i,j} = p\{x := a_i a_j\}$ for each $(i, j) \in M$. Obviously, each $p_{i,j}$ contains just n variables, and $S_2(p_{i,j}) \subseteq L(Q)$ holds. For each $t \in K$, we put $M_t = \{(i, j) \in M \mid p_{i,j} \preceq q_t\}$. Then by the hypothesis of induction, for any $(i, j) \in M$, there is an index $t \in K$ such that $p_{i,j} \preceq q_t$, and so $\bigcup_{t \in K} M_t = M$ must hold. Hereafter, we will show that $\bigcup_{t \in K} M_t \neq M$ under the assumption $p \not\preceq q_t$ for any $t \in K$.

Claim A. For every $t \in K$, the set M_t satisfies at least one of the following conditions, where $R_i = \{(i, j) \mid j \in I\}$ and $C_j = \{(i, j) \mid i \in I\}$ for $i, j \in I$:
(1) $\exists (i_t, j_t) \in M$ s.t. $M_t \subseteq R_{i_t} \cup C_{j_t} \cup \{(j_t, i_t)\}$,
(2) $\exists (i_t, j_t), (i'_t, j'_t) \in M$ s.t. $i_t \neq i'_t, j_t \neq j'_t, M_t \subseteq R_{i_t} \cup \{(i'_t, j_t), (i'_t, j'_t)\}$,
(3) $\exists (i_t, j_t), (i'_t, j'_t) \in M$ s.t. $j_t \neq j'_t, i_t \neq i'_t, M_t \subseteq C_{j_t} \cup \{(i_t, j'_t), (i'_t, j'_t)\}$.

The proof of the claim A. Let $t \in K$ be an arbitrary fixed index. It is enough to show that if M_t does not satisfy the condition (2) or (3), then the set satisfies the remaining condition (1). Assume that M_t does not satisfy the conditions (2) or (3). If $\sharp M_t < 3$, the condition (2) and (3) hold and it leads a contradiction. Thus $\sharp M_t \geq 3$. Let us put $R_{i,t} = R_i \cap M_t$ and $C_{j,t} = C_j \cap M_t$

for $i, j \in I$. By Lemma 5, $\sharp R_{i,t} \geq 3$ implies $p_1(a_i x_1)p_2 \preceq q_t$. If $\sharp R_{i,t} \geq 3$ for two or more i 's, by Lemma 6, $p \preceq q_t$ holds, and a contradiction. Thus $\sharp R_{i,t} \geq 3$ is possible for at most one i. Similarly, we have $\sharp C_{j,t} \geq 3$ for at most one j. The above mean only the following cases to be possible:

Case 1. $\sharp R_{i_t,t} \geq 3$ and $\sharp C_{j_t,t} \geq 3$ only for some $i_t, j_t \in I$, and $\sharp R_{i,t} \leq 2$ and
   $\sharp C_{j,t} \leq 2$ for any $i \neq i_t$ and $j \neq j_t$.
Case 2. $\sharp R_{i_t,t} \geq 3$ only for some i_t, $\sharp R_{i,t} \leq 2$ and $\sharp C_{j,t} \leq 2$ for any $i(\neq i_t), j$.
Case 3. $\sharp C_{j_t,t} \geq 3$ only for some j_t, $\sharp R_{i,t} \leq 2$ and $\sharp C_{j,t} \leq 2$ for any i, $j(\neq j_t)$.
Case 4. $\sharp R_{i,t} \leq 2$ and $\sharp C_{j,t} \leq 2$ for any $i, j \in I$.

Under the assumption $p \not\preceq q_t$, we show that M_t satisfies the condition (1) for the case 1 while the other cases do not happen.
Case 1. By Lemma 5, $p_1(a_{i_t} x_1)p_2 \preceq q_t$ and $p_1(x_2 a_{j_t})p_2 \preceq q_t$ hold. Since $p \not\preceq q_t$, by Lemma 7, $M_t - (R_{i_t} \cup C_{j_t})$ contains at most one (j_t, i_t). Hence for this case M_t satisfies the condition (1).
Case 2. In this case, Lemma 5 implies $p_1(a_{i_t} x_1)p_2 \preceq q_t$, and clearly $p_1(a_i x_1)p_2 \not\preceq q$ and $p_1(x_2 a_j)p_2 \not\preceq q$ hold for any $i(\neq i_t), j \in I$. Since M_t does not satisfy the condition (2), there are at least two pairs $(i_1, j_1), (i_2, j_2) \in M_t$ such that i_t, i_1, i_2 are distinct. Since $p_1(x_2 a_j)p_2 \not\preceq q_t$, appealing Lemma 8(i), $j_1 = j_2$ must hold. It means together with $(i_t, j) \in M_t$ for any j that three pairs $(i_t, j_1), (i_1, j_1)$ and (i_2, j_1) belong to M_t. It implies that $\sharp C_{j_1,t} \geq 3$, and a contradiction.
Case 3. Similarly to the case 2, it leads a contradiction.
Case 4. In this case, $p_1(a_i x_1)p_2 \not\preceq q_t$ and $p_1(x_2 a_j)p_2 \not\preceq q_t$ hold for any $i, j \in I$. Remember that M_t does not satisfy the condition (2) or (3). It can be easily shown that there are distinct i_1, i_2, i_3 and distinct j_1, j_2, j_3 satisfying $(i_s, j_s) \in M_t(s = 1, 2, 3)$. However, by Lemma 9, it leads a contradiction.

By the above, the proof of the claim A is completed.

By the claim A, there are three subsets K_1, K_2 and K_3 of K such that $K_1 \cup K_2 \cup K_3 = K$, they are mutually disjoint and for any $t \in K_s$, M_t satisfies the condition (s) for $s = 1, 2, 3$. For $t \in K_1$, let (i_t, j_t) be a pair satisfying the condition (1).

We first modify the sets K_s as follows: If $i_{t_1} = i_{t_2}$ for some distinct $t_1, t_2 \in K_1$, then $M_{t_1} \cup M_{t_2} = M_{t_1} \cup (M_{t_2} - R_{i_{t_2}})$ holds, and moreover, $(M_{t_2} - R_{i_{t_2}})$ satisfies the condition (3), i.e., $(M_{t_2} - R_{i_{t_2}}) \subseteq C_{j_{t_2}} \cup \{(i_{t'_2}, j_{t'_2})\}$ with $i_{t'_2} = j_{t_2}, j_{t'_2} = i_{t_2}$. It means that the set $\bigcup_{t \in K_1 \cup K_2 \cup K_3} M_t$ is invariant for deleting t_2 from K_1 and adding it to K_3. Let K'_1 and K'_3 be a subset of K_1 and a superset of K_3, respectively, obtained by repeating such operations until the indexes i_t's, $(t \in K'_1)$ are distinct. Similarly, let K''_1 and K'_2 be a subset of K'_1 and a superset of K_2 obtained by repeating similar operations for j_t's until the indexes j_t's, $(t \in K''_1)$ are distinct. We denote these new sets by K_1, K_2 and K_3, simply. For simplicity, we put $K_1 = \{1, 2, \cdots, l\}, K_2 = \{l + 1, \cdots, l + m\}$ and $K_3 = \{l + m + 1, \cdots, l + m + n\}$, where $\sharp K_1 = l, \sharp K_2 = m, \sharp K_3 = n$ and $l + m + n = k$.

Let (i_t, j_t) be the first pair satisfying the condition (s) for $s = 1, 2, 3$, and let (i'_t, j'_t) be the second pair given in the condition (s) for $s = 2, 3$. Then we define subsets of M as follows:

$$H_1 = (\bigcup_{t \in K_1 \cup K_2} R_{i_t}) \cup (\bigcup_{t \in K_1 \cup K_3} C_{j_t}),$$
$$H_2 = (\bigcup_{t \in K_2} \{(i_t^t, j_t), (i_t', j_t')\}) \cup (\bigcup_{t \in K_3} \{(i_t, j_t'), (i_t', j_t')\}),$$
$$H_3 = \{(j_t, i_t) \mid t \in K_1\},$$

Then by the claim A, we have $\bigcup_{t \in K} M_t \subseteq H_1 \cup H_2 \cup H_3$. We now prove the following claim:

Claim B. $\sharp(H_1 \cup H_2 \cup H_3) \le (k+2)^2 - 2$.

The proof of the Claim B. Let us put $n_r = \sharp(\{i_1, \cdots, i_l\} \cup \{i_{l+m+1}, \cdots, i_k\})$ and $n_c = \sharp(\{j_{l+1}, \cdots, j_{l+m}\} \cup \{j_{l+m+1}, \cdots, j_k\})$. Then as easily seen, $n_r \le l + m$, $n_c \le l + n$ and

$$\sharp H_1 = (k+2)^2 - (k+2-n_r)(k+2-n_c) \quad \text{and} \quad \sharp H_2 \le 2(m+n).$$

Here we consider about the number of elements in $H_3 - H_1$. Let $(j_t, i_t), (j_{t'}, i_{t'})$ be any distinct pairs in $H_3 - H_1$. Then by the definition of H_3, $t, t' \in K_1$. Thus by the choice of K_1, we have $j_t \ne j_{t'}$ and $i_t \ne i_{t'}$. Moreover, since $(j_t, i_t) \notin H_1$ means $j_t \ne i_1, \cdots, i_l, i_{l+m+1}, \cdots, i_k$ and $i_t \ne j_{l+1}, \cdots, j_k$, it implies that $\sharp(H_3 - H_1) \le \min\{k+2-n_r, k+2-n_c\}$.

A case of $n_c \le n_r$. In this case, $\sharp(H_3 - H_1) \le k+2-n_r$ holds. From the above, we obtain

$$\sharp(H_1 \cup H_2 \cup H_3) \le \sharp H_1 + \sharp H_2 + \sharp(H_3 - H_1)$$
$$\le [(k+2)^2 - (k+2-n_r)(k+2-n_c)] + 2(l+m) + (k+2-n_r)$$
$$= (k+2)^2 - [(k+2-n_r)(k+1-n_c) - 2(l+m)].$$

Let us put $A = (k+2-n_r)(k+1-n_c) - 2(l+m)$. Then it is enough to show that $A \ge 2$. Since $m \le k - n_r$ and $l \le k - n_c$, we have

$$A \ge (m+2)(l+1) - 2(l+m) \ge (l-1)m + 2.$$

Hence, if $l \ge 1$ then $A \ge 2$ holds. Otherwise, i.e., $l = 0$, since $m \le k - n_r \le k - n_c$, we have $A = (k+2-n_r)(k+1-n_c) - 2m \ge (m+2)(m+1) - 2m \ge 2$.

Similarly we can prove for the case of $n_r < n_c$.

Consequently, the claim B is valid.

By the claim B, since $\sharp(\bigcup_{t \in K} M_t) \le \sharp(H_1 \cup H_2 \cup H_3) \le (k+2)^2 - 2$, it implies that there is a pair $(i, j) \in M$ such that $p_{i,j} \npreceq q$ for any $q \in Q$. This is a contradiction. Hence $p \preceq q$ holds for some $q \in Q$. $\square$

Arimura and Shinohara[4] showed that if $\sharp \Sigma \le k+1$, the class $\mathcal{RP}^k$ does not have compactness, and gave the following counter example:

Let $\Sigma = \{a_1, a_2, \cdots, a_{k+1}\}$, $p = a_1 a_1 x_1 a_{k+1} a_{k+1}$ and $q_i = x_1 a_1 a_i x_2$ for $i = 1, 2, \cdots k$. Then $L(p) \subseteq \bigcup_{i=1}^k L(q_i)$, but $p \npreceq q_i$ for any i. Thus we have:

Theorem 4. *Let $k \ge 1$. The class $\mathcal{RP}^k$ has compactness w.r.t. containment if and only if $\sharp \Sigma \ge k+2$.*

Note that Sato et al.[13] proved the class of sets of k *nonerasing* regular patterns to have compactness if and only if $\sharp \Sigma \ge 2k+1$ for $k \ge 3$ and $\sharp \Sigma \ge 4$ for $k = 2$. By Theorem 4, it immediately follows that:

Corollary 2. *Suppose* $\sharp \Sigma \geq k + 2$. *Let* $P \in \mathcal{RP}^k$. *Then the set* $S_2(P)$ *is a characteristic set for the language* $L(P)$ *within* $\mathcal{RP}^k$.

5   Learning of Unions of Regular Patterns Languages

5.1   Inductive Inference from Positive Examples

We first give the notion of identification in the limit from positive examples ([6]).

A language class $\mathcal{L} = L_0, L_1, \cdots$ over Σ is an *indexed family of recursive languages* if there is a computable function $f : N \times \Sigma^* \to \{0, 1\}$ such that $f(i, w) = 1$ if $w \in L_i$, otherwise 0. The function f is called a *membership* function. Hereafter we confine ourselves to indexed families of recursive languages.

An infinite sequence of strings $w_1, w_2, \cdots$ over Σ is a *positive presentation* of a language L, if $L = \{w_n \mid n \geq 1\}$ holds. An *inference machine* is an effective procedure M that runs in stages $1, 2, \cdots$, and requests an *example* and produces a *hypothesis* in N based on the examples so far received. Let M be an inference machine and $\sigma = w_1, w_2, \cdots$ be an infinite sequence of strings. We denote by h_n the hypothesis produced by M at stage n after the examples $w_1, \cdots, w_n$ are fed to M. M is *consistent* if $\{w_1, \cdots, w_n\} \subseteq L_{h_n}$, and is *conservative* if $h_{n-1} \neq h_n$ only if $w_n \notin L_{h_{n-1}}$. M is *polynomial time updating* if after receiving w_n M produces h_n within a polynomial time of $|w_1| + \cdots + |w_n|$. M on input σ *converges* to h if there is an integer $n_0 \in N$ such that $h_n = h$ for every $n \geq n_0$. M *identifies in the limit* or *infers* a language L *from positive examples*, if for any positive presentation σ of L, M on input σ converges to h with $L = L_h$. A class of languages $\mathcal{L}$ is *inferable from positive examples* if there is an inference machine that infers any language in $\mathcal{L}$ from positive examples. A class $\mathcal{L}$ is *polynomial time inferable from positive examples* if there is a consistent, conservative and polynomial time updating inference machine that infers the class $\mathcal{L}$ from positive examples.

Anguluin[2] gave a characterising theorem for a language class to be inferable from positive examples, and a very useful sufficient condition for inferability called *finite thickness* defined as follows: A class $\mathcal{L}$ has *finite thickness*, if $\sharp\{L \in \mathcal{L} \mid S \subseteq L\}$ is finite for any nonempty finite subset $S \subseteq \Sigma^*$.

The class $\mathcal{RPL}$ of regular pattern languages discussed in this paper was shown to have finite thickness as well as the class of nonerasing regular pattern languages by Shinohara[14]. Wright[16] introduced another sufficient condition for inferability called *finite elasticity* to be more general than finite thickness ([10]). A class $\mathcal{L}$ has *finite elasticity*, if there is no infinite sequence of strings $w_0, w_1, \cdots$ and no infinite sequence of languages $L_0, L_1, \cdots$ in $\mathcal{L}$ satisfying $\{w_0, w_1, \cdots, w_{n-1}\} \subseteq L_n$ but $w_n \notin L_n$ for every $n \in N$. Finite elasticity is a good property in a sense that it is closed under various class operations such as union, intersection and so on (Wright[16], Moriyama et al.[9], Sato[12]). Hence the class $\mathcal{RPL}^k$ has finite elasticity for every k. For a class with finite elasticity, a sufficient condition for polynomial time inferability from positive examples was given as follows: For a given nonempty finite set $S \subseteq \Sigma^*$, the MINL problem is to find an positive integer (or description like pattern) for one of the minimal languages containing the set S within $\mathcal{L}$.

Theorem 5 (Angluin[1], Arimura et al.[5]). *If a class $\mathcal{L}$ has finite elasticity and the MINL problem for $\mathcal{L}$ is computable, the procedure INFER below infers $\mathcal{L}$ from positive examples. Furthermore, if the membership function and the MINL problem for $\mathcal{L}$ are polynomial time computable, then $\mathcal{L}$ is polynomial time inferable from positive examples by INFER.*

Procedure INFER
begin
$S := \{w_1\}$; $h_1 := \text{MINL}(S)$; $n := 1$;
repeat
$n := n + 1$; read the next example w_n; $S := S \cup \{w_n\}$;
if $w_n \in L_{h_{n-1}}$ **then** $h_n := h_{n-1}$ **else** $h_n := \text{MINL}(S)$; **output** h_n
forever
end

Since the class $\mathcal{RPL}^k$ has finite elasticity, by the above theorem, if the membership function and the MINL problem are both polynomial computable, then the class is polynomial time inferable from positive examples.

5.2   Efficient Learning of Unions of Erasing Regular Pattern Languages

We first consider the membership problem for the class $\mathcal{RPL}^k$. Shinohara[14] showed that for given regular patterns $p, q \in \mathcal{RP}$, to decide whether $p \preceq q$ or not is computable in time $O(|p| + |q|)$. Thus the membership problem for regular pattern languages is polynomial time computable. By it, we have the following:

Lemma 10. *The membership problem for $\mathcal{RPL}^k$ is polynomial time computable.*

Next, we consider the MINL problem for $\mathcal{RPL}^k$. Arimura et al.[5] gave an efficient algorithm for the problem in terms of generalization systems. The efficient algorithm works well as a correct MINL algorithm for our class $\mathcal{RP}^k$ under the following conditions (A) and (B):
(A) (i) $p \preceq q \iff L(p) \subseteq L(q)$, and $(\mathcal{RP}, \preceq)$ is *efficient* in sense that
(ii) $\preceq$ is polynomial time computable and
(iii) there is a polynomial time computable function $size : \mathcal{RP} \to N$ such that
• $p \prec q \Rightarrow size(p) > size(q)$ for any $p, q \in \mathcal{RP}$,
• for almost all $p \in \mathcal{RP}$, $size(p) \leq h(|p|)$ and $|p| \leq h'(size(p))$ for some polynomials h and h',
• $\{p \in \mathcal{RP} \mid size(p) \leq n\}$ is finite and polynomial time computable for any $n \geq 0$,
• the MINL problem for $\mathcal{RP}$ is polynomial time computable.
(B) The class $\mathcal{RP}^k$ has compactness w.r.t. containment.

By Theorem 1 and the above mentioned, (i) and (ii) are valid. We consider the condition (iii) of (A). Let us define $size$ as follows: $size(p) = 3|p|_c - |p|_v + 1$, where

$|p|_c$ and $|p|_v$ are the numbers of constant symbols and of variables in p. Then clearly $p \preceq q$ implies $size(p) < size(q)$, and the set $\{p \in \mathcal{RP} \mid size(p) \leq n\}$ is finite and polynomial time computable. Moreover, let h and h' be functions from N to itself as follows: $h(x) = 3x+1, h'(x) = x+1$. Then obviously these functions are polynomials, and by the above, $size(p) \leq h(|p|)$ and $|p| \leq h'(size(p))$.

Concerning the MINL problem for $\mathcal{RP}$, the following was shown by Shinohara[14]: A string $w \in \Sigma^*$ is a *common subsequence* of a sample S, if $w \preceq' u$ for every $u \in S$, and a *maximal common subsequence* (*MCS* for short) of S, if w is a common subsequence of S and there is no common subsequence $w'(\neq w)$ of S such that $w \preceq' w'$. By MCS(S), we mean the set of MCS of a sample S.

Lemma 11 (Shinohara[14]). *Let $S \subseteq \Sigma^*$ be a sample and $w \in MCS(S)$. Then the problem for finding one of the regular patterns defining minimal languages containing S within the class $\mathcal{RPL}$ is computable in time $O(l^2 n)$, where l is the maximal length of strings in S and $n = \sharp S$.*

Note that the procedure to compute the MINL(S) given in Shinohara[14] outputs a regular pattern p satisfying $c(p) = w$ for a given $w \in$ MCS(S). Thus the MINL problem for $\mathcal{RPL}$ is very closed to that for finding one of the maximal common subsequences(MCS) for a given sample.

Lemma 12 (Fraser et al.[7]). *Let S be a sample. Then the problem of finding an element of $MCS(S)$ is computable in time $O(ln)$, where l and n are defined in Lemma 11.*

By these lemmas, the MINL problem for $\mathcal{RPL}$ is polynomial time computable. Consequently, by Theorem 3 and Theorem 5, we have the following main result:

Theorem 6. *Suppose $\sharp \Sigma \geq k + 2$. Then the class $\mathcal{RPL}^k$ is polynomial time inferable from positive examples.*

6   Conclusions

In this paper, we gave a necessary and sufficient condition for the class $\mathcal{RP}^k$ to have compactness w.r.t. containment. Furthermore, by applying the efficient algorithm for the MINL problem due to Arimura et al.[5], the class $\mathcal{RPL}^k$ is shown to be polynomial time inferable from positive examples under the condition $\sharp \Sigma \geq k + 2$. As noted in the section 5.2, the MINL problem for $\mathcal{RPL}$ is very closed to that for finding one of the maximal common subsequences(MCS) for a given sample. The minimality of the former can be reduced to that under the syntactic relation $\preceq$, while the *maximality* of the latter is that under $\preceq'$. As a generalization of $\preceq'$, define a relation $\sqsubseteq'$ for two finite subsets of Σ^* such that $S \sqsubseteq' T \iff \forall w \in S, \exists u \in T$ s.t. $w \preceq' u$. As easily seen, if $L(P)$ is a language containing a sample S, then $S \sqsubseteq' T_P$, where $T_P = \{c(p) \mid p \in P\}$. We are interested in the *maximal multiple common subsequences* for a sample S under $\sqsubseteq'$, in the class of finite sets $T \subseteq \Sigma^*$ satisfying $S \sqsubseteq' T$ and $\sharp T \leq k$. Further work will establish the relation between such a generalized MCS problem and the MINL problem for the class $\mathcal{RP}^k$.

References

[1] D. Angluin: *Finding patterns common to a set of strings*, Information and Control, **21**, 46–62, (1980).

[2] D. Angluin: *Inductive inference of formal languages form positive data*, Information and Control, **45**, 117–135, (1980).

[3] D. Angluin: *Inference of reversible language*, Journal of the Association for Computing Machinery, **29(3)**, 741–765, (1982).

[4] H. Arimura and T. Shinohara: *Compactness for unions of regular pattern languages*, Proc. of Symposium on Language and Automaton, Research on Computational Models and Complexity, RIMS Koukyuroku, **950**, 246–249, (1996), (in Japanese).

[5] H. Arimura, T. Shinohara and S. Otsuki: *Finding minimal generalizations for unions of pattern languages and its application to inductive inference from positive data*, Lecture Notes in Computer Science, **775**, 646–660, (1994).

[6] E. M. Gold: *Language identification in the limit*, Information and Control, **10**, 447–474, (1967).

[7] C. B. Fraser, R.W. Irving and M. Middendorf: *Maximal common subsequences and minimal common supersequences*, Information and Computation, **124**, 145–153, (1996).

[8] D. Maier: *The Complexity of Some Problems on Subsequences and Supersequences*, JACM, **25**, 322–336, (1978).

[9] T. Moriyama and M. Sato: *Properties of language classes with finite elasticity*, IEICE Transactions on Information and Systems, **E78-D(5)**, 532–538, (1995).

[10] T. Motoki, T. Shinohara and K. Wright: *The correct definition of finite elasticity: Corrigendum to identification of unions*, Proc. of the 4th Annual Workshop on Computational Learning Theory, 375, (1991).

[11] Y.Mukouchi: *Containment problems for pattern languages*, IEICE Transactions on Information and Systems, **E75-D(4)**, 420–425, (1992).

[12] M. Sato: *Inductive Inference of Formal Languages*, Bulletin of Informatics and Cybernetics, **27(1)**, 85–106, (1995).

[13] M. Sato, Y. Mukouchi and D. Zheng: *Characteristic sets for unions of regular pattern languages and compactness*, Lecture Notes in Artificial Intelligence, **1501**, 220–233, (1998).

[14] T. Shinohara: *Polynomial time inference of extended regular pattern languages*, Proc. of RIMS Symposia on Software Science and Engineering, Lecture Notes in Computer Science, **147**, 115–127, (1982).

[15] T. Shinohara and H. Arimura: *Inductive inference of unbounded unions of pattern languages from positive data*, Proc. of the 7th International Workshop on Algorithmic Learning Theory, Lecture Notes in Artificial Intelligence, **1160**, 256–271, (1996).

[16] K. Wright: *Identification of unions of languages drawn from positive data*, Proc. of the 2nd Annual Workshop on Computational Learning Theory, 328–333, (1989).

A Negative Result on Inductive Inference of Extended Pattern Languages

Daniel Reidenbach

Fachbereich Informatik, Universität Kaiserslautern,
Postfach 3049, 67653 Kaiserslautern, Germany
reidenba@rhrk.uni-kl.de

Abstract. The question of learnability of the class of extended pattern languages is considered to be one of the eldest and outstanding open problems in inductive inference of formal languages. This paper provides an appropriate answer presenting a subclass – the terminal-free extended pattern languages – that is not learnable in the limit. In order to achieve this result we will have to limit the respective alphabet of terminal symbols to exactly two letters.

In addition we will focus on the impact of ambiguity of pattern languages on inductive inference of terminal-free extended pattern languages. The conventional view on nondeterminism in patterns inspired by formal language theory is transformed into an approach that meets the requirements of inductive inference. These studies will lead to some useful learnability criteria for classes of terminal-free extended pattern languages.

1   Introduction

The analysis of learnability of formal languages – originating in [Gol67] – is one of the main subjects in inductive inference. Meanwhile there exist some powerful criteria on language identification in the limit (like in [Ang80], [Wri89] and [BCJ99]) deriving from these studies. Contrary to the discouraging findings concerning *super-finite* classes of languages, learnability of the class of *pattern languages* was shown by Angluin ([Ang79] and [Ang80]). In the sequel there has been a variety of additional studies (e.g. in [LW91], [WZ94]) concerning complexity of learning algorithms, consequences of different input data, and so on.

Pattern languages in the sense of Angluin disallow any empty substitution of variables. The question whether the class of *extended pattern languages* – tolerating empty substitutions and also known as *erasing pattern languages* or *E-pattern languages* – is learnable has proven to be more complicated than that of "standard" pattern languages. It has been the focus of attention since 1982 when Shinohara was the first to deal with extended pattern languages and it was characterized as "one of the outstanding open problems of inductive inference" by Mitchell in 1998 (cf. [Mit98]). Up to the present there are only two non-trivial subclasses of extended pattern languages known to be learnable, both of them

N. Cesa-Bianchi et al. (Eds.): ALT 2002, LNAI 2533, pp. 308–320, 2002.

restricting the occurrences of variables. In detail, the class of extended pattern languages where the patterns contain at most m distinct variables ([Wri89]) and the class of *quasi-regular pattern languages*, with every variable occurring exactly m times (first shown in [Shi82a] for $m = 1$, the general case shown by Mitchell in [Mit98]), can be mentioned. Mitchell also pointed out that the full class of extended pattern languages is learnable in the limit if the respective alphabet of terminal symbols is infinite or singular. The research on extended pattern languages within the scope of formal language theory was initiated in [JKS+94] and led among others to some interesting findings concerning the decidability of inclusion.

In order to take an undisguised look at the difficulties leading to the restrictions in the approaches of Shinohara, Wright and Mitchell we will focus in the following sections on terminal-free extended pattern languages. The main result of this paper will state that the class of extended pattern languages – and also that of terminal-free extended pattern languages – is not learnable in the limit if the respective terminal alphabet consists of exactly two letters. Subsequent to this the impact of nondeterminism of pattern languages on the questions of learning theory will be analysed, but first a sufficiently precise definition of the concepts to be used will be given.

2   Preliminaries

For standard mathematical notions and recursion-theoretic terms not defined explicitly in this paper we refer to [Rog92]. Let Σ be an alphabet of *terminal* symbols and $X = \{x_1, x_2, x_3, \cdots\}$ an infinite alphabet of *variables*, $\Sigma \cap X = \emptyset$. If we are talking just of an *alphabet* we mean an alphabet of terminals. If A is an arbitrary alphabet then A^+ denotes the set of all non-empty words over A and A^* the set of all (empty and non-empty) words over A. We will use lower case letters from the end of the Latin alphabet in order to name words of terminal symbols. We designate the *empty* word as e. $|\cdot|$ denotes the size of an alphabet or the length of a word, respectively, and $|w|_a$ the frequency of a letter a in a word w. A *pattern* is a word over $\Sigma \cup X$, a *terminal-free pattern* is a word over X; naming patterns we will use lower case letters from the beginning of the Greek alphabet. $\text{var}(\alpha)$ denotes the set of all variables of a pattern α.

A *substitution* is a morphism $\sigma : (\Sigma \cup X)^* \longrightarrow \Sigma^*$ such that $\sigma(a) = a$ for all $a \in \Sigma$. An *inverse substitution* is a morphism $\overline{\sigma} : \Sigma^* \longrightarrow X^*$. The *extended pattern language* of a pattern α is defined as

$$L_\Sigma(\alpha) := \{w \in \Sigma^* \mid \exists \sigma : \sigma(\alpha) = w\}.$$

If there is no need to give emphasis to the concrete shape of Σ we denote the extended pattern language of a pattern α simply as $L(\alpha)$. Each function $t : \mathbb{N} \longrightarrow \Sigma^*$ satisfying $\{t(n) \mid n \geq 0\} = L(\alpha)$ is called a *text* for $L(\alpha)$.

Following [Mit98] we designate a pattern α as *succinct* if and only if for all patterns β

$$L(\beta) = L(\alpha) \implies |\alpha| \leq |\beta|.$$

According to the studies of Mateescu and Salomaa ([MS94]) we denote a word w as *ambiguous* (in respect of a pattern α) if and only if there exist two substitutions σ and σ' such that $\sigma(x_i) \neq \sigma'(x_i)$ for some $x_i \in \text{var}(\alpha)$, but $\sigma(\alpha) = w = \sigma'(\alpha)$. We call a word *unambiguous* (in respect of a pattern α) if it is not ambiguous.

In [JSSY95] it is shown that the inclusion of two arbitrary extended pattern languages is not decidable. Fortunately this fact does not hold true for terminal-free extended pattern languages. As this is of great importance for the following studies we now cite a respective theorem of [JSSY95]:

Fact 1. *Let* $\alpha, \beta \in X^*$ *be two arbitrarily given terminal-free patterns. Then* $L(\beta) \subseteq L(\alpha)$ *if and only if there exists a morphism* $\phi : X^* \longrightarrow X^*$ *such that* $\phi(\alpha) = \beta$.

We investigate the identification of extended pattern languages in Gold's learning model (cf. [Gol67]), so we have to agree on the corresponding notions. Let S be any total computable function reading initial segments of texts and returning patterns. Each such function is called a *strategy*. If α is a pattern and t a text for $L(\alpha)$ we say that S *identifies* $L(\alpha)$ *from* t, iff the sequence of patterns returned by S, when reading t, converges to a pattern β, such that $L(\beta) = L(\alpha)$. Any set PAT* of extended pattern languages is *learnable in the limit* (or: *inferrable from positive data*) iff there is a strategy S identifying each language $L \in$ PAT* from any corresponding text.

The learnability characterization used in this paper originates from Angluin. In fact it combines Condition 1 and Theorem 1 of [Ang80]:

Fact 2. *An arbitrary subclass* PAT* *of extended pattern languages is inferrable from positive data iff there exists an effective procedure that enumerates for every pattern* α *with* $L(\alpha) \in$ PAT* *a set* T_α *such that*

- $T_\alpha \subseteq L(\alpha)$,
- T_α *is finite, and*
- $T_\alpha \not\subseteq L(\beta)$ *for all* $L(\beta) \in$ PAT* *with* $L(\beta) \subset L(\alpha)$.

T_α *is called a* telltale *(in respect of* α *and* PAT*).*

The second learnability criterion we will use also derives from Angluin (combining Condition 2, Condition 4 and Corollary 3 of [Ang80]):

Fact 3. *Let* PAT* *be an arbitrary subclass of extended pattern languages such that the inclusion problem for* PAT* *is decidable. Then* PAT* *is inferrable from positive data if there exists for every pattern* α *with* $L(\alpha) \in$ PAT* *a set* T_α *such that*

- $T_\alpha \subseteq L(\alpha)$,
- T_α *is finite, and*
- $T_\alpha \not\subseteq L(\beta)$ *for all* $L(\beta) \in$ PAT* *with* $L(\beta) \subset L(\alpha)$.

3   A Non-learnable Subclass of Extended Pattern Languages

In this section we will present a specific and simply structured extended pattern language that does not have a telltale. This fact entails the conclusion that the class of extended pattern languages is not learnable in the limit.

Our argumentation will lead to conflicting presumptions; on the one hand elements with such a feature seem to be quite frequent among the set of all patterns, on the other hand we will have to limit the used alphabet to exactly two letters, turning the examined class of languages into a rather peculiar one.

To begin with we will name a well known type of pattern that is as useful for our line of reasoning as it is inconvenient for the needs of inductive inference:

Definition 1 (Passe-partout). *Let α be a pattern and $W \subset L(\alpha)$ a finite set of words. Let β be a pattern, such that*

- *$W \subseteq L(\beta)$ and*
- *$L(\beta) \subset L(\alpha)$.*

We then say that β is a passe-partout (for α and W).

Note that if there exists a passe-partout for a pattern α and a set of words W, then W is not a telltale for $L(\alpha)$.

Now we will present the crucial lemma of this section:

Lemma 1. *Let $\Sigma = \{a, b\}$ be an alphabet and*

$$\alpha := x_1 x_1 \ x_2 x_2 \ x_3 x_3$$

a pattern. Then for any finite $W \subset L_\Sigma(\alpha)$ there exists a terminal-free passe-partout.

Proof. If W is empty the above statement is trivially true. Given an arbitrary non-empty $W = \{w_1, w_2, \cdots, w_n\} \subset L(\alpha)$, the following procedure constructs a passe-partout β:

As an inverse substitution we define for every w_i a morphism $\overline{\sigma}_i : \Sigma^* \longrightarrow X^*$ by

$$\overline{\sigma}_i(c) := \begin{cases} x_{2i-1} & , \quad c = a, \\ x_{2i} & , \quad c = b. \end{cases}$$

As $W \subset L(\alpha)$, for every w_i, $1 \leq i \leq n$, there exists a substitution σ_i satisfying $\sigma_i(\alpha) = w_i$. Constructing a set of $3n$ strings $\gamma_{i,k} \in X^*$ we now will identify the necessary elements of β.

Case (i) $\sigma_i(x_3) = v_1 \, \text{a} \, v_2$, $v_1, v_2 \in \{\text{b}\}^*$ $\wedge$ $\sigma_i(x_1), \sigma_i(x_2) \in \{\text{b}\}^*$ or
$\sigma_i(x_3) = v_1 \, \text{b} \, v_2$, $v_1, v_2 \in \{\text{a}\}^*$ $\wedge$ $\sigma_i(x_1), \sigma_i(x_2) \in \{\text{a}\}^*$.
Thus, $\sigma_i(x_3)$ contains a letter exactly once and w_i contains this letter exactly twice. In this case we define

$$\gamma_{i,1} := \overline{\sigma}_i \left(\sigma_i(x_1) \, \sigma_i(x_2) \right),$$
$$\gamma_{i,2} := \overline{\sigma}_i \left(\sigma_i(x_3) \right),$$
$$\gamma_{i,3} := e.$$

Note that in (i) w_i is ambiguous, so that the above definition provides a pattern $\gamma_i := \gamma_{i,1} \, \gamma_{i,1} \, \gamma_{i,2} \, \gamma_{i,2} \, \gamma_{i,3} \, \gamma_{i,3}$ with $w_i \in L(\gamma_i)$.

Case (ii) $\sigma_i(x_3)$ is empty or w_i contains every letter of $\sigma_i(x_3)$ at least four times.
In this case we simply define

$$\gamma_{i,k} := \overline{\sigma}_i \left(\sigma_i(x_k) \right), \ 1 \leq k \leq 3.$$

Obviously (ii) also provides a pattern $\gamma_i := \gamma_{i,1} \, \gamma_{i,1} \, \gamma_{i,2} \, \gamma_{i,2} \, \gamma_{i,3} \, \gamma_{i,3}$ with $w_i \in L(\gamma_i)$.

Combining the fragments of all γ_i in an appropriate manner we now compose the resulting pattern of the procedure:

$$\beta := \underbrace{\gamma_{1,1} \, \gamma_{2,1} \, \cdots \, \gamma_{n,1}}_{\sim x_1} \, \underbrace{\gamma_{1,1} \, \gamma_{2,1} \, \cdots \, \gamma_{n,1}}_{\sim x_1} \, \underbrace{\gamma_{1,2} \, \gamma_{2,2} \, \cdots \, \gamma_{n,2}}_{\sim x_2} \, \underbrace{\gamma_{1,2} \, \gamma_{2,2} \, \cdots \, \gamma_{n,2}}_{\sim x_2}$$
$$\underbrace{\gamma_{1,3} \, \gamma_{2,3} \, \cdots \, \gamma_{n,3}}_{\sim x_3} \, \underbrace{\gamma_{1,3} \, \gamma_{2,3} \, \cdots \, \gamma_{n,3}}_{\sim x_3} \cdot$$

In order to conclude the proof we now show that β indeed is a passe-partout for α and W:

1. We define a substitution $\sigma_i' : X^* \longrightarrow \Sigma^*$ by

$$\sigma_i'(x_j) := \begin{cases} \text{a} & , \quad j = 2i - 1, \\ \text{b} & , \quad j = 2i, \\ e & , \quad \text{else.} \end{cases}$$

Obviously $\sigma_i'(\beta) = w_i$, and thus $W \subseteq L(\beta)$.

2. α and β are both terminal-free patterns, and due to the above depicted shape of these patterns there exists a morphism $\phi : X^* \longrightarrow X^*$ with $\phi(\alpha) = \beta$. Thus, $L(\beta)$ is a subset of $L(\alpha)$ (according to the inclusion criterion in [JSSY95] described in Fact 1).
On the other hand there exists no morphism $\psi : X^* \longrightarrow X^*$ with $\psi(\beta) = \alpha$, as $\gamma_{i,3} \neq \delta_1 \, x_j \, \delta_2$, $1 \leq i \leq n$, if $x_j \notin \text{var}(\delta_k)$, $1 \leq k \leq 2$, and $x_j \notin \text{var}(\gamma_{i,l})$, $1 \leq l \leq 2$. Because of this fact

$$\beta \neq \cdots x_p \cdots x_p \cdots x_q \cdots x_q \cdots x_r \cdots x_r \cdots$$

if there are no other occurrences of at least one of these variables in β.
$\implies L(\beta) \subset L(\alpha)$ $\qquad\qquad\qquad\qquad\qquad\qquad\qquad\qquad\qquad\qquad$ $\square$

Obviously every variable of α occurs exactly twice. Ironically its language thus belongs to a class that – according to [Mit98] – is learnable in the limit. Nevertheless, the findings of Mitchell and Lemma 1 are consistent as β not necessarily is quasi-regular. Accordingly the quasi-regular pattern languages to some extent are not learnable on account of their shape as such but as they do not include all possible passe-partouts.

In addition we want to point out that ambiguity of words plays a major role in the proof of Lemma 1: a telltale for an extended pattern language has to include words with a substitution of variables containing a unique letter – as taken into consideration in case (i). If the alphabet consists of just two letters these specific words may turn out to be ambiguous, leading to a decisive loss of significance. We will revert to this aspect in the next section.

Referring to Angluin the impact of Lemma 1 on inductive inference can be stated with little effort:

Theorem 1. *The class of terminal-free extended pattern languages is not inferrable from positive data if the respective alphabet consists of exactly two letters.*

Proof. Let Σ be an alphabet, $|\Sigma| = 2$. Lemma 1 provides a terminal-free pattern α, such that for any finite set $W \subset L_\Sigma(\alpha)$ there exists a passe-partout. Therefore the class of terminal-free extended pattern languages does not satisfy Angluin's Condition 1, and according to Theorem 1 of [Ang80] it is not inferrable from positive data (as presented in Fact 2). □

Theorem 1 entails the finding, that all positive results on inductive inference of extended pattern languages cited in the introduction follow the only practicable course: any learnable (sub-)class of these languages has to be provided with some restrictions on the shape of the variables or the alphabet of terminal symbols.

Finally we now explicitly will formulate the trivial conclusion of Theorem 1:

Corollary 1. *The class of extended pattern languages is not inferrable from positive data if the respective alphabet consists of exactly two letters.*

As explained in section 2 we investigate in this paper the standard learning model of inductive inference regarding a class of languages as learnable if, roughly speaking, for every of its elements a syntactical convergence of hypotheses can be achieved. A second, widely analysed model – known as *behaviourally correct* learning or BC-learning – replaces this aspect by the weaker claim of a semantic convergence (cf. [CL82], [OW82] and concerning the inference of functions [Bar74]). According to [BCJ96] Angluin's Condition 2 (cf. [Ang80]) fully characterizes any BC-learnable class of languages. Hence it is obvious that the class of extended pattern languages (and that of terminal-free extended pattern languages as well) is not BC-learnable, either, since Lemma 1 presents a certain terminal-free extended pattern language for which there does not *exist* any telltale. In addition we want to point out that – due to the decidability of inclusion – every result in Gold's model concerning the learnability of terminal-free extended pattern languages directly can be interpreted as a statement on BC-learning.

4   The Importance of Unambiguous Words

As already mentioned above ambiguity of words is the core of the construction of a passe-partout in the proof of Lemma 1. In this section we will return to that point with a more general view.

Nondeterminism of pattern languages has been examined by Mateescu and Salomaa in [MS94]. Within the scope of learning theory however it seems to be useful to focus on a slightly different aspect of nondeterminism. Instead of searching for the maximum ambiguity of a pattern and its words we conjecture that it is beneficial to analyse the minimum ambiguity of the words of extended pattern languages. Being more precisely we suggest to pose the question, whether there exist certain unambiguous words in every terminal-free extended pattern language. This approach is inspired by the special needs of inductive inference concerning the analysis of subset relations of languages.

The following Theorem – providing a criterion for the learnability of terminal-free extended pattern languages – will specify our intention:

Theorem 2. *Let Σ be an alphabet. Let $\mathrm{Pat}^{\star}_{\mathrm{tf}}$ be a set of terminal-free patterns and $\mathrm{PAT}^{\star}_{\mathrm{tf}}$ the corresponding class of extended pattern languages. If for any $\alpha \in \mathrm{Pat}^{\star}_{\mathrm{tf}}$ there exists a finite set of substitutions $\{\sigma_1, \sigma_2, \cdots, \sigma_n\}$ such that*

1. for every i, $1 \leq i \leq n$, $\sigma_i(\alpha)$ is unambiguous in respect of α and
2. for every $x_j \in \mathrm{var}(\alpha)$ there exists an i, $1 \leq i \leq n$, and an $\mathbf{a} \in \Sigma$ such that $|\sigma_i(x_j)|_{\mathbf{a}} = 1$ and $|\sigma_i(\alpha)|_{\mathbf{a}} = |\alpha|_{x_j}$

then $\mathrm{PAT}^{\star}_{\mathrm{tf}}$ is inferrable from positive data.

Proof. Given $\alpha \in \mathrm{Pat}^{\star}_{\mathrm{tf}}$, we define a set T_α of words over Σ by

$$T_\alpha := \{w_i \mid 1 \leq i \leq n \ \wedge \ \sigma_i(\alpha) = w_i\}.$$

We now will show that T_α is a telltale for $L(\alpha)$ in respect of $\mathrm{PAT}^{\star}_{\mathrm{tf}}$. For that purpose assume $T_\alpha \subseteq L(\beta) \subseteq L(\alpha)$ for some $\beta \in \mathrm{Pat}^{\star}_{\mathrm{tf}}$. Then – according to the inclusion criterion of [JSSY95] described in Fact 1 – there exists a morphism

$\phi : X^* \longrightarrow X^*$ such that $\phi(\alpha) = \beta$. Moreover, there exists a second set of substitutions $\{\sigma'_1, \sigma'_2, \cdots, \sigma'_n\}$ with $\sigma'_i(\beta) = w_i$ for all i, $1 \le i \le n$. Consequently, the following diagram illustrates the relationship of α, β, and w_i for every i, $1 \le i \le n$:

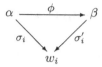

Hence it is obvious that

$$\sigma_i(x_j) = \sigma'_i(\phi(x_j)) \text{ for all } x_j \in \text{var}(\alpha) \text{ and } 1 \le i \le n$$

as every w_i is unambiguous in respect of α. Because of this fact (and because of condition 2) $\phi(x_j)$ must have the following shape:

$$\phi(x_j) = \gamma_1 \, x_{j'} \, \gamma_2 \text{ for all } x_j \in \text{var}(\alpha)$$

with $\gamma_1, \gamma_2 \in X^*$ and $|\beta|_{x_{j'}} = |\alpha|_{x_j}$. Thus, the morphism $\psi : X^* \longrightarrow X^*$ defined by

$$\psi(x_k) := \begin{cases} x_j & , \quad k = j', \\ e & , \quad \text{else} \end{cases}$$

leads to $\psi(\beta) = \alpha$ and – according to Fact 1 – $L(\beta) = L(\alpha)$. Consequently, $\text{PAT}^\star_{\text{tf}}$ satisfies the conditions of Fact 3 as T_α is a telltale for $L(\alpha)$ in respect of $\text{PAT}^\star_{\text{tf}}$.
$\Longrightarrow \text{PAT}^\star_{\text{tf}}$ is inferrable from positive data. $\square$

As a consequence of Theorem 2 of [MS94] – dealing with changing degrees of ambiguity of the same extended pattern language depending on the question of whether the respective pattern is succinct or not – we consider it as vital to restrict the search for unambiguous words on a set of succinct patterns. In addition we may see the results of the previous section as a hint that – depending on the concrete shape of the class of pattern languages to be examined – an alphabet of at least three letters is necessary in order to construct a set of unambiguous words.

The following example demonstrates the way how Theorem 2 might be used:

Example 1. Following Shinohara (cf. [Shi82b]) we define:

Definition 2 (Terminal-free non-cross patterns). *A pattern α is called a terminal-free non-cross pattern if and only if it satisfies*

$$\alpha = x_1^{e_1} \, x_2^{e_2} \, x_3^{e_3} \cdots x_n^{e_n}$$

for some n and numbers $e_1, e_2, \cdots, e_n$ with $n \ge 1$ and $e_i \ge 1$, $1 \le i \le n$.
We denote an extended pattern language $L(\alpha)$ as terminal-free extended non-cross pattern language if and only if α is a terminal-free non-cross pattern.

We state without proof that the class of terminal-free extended non-cross pattern languages is inferrable from positive data for any finite alphabet Σ with at least two letters. To this end let α be an arbitrarily chosen terminal-free non-cross pattern and $\{\mathsf{a},\mathsf{b}\} \subseteq \Sigma$. Given the substitution σ by

$$\sigma(x_j) := \mathsf{a}\,\mathsf{b}^j$$

the set T_α defined by

$$T_\alpha := \begin{cases} \{\mathsf{a}\} & , \quad \exists\, i : 1 \le i \le n \wedge e_i = 1, \\ \{\sigma(\alpha)\} & , \quad \text{else.} \end{cases}$$

is a telltale for α. Note that the absence of possible passe-partouts among the terminal-free non-cross patterns again is the *conditio sine qua non* for this conclusion. As – according to [Mit98] – the full class of extended pattern languages is learnable in the limit if the respective alphabet is infinite or consists of just one letter, the above statement implies the learnability of the class of terminal-free extended non-cross pattern languages for any alphabet.

For the purpose of this paper however our example looks different: Let again α be a terminal-free non-cross pattern and Σ a finite alphabet, $\{\mathsf{a},\mathsf{b},\mathsf{c}\} \subseteq \Sigma$. Then the set of substitutions $\{\sigma_1^{nc}, \sigma_2^{nc}, \cdots, \sigma_n^{nc}\}$ given by

$$\sigma_k^{nc}(x_j) := \begin{cases} \mathsf{b}^{f_j}\mathsf{b}^{f_j} & , \quad k \ne j \wedge j \text{ is odd,} \\ \mathsf{c}^{f_j}\mathsf{c}^{f_j} & , \quad k \ne j \wedge j \text{ is even,} \\ \mathsf{b}^{f_j}\,\mathsf{a}\,\mathsf{b}^{f_j} & , \quad k = j \wedge j \text{ is odd,} \\ \mathsf{c}^{f_j}\,\mathsf{a}\,\mathsf{c}^{f_j} & , \quad k = j \wedge j \text{ is even,} \end{cases}$$

$1 \le j \le n$ and $1 \le k \le n$, with

$$f_j := \begin{cases} 1 & , \quad j = 1, \\ \prod\limits_{i=1}^{j-1} e_i & , \quad j > 1 \end{cases}$$

satisfies the conditions of Theorem 2 if $L(\alpha) \ne L(x_1)$. The set $\{\mathsf{a}\}$ serves as a telltale for $L(x_1)$. Thus, choosing this approach leads to the conclusion that the class of terminal-free extended non-cross pattern languages is inferrable from positive data if Σ is finite and consists of at least three letters.

Consequently, in the present example Theorem 2 does not lead to an optimal result. Thus, we suggest to examine the use of Theorem 2 for those classes of terminal-free extended pattern languages that turn out to be not learnable in the limit if the corresponding alphabet consists of two letters, such as the full class of terminal-free extended pattern languages (cf. Theorem 1).

5 Diffuse Words

In Theorem 2 we use unambiguous words in order to guarantee fixed spheres of responsibility for every variable when generating a word. We now will present an – in a sense – weaker claim leading to a comparable result concerning the existence of a telltale in a terminal-free extended pattern language.

We will start with a precise explanation of the concept to be used:

Definition 3 (Diffuse). *Let α be a pattern, $|\alpha| := n$, and σ a substitution. If $m \leq n$ let $\alpha^m = x_{i_1} x_{i_2} \cdots x_{i_m}$ be the initial segment of length m of α. Let ϵ be the smallest natural number such that for every substitution σ' with $\sigma'(\alpha) = \sigma(\alpha)$ and for every m, $1 \leq m \leq n$,*

$$|\sigma(\alpha^m)| - \epsilon < |\sigma'(\alpha^m)| \leq |\sigma(\alpha^m)| + \epsilon.$$

If $|\sigma(x_i)| \geq 2\epsilon + 1$ for all $x_i \in \text{var}(\alpha)$ then we call the word $\sigma(\alpha)$ diffuse (of degree ϵ)(in respect of α).

Thus, a diffuse word contains certain letters that – regarding all possible substitutions – have to be generated by distinct variables. Note that all words being diffuse of degree 0 are unambiguous but not every unambiguous word necessarily has to be diffuse of degree 0 (because of the condition $|\sigma(x_i)| \geq 1$ for all x_i).

The following example illustrates Definition 3:

Example 2. We define a pattern α by

$$\alpha = x_1 \, x_2 \, x_3 \, x_4 \, x_1 \, x_4 \, x_3 \, x_2.$$

Obviously α is terminal-free and succinct. We examine the substitution σ given by

$$\sigma(x_1) := \text{baa}, \ \sigma(x_2) := \text{aba}, \ \sigma(x_3) := \text{bba}, \ \sigma(x_4) := \text{bbb}.$$

There exists only one different substitution σ' such that $\sigma'(\alpha) = \sigma(\alpha)$, σ' given by

$$\sigma'(x_1) = \text{ba}, \ \sigma'(x_2) = \text{aaba}, \ \sigma'(x_3) = \text{bb}, \ \sigma'(x_4) = \text{abbb}.$$

Taking a look at the resulting word of both substitutions

$$\sigma(\alpha)$$

| b | a | a | a | b | a | b | b | a | b | b | b | b | a | a | b | b | b | b | b | a | a | b | a |

| b | a | a | a | b | a | b | b | a | b | b | b | b | a | a | b | b | b | b | b | a | a | b | a |

$$\sigma'(\alpha)$$

it is obvious that $\sigma(\alpha)$ is diffuse of degree 1.

The learning criterion for terminal-free extended pattern languages based on diffuse words reads as follows:

Theorem 3. *Let Σ be an alphabet. Let $\mathrm{Pat}_{\mathrm{tf}}^\star$ be a set of terminal-free patterns and $\mathrm{PAT}_{\mathrm{tf}}^\star$ the corresponding class of extended pattern languages. If for every $\alpha \in \mathrm{Pat}_{\mathrm{tf}}^\star$ there exist natural numbers $\epsilon_1, \epsilon_2, \cdots, \epsilon_n \geq 0$ and a finite set of substitutions $\{\sigma_1, \sigma_2, \cdots, \sigma_n\}$ such that*

1. *for every i, $1 \leq i \leq n$, $\sigma_i(\alpha)$ is diffuse of degree ϵ_i in respect of α and*
2. *for every $x_j \in \mathrm{var}(\alpha)$ there exists an i, $1 \leq i \leq n$, such that*

$$\sigma_i(x_j) = v_{i_1}\, v_{i_2}\, \mathbf{a}\, v_{i_3}\, v_{i_4}$$

for a letter $\mathbf{a} \in \Sigma$ and some $v_{i_1}, v_{i_2}, v_{i_3}, v_{i_4} \in \Sigma^*$, $|v_{i_1}| = \epsilon_i = |v_{i_4}|$, such that $|\sigma_i(\alpha)|_{\mathbf{a}} = |\alpha|_{x_j}$

then $\mathrm{PAT}_{\mathrm{tf}}^\star$ is inferrable from positive data.

Proof. Given $\alpha \in \mathrm{Pat}_{\mathrm{tf}}^\star$, we define a set T_α of words over Σ by

$$T_\alpha := \{w_i \mid 1 \leq i \leq n \wedge \sigma_i(\alpha) = w_i\}.$$

We now will show that T_α is a telltale for $L(\alpha)$ in respect of $\mathrm{PAT}_{\mathrm{tf}}^\star$. For that purpose assume $T_\alpha \subseteq L(\beta) \subseteq L(\alpha)$ for some $\beta \in \mathrm{Pat}_{\mathrm{tf}}^\star$. Then – according to Fact 1 – there exists a morphism $\phi : X^* \longrightarrow X^*$ such that $\phi(\alpha) = \beta$. Moreover, there exists a second set of substitutions $\{\sigma_1', \sigma_2', \cdots, \sigma_n'\}$ with $\sigma_i'(\beta) = w_i$ for all i, $1 \leq i \leq n$.

Because every w_i, $1 \leq i \leq n$, is diffuse in respect of α and because of condition 2 we may conclude that for every $x_j \in \mathrm{var}(\alpha)$ there exists a σ_i' such that

$$\sigma_i'(\phi(x_j)) = u_1\, v_{i_2}\, \mathbf{a}\, v_{i_3}\, u_2$$

for a letter $\mathbf{a} \in \Sigma$, some words $u_1, u_2 \in \Sigma^*$ and v_{i_2}, v_{i_3} deriving from $\sigma_i(x_j)$. In addition it is obvious that $|\sigma_i'(\beta)|_{\mathbf{a}} = |\alpha|_{x_j}$ can be stated for this σ_i'. Therefore – like in the proof of Theorem 2 – ϕ must have the shape

$$\phi(x_j) = \gamma_1\, x_{j'}\, \gamma_2 \text{ for all } x_j \in \mathrm{var}(\alpha)$$

with $\gamma_1, \gamma_2 \in X^*$ and $|\beta|_{x_{j'}} = |\alpha|_{x_j}$. Thus, the morphism $\psi : X^* \longrightarrow X^*$ defined by

$$\psi(x_k) := \begin{cases} x_j & , \quad k = j', \\ e & , \quad \text{else} \end{cases}$$

leads to $\psi(\beta) = \alpha$ and $L(\beta) = L(\alpha)$. Consequently, $\mathrm{PAT}_{\mathrm{tf}}^\star$ satisfies the conditions of Fact 3 as T_α is a telltale for $L(\alpha)$ in respect of $\mathrm{PAT}_{\mathrm{tf}}^\star$.
$\Longrightarrow \mathrm{PAT}_{\mathrm{tf}}^\star$ is inferrable from positive data. $\qquad\qquad\Box$

Note that Example 1 is valid for Theorem 3 as well, since all of the words generated by the given substitutions are diffuse of degree 0 in respect of any terminal-free non-cross pattern. Additionally, we generally suggest to restrict the search for substitutions satisfying the conditions of Theorem 3 on succinct patterns and an alphabet of at least three letters.

6   Concluding Remarks

Since we focus in the present paper on terminal-free patterns it seems worth mentioning that many aspects of the previous two sections may also be expressed using the terms of Post's correspondence problem (as it is revealed by Example 2).

Finally we presume that for every succinct terminal-free pattern there exists a set of substitutions satisfying the conditions of Theorem 2 (or Theorem 3, respectively), if the corresponding alphabet consists of at least three letters. Thus, we conjecture (referring to Theorem 1 and the results from [Mit98]) that the class of terminal-free extended pattern languages is inferrable from positive data if and only if the respective alphabet does not consist of exactly two letters.

Acknowledgements. The results of this paper are part of a diploma thesis at the University of Kaiserslautern. The author wishes to thank Sandra Zilles for her extraordinary support, Jochen Nessel for some useful hints, and Rolf Wiehagen for his inspiring introduction to inductive inference and continuous advice.

References

[Ang79]   D. Angluin. Finding patterns common to a set of strings. In *Proceedings, 11th Annual ACM Symposium on Theory of Computing*, pages 130–141, 1979.

[Ang80]   D. Angluin. Inductive inference of formal languages from positive data. *Information and Control*, 45:117–135, 1980.

[Bar74]   J. Barzdin. Two theorems on the limiting synthesis of functions. *Theory of Algorithms and Programs, Latvian State University, Riga*, 210:82–88, 1974.

[BCJ96]   G.R. Baliga, J. Case, and S. Jain. Synthesizing enumeration techniques for language learning. In *Proceedings of the Ninth Annual Conference on Computational Learning Theory*, pages 169–180, 1996.

[BCJ99]   G.R. Baliga, J. Case, and S. Jain. The synthesis of language learners. *Information and Computation*, 152:16–43, 1999.

[CL82]   J. Case and L. Lynes. Machine inductive inference and language identification. In *Lecture Notes in Computer Science*, volume 140, pages 107–115. Proceedings of the 9th International Colloquium on Automata, Languages and Programming, 1982.

[Gol67]   E.M. Gold. Language identification in the limit. *Information and Control*, 10:447–474, 1967.

[JKS+94]   T. Jiang, E. Kinber, A. Salomaa, K. Salomaa, and S. Yu. Pattern languages with and without erasing. *Intern. J. Computer Math.*, 50:147–163, 1994.

[JSSY95]   T. Jiang, A. Salomaa, K. Salomaa, and S. Yu. Decision problems for patterns. *Journal of Computer and System Science*, 50:53–63, 1995.

[LW91]   S. Lange and R. Wiehagen. Polynomial-time inference of arbitrary pattern languages. *New Generation Computing*, 8:361–370, 1991.

[Mit98]   A.R. Mitchell. Learnability of a subclass of extended pattern languages. In *Proceedings of the Eleventh Annual Conference on Computational Learning Theory*, pages 64–71, 1998.

[MS94]   A. Mateescu and A. Salomaa. Nondeterminism in patterns. In *Lecture Notes in Computer Science*, volume 775, pages 661–668. STACS 94, 11th Annual Symposium on Theoretical Aspects of Computer Science, 1994.

[OW82]   D. Osherson and S. Weinstein. Criteria of language learning. *Information and Control*, 52:123–138, 1982.

[Rog92]   H. Rogers. *Theory of Recursive Functions and Effective Computability*. MIT Press, 1992. 3. print.

[Shi82a]   T. Shinohara. Polynomial time inference of extended regular pattern languages. In *Lecture Notes in Computer Science*, volume 147, pages 115–127. RIMS Symposia on Software Science and Engineering, Proceedings, Kyoto, 1982.

[Shi82b]   T. Shinohara. Polynomial time inference of pattern languages and its application. In *Proceedings of the 7th IBM Symposium on Mathematical Foundations of Computer Science*, pages 191–209, 1982.

[Wri89]   K. Wright. Identification of unions of languages drawn from an identifiable class. In *Proceedings of the Second Annual Workshop on Computational Learning Theory*, pages 328–333, 1989.

[WZ94]   R. Wiehagen and T. Zeugmann. Ignoring data may be the only way to learn efficiently. *Journal of Experimental and Theoretical Artificial Intelligence*, 6:131–144, 1994.

RBF Neural Networks and Descartes' Rule of Signs*

Michael Schmitt

Lehrstuhl Mathematik und Informatik, Fakultät für Mathematik
Ruhr-Universität Bochum, D–44780 Bochum, Germany
www.ruhr-uni-bochum.de/lmi/mschmitt/
mschmitt@lmi.ruhr-uni-bochum.de

Abstract. We establish versions of Descartes' rule of signs for radial basis function (RBF) neural networks. These RBF rules of signs provide tight bounds for the number of zeros of univariate networks with certain parameter restrictions. Moreover, they can be used to derive tight bounds for the Vapnik-Chervonenkis (VC) dimension and pseudo-dimension of these networks. In particular, we show that these dimensions are no more than linear. This result contrasts with previous work showing that RBF neural networks with two and more input nodes have superlinear VC dimension. The rules give rise also to lower bounds for network sizes, thus demonstrating the relevance of network parameters for the complexity of computing with RBF neural networks.

1 Introduction

First published in 1637, Descartes' rule of signs is an astoundingly simple and yet powerful method to estimate the number of zeros of a univariate polynomial [6,22]. Precisely, the rule states that the number of positive zeros of every real univariate polynomial is equal to the number of changes of sign occurring in the sequence of its coefficients, or is less than this number by a multiple of two (see, e.g., [9]).

In this contribution we show that versions of Descartes' rule of signs can be established for radial basis function (RBF) neural networks. We focus on networks with standard, that is, Gaussian hidden units with parameters satisfying certain conditions. In particular, we formulate RBF rules of signs for networks with uniform widths, that is, where each hidden unit has the same width. In the strongest version, the RBF rules of signs yield that for every univariate function computed by these networks, the number of zeros is not larger than the number of changes of sign occurring in a specific sequence of the output weights. A similar rule is stated for networks with uniform centers. We further show that the bounds given by these rules are tight, a fact that has recently been established

---

* This work has been supported in part by the ESPRIT Working Group in Neural and Computational Learning II, NeuroCOLT2, No. 27150.

N. Cesa-Bianchi et al. (Eds.): ALT 2002, LNAI 2533, pp. 321–335, 2002.

also for the original Descartes' rule [1,8]. The RBF rules of signs are presented in Section 2.

Furthermore, we employ the rules to derive bounds on the Vapnik-Chervonenkis (VC) dimension and the pseudo-dimension of RBF neural networks. These dimensions measure the diversity of a function class and are fundamental concepts studied in theories of learning and generalization (see, e.g., [3]). The pseudo-dimension has also applications in approximation theory [7,14]. We show that the VC dimension and the pseudo-dimension of RBF neural networks with a single input node and uniform widths is no more than linear in the number of parameters. The same fact holds for networks with uniform centers. These results nicely contrast with previous work showing that these dimensions grow superlinearly for RBF neural networks with more than one input node and at least two different width values [20,21]. In particular, the bound established in that work is $\Omega(W \log k)$, where W is the number of parameters and k the number of hidden units. Further, for networks with a single input variable, the linear upper bound improves a result of Bartlett and Williamson [4] who have shown that Gaussian RBF neural networks restricted to discrete inputs from $\{-D, \ldots, D\}$ have VC dimension and pseudo-dimension bounded by $O(W \log(WD))$. Moreover, the linear bounds are tight and considerably smaller than the bound $O(W^2 k^2)$ known for Gaussian RBF neural networks with an unrestricted number of layers [10]. We establish the linear bounds on the VC dimension and the pseudo-dimension in Section 3.

The computational power of neural networks is a well recognized and frequently studied phenomenon. Not so well understood, however, is the question how large a network must be to be capable of performing a desired task. The rules of signs and the VC dimension bounds provided here give partly rise to answers in terms of lower bounds on the size of RBF networks. These bounds cast light on the relevance of network parameters for the complexity of computing with networks having uniform widths. In particular, we show that a network with zero bias must be more than twice as large to be as powerful as a network with variable bias. Further, to have the capabilities of a network with nonuniform widths, it must be larger in size by a factor of nearly two. The latter result is of particular significance since, as shown by Park and Sandberg [17], the universal approximation capabilities of RBF networks hold even for networks with uniform widths (see also [18]). The bounds for the complexity of computing are derived in Section 4.

The results presented here are concerned with networks having a single input node. Networks of this type are not, and have never been, of minor importance. This is evident from the numerous simulation experiments that have been performed to assess the capabilities of neural networks for approximating univariate functions. For instance, Broomhead and Lowe [5], Moody and Darken [16], Mel and Omohundro [15], Wang and Zhu [23], or Li and Leiss [13] have done such studies using RBF networks. Moreover, the largest known lower bound for the VC dimension of neural networks, being quadratic in the number of parameters, holds, among others, for univariate networks [12]. Thus, the RBF rules of signs provide new insights for a neural network class that is indeed relevant in theory and practice.

2   Rules of Signs for RBF Neural Networks

We consider a type of RBF neural network known as Gaussian or standard RBF neural network.

Definition 1. *A radial basis function (RBF) neural network computes functions over the reals of the form*

$$w_0 + w_1 \exp\left(-\frac{\|x - c_1\|^2}{\sigma_1^2}\right) + \cdots + w_k \exp\left(-\frac{\|x - c_k\|^2}{\sigma_k^2}\right) ,$$

where $\|\cdot\|$ denotes the Euclidean norm. Each exponential term corresponds to a hidden unit with center c_i and width σ_i, respectively. The input nodes are represented by x, and $w_0, \ldots, w_k$ denote the output weights of the network. Centers, widths, and ouptut weights are the network parameters. The network is said to have uniform widths if $\sigma_1 = \cdots = \sigma_k$ is satisfied; it has uniform centers if $c_1 = \cdots = c_k$ holds. The parameter w_0 is also referred to as the bias or threshold of the network.

Note that the output weights and the widths are scalar parameters, whereas the input x and the centers are tuples if the network has more than one input node. Throughout this paper, all functions have a single input variable unless indicated otherwise.

Definition 2. *Given a finite sequence $w_1, \ldots, w_k$ of real numbers, a change of sign occurs at position j if there is some $i < j$ such that the conditions*

$$w_i w_j < 0$$

and

$$w_l = 0 \quad for \ i < l < j ,$$

are satisfied.

Thus we can refer to the number of changes of sign of a sequence as a well defined quantity.

2.1   Uniform Widths

We first focus on networks with zero bias and show that the number of zeros of a function computed by an RBF network with uniform widths does not exceed the number of changes of sign occurring in a sequence of its output weights. Moreover, the difference of the two quantities is always even. Thus, we obtain for RBF networks a precise rephrasing of Descartes' rule of signs for polynomials (see, e.g., [9, Theorem 6.2d]). We call it the strong RBF rule of signs. In contrast to Descartes' rule, the RBF rule is not confined to the strictly positive numbers, but valid for whole real domain. Its derivation generalizes Laguerre's proof of Descartes' rule [19, Part V, Chapter 1, No. 77].

Theorem 3 (Strong RBF Rule of Signs for Uniform Widths). *Consider a function* $f : \mathbb{R} \to \mathbb{R}$ *computed by an RBF neural network with zero bias and* k *hidden units having uniform width. Assume that the centers be ordered such that* $c_1 \leq \cdots \leq c_k$ *and let* $w_1, \ldots, w_k$ *denote the associated output weights. Let* s *be the number of changes of sign of the sequence* $w_1, \ldots, w_k$ *and* z *the number of zeros of* f. *Then* $s - z$ *is even and nonnegative.*

Proof. Without loss of generality, let k be the smallest number of RBF units required for computing f. Then we have $w_i \neq 0$ for $1 \leq i \leq k$, and due to the equality of the widths, $c_1 < \cdots < c_k$. We first show by induction on s that $z \leq s$ holds.

Obviously, if $s = 0$ then f has no zeros. Let $s > 0$ and assume the statement is valid for $s-1$ changes of sign. Suppose that there is a change of sign at position i. As a consequence of the assumptions above, $w_{i-1} w_i < 0$ holds and there is some real number b satisfying $c_{i-1} < b < c_i$. Clearly, f has the same number of zeros as the function g defined by

$$g(x) = \exp\left(\frac{x^2 - 2bx}{\sigma^2}\right) \cdot f(x) \ ,$$

where σ is the common width of the hidden units in the network computing f. According to Rolle's theorem, the derivative g' of g must have at least $z - 1$ zeros. Then, the function h defined as

$$h(x) = \exp\left(-\frac{x^2 - 2bx}{\sigma^2}\right) \cdot g'(x)$$

has at least $z - 1$ zeros as well. We can write this function as

$$h(x) = \sum_{\lambda=1}^{k} w_\lambda \frac{2(c_\lambda - b)}{\sigma^2} \exp\left(-\frac{(x - c_\lambda)^2}{\sigma^2}\right) \ .$$

Hence, h is computed by an RBF network with zero bias and k hidden units having width σ and centers $c_1, \ldots, c_k$. Since b satisfies $c_{i-1} < b < c_i$ and the sequence $w_1, \ldots, w_k$ has a change of sign at position i, there is no change of sign at position i in the sequence of the output weights

$$w_1 \frac{2(c_1 - b)}{\sigma^2}, \ldots, w_{i-1} \frac{2(c_{i-1} - b)}{\sigma^2}, w_i \frac{2(c_i - b)}{\sigma^2}, \ldots, w_k \frac{2(c_k - b)}{\sigma^2} \ .$$

At positions different from i, there is a change of sign if and only if the sequence $w_1, \ldots, w_k$ has a change of sign at this position. Hence, the number of changes of sign in the output weights for h is equal to $s - 1$. By the induction hypothesis, h has at most $s - 1$ zeros. As we have argued above, h has at least $z - 1$ zeros. This yields $z \leq s$, completing the induction step.

It remains to show that $s - z$ is even. For $x \to +\infty$, the term

$$w_k \exp\left(-\frac{(x - c_k)^2}{\sigma^2}\right)$$

becomes in absolute value larger than the sum of the remaining terms so that its sign determines the sign of f. Similarly, for $x \to -\infty$ the behavior of f is governed by the term

$$w_1 \exp\left(-\frac{(x - c_1)^2}{\sigma^2}\right) .$$

Thus, the number of zeros of f is even if and only if both terms have the same sign. And this holds if and only if the number of sign changes in the sequence $w_1, \ldots, w_k$ is even. This proves the statement.   □

The above result establishes the number of sign changes as upper bound for the number of zeros. It is easy to see that this bound cannot be improved. If the width is sufficiently small or the intervals between the centers are sufficiently large, the sign of the output of the network at some center c_i is equal to the sign of w_i. Thus we can enforce a zero between any pair of adjacent centers c_{i-1}, c_i through $w_{i-1} w_i < 0$.

Corollary 4. *The parameters of every univariate RBF neural network can be chosen such that all widths are the same and the number of changes of sign in the sequence of the output weights $w_1, \ldots, w_k$, ordered according to $c_1 \leq \cdots \leq c_k$, is equal to the number of zeros of the function computed by the network.*

Next, we consider networks with freely selectable bias. The following result is the main step in deriving a bound on the number of zeros for these networks. It deals with a more general network class where the bias can be an arbitrary polynomial.

Theorem 5. *Suppose $p : \mathbb{R} \to \mathbb{R}$ is a polynomial of degree l and $g : \mathbb{R} \to \mathbb{R}$ is computed by an RBF neural network with zero bias and k hidden units having uniform width. Then the function $p + g$ has at most $l + 2k$ zeros.*

Proof. We perform induction on k. For the sake of formal simplicity, we say that the all-zero function is the (only) function computed by the network with zero hidden units. Then for $k = 0$ the function $p + g$ is a polynomial of degree l that, by the fundamental theorem of algebra, has no more than l zeros.

Now, let g be computed by an RBF network with $k > 0$ hidden units, so that $p + g$ can be written as

$$p + \sum_{i=1}^{k} w_i \exp\left(-\frac{(x - c_i)^2}{\sigma^2}\right) .$$

Let z denote the number of zeros of this function. Multiplying with $\exp((x - c_k)^2/\sigma^2)$, we obtain the function

$$\exp\left(\frac{(x-c_k)^2}{\sigma^2}\right) p + w_k + \sum_{i=1}^{k-1} w_i \exp\left(-\frac{(x-c_i)^2 - (x-c_k)^2}{\sigma^2}\right)$$

that must have z zeros as well. Differentiating this function with respect to x yields

$$\exp\left(\frac{(x-c_k)^2}{\sigma^2}\right)\left(\frac{2(x-c_k)}{\sigma^2}p + p'\right)$$

$$+ \sum_{i=1}^{k-1} w_i \frac{2(c_i - c_k)}{\sigma^2} \exp\left(-\frac{(x-c_i)^2 - (x-c_k)^2}{\sigma^2}\right) ,$$

which, according to Rolle's theorem, must have at least $z - 1$ zeros. Again, multiplication with $\exp(-(x - c_k)^2/\sigma^2)$ leaves the number of zeros unchanged and we get with

$$\frac{2(x-c_k)}{\sigma^2}p + p' + \sum_{i=1}^{k-1} w_i \frac{2(c_i - c_k)}{\sigma^2} \exp\left(-\frac{(x-c_i)^2}{\sigma^2}\right)$$

a function of the form $q + h$, where q is a polynomial of degree $l + 1$ and h is computed by an RBF network with zero bias and $k - 1$ hidden units having uniform width. By the induction hypothesis, $q + h$ has at most $l + 1 + 2(k - 1) = l + 2k - 1$ zeros. Since $z - 1$ is a lower bound, it follows that $z \le l + 2k$ as claimed. □

From this we immediately have a bound for the number of zeros for RBF networks with nonzero bias. We call this fact the weak RBF rule of signs. In contrast to the strong rule, the bound is not in terms of the number of sign changes but in terms of the number of hidden units. The naming, however, is justified since the proofs for both rules are very similar. As for the strong rule, the bound of the weak rule cannot be improved.

Corollary 6 (Weak RBF Rule of Signs for Uniform Widths). *Let function $f : \mathbb{R} \to \mathbb{R}$ be computed by an RBF neural network with arbitrary bias and k hidden units having uniform width. Then f has at most $2k$ zeros. Furthermore, this bound is tight.*

Proof. The upper bound follows from Theorem 5 since $l = 0$. The lower bound is obtained using a network that has a negative bias and all other output weights positive. For instance, -1 for the bias and 2 for the weights are suitable. An example for $k = 3$ is displayed in Figure 1. For sufficiently small widths and large intervals between the centers, the output value is close to 1 for inputs close to a center and approaches -1 between the centers and toward $+\infty$ and $-\infty$. Thus, each hidden unit gives rise to two zeros. □

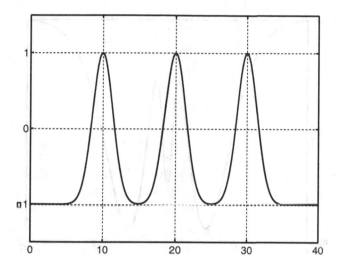

Fig. 1. Optimality of the weak RBF rule of signs for uniform widths: A function having twice as many zeros as hidden units

The function in Figure 1 has only one change of sign: The bias is negative, all other weights are positive. Consequently, we realize that a strong rule of signs does not hold for networks with nonzero bias.

2.2 Uniform Centers

We now establish a rule of signs for networks with uniform centers. Here, in contrast to the rules for uniform widths, the bias plays a role in determining the number of sign changes.

Theorem 7 (RBF Rule of Signs for Uniform Centers). *Suppose $f : \mathbb{R} \to \mathbb{R}$ is computed by an RBF neural network with arbitrary bias and k hidden units having uniform centers. Assume the ordering $\sigma_1^2 \leq \cdots \leq \sigma_k^2$ and let s denote the number of sign changes of the sequence $w_0, w_1, \ldots, w_k$. Then f has at most $2s$ zeros.*

Proof. Given f as supposed, consider the function g obtained by introducing the new variable $y = (x - c)^2$, where c is the common center. Then

$$g(y) = w_0 + w_1 \exp(-\sigma_1^{-2} y) + \cdots + w_k \exp(-\sigma_k^{-2} y) \ .$$

Let z be the number of zeros of g and s the number of sign changes of the sequence $w_0, w_1, \ldots, w_k$. Similarly as in Theorem 3, we deduce $z \leq s$ by induction on s.

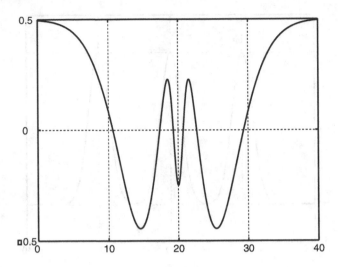

Fig. 2. Optimality of the RBF rule of signs for uniform centers: A function having twice as many zeros as sign changes

Assume there is a change of sign at position i and let b satisfy $\sigma_{i-1}^{-2} < b < \sigma_i^{-2}$. (Without loss of generality, the widths are all different.) By Rolle's theorem, the derivative of the function $\exp(by) \cdot g(y)$ has at least $z - 1$ zeros. Multiplying this derivative with $\exp(-by)$ yields

$$w_0 b + w_1(b - \sigma_1^{-2})\exp(-\sigma_1^{-2}y) + \cdots + w_k(b - \sigma_k^{-2})\exp(-\sigma_k^{-2}y)$$

with at least $z - 1$ zeros. Moreover, this function has at most $s - 1$ sign changes. (Note that $b > 0$.) This completes the induction.

Now, each zero $y \neq 0$ of g gives rise to exactly two zeros $x = c \pm \sqrt{y}$ for f. (By definition, $y \geq 0$.) Further, $g(0) = 0$ if and only if $f(c) = 0$. Thus, f has at most $2s$ zeros. $\qquad\square$

That the bound is optimal can be seen from Figure 2 showing a function having three hidden units with center 20, widths $\sigma_1 = 1, \sigma_2 = 4, \sigma_3 = 8$, and output weights $w_0 = 1/2, w_1 = -3/4, w_2 = 2, w_3 = -2$. The example can easily be generalized to any number of hidden units.

3   Linear Bounds for VC Dimension and Pseudo-Dimension

We apply the RBF rules of signs to obtain bounds for the VC dimension and the pseudo-dimension that are linear in the number of hidden units. First, we give the definitions.

A set S is said to be shattered by a class $\mathcal{F}$ of $\{0,1\}$-valued functions if for every dichotomy (S_0, S_1) of S (where $S_0 \cup S_1 = S$ and $S_0 \cap S_1 = \emptyset$) there is some $f \in \mathcal{F}$ such that $f(S_0) \subseteq \{0\}$ and $f(S_1) \subseteq \{1\}$. Let $\mathrm{sgn} : \mathbb{R} \to \{0,1\}$ denote the function satisfying $\mathrm{sgn}(x) = 1$ if $x \geq 0$, and $\mathrm{sgn}(x) = 0$ otherwise.

Definition 8. *Given a class $\mathcal{G}$ of real-valued functions, the VC dimension of $\mathcal{G}$ is the largest integer m such that there exists a set S of cardinality m that is shattered by the class $\{\mathrm{sgn} \circ g : g \in \mathcal{G}\}$. The pseudo-dimension of $\mathcal{G}$ is the VC dimension of the class $\{(x,y) \mapsto g(x) - y : g \in \mathcal{G}\}$.*

We extend this definition to neural networks in the obvious way: The VC dimension of a neural network is defined as the VC dimension of the class of functions computed by the network (obtained by assigning all possible values to its parameters); analogously for the pseudo-dimension. It is evident that the VC dimension of a neural network is not larger than its pseudo-dimension.

3.1   Uniform Widths

The RBF rules of signs give rise to the following VC dimension bounds.

Theorem 9. *The VC dimension of every univariate RBF neural network with k hidden units, variable but uniform widths, and zero bias does not exceed k. For variable bias, the VC dimension is at most $2k + 1$.*

Proof. Let $S = \{x_1, \dots, x_m\}$ be shattered by an RBF neural network with k hidden units. Assume that $x_1 < \cdots < x_m$ and consider the dichotomy (S_0, S_1) defined as

$$x_i \in S_0 \iff i \text{ even} \ .$$

Let f be the function of the network that implements this dichotomy. We want to avoid that $f(x_i) = 0$ for some i. This is the case only if $x_i \in S_1$. Since $f(x_i) < 0$ for all $x_i \in S_0$, we can slightly adjust some output weight such that the resulting function g of the network still induces the dichotomy (S_0, S_1) but does not yield zero on any element of S. Clearly, g must have a zero between x_i and x_{i+1} for every $1 \leq i \leq m - 1$. If the bias is zero then, by Theorem 3, g has at most $k - 1$ zeros. This implies $m \leq k$. From Corollary 6 we have $m \leq 2k + 1$ for nonzero bias. $\square$

As a consequence of this result, we now know the VC dimension of univariate uniform-width RBF neural networks exactly. In particular, we observe that the use of a bias more than doubles their VC dimension.

Corollary 10. *The VC dimension of every univariate RBF neural network with k hidden units and variable but uniform widths equals k if the bias is zero, and $2k + 1$ if the bias is variable.*

Proof. Theorem 9 has shown that k and $2k + 1$ are upper bounds, respectively. The lower bound k for zero bias is implied by Corollary 4. For nonzero bias, consider a set S with $2k + 1$ elements and a dichotomy (S_0, S_1). If $|S_1| \leq k$, we put a hidden unit with positive output weight over each element of S_1 and let the bias be negative. Figure 1, for instance, implements the dichotomy $(\{5, 15, 25, 35\}, \{10, 20, 30\})$. If $|S_0| \leq k$, we proceed the other way round with negative output weights and a positive bias. $\qquad\qquad\square$

It is easy to see that the result holds also if the widths are fixed. This observation is helpful in the following where we address the pseudo-dimension and establish linear bounds for networks with uniform and fixed widths.

Theorem 11. *Consider a univariate RBF neural network with k hidden units having the same fixed width. For zero bias, the pseudo-dimension d of the network satisfies $k \leq d \leq 2k$; if the bias is variable then $2k + 1 \leq d \leq 4k + 1$.*

Proof. The lower bounds follow from the fact that the VC dimension is a lower bound for the pseudo-dimension and that Corollary 10 is also valid for fixed widths. For the upper bound we use an idea that has been previously employed by Karpinski and Werther [11] and Andrianov [2] to obtain pseudo-dimension bounds in terms of zeros of functions. Let $\mathcal{F}_{k,\sigma}$ denote the class of functions computed by the network with k hidden units and width σ. Assume the set $S = \{(x_1, y_1), \ldots, (x_m, y_m)\} \subseteq \mathbb{R}^2$ is shattered by the class

$$\{(x, y) \mapsto \mathrm{sgn}(f(x) - y) : f \in \mathcal{F}_{k,\sigma}\} .$$

Let $x_1 < \cdots < x_m$ and consider the dichotomy (S_0, S_1) defined as

$$(x_i, y_i) \in S_0 \iff i \text{ even} .$$

Since S is shattered, there exist functions $f_1, f_2 \in \mathcal{F}_{k,\sigma}$ that implement the dichotomies (S_0, S_1) and (S_1, S_0), respectively. That is, we have for $i = 1, \ldots, m$

$$f_2(x_i) \geq y_i > f_1(x_i) \iff i \text{ even} ,$$

$$f_1(x_i) \geq y_i > f_2(x_i) \iff i \text{ odd} .$$

This implies

$$(f_1(x_i) - f_2(x_i)) \cdot (f_1(x_{i+1}) - f_2(x_{i+1})) < 0$$

for $i = 1, \ldots, m - 1$. Therefore, $f_1 - f_2$ must have at least $m - 1$ zeros. On the other hand, since $f_1, f_2 \in \mathcal{F}_{k,\sigma}$, the function $f_1 - f_2$ can be computed by an RBF network with $2k$ hidden units having equal width. Considering networks with zero bias, it follows from the strong RBF rule of signs (Theorem 3) that $f_1 - f_2$ has at most $2k - 1$ zeros. For variable bias, the weak rule of signs (Corollary 6) bounds the number of zeros by $4k$. This yields $m \leq 2k$ for zero and $m \leq 4k + 1$ for variable bias. $\qquad\qquad\square$

3.2   Uniform Centers

Finally, we state the linear VC dimension and pseudo-dimension bounds for networks with uniform centers.

Corollary 12. *The VC dimension of every univariate RBF neural network with k hidden units and variable but uniform centers is at most $2k + 1$. For networks with uniform and fixed centers, the pseudo-dimension is at most $4k + 1$.*

Proof. Using the RBF rule of signs for uniform centers (Theorem 7), the VC dimension bound is derived following the proof of Theorem 9, the bound for the pseudo-dimension is obtained as in Theorem 11.   □

Employing techniques from Corollary 10, it is not hard to derive that k is a lower bound for the VC dimension of these networks and, hence, also for the pseudo-dimension.

4   Computational Capabilities

In this section we demonstrate how the above results can be used to derive lower bounds on the size of networks required for simulating other networks that have more parameters. We focus on networks with uniform widths. Lower bounds for networks with uniform centers can be obtained analogously.

We know from Corollary 10 that introducing a variable bias increases the VC dimension of uniform-width RBF networks by a factor of more than two. As an immediate consequence, we have a lower bound on the size of networks with zero bias for simulating networks with nonzero bias. It is evident that a network with zero bias cannot simulate a network with nonzero bias on the entire real domain. The question makes sense, however, if the inputs are restricted to a compact subset, as done in statements about uniform approximation capabilities of neural networks.

Corollary 13. *Every univariate RBF neural network with variable bias and k hidden units requires at least $2k + 1$ hidden units to be simulated by a network with zero bias and uniform widths.*

In the following we show that the number of zeros of functions computed by networks with zero bias and nonuniform widths need not be bounded by the number of sign changes. Thus, the strong RBF rule of signs does not hold for these networks.

Lemma 14. *For every $k \geq 2$ there is a function $f_k : \mathbb{R} \to \mathbb{R}$ that has at least $2k - 2$ zeros and can be computed by an RBF neural network with zero bias, k hidden units and two different width values.*

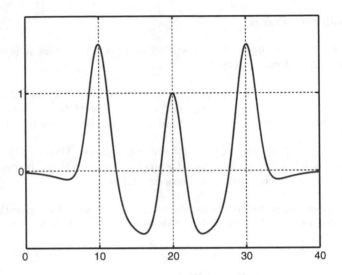

Fig. 3. Function f_4 of Lemma 14 has six zeros and is computed by an RBF network with four hidden units using two different widths

Proof. Consider the function

$$f_k(x) = w_1 \exp\left(\frac{(x - c_1)^2}{\sigma_1^2}\right) + \sum_{i=2}^{k} w_i \exp\left(\frac{(x - c_i)^2}{\sigma_2^2}\right) .$$

Clearly, it is computed by a network with zero bias and k hidden units having widths σ_1 and σ_2. It can also immediately be seen that the parameters can be instantiated such that f_k has at least $2k - 2$ zeros. An example for $k = 4$ is shown in Figure 3. It arises from a network with three positive units by adding a negative unit with large width simulating a bias, such that the baseline is pulled into the negative domain. Precisely, the centers are $c_1 = 20, c_2 = 10, c_3 = 20, c_4 = 30$, the widths are $\sigma_1 = 10, \sigma_2 = 2$, and the output weights are $w_1 = -1, w_2 = w_3 = w_4 = 2$. Examples for larger values of k are easily obtained. □

For zero bias, the family of functions constructed in the previous proof gives rise to a lower bound on the size of networks with uniform widths simulating networks with nonuniform widths. In particular, uniform-width networks must be a factor of almost two larger to be as powerful as nonuniform-width networks. This separates the computational capabilities of the two network models and demonstrates the power of the width parameter.

Corollary 15. *A univariate zero-bias RBF neural network with k hidden units of arbitrary width cannot be simulated by a zero-bias network with uniform widths and less than $2k - 1$ hidden units. This holds even if the nonuniform-width network uses only two different width values.*

Proof. Consider again the functions f_k defined in the proof of Lemma 14. Each f_k is computed by a network with k hidden units using two different width values and has $2k - 2$ zeros. By virtue of the strong RBF rule of signs (Theorem 3), at least $2k - 1$ hidden units are required for a network with uniform widths to have $2k - 2$ zeros. □

The lower bounds derived here are concerned with zero-bias networks only. We remark at this point that it remains open whether and to what extent nonuniform widths increase the computational power of networks with nonzero bias.

5   Conclusion

We have derived rules of signs for various types of univariate RBF neural networks. These rules have been shown to yield tight bounds for the number of zeros of functions computed by these networks. Two quantities have turned out to be crucial: On the one hand, the number of sign changes in a sequence of the output weights for networks with zero bias and uniform widths and for networks with uniform centers; on the other hand, the number of hidden units for networks with nonzero bias and uniform widths. The first quantity lead to the strong RBF rule of signs for uniform widths and to the RBF rule of signs for uniform centers; the second quantity gave rise to the weak RBF rule of signs for uniform widths. The most challenging open problem that results from this work is to find a rule of signs for networks with nonuniform widths and nonuniform centers.

Using the introduced rules of signs, linear bounds on the VC dimension and pseudo-dimension of the studied networks have been established. The smallest bound has been found for networks with zero bias and uniform widths, for which the VC dimension was shown to be equal to the number of hidden units and, hence, less than half the number of parameters. Further, introducing one additional parameter, the bias, more than doubles this VC dimension. The pseudo-dimension bounds have been obtained for networks with fixed width or fixed centers only. In view of these results, the question arises how such bounds can be derived for networks that do not have these restrictions. Since the pseudo-dimension is defined via the VC dimension using one more variable, we suspect that getting bounds for more general networks is a matter of looking at higher input dimensions.

Finally, we have calculated lower bounds for sizes of networks simulating other networks with more parameters. These results assume that the simulations are performed exactly. In consideration of the well-established approximation capabilities of neural networks it is desirable to have such bounds also for notions of approximative computation.

References

[1] Bruce Anderson, Jeffrey Jackson, and Meera Sitharam. Descartes' rule of signs revisited. *American Mathematical Monthly*, 105:447–451, 1998.

[2] Alexander Andrianov. On pseudo-dimension of certain sets of functions. *East Journal on Approximations*, 5:393–402, 1999.

[3] Martin Anthony and Peter L. Bartlett. *Neural Network Learning: Theoretical Foundations*. Cambridge University Press, Cambridge, 1999.

[4] Peter L. Bartlett and Robert C. Williamson. The VC dimension and pseudodimension of two-layer neural networks with discrete inputs. *Neural Computation*, 8:625–628, 1996.

[5] D. S. Broomhead and David Lowe. Multivariable functional interpolation and adaptive networks. *Complex Systems*, 2:321–355, 1988.

[6] René Descartes. *The Geometry of René Descartes with a Facsimile of the First Edition*. Dover Publications, New York, NY, 1954. Translated by D. E. Smith and M. L. Latham.

[7] Dinh Dung. Non-linear approximations using sets of finite cardinality or finite pseudo-dimension. *Journal of Complexity*, 17:467–492, 2001.

[8] David J. Grabiner. Descartes' rule of signs: Another construction. *American Mathematical Monthly*, 106:854–856, 1999.

[9] Peter Henrici. *Applied and Computational Complex Analysis 1: Power Series, Integration, Conformal Mapping, Location of Zeros*. Wiley, New York, NY, 1974.

[10] Marek Karpinski and Angus Macintyre. Polynomial bounds for VC dimension of sigmoidal and general Pfaffian neural networks. *Journal of Computer and System Sciences*, 54:169–176, 1997.

[11] Marek Karpinski and Thorsten Werther. VC dimension and uniform learnability of sparse polynomials and rational functions. *SIAM Journal on Computing*, 22:1276–1285, 1993.

[12] Pascal Koiran and Eduardo D. Sontag. Neural networks with quadratic VC dimension. *Journal of Computer and System Sciences*, 54:190–198, 1997.

[13] S.-T. Li and E. L. Leiss. On noise-immune RBF networks. In R. J. Howlett and L. C. Jain, editors, *Radial Basis Function Networks 1: Recent Developments in Theory and Applications*, volume 66 of *Studies in Fuzziness and Soft Computing*, chapter 5, pages 95–124. Springer-Verlag, Berlin, 2001.

[14] V. Maiorov and J. Ratsaby. On the degree of approximation by manifolds of finite pseudo-dimension. *Constructive Approximation*, 15:291–300, 1999.

[15] Bartlett W. Mel and Stephen M. Omohundro. How receptive field parameters affect neural learning. In Richard P. Lippmann, John E. Moody, and David S. Touretzky, editors, *Advances in Neural Information Processing Systems 3*, pages 757–763. Morgan Kaufmann, San Mateo, CA, 1991.

[16] John Moody and Christian J. Darken. Fast learning in networks of locally-tuned processing units. *Neural Computation*, 1:281–294, 1989.

[17] J. Park and I. W. Sandberg. Universal approximation using radial-basis-function networks. *Neural Computation*, 3:246–257, 1991.

[18] Jooyoung Park and Irwin W. Sandberg. Approximation and radial-basis-function networks. *Neural Computation*, 5:305–316, 1993.

[19] George Pólya and Gabor Szegő. *Problems and Theorems in Analysis II: Theory of Functions. Zeros. Polynomials. Determinants. Number Theory. Geometry.* Springer-Verlag, Berlin, 1976.

[20] Michael Schmitt. Radial basis function neural networks have superlinear VC dimension. In David Helmbold and Bob Williamson, editors, *Proceedings of the 14th Annual Conference on Computational Learning Theory COLT 2001 and 5th European Conference on Computational Learning Theory EuroCOLT 2001*, volume 2111 of *Lecture Notes in Artificial Intelligence*, pages 14–30, Springer-Verlag, Berlin, 2001.

[21] Michael Schmitt. Neural networks with local receptive fields and superlinear VC dimension. *Neural Computation*, 14:919–956, 2002.

[22] D. J. Struik, editor. *A Source Book in Mathematics, 1200–1800.* Princeton University Press, Princeton, NJ, 1986.

[23] Zheng-ou Wang and Tao Zhu. An efficient learning algorithm for improving generalization performance of radial basis function neural networks. *Neural Networks*, 13:545–553, 2000.

Asymptotic Optimality of Transductive Confidence Machine

Vladimir Vovk

Computer Learning Research Centre, Department of Computer Science,
Royal Holloway, University of London, Egham, Surrey TW20 0EX, UK
vovk@cs.rhul.ac.uk

Abstract. Transductive Confidence Machine (TCM) is a way of converting standard machine-learning algorithms into algorithms that output predictive regions rather than point predictions. It has been shown recently that TCM is well-calibrated when used in the on-line mode: at any confidence level $1 - \delta$, the long-run relative frequency of errors is guaranteed not to exceed δ provided the examples are generated independently from the same probability distribution P. Therefore, the number of "uncertain" predictive regions (i.e., those containing more than one label) becomes the sole measure of performance. The main result of this paper is that for any probability distribution P (assumed to generate the examples), it is possible to construct a TCM (guaranteed to be well-calibrated even if the assumption is wrong) that performs asymptotically as well as the best region predictor under P.

1 Region Predictors

The notion of TCM was introduced in [5] and [8] (our exposition is, however, self-contained). Before we define TCM (in §3) we discuss general properties of region predictors.

In our learning protocol, Nature outputs pairs $(x_1, y_1), (x_2, y_2), \ldots$ called *examples*. Each example (x_i, y_i) consists of an *object* x_i and its *label* y_i; the objects are chosen from a measurable space $\mathbf{X}$ called the *object space* and the labels are elements of a measurable space $\mathbf{Y}$ called the *label space*. In this paper we assume that $\mathbf{Y}$ is finite (and endowed with the σ-algebra of all subsets). The protocol includes variables Err_n (the total number of errors made up to and including trial n) and err_n (the binary variable showing if an error is made at trial n); it also includes analogous variables Unc_n and unc_n for uncertain predictions:

> $\mathrm{Err}_0 := 0; \quad \mathrm{Unc}_0 := 0;$
> FOR $n = 1, 2, \ldots$:
> > Nature outputs $x_n \in \mathbf{X}$;
> > Predictor outputs $\Gamma_n \subseteq \mathbf{Y}$; Nature outputs $y_n \in \mathbf{Y}$;
> > $\mathrm{err}_n := \begin{cases} 1 \text{ if } y_n \notin \Gamma_n \\ 0 \text{ otherwise} \end{cases}$; $\quad \mathrm{Err}_n := \mathrm{Err}_{n-1} + \mathrm{err}_n$;

N. Cesa-Bianchi et al. (Eds.): ALT 2002, LNAI 2533, pp. 336–350, 2002.

$$\text{unc}_n := \begin{cases} 1 \text{ if } |\Gamma_n| > 1 \\ 0 \text{ otherwise} \end{cases} ; \quad \text{Unc}_n := \text{Unc}_{n-1} + \text{unc}_n;$$

END FOR.

We will use the notation $\mathbf{Z} := \mathbf{X} \times \mathbf{Y}$ for the *example space*; Γ_n will be called a *predictive region* (or just *prediction*).

We will be assuming that each example $z_n = (x_n, y_n)$, $n = 1, 2, \ldots$, is output according to a probability distribution P in $\mathbf{Z}$ and the examples are independent of each other (so the sequence $z_1 z_2 \ldots$ is output by the power distribution P^∞). This is Nature's randomised strategy.

A *region predictor* is a family (indexed by $\gamma \in [0, 1]$) of Predictor's strategies Γ_γ such that $\Gamma_\gamma(x_1, y_1, \ldots, x_{n-1}, y_{n-1}, x_n)$ is a measurable function of Nature's moves and $\Gamma_{\gamma_1}(x_1, y_1, \ldots, x_{n-1}, y_{n-1}, x_n) \subseteq \Gamma_{\gamma_2}(x_1, y_1, \ldots, x_{n-1}, y_{n-1}, x_n)$ if $\gamma_1 \leq \gamma_2$. Since we are interested in prediction with confidence, the predictor is given an extra input $\gamma = 1 - \delta \in [0, 1]$, which we call the *confidence level* (typically it is close to 1, standard values being 95% and 99%); the complementary value δ is called the *significance level*.

To provide the reader with an intuition about region prediction, we present results for Predictor's particular strategy ("1-Nearest Neighbour TCM"; for details, see [10]) on the USPS data set (as described in [7], §12.2, but randomly permuted). Figure 1 shows the cumulative number of errors Err_n plotted against $n = 0, 1, \ldots, 9298$ (solid line), the cumulative number Unc_n of uncertain predictions Γ_n, and that of empty predictions (for which $|\Gamma_n| = 0$). Figure 2 (left) gives the *empirical calibration curve*

$$\delta \mapsto \text{Err}_N(\text{USPS}, \Gamma_{1-\delta})/N$$

and the *empirical performance curve*

$$\delta \mapsto \text{Unc}_N(\text{USPS}, \Gamma_{1-\delta})/N$$

for this region predictor; we use the strategies followed by Nature (the randomly permuted USPS data set) and Predictor (corresponding to significance level δ) as arguments for Err and Unc; $N = 9298$ is the size of the USPS data set.

2 Well-Calibrated and Asymptotically Optimal Region Predictors

Suppose we know the true distribution P in $\mathbf{Z}$ generating the examples. In this section we will construct a region predictor optimal under P; we will often omit P from our notation.

Let $P_{\mathbf{X}}$ be the marginal distribution of P in $\mathbf{X}$ (i.e., $P_{\mathbf{X}}(E) := P(E \times \mathbf{Y})$) and $P_{\mathbf{Y}|\mathbf{X}}(y \mid x)$ be the conditional probability that, for a random example (X, Y) chosen from P, $Y = y$ provided $X = x$ (we fix arbitrarily a regular version of this conditional probability). We will often omit subindices $\mathbf{X}$ and $\mathbf{Y} \mid \mathbf{X}$.

The *predictability* of an object $x \in \mathbf{X}$ is

$$f(x) := \max_{y \in \mathbf{Y}} P(y \mid x)$$

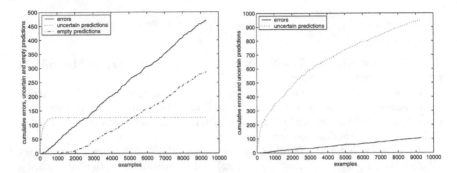

Fig. 1. On-line performance of the Nearest Neighbour TCM on the USPS data set (9298 hand-written digits, randomly permuted) for the confidence level 95% (**left**) and 99% (**right**). The solid line shows the cumulative number of errors, dotted the cumulative number of uncertain predictions, and dashdot the cumulative number of empty predictions (inevitably leading to an error). For 99%, the dashdot line coincides with the horizontal axis (there are no empty predictions) and so is invisible. This and following figures are not significantly affected by statistical variation (due to the random choice of the permutation of the data set).

and the *predictability distribution function* is the function $F : [0,1] \to [0,1]$ defined by

$$F(\beta) := P\{x : f(x) \le \beta\}.$$

An example of such a function F is given in Figure 3 (left); the graph of F is the thick line, and the unit box is also shown. The intuition behind some constructions in this paper will become clearer if the case of finite $\mathbf{X}$ with equiprobable objects is considered first; see Figure 3, right.

The *success curve* $\mathbf{S}$ of P is defined by the equality

$$\mathbf{S}(\delta) = \inf \left\{ B \in [0,1] : \int_0^1 (F(\beta) - B)^+ d\beta \le \delta \right\},$$

where t^+ stands for $\max(t, 0)$; the function $\mathbf{S}$ is also of the type $[0,1] \to [0,1]$. (Why the terminology introduced here and below is natural will become clear from Theorems 1 and 2.) Geometrically, $\mathbf{S}$ is defined from the graph of F as follows (see Figure 3, left): move the point B from A to Z until the area of the curvilinear triangle ABC becomes δ (assuming this area does become δ eventually, i.e., δ is not too large); the ordinate of B is then $\mathbf{S}(\delta)$. The intuition in the case of finite $\mathbf{X}$ (Figure 3, right) is that $1 - \mathbf{S}(\delta)$ is the maximum fraction of objects that are "easily predictable" in the sense that their cumulative lack of predictability does not exceed δ (where the lack of predictability $1 - f(x)$ of each object is taken with the weight $1/|\mathbf{X}|$). Notice that the value $\mathbf{S}(\delta)$ in fact satisfies the equality

$$\int_0^1 (F(\beta) - \mathbf{S}(\delta))^+ d\beta = \delta$$

provided δ does not exceed the *critical significance level*

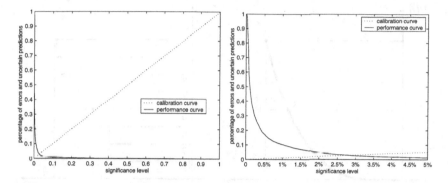

Fig. 2. The empirical calibration and performance curves for the Nearest Neighbour TCM on the USPS data set (**left**); their left edges stretched horizontally (**right**).

$$\delta_0 := \int_0^1 F(\beta)d\beta \tag{1}$$

(the area under the thick curve in Figure 3, left; we will later see that this coincides with what is sometimes called *Bayes error* or *Bayes risk*—see, e.g., [2], §2.1).

So far we have defined some characteristics of the distribution P itself; now we will give definitions related to individual region predictors. The most natural class of region predictors is that of *permutationally invariant region predictors* Γ, for which $\Gamma_{1-\delta}(z_1,\dots,z_n,x)$ does not depend on the order of $z_1,\dots,z_n$ (we know the examples are i.i.d., so knowing the order should not help).

The *calibration curve* of a region predictor Γ under P is the following function of the type $[0,1] \to [0,1]$:

$$\mathbf{C}(\delta) := \inf \left\{ \beta : \mathbb{P}\left\{ \limsup_{n\to\infty} \frac{\mathrm{Err}_n(P^\infty, \Gamma_{1-\delta})}{n} \le \beta \right\} = 1 \right\} \tag{2}$$

($\mathbb{P}(E)$ stands for the probability of event E). By the Hewitt–Savage zero-one law (see, e.g., [6], Theorem IV.1.3) in the case of permutationally invariant region predictors this definition will not change if "$= 1$" is replaced by "> 0" in (2). The *performance curve* of Γ under P is defined by

$$\mathbf{P}(\delta) := \inf \left\{ \beta : \mathbb{P}\left\{ \limsup_{n\to\infty} \frac{\mathrm{Unc}_n(P^\infty, \Gamma_{1-\delta})}{n} \le \beta \right\} = 1 \right\} ; \tag{3}$$

this is again a function of the type $[0,1] \to [0,1]$. The Hewitt–Savage zero-one law again implies that for permutationally invariant Γ this will not change if "$= 1$" is replaced by "> 0".

We will say that a region predictor Γ is *well-calibrated* under P if its calibration curve $\mathbf{C}(\delta)$ is below the diagonal: $\mathbf{C}(\delta) \le \delta$ for any significance level δ. It is *asymptotically optimal* under P if its performance curve coincides with the success curve: $\mathbf{P}(\delta) = \mathbf{S}(\delta)$ for all δ.

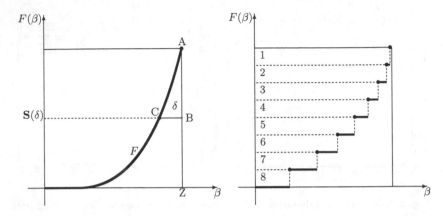

Fig. 3. Left: The predictability distribution function F. The function F is non-decreasing, continuous on the right, and $F(1/|\mathbf{Y}|) = 0$. For a possibly more realistic example of a predictability distribution function, see Figure 6. **Right:** The predictability distribution function (thick line) in the case where the object space $\mathbf{X}$ is finite and all objects $x \in \mathbf{X}$ have the same probability. The objects are numbered, from 1 to 8 in this case, in the order of decreasing predictability.

Theorem 1. *Let P be a probability distribution in $\mathbf{Z}$ with success curve $\mathbf{S}$. If a region predictor Γ is well-calibrated under P, its performance curve $\mathbf{P}$ is above $\mathbf{S}$: for any δ, $\mathbf{P}(\delta) \geq \mathbf{S}(\delta)$. Moreover, for any significance level δ,*

$$\liminf_{n \to \infty} \frac{\mathrm{Unc}_n(P^\infty, \Gamma_{1-\delta})}{n} \geq \mathbf{S}(\delta) \qquad a.s. \tag{4}$$

Let us now assume, for simplicity, that the distribution P is *regular*, in the sense that the predictability distribution function F is continuous. (The general case will be considered in §5 and will involve randomised region predictors.)

The main result of this paper (Theorem 2, strengthened in Theorem 2r) is that one can construct an asymptotically optimal TCM (which is well-calibrated automatically, by [10]). If, however, we know for sure that the true distribution is P it is very easy to construct a well-calibrated and asymptotically optimal region predictor. Fix a *choice function* $\hat{y} : \mathbf{X} \to \mathbf{Y}$ such that

$$\forall x \in \mathbf{X} : f(x) = P(\hat{y}(x) \,|\, x)$$

(to put it differently, $\hat{y}(x) \in \arg\max_y P(y \,|\, x)$). Define the *$P$-Bayesian* region predictor Γ by

$$\Gamma_{1-\delta}(z_1, \ldots, z_n, x) := \begin{cases} \{\hat{y}(x)\} & \text{if } F(f(x)) \geq \mathbf{S}(\delta) \\ \mathbf{Y} & \text{otherwise,} \end{cases}$$

for all significance levels δ and data sequences $(z_1, \ldots, z_n, x) \in \mathbf{Z}^n \times \mathbf{X}$, $n = 0, 1, \ldots$. It can be shown that the P-Bayesian region predictor is well-

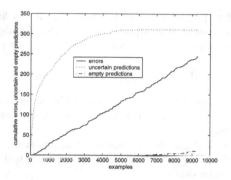

Fig. 4. On-line performance of the Nearest Neighbour TCM on the USPS data set for the confidence level 97.5%. (This figure cannot be directly compared to the error rate of 2.5% for humans reported in [7], since this experiment has been carried out on the randomly permuted data set, whereas the test part of the USPS data set is known to be especially hard.)

calibrated and asymptotically optimal under P. (Our definition of the P-Bayesian region predictor is arbitrary in several respects; in principle, different choice functions can be used at different trials, the prediction can be arbitrary when $F(f(x)) = \mathbf{S}(\delta)$, and $\mathbf{Y}$ can be replaced by any $E \subseteq \mathbf{Y}$ such that $P(E \mid x) := \sum_{y \in E} P(y \mid x) = 1$.)

The critical significance level (1) is an important characteristic of the probability distribution P generating the examples. If $\delta > \delta_0$, an optimal region predictor will always output certain predictions and, if forced to achieve the error rate δ, will sometimes have to output empty predictions. If, on the other hand, $\delta < \delta_0$, there will be uncertain predictions but no empty predictions. Figure 1 suggests that the critical significance level for the USPS data set is between 1% and 5%. This agrees with the observation that the critical significance level is just the error rate of the Bayesian point predictor (which is restricted to outputting Γ_n with $|\Gamma_n| = 1$ and minimises the expected number of errors) and the fact (reported in [7]) that the error rate achieved by humans on the USPS data set is 2.5%. Notice that in Figure 1 (left) the onset of empty predictions closely follows the point where all predictions become certain; see also Figures 4 and 5.

3   Transductive Confidence Machine

The procedure at the end of §2 works well when P is known. If, however, P is only a convenient benchmark, the Bayesian region predictor can give very misleading results [4]. In the rest of this paper we will discuss how to ensure well-calibratedness under any distribution in $\mathbf{Z}$ without losing the asymptotic performance of the Bayesian predictor if P happens to be the true distribution.

Transductive Confidence Machine (TCM) is a way of transition from what we call an "individual strangeness measure" to a region predictor. A family of measurable functions $\{A_n : n = 1, 2, \ldots\}$, where $A_n : \mathbf{Z}^n \to \mathbb{R}^n$ for all n and $\mathbb{R}$ is the set of all real numbers (equipped with the Borel σ-algebra), is called an *individual strangeness measure* if, for any $n = 1, 2, \ldots$, each α_i in

$$A_n : (z_1, \ldots, z_n) \mapsto (\alpha_1, \ldots, \alpha_n) \tag{5}$$

is determined by z_i and the bag $\lceil z_1, \ldots, z_n \rfloor$. (The difference between the bag $\lceil z_1, \ldots, z_n \rfloor$ and the set $\{z_1, \ldots, z_n\}$ is that the former can contain several copies of the same element.)

The *TCM associated with the individual strangeness measure A_n* is the following region predictor: $\Gamma_{1-\delta}(x_1, y_1, \ldots, x_{n-1}, y_{n-1}, x_n)$ is defined to be the set of all labels $y \in \mathbf{Y}$ such that

$$\frac{\#\{i = 1, \ldots, n : \alpha_i \geq \alpha_n\}}{n} > \delta \;, \tag{6}$$

where

$$(\alpha_1, \ldots, \alpha_n) := A_n((x_1, y_1), \ldots, (x_{n-1}, y_{n-1}), (x_n, y)) \;. \tag{7}$$

In general, a *TCM* is the TCM associated with some individual strangeness measure. It is shown in [10] that TCM is well-calibrated under any P (the technical report [10] also contains stronger assertions: for example, TCM is still well-calibrated, in a natural sense, when the confidence level $1 - \delta$ is allowed to depend on n).

4   Asymptotically Optimal TCM

If we suspect that the probability distribution in $\mathbf{Z}$ generating the examples might be P, we can define the individual strangeness measure (5) by

$$\alpha_i := \begin{cases} 0 & \text{if } y_i = \hat{y}(x_i) \\ P(\hat{y}(x_i) \mid x_i) & \text{otherwise} \;. \end{cases} \tag{8}$$

The corresponding TCM will be called the *P-TCM* (cf. [9]). We say that a region predictor is *universally well-calibrated* if it is well-calibrated under any probability distribution P in $\mathbf{Z}$.

Theorem 2. *Let P be a regular probability distribution in $\mathbf{Z}$. The P-TCM is (a) universally well-calibrated and (b) asymptotically optimal under P.*

5   Randomised Region Predictors

In this section we will remove the assumption that the probability distribution P generating examples is regular. The price we will have to pay is that we will have to generalise the notion of region predictor in general, and TCM in particular, to allow using a generator of random numbers (as in [10]).

The generator that we consider generates a sequence τ_n, $n = 1, 2, \ldots$, of uniformly distributed independent random numbers in the interval $[0, 1]$; τ_n will be used by Predictor at trial n of our basic protocol (see §1). Formally, a *randomised region predictor* Γ is a family, indexed by $n = 1, 2, \ldots$ and $\gamma \in [0, 1]$, of measurable functions $\Gamma_\gamma(z_1, \tau_1, \ldots, z_{n-1}, \tau_{n-1}, x_n, \tau_n)$, where the $z_i \in \mathbf{Z}$, $i = 1, \ldots, n-1$, are examples, $\tau_i \in [0, 1]$, $i = 1, \ldots, n$, and $x_n \in \mathbf{X}$ is an object, which satisfies

$$\Gamma_{\gamma_1}(z_1, \tau_1, \ldots, z_{n-1}, \tau_{n-1}, x_n, \tau_n) \subseteq \Gamma_{\gamma_2}(z_1, \tau_1, \ldots, z_{n-1}, \tau_{n-1}, x_n, \tau_n)$$

whenever $\gamma_1 \leq \gamma_2$. The notation err_n, unc_n, etc., will be continued to be used in the randomised case as well; it should be remembered that these now depend on $\tau_1, \tau_2, \ldots$. We can strengthen Theorem 1 as follows.

Theorem 1r. *Let P be a probability distribution in $\mathbf{Z}$ with success curve $\mathbf{S}$. If a randomised region predictor Γ is well-calibrated under P, then for any significance level δ,*

$$\liminf_{n \to \infty} \frac{\mathrm{Unc}_n(P^\infty, \Gamma_{1-\delta})}{n} \geq \mathbf{S}(\delta) \quad a.s.$$

The "a.s." in this theorem refers to the probability distribution $(P \times \mathbf{U})^\infty$ generating the sequence $z_1, \tau_1, z_2, \tau_2, \ldots$, with $\mathbf{U}$ standing for the uniform distribution in $[0, 1]$.

Next we introduce a randomised version of TCM. The *randomised Transductive Confidence Machine (rTCM)* associated with an individual strangeness measure A_n is the following randomised region predictor $\Gamma_{1-\delta}$: at any trial n and for any label $y \in \mathbf{Y}$,

1. if $\#\{i = 1, \ldots, n : \alpha_i > \alpha_n\}/n > \delta$ (as before, the αs are defined by (7)), the label y is included in $\Gamma_{1-\delta}$;
2. if $\#\{i = 1, \ldots, n : \alpha_i \geq \alpha_n\}/n \leq \delta$, y is not included in $\Gamma_{1-\delta}$;
3. otherwise, y is included in $\Gamma_{1-\delta}$ if

$$\tau_n < \frac{\#\{i = 1, \ldots, n : \alpha_i \geq \alpha_n\} - n\delta}{\#\{i = 1, \ldots, n : \alpha_i = \alpha_n\}}. \tag{9}$$

We say that a randomised region predictor Γ is *perfectly calibrated* if, under any probability distribution P, its calibration curve $\mathbf{C}(\delta)$ coincides with the diagonal: $\mathbf{C}(\delta) = \delta$ for any significance level δ. (Formally, this definition can also be given for deterministic predictors as well, but it would be impossible to satisfy in some cases.) The P-rTCM is defined to be the rTCM associated with the individual strangeness measure (8).

Theorem 2r. *Let P be a probability distribution in $\mathbf{Z}$. The P-rTCM is perfectly calibrated and, under P, asymptotically optimal.*

Notice that the rTCM makes at least as many errors as the TCM associated with the same individual strangeness measure. It is shown in [10] that rTCM's errors are independent and happen with probability δ at any confidence level $1 - \delta$. The difference between TCM and rTCM is typically negligible after the first several hundred trials; cf. the dotted line in Figure 2 (left).

6 Conclusion

In this paper we defined two desiderata for region predictors: being well-calibrated and asymptotic optimality. Being well-calibrated is the first priority: without it, the meaning of confidence levels is lost and it does not make sense to talk about optimality. If the probability distribution P generating individual examples is known, the Bayesian region predictor is well-calibrated and asymptotically optimal. But even in the situation where P is just a convenient guess that we are unwilling to take too seriously, there exists a region predictor (a TCM) which is universally well-calibrated and asymptotically optimal under P.

Acknowledgments. I am grateful to Alex Gammerman, Philip Dawid and anonymous referees for helpful suggestions. This work was partially supported by EPSRC (grant GR/R46670/01 "Complexity Approximation Principle and Predictive Complexity: Analysis and Applications"), BBSRC (grant 111/BIO14428 "Pattern Recognition Techniques for Gene and Promoter Identification and Classification in Plant Genomic Sequences"), and EU (grant IST-1999-10226 "EurEdit: The Development and Evaluation of New Methods for Editing and Imputation").

References

[1] Bourbaki, N.: Eléments de mathématique, Livre IV, Fonctions d'une variable réelle (théorie élémentaire). 2nd edn. Hermann, Paris (1958)

[2] Devroye, L., Györfi, L., Lugosi, G.: A Probabilistic Theory of Pattern Recognition. Springer, New York (1996)

[3] Lehmann, E.: Testing Statistical Hypotheses. Wiley, New York (1959)

[4] Melluish, T., Saunders, C., Nouretdinov, I., Vovk, V.: Comparing the Bayes and typicalness frameworks. In: De Raedt, L., Flash, P. (eds.): Machine Learning: ECML 2001. Proceedings of the 12th European Conference on Machine Learning. Lecture Notes in Artificial Intelligence, Vol. 2167, Springer (2001) 360–371. Full version published as Technical Report CLRC-TR-01-05, Computer Learning Research Centre, Royal Holloway, University of London, http://www.clrc.rhul.ac.uk

[5] Saunders, C., Gammerman, A., Vovk, V.: Transduction with confidence and credibility. In: Proceedings of the 16th International Joint Conference on Artificial Intelligence (1999) 722–726

[6] Shiryaev, A. N.: Probability. 2nd edn. Springer, New York (1996)

[7] Vapnik, V. N.: Statistical Learning Theory. Wiley, New York (1998)

[8] Vovk, V., Gammerman, A., Saunders, C.: Machine-learning applications of algorithmic randomness. In: Proceedings of the 16th International Conference on Machine Learning (1999) 444–453

[9] Vovk, V.: De-Bayesing Bayesian prediction algorithms. Manuscript (June 2000)

[10] Vovk, V.: On-line Confidence Machines are well-calibrated. In: Proceedings of FOCS'2002. Full version published as Technical Report CLRC-TR-02-01, Computer Learning Research Centre, Royal Holloway, University of London, http://www.clrc.rhul.ac.uk (April 2002). Additional information can be found at http://www.cs.rhul.ac.uk/~vovk/cm

Appendix: Proofs

First we establish some simple properties of the predictability distribution function and success curve.

Lemma 1. *The predictability distribution function F satisfies the following properties:*

1. *$F(\epsilon) = 0$ for some $\epsilon > 0$ and $F(1) = 1$;*
2. *F is non-decreasing;*
3. *F is continuous on the right.*

If a function $F : [0, 1] \to [0, 1]$ satisfies these properties, there exist a measurable space $\mathbf{X}$, a finite set $\mathbf{Y}$, and a probability distribution P in $\mathbf{X} \times \mathbf{Y}$ for which F is the predictability distribution function.

Proof. Properties 1 (cf. the caption to Figure 3), 2, and 3 are obvious (and the last two are well-known properties of all distribution functions). The fact that these three properties characterise predictability distribution functions easily follows from the fact that the last two properties plus $F(-\infty) = 0$ and $F(\infty) = 1$ characterise distribution functions (see, e.g., [6], Theorem II.3.1). □

We will use the notations g'_{left} and g'_{right} for the left and right derivatives, respectively, of a function g.

Lemma 2. *The success curve $\mathbf{S} : [0, 1] \to [0, 1]$ always satisfies these properties:*

1. *$\mathbf{S}$ is convex.*
2. *There is a point $\delta_0 \in [0, 1]$ (the critical significance level) such that $\mathbf{S}(\delta) = 0$ for $\delta \geq \delta_0$ and $\mathbf{S}'_{\text{left}}(\delta_0) < -1$; therefore, $\mathbf{S}'_{\text{left}} < -1$ and $\mathbf{S}'_{\text{right}} < -1$ to the left of δ_0, and the function $\mathbf{S}$ is decreasing before it hits the δ-axis at δ_0.*
3. *$\mathbf{S}$ is continuous at $\delta = 0$; therefore, it is continuous everywhere in $[0, 1]$.*

If a function $\mathbf{S} : [0, 1] \to [0, 1]$ satisfies these properties, there exist a measurable space $\mathbf{X}$, a finite set $\mathbf{Y}$, and a probability distribution P in $\mathbf{X} \times \mathbf{Y}$ for which $\mathbf{S}$ is the success curve.

Proof. For the basic properties of convex functions and their left and right derivatives, see, e.g., [1], §I.4. The statement of the lemma follows from the fact that the success curve $\mathbf{S}$ can be obtained from the predictability distribution function F using these steps (labelling the horizontal and vertical axes as x and y respectively):

1. Invert F: $F_1 := F^{-1}$.
2. Flip F_1 around the line $x = 0.5$ and then around the line $y = 0.5$: $F_2(x) := 1 - F_1(1 - x)$.
3. Integrate F_2: $F_3(x) := \int_0^x F_2(t) dt$.
4. Invert F_3: $F_4 := F_3^{-1}$.
5. Flip F_4 around the line $y = 0.5$: $F_5 := 1 - F_4$.

It can be shown that $\mathbf{S} = F_5$, no matter which of the several natural definitions of the operation $g \mapsto g^{-1}$ is used; for concreteness, we can define $g^{-1}(y) := \sup\{x : g(x) \leq y\}$ for non-decreasing g (so that g^{-1} is continuous on the right). □

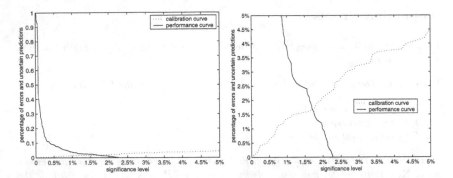

Fig. 5. Left: Picture analogous to Figure 2 (right) for the last one thousand examples. Notice a different behaviour of the empirical performance curve as it approaches the horizontal axis as compared with Figure 2 (right). The unexpected behaviour of the empirical performance curve as it approaches the vertical axis may be explained (at least partially) by the "granularity" of TCM: for example, the "realised p-value" given by the left-hand side of (6) can never be less than $1/9298 > 0.01\%$; this behaviour may become more regular for randomised TCM. **Right:** The bottom part of the picture on the left stretched vertically. Notice that the slope of the empirical performance curve is at least 1 in absolute value before it hits the horizontal axis; this agrees with Lemma 2 on p. 345. This figure suggests that, if the 1-NN TCM were an optimal region predictor, the critical significance level for the USPS data set would be close to 2.3.

Visually the empirical performance curve in Figure 2 seems to satisfy the properties listed in Lemma 2 for significance levels that are not too large or too small (approximately in the range 0.1%–5%); for an even better agreement, see Figure 5.

A natural idea is to reverse the process of transforming F into **S** and try to obtain an estimate of the predictability distribution function F from an empirical performance curve. Figure 6 shows the result of such an attempt. Such pictures, however, should not be taken too seriously, since the differentiation operation needed in finding F is known to be unstable (see, e.g., [7], §1.12).

Proof of Theorems 1 and 1r. Let us check first that (4) indeed implies $\mathbf{P}(\delta) \geq \mathbf{S}(\delta)$. Since probability measures are σ-additive, (3) implies

$$\limsup_{n\to\infty} \frac{\mathrm{Unc}_n(P^\infty, \Gamma_{1-\delta})}{n} \leq \mathbf{P}(\delta) \quad \text{a.s.} ,$$

and so we obtain from (4):

$$\mathbf{P}(\delta) \geq \limsup_{n\to\infty} \frac{\mathrm{Unc}_n(P^\infty, \Gamma_{1-\delta})}{n} \geq \liminf_{n\to\infty} \frac{\mathrm{Unc}_n(P^\infty, \Gamma_{1-\delta})}{n} \geq \mathbf{S}(\delta)$$

almost surely; since the two extreme terms are deterministic, we have $\mathbf{P}(\delta) \geq \mathbf{S}(\delta)$.

We start the actual proof with alternative definitions of calibration and performance curves. Complement the protocol of §1 in which Nature plays P^∞ and Predictor plays

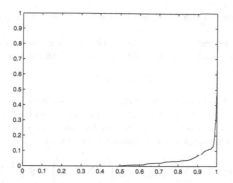

Fig. 6. An attempt to reverse engineer the predictability distribution function of the hand-written digits in the USPS data set. This picture was obtained from the solid line in Figure 5 (left) by reversing the list in the proof of Lemma 2.

$\Gamma_{1-\delta}$ with the following variables:

$$\overline{\mathrm{err}}_n := (P \times \mathbf{U})\Big\{(x, y, \tau): y \notin \Gamma_{1-\delta}(x_1, \tau_1, y_1, \dots, x_{n-1}, \tau_{n-1}, y_{n-1}, x, \tau)\Big\},$$

$$\overline{\mathrm{unc}}_n := (P_{\mathbf{X}} \times \mathbf{U})\Big\{(x, \tau): |\Gamma_{1-\delta}(x_1, \tau_1, y_1, \dots, x_{n-1}, \tau_{n-1}, y_{n-1}, x, \tau)| > 1\Big\},$$

$$\overline{\mathrm{Err}}_n := \sum_{i=1}^{n} \overline{\mathrm{err}}_i, \qquad \overline{\mathrm{Unc}}_n := \sum_{i=1}^{n} \overline{\mathrm{unc}}_i$$

(we are not always consistent in the order of arguments of the function $\Gamma_{1-\delta}$). The *prequential calibration curve* of Γ under P is defined by

$$\overline{\mathbf{C}}(\delta) := \inf\left\{\beta : \mathbb{P}\left\{\limsup_{n \to \infty} \frac{\overline{\mathrm{Err}}_n(P^\infty, \Gamma_{1-\delta})}{n} \leq \beta\right\} = 1\right\}$$

and the *prequential performance curve* of Γ under P by

$$\overline{\mathbf{P}}(\delta) := \inf\left\{\beta : \mathbb{P}\left\{\limsup_{n \to \infty} \frac{\overline{\mathrm{Unc}}_n(P^\infty, \Gamma_{1-\delta})}{n} \leq \beta\right\} = 1\right\},$$

where $\mathbb{P}$ refers to the probability distribution $(P \times \mathbf{U})^\infty$ over the examples $z_1, z_2, \dots$ and random numbers $\tau_1, \tau_2, \dots$. By the martingale strong law of large numbers the prequential versions of the calibration and performance curves coincide with the original versions: indeed, since $\mathrm{Err}_n - \overline{\mathrm{Err}}_n$ and $\mathrm{Unc}_n - \overline{\mathrm{Unc}}_n$ are martingales (with increments bounded by 1 in absolute value) with respect to the filtration $\mathcal{F}_n$, $n = 0, 1, \dots$, where each $\mathcal{F}_n$ is generated by $z_1, \dots, z_n$ and $\tau_1, \dots, \tau_n$, we have

$$\lim_{n \to \infty} \frac{\mathrm{Err}_n - \overline{\mathrm{Err}}_n}{n} = 0 \qquad \mathbb{P}\text{-a.s.}$$

and

$$\lim_{n \to \infty} \frac{\mathrm{Unc}_n - \overline{\mathrm{Unc}}_n}{n} = 0 \qquad \mathbb{P}\text{-a.s.}$$

(see, e.g., [6], Theorem VII.5.4). It is also clear that we can replace Unc_n by $\overline{\text{Unc}}_n$ in (4).

Without loss of generality we can assume that Nature's move Γ_n at trial n is either $\{\hat{y}(x_n)\}$ or the whole label space $\mathbf{Y}$. Furthermore, we can assume that

$$\overline{\text{unc}}_n = \mathbf{S}(\overline{\text{err}}_n) \tag{10}$$

at every trial, since the best way to spend the allowance of $\overline{\text{err}}_n$ is to be certain on objects x with the largest (topmost in Figure 3) representations $F(f(x))$. (For a formal argument, see the end of this proof.) Using the fact that the success curve $\mathbf{S}$ is convex, non-increasing, and continuous (see Lemma 2), we obtain

$$\frac{\overline{\text{Unc}}_n}{n} = \frac{1}{n} \sum_{i=1}^{n} \overline{\text{unc}}_i = \frac{1}{n} \sum_{i=1}^{n} \mathbf{S}(\overline{\text{err}}_i) \geq \mathbf{S}\left(\frac{1}{n}\sum_{i=1}^{n} \overline{\text{err}}_i\right) = \mathbf{S}\left(\frac{\overline{\text{Err}}_n}{n}\right) \geq \mathbf{S}(\delta) - \epsilon\,,$$

the last inequality holding almost surely for an arbitrary $\epsilon > 0$ from some n on and δ being the significance level used.

It remains to prove formally that $\overline{\text{unc}}_n \geq \mathbf{S}(\overline{\text{err}}_n)$ (which is the part of (10) that we actually used). Let us fix $1 - \delta$ and $x_1, \tau_1, y_1, \ldots, x_{n-1}, \tau_{n-1}, y_{n-1}$; we will write

$$\Gamma(x, \tau) := \Gamma_{1-\delta}(x_1, \tau_1, y_1, \ldots, x_{n-1}, \tau_{n-1}, y_{n-1}, x, \tau)\,,$$

omitting the fixed arguments. Without loss of generality we are assuming that either $\Gamma(x, \tau) = \hat{y}(x)$ or $\Gamma(x, \tau) = \mathbf{Y}$. Set

$$p(x) := \mathbf{U}\{\tau : \Gamma(x, \tau) = \{\hat{y}(x)\}\}\,, \qquad \delta := \overline{\text{err}}_n\,.$$

Our goal is to show that $\overline{\text{unc}}_n \geq \mathbf{S}(\delta)$; without loss of generality we assume $0 < \delta < \delta_0$. To put it differently, we are required to show that the value of the optimisation problem

$$\int_{\mathbf{X}} p(x)P(dx) \to \max \tag{11}$$

subject to the constraint

$$\int_{\mathbf{X}} (1 - f(x))p(x)P(dx) = \delta$$

is $1 - \mathbf{S}(\delta)$ at best. By the Neyman–Pearson lemma (see, e.g., [3]) there exist constants $c > 0$ and $d \in [0, 1]$ such that

$$p(x) = \begin{cases} 1 & \text{if } f(x) > c \\ d & \text{if } f(x) = c \\ 0 & \text{if } f(x) < c\,. \end{cases} \tag{12}$$

The constants c and d are defined (c uniquely and d uniquely unless the probability of $f(x) = c$ is zero) from the condition

$$\int_{x:f(x)>c} (1 - f(x))P(dx) + d\int_{x:f(x)=c} (1 - c)P(dx) = \delta\,,$$

which is equivalent, by Fubini's theorem (applied to the indicator function of the subgraph of F; see Figure 3, left), to

$$\int_0^1 (F(\beta) - F(c))^+ d\beta + d(1 - c)(F(c) - F(c-)) = \delta\,,$$

where $F(c-)$ is defined as $\lim_{\beta \uparrow c} F(\beta)$. From this it is easy to obtain that the value of the optimal problem (11) is indeed $1 - \mathbf{S}(\delta)$: using the notation $p_d(x)$ for the right-hand side of (12), we have

$$
\begin{aligned}
\int_{\mathbf{X}} p_d(x) P(dx) &= d \int p_1(x) P(dx) + (1-d) \int p_0(x) P(dx) \\
&= dP\{x : f(x) \geq c\} + (1-d)P\{x : f(x) > c\} \\
&= d(1 - F(c-)) + (1-d)(1 - F(c)) \\
&= 1 - F(c) + d(F(c) - F(c-)) \\
&= 1 - \mathbf{S}(\delta) \ .
\end{aligned}
$$

This completes the proof of Theorem 1r; since Theorem 1 is a special case, it is also proved.

Proof of Theorems 2 and 2r. The fact that every rTCM Γ is perfectly calibrated is proved in [10], so we are only required to show that Γ is asymptotically optimal under P. Fix a confidence level $1 - \delta$; we will show that

$$
\limsup_{n \to \infty} \frac{\overline{\mathrm{Unc}}_n(P^\infty, \Gamma_{1-\delta})}{n} \leq \mathbf{S}(\delta) \tag{13}
$$

almost surely (the underlying probability distribution $\mathbb{P}$ being the product $(P \times \mathbf{U})^\infty$). Without loss of generality we assume $\mathbf{S}(\delta) < 1$ ((13) holds trivially when $\mathbf{S}(\delta) = 1$). Set

$$
c := \sup\{\beta : F(\beta) \leq \mathbf{S}(\delta)\} \ .
$$

The case $c = 1$ is simple: it means that $P\{x : f(x) < 1\} \leq \mathbf{S}(\delta)$; since, almost surely, $\mathrm{unc}_n = 0$ at trials where $f(x_n) = 1$, by Borel's strong law of large numbers we immediately obtain (13). Therefore, we assume $c < 1$ in the rest of the proof.

First we consider the case $F(c) = \mathbf{S}(\delta)$ (this will be sufficient to prove Theorem 2, since $F(c) = \mathbf{S}(\delta)$ is implied by $F(c) = F(c-)$ and the rTCM constructed in this part of the proof will be deterministic). Notice that $F(c + \epsilon) > F(c)$ for any $0 < \epsilon \leq 1 - c$ (we are assuming $\epsilon \leq 1 - c$ so that $F(c + \epsilon)$ is defined). We will prove that, for any $0 < \epsilon \leq 1 - c$ and from some n on,

$$
\mathbb{P}(\mathrm{unc}_n \mid \mathcal{F}_{n-1}) \leq F(c + \epsilon) \quad \text{a.s.} \tag{14}
$$

(we are using the same notation for an event and for its indicator function). This will imply

$$
\limsup_{n \to \infty} \frac{\overline{\mathrm{Unc}}_n}{n} \leq F(c + \epsilon)
$$

almost surely; since $\lim_{\epsilon \downarrow 0} F(c + \epsilon) = \mathbf{S}(\delta)$, this will prove (13).

Fix $0 < \epsilon \leq 1 - c$; without loss of generality assume that F is continuous at $c + \epsilon$. Let us prove (14), assuming n is large enough. Suppose the examples observed before trial n are $(z_1, \ldots, z_{n-1}) = ((x_1, y_1), \ldots, (x_{n-1}, y_{n-1}))$. Let us say that an example $(x, y) \in \mathbf{Z}$ is *wrongly classified* if $y \neq \hat{y}(x)$. Remember that according to the individual strangeness measure (8) the strange elements in every bag of examples are those that are wrongly classified, and the more predictable they are the stranger. Notice that the prediction for the new object x_n will be certain if (a) the new object x_n is to the right of $\beta = c + \epsilon$ in Figure 3 (left), in the sense $f(x_n) \geq c + \epsilon$, and (b) the number of the wrongly classified objects x_i, $i = 1, \ldots, n - 1$, to the right of $\beta = c + \epsilon$ is less than $n\delta - 10$. The probability (conditional on $\mathcal{F}_{n-1}$) of (a) is $1 - F(c+\epsilon)$, so to prove (14) it is sufficient to show that the event (b) (remember that it is measurable w.r. to $\mathcal{F}_{n-1}$) happens from some n on almost surely. The probability that an object is wrongly classified and to the right of $\beta = c + \epsilon$ is

$$b := \int_0^1 (F(\beta) - F(c + \epsilon))^+ d\beta < \delta \ .$$

By Hoeffding's inequality (see, e.g., [2], Theorem 8.1) the probability that the event (b) will fail to happen is bounded from above by

$$e^{-2(n\delta - 10 - (n-1)b)^2/(n-1)} \le e^{-\kappa n} , \qquad (15)$$

for some positive constant κ and from some n on. Since $\sum_n e^{-\kappa n} < \infty$, the Borel–Cantelli lemma implies that (b) will almost surely happen from some n on. This completes the proof in the case $F(c) = \mathbf{S}(\delta)$.

Now we consider the case $F(c) > \mathbf{S}(\delta)$ (which is the only remaining possibility). In the remaining part of the proof it will be important that we consider rTCM rather than TCM.

Let $\epsilon > 0$ satisfy $\epsilon < F(c) - \mathbf{S}(\delta)$. We will prove that, from some n on,

$$\mathbb{P}(\mathrm{unc}_n \mid \mathcal{F}_{n-1}) \le \mathbf{S}(\delta) + \epsilon \qquad \text{a.s.} \qquad (16)$$

This will imply

$$\limsup_{n \to \infty} \frac{\overline{\mathrm{Unc}_n}}{n} \le \mathbf{S}(\delta) + \epsilon$$

almost surely, and so prove (13).

We say that an object and random number $(x, \tau) \in \mathbf{X} \times [0, 1]$ (such a pair will be called an *extended object*) is *above the line* $\mathbf{S}(\delta) + \epsilon$ (cf. Figure 3, left) if either $f(x) > c$ or

$$f(x) = c \ \& \ \tau \ge \frac{\mathbf{S}(\delta) + \epsilon - F(c-)}{F(c) - F(c-)}$$

(this definition corresponds to representing each extended object (x, τ) by the point

$$(f(x), \tau F(f(x)) + (1 - \tau)F(f(x)-))$$

in Figure 3, left).

Let us prove (16), assuming n is large enough. Suppose the extended objects observed before trial n are $(x_1, \tau_1, \ldots, x_{n-1}, \tau_{n-1})$. Now the prediction for the new object x_n will be certain if (a) the new extended object (x_n, τ_n) is above $\mathbf{S}(\delta) + \epsilon$, and (b) the number of the wrongly classified extended objects (x_i, τ_i), $i = 1, \ldots, n - 1$, above $\mathbf{S}(\delta) + \epsilon$ is less than $n\delta - 10$. (We say that (x, τ) is wrongly classified if x is.) The probability (conditional on $\mathcal{F}_{n-1}$) of (a) is $1 - \mathbf{S}(\delta) - \epsilon$, so to prove (16) it is sufficient to show that the event (b) happens from some n on almost surely. The probability that an extended object is wrongly classified and above $\mathbf{S}(\delta) + \epsilon$ is

$$b := \int_0^1 (F(\beta) - \mathbf{S}(\delta) - \epsilon)^+ d\beta < \delta \ .$$

The proof is completed literally as before: apply Hoeffding's inequality to obtain upper bound (15) and then apply the Borel–Cantelli lemma.

An Efficient PAC Algorithm for Reconstructing a Mixture of Lines

Sanjoy Dasgupta[1], Elan Pavlov[2], and Yoram Singer[2]

[1] University of California
Berkeley, CA 94720
dasgupta@cs.berkeley.edu
[2] School of Computer Science & Engineering
Hebrew University, Jerusalem 91904, Israel
{elan,singer}@cs.huji.ac.il

Abstract. In this paper we study the learnability of a mixture of lines model which is of great importance in machine vision, computer graphics, and computer aided design applications. The mixture of lines is a partially-probabilistic model for an image composed of line-segments. Observations are generated by choosing one of the lines at random and picking a point at random from the chosen line. Each point is contaminated with some noise whose distribution is unknown, but which is bounded in magnitude. Our goal is to discover efficiently and rather accurately the line-segments that generated the noisy observations. We describe and analyze an efficient probably approximately correct (PAC) algorithm for solving the problem. Our algorithm combines techniques from planar geometry with simple large deviation tools and is simple to implement.

1 Introduction

Mixture models are a very popular tool in statistics and related fields, and are used in a wide range of applications. For an excellent source of information on these models see the book by Titterington, Smith, and Makov [9]. Recently, PAC learnability of mixture models, more specifically mixture of Gaussians, have been analyzed using learning-theoretic tools [3,1]. The work, which provided new algorithms for learning mixtures of Gaussians, builds upon rather general algebraic properties of the mixture components. The generality of mixture models, and of the algorithms for learning them, have made it convenient to apply them to a diverse variety of problems ranging from astrophysics to zoology. However, this generality might also be a limiting factor when the problem on hand has a specific structure that can be exploited.

Many applications in machine vision, computer graphics, and computer aided design can be cast as problems of learning mixture models. See for instance the survey by Stewart [8] and the work in [4,7,5] for such approaches. The models described and studied in these papers explicitly exploit geometrical knowledge in order to build algorithms that find a compact geometrical representation

N. Cesa-Bianchi et al. (Eds.): ALT 2002, LNAI 2533, pp. 351–364, 2002.

to a set of observations. Such representations are often equivalent to mixture models where the individual components are simple geometric shapes that are accompanied with a noise (assumed typically to be Gaussian).

In this paper we study a learning algorithm that borrows from the seemingly disparate disciplines above. Specifically, the model we study is a mixture of line-segments model in which each point is generated by one of k unknown line-segments and is subsequently corrupted by some noise, whose distribution is unknown. We describe an efficient PAC algorithm for finding the unknown line-segments generating the observations. The algorithms is composed of a few stages. It first identifies relationships between points which might indicate that the points are from the same line. These relationships are then embedded in a graph whose connected components represent the line-segments. As a final stage the algorithm reconstructs the lines from the individual large connected components. The result is an efficiently provably correct algorithm which is also simple to implement.

Our analysis is based on simple large deviation techniques with straight-forward planar geometrical properties. The time and sample complexity of the algorithm grow quadratically in the number of different lines but are, under mild conditions, independent of the number of observations.

In computer vision, one standard algorithm for inferring a set of line-segments is the *Hough transform* [5]. The idea is to pick pairs of points from the image (maybe *all* pairs), and to generate a candidate line from each pair. These candidates are then bucketed into a discretized version of the space of all possible lines. The fullest buckets are chosen as the final lines. In terms of formally analyzing this technique, many questions need to be answered – for instance, what is the tradeoff between the levels of noise and discretization? Our algorithm is based on a similar principle – clustering lines – but addresses these issues in its proof of correctness, and achieves further efficiency through sampling techniques.

The Hough transform can also be applied to higher-order curves, and here the error introduced by discretization is potentially a lot more problematic. Independent of our work, Arora and Khot [2] have demonstrated how a degree-d polynomial can be efficiently learned from $O(d^2)$ noisy points; to learn a mixture of such polynomials, one can then sample subsets of size $O(d^2)$. In this paper, we only handle the case $d = 1$ (i.e. lines) and focus on the efficiency of the overall procedure. The end result is a simple and robust algorithm that takes 20 lines of Matlab code to implement.

The paper is organized as follows. In Sec. 2 we formally introduce the mixture of lines model and pose assumptions that we deem required for efficient PAC learning of the model. In Sec. 3 we give a high level of the algorithm which is then followed in Sec. 4 by a more formal description and the main PAC-learnability theorem. In Sec. 5 we prove the main theorem. We give an illustrative example of the behavior of our algorithm using synthetic data in Sec. 6. We conclude and describe possible extensions in Sec. 7.

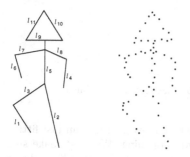

Fig. 1. An illustration of the model of mixture of lines. Left: the original mixture of lines. Right: the noisy set of observed points.

2   Model and Assumptions

Our model is that the data is generated by a mixture of line segments, where the number of lines k is unknown, and that each data point is subsequently corrupted by some bounded but otherwise arbitrary noise. A point is generated by first choosing a line segment (the ith line segment is chosen with probability w_i), picking a point uniformly at random from this line, and then adding noise to it. See also Fig. 2 for an illustration of the model. Whenever it is clear from the context we will refer to line segments simply as lines.

Given this noisy data, we then wish to determine the number of lines and to reconstruct them. To avoid dealing with arbitrarily small lines, we start with a simple normalizing assumption.

Assumption A: All lines have length *at least* one.

We also put a bound on the amount of noise to which data points can be subjected. Each point can be perturbed by an Euclidean distance of at most ξ.

Assumption B: An upper bound ξ on the maximum noise is known.

One particular feature of our setting is that the number of points from a line does not depend upon the length of the line. For instance, the mixing weights w_i might all be equal, even if some lines are much longer than others. What is the best we can hope to achieve given such limited information?

Fig. 2. The 5 lines on the left may appear as only 4 horizontal lines by a noisy sample.

There are certain identifiability issues which arise, and which will motivate the assumptions we make. In Fig. 2, given just a few points from each line, it might well appear that there are only four lines, namely the horizontal ones. This is because the points from the vertical line might lie sufficiently close to the continuations of the horizontal lines, that they can be explained by these lines.

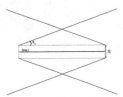

Fig. 3. The θ_0-cones of a line l.

Since we are interested in actually finding the true lines (rather than just fitting lines to the data), we must prevent this from happening. We must make sure that at least some portion of each line cannot be explained by other lines. To do this, we start by defining a pair of cones associated with each line. Recall that our lines are in effect rectangles of width 2ξ on account of the noise process.

Definition. For a line l, denote by C_l the union of the two cones which subtend an angle of θ_0 at the rectangle corresponding to line l: see Fig. 3. We will call each of these cones a θ_0-*cone* of line l. Here θ_0 is some small constant angle.

We will think of C_l as the set of points which can roughly be explained by line l. From this point of view, the region of space which can be explained by all lines other than l is $D_l = \bigcup_{l' \neq l} C_{l'}$. We must make sure that at least some portion of each line l lies outside D_l. One way to phrase this would be to say something like: "at most half of any line l lies in D_l". But in order to identify where line l starts and ends, we particularly need these parts of the line to be exposed (to lie outside D_l).

Assumption C: For each line l, the starting δ-fraction of the line and the terminating δ-fraction of the line lie outside D_l, where $\delta \in (0, \frac{1}{4})$ is a small constant.

We need three more assumptions. The first follows from the observation that the sample complexity will inevitably depend upon the smallest mixing weight.

Assumption D: A lower bound w_{min} on the mixing weights is known.

Next, we place some upper bounds on the noise; in particular, we require that the noise be much smaller than the mixing weights.

Assumption E: $\xi \leq \frac{\sin\theta_0}{128e^2} \cdot w_{min}$ and $\xi \leq \frac{1}{16} - \frac{1}{4}\delta$.

It appears from Assumption E that there is a tradeoff between the maximal noise ξ the fraction of the line that is not covered by other lines, δ. In cases where $\xi \geq \frac{1}{16} - \frac{1}{4}\delta$, it is possible to consider only a $\delta' = \frac{1}{4} - 4\xi$ fraction, and to increase the sample complexity accordingly.

The final assumption makes sure that if two lines come close to one another, their angle of intersection should be significant (that is, one should not look like a continuation of the other).

Assumption F: If two lines l_1 and l_2 are close in that they encroach upon each other's $(2\theta_0 + 4\sin^{-1} 8\xi)$-cones, then the (acute) angle between them must be at least $4\theta_0 + 6\sin^{-1} 8\xi$.

3   A High-Level View

The algorithm proceeds in four phases.

1. By looking at pairs of points (x, y), we can get an idea of the various directions along which lines might lie. Most of these are spurious, so we start by pruning them: we select only those pairs (x, y) for which there seem to be a lot of collinear triples (x, y, z).
2. For each point x, the pairs (x, y) that we have chosen tell us the possible slopes of the line on which x lies. Some points x might lie near the intersection of two lines; such points are noisy. By Assumption C, at most about a $(1-2\delta)$ fraction of the points on each line are noisy.

   So for each point x, look at the slopes of the chosen pairs (x, y). If they are all about the same, then this value is close to the slope of the true line on which x lies. Let X denote the set of points whose slopes are unambiguous in this way.
3. If points x and y are unambiguous, then they lie on the same line if and only if their slopes are almost the same, and if there are strong collinearity relationships between the two (as determined in the first step). This enables us to cluster the points of X according to their respective lines.
4. At this stage, we have a few points from each line, including the points at the extreme ends of the line. We need only reconstruct the lines from these points.

4   The Algorithm and Main Theorem

The algorithm requires a bit of notation, which we now present. Let $l(a, b)$ denote the line connecting points a and b, and denote by $d(\cdot, \cdot)$ the normal Euclidean distance from a point to a line. The first definition addresses the issue of approximate collinearity.

Definition. Points x, y, z are called ϵ-*collinear* if

$$\min \{d(x, l(y, z)),\ d(y, l(x, z)),\ d(z, l(x, y))\} \leq \epsilon .$$

Definition. Let collinearity$(x, y) = |\{z : x, y, z \text{ are } 2\xi\text{-collinear, and } \min(\|z - x\|, \|z - y\|) \leq 2\|x - y\|\}|$. In other words: the number of points approximately collinear with x and y, and not too far from them.

The second phase of the algorithm measures slopes of various lines.

Definition. For a line segment l, let $\theta(l)$ denote the angle subtended by it line segments. In both cases, angles are measured so as to always be in the range $(-\pi/2, \pi/2]$.

Let m denote the number of data points. The algorithm is shown in Fig. 4. Its principal performance guarantee is summarized in the following main theorem. The constants in it are atrocious; no attempt has been made to optimize them.

Phase One – Collinearity:
/* For each x: */
/*   determine a set $N(x)$ of other points with which it might be collinear */
For each pair of points x, y:
  Compute collinearity(x, y).
For each point x:
  $N(x) = \{y : \text{collinearity}(x, y) \geq \frac{1}{8}mw_{min}, \text{ and } \|x - y\| \geq \frac{1}{4}\}$

Phase Two – Angles:
/* Determine a set X of points of unambiguous slope. */
For each point x:
  $A(x) = \{\theta(\overline{xy}) : y \in N(x)\}$
  $\Delta(x) = \max A(x) - \min A(x)$
$X = \{x : \Delta(x) \leq 2\max(\theta_0, \sin^{-1} 8\xi)\}$

Phase Three – Clustering:
/* Find a few points from each line. */
Construct graph G on vertices X,
  placing an edge (x, y) if both $x \in N(y)$ and $y \in N(x)$.
Find the connected components X_i of G.

Phase Four – Reconstruction:
/* Put the lines together. */
For each set X_i:
  Find the two points $x_i, y_i \in X_i$ which are farthest apart.
  Return line $l(x_i, y_i)$.

Fig. 4. Algorithm for learning a mixture of lines.

Theorem 1 *If Assumptions A-F hold, and* $m \geq \frac{2}{\delta w_{min}}$*, then with probability*

$$1 - 8\left(\frac{64e}{\delta w_{min}} \ln \frac{64e}{\delta w_{min}}\right)^2 \cdot e^{-mw_{min}^2 \delta^2 / 256} - \frac{1}{2}m^2 e^{-mw_{min}/8} ,$$

the algorithm will return k *line segments* $l(x_i, y_i)$*, where* x_i, y_i *are the farthest apart points generated from* l_i*.*

5   Proof of Correctness

We start by establishing some properties of collinearity$(\cdot, \cdot)$. In order to do this, we need to ensure that each interval of each line gets approximately the expected number of points. This follows immediately from a VC dimension argument [6].

Lemma 1. *Fix any constant* $\epsilon_0 > 0$*. Let* $\pi(\cdot)$ *denote the distribution over the plane specified by the true mixture* $w_1 l_1 + \cdots + w_k l_k$*. Let* $\widehat{\pi}(\cdot)$ *be the empirical distribution before noise. Then with probability of at least*

$$1 - 8 \left(\frac{32e}{\epsilon_0} \ln \frac{32e}{\epsilon_0} \right)^2 e^{-\epsilon_0^2 m/64} ,$$

for every interval I of every line l_i, the empirical probability $\hat{\pi}(I)$ differs from the true probability $\pi(I)$ by at most ϵ_0.

Comments:

- We will use $\epsilon_0 = \frac{1}{2}\delta w_{min}$, resulting in a sample complexity which depends quadratically on $\frac{1}{w_{min}}$. We would like to note in passing the quadratic dependency on w_{min} is not optimal. We plan to give improved sample complexity in the full version.
- Lemma 1 above the following lemmas show that certain favorable conditions hold with high probability. We will henceforth assume these conditions hold for sure, until the end, when we will take stock of probabilities.

The next lemma is quite simple to establish and implies that for most pairs of points x, y from line l_i, collinearity(x, y) is $\Omega(m w_i)$.

Lemma 2. *If points x, y come from line l_i, then*

$$collinearity(x, y) \geq m \left(\frac{\|x - y\| - 2\xi}{\|l_i\|} w_i - \epsilon_0 \right) .$$

Proof. Points x and y are the noisy versions of some original points x^* and y^* which actually lie on line l_i. We know $\|x^* - y^*\| \geq \|x - y\| - 2\xi$. Any point drawn from the open interval (x^*, y^*) contributes to collinearity(x, y). The rest follows from Lemma 1.

Corollary 2 *If points x, y come from line l_i, and $\|x - y\| \geq \frac{1}{4}\|l_i\|$, then*

$$collinearity(x, y) \geq m \left(\left(\frac{1}{4} - 2\xi \right) w_i - \epsilon_0 \right) \geq \frac{1}{8} m w_{min} .$$

We need to be able to say something about collinearity(x, y) when x and y are not from the same line. This is tough to answer if they lie in each other's cones. But:

Lemma 3. *The following holds with probability at least $1 - \frac{1}{2}m^2 e^{-m w_{min}/8}$. Pick any x, y from distinct lines l_1, l_2 respectively, such that $x \notin D_{l_1}$ (i.e. x lies outside the cones of other lines). Then: either (1) $y \in C_{l_1}$ or (2) collinearity$(x, y) < \frac{1}{8}m w_{min}$.*

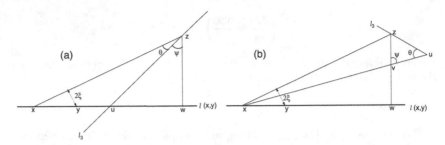

Fig. 5. Case I of Lemma 3.

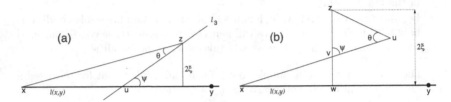

Fig. 6. Case II of Lemma 3.

Proof. Consider z from some line l_3 such that x, y, z are 2ξ-collinear. We'll show that, unless $y \in C_{l_1}$, at most an $\frac{16\xi}{\sin\theta_0}$ fraction of any line l_3 can contribute such a point z. In other words, the expected value of collinearity(x, y) is at most $\frac{16\xi}{\sin\theta_0} \cdot m$. We will then apply a large deviation bound (followed by a union bound over all pairs x, y) to show that even with our limited number of samples, collinearity(x, y) will remain small, less than $\frac{1}{8}mw_{min}$. We could use Lemma 1 here; however, that bound is rather weak when dealing with these very low-probability events. There are three cases.

<u>Case I</u>: $l_3 \neq l_1, l_2$; and y lies between x and z.

This can happen in two ways, corresponding to Fig. 5(a) and 5(b). Let's start with the first of these. Pretend for the time being that points z from l_3 must actually lie on the line segment l_3 (that is, there is no noise). The portion $\overline{uz}$ of line l_3 is *bad*: it will get included in collinearity(x, y). We must show that it is short, specifically that it is $O(\xi)$.

By similar triangles, $\|\overline{wz}\|/\|\overline{xz}\| = 2\xi/\|\overline{xy}\|$, and so

$$\|\overline{wz}\| = 2\xi \cdot \frac{\|\overline{xz}\|}{\|\overline{xy}\|} \leq 2\xi \cdot \frac{\|\overline{xy}\| + \|\overline{yz}\|}{\|\overline{xy}\|} \leq 2\xi \cdot \frac{\|\overline{xy}\| + 2\|\overline{xy}\|}{\|\overline{xy}\|} = 6\xi,$$

where the last inequality is from the definition of collinearity. Therefore we can bound the length of the bad portion $\overline{uz}$:

$$\|\overline{uz}\| = \frac{\|\overline{wz}\|}{\cos\psi} \leq \frac{6\xi}{\cos\psi} = \frac{6\xi}{\sin(\frac{\pi}{2} - \psi)} \leq \frac{6\xi}{\sin\theta} \leq \frac{6\xi}{\sin\theta_0},$$

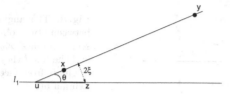

Fig. 7. Case III of Lemma 3.

since $\theta \geq \theta_0$ (by hypothesis, $x \notin D_l$). Therefore at most an $\frac{6\xi}{\sin \theta_0}$ fraction of line l_3 can contribute to collinearity(x, y) (by Assumption A, all lines have length at least one). In this analysis we ignored the fact that z is subject to noise of magnitude up-to ξ. This "edge effect" can increase the bad portion of line l_3 by at most $\frac{2\xi}{\sin \theta_0}$.

Now we move on to Fig. 5(b). As before $\|\overline{wz}\| \leq 6\xi$. But now, the bad portion $\overline{uz}$ needs to be bounded differently:

$$\|\overline{uz}\| = \|\overline{vz}\| \cdot \frac{\sin \psi}{\sin \theta} \leq \|\overline{wz}\| \cdot \frac{1}{\sin \theta} \leq \frac{\|\overline{wz}\|}{\sin \theta_0} \leq \frac{6\xi}{\sin \theta_0},$$

and as before, noise-related effects add another $\frac{2\xi}{\sin \theta_0}$ to the length of this bad portion.

In each of these two scenarios, we have bounded the bad portion of l_3 either above or below the line $l(x, y)$. Combining, we find that the total bad portion of l_3 has length at most $\frac{16\xi}{\sin \theta_0}$.

Case II: $l_3 \neq l_1, l_2$; and z lies between x and y.

See Figs. 6(a) and 6(b). We start with the first of them; since $\theta \leq \psi$,

$$\|\overline{uz}\| = \frac{2\xi}{\sin \psi} \leq \frac{2\xi}{\sin \theta} \leq \frac{2\xi}{\sin \theta_0},$$

As before, the fact that z is subject to noise can effectively add up-to $\frac{2\xi}{\sin \theta_0}$ to this bad length.

In Fig. 6(b), we notice that $\|\overline{vz}\| \leq \|\overline{wz}\| \leq 2\xi$, and so

$$\|\overline{uz}\| = \|\overline{vz}\| \cdot \frac{\sin \psi}{\sin \theta} \leq \frac{2\xi}{\sin \theta} \leq \frac{2\xi}{\sin \theta_0},$$

with noise contributing another $\frac{2\xi}{\sin \theta_0}$.

Again, by combining the bad portions of l_3 above and below $l(x, y)$, we get a total of $\frac{8\xi}{\sin \theta_0}$.

Case III: $l_3 = l_1$ (i.e. $z \in l_1$).

In this case, either $y \in C_{l_1}$ or we have the situation depicted in Fig. 7. The bad stretch along l_1 has length

$$\frac{2\xi}{\sin \theta} \leq \frac{2\xi}{\sin \theta_0}$$

plus the usual $\frac{2\xi}{\sin \theta_0}$ compensation for noise.

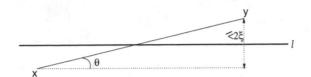

Fig. 8. The angle between two observed points x,y and the line l they originate from (see Lemma 5(a)).

At this stage, we have shown that the points from any line l_3 which contribute to collinearity(x, y) come from a small portion of l_3, of length at most $\frac{16\xi}{\sin\theta_0}$. The combined probability mass of these portions of lines (summed over all l_3) is then $\frac{16\xi}{\sin\theta_0}$, and this is an upper bound on the expected value of $\frac{1}{m}$collinearity(x, y). We now apply a simple large deviation bound for a fixed pair x, y meeting the hypotheses of this lemma:

$$\mathbf{P}\left(\text{collinearity}(x, y) \geq \frac{1}{8}mw_{min}\right) \leq \left(\frac{m}{\frac{1}{8}mw_{min}}\right) \cdot \left(\frac{16\xi}{\sin\theta_0}\right)^{\frac{1}{8}mw_{min}}$$

$$\leq \left(\frac{e}{\frac{1}{8}w_{min}}\right)^{\frac{1}{8}mw_{min}} \cdot \left(\frac{16\xi}{\sin\theta_0}\right)^{\frac{1}{8}mw_{min}}$$

$$\leq \exp\left(-\frac{1}{8}mw_{min}\right),$$

where the last inequality follows from Assumption E. To complete the lemma take a union bound over all pairs x, y.

As in the algorithm description, let $N(x)$ designate all points y with which x has strong collinearity, and whose distance from x is at least $\frac{1}{4}$. It follows from Corollary 2 and the previous lemma that:

Lemma 4. (a) *If x is from line l, then the set $N(x)$ includes all points from l which are at distance at least $\frac{1}{4}\|l\|$ from x.* **(b)** *If x is from l and $x \notin D_l$ then $N(x)$ consists entirely of points from line l or in the pair of cones C_l.*

This completes the analysis of Phase One of the algorithm. For Phase Two we need to establish some conditions on the angles between the true lines l_i and the line segments $l(x, y)$ which are generated by pairs of points.

Lemma 5. (a) *If x and y are from line l, then $\theta(\overline{xy}, l) \leq \sin^{-1}(2\xi/\|x - y\|)$.* **(b)** *If x is from line l and y comes from a different line but nonetheless lies in C_l, then $\theta(\overline{xy}, l) \leq \theta_0$.*

Proof. In part (a), both x and y are within distance ξ of line l. Therefore (Fig. 8),

$$\sin\theta(\overline{xy}, l) \leq \frac{2\xi}{\|x - y\|}.$$

Part (b) corresponds to Case III of Lemma 3. In order for collinearity(x, y) to be significant, we need the angle between $\overline{xy}$ and l to be at most θ_0.

For each point x, recall that $A(x)$ is the set of angles subtended by points in $N(x)$ and that $\Delta(x)$ is an indication of the range of $A(x)$. We can think of a point x as having an unambiguous slope associated with it if $\Delta(x)$ is small. The following is an immediate consequence of the previous two lemmas.

Lemma 6. (a) *If x comes from line l and $x \notin D_l$, then*

$$\Delta(x) \leq 2 \max(\theta_0, \sin^{-1} 8\xi) \,,$$

and so $x \in X$.
(b) *For each line l_i, the points from the starting δ-fraction of the line and the ending δ-fraction of the line must lie in X. There are at least $\frac{1}{2}\delta m w_i$ such points from each of the two endpoints.*

Proof. (a) By Lemma 4(b), all of $N(x)$ comes either from line l or lies in C_l. Therefore, by Lemma 5, for all $y \in N(x)$, we know $\theta(\overline{xy}, l) \leq \max(\theta_0, \sin^{-1} 8\xi)$. This implies the bound on $\Delta(x)$.
(b) By Assumption C, these points lie outside D_l and must therefore be in X. The number of such points at one given endpoint of l_i is $\geq m(w_i\delta - \epsilon_0)$ (by Lemma 1), which is at least $\frac{1}{2}\delta m w_i$ by the choice of ϵ_0.

Can points from different lines have unambiguous slopes and yet lie in each other's neighborhoods? This cannot be the case, on account of Assumption F.

Lemma 7. (a) *If point $x \in X$ comes from line l, and $y \in N(x)$, then*

$$\theta(\overline{xy}, l) \leq 2 \max(\theta_0, \sin^{-1} 8\xi) + \sin^{-1} 8\xi \,.$$

(b) *Suppose $x, y \in X$ come from different lines l_1 and l_2 respectively. Then it cannot be the case that both $x \in N(y)$ and $y \in N(x)$.*

Proof. (a) By the previous lemma, $N(x)$ must contain some point z from l with $\|x - z\| \geq \frac{1}{4}$. Then, by Lemma 5(a), $\theta(\overline{xz}, l) \leq \sin^{-1} 8\xi$. By definition of X, $\theta(\overline{xy}, \overline{xz}) < 2 \max(\theta_0, \sin^{-1} 8\xi)$. Now use $\theta(\overline{xy}, l) < \theta(\overline{xy}, \overline{xz}) + \theta(\overline{xz}, l)$.
(b) From the previous part, we know that both

$$\theta(\overline{xy}, l_1) \leq 2 \max(\theta_0, \sin^{-1} 8\xi) + \sin^{-1} 8\xi$$

and

$$\theta(\overline{xy}, l_2) \leq 2 \max(\theta_0, \sin^{-1} 8\xi) + \sin^{-1} 8\xi \,.$$

Therefore, $\theta(l_1, l_2) \leq 4 \max(\theta_0, \sin^{-1} 8\xi) + 2\sin^{-1} 8\xi$. This violates Assumption F.

We can now wrap up the details of the clustering phase of the algorithm.

Lemma 8. *The third phase of the algorithm returns k connected components, each corresponding to a particular line l_i. The component X_i for line l_i only contains points from l_i, and, provided $m \geq \frac{2}{\delta w_{min}}$, includes the two most extreme points from this line (i.e. the empirical endpoints).*

Proof. From Lemma 7(b), we know that points from different lines will not be connected in graph G. At the same time, we know from Lemma 6(b) that X includes at least $\delta m w_i$ points from each line l_i, including the extreme points of the line. Pick any two of these points from l_i. By Lemmas 4(a) and 6(b), these two points are connected in G, by a path of length at most two.

Lemma 9. *For a sample of size* $m = \frac{1}{2}\delta w_{min}^{-2}$ *and any line* ℓ_i *the endpoints of the approximated line are an expected distance from the original line of*

$$\frac{9}{(w_{min}^{-1} + 2)(w_{min}^{-1} + 4)} + 2\xi .$$

Proof. Note that for any line the expected number of points that are *not* in D_ℓ is at least $\frac{1}{2}w_{min}^{-1}$. Therefore, for one of the endpoints the probability of being a distance a is $(1 - a)^{\frac{1}{2w_{min}}}$. Integrating to calculate the expectation, we get an expected distance of $\frac{4}{(w_{min}^{-1}+2)(w_{min}^{-1}+4)}$. We can therefore bound expected distance from both endpoints. Since the point can have an additional noise of ξ we get the total expected distance of

$$\frac{8}{(w_{min}^{-1} + 2)(w_{min}^{-1} + 4)} + 2\xi .$$

6   Illustrative Example

In this section we give an illustration of the running stages of the algorithm. We implemented in Matlab the code described in Fig. 4. We set the coordinates system to be $[0, 1] \times [0, 1]$. We then picked at random five lines and sampled uniformly from the lines, choosing each of the lines with equal probability. Each sample point was then displaced by adding a noise which was distributed uniformly in a circle of radius 0.05, hence the noise level was 5%. We also generated 5% of random points that do not belong to any of the lines. This data along with the generating lines is depicted on the top left plot in Fig. 9. The reconstructed lines along with all the points are shown on the top right part of the same figure.

On the bottom part of Fig. 9 we illustrate the stages of the algorithm. For the clarity of the illustration we re-ordered the sample points so that each line constitute a consecutive points in the illustration. On the bottom left plot of the figure we show the value of *collinearity*(x, y) for each pair of point x, y. We used a gray scale color coding to designate the magnitude. (White represents a value of 0 and black the maximum number of points in the figure.) It is clear that the first stage of the algorithm already captures the structure induced by the generating lines. In the middle bottom figure we show the sets $N(x)$ for each sample point x which is represented as a row in the figure. For each point $y \neq x$ we set the corresponding pixel in the figure to black if $y \in N(x)$ and to white otherwise. The picture becomes clearer – the matrix is almost block diagonal with scatter black pixels corresponding to points that are in the intersection of the lines and

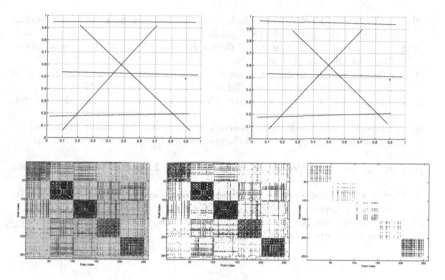

Fig. 9. Top left: original synthetic data with generating lines. Top right: reconstructed lines. Bottom: illustration of the running stages of the algorithm.

noisy points that are close to one of the lines. Finally, on the bottom right part of Fig. 9 we show that *closure* of the graph G from Phase Three (obtained after discarding points with ambiguous slopes). It is clear that G is block diagonal. Although the algorithm discarded some of the points residing on the lines as well, the remaining points suffice to provide a reliable reconstruction.

7   Conclusions

In this paper we described a simple and efficient algorithm for reconstructing the arrangement of line-segments from noisy observations. We hope that our algorithm will also provide a practical tool in the fields of computer vision and computer graphics. However, since we confined the algorithm and its analysis to the model of lines in the two dimensional plane, some extensions and generalizations might be needed in order to make the algorithm applicable to real-world problems. First, we will need to generalize the algorithm for line segments in $\Re^n$ where n can be 3 or 4. Second, we would like to be able to handle sources more complex than line-segments, such as circle or even general algebraic functions.

References

[1] S. Arora and R. Kannan, *A polynomial time algorithm to learn a mixture of general gaussians*, ACM Symposium on Theory of Computing (STOC), 2001.

[2] S. Arora and S. Khot, *Fitting algebraic curves to noisy data*, ACM Symposium on Theory of Computing (STOC), 2002.

[3] S. Dasgupta, *Learning mixtures of Gaussians*, IEEE Symposium on Foundations of Computer Science (FOCS), 1999.

[4] M. Fischler and R. Bolles, *Random Sample Consensus: A Paradigm for Model fitting*, Communications of the ACM (CACM), 24(5), pp. 381–395, 1981.

[5] D. Forsyth and J. Ponce, *Computer Vision – a modern approach*, Manuscript, 2002.

[6] D. Haussler, *Decision-theoretic generalizations of the PAC model for neural net and other learning applications*, Information and Computation, Vol. 100, pp. 78–150, 1992.

[7] P. Roosseeuw, *Least Median of Squares Regression*, Journal of American Statistical Association, 58, pp. 1–22, 1993.

[8] C. Stewart, *Robust Parameter Estimation on Computer Vision*, Society for Industrial and Applied Mathematics, SIAM 41(3), pp. 513–537, 1985.

[9] D.M. Titterington, A.F.M. Smith and U.E. Makov, *Statistical Analysis of Finite Mixture Distributions*, John Wiley & Sons, 1985.

Constraint Classification: A New Approach to Multiclass Classification

Sariel Har-Peled, Dan Roth, and Dav Zimak

Department of Computer Science,
University of Illinois,
Urbana, IL 61801,
{sariel,danr,davzimak}@uiuc.edu

Abstract. In this paper, we present a new view of multiclass classification and introduce the constraint classification problem, a generalization
that captures many flavors of multiclass classification. We provide the
first optimal, distribution independent bounds for many multiclass learning algorithms, including winner-take-all (WTA). Based on our view, we
present a learning algorithm that learns via a single linear classifier in
high dimension. In addition to the distribution independent bounds, we
provide a simple margin-based analysis improving generalization bounds
for linear multiclass support vector machines.

1 Introduction

Multiclass classification is a central problem in machine learning, as applications
that require a discrimination among many classes are ubiquitous. Examples studied in machine learning include handwritten character recognition [LS97,LB+89],
part-of-speech tagging [Bri94,RZ98], speech recognition [Jel98] and text page
classification [ADW94,DKR97].

Learning approaches for these tasks often use a winner-take-all (WTA) strategy at some point in the decision process. As input, the WTA uses several real
valued functions and returns the index of the function with the highest value.
Classifiers making use of WTA exist in many sub-fields of of machine learning,
such as neural networks [AB99], self-organizing maps[Koh01] and, more recently,
networks of linear threshold functions such as SNoW [CCRR99,Rot98] and multiclass support vector machines [CS01a,ASS00,Sch97,WW99].

Currently there is only a limited understanding of multiclass classification.
It is known, for example, that WTA is a powerful classifier in terms of expres-
sivitiy [Maa00]: neural network using a single WTA unit as its only nonlinear
computational element can, with enough inputs, approximate arbitrary continuous functions. However, little is known about generalization properties and
convergent algorithmic approaches. A PAC-style analysis of multiclass functions
that uses an extended notion of VC-dimension for multiclass case [BCHL95]

N. Cesa-Bianchi et al. (Eds.): ALT 2002, LNAI 2533, pp. 365–379, 2002.

provides poor bounds on generalization for WTA, and the current best bounds rely on a generalized notion of margin [ASS00]. However, the more fundamental question about deriving such bounds directly has not been investigated.

Algorithmically, most approaches to multiclass classification make use of "standard" binary classifiers to encode and train the output labels. The most commonly used scheme makes a "one versus all" (OvA) assumption, dictating that for each class there exists a single separator between that class and all other classes. "All versus all" (AvA, or pairwise) classification [HT98] is a more expressive alternative which assumes the existence of a separator between any two classes (but requires training a quadratic number of Boolean classifiers).

This work is motivated by several successful practical approaches, such as multiclass SVM and SNoW that rely on WTA-style strategies over linear functions (that produce a decision surface consisting of linear boundaries). In this paper, we introduce a new constraint classification problem that generalizes many interesting variants of multiclass classification and derive both VC-dimension and margin-based generalization bounds. The VC-dimension bounds are optimal for the case of WTA classifiers over linear functions.

Underlying our results is a new view of multiclass classification based on a simple transformation. In Subsection 3.2, we present a new algorithm that transforms an example set into higher dimensional space and learns a simple separating hyperplane in this space. Our algorithm suggests a way to fix the popular "one-vs-all" training scheme so that it will guarantee consistent classification. This algorithm turns out to be similar to the ultraconservative online algorithm for multiclass problems introduced in [CS01b].

In Section 4, we use the high dimensional view of multiclass classification and standard bounds for learning separating hyperplanes to develop generalization bounds. Distribution independent bounds are developed using a multiclass version of the standard growth function, and margin-based bounds are given that improve over previous bounds.

2   Learning Problems

Learning problems often assume that examples, $(x, y) \in \mathcal{X} \times \mathcal{Y}$, are drawn *i.i.d.* from a fixed probability distribution, $\mathcal{D}_{\mathcal{X} \times \mathcal{Y}}$, over $\mathcal{X} \times \mathcal{Y}$. $\mathcal{X}$ is referred to as the instance space and $\mathcal{Y}$ is referred to as the output space (*label set*). The learning algorithm is presented with m training examples, P, drawn in such a fashion from $\mathcal{D}_{\mathcal{X} \times \mathcal{Y}}$ and attempts to output a function (*hypothesis*) $h : \mathcal{X} \to \mathcal{Y}$ from the set of all functions (hypotheses) $\mathcal{H}$ that minimizes the *empirical error* on P.

Definition 1 (Permutations.) Denote the set of full orders over $\{1, \ldots, k\}$ as S^k, consisting of all permutations of $\{1, \ldots, k\}$. Similarly, $\bar{S}^k$ denotes the set of all partial orders over $\{1, \ldots, k\}$. A partial order, $c \in \bar{S}^k$, defines a binary relation, $\prec_c$ and can be represented by set of pairs on which $\prec_c$ holds, $c = \{(i, j) | i \prec_c j\}$. In addition, for any set of pairs $c = \{(i_1, j_1), \ldots, (i_n, j_n)\}$, we refer to c both as a set of pairs and as the partial order produced by the transitive closure of c with respect to $\prec_c$. Given two partial orders $a, b \in \bar{S}^k$, a is *consistent* with b (denoted $a \sqsubseteq b$) if for every $(i, j) \in \{1, \ldots, k\}^2$, $i \prec_b j$ holds whenever $i \prec_a j$. If $c \in S^k$ is a full order, then it can be represented by a list of k integers where $i \prec_c j$ if i precedes j in the list, and is refered to as a *ranking*. The size of a partial order, $|c|$ is the number of pairs specified in c.

Definition 2 (Learning.) Given m examples, $P = ((x_1, y_1), \ldots, (x_m, y_m))$, drawn *i.i.d.* from $\mathcal{D}_{\mathcal{X} \times \mathcal{Y}}$, a hypothesis class $\mathcal{H}$ and an error function $\mathcal{E} : \mathcal{X} \times \mathcal{Y} \times \mathcal{H} \to \{0, 1\}$, a learning algorithm $\mathcal{L}(P, \mathcal{H})$ outputs a function $h \in \mathcal{H}$, where $h : \mathcal{X} \to \mathcal{Y}$.

Typically learning algorithms try to output the hypothesis $h \in \mathcal{H}$ that minimizes the expected error on a randomly drawn example. The particular algorithm used may vary. We propose a framework that allows for any binary learning algorithm to be used, including support vector machines.

Many interesting learning problems can be expressed in this general learning framework simply by changing the type of output space, $\mathcal{Y}$. Binary classification, for example, setts $\mathcal{Y} = \{-1, 1\}$, whereas multiclass classification sets $\mathcal{Y} = \{1, \ldots, k\}$.

In this paper, algorithms and generalization bounds are provided for the following learning problems (of course, the actual function classes used for classification must be restricted to produce a generalization bound).

Binary Classification. Set $\mathcal{Y} = \{-1, 1\}$.

Multiclass Classification. Set $\mathcal{Y} = \{1, \ldots, k\}$.

The most commonly used multiclass classification scheme is the *winner-take-all (WTA)* strategy, where each class $i \in \mathcal{Y}$ is represented with a real-valued function $f_i : \mathcal{X} \to \mathbb{R}$. WTA outputs $y^* = \mathrm{argmax}_{\{1,\ldots,k\}} f_i(x)$ as the final class. Notice that binary classification is a special case of multiclass classification where $k = 2$.

l-Multilabel Classification. Set $\mathcal{Y} = \{1, \ldots, k\}^l$.

In practice, it is common for examples to be labeled with more than one class from $\{1, \ldots, k\}$. When classifying web pages, for example, a single page might be a "homepage", a "faculty page", *and* a "machine learning page," in which case a web classification system should be able to produce all three labels as output. Clearly multiclass classification and binary classification are special cases of l-multilabel classification.

Just as the WTA function is used for multiclass classification, the l-WTA function can be used for l-multiclass classification. l-WTA outputs l labels from $\mathrm{argmax}^l_{\{1,\ldots,k\}} f_i(x)$, where argmax^l outputs a set of consisting of the l highest values of $f_i(x)$.

Ranking Classification. Set $\mathcal{Y} = S^k$.

A ranking classifier returns a full order, or permutation, of $\{1, \ldots, k\}$ from the set S^k. In some settings, class i might be "preferred" over class j. Often i precedes j when $f_i(x) > f_j(x)$.

Constraint Classification. Set $\mathcal{Y} = \bar{S}^k$.

Constraint classification is a direct generalization of ranking classification where the classifier must output a partial order from $\bar{S}^k$, the set of all partial orders of $\{1, \ldots, k\}$.

c-**Constraint Classification.** Set $\mathcal{Y} = \bar{S}_c^k$.

The set $\bar{S}_c^k$ is simply a subset of $\bar{S}^k$ where for all $y \in \bar{S}_c^k$, $|y| \leq c$. Clearly constraint classification is a special case of c-constraint classification where $c = \binom{k}{2}$.

Constraint classification is very general and powerful since every example can have its own specific set of constraints. The distribution $\mathcal{D}_{\mathcal{X} \times \bar{S}^k}$ may be constrained based on a strong relationship among the classes $\{1, \ldots, k\}$, or even on the example, x, at hand. For example, suppose every constraint $(i, j) \in y$ is such that i and j are either both even or both odd. Unfortunately, this type of information is unknown to the learning algorithm a-priori and might be difficult to learn. Therefore, a hypothesis is acceptable if it is consistent with the examples. This notion is captured in the error function.

Definition 3 (Error Indicator Function.) For any $(x, y) \in \mathcal{X} \times \bar{S}^k$, and hypothesis $h : \mathcal{X} \to \bar{S}^k$, the *indicator function* $\mathcal{E}(x, y, h)$ indicates an error on example x, $\mathcal{E}(x, y, h) = 1$ if $y \not\sqsubseteq h(x)$, and 0 otherwise.

Given a set of m labeled examples $P = ((x_1, y_1), \ldots, (x_m, y_m)) \in \{\mathcal{X} \times \mathcal{Y}\}^m$, the *indicator vector* for a function $h \in \mathcal{H}$,

$$\mathcal{E}(P, h) = (\mathcal{E}(x_1, y_1, h), \mathcal{E}(x_2, y_2, h), \ldots, \mathcal{E}(x_m, y_m, h))$$

indicates which examples were classified incorrectly. Finally, we define

$$\mathcal{E}(P, \mathcal{H}) = \left\{ \mathcal{E}(P, h) \mid h \in \mathcal{H} \right\}$$

to be the set of all possible indicator vectors for $\mathcal{H}$.

For example, if $k = 4$ and the example $(x, \{(2, 3), (2, 4)\})$, $h_1(x) = (2, 3, 1, 4)$, and $h_2(x) = (4, 2, 3, 1)$, then h_1 is correct since 2 precedes 3 and 2 precedes 4 in the full order $(2, 3, 1, 4)$ whereas h_2 is incorrect since 4 precedes 2 in $(4, 2, 3, 1)$.

Definition 4 (Error.) Given an example (x, y) drawn *i.i.d.* from $\mathcal{D}_{\mathcal{X} \times \mathcal{Y}}$, the *true error* of $h \in \mathcal{H}$, where $h: \mathcal{X} \to \mathcal{Y}$ is defined to be $err(h) = \Pr_{\mathcal{D}}[\mathcal{E}(x, y, h) = 1]$. Given $P = ((x_1, y_1), \ldots, (x_m, y_m))$ drawn from $EX(\mathcal{D}_{\{\mathcal{X} \times \mathcal{Y}\}})$, the *empirical error* of $h \in \mathcal{H}$ with respect to P is defined to be $err(P, h) = \frac{1}{|P|} \sum_{i=1 \ldots m} \mathcal{E}(x_i, y_i, h)$.

Throughout the rest of this paper, the each hypothesis from $\mathcal{H}$ consists of a collection of linear functions over $\mathcal{X} = \mathbb{R}^d$. Specifically, hypothesis $h \in \mathcal{H}$ can be represented as k weight vectors $w_1, \ldots, w_k \in \mathbb{R}^d$, where w_i is associated with class i. Given an example x, $(w_i \cdot x)$ represents the "strength" or "confidence" of class i. With this assumption each of the above learning problems takes on a specific form, and furthermore, can be represented within the constraint classification setting. Table 1 shows their representation space and hypothesis classes.

Table 1. Learning problems differ based on their output space and on their internal representation. Definitions for each of the problems considered in this paper (*notice that the output space for the constraint classification problems is different than the range of the hypothesis space). argmax^l is a variant of argmax that returns the indices of the weight vectors that give the l largest values of $w_i \cdot x$ instead of only the largest. argsort is a linear sorting function (see Definition 5).

Problem	Internal Representation	Output Space ($\mathcal{Y}$)	Hypothesis
binary	$w \in \mathbb{R}^d$	$\{-1, 1\}$	$\text{sign}\, w \cdot x$
multiclass	$(w_1, \ldots, w_k) \in \mathbb{R}^{kd}$	$\{1, \ldots, k\}$	$\text{argmax}_{\{1,\ldots,k\}}\, w_i \cdot x$
l-multiclass	$(w_1, \ldots, w_k) \in \mathbb{R}^{kd}$	$\{1, \ldots, k\}^l$	$\text{argmax}^l_{\{1,\ldots,k\}}\, w_i \cdot x$
ranking	$(w_1, \ldots, w_k) \in \mathbb{R}^{kd}$	S^k	$\text{argsort}_{\{1,\ldots,k\}}\, w_i \cdot x$
constraint*	$(w_1, \ldots, w_k) \in \mathbb{R}^{kd}$	$\bar{S}^k$	$\text{argsort}_{\{1,\ldots,k\}}\, w_i \cdot x$
c-constraint*	$(w_1, \ldots, w_k) \in \mathbb{R}^{kd}$	$\bar{S}^k_c$	$\text{argsort}_{\{1,\ldots,k\}}\, w_i \cdot x$

The relationships among all of these problems can be made explicit. For example, 2-class multiclass classification is equivalent to binary classification since $\text{argmax}_{\{1,2\}}\, w_i \cdot x = 1$ exactly when $(w_1 \cdot x - w_2 \cdot x) = (w_1 - w_2) \cdot x > 0$; both problems compute separating hyperplanes in $\mathbb{R}^d$. Furthermore, constraint classification can capture all of the problems in Table 1.

Definition 5 (Linear Sorting Function.) Let $w = (w_1, \ldots, w_k)$ be a set of k vectors, where $(w_1, \ldots, w_k) \in \mathbb{R}^d$. Given $x \in \mathbb{R}^d$, a *linear sorting classifier* is a function $h : \mathbb{R}^d \to S^k$ computed in the following way:

$$h(x) = \underset{i=1\ldots k}{\text{argsort}}\, w_i \cdot x,$$

where argsort returns a permutation of $\{1, \ldots, k\}$ where i precedes j if $w_i \cdot x > w_j \cdot x$. In the case that $w_i \cdot x = w_j \cdot x$, i precedes j if $i < j$.

Lemma 1 (Problem mappings.). *All of the learning problems in Table 1 can be expressed as constraint classification problems.*

Proof. Because binary and multilabel classification are special cases of l-multilabel classification, and ranking and constraint classification are special cases of c-constraint classification, it suffices to show that l-multilabel classification can be expressed as a c-constraint classification problem.

Given an example $(x, y) \in \mathbb{R}^d \times \{1, \ldots, k\}^l$, define a new example $(x, y_c) \in \mathbb{R}^d \times \bar{S}^k_{l(k-l)}$ (notice that y is a set of integers and y_c is a set of integer pairs), where

$$y_c = \left\{ (i, j) \,\middle|\, i \in y, j \in \{1, \ldots, k\} \setminus y \right\}.$$

Any l-multilabel classifier $h_l(x) = \text{argmax}^l_{\{1,\ldots,k\}}\, w_i \cdot x$ will err on example (x, y) exactly when the c-constraint classifier $h_c(x) = \text{argsort}_{\{1,\ldots,k\}}\, w_i \cdot x$ errs, and the indicator functions for the two classifiers are equal, $\mathcal{E}(x, h_l) = \mathcal{E}(x, h_c)$.

The size of the constraint sets for each of the problem mappings appears up in the margin-based generalization bound in Subsection 4.2. Binary classification becomes a 2-constraint classification problem and multiclass classification is transformed into a $(k-1)$-constraint classification problem. Ranking classification becomes a $(k-1)$-constraint classification problem by noticing that any full order from S^k can be represented by only $k-1$ constraints, namely $(i,j) \in y_c$ if i precedes j in y.

Consider a 4-class multiclass example, $(x, 3)$. It is transformed into the 3-constraint example, $(x, \{(3, 1), (3, 2), (3, 4)\})$. If we find a constraint classifier that correctly labels x according to the given constraints ($w_3 \cdot x > w_1 \cdot x$, $w_3 \cdot x > w_2 \cdot x$, and $w_3 \cdot x > w_4 \cdot x$), then $3 = \mathrm{argmax}_{1,2,3,4}\, w_i \cdot x$.

The goal of a learning algorithm for constraint classification is to return a linear sorting function that has small error on the training data.

3   Learning

In this section, the k-class constraint classification problem is transformed into a binary classification problem in higher dimension. Each example $(x, y) \in \mathbb{R}^d \times \bar{S}^k$ is transformed into a set of examples in $\mathbb{R}^{kd} \times \{-1, 1\}$ based on the information contained in y. Then, a single separating hyperplane in $\mathbb{R}^{kd}$ can be interpreted as a collection of k weight vectors, in $\mathbb{R}^d$, of a linear sorting classifier.

It is important to point out the connection to optimization when using linear sorting functions. Weston and Watkins'[WW99] transformation of multiclass classification to an optimization problem is easily extended to constraint classification.

The goal of the (hard) optimization problem is to minimize

$$\Phi(w_1, \ldots, w_k),$$

subject to constraints derived from examples in P,

$$w_i \cdot x > w_j \cdot x,$$

$$\forall (x, y) \in P, \forall (i, j) \in y.$$

The solution $w^* = (w_1^*, \ldots, w_k^*)$ that minimizes $\Phi(\cdot)$ is a point in $\mathbb{R}^{kd}$ that can be interpreted as the coefficients of a linear sorting classifier consistent with the constraints given in a constraint classification problem. While w^* is certainly one feasible solution, there are many others. By viewing the constraint classification problem as a feasibility problem rather than an optimization problem, any standard learning algorithm for binary classification can be used – including perceptron, winnow, and kernel-based SVM's.

3.1   Transformation

Here, a dual version of the above feasibility problem is described in detail to highlight the fact that the constraint classification problem is being transformed into an equivalent binary classification problem.

Definition 6 (Chunk.) A vector $\mathbf{v} = (v_1, \ldots, v_{kd}) \in \mathbb{R}^{kd} = \mathbb{R}^d \times \cdots \times \mathbb{R}^d$, is broken into k *chunks* $(\mathbf{v}_1, \ldots, \mathbf{v}_k)$ where the i-th chunk, $\mathbf{v}_i = (v_{(i-1)*d+1}, \ldots, v_{i*d})$.

Definition 7 (Expansion.) Let $\text{Vec}(x, i)$ be a vector $x \in \mathbb{R}^d$ embedded in kd dimensions, by writing the coordinates of x in the i-th chunk of a vector in $\mathbb{R}^{k(d+1)}$. Denote by $\mathbf{0}^l$ the zero vector of length l. Then $\text{Vec}(x, i)$ can be written formally as the concatenation of three vectors, $\text{Vec}(x, i) = (\mathbf{0}^{(i-1)*d}, x, \mathbf{0}^{(k-i)*d}) \in \mathbb{R}^{kd}$. Finally, $\text{Vec}(x, i, j) = \text{Vec}(x, i) - \text{Vec}(x, j)$, as the embedding of x in the i-th chunk and $-x$ in the j-th chunk of a vector in $\mathbb{R}^{kd}$.

Definition 8 (Expanded Example Sets.) Given an example (x, y), where $x \in \mathbb{R}^d$ and $y \in \bar{S}^k$, we define the *expansion* of (x, y) into a set of examples as follows,

$$\mathbf{P}_+(x, y) = \left\{ (\text{Vec}(x, i, j), 1) \,\middle|\, (i, j) \in y \right\} \subseteq \mathbb{R}^{kd} \times \{1\},$$

A set of negative examples is defined as the reflection of each expanded example through the origin, specifically

$$\mathbf{P}_-(x, y) = \left\{ (-\mathbf{x}, -1) \,\middle|\, (\mathbf{x}, 1) \in \mathbf{P}_+(x, y) \right\} \subseteq \mathbb{R}^{kd} \times \{-1\},$$

and the set of both positive and negative examples is denoted by $\mathbf{P}(x, y) = \mathbf{P}_+(x, y) \cup \mathbf{P}_-(x, y)$. The expansion of a set of examples, P, is defined as the union of all of the expanded examples in the set,

$$\mathbf{P}(P) = \bigcup_{(x,y) \in P} \mathbf{P}(x, y) \subseteq \mathbb{R}^{kd} \times \{-1, 1\}.$$

For example, consider the example $((x_1, x_2), \{(2, 3), (2, 4)\})$. Set

$$\mathbf{P}_+((x_1, x_2), \{(2, 3), (2, 4)\}) = \{\ ((0, 0, x_1, x_2, -x_1, -x_2, 0, 0), 1)\ ,$$
$$((0, 0, x_1, x_2, 0, 0, -x_1, -x_2), 1)\ \},$$

and

$$\mathbf{P}_-((x_1, x_2), \{(2, 3), (2, 4)\}) = \{\ ((0, 0, -x_1, -x_2, x_1, x_2, 0, 0), -1)\ ,$$
$$((0, 0, -x_1, -x_2, 0, 0, x_1, x_2), -1)\ \}.$$

3.2   Algorithm

Given a set of examples P, compute the expanded examples $\mathbf{P}(P)$ and learn a separating hyperplane, $\mathbf{v} \in \mathbb{R}^{kd}$, using any linear classification algorithm. If the learning algorithm is successful in finding a vector $\mathbf{v}$ that correctly classifies all points in $\mathbf{P}(P)$, then $h(x) = \text{argsort}_{1,\ldots,k} \mathbf{v}_i \cdot x$ is also consistent with all constraints from all examples in P.

The significance of framework in multiclass classification is the observation that the hypothesis learned above is more expressive than the one learned by using the OvA assumption.

3.3   Comparison to "One vs. All"

A common approach to multiclass classification $(\mathcal{Y} = \{1, \ldots, k\})$ is to make the *one-versus-all (OvA)* assumption, that each class can be separated from the rest using a binary classification algorithm. Learning proceeds by learning k binary classifiers, each trained separately, where for example (x, y), x is considered a positive example for classifier i if $y = i$ and as a negative example if $y \neq i$. Although a consistent classifier can be found for any set of training data when arbitrarily complex hypotheses are used, it will suffer poor generalization error.

Definition 9 (OvA Assumption.) Let $\mathcal{L}^*(P, \mathcal{H})$ be an "optimal" learning algorithm in the sense that $h^* = \mathcal{L}^*(P, \mathcal{H})$ is a hypothesis, $h^* \in \mathcal{H}$, that has minimum error on P, $err(P, h^*) = \min_{h \in \mathcal{H}} err(P, h)$.

Given a set of examples $P = ((x_1, y_1), \ldots, (x_m, y_m)) \in \mathbb{R}^d \times \{1, \ldots, k\}$, define $P_i = ((x_1, eq(y_1, i)), \ldots, (x_m, eq(y_m, i))) \in \mathbb{R}^d \times \{-1, 1\}$, where $eq(a, b) = 1$ if $a = b$, and $eq(a, b) = -1$ otherwise. Let $\mathcal{H}$ be the class of linear threshold functions where for all $h \in \mathcal{H}$, $h(x) = \text{sign}(w \cdot x)$, $w, x \in \mathbb{R}^d$, where $\text{sign}(a) = 1$ if $a > 0$ and $\text{sign} = -1$ otherwise. Set $h_i^* = \mathcal{L}^*(P_i, \mathcal{H})$. The final WTA hypothesis trained on P is $h^{WTA}(x) = \text{argmax}_{\{1, \ldots, k\}} w_i^* \cdot x$.

The above assumption is commonly used in practice[Rot98,AB99] where convergence is guaranteed only if each class is linearly separable from all other classes. However, this is often not the case and convergence may not occur even though a consistent multiclass classifier exists (see Figure 1 and Theorem 10).

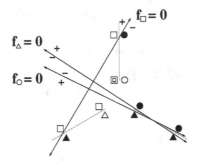

Fig. 1. An example in $\mathbb{R}^2$ showing that one-versus-all (OvA) will not converge to a consistent hypothesis. A three class classification problem (squares, triangles, and circles), where the solid points have weight 10 times that of the hollow points. The weighted points restrict the minimum error OvA separating hyperplanes. The square-classifier will predict the point outlined with a double square as negative while the circle-classifier will predict it as positive. Therefore, the final prediction for this point will be incorrect. One can verify the existence of a consistent WTA classifier for this pointset.

Theorem 10. *Winner-take-all classifiers over linear functions trained according to the one-versus-all assumptions in Definition 9 can not learn all data sets consistent with some winner-take-all hypothesis.*

Proof. see Figure 1.

3.4 Comparison to Networks of Linear Threshold Gates (Perceptron)

It is possible to rewrite the constraint classification algorithm in Section 3.2 in a way that allows a network of linear classifiers (e.g., SNoW, or a multiclass SVM) to run it, with only a slight modification to the update rule. Such a network has $x \in \mathbb{R}^d$ as input and k outputs where the i-th output computes $\mathbf{v}_i \cdot x$.

Specifically, in an on-line case such as Perceptron or Winnow, given (x, y), the update rule cycles through the outputs from 1 to k and when $w_i \cdot x > w_y \cdot x$, it "demotes" weights connected to output i and "promotes" weights connected to output y, while updating $w_y \cdot x$ along the way.

Using a network in this way results in an algorithm very similar to the ultraconservative online algorithms presented in [CS01b]. Instead of viewing an example as positive for one class and negative for all others and training each output independently, as in OvA, only those outputs that have a higher value than the correct index are changed.

4   Generalization Bounds

When considering $\mathcal{H}$ to be the class of linear sorting functions, a consistent classifier for constraint classification can be found via the use of a hyperplane to separate randomly generated points in $\mathbb{R}^{kd}$. Both VC-dimension-based (based on growth function), and margin-based bounds for the class of hyperplanes in $\mathbb{R}^{kd}$ have been heavily studied[Vap98,AB99]. Unfortunately, these results cannot directly be applied here since the transformation produces points in $\mathbb{R}^{kd}$ that are random, but not *independently* drawn. In this section, generalization bounds for linear threshold functions are used to indirectly bound generalization error of the original, low dimension, constraint classification problem.

4.1   Growth Function-Based Bounds

Although VC-dimension cannot be used explicitly for constraint classification problems, bounds based on the growth function can be used.

Preliminaries

Definition 11 (Prediction Vector.) Let $\mathcal{H}$ be a class of functions $h : \mathcal{X} \to \mathcal{Y}$. Given a set of m unlabeled examples $P = (x_1, \ldots, x_m) \in \mathcal{X}^m$ we denote the *prediction vector* for a function h as $h(P) = (h(x_1), \ldots, h(x_m))$. The set of all prediction vectors for $\mathcal{H}$ is $\mathcal{H}(P) = \left\{ h(P) \mid h \in \mathcal{H} \right\}$.

The growth function is usually defined when labels come from $\{-1, 1\}$, however, the definition holds in more general settings as well.

Definition 12 (Growth Function.) Let $\mathcal{H}$ be a hypothesis class where $h \in \mathcal{H}$ is a function $h : \mathcal{X} \to \mathcal{Y}$. The number of assignments to a set of *unlabeled* examples, $P = (x_1, \ldots, x_m) \in \mathcal{X}^m$, by hypothesis class $\mathcal{H}$ can be measured by the size of $\mathcal{H}(P)$ as it gives the set of all possible labeling for a particular sample. We define this number as $\mathcal{N}_{\mathcal{H}}(P) = |\mathcal{H}(P)|$. The *growth function* for $\mathcal{H}$ is $\mathcal{G}_{\mathcal{H}}(m) = \sup_{P \in \mathcal{X}^m} \log \mathcal{N}_{\mathcal{H}}(P)$.

Similarly, the number of (binary) assignments to a set of *labeled* examples $P = ((x_1, y_1), \ldots, (x_m, y_m)) \in \{\mathcal{X} \times \mathcal{Y}\}^m$ by $\mathcal{E}(\cdot)$, an indicator function for $\mathcal{H}$, can be measured by the size of $\mathcal{E}(P, \mathcal{H})$. We define this number as $\mathcal{N}_{\mathcal{E}}(P) = |\mathcal{E}(P, \mathcal{H})|$. The *growth function* for $\mathcal{E}(\cdot)$ is $\mathcal{G}_{\mathcal{E}}(m) = \sup_{P \in \mathcal{X}^m} \log \mathcal{N}_{\mathcal{E}}(P)$.

Observation 13 *For a given set of m labeled examples, $P = ((x_1, y_1), \ldots, (x_m, y_m)) \in \{\mathcal{X} \times \mathcal{Y}\}^m$ and a hypothesis class $\mathcal{H}$, the size of the set of all indicator vectors is smaller than the size of the set of all prediction vectors, $\mathcal{N}_{\mathcal{E}}(P) = |\mathcal{E}(P, \mathcal{H})| \leq |\mathcal{H}(P_{\mathcal{X}})| = \mathcal{N}_{\mathcal{H}}(P_{\mathcal{X}})$, where $P_{\mathcal{X}} = (x_1, \ldots, x_m)$ are the examples from P without their labels. Therefore, the maximum number of assignments by the indicator functions is bounded by the maximum number of assignments by $\mathcal{H}$. Namely,*

$$\sup_{P \in \{\mathcal{X} \times \mathcal{Y}\}^m} \mathcal{N}_{\mathcal{E}}(P) = \sup_{P \in \{\mathcal{X} \times \mathcal{Y}\}^m} |\mathcal{E}(P, \mathcal{H})| \leq \sup_{P \in \mathcal{X}^m} |\mathcal{H}(P)| = \sup_{P \in \mathcal{X}^m} \mathcal{N}_{\mathcal{H}}(P).$$

Thus, $\mathcal{G}_{\mathcal{E}}(m) \leq \mathcal{G}_{\mathcal{H}}(m)$. Furthermore, notice when $\mathcal{H}$ is the class of linear sorting functions the indicator function, $\mathcal{E}(P, \mathcal{H})$, can be interpreted in the constraint classification setting. In this case, the above inequalities still hold.

As a consequence of Sauer's lemma, the following lemma holds, as stated in[AB99].

Lemma 2 (Corollary 3.8[AB99]). *For a function class $\mathcal{H}$ with VC-dimension d, if $m > d$, then*

$$d < G_H(m) < d \log_2(em/d)$$

Growth Function for Linear Sorting Functions. When considering binary classification tasks, the fundamental characteristic of a hypothesis class $\mathcal{H}$ used to bound generalization error is that for any set of examples there exists only a finite number of *effective* hypotheses. That is, there are only limited number of ways that a set of m examples can be labeled according to $\mathcal{H}$. This property is what facilitates the usage of $\mathcal{G}_{\mathcal{H}}(m)$ (recall Definition 12) to bound generalization error. When assigning labels from $\{-1, 1\}$, the trivial bound for the number of possible assignments is 2^m, which can be extended easily to $(k!)^m$ when assigning labels from S^k. In this section, we show that there exists a bound of $(emk/d)^{kd}$ when $\mathcal{H}$ is the class of linear sorting functions.

It is also important to notice that all generalization bounds presented in this subsection are fundamentally based on $\mathcal{G}_{\mathcal{E}}(m)$, and only by Observation 13, on $\mathcal{G}_{\mathcal{H}}(m)$.

Lemma 3. *Let* $\mathcal{H}$ *be the class of linear sorting functions over* k *weight vectors, each in* $\mathbb{R}^d$, *then* $\mathcal{G}_{\mathcal{H}}(m) \leq kd \log(emk/d)$.

Proof. Let $P = (x_1, \ldots, x_m)$ be a set of m unlabeled examples where $x_i \in \mathbb{R}^d$. Similar to the definition of $\mathbf{P}(x, y)$ in Definition 8, $\mathbf{P}^U(x)$ is defined for unlabeled examples as

$$\mathbf{P}^U(x) = \left\{ (\mathrm{Vec}(x, i, j)) \,\middle|\, (i, j) \in \{1, \ldots, k\} \times \{1, \ldots, k\} \right\} \setminus \mathbf{0}^{kd},$$

and $\mathbf{P}^U(P) = \bigcup_{x \in P} \mathbf{P}^U(x)$.

Let $\mathcal{H}'$ be the class of separating hyperplanes in $\mathbb{R}^{kd}$. For every linear sorting function $h \in \mathcal{H}$, there is a linear threshold function $h' \in \mathcal{H}'$ which labels $\mathrm{Vec}(x, i, j)$ as positive iff i precedes j in $h(x)$. If $h(x) = \mathrm{argsort}_{\{1,\ldots,k\}} w_i \cdot x$, then $h'(x') = (w_1, \ldots, w_k) \cdot x'$, where $x' \in \mathbb{R}^{kd}$, satisfies this property. Notice that $h'(\mathrm{Vec}(x, i, j)) = w_i \cdot x - w_j \cdot x > 0$ when $w_i \cdot x > w_j \cdot x$, precisely when i precedes j according to $h(x)$.

Therefore, we can bound $\mathcal{G}_{\mathcal{H}}(m)$ by $\mathcal{G}_{\mathcal{H}'}((k-1)^2 m)$ since the number of examples in $\mathbf{P}^U(P)$ is $(k-1)^2 m$. Of course $\mathcal{G}_{\mathcal{H}'}((k-1)^2 m)$ is an over estimate since not all points in $\mathbb{R}^{kd}$ can be examples in $\mathbf{P}^U(P)$ (every example in $\mathbf{P}^U(P)$ has $(k-1) * d$ zeros, for example). Since the VC-dimension of $\mathcal{H}'$ is $kd - 1$, by Lemma 2 and simple algebra,

$$kd < \mathcal{G}_{\mathcal{H}'}((k-1)^2 m) < kd \log(emk/d)$$

Theorem 14. *For any* $0 < \delta < 1$, *any* $h \in \mathcal{H}$, *the class of linear sorting functions over* k *linear functions in* $\mathbb{R}^d$, *where* $h : \mathbb{R}^d \to S^k$, *given* $P = ((x_1, y_1), \ldots, (x_m, y_m))$, *a sample of size* m *drawn i.i.d. from* $\mathcal{D}_{\mathbb{R}^d \times S^k}$, *with probability at least* $1 - \delta$,

$$err(h) \leq err(P, h) + \sqrt{4 \frac{kd \log(2emk/d) - \log \delta/4}{m}} + \frac{1}{m}$$

Proof. The proof follows from proof of [Vap98, Theorem 4.1]. This bound is a consequence of bounding the probability that any hypothesis taken from $\mathcal{H}$ will differ by more than ε on two finite half-samples. Since we are bounding the probability that the two errors will differ, it suffices to consider only how many different possible error vectors might be generated when allowed to choose any $h \in \mathcal{H}$. Since the number of ways that $\mathcal{H}$ can err on any given example set is less than the total possible assignments of labels from $\mathcal{H}$ on that set, it is possible to phrase the generalization bounds based on the multiclass growth function as well as the binary growth function as is done by Vapnik. In particular, interpreting the bound of Lemma 3 as a bound on the number of indicator vectors generated by $\mathcal{H}$ on a sample of size m, as suggested in Observation 13, and plugging it into Vapnik's proof, results in the required bound. Indeed,

$$err(h) \leq err(P, h) + \sqrt{4 \frac{\mathcal{G}_{\mathcal{H}}(2m) - \log \delta/4}{m}} + \frac{1}{m}$$

$$\leq err(P, h) + \sqrt{4 \frac{kd \log(2emk/d) - \log \delta/4}{m}} + \frac{1}{m}$$

The bound of Theorem 14 can be extended also for the case where there is no error on the sample (i.e. $err(P,h) = 0$).

Theorem 15. *For any $0 < \delta < 1$, any $h \in \mathcal{H}$, the class of linear sorting functions over k linear functions in $\mathbb{R}^d$, where $h : \mathbb{R}^d \rightarrow S^k$, given $P = ((x_1, y_1), \ldots, (x_m, y_size))$, a sample of size m drawn i.i.d. from $\mathcal{D}_{\mathbb{R}^d \times S^k}$, with probability at least $1 - \delta$, the inequality*

$$err(h) \leq err(P,h) + 2\frac{\mathcal{G}_{\mathcal{H}}(2m) - \log \delta/4}{m}\left(1 + \sqrt{\left(1 + \frac{m \cdot err(P,h)}{\mathcal{G}_{\mathcal{H}}(2m) - \log \delta/4}\right)}\right)$$

holds true, where $\mathcal{G}_{\mathcal{H}}(2m) = kd\log(2emk/d)$ (see Definition 12).

Proof. Omitted, as it follows by the same argumentation used in Theorem 14 and modification to the proof of [Vap98, Theorem 4.2] in a straightforward fashion.

Corollary 1. *To guarantee that the sampled error differ from the true error by less than ε with probability at least $1 - \delta$, it is sufficient to draw $m > m(\varepsilon, \delta)$ examples drawn i.i.d. from $\mathcal{D}_{\mathbb{R}^d \times S^k}$ where, $m(\varepsilon, \delta) = O\left(\frac{1}{\varepsilon^2}\max\left(kd\log\frac{kd}{\varepsilon^2}, \log\frac{1}{\delta}\right)\right)$.*

If we are able to find a classifier h which is consistent on all the examples (i.e. $err(P,h) = 0$), then to achieve true error less than ε, we need to pick $m > m_1(\varepsilon, \delta)$, where $m_1(\varepsilon, \delta) = O\left(\frac{1}{\varepsilon}\max\left(kd\log\frac{kd}{\varepsilon^2}, \log\frac{1}{\delta}\right)\right)$.

Proof. Follows by simple algebra from Theorem 14 and Theorem 15.

4.2   Margin-Based Generalization Bounds

A multiclass support vector machine can be implemented by learning a maximal margin hyperplane in $\mathbb{R}^{kd}$ for the expanded point set defined in Definition 8. This hyperplane will maximize a notion of margin defined below that is also used in previous multiclass support vector machine work[CS00,WW99]. This subsection develops generalization bounds for our simple multiclass SVM implementation.

Definition 16 (Binary Margin.) The margin of an example (x_i, y_i), where $(x_i, y_i) \in \mathbb{R}^d \times \{-1, 1\}$, with respect to a separating hyperplane, $h(x) = w \cdot x$, where $w, x \in \mathbb{R}^d$, is defined to be

$$\gamma_i = y_i h(x_i) = y_i(w \cdot x_i).$$

The minimal margin over a set of examples, $P = ((x_1, y_1), \ldots, (x_m, y_m))$, is defined to be

$$\text{mar}(h) = \min_{(x_i, y_i) \in P} \gamma_i.$$

In light of the transformation described in Subsection 3.1, a natural extension of binary margin to the constraint case can be derived. The constraint margin of a set of a set of examples, P, is simply the binary margin of a hyperplane in high dimension of $\mathbf{P}(P)$.

Definition 17 (Constraint Margin.) The margin of an example (x_i, y_i), where $(x_i, y_i) \in \mathbb{R}^d \times \bar{S}^k$, with respect to a linear sorting function, $h(x) = \text{argsort}_{\{1,\dots,k\}} w_i \cdot x$, where $w_i, x \in \mathbb{R}^d$, is defined to be

$$\gamma_i = \min_{(j,j') \in y_i} (w_j \cdot x_i - w_{j'} \cdot x_i).$$

The minimal margin over a set of examples, $P = ((x_1, y_1), \dots, (x_m, y_m))$, is defined to be

$$\text{mar}_P(h) = \min_{(x_i, y_i) \in P} \gamma_i.$$

Given some linear threshold function acheiving large margin ($\geq \gamma$) on m randomly drawn input data, standard generalization bounds are known [CST00]. With probability $1 - \delta$, generalization error is less than

$$err_D(h) = epsilon(\gamma, m, \delta, R) \leq \frac{2}{m} \left(\frac{64R^2}{\gamma^2} \log \frac{em\gamma}{8R^2} \log \frac{32m}{\gamma^2} + \log \frac{4}{\delta} \right), \quad (1)$$

where the size of any example is less than R.

Theorem 18 (Constraint Margin Bound). *Consider real-valued linear sorting functions $\mathcal{H}$ with $\sum_{i=1,\dots,k} \|w_1\| = 1$, where $h : \mathbb{R}^d \to S^k$, and fix $\gamma \in \mathbb{R}^+$. For any probability distribution $\mathcal{D}$ on $\mathbb{R}^d \times \bar{S}_C^k$ with support in a ball of radius R around the origin, with probability $1 - \delta$ over m random examples P, any hypothesis $h \in \mathcal{H}$ that has constraint margin $\text{mar}_P(h) \geq \gamma$ on P has error no more than*

$$err_D(h) = \epsilon(\gamma, m, \delta, R, C) \leq \frac{2C}{m} \left(\frac{256R^2}{\gamma^2} \log \frac{em\gamma}{32R^2} \log \frac{32m}{\gamma^2} + \log \frac{4}{\delta} \right)$$

provided $m > \frac{2}{\epsilon}$ and $\frac{256R^2}{\gamma^2} < m$.

Proof. Consider $\mathbf{P}(P)$ in $\mathbb{R}^{kd} \times \{-1, 1\}$ and notice that $|\mathbf{P}(P)| \leq Cm$. It is not possible to apply Equation 1 directly because examples in $\mathbf{P}(P)$ are not independently generated. Therefore, a new distribution $\mathcal{D}'$ over examples in $\mathbb{R}^{kd}$ is used to generate a set of m examples, $\mathbf{P}'(P)$, in $\mathbb{R}^{kd} \times \{-1, 1\}$ based on the original set P.

For each example $(x, y) \in P$, define $\mathbf{P}'(x, y)$ as a single point in $\mathbb{R}^{kd} \times \{-1, 1\}$ chosen uniformly at random from $\mathbf{P}(x, y)$. Then define

$$\mathbf{P}'(P) = \bigcup_{(x,y) \in P} \mathbf{P}'(x, y).$$

For each example generated randomly according to $\mathcal{D}'$, Equation 1 can be applied to bound the chance of making an error. Furthermore, since an error is made on example (x, y) if any example from $\mathbf{P}(x, y)$ is classified incorrectly, it is necessary to guarantee that no error is made. If C is the maximum number of constraints per example, then by the union bound and by noticing that the size of any example in $\mathbf{P}(x, y)$ is less than $2R$, the theorem follows.

Observation 19 *Because all learning problems described in Table 1 can be mapped to constraint classification with a fixed number of constraints, the bound in Theorem 18 applies. For multiclass classification, there are $k - 1$ constraints and the above bound is similar to those given in[CS00, WW99]. The number of constraints may also be limited by the problem at hand, as is the case with context-sensitive spelling correction where each example may have at most three or four constraints, and the bounds will be vastly improved.*

5   Conclusions

The view of multiclass classification presented here simplifies the implementation, analysis, and understanding of many preexisting approaches. Multiclass support vector machines, ultraconservative online algorithms, and traditional one-versus-all approach can be cast in this framework. Furthermore, this view allows for a very natural extension of multiclass classification to constraint classification – capturing within it complex learning tasks such as multilabel classification and ranking problems. Because constraint classification is a very intuitive approach and it's implementation can be carried out by any discriminant technique and not only optimization techniques, we think it will have useful real-world applications.

References

[AB99]   M. Anthony and P. Bartlett. *Neural Network Learning: Theoretical Foundations.* Cambridge University Press, Cambridge, England, 1999.

[ADW94]   Chidanand Apte, Fred Damerau, and Sholom M. Weiss.   Automated learning of decision rules for text categorization. *Information Systems*, 12(3):233–251, 1994.

[ASS00]   E. Allwein, R.E. Schapire, and Y. Singer. Reducing multiclass to binary: A unifying approach for margin classifiers. In *Proc. 17th International Conf. on Machine Learning*, pages 9–16. Morgan Kaufmann, San Francisco, CA, 2000.

[BCHL95]   S. Ben-David, N. Cesa-Bianchi, D. Haussler, and P. Long. Characterizations of learnability for classes of $0, ..., n$- valued functions. *J. Comput. Sys. Sci.*, 50(1):74–86, 1995.

[Bri94]   E. Brill. Some advances in transformation-based part of speech tagging. In *AAAI, Vol. 1*, pages 722–727, 1994.

[CCRR99]   A. Carlson, C. Cumby, J. Rosen, and D. Roth. The SNoW learning architecture. Technical Report UIUCDCS-R-99-2101, UIUC Computer Science Department, May 1999.

[CS00]   K. Crammer and Y. Singer. On the learnability and design of output codes for multiclass problems. In *Computational Learing Theory*, pages 35–46, 2000.

[CS01a]   K. Crammer and Y. Singer. On the algorithmic implementation of multiclass kernel-based vector machines. *J. Machine Learning Research*, 2 (December):265–292, 2001.

[CS01b]   K. Crammer and Y. Singer. Ultraconservative online algorithms for mul-
            ticlass problems. In *COLT/EuroCOLT*, pages 99–115, 2001.

[CST00]   Nello Cristianini and John Shawe-Taylor. *An Introduction to Support Vec-
            tor Machines and Other Kernel-Based Learning Methods*. Cambridge Uni-
            versity Press, 2000.

[DKR97]   I. Dagan, Y. Karov, and D. Roth. Mistake-driven learning in text catego-
            rization. In *EMNLP-97, The Second Conference on Empirical Methods in
            Natural Language Processing*, pages 55–63, 1997.

[HT98]   T. Hastie and R. Tibshirani. Classification by pairwise coupling. In *NIPS-
            10, The 1997 Conference on Advances in Neural Information Processing
            Systems*, pages 507–513. MIT Press, 1998.

[Jel98]   F. Jelinek. *Statistical Methods for Speech Recognition*. The MIT Press,
            Cambridge, Massachusetts, 1998.

[Koh01]   T. Kohonen. *Sel-Organizing Maps*. Springer Verlag, New York, 3rd edition,
            2001.

[LB+89]   Y. Le Cun, B. Boser, J. Denker, D. Hendersen, R. Howard, W. Hubbard,
            and L. Jackel. Backpropagation applied to handwritten zip code recogni-
            tion. *Neural Computation*, 1:pp 541, 1989.

[LS97]   D. Lee and H. Seung. Unsupervised learning by convex and conic coding.
            In Michael C. Mozer, Michael I. Jordan, and Thomas Petsche, editors,
            Advances in Neural Information Processing Systems, volume 9, page 515.
            The MIT Press, 1997.

[Maa00]   W. Maass. On the computational power of winner-take-all. *Neural Com-
            putation*, 12(11):2519–2536, 2000.

[Rot98]   D. Roth. Learning to resolve natural language ambiguities: A unified ap-
            proach. In *Proc. of AAAI*, pages 806–813, 1998.

[RZ98]   D. Roth and D. Zelenko. Part of speech tagging using a network of linear
            separators. In *COLING-ACL 98, The 17th International Conference on
            Computational Linguistics*, pages 1136–1142, 1998.

[Sch97]   R.E. Schapire. Using output codes to boost multiclass learning problems.
            In *Proc. 14th Internat. Conf. on Machine Learning*, pages 313–321. Morgan
            Kaufmann, 1997.

[Vap98]   V. Vapnik. *Statistical Learning Theory*. Wiley, 605 Third Avenue, New
            York, New York, 10158-0012, 1998.

[WW99]   J. Weston and C. Watkins. Support vector machines for multiclass pat-
            tern recognition. In *Proceedings of the Seventh European Symposium On
            Artificial Neural Networks*, 4 1999.

How to Achieve Minimax Expected Kullback-Leibler Distance from an Unknown Finite Distribution[*]

Dietrich Braess[1], Jürgen Forster[2], Tomas Sauer[3], and Hans U. Simon[2]

[1] Fakultät für Mathematik, Ruhr-Universität Bochum, D-44780 Bochum
braess@num.ruhr-uni-bochum.de
[2] Fakultät für Mathematik, Ruhr-Universität Bochum, D-44780 Bochum
{forster,simon}@lmi.ruhr-uni-bochum.de
[3] Mathematisches Institut, Universität Giessen, D-35392 Giessen

Abstract. We consider a problem that is related to the "Universal Encoding Problem" from information theory. The basic goal is to find rules that map "partial information" about a distribution X over an m-letter alphabet into a guess $\widehat{X}$ for X such that the Kullback-Leibler divergence between X and $\widehat{X}$ is as small as possible. The cost associated with a rule is the maximal expected Kullback-Leibler divergence between X and $\widehat{X}$. First, we show that the cost associated with the well-known add-one rule equals $\ln(1 + (m-1)/(n+1))$ thereby extending a result of Forster and Warmuth [3,2] to $m \geq 3$. Second, we derive an absolute (as opposed to asymptotic) lower bound on the smallest possible cost. Technically, this is done by determining (almost exactly) the Bayes error of the add-one rule with a uniform prior (where the asymptotics for $n \to \infty$ was known before). Third, we hint to tools from approximation theory and support the conjecture that there exists a rule whose cost asymptotically matches the theoretical barrier from the lower bound.

1   Introduction

We consider a problem that is related to the "Universal Encoding Problem" from information theory. Loosely speaking, the basic goal is to find rules that map "partial information" about a distribution X over an m-letter alphabet into a guess $\widehat{X}$ for X such that the Kullback-Leibler divergence between X and $\widehat{X}$ is as small as possible. We mainly consider a variant of the problem (first proposed by Krichevskiy), where the partial information about X consists of a sample word drawn at random according to X^n. The cost associated with a rule is the maximal expected Kullback-Leibler divergence between X and $\widehat{X}$, where maximization ranges over all possible choices for X and expectation is taken over all words of length n drawn at random according to X^n.

---

[*] This work has been supported in part by the ESPRIT Working Group in Neural, Computational Learning II, NeuroCOLT2, No. 27150 and by the Deutsche Forschungsgemeinschaft Grant SI 498/4-1.

N. Cesa-Bianchi et al. (Eds.): ALT 2002, LNAI 2533, pp. 380–394, 2002.

The problem whose roots trace back to Laplace has a long history and their is a fair amount of knowledge about it. The reader interested in a broader introduction is therefore referred to [6,7,9,10] and the references given there.

The problem has been treated in considerable depth in the information-theoretic literature because its significance for code design. According to Shannon's Noiseless Coding Theorem [8], the minimal expected code-length for an alphabet with distribution X coincides (up to rounding) with the entropy $H(X)$ of X. If X is known, the optimal code can be efficiently designed [5]. A problem arises if X is not completely known and, given our current knowledge about X, approximated by $\widehat{X}$. Suppose we use a code that is optimal for outputs drawn according to $\widehat{X}$ in order to encode outputs drawn according to X. Then the Kullback-Leibler distance between X and $\widehat{X}$, denoted as $D(X\|\widehat{X})$ and sometimes called relative entropy, measures how many additional bits we use compared to an optimal code for X. This motivates the general goal of finding rules mapping partial knowledge about X to a guess that exhibits a small Kullback-Leibler distance to X.

Before the problem was exposed to a worst case analysis (as in our paper), it had been investigated in a Bayesean setting, where X itself is assumed to be randomly chosen according to a (known) prior distribution. In this setting, the cost associated with a rule is the expected Kullback-Leibler distance between X and $\widehat{X}$, where expectation is taken over all X (distributed according to the prior) and all words of length n (distributed according to X^n). Cover [1] investigated the family of add-β rules, which make the estimated probability of a letter occurring k-times in the sample word proportional to $k + \beta$. He proved that the add-β rule is the Bayes rule for the Dirichlet prior with parameters $(\beta, \ldots, \beta)$. For instance, the add-one rule (sometimes named Laplace's law of succession) is the Bayes rule for the uniform prior; the add-half rule (sometimes named Jeffrey's rule) is the Bayes rule for Jeffrey's prior.

The problem with Bayesean analysis is that the choice of the prior often appears quite arbitrary. Krichevskiy was the first who exposed the problem to a worst case analysis (as we do in our paper). In [6] he showed that Jeffrey's rule is asymptotically best for many-letter prediction, where one does not only probabilistically predict a single letter (by guessing its probability) but many letters (by guessing the probability of a "long" word).[1] The results of Xie and Barron [9,10] go in a similar direction. For single-letter prediction however, the situation is quite different. In [7], Krichevskiy showed the following results:

1. The cost of any rule is asymptotically bounded from below by $(m-1)/(2n) = 0.5(m-1)/n$ when n approaches infinity.
2. The best rule within the family of add-β rules is the add-β_0 rule for $\beta_0 = 0.50922\cdots$ whose cost asymptotically equals $\beta_0(m-1)/n$ (falling short of the theoretical barrier $0.5(m-1)/n$). The cost associated with any other rule from the add-β family is asymptotically strictly larger.

---

[1] Many-letter prediction can also be viewed as on-line prediction with cumulative relative entropy loss.

Thus, Jeffrey's rule is asymptotically optimal for many-letter prediction, but due to the results above it is not asymptotically optimal for single-letter prediction.

For $m = 2$, Forster and Warmuth [3,2] have shown that the cost associated with the add-one rule equals $\ln(1 + 1/(n+1)) < 1/(n+1)$. Note that this result holds for all n, m (not just asymptotically when n approaches infinity).

Structure of the paper: Section 2 reviews the main problem in this paper in a more formal notation. In section 3, we generalize the result of Forster and Warmuth concerning the cost associated with the add-one rule to arbitrary values of m. In section 4, we provide an absolute lower bound on the smallest possible cost (which, of course, asymptotically matches the asymptotic lower bound provided by Krichevskiy). For this purpose, we determine sharp bounds of the Bayes error of the add-one rule. In section 5, we proceed in the framework of asymptotics as Krichevskiy [7] and hint to a connection with the approximation by Bernstein polynomials. By modifying an add-β rule we establish a rule whose cost seems to match asymptotically the theoretical barrier $(m-1)/(2n)$.

A technical simplification of the problem: A simple symmetry argument shows that each rule can be "normalized" without increasing its cost such that, after normalization, it depends on the sample word w of length n only through the frequencies $(k_1, \ldots, k_m)$, where k_j denotes the number of occurrences of the j-th letter in w. In other words, one has only to count frequencies of letters and need not remember their ordering.

2   Notations and Reformulations of the Problem

Throughout this paper, $\mathcal{X}_m$ denotes the $(m-1)$-dimensional "probability simplex" in $\mathbb{R}^m$:

$$\mathcal{X}_m = \left\{ x \in \mathbb{R}^m : (\forall i = 1, \ldots, m : x_i \geq 0) \text{ and } \sum_{i=1}^{m} x_i = 1 \right\}.$$

$\mathcal{K}_{m,n}$ denotes the subset of $\mathbb{Z}^m$ that contains the grid points of $n \cdot \mathcal{X}_m$:

$$\mathcal{K}_{m,n} = \left\{ k \in \mathbb{Z}^m : (\forall i = 1, \ldots, m : k_i \geq 0) \text{ and } \sum_{i=1}^{m} k_i = n \right\}.$$

A point in $\mathcal{X}_m$ represents an unknown distribution X on an m-letter alphabet and a point in $\mathcal{K}_{m,n}$ represents the frequencies that one can extract from a sample word of length n. If the sample word is generated randomly according to X^n, then the corresponding grid-point $k \in \mathcal{K}_{m,n}$ is multinomially distributed. In the sequel, we will use the shorthands with multi-indices

$$\binom{n}{k} = \frac{n!}{k_1! \cdots k_m!} \quad \text{and} \quad x^k = x_1^{k_1} \cdots x_m^{k_m}.$$

In this notation, the probability assigned to k by the distribution X equals $\binom{n}{k}x^k$.

A *rule* is a function of the form $Q : \mathcal{K}_{m,n} \to \mathcal{X}_m$. It maps a vector $k \in \mathcal{K}_{m,n}$ of absolute letter-frequencies to a point in $Q(k) \in \mathcal{X}_m$, which represents the "guess" for the unknown x. In particular, the *add-β rule* is given by

$$Q_i^\beta(k) = \frac{k_i + \beta}{n + m\beta} \quad \text{for} \quad i = 1, \ldots, m, \tag{1}$$

where Q_i denotes the i-th component of Q. For $\beta = 1$, we obtain the add-one rule (Laplace's law of succession), and for $\beta = 1/2$ the add-half-rule (Jeffrey's rule).

The *Kullback-Leibler divergence* between two distributions $x, y \in \mathcal{X}_m$ is defined as

$$D(x\|y) = \sum_{i=1}^m x_i \ln \frac{x_i}{y_i} \; .$$

The expected Kullback-Leibler divergence between x and $Q(k)$, where the expectation value is taken over the multinomially distributed random variable k, is then

$$C_{m,n}^Q(x) = \sum_{k \in \mathcal{K}_{m,n}} \binom{n}{k} x^k D(x\|Q(k)) \; . \tag{2}$$

The *cost associated with rule Q* is given by

$$C_{m,n}^Q = \sup_{x \in \mathcal{X}_m} C_{m,n}^Q(x) \; . \tag{3}$$

As already mentioned, we aim at finding a rule whose cost is as small as possible and at determining

$$\inf_{Q:\mathcal{K}_{m,n} \to \mathcal{X}_m} C_{m,n}^Q \; .$$

In the Bayesean approach, the supremum over all $x \in \mathcal{X}_m$ is replaced by averaging over all $x \in \mathcal{X}_m$ according to a (given) prior distribution D on $\mathcal{X}_m$. We will refer only to the uniform prior. Since $\mathcal{X}_m$ has volume $1/(m-1)!$, the resulting Bayes error is

$$\bar{C}_{m,n} = (m-1)! \inf_{Q:\mathcal{K}_{m,n} \to \mathcal{X}_m} \int_{\mathcal{X}_m} C_{m,n}^Q(x)\,dx \; , \tag{4}$$

and, according to Cover's result [1], the infimum is attained at $Q = Q^1$. Since

$$\inf_{Q:\mathcal{K}_{m,n} \to \mathcal{X}_m} C_{m,n}^Q \geq \bar{C}_{m,n} \; ,$$

the Bayesean approach can be used to derive lower bounds on $\inf_{Q:\mathcal{K}_{m,n} \to \mathcal{X}_m} C_{m,n}^Q$.

We now briefly mention some other useful reformulations of the basic equation (2).

Extraction of the entropy-term: Using the formula

$$\forall x \in \mathcal{X}_m : \sum_{k \in \mathcal{K}_{m,n}} \binom{n}{k} x^k = 1 \tag{5}$$

and the definition of the well-known entropy function

$$H(x) = -\sum_{i=1}^{m} x_i \ln x_i ,$$

we immediately get

$$C_{m,n}^{Q}(x) = \sum_{k \in \mathcal{K}_{m,n}} \binom{n}{k} x^k \sum_{i=1}^{m} x_i \ln \frac{1}{Q_i(k)} - H(x) . \tag{6}$$

An easy algebraic manipulation: Define

$$k_j^{\uparrow i} = \begin{cases} k_i + 1 & \text{if } j = i , \\ k_j & \text{otherwise} , \end{cases} \quad \text{and} \quad k_j^{\downarrow i} = \begin{cases} k_i - 1 & \text{if } j = i , \\ k_j & \text{otherwise} . \end{cases}$$

The inner sums in (6) are now reorganized:

$$\sum_{k \in \mathcal{K}_{m,n}} \binom{n}{k} x^k \cdot x_i \ln \frac{x_i}{Q_i(k)} = \sum_{k \in \mathcal{K}_{m,n}} \binom{n+1}{k^{\uparrow i}} x^{k^{\uparrow i}} \cdot \frac{k_i + 1}{n+1} \ln \frac{x_i}{Q_i(k)}$$

$$= \sum_{k \in \mathcal{K}_{m,n+1}} \binom{n+1}{k} x^k \cdot \frac{k_i}{n+1} \ln \frac{x_i}{Q_i(k^{\downarrow i})} .$$

Thus, we have

$$C_{m,n}^{Q}(x) = \sum_{k \in \mathcal{K}_{m,n+1}} \binom{n+1}{k} x^k \cdot \sum_{i=1}^{m} \frac{k_i}{n+1} \ln \frac{x_i}{Q_i(k^{\downarrow i})} . \tag{7}$$

Clearly, this algebraic manipulation can be combined with the extraction of the entropy-term to obtain

$$C_{m,n}^{Q}(x) = \sum_{k \in \mathcal{K}_{m,n+1}} \binom{n+1}{k} x^k \cdot \sum_{i=1}^{m} \frac{k_i}{n+1} \ln \frac{1}{Q_i(k^{\downarrow i})} - H(x) . \tag{8}$$

3   The Cost Associated with the Add-One Rule

The cost associated with the add-one rule can be calculated in a surprisingly simple manner:

Theorem 1. $C_{m,n}^{Q^1} = \ln\big(1 + \frac{m-1}{n+1}\big)$.

Proof. We substitute $n - 1$ for n and show that $C_{m,n-1}^{Q^1} = \ln(1 + (m-1)/n)$.
It is easy to check that $C_{m,n-1}^{Q^1}(x) = \ln(1 + (m-1)/n)$ for each corner x of the
probability simplex $\mathcal{X}_m$. For instance, $C_{m,n-1}^{Q^1}(1, 0, \ldots, 0) = \ln(1 + (m-1)/n)$.
Thus, $C_{m,n-1}^{Q^1} \geq \ln(1 + (m-1)/n)$.

In order to show the converse direction, we first observe that any rule Q satisfies

$$C_{m,n-1}^{Q}(x) \overset{(7)}{=} \sum_{k \in \mathcal{K}_{m,n}} \binom{n}{k} x^k \cdot \sum_{i=1}^{m} \frac{k_i}{n} \ln \frac{x_i}{Q_i(k^{\downarrow i})} \tag{9}$$

$$\leq \sum_{k \in \mathcal{K}_{m,n}} \binom{n}{k} x^k \cdot \sum_{i=1}^{m} \frac{k_i}{n} \ln \frac{k_i/n}{Q_i(k^{\downarrow i})} \ . \tag{10}$$

The last inequality holds because the term $\sum_{i=1}^{m} \frac{k_i}{n} \ln \frac{x_i}{Q_i(k^{\downarrow i})}$ attains its maximal
value at $x_i = k_i/n$ since $x \in \mathcal{X}_m$ implies the constraint $\sum_{i=1}^{m} x_i = 1$. We proceed
with the add-one rule Q^1. Recalling (1), (5), and $\sum_{i=1}^{m} k_i = n$, we obtain

$$C_{m,n-1}^{Q^1}(x) \leq \sum_{k \in \mathcal{K}_{m,n}} \binom{n}{k} x^k \cdot \sum_{i=1}^{m} \frac{k_i}{n} \ln \frac{k_i/n}{Q_i^1(k^{\downarrow i})}$$

$$= \sum_{k \in \mathcal{K}_{m,n}} \binom{n}{k} x^k \cdot \sum_{i=1}^{m} \frac{k_i}{n} \ln \frac{n+m-1}{n}$$

$$= \ln\left(1 + \frac{m-1}{n}\right) \ .$$

$\bullet$

4   A Lower Bound on the Smallest Possible Cost

We establish a lower bound on $\inf_Q C_{m,n}^{Q}$ by applying the Bayesean approach
for the uniform prior and calculating a sharp lower bound on $\bar{C}_{m,n}$. In a first
step, we show that $\bar{C}_{m,n} = \widehat{H}_{m,n} - \bar{H}_m$ with

$$\widehat{H}_{m,n} = |\mathcal{K}_{m,n}|^{-1} \sum_{k \in \mathcal{K}_{m,n}} H\left(\frac{k+1}{n+m}\right) = \binom{n+m-1}{m-1}^{-1} \sum_{k \in \mathcal{K}_{m,n}} H\left(\frac{k+1}{n+m}\right) ,$$

$$\bar{H}_m = (m-1)! \int_{\mathcal{X}_m} H(x) dx \ ,$$

and $k/(n+m) = [k_1/(n+m), \ldots, k_m/(n+m)]$. Note that $\bar{H}_m$ is the expected
entropy when we average uniformly over all $x \in \mathcal{X}_m$. Similarly, $\widehat{H}_{m,n}$ is the
expected entropy when we average uniformly over all $(k+1)/(n+m)$ with
$k \in \mathcal{K}_{m,n}$. The Bayes error $\bar{C}_{m,n}$ can therefore be viewed as the excess of the
"discrete average entropy" (associated with the grid $\mathcal{K}_{m,n}$) over the "continuous
average entropy".

In the proof of Theorem 2 below, we will refer to a well-known formula for integrals over simplices:

Lemma 1. *For each $k \in \mathbb{N}_0^m$ and $n = \sum_{j=1}^m k_j$, the following integration rule holds:*

$$\int_{\mathcal{X}_m} x^k dx = \frac{k_1! \cdots k_m!}{(n+m-1)!} .$$

Theorem 2. *Let $\bar{C}_{m,n}$ be defined by (4). Then, $\bar{C}_{m,n} = \hat{H}_{m,n} - \bar{H}_m$.*

Proof. From Lemma 1 and (6), it follows that

$$(m-1)! \int_{\mathcal{X}_m} C_{m,n}^Q(x) dx$$

$$= (m-1)! \sum_{k \in \mathcal{K}_{m,n}} \binom{n}{k} \sum_{i=1}^m \ln \frac{1}{Q_i(k)} \int_{\mathcal{X}_m} x_i x^k dx - (m-1)! \int_{\mathcal{X}_m} H(x) dx$$

$$= \frac{(m-1)! \cdot n!}{(n+m-1)!} \sum_{k \in \mathcal{K}_{m,n}} \sum_{i=1}^m \frac{k_i+1}{n+m} \ln \frac{1}{Q_i(k)} - \bar{H}_m$$

The inner sums are minimal when $Q_i(k) = (k_i+1)/(n+m)$, i.e. when $Q = Q^1$; cf. [1]. Hence,

$$\bar{C}_{m,n} = \binom{n+m-1}{m-1}^{-1} \sum_{k \in \mathcal{K}_{m,n}} \sum_{i=1}^m \frac{k_i+1}{n+m} \ln \frac{n+m}{k_i+1} - \bar{H}_m$$

$$= \hat{H}_{m,n} - \bar{H}_m .$$

$\bullet$

The entropy term $\bar{H}_m$ is related to the Harmonic number $\approx_m = \sum_{j=1}^m 1/j$ as follows:

Lemma 2. $\bar{H}_m = \sum_{j=2}^m \frac{1}{j} = \approx_m - 1.$

The proof of Lemma 2 will be given in subsection 4.1.

The Bayes error can now be bounded from below as follows:

Theorem 3. *$\bar{C}_{m,n}$ is larger than*

$$\frac{m-1}{2(n+m)} + \frac{1}{12(n+m)^2} - \frac{(m-1)m}{12(n+m)(n+1)} (\approx_{n+m-1} - \approx_{m-2}) - \frac{1}{120(n+m)^4} .$$

The proof of Theorem 3 will be given in subsection 4.2. In the full version of this paper, we will provide an upper bound on $\bar{C}_{m,n}$ which differs from the lower bound by a term of order $\ln(n)/n^2$. We conjecture that the upper bound can be strengthened such that it differs from the lower bound only by a term of order $\ln(n)/n^4$.

The reader who is not interested in the technical details of the proofs may now immediately pass to section 5 without loss of continuity.

4.1   Proof of Lemma 2

Since the domain $\mathcal{X}_m$ and the function H are symmetric in $x_1, \ldots, x_m$, we can reduce $\int_{\mathcal{X}_m} H(x)dx$ to a one-dimensional integral. Moreover, we note that the volume of the $(m-2)$-dimensional polytope $\{x \in \mathcal{X}_m : x_1 = 1 - t\}$ equals $t^{m-2}/(m-2)!$:

$$\bar{H}_m = (m-1)! \int_{\mathcal{X}_m} H(x)dx$$

$$= -m! \int_{\mathcal{X}_m} x_1 \ln(x_1)dx$$

$$= -m(m-1) \int_0^1 t^{m-2}(1-t)\ln(1-t)dt$$

$$= -m(m-1) \int_0^1 (t^{m-2} \quad t^{m-1})\ln(1-t)dt.$$

Next we perform partial integration such that boundary terms vanish:

$$\bar{H}_m = -m(m-1) \left[\left(\frac{t^{m-1}-1}{m-1} - \frac{t^m-1}{m} \right) \ln(1-t) \right]_0^1$$

$$- m(m-1) \int_0^1 \left[\frac{t^{m-1}-1}{m-1} - \frac{t^m-1}{m} \right] \frac{1}{1-t} dt$$

$$= \int_0^1 \left[\frac{m(t^{m-1}-1)}{t-1} - \frac{(m-1)(t^m-1)}{t-1} \right] dt$$

$$= \int_0^1 \left[m \sum_{j=0}^{m-2} t^j - (m-1) \sum_{j=0}^{m-1} t^j \right] dt$$

$$= \int_0^1 \left[\sum_{j=0}^{m-2} t^j - (m-1)t^{m-1} \right] dt$$

$$= \sum_{j=0}^{m-2} \frac{1}{j+1} - \frac{m-1}{m} = \sum_{j=2}^{m} \frac{1}{j} \; .$$

4.2   Proof of Theorem 3

For ease of reference, we first mention some useful facts that will be needed in the course of the proof:

1. For each $n \geq 1$, there exists $0 < \varepsilon < 1$ such that

$$\approx_n = \ln n + \gamma + \frac{1}{2n} - \frac{1}{12n^2} + \frac{\varepsilon}{120n^4} \; , \tag{11}$$

where $\gamma = 0.5772156649 \cdots$ denotes Euler's constant.
2. The following formulas hold for binomial coefficients:

$$\sum_{i=0}^{n} \binom{i}{m} = \binom{n+1}{m+1} , \tag{12}$$

$$\binom{n+1}{i+1} = \frac{n+1}{i+1}\binom{n}{i} , \tag{13}$$

$$\sum_{j=i}^{n+1} j\binom{n+m-j-1}{m-2} = \frac{n+(m-1)i+1}{m}\binom{n+m-i}{m-1} , \tag{14}$$

$$\sum_{j=1}^{n+1} j\binom{n+m-j-1}{m-2} = \binom{n+m}{m} , \tag{15}$$

$$\binom{m+n}{m}^{-1}\sum_{j=1}^{n} \frac{1}{j}\binom{n+m-j}{m} = \widetilde{\approx}_{n+m} - \widetilde{\approx}_m . \tag{16}$$

Formulas (11), (12), and (13) are well-known as Euler's summation rule, as the rule of upper summation, and as the rule of absorption, resp., and can be found, for instance, in [4]. Formula (15) is an immediate consequence of formula (14), specialized to $i = 1$, and formula (13). The proofs for formulas (14) and (16) are found in the full version of this paper.

We are now ready to sketch the proof of Theorem 3. We first bring $\widehat{H}_{m,n}$ into another form that will be more convenient for our purpose. In the following computation, we mainly exploit (11), (13), and (15) and the fact that

$$|\{k \in \mathcal{K}_{m,n} : k_i = j\}| = \binom{n+m-j-2}{m-2}$$

for each fixed $i \in \{1,\ldots,m\}$ and each fixed $j \in \{0,\ldots,n\}$:

$$\begin{aligned}
\widehat{H}_{m,n} &= -\binom{n+m-1}{m-1}^{-1}\sum_{k \in \mathcal{K}_{m,n}}\sum_{i=1}^{m} \frac{k_i+1}{n+m} \cdot \ln\frac{n+m}{k_i+1} \\
&= -\binom{n+m-1}{m-1}^{-1}\sum_{i=1}^{m}\sum_{j=0}^{n}\binom{n+m-j-2}{m-2}\frac{j+1}{n+m}\ln\frac{n+m}{j+1} \\
&= \frac{m}{n+m}\binom{n+m-1}{m-1}^{-1}\sum_{j=0}^{n}\binom{n+m-j-2}{m-2}(j+1)\ln\frac{n+m}{j+1} \\
&\stackrel{(13)}{=} \binom{n+m}{m}^{-1}\sum_{j=1}^{n+1}\binom{n+m-j-1}{m-2}j\ln\frac{n+m}{j} \\
&= A - B ,
\end{aligned}$$

where

$$A = \ln(n+m)\binom{n+m}{m}^{-1}\sum_{j=1}^{n+1} j\binom{n+m-j-1}{m-2}$$

$$\overset{(15)}{=} \ln(n+m)$$

$$\overset{(11)}{>} \approx_{n+m} - \gamma - \frac{1}{2(n+m)} + \frac{1}{12(n+m)^2} - \frac{1}{120(n+m)^4}$$

and

$$B = \binom{n+m}{m}^{-1} \sum_{j=1}^{n+1} j \binom{n+m-j-1}{m-2} \ln j$$

$$\overset{(11)}{<} \binom{n+m}{m}^{-1} \sum_{j=1}^{n+1} j \binom{n+m-j-1}{m-2} \left(\approx_j - \gamma - \frac{1}{2j} + \frac{1}{12j^2} \right) .$$

Thus, $B < B_1 - B_2 - B_3 + B_4$ for

$$B_1 = \binom{n+m}{m}^{-1} \sum_{j=1}^{n+1} j \binom{n+m-j-1}{m-2} \approx_j ,$$

$$B_2 = \gamma \binom{n+m}{m}^{-1} \sum_{j=1}^{n+1} j \binom{n+m-j-1}{m-2}$$

$$\overset{(15)}{=} \gamma ,$$

$$B_3 = \frac{1}{2} \binom{n+m}{m}^{-1} \sum_{j=1}^{n+1} \binom{n+m-j-1}{m-2}$$

$$= \frac{1}{2} \binom{n+m}{m}^{-1} \sum_{j=0}^{n+m-2} \binom{j}{m-2}$$

$$\overset{(12)}{=} \frac{1}{2} \binom{n+m}{m}^{-1} \binom{n+m-1}{m-1}$$

$$= \frac{m}{2(n+m)} ,$$

$$B_4 = \frac{1}{12} \binom{n+m}{m}^{-1} \sum_{j=1}^{n+1} \frac{1}{j} \binom{n+m-1-j}{m-2}$$

$$= \frac{(m-1)m}{12(n+m)(n+1)} \binom{n+m-1}{m-2} \sum_{j=1}^{n+1} \frac{1}{j} \binom{n+m-1-j}{m-2}$$

$$\overset{(16)}{=} \frac{(m-1)m}{12(n+m)(n+1)} (\approx_{n+m-1} - \approx_{m-2}) .$$

Here, formula (16) is applied to parameters $n-1$ in the role of n and $m-2$ in the role of m.

We move on to the computation of B_1. We start by rewriting this term as follows:

$$B_1 = \binom{n+m}{m}^{-1} \sum_{j=1}^{n+1} j \binom{n+m-j-1}{m-2} \sum_{i=1}^{j} \frac{1}{i}$$

$$= \binom{n+m}{m}^{-1} \sum_{i=1}^{n+1} \frac{1}{i} \sum_{j=i}^{n+1} j \binom{n+m-j-1}{m-2}$$

$$\overset{(14)}{=} \binom{n+m}{m}^{-1} \sum_{i=1}^{n+1} \frac{1}{i} \frac{n+(m-1)i+1}{m} \binom{n+m-i}{m-1}$$

$$= B_1' + B_1'' \ ,$$

where

$$B_1' = \binom{n+m}{m}^{-1} \frac{m-1}{m} \sum_{i=1}^{n+1} \binom{n+m-i}{m-1}$$

$$= \left(1-\frac{1}{m}\right) \binom{n+m}{m}^{-1} \sum_{i=0}^{n+m-1} \binom{i}{m-1}$$

$$\overset{(12)}{=} \left(1-\frac{1}{m}\right) \binom{n+m}{m}^{-1} \binom{n+m}{m}$$

$$= 1 - \frac{1}{m} \ ,$$

$$B_1'' = \binom{n+m}{m}^{-1} \frac{n+1}{m} \sum_{i=1}^{n+1} \frac{1}{i} \binom{n+m-i}{m-1}$$

$$= \binom{n+m}{m-1}^{-1} \sum_{i=1}^{n+1} \frac{1}{i} \binom{n+m-i}{m-1}$$

$$\overset{(16)}{=} \widetilde{\sim}_{n+m} - \widetilde{\sim}_{m-1} \ .$$

Here, formula (16) is applied to $n+1$ in the role of n and $m-1$ in the role of m. We may now conclude that B_1 satisfies equation

$$B_1 = 1 + \widetilde{\sim}_{n+m} - \widetilde{\sim}_m \ .$$

We finally observe that

$$\widehat{H}_{m,n} - \bar{H}_m = A - B - \bar{H}_m$$
$$= A - B_1 + B_2 + B_3 - B_4 - \bar{H}_m$$

$$> \left(\approx_{n+m} - \gamma - \frac{1}{2(n+m)} + \frac{1}{12(n+m)^2} - \frac{1}{120(n+m)^4} \right)$$
$$- (1 + \approx_{n+m} - \approx_m) + \gamma + \frac{m}{2(n+m)}$$
$$- \left(\frac{(m-1)m}{12(n+m)(n+1)} (\approx_{n+m-1} - \approx_{m-2}) \right) - (\approx_m - 1)$$
$$= \frac{m-1}{2(n+m)} + \frac{1}{12(n+m)^2} - \frac{(m-1)m}{12(n+m)(n+1)} (\approx_{n+m-1} - \approx_{m-2})$$
$$- \frac{1}{120(n+m)^4} ,$$

which concludes the proof of Theorem 3.

5   An Asymptotically Optimal Rule?

In this section, we will propose a rule Q^* whose cost seems to match asymptotically the lower bound $(m-1)/(2n)$. To this end, we will modify the add-0.8 rule $Q^{0.8}(k)$ at $k = 0, 1, n-1, n$ as specified in (24) below for the special case $m = 2$.

We start with some preliminary considerations. The computation of the cost associated with an add-β rule may start like the computation of the cost associated with the add-one rule in section 3 up to the following notable exception: we aim at controlling the deficit when we pass from (9) to (10). This deficit does not depend on Q. It equals the absolute difference between the entropy function H and its approximation by Bernstein polynomials. By exploiting this observation, we show in the full paper (focusing on the case $m = 2$) that

$$C_{2,n}^{Q^\beta}(x, 1-x) \le \frac{1}{2n} \left(1 + \frac{1}{3nx(1-x) + 1} \right) \tag{17}$$

for $1/2 \le \beta \le 1$. Note that this upper bound will match asymptotically the lower bound $1/(2n)$, if x is "separated away" from 0 and 1 in the sense that $x \in [\delta_n, 1 - \delta_n]$ for a sequence $\delta_n = \omega(1/n)$. For instance, the upper bound (17) is already satisfactory for $x \in [1/\sqrt{n}, 1 - 1/\sqrt{n}]$. (Observe that the special choice of β does not matter very much, when x is separated away from 0 and 1.)

In order to control the cost of the add-β rule when x is *not* separated away from 0 and 1, we follow Krichevskiy [7] who introduced the characteristic function

$$\Phi(\beta, z) = \beta + z \ln z - z e^{-z} \sum_{j=0}^{\infty} \frac{z^j}{j!} \ln(j + \beta) . \tag{18}$$

For $m = 2$ and each fixed z, the relation between Φ and the cost-terms that we are interested in is as follows:

$$\Phi(\beta, z) = \lim_{n \to \infty} n C_{2,n}^{Q^\beta}(z/n, 1 - z/n) . \tag{19}$$

Krichevskiy showed that $C_{m,n}^{Q^{\beta_0}} \approx \beta_0/n$ for $\beta_0 = 0.50922 \cdots$ by analyzing Φ at β_0; cf. Fig. 1.

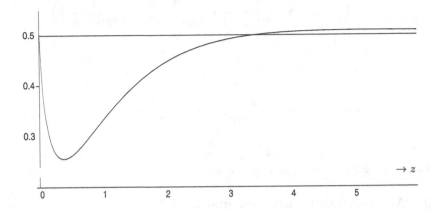

Fig. 1. Characteristic function at $\beta_0 = 0.50922\cdots$ from Krichevskiy's solution. The maximum is attained at $z \approx 5.3$.

Details of the modification for the case $m = 2$: For $m = 2$, we will use a simplified notation from now on. First, we we write C_n^Q instead of $C_{2,n}^Q$. Second, we write $Q(k)$ instead of $Q(k, n - k)$ and $C_n^Q(x)$ instead of $C_n^Q(x, 1 - x)$. The function in (2) can now be written in the form

$$C_n^Q(x) = \sum_{k=0}^{n} \binom{n}{k} x^k (1 - x)^{n-k} \left\{ x \ln \frac{x}{Q(k)} + (1 - x) \ln \frac{1 - x}{1 - Q(k)} \right\} . \qquad (20)$$

In the following, Q denotes a modification of Q^β that differs from Q^β only at $k = 0, 1, n - 1, n$ and satisfies

$$Q(0) < Q(1) \le 3/n \text{ and } Q(0) + Q(n) = Q(1) + Q(n - 1) = 1 . \qquad (21)$$

Due to a symmetry argument, we restrict ourselves to $x \le 0.5$. In this part of the domain, the differences between the two rules at $k = n - 1, n$ contribute only $O(2^{-n})$ to the difference between the associated cost-terms:

$$C_n^Q(x) - C_n^{Q^\beta}(x) = (1 - x)^n \left\{ x \ln \frac{Q^\beta(0)}{Q(0)} + (1 - x) \ln \frac{1 - Q^\beta(0)}{1 - Q(0)} \right\}$$
$$+ nx(1 - x)^{n-1} \left\{ x \ln \frac{Q^\beta(1)}{Q(1)} + (1 - x) \ln \frac{1 - Q^\beta(1)}{1 - Q(1)} \right\} + O(2^{-n}) . \qquad (22)$$

Since $Q(0)$ and $Q(1)$ are smaller than $3/n$, we get

$$\ln \frac{1 - Q^\beta(k)}{1 - Q(k)} = \ln\left\{ 1 + \frac{Q(k) - Q^\beta(k)}{1 - Q(k)} \right\}$$
$$= Q(k) - Q^\beta(k) + O(n^{-2}) \quad \text{for } k = 0, 1 .$$

Now we proceed from the Bernoulli distribution to the Poisson distribution (as done by Krichevskiy), or equivalently, setting $z = nx$ we have, for each fixed z,

$(1 - z/n)^n = e^{-z} + O(1/n)$ and

$$n\{C_n^Q(z/n) - C_n^{Q^\beta}(z/n)\} = e^{-z}\{z \ln \tfrac{Q^\beta(0)}{Q(0)} + Q(0) - Q^\beta(0)\}$$
$$+ ze^{-z}\{z \ln \tfrac{Q^\beta(1)}{Q(1)} + Q(1) - Q^\beta(1)\} + O(n^{-1}). \tag{23}$$

Finally, we define our candidate rule Q^* as the following modification of the add-0.8 rule:

$$Q^*(k) = \begin{cases} \frac{k+1/2}{n+1} & \text{if } k = 0, n \ , \\[2mm] \frac{k+1.05}{n+2.1} & \text{if } k = 1, n-1 \ , \\[2mm] \frac{k+0.8}{n+1.6} & \text{otherwise} \ . \end{cases} \tag{24}$$

Note that Q^* coincides with the add-half rule at $k = 0, n$, with the add-1.05 rule at $k = 1, n-1$, and with the add-0.8 rule everywhere else. Furthermore, Q^* satisfies (21). Combining (23) and a convergence condition similar[2] to (19), we show in the full paper that

$$nC_n^{Q^*}(\tfrac{z}{n}) = \Phi(0.8, z)$$
$$+ e^{-z}\left\{-0.3 + z(\ln(1.6) + 0.25) - z^2 \ln \tfrac{2.05}{1.8}\right\} + O(n^{-1/2}) \tag{25}$$

holds uniformly for all $0 \leq z \leq n^{1/4}$. An interesting part of that function is shown in Fig. 2. The values do not exceed $1/2$, i.e., the number given by the lower bound (something that we have checked numerically up to $z = 20$). Moreover, the additional term $e^{-z}\left\{-0.3 + z(\ln(1.6) + 0.25) - z^2 \ln \tfrac{2.05}{1.8}\right\}$ on the right-hand side of (25) is negative for $z \geq 6$. We note that the cost associated with Q^* would

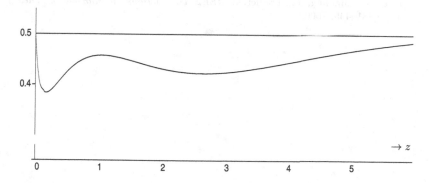

Fig. 2. A plot of the right-hand side of equation (25) for $z \in [0, 6]$, except that the vanishing term of order $n^{-1/2}$ is ignored.

---

[2] Actually, we need a sort of uniform convergence.

provably asymptotically match the lower bound $1/(2n)$ if we could guarantee that the right-hand side of (25) does not exceed $1/2$ for $20 \leq z \leq n^{1/4}$. For larger z, we may appeal to (17).

The Case $m \geq 3$: The case $m \geq 3$ can be treated analogously except for the complication that special care must be taken to guarantee the condition $\sum_{i=1}^{m} Q_i^*(k) = 1$ for each $k \in \mathcal{K}_{m,n}$. More details can be found in the full paper.

References

[1] T. M. Cover. Admissibility properties of Gilbert's encoding for unknown source probabilities. *IEEE Transactions on Information Theory*, 18:216–217, 1971.

[2] Jürgen Forster and Manfred Warmuth. Relative expected instantaneous loss bounds. *Journal of Computer and System Sciences*. To appear.

[3] Jürgen Forster and Manfred Warmuth. Relative expected instantaneous loss bounds. In *Proceedings of the 13th Annual Conference on Computational Learning Theory*, pages 90–99. Morgan Kaufmann, 2000.

[4] Ronald L. Graham, Donald E. Knuth, and Oren Patashnik. *Concrete Mathematics*. Addison Wesley, 1989.

[5] D. A. Huffman. A method for the construction of minimum redundancy codes. *Proc. IRE*, 40(10):1098–1101, 1952.

[6] Rafail E. Krichevskiy. *Universal Compression and Retrieval*. Kluwer Academic Publishers, 1994.

[7] Rafail E. Krichevskiy. Laplace's law of succession and universal encoding. *IEEE Transactions on Information Theory*, 44(1):296–303, 1998.

[8] Claude E. Shannon. A mathematical theory of communication. *The Bell System Technical Journal*, 27:379–423,623–656, 1948.

[9] Qun Xie and Andrew R. Barron. Minimax redundancy for the class of memoryless sources. *IEEE Transactions on Information Theory*, 43(2):646–657, 1997.

[10] Qun Xie and Andrew R. Barron. Asymptotic minimax regret for data compression, gambling, and prediction. *IEEE Transactions on Information Theory*, 46(2):431–445, 2000.

Classification with Intersecting Rules

Tony Lindgren and Henrik Boström

Department of Computer and Systems Sciences,
Stockholm University and Royal Institute of Technology,
Forum 100,
164 40 Kista, Sweden
{tony,henke}@dsv.su.se
http://www.dsv.su.se

Abstract. Several rule induction schemes generate hypotheses in the form of unordered rule sets. One important problem that has to be addressed when classifying examples with such hypotheses is how to deal with overlapping rules that predict different classes. Previous approaches to this problem calculate class probabilities based on the union of examples covered by the overlapping rules (as in CN2) or assumes rule independence (using naive Bayes). It is demonstrated that a significant improvement in accuracy can be obtained if class probabilities are calculated based on the intersection of the overlapping rules, or in case of an empty intersection, based on as few intersecting regions as possible.

1 Introduction

Methods for rule induction have been studied for more than two decades within the field of machine learning. They include various techniques such as divide-and-conquer (recursive partitioning), that generates hierarchically organized rules (decision trees) [4], and separate-and-conquer (covering) that generates overlapping rules. The sets of rules generated by separate-and-conquer may either be treated as ordered (decision lists) [5] or unordered [3,2]. In case of inducing decision trees or decision lists, there is no need for resolving classification conflicts among the rules. In the former case this is due to that the rules are non-overlapping and hence there is only one single rule that is applicable to any given problem. In the latter case, this is due to that the first applicable rule in the list is always used.

In this work we focus on the problem of how to deal with overlapping rules that predict different classes in unordered rule sets. Previous approaches to this problem calculate class probabilities based on the union of examples covered by the overlapping rules (as in CN2 [2]) or assumes rule independence (using naive Bayes). We propose a novel approach to this problem that bases the calculation of class probabilities on the intersection, rather than the union, of the overlapping rules, or in case of an empty intersection, on as few intersecting regions as possible. The new method, called *intersection-based classification*, is compared to the two previous methods in an empirical evaluation.

N. Cesa-Bianchi et al. (Eds.): ALT 2002, LNAI 2533, pp. 395–402, 2002.

The paper is organized as follows. In the next section, we briefly describe the two previous methods, which are here referred to as *union-based classification* and *naive Bayes classification*, together with an informal presentation of the novel method, *intersection-based classification*. In section three, we describe the algorithm in more detail and briefly present the system in which it has been implemented. The empirical evaluation is given in section four, and finally, in section five, we give some concluding remarks and point out directions for future research.

2   Ways of Resolving Classification Conflicts

In this section, we first recall two previous methods for resolving classification conflicts among overlapping rules and then introduce a new method.

2.1   Union-Based Classification

The system CN2 [2] resolves classification conflicts among rules in the following way. Given the examples in figure 1, the class frequencies in union of the rules that covers the example to be classified is calculated:

$$C(+) = covers(R_1, +) + covers(R_2, +) + covers(R_3, +) = 32$$

and

$$C(-) = covers(R_1, -) + covers(R_2, -) + covers(R_3, -) = 33$$

where $covers(R, C)$ gives the number of examples of class C that are covered by R. This means that CN2 would classify the example as belonging to the negative class (-). More generally:

$$UnionBasedClassification = argmax_{Class_i \in Classes} \sum_{j=1}^{|CovRules|} covers(R_j, C_i)$$

where $CovRules$ is the set of rules that cover the example to be classified, and $covers$ is the function defined above.

2.2   Naive Bayes Classification

Bayes theorem is as follows:

$$P(H|E) = P(H)\frac{P(E|H)}{P(E)}$$

where H is a hypotesis (in our case, a class label for the example to be classified) and E is our evidence (the rules that cover the example). As usual, since $P(E)$

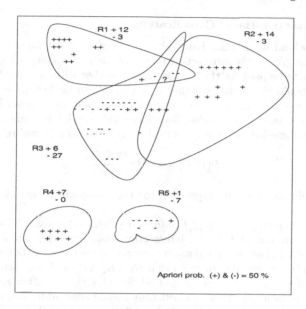

Fig. 1. Three rules covering an example to be classified (marked with ?). The training examples are labeled with their respective classes (+ and -).

does not affect the relative order of different hypotheses according to probability, it is ignored.

The naive Bayes assumption is that each piece of evidence is conditionally independent in relation to other evidence given the hypotesis. Hence, the maximum a posteriori probable hypotesis (MAP) according to the naive Bayes assumption is:

$$h_{MAP} = argmax_{Class_i \in Classes} P(Class_i) \prod_{Rj \in Rules}^{|Rules|} P(R_j|Class_i)$$

where *Rules* is the set of rules that cover the example to be classified.
If we again consider the example shown in figure 1 we get:

$$P(+|R_1 \wedge R_2 \wedge R_3) = P(+) * P(R_1|+) * P(R_2|+) * P(R_3|+) =$$

$$40/80 * 12/40 * 14/40 * 6/40 = 0.0079$$

$$P(-|R_1 \wedge R_2 \wedge R_3) = P(-) * P(R_1|-) * P(R_2|-) * P(R_3|-) =$$

$$40/80 * 3/40 * 3/40 * 27/40 = 0.0019$$

This means that naive Bayes classification results in that the example with unknown class label is classified as belonging to the positive (+) class.

2.3   Intersection-Based Classification

The idea behind intersection-based classification is that if we are given some training examples in the intersecting region of the overlapping rules, this information should be used for the classification together with Bayes rule. In other words, it should be checked whether it is possible to be less naive than naive Bayes. In case there are some training examples that are covered by all rules that cover the example to be classified, Bayes rule can be used directly without having to assume independence of all rules. That is, from Bayes' rule:

$$P(H|E) = P(H)\frac{P(E|H)}{P(E)}$$

we obtain the following expression for the maximum a posteriori probable hypothesis:

$$h_{MAP} = argmax_{Class_i \in Classes} P(Class_i)P(Rule_1 \wedge Rule_2 \wedge \ldots \wedge Rule_n | Class_i)$$

If we again look at figure 1, intersection-based classification would assign the negative (-) class to the unknown example, since there exists a negative (-) example in the intersection between rule $R_1 \wedge R_2 \wedge R_3$ and the apriori is 40/80. This gives the negative class a value of $40/80 * (1+1)/(40+2) = 2.4e - 2$ using Laplace correction (i.e., it is assumed that there is one additional example for each class that is covered by all rules), while the positive class gets a value of $40/80 * 1/(40+2) = 1.2e - 2$.

However, if there are no training examples at all in the intersection, we can check whether a small number of (non-empty) intersecting regions can be formed.

Assume that there is no negative (-) training example in the intersection of $R_1 \cap R_2 \cap R_3$ in figure 1. The smallest number of elements in a partition of this set, such that the intersecting region of each element (subset) covers a non-empty set of training examples, is two. There are three possible partitions of this size, such that each intersection covers a non-empty sets of training examples: [[1],[2,3]],[[2],[1,3]] and [[3],[1,2]].

The probability values for partition one are:

$$Pos = 40/80 * (12+1)/(40+2) * (2+1)/(40+2) = 0.0111$$

$$Neg = 40/80 * (3+1)/(40+2) * (2+1)/(40+2) = 0.0034$$

The probability values for partition two are:

$$Pos = 40/80 * (14+1)/(40+2) * (1+1)/(40+2) = 0.0085$$

$$Neg = 40/80 * (3+1)/(40+2) * (2+1)/(40+2) = 0.0034$$

The probability values for partition three are:

$$Pos = 40/80 * (6+1)/(40+2) * (0+1)/(40+2) = 0.0020$$

$$Neg = 40/80 * (27+1)/(40+2) * (2+1)/(40+2) = 0.0238$$

The highest probability value is obtained for the negative class (-), which is the class that will be assigned to the example by the intersection-based classification method.

3 Algorithm for Intersection-Based Classification

In this section we first give pseudo-code for the intersection-based classification algorithm, and then explain some parts of the algorithm in more detail.

Table 1. Pseudo-code for the Intersection-based Classification Algorithm.

```
IntersectionBasedClassification(Rules,Classes)
  begin {
    BestClassFreq := 0
    ClassFreq := 1
    NoElements := 0
    repeat
      NoElements := NoElements + 1
      NewPartitions := make_part(NoElements,Rules)
    until not_empty(NewPartitions)
    for each Partition in NewPartitions do {
      for each Class in Classes do {
        for each Part in Partition do
          ClassFreq := ClassFreq * covers(Part,Class)
        ClassFreq  := apriori(Class) * ClassFreq
        if ClassFreq > BestClassFreq then {
          BestClass := Class
          BestClassFreq := ClassFreq
        }
      }
    }
    return BestClass
  }
```

The intersection based classification algorithm takes as input the rules that are applicable to the example to be classified as well as the classes in the current domain.

The make_part function takes two arguments: the first argument tells how many elements the make_part function should generate in the partition of the applicable rules (which are given as the second argument). The make_part function is called in an iterative deepening fashion starting with the number of elements set to one.

The function not_empty goes through the partitions made and returns true if there is some partition for which the intersection of the rules in each subset is non-empty (i.e., contains at least one training example).

The algorithm finally computes the class probability for all generated partitions and returns the class label with maximum probability.

It should be noted that the algorithm may degrade to become identical to naive Bayes, in case none of the rules overlap on the training examples. In that case, all elements in the generated partition will consist of single rules.

4   Empirical Evaluation

Intersection-based classification has been implemented in the system Virtual Predict [1], which is a platform for experimenting with various rule induction techniques, e.g., both separate-and-conquer and divide-and-conquer may be employed, and both ordered and unordered rule sets may be generated. The novel method is compared to naive Bayes and union-based classification. We first present the parameter settings that were used in Virtual Predict and describe the data sets that were used in the evaluation, and then give the experimental results.

Table 2. Virtual Predict settings used in the experiment

Parameter	Value
Strategy	Separate and Conquer (SAC)
Probability estimate	M estimate, with $M = 2$
Structure cost	0.5
Measure	Information gain
Incremental reduced error pruning	Most Compressive
Experiment type	10 fold cross validation

4.1   Experimental Setting

There are several parameters that can be adjusted in Virtual Predict. The settings used in our experiments are shown in Table 2, and they all determine how rules are induced. All data sets used were taken from the UCI Machine Learning Repository except the King-Rook-King-Illegal (KRKI) database which comes from the Machine Learning group at the University of York. In Table 3 the domains used in the experiment is shown, as well as their main characteristics. The datasets were choosen to be as diverse as possible with respect to both size and difficulty.

4.2   Experimental Results

The results from the eleven domains are shown in Table 4, where the result for each domain has been obtained by ten-fold cross-validation. Exactly the same folds and generated rules are used by the three classification methods. The last

Table 3. The domains used in the experiment

Domain	Classes	Class distribution	Examples
Shuttle Landing Control	2	47.8, 52.2	278
Car Evaluation	4	4, 4, 22, 70	1728
Balance Scale	3	8, 46, 46	625
Dermatology	6	5.5, 13.3, 14.2, 16.7, 19.7, 30.6	366
The Glass	2	24.1, 75.9	112
Congressional Votes	2	45.2, 54.8	435
KRKI	2	34, 66	1000
Liver-disorders	2	42, 58	345
Ionosphere	2	36, 64	351
Breast Cancer	2	29.7, 70.3	286
Lymphography	4	1.4, 2.7, 41.2, 54.7	148

column shows the percentage of all predictions for which at least two conflicting rules overlap on training data (this gives an upper bound on the amount of
examples for which Intersection-based classification may perform in a less naive
way than naive Bayes). The p-values according to an exact version of McNe-
mar's test for obtaining the observed difference between the novel method and
the two others are given in the columns after their accuracies. It can be seen that
Intersection-based classification outperforms both Union-based and naive Bayes
classification in all eleven domains. Even when considering only statistically significant differences ($p < 0.05$), intersection-based classification is more accurate
in seven out of seven domains. The probability of obtaining this difference (7
wins and 0 losses), given that two methods are equally good, is 0.0078 according
to a sign test. This means that the null hypothesis (no improvement is obtained
with the new method) can be rejected at a 0.05 significance level.

5   Discussion

Previous approaches to the problem of classifying examples using conflicting
rules calculate class probabilities based on the union of examples covered by
the overlapping rules (union-based classification) or assumes rule independence
(naive Bayes classification). We have demonstrated that a significant improvement in accuracy can be obtained if class probabilities are calculated based on
the intersection of the overlapping rules, or in case of an empty intersection,
based on as few intersecting regions as possible.

Union-based classification just sums all the covered classes and returns the
class with the highest frequency. Note that this means that this strategy weights
the examples in the intersection as more important than the rest of the examples.
This follows from that the examples in the intersection are counted as many times
as the number of conflicting rules. Naive Bayes does also weight the examples

Table 4. Intersecting rules compared with naive Bayes and Intersecting rules compared with Union based classification

Data Set	Inter.	naive B.	Sign.	Union-b.	Sign.	No. Conf.	Prediction
Shuttle	99.64	98.20	0.125	98.56	0.250	1.0	3.6 %
Car	93.75	93.17	4.139e-002	93.23	3.515e-002	25.1	14.5 %
Balance Scale	90.88	84.64	2.706e-007	86.08	5.704e-005	22.0	35.2 %
Dermatology	96.08	94.12	1.563e-002	93.28	1.953e-003	5.6	15.7 %
The Glass	94.64	92.86	0.500	92.86	0.500	0.6	5.4 %
C. Votes	96.78	95.40	7.031e-002	95.86	0.388	7.1	16.3 %
KRKI	99.50	99.20	0.375	95.80	1.455e-010	8.8	8.6 %
Liver-disorders	77.68	69.57	4.056e-005	68.99	1.522e-005	14.8	42.9 %
Ionosphere	92.02	89.46	2.246e-002	89.17	3.088e-002	4.7	13.4 %
Breast Cancer	77.62	71.68	4.883e-004	72.73	5.188e-004	6.1	21.3 %
Lymphography	84.46	77.03	7.385e-003	81.08	0.180	5.7	38.5 %

in the intersection in a similar fashion. Intersection-based classification take this notion to it's extreme and considers examples in the intersection only (if there are any, otherwise it tries to find a partition of the rules in conflict with as few elements as possible, where the intersection of each element covers some examples). The experiment supports the hypothesis that the most important information actually resides in the intersection of the rules.

The number of possible partitions to consider in the worst-case grows exponentially with the number of rules. Hence, using this method together with very large rule sets (e.g., as generated by ensemble learning techniques such as bagging or randomization), calls for more efficient (greedy) methods for partitioning the set of conflicting rules. However, in the current experiment the partitioning did not occur to a large extent, and the maximum number of rules that were applicable to any example was not very high (less than ten), keeping the computational cost at a reasonable level.

References

[1] Henrik Boström. *Virtual Predict User Manual.* Virtual Genetics Laboratory, 2001.
[2] P. Clark and R. Boswell. Rule induction with CN2: Some recent improvements. In *Proc. Fifth European Working Session on Learning*, pages 151–163, Berlin, 1991. Springer.
[3] P. Clark and T. Niblett. The cn2 induction algorithm. *Machine Learning, 3, 261–283*, 1989.
[4] J.R. Quinlan. Induction of decision trees. *Machine Learning, 1, 81–106*, 1986.
[5] R. Rivest. Learning decision lists. *Machine Learning, 2(3), 229–246*, 1987.

Feedforward Neural Networks in Reinforcement Learning Applied to High-Dimensional Motor Control

Rémi Coulom

Laboratoire Leibniz-IMAG, Grenoble, France

Abstract. Local linear function approximators are often preferred to feedforward neural networks to estimate value functions in reinforcement learning. Still, motor tasks usually solved by this kind of methods have a low-dimensional state space. This article demonstrates that feedforward neural networks can be applied successfully to high-dimensional problems. The main difficulties of using backpropagation networks in reinforcement learning are reviewed, and a simple method to perform gradient descent efficiently is proposed. It was tested successfully on an original task of learning to swim by a complex simulated articulated robot, with 4 control variables and 12 independent state variables.

1 Introduction

Reinforcement learning [20,8] has been successfully applied to numerous motor control problems, either simulated or real [1,6,11,19]. These results are rather spectacular, but successes are restricted to the control of mechanical systems with few degrees of freedom, such as the cart-pole task or the acrobot. Schaal *et. al.* [15,16] successfully taught robots with many degrees of freedom to perform motor tasks, but the learning consisted only in estimating a model of state dynamics, and no value function was estimated (a linear-quadratic regulator was used to generate controls). As far as I know, no value function with more than 6 input variables has been successfully approximated in non-trivial dynamic motor-control tasks.

The reasons of this restriction is that linear functions approximators are struck by the curse of dimensionality [3]: the cost of approximating a function is exponential with the dimension of the input space. Although some linear approximation schemes such as tile coding [20] can alleviate the curse of dimensionality when their architectures are carefully designed with well-chosen features, they are still very hard to use in practice when there are many input variables, and when there is no good way to guess the right features.

Another way to approximate value functions in reinforcement learning consists in using feedforward neural networks. Tesauro [21] obtained very spectacular successes with these function approximators in his famous backgammon player. An advantage of feedforward neural networks is that they can handle high-dimensional inputs more easily. Barron proved that, to approximate a function

N. Cesa-Bianchi et al. (Eds.): ALT 2002, LNAI 2533, pp. 403–413, 2002.

in a general class, neural networks with sigmoidal units do not suffer from the curse of dimensionality, whereas parametric linear approximators do [2].

Nevertheless, linear function approximators have been often preferred. The main advantage of linear function approximators is that they can have a better locality, that is to say it is possible to adjust the value in a small area of the input space without interfering with values outside this small area. This prevent the approximation scheme from "unlearning" past experience and allows reinforcement learning algorithms to make an efficient incremental use of learning data.

In this paper, we demonstrate that it is worth trying to overcome the difficulties of feedforward neural networks, because they can solve problems that have a higher dimensionality than those previously tackled with linear function approximators. In the first section, the continuous TD(λ) algorithm that was used to train the neural network is presented. The second section deals with issues that have to be solved to perform gradient descent efficiently with feedforward neural networks. The third section presents experimental results obtained on a swimmer with 12 state variables and 4 control variables.

2   Continuous TD(λ)

The algorithm used in experiments reported in this paper is Doya's [6] continuous TD(λ). It is a continuous version of Sutton's discrete algorithm [18] that is adapted to problems in continuous time and space such as motor-control problems.

2.1   Problem Definition

In general, we will suppose that we are to solve motor problems defined by:

- States $x \in S \subset \mathbb{R}^p$ (p real values define the state of the system).
- Controls $u \in U \subset \mathbb{R}^q$ (the system can be controlled via q real values).
- System dynamics $f : S \times U \mapsto \mathbb{R}^p$. This function maps states and actions to derivatives of the state with respect to time. That is to say $\dot{x} = f(x, u)$.
- A reward function $r : S \times U \mapsto \mathbb{R}$. The problem consists in maximizing the cumulative reward as detailed below.
- A shortness factor $s_\gamma \geq 0$. This factor measures the short-sightedness of the optimization. It can be related to the traditional γ in discrete reinforcement learning by $\gamma = e^{-s_\gamma \delta t}$.

A *strategy* or *policy* is a function $\pi : S \mapsto U$ that maps states to controls. Applying a policy from a starting state x_0 at time t_0 produces a trajectory $x(t)$ defined by the ordinary differential equation

$$\forall t \geq t_0 \quad \dot{x} = f(x, \pi(x)) \ ,$$

$$x(t_0) = x_0 \ .$$

The value function of π is defined by

$$V^\pi(\boldsymbol{x}_0) = \int_{t=t_0}^{\infty} e^{-s_\gamma(t-t_0)} r\Big(\boldsymbol{x}(t), \pi\big(\boldsymbol{x}(t)\big)\Big) dt \ . \tag{1}$$

The goal is to find a policy that maximizes the total amount of reward over time, whatever the starting state $\boldsymbol{x}_0$. More formally, problem consists in finding π^* so that

$$\forall \boldsymbol{x}_0 \in S \quad V^{\pi^*}(\boldsymbol{x}_0) = \max_{\pi:S \mapsto U} V^\pi(\boldsymbol{x}_0) \ .$$

V^{π^*} does not depend on π^* and is denoted V^*.

2.2   Learning Algorithm

We will suppose we are to approximate the optimal value function V^* with a parametric function approximator $V_{\boldsymbol{w}}$, where $\boldsymbol{w}$ is the vector of weights (parameters). The continuous TD(λ) algorithm consists in integrating an ordinary differential equation:

$$\begin{cases} \dot{\boldsymbol{w}} = \eta \mathcal{H} \boldsymbol{e} \ , \\ \dot{\boldsymbol{e}} = -(s_\gamma + s_\lambda) \boldsymbol{e} + \frac{\partial V_{\boldsymbol{w}}(\boldsymbol{x})}{\partial \boldsymbol{w}} \ , \\ \dot{\boldsymbol{x}} = f\big(\boldsymbol{x}, \pi(\boldsymbol{x})\big) \ , \end{cases} \tag{2}$$

with

$$\mathcal{H} = r\big(\boldsymbol{x}, \pi(\boldsymbol{x})\big) - s_\gamma V_{\boldsymbol{w}}(\boldsymbol{x}) + \frac{\partial V_{\boldsymbol{w}}}{\partial \boldsymbol{w}} \cdot f\big(\boldsymbol{x}, \pi(\boldsymbol{x})\big) \ .$$

$\mathcal{H}$ is the Hamiltonian and is a continuous equivalent of Bellman's residual. $\mathcal{H} > 0$ indicates a "good surprise" and causes and increase in the past values, whereas $\mathcal{H} < 0$ is a "bad surprise" and causes a decrease in the past values. The magnitude of this change is controlled by the learning rate η, and its time extent in the past is defined by the parameter s_λ. s_λ can be related to the traditional λ parameter in the discrete algorithm by $\lambda = e^{-s_\lambda \delta t}$. $\boldsymbol{e}$ is the vector of eligibility traces. Learning is decomposed into several episodes, each starting from a random initial state, thus insuring exploration of the whole state space. During these episodes, the policy π is chosen to be greedy with respect to the current value estimate $V_{\boldsymbol{w}}$.

3   Efficient Gradient Descent

The basic continuous TD(λ) algorithm presented in the previous section trains the parametric function estimator by applying the steepest-descent method. This kind of method usually does not work efficiently with feedforward neural networks, because it can be struck hard by ill-conditioning. Ill-conditioning means that the output of the value function may be much more sensitive to some weights than to some others. As a consequence, a global learning coefficient that would be good for one weight is likely to be too high for some and too low for others.

Many numerical methods to deal with ill-conditioning have been proposed in the framework of supervised learning [5]. Most of the classical advanced methods that are able to deal with this difficulty are batch algorithms (scaled conjugate gradient [10], Levenberg Marquardt, RPROP [14], QuickProp [7], ...). TD(λ) is incremental by nature since it handles a continuous infinite flow of learning data, so these batch algorithms are not well adapted.

It is possible, however, to use second order ideas in on-line algorithms [13, 17]. Le Cun et al. [9] recommend a "stochastic diagonal Levenberg Marquardt" method for supervised classification tasks that have a large and redundant training set. TD(λ) is not very far from this situation, but using this method is not easy because of the special nature of the gradient descent used in the TD(λ) algorithm. Evaluating the diagonal terms of the Hessian matrix would mean differentiating with respect to each weight the total error gradient over one trial, which is equal to

$$\int_{t_0}^{t_f} -\mathcal{H}(t)e(t)dt \ .$$

This is not impossible, but still a bit complicated. In particular, $\mathcal{H}$ depends on w in a very complex way, since it depends on the gradient of the output of the network with respect to its input.

Another method, the Vario-η algorithm [12], was used instead. It is well adapted for the continuous TD(λ) algorithm, and it is both virtually costless in terms of CPU time and extremely easy to implement.

3.1 Principle

Figure 1 shows the typical variations of two weights during learning. In this figure, the basic algorithm (derived from (2)) was applied to a simple control problem and no special care was taken to deal with ill-conditioning. Obviously, the error function was much more sensitive to w_1 than to w_2. w_2 varied very slowly, whereas w_1 converged rapidly. This phenomenon is typical of ill-conditioning.

Another effect of these different sensitivities is that w_1 looks much more noisy than w_2. The key idea of Vario-η consists in measuring this noise to estimate the sensitivity of the error with respect to each weight, and scale individual learning rates appropriately. That is to say, instead of measuring ill-conditioning of the Hessian matrix, which is the traditional approach of efficient gradient-descent algorithms, ill-conditioning is measured on the covariance matrix.

3.2 Algorithm

In theory, it would be possible to obtain a perfect conditioning by performing a principal component analysis with the covariance matrix. This approach is not practical because of its computational cost, so a simple analysis of the diagonal is performed:

$$v_i(k+1) = (1-\beta)v_i(k) + \beta\left(\frac{w_i(k+1) - w_i(k)}{\eta_i(k)}\right)^2 ,$$

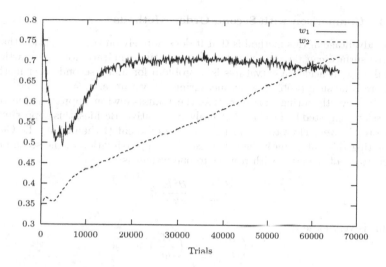

Fig. 1. Variations of two weights when applying the basic TD(λ). A value is plotted every 100 trials. The function approximator used is a 66-weight feedforward neural network.

$$\eta_i(k) = \frac{\eta}{\sqrt{v_i(k)} + \varepsilon} \ .$$

k is the trial number. $v_i(0)$ is a large enough value. β is the variance decay coefficient. A typical choice is $1/100$. ε is a small constant to prevent division by zero. $\eta_i(k)$ is the learning rate for weight w_i. This formula assumes that the standard deviation of the gradient is large in comparison to its mean, which was shown to be true empirically in experiments.

3.3   Results

Experiments were run with fully-connected cascade feedforward networks, with a linear output unit, and sigmoidal hidden units. Observations during reinforcement learning indicated that the variances of weights on connections to the linear output unit were usually n times larger than those on internal connections, n being the total number of neurons. The variances of internal connections are all of the same order of magnitude (we have yet to find a good theoretical explanation for this). This means that good conditioning can be simply obtained by scaling the learning rate of the output unit by $1/\sqrt{n}$. This allows to use a global learning rate that is $\sqrt{n}$ times larger and provides a speed-up of about $\sqrt{n}$. The network used in experiments had 60 neurons, so this was a very significant acceleration.

3.4   Comparison with Second-Order Methods

An advantage of this method is that it does not rely on the assumption that the error surface can be approximated by a positive quadratic form. In particular, dealing with negative curvatures is a problem for many second-order methods. There is no such problem when measuring the variance.

It is worth noting, however, that the Gauss-Newton approximation of the Hessian suggested by Le Cun *et al.* is always positive. Besides, this approximation is formally very close to the variance of the gradient (I thank Yann Le Cun for pointing this out to me): the Gauss-Newton approximation of the second order derivative of the error with respect to one weight is

$$\frac{\partial^2 E}{\partial w_{ij}^2} \approx \frac{\partial^2 E}{\partial a_i^2} y_j^2 \ .$$

This is very close to

$$\left(\frac{\partial E}{\partial w_{ij}}\right)^2 = \left(\frac{\partial E}{\partial a_i}\right)^2 y_j^2 \ .$$

A major difference between the two approaches is that there is a risk that the variance goes to zero as weights approach their optimal value, whereas the estimate of the second order derivative of the error would stay positive. That is to say, the learning rate increases as the gradient of the error decreases, which may be a cause of instability, especially if the error becomes zero. This was not a problem at all in the reinforcement learning experiments that were run, because the variance actually *increased* during learning, and was never close to zero.

4   Experiments with Swimmers

Experiments where run with a mechanical system made of 5 articulated segments, controlled with 4 torques, and moving in a two-dimensional fluid. This system has 12 state variables and 4 control variables. Full details about the simulation can be found in Appendix A.

A 60-neuron feedforward neural network was used, with a fully connected cascade architecture (that is to say, neuron number i was connected to all neurons $j > i$). Inputs were the 5 angles of the 5 segments, their 5 derivatives with respect to time, and the velocity of the center of mass (so, 12 independent variables). The learning rate was $\eta = 0.01$ and it was scaled down in the output unit as explained in Section 3.3. The learning algorithm was integrated with the Euler method, using a time step of 0.01 seconds.

Figure 2 shows how learning progressed. It took about 2.5 million trials of 5 seconds to obtain top performance. This simulation took about one week of CPU time on a 800 MHz PC. The fact that it took such a long time to learn is one of the limitations of this methods: it requires a lot of training data.

After some more training time, performance collapses. The reasons of this drop in performance are not very well understood yet, and some investigations remain to be done. This lack of stability is another limitation of this method.

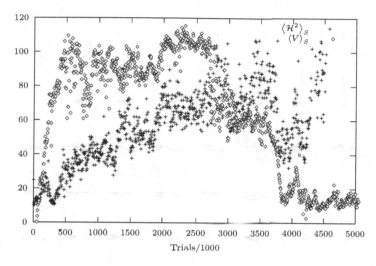

Fig. 2. Progress of learning. $\langle \mathcal{H}^2 \rangle_S$ is the mean squared Hamiltonian estimated over the state space. $\langle V \rangle_S$ is the mean value over the state space.

The swimming technique obtained after 2.5 million trials is presented on Fig. 3. Visualizing the swimmer movements on this figure might not be very easy. Animations can be downloaded from the author's web page (`http://remi.coulom.free.fr/Thesis/`), and can give a better feeling of how the swimmer moves.

5   Conclusion

In this paper, a method for the efficient use of feedforward neural networks has been presented, and tested successfully on a difficult motor-control task. This result indicates that continuous model-based reinforcement learning with feedforward neural networks can handle motor control problems that are significantly more complex than those that have been solved with linear function approximators so far.

The main limits of this method are that it requires a lot of training data, and convergence is no guaranteed. Refining the learning algorithm to deal with these problems seems to be an interesting direction for further research. Weaver *et al's* [22] method to make feedforward neural networks local might be a possibility, but its efficiency on real problems remains to be established. Another interesting possibility to make a more efficient use of learning data consists in "recycling trajectories" [4], that is to say reusing past trajectories several times.

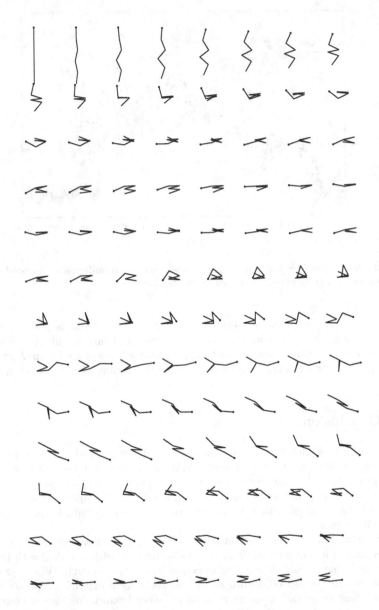

Fig. 3. A 5-segment swimmer trained with a 60-neuron network. In the first 5 lines of this animation, the target direction is to the right. In the last 8, it is reversed to the left. Swimmers are plotted every 0.1 seconds, reading from left to right and from top to bottom.

References

[1] Charles W. Anderson. Strategy learning with multilayer connectionist representations. In *Proceedings of the Fourth International Workshop on Machine Learning*, pages 103–114, Irvine, CA, 1987. Morgan Kaufmann.

[2] Andrew R. Barron. Universal approximation bounds for superpositions of a sigmoidal function. *IEEE Transactions on Information Theory*, 39(3):930–945, May 1993.

[3] Richard Bellman. *Dynamic Programming*. Princeton University Press, Princeton, New Jersey, 1957.

[4] Dimitri P. Bertsekas and John N. Tsitsiklis. *Neuro-Dynamic Programming*. Athena Scientific, Belmont, MA, 1996.

[5] Christopher M. Bishop. *Neural Networks for Pattern Recognition*. Oxford University Press, 1995.

[6] Kenji Doya. Reinforcement learning in continuous time and space. *Neural Computation*, 12:243–269, 2000.

[7] Scott E. Fahlman. An empirical study of learning speed in back-propagation networks. Technical Report CMU-CS-88-162, Carnegie-Mellon University, 1988.

[8] Leslie Pack Kaelbling, Michael L. Littman, and Andrew W. Moore. Reinforcement learning: A survey. *Journal of Artificial Intelligence Research*, 4:237–285, 1996.

[9] Yann Le Cun, Leon Bottou, Genevieve B. Orr, and Klaus-Robert Müller. Efficient BackProp. In Genevieve B. Orr and Klaus-Robert Müller, editors, *Neural Networks: Tricks of the Trade*. Springer, 1998.

[10] Martin F. Møller. A scaled conjugate gradient algorithm for fast supervised learning. *Neural Networks*, 6:525–533, 1993.

[11] Jun Morimoto and Kenji Doya. Hierarchical reinforcement learning of low-dimensional subgoals and high-dimensional trajectories. In *Proceedings of the Fifth International Conference on Neural Information Processing*, pages 850–853, 1998.

[12] Ralph Neuneier and Hans-Georg Zimmermann. How to train neural networks. In Genevieve B. Orr and Klaus-Robert Müller, editors, *Neural Networks: Tricks of the Trade*. Springer, 1998.

[13] Genevieve B. Orr and Todd K. Leen. Using curvature information for fast stochastic search. In *Advances in Neural Information Processing Systems 9*. MIT Press, 1997.

[14] Martin Riedmiller and Heinrich Braun. A direct adaptive method for faster back-propagation learning: The RPROP algorithm. In *Proceedings of the IEEE International Conference on Neural Networks*, 1993.

[15] Stefan Schaal and Christopher G. Atkeson. Robot juggling: An implementation of memory-based learning. *Control Systems Magazine*, 14:57–71, 1994.

[16] Stefan Schaal, Christopher G. Atkeson, and Sethu Vijayakumar. Real-time robot learning with locally weighted statistical learning. In *International Conference on Robotics and Automation (ICRA2000)*, 2000.

[17] Nicol N. Schraudolph. Local gain adaptation in stochastic gradient descent. In *Proceedings of the 9th International Conference on Artificial Neural Networks*, London, 1999. IEE.

[18] Richard S. Sutton. Learning to predict by the methods of temporal differences. *Machine Learning*, 3:9–44, 1988.

[19] Richard S. Sutton. Generalization in reinforcement learning: Successful examples using sparse coarse coding. In *Advances in Neural Information Processing Systems 8*, pages 1038–1044. MIT Press, 1996.

[20] Richard S. Sutton and Andrew G. Barto. *Reinforcement Learning: An Introduction.* MIT Press, Cambridge, MA, 1998.

[21] Gerald Tesauro. Temporal difference learning and TD-Gammon. *Communications of the ACM*, 38(3):58–68, March 1995.

[22] Scott E. Weaver, Leemon C. Baird, and Marios M. Polycarpou. Preventing unlearning during on-line training of feedforward networks. In *Proceedings of the International Symposium of Intelligent Control*, 1998.

A   Swimmer Model

This section gives a description of the Swimmer model. The C++ source code of the simulator can be obtained from the author on request.

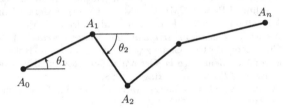

Fig. 4. Swimmer model

A.1   Variables and Parameters

State variables:

- A_0: position of first point
- θ_i: angle of part i with respect to the x axis
- $\dot{A}_0, \dot{\theta}_i$: their derivatives with respect to time

Control variables:

- $(u_i)_{i \in \{1...n-1\}}$, torques applied between body parts, constrained by $|u_i| < U_i$

Problem parameters:

- n: number of body parts
- m_i: mass of part i ($i \in \{1...n\}$)
- l_i: length of part i ($i \in \{1...n\}$)
- k: viscous-friction coefficient

A.2   Model of Viscous Friction

The model of viscous friction used consists in supposing that a small line of length $d\lambda$ with a normal vector $\boldsymbol{n}$ and moving at velocity $\boldsymbol{v}$ receives a small force of value $d\boldsymbol{F} = -k(\boldsymbol{v} \cdot \boldsymbol{n})\boldsymbol{n}d\lambda$. The total force applied to part i is equal to $\boldsymbol{F}_i = -kl_i(\dot{G}_i \cdot \boldsymbol{n}_i)\boldsymbol{n}_i$, with $G_i = (A_{i-1} + A_i)/2$. The Total moment at G_i is $\mathcal{M}_i = -k\dot{\theta}_i l_i^3/12$.

A.3   System Dynamics

Let $\boldsymbol{f}_i$ be the force applied by part $i+1$ to part i.

$$\forall i \in \{1,\ldots,n\}   -\boldsymbol{f}_{i+1} + \boldsymbol{f}_i + \boldsymbol{F}_i = m_i\ddot{G}_i$$

These equations allow to express the $\boldsymbol{f}_i$'s as a function of state variables:

$$\boldsymbol{f}_0 = \boldsymbol{0}$$
$$\forall i \in \{1,\ldots,n\}   \boldsymbol{f}_i = \boldsymbol{f}_{i-1} - \boldsymbol{F}_i + m_i\ddot{G}_i$$

We end up with a set of $n+2$ linear equations with $n+2$ unknowns:

$$\begin{cases} \boldsymbol{f}_n = \boldsymbol{0}, \\ m_i\frac{l_i}{12}\ddot{\theta}_i = \det(\overrightarrow{G_iA_i}, \boldsymbol{f}_i + \boldsymbol{f}_{i-1}) + \mathcal{M}_i - u_i + u_{i-1} \,. \end{cases}$$

Unknowns are $\ddot{G}_0$ (or any $\ddot{G}_i$) and all the $\ddot{\theta}_i$'s. Solving this set of equations gives state dynamics.

A.4   Reward

$r(\boldsymbol{x}, \boldsymbol{u}) = \dot{G}_x$ (G_x is the abscissa of the center of mass)

A.5   Numerical Values (SI Units)

$m_i = 1, l_i = 1, k = 10, U_i = 5$

Author Index

Lecture Notes in Artificial Intelligence (LNAI)

Lecture Notes in Computer Science